# ROOSEVELT
## FROM MUNICH
## TO PEARL HARBOR

A Da Capo Press Reprint Series

# FRANKLIN D. ROOSEVELT
# AND THE ERA OF THE NEW DEAL

GENERAL EDITOR: FRANK FREIDEL
*Harvard University*

# ROOSEVELT

## FROM MUNICH
## TO PEARL HARBOR

*A Study
in the Creation of a Foreign Policy*

*by*
### BASIL RAUCH

DA CAPO PRESS • NEW YORK • 1975

Library of Congress Cataloging in Publication Data

Rauch, Basil, 1908-
   Roosevelt, from Munich to Pearl Harbor.

   (Franklin D. Roosevelt and the era of the New Deal)
   Reprint of the ed. published by Barnes & Noble,
New York.
   Bibliography: p.
   1. Roosevelt, Franklin Delano, Pres. U. S.,
1882-1945.   2. United States—Foreign relations—
1933-1945.   I. Title.   II. Series.
[E807.R3   1975]            327.73            74-34446
ISBN 0-306-70739-X

MB

This Da Capo Press edition of *Roosevelt: From Munich to Pearl Harbor* is an
unabridged republication of the second edition published in New York in 1967.
It is reprinted with the permission of the author.

Published by Da Capo Press, Inc.
A Subsidiary of Plenum Publishing Corporation
227 West 17th Street, New York, N.Y. 10011

# ROOSEVELT
## FROM MUNICH
## TO PEARL HARBOR

*The History of the New Deal: 1933 – 1938*

*American Interest in Cuba: 1848 – 1855*

# ROOSEVELT

## FROM MUNICH
## TO PEARL HARBOR

*A Study*

*in the Creation of a Foreign Policy*

*by*

## BASIL RAUCH

*Professor of History, Barnard College,*
*Columbia University*

BARNES & NOBLE, Inc.
NEW YORK
PUBLISHERS & BOOKSELLERS SINCE 1873

*For Elizabeth*

# Preface to Barnes & Noble Edition

AMERICANS ARE SAID ALWAYS TO PRODUCE A MOVEMENT OF repentance after they have won a war. Historians "revise" the noble official reasons why we went to war. Perhaps they satisfy many Americans' doubt that government can be honest.

One might have thought that the Japanese sneak attack on the United States Pacific Fleet at Pearl Harbor was *casus belli* clear enough to quiet doubts. Not at all. Charges that the Roosevelt administration rather than the Japanese militarists bears responsibility for Pearl Harbor persist to this day. This book is an effort to refute the revisionists.

The dispute has not been fruitless. Historians have explored the implications and evidence for particular positions and have worked out larger meanings for national policy and international relations. The controversy has now moved through three stages. The revisionists opened with their biggest gun: the two books by Charles A. Beard which are countered in the present volume. Beard was too canny a polemicist to accuse Roosevelt of "plotting" Pearl Harbor. But his books left his readers with a dense cloud of suspicions about the motives of Roosevelt and his aides.

Beard died before the present book appeared. Thereafter lesser writers tried to keep his arguments alive. Harry Elmer Barnes thrashed about making every sort of attack on this book (and its author) except the only one that mattered: a refutation of points at issue based on evidence. Nor did Charles C. Tansill refute them in his book *Back Door to War* (1952). Tansill tried to make up for Beard's neglect to notice the bearing of the rise of Axis aggression on American entry into the war. But his overt sympathy with the policy of collaboration with Hitler Germany and militarist Japan made his book an embarrassment to the revisionist cause.

The first stage of the controversy then reached nadir in a growling outburst by Rear Admiral Robert A. Theobald, *The Final Secret of Pearl Harbor* (1954). The "final secret" was Roosevelt's purpose to get the battleships at Pearl Harbor bombed by the Japanese. Theobald wants to defend his friend Admiral Husband E. Kimmel, in command of the Pacific Fleet, against the charge of negligence. He goes farther than Kimmel does in his own memoirs. His argument depends on his assurance to readers that "no naval officer" would do certain things of which Kimmel was accused. He flays Roosevelt and General George C. Marshall. He is also forced by the logic of his case to accuse Admiral Stark of conniving with Roosevelt in a plot so monstrous that one wants not only some evidence but an explanation of why anyone, let alone a naval officer, would do it. Theobald is unfamiliar with the rule that evidence is necessary to support inference.

The second stage of the controversy brought under scrutiny the question of responsibility on the American side for the success of Japan's surprise attack. A great deal of confusion, distortion, and vague speculation ended when Roberta Wohlstetter published *Pearl Harbor: Warning and Decision* (1962). She demonstrates that flukes, most of them failures to read the future in imprecise "signals" amid a roar of "noise," and a few of them the result of incompetence and service rivalries, laid the Pacific Fleet open to sneak attack. The book reveals Americans' marvellous feats in gathering intelligence and their great weakness, stemming from suspicion of intellectuality, in evaluating it. There is no evidence that anyone on our side knew anything about the actual Japanese plan to attack Pearl Harbor. Information that looks indicative in hindsight was not so in its context.

Far more difficult to answer is the charge around which the third stage of the controversy revolves: that the Roosevelt administration made a mistake in holding to the "hard" line in relations with Japan. George F. Kennan and Hans Morgenthau test foreign policies by applying a litmus paper that turns one color when too much idealism is present, and another color in the presence of a satisfactory amount of realism. Power is the determinant of realism. Idealism is particularly foolish in those American policies which preached good behavior to nations without committing power enough to enforce it. Following Kennan and Morgenthau, some writers now argue that it was hopelessly unrealistic of Roosevelt and Hull to require the Japanese warlords to get out of China if they wanted the United States to lift the embargo of July, 1941.

An effective exploration of this view is by Paul W. Schroeder, *The Axis Alliance and Japanese-American Relations* (1958). It illustrates the point that realism-versus-idealism is an intellectual instrument of strictly limited utility. This instrument polarizes abstractions to an extreme. It obscures the subtle inter-relations between idealism and realism, in this case, the possibility that United States refusal to supply Japan with means to conquer China served both the cause of morality and the power interests of the United States. Nor are mistakes at Yalta in 1945 that favored Russia a reason to urge that a mistake favoring Japan should have been made in 1941.

It will not do to equate the United States foreign policy of anti-aggression with impractical idealism. The principles which Roosevelt and Hull asked Japan to agree to in action as well as in promises served not only the cause of peace, not only the self-interest of the United States; they also served the real interests of the Japanese nation. This has been proved during the past twenty years. Shorn of her empire, Japan has progressed economically and socially faster than ever before, precisely by following the principles urged by American statesmanship in 1941.

So we are back at the starting point. What was the foreign policy of the Roosevelt administration? A student of this question must consult the admirable books by Herbert Feis and by William L. Langer and S. Everett Gleason. It is the question to which the present book is addressed within the particular framework of Roosevelt's and Hull's intentions. It is far more difficult than the questions controverted earlier; indeed, it is scarcely subject to a final answer. But it lifts the study of Pearl Harbor out of the realms of melodrama and bureaucratic procedure onto the level where the historian strives to perform his highest function, which is the judgment of policy.

BASIL RAUCH

*Outer Island*
*Stony Creek*
*Connecticut*
*June 21, 1966*

# Preface

THE ORIGINAL PLAN FOR THIS BOOK WAS TO SURVEY WITH-
out any particular interpretation the history of our foreign relations during the administration of President Franklin D. Roosevelt. Perhaps the year 1945, when this plan took shape, explains
its simplicity. In that year of victory over the Axis and of American entry into the United Nations, the pre-Pearl Harbor quarrels
between isolationists and internationalists seemed to have been
generally resolved in favor of the internationalists. When an issue
ceases to exist, the time is ripe for an historical obituary.

But in this case an obituary would have been premature. Besides showing signs of life in the political arena since 1945, isolationism has found champions among historians, led by the late
Dr. Charles A. Beard, who deny that internationalism vanquished
their cause. They offer seemingly valid evidence to support the
view that the President plotted to carry the United States into the
Second World War contrary to his public professions of peaceful
intent, in violation of constitutional limits on his authority, and
contrary to the desire of the Axis leaders to avoid war with the
United States. Confronted by this challenging interpretation, I
studied the evidence, trying to discover whether it had been fairly
treated by the isolationists.

My examination of the evidence convinced me that their thesis
is based on omissions, distortions, and falsifications. Therefore I
abandoned my original plan and turned to write not merely a
factual account of events but also a point-by-point refutation of
the isolationist thesis, and to present the internationalist argument
in favor of President Roosevelt's conduct of foreign relations.

It is not difficult to establish the essential facts regarding American foreign relations during the years before Pearl Harbor or to find the evidence that refutes the isolationist thesis. Documents which governments normally keep secret have been made public in vast quantity by such bodies as the Congressional Joint Committee to Investigate the Pearl Harbor Attack. Several of the most intimate associates of President Roosevelt have written memoirs which provide insight to his thinking and that of his subordinates. The nature of the evidence now available seems to rule out the possibility of further revelations of an importance to compare with the secret protocols of the Yalta Agreement. For example, the voluminous evidence showing that British leaders continued, until the moment of the Pearl Harbor attack, to ask President Roosevelt for a commitment that the United States would go to war even if it was not attacked, seems to rule out the possibility that evidence of such a commitment lies hidden somewhere out of our sight.

Still a stupendous quantity of documentation is at this writing kept out of the searcher's reach at the Roosevelt Library in Hyde Park, in the archives of the Department of State, in the British archives, and in many other personal and official files. When this material is made available to students it will provide understanding of the way in which decisions were reached and of the way in which policies were carried out. But it will probably not greatly alter our present knowledge of the objective meaning of major policies and actions. This book is concerned with such meanings and, although the period mainly treated is only the three years from 1938 to 1941, the embarrassment has been one not of poverty but of riches in the material available. A bibliography has not been thought worthwhile because the sources used are well known and readily available to any reader. They are set forth in the citations at the end of the book.

Permissions to quote copyright material have been granted by the Honorable Cordell Hull and The Macmillan Company: *Memoirs of Cordell Hull,* copyright, 1948, by Cordell Hull; The American National Red Cross: *Wartime Correspondence between President Roosevelt and Pope Pius XII,* introduction and notes by Myron C. Taylor (published by The Macmillan Company); Macmillan and Co., Ltd.: Keith Feiling, *Life of Neville Chamber-*

*lain;* Harper and Brothers: Sumner Welles, *The Time for Decision,* and Henry L. Stimson and McGeorge Bundy, *Active Service in Peace and War;* Yale University Press: Charles A. Beard, *President Roosevelt and the Coming of the War;* Houghton Mifflin Company: Winston S. Churchill, *Their Finest Hour.*

Valuable suggestions were given to me by Professor Thomas P. Peardon of Barnard College, Professor Allan Nevins of Columbia University, and Professor Samuel Eliot Morison of Harvard University. It is a pleasure to thank them and a duty to absolve them of responsibility for the shortcomings of this book.

I wish also to thank Mr. John B. Stabler for his expert assistance in preparing the manuscript for publication, and Miss Renée Lamouree for her skillful secretarial work.

B. R.

*Pike's Falls*
*Jamaica, Vermont*
*1946–1949*

# Contents

# 1.

## Introduction

During the decade 1933–1942, world events and president Franklin D. Roosevelt led the American people and their government to adopt collective security as the foreign policy of the United States. The late Dr. Charles A. Beard is the only historian who has written on the process by which the nation abandoned isolationism and turned to internationalism. His two books, *American Foreign Policy in the Making: 1932–1940: A Study in Responsibilities*,[1] and *President Roosevelt and the Coming of the War: 1941: A Study in Appearances and Realities*[2] frankly aim to destroy the faith of Americans in the honesty of President Roosevelt in planning the new foreign policy.

These books propose a revisionist interpretation of the causes of American entry into the Second World War. After the First World War, revisionist historians won over the American public to their view that the United States had entered that war not because Germany committed aggression against it, but because American bankers and munitions manufacturers plotted entry for their own profit. The thesis provided justification for the return to isolationism. Beard's purpose was to create a similar disillusionment regarding the reasons for American entry into the recent war, and a similar revulsion against the foreign policy of internationalism.[3]

The villain in Beard's plot is not an economic group with a vested interest in war, but the President of the United States acting for motives which are not defined. The picture of President Roosevelt engaged in a colossal and profoundly immoral plot to deceive the American people into participating in the war unnecessarily and contrary to their interests might be thought so overdrawn as to be unconvincing. But Beard relies upon the effects of the twelve and more years of widely publicized hatred of Roosevelt by a minority of the public and the majority of the press to make the familiarity of his characterization overcome its implausibility.

An indication of Beard's desire to capitalize on anti-Roosevelt feeling is that in his two books he almost completely ignores the part Secretary of State Hull played in the making of administration foreign policy. Hull's work was certainly second in importance only to that of the President himself, and in details it was more revealing than Roosevelt's. But, because Hull was generally regarded as an honest and safe leader, his presence on Beard's stage as Roosevelt's partner would have been an inartistic contradiction of Beard's image of Roosevelt pursuing a sinister plot.

This is only one of the many artful exclusions Beard practices. More important is his exclusion of any data on the objective course of world events which might suggest that the United States, confronted by rising Axis power, did actually face danger to its own security. In Beard's books, not policies of Hitler or Japan but the policies of Roosevelt created first the danger and then the fact of United States participation in the Second World War. In the early pages of *American Foreign Policy in the Making*, Beard shows admirable, perhaps even excessive, respect for the complexities of problems of historical causation, but only in order to justify his own failure to assess the part of the aggressor nations in causing the Second World War.[4] Thereafter Beard proceeds in the remainder of that book and throughout his second one to make a masterpiece of oversimplification in order to lay responsibility for war upon Roosevelt.

Besides excluding material essential for the understanding of Roosevelt's foreign policy, Beard violently distorts the material he does use. His principal distortions are two: that internationalists, led by Roosevelt during the thirties, wanted the United States to go to war; and that Roosevelt practiced deception on the American people regarding the nature and aims of his foreign policy.

The first of these distortions depends upon a perverse definition of internationalism. Beard lifts his definition from the lexicon of isolationism and uses it in both his books as axiomatic truth. His complete definition follows:

Here and in the following pages the term *internationalism* is used as meaning: World peace is desirable and possible; it is indivisible and can be secured for the United States only by entering into a positive connection with a league, or association, of nations, empowered to make pacific adjustments of international conflicts and to impose peace, by effective sanctions or by force, on aggressors or peace breakers; the United States cannot maintain neutrality in case of any major war among European and Asiatic powers.[5]

This definition is fair enough up to the word "only," which, strengthened as it is by the word "positive," falsifies the program of American internationalists, especially of the time when President Roosevelt came to office, as if the *ultimate* step by the United States in the direction of collective security, that is, "a positive connection with a league, or association, of nations," was the "only" and therefore the *first* step they advocated. The Roosevelt administration never advocated United States entry into the League of Nations. It did advocate parallel action with the League in particular cases, after the United States should have first decided independently in each case that the action of the League corresponded to the interests and policy of the United States. Whether independent and parallel action with the League of Nations may be termed a "positive connection with a league" is debatable, but it is also beside the point.

The heart of the argument was that isolationists during the period between the two World Wars asserted the impossibility of the United States taking part in collective action against an aggressor without forming "entangling alliances" and making "prior commitments" which would destroy the sovereignty of the United States and permit other nations to determine its policy and even plunge it into war against its will. This was the chief argument against joining the League after the First World War. Henry L. Stimson, President Hoover's Secretary of State, President Roosevelt, and Secretary Hull were, nonetheless, internationalists even though they conceded to the power of this argument. Their statesmanship consisted in devising techniques which would permit the United States to take part in international action for collective security without forming entangling alliances or making prior commitments. One such was the technique of "parallel action"; another was "consultation," whereby the United States promised to consult with other nations when aggression occurred, but reserved the right to judge for itself in each case whether it should take action against the aggressor; a third was a discriminatory arms embargo against aggressors; a fourth was Lend Lease; a fifth was the "veto power" of the United States in the Security Council of the United Nations, which not only avoids prior commitment by the United States to take action in any particular case, but enables the United States to prevent the Security Council itself from taking action.

The development of such techniques is of supreme importance in the history of collective security as an American policy. It is sometimes argued that these techniques compromised the policy of collective security to the point of obliteration. In this view, the effective policy of the United States under Roosevelt shifted not from isolation to collective security but from isolation to participation in world politics to protect the United States and increase its power at the expense of other powers. Whether this is indeed a fair statement of the "inner meaning" of Roosevelt's policy will be discussed hereafter. In either case, Roosevelt's method was cooperation with some powers against others; the method was supported by internationalists and the development certainly marked a change in United States foreign policy. Whatever the "inner meaning" of this development, isolationists denied that national sovereignty could be preserved by any method except abstinence from cooperation with other governments; they asserted that the object of the new policy was not peace but war, and Beard perpetuates their distortions as "truths of history."

The new techniques enabled Roosevelt and other leaders to go before the country and plead for collective security, and at the same time promise in good faith that they did not contemplate entangling alliances or prior commitments and that they had as their greatest purpose avoidance of United States participation in war. Throughout his two books, Beard calls such promises "retreats" from the policy of collective security or "denials" of that policy and examples of how Roosevelt "misled" the people. Evidently parallel action, consultation, and a discriminatory arms embargo do not constitute for Beard a "positive connection with a league." Positive or not, these techniques constituted the program of American internationalism during the thirties, and Beard's definition of that word evades, as isolationists generally evaded, that fact, in order to make the false charge that internationalism did involve entangling alliances and prior commitments—and war.

Collective security, the isolationists charged, would involve the United States in war. It would be a most evil war because entangling alliances and prior commitments would make it an "offensive" war, one that was "none of our business," fought by the United States "against our will," "to pull other people's chestnuts out of the fire." The President was accused of advocating internationalism *because* it would involve the United States in war. Beard arranges his definition of internationalism to lead his readers into acceptance of the charge as truth. The central argument of internationalists, that collective security is precisely the only means whereby the United States can *avoid* war, he distorts into a charge that they believe in using force, not solely as a last recourse *after* peaceful moral, diplomatic, economic, and political sanctions have failed to halt an aggressor, but at the outset, as an *alternative* to other sanctions. The word "or" in Beard's definition ". . . impose peace, by effective sanctions or by force, . . ." mashes into one lump the series of measures, carefully graded from less to more coercive, with which internationalists believe an aggressor should be faced—those measures to be applied successively, with the hope and reasonable expectation that the threat of stronger measures would, at a stage short of war, stop the aggressor. No reasonable observer is likely to argue that, if all the allied and associated powers that ultimately combined to win the First and Second World Wars had combined before those wars began and faced Germany and its allies with the certainty of their collective action, those wars would have occurred.

A fair definition of internationalism must specify that the policy involves a series of collective measures, graded from less to more coercive, by a group of nations having a large share of world power, and the reasoned conviction of internationalists that the threat of these measures will stop aggression before the last one, force, is reached. Thus the central, simple fact may be understood: internationalists support collective measures against aggression as the best means of securing world peace.

Beard's other chief distortion—that Roosevelt practiced deception on the American people regarding the nature and aims of his foreign policy—depends upon his distorted definition of internationalism. Beard proves in great detail that Roosevelt repeatedly assured the American people that his policy was to avoid entangling alliances, prior commitments, and war. He finds deception in these assurances because an internationalist policy, in Beard's view, could not avoid entangling alliances, prior commitments, and war.

His thesis is maintained by butchering the record and throwing out its most vital parts. Roosevelt, from his first to his last days in office, not only repeatedly assured the American people that his policy was to avoid entangling alliances, prior commitments and war, but he devised and repeatedly urged upon the public and Congress techniques of collective security which, while avoiding entangling alliances and prior commitments, he as an internationalist was convinced were the best means of preventing United States involvement in war.

A shift that occurred in January, 1939, was not a shift in policy but in emphasis. Before his Annual Message of that year, President Roosevelt placed primary emphasis on the achievement of domestic reforms and only secondary emphasis on the achievement of collective security as the foreign policy of the United States. From 1933 to November, 1939, every attempt to achieve the latter outside the Western Hemisphere was defeated by Congress. The Munich crisis of September, 1938, and Roosevelt's conviction that the "settlement" made war certain, motivated a shift. In his Message of January, 1939, Roosevelt announced that the order of emphasis was reversed: thenceforth the administration would seek no new domestic reforms but would place the achievement of collective security first on its program.

A change in administration policy did occur in the field of economic, as opposed to political, foreign policy. From 1933 to about 1935 the Roosevelt administration was led by the domestic economic crisis to pursue foreign policies of economic nationalism designed to support such measures as the National Industrial Recovery Act and the Agricultural Adjustment Act. These economic foreign policies contradicted and weakened the first efforts at collective security in political foreign relations. Secretary Hull opposed them, but the President assured him they were temporary expedients, and Hull's patience and persistence were rewarded when the President kept his promise, reversed himself, and, between 1934 and 1936, installed the entire Hull program of economic internationalism. Both Hull and Roosevelt never lost sight of the truth that economic internationalism is a necessary and solid foundation for political internationalism and, therefore, world peace.

The new American economic policy led the peaceful nations of the world to liquidate economic rivalries among themselves and form ties of great political and military as well as economic significance in opposition to the Axis nations. In perspective, the Roosevelt administration's internationalist economic policy may be called the taproot of the political and military united front which the peaceful nations organized too late to prevent the Second World War but in time to win it and make their victory a victory for collective security and the United Nations.

Beard, whose most valuable contribution to the understanding of American history was his exploration of the influence of economics on politics, might be expected to admit that a definition of internationalism which neglects economic policy is inadequate. His own writings suggest that certain nationalist economic doctrines [6] influenced his political isolationism and make his elimination of the economic category from his presentation of internationalism the more astonishing.

The policy of internationalism also includes much that lies beyond the economic and political spheres. It involves attitudes of respect towards foreign peoples and cultures and their governments, no matter how weak they may be in material power. It is the opposite of provincialism, chauvinism, and imperialism. One needs only to think of the attitudes and policies of Hitler, whom no one will accuse of being an internationalist, to understand what internationalism is by its opposites. When American isolationists adopted the slogan "America First" as the name of their directing committee, they implied that internationalists do not place the interests of their own country first, which is not true, but isolationists' actual policy and propaganda was "America First and Last—Other Nations and Peoples Nowhere," and this did distinguish them from internationalists.

An internationalist welcomes the diversities and contributions of peoples other than his own group as enrichments of his thinking and living. He is free of those attitudes of inferiority and insecurity which lead an isolationist to struggle to exclude from his thinking and living influences tainted by "foreignness" as threats to his identity. Fear, suspicion, hatred, and contempt of foreign peoples and cultures were remarkably absent among the leaders of the Roosevelt administration and the President set a tone thoroughly internationalist in spirit. By way of contrast, one may recall the contemptuous epithets President Theodore Roosevelt commonly hurled at foreigners, especially those not of "Teutonic" race. Innumerable trivial and important activities of the Franklin D. Roosevelt administration illustrated the spiritual and material values of internationalism in spheres ramified beyond, yet organically related to, internationalist economic and political programs.

While it will be impossible in this book to pursue further these broadest aspects of Rooseveltian internationalism, it will be useful to notice two of its corollaries as amplifications of the meaning of internationalism. The first is that internationalism is incompatible with imperialism. Historical reason exists for the common identification of the two. During the McKinley-Theodore Roosevelt era, United States policy was frankly imperialist, and anti-imperialists were reasonably designated "isolationists" because their argument was that "we should stop meddling in foreign countries and come home and mind our own business." Anti-imperialists came to power with Woodrow Wilson and again with Franklin D. Roosevelt, but they were not content merely to liquidate imperialist positions established by McKinley and Theodore Roosevelt and to retire into isolation. They worked for foreign policies of international cooperation that called for even more "meddling" even farther "away from home" than did imperialism. Their conversion of those imperialist positions which they did not liquidate into supports for policies of international cooperation made the application of correct labels quite difficult. Thus the naval policies of the two Roosevelts seemed identical because they both "loved the Navy," both built "big" navies, and they both used these spectacular instruments with considerable freedom to support their foreign policies. But a surgeon's knife can be used either to cure or to kill. The two Roosevelts used the United States Navy for opposite purposes—the one imperialist and the other internationalist.

When internationalists controlled an administration the imperialists used the arguments of, and were called, isolationists. In short, isolationism is the policy of the "outs" and no administration in this century has actually practiced it. The Harding-Coolidge administrations, caught between the unpopularity of imperialism and the temporary defeat of internationalism, came closest, but with a margin in favor of imperialism, especially of the more cryptic economic varieties.

The public rejection, first of imperialism and then of isolationism, has made the two words semantically poisonous for political use. Those isolationists of the thirties who, unlike pacifists and doctrinaires, were aware of the impossibility of isolation and wished for an imperialist program found it necessary to devise phrases with which they could smuggle their cause into the good graces of unwary internationalists. They spoke of the necessity of the United States assuming its rightful international responsibilities.

In theoretical debate both imperialism and internationalism are opposites of isolation, and this enables the unpopular cause of imperialism to masquerade as internationalism. These two are, in fact, also opposites of each other, and in the practical conduct of the United States government's foreign relations they are the only alternatives. The seemingly objective test of whether an administration retains or acquires territorial positions is useless because such positions may be used, as were the American bases acquired from Britain in 1940, for thoroughly anti-imperialist purposes and to support the policy of internationalism. The best available test of whether an administration is imperialist or internationalist is found in its attitudes towards foreign peoples and their governments, because these attitudes determine whether the use that is made of power wielded outside the national boundaries will be favorable or unfavorable to foreign rights and interests. The Roosevelt administration illustrated the incompatibility of internationalism and imperialism and effectively installed the former as the policy of the United States.

The other corollary of Rooseveltian internationalism is that it placed the administration in the main stream of the American tradition of democratic idealism. This won support for the policy from many at home who were still dubious of political and economic internationalism, as well as devotion from the rank and file of peoples throughout the world. It was one of several respects in which Roosevelt revived creative democratic, as opposed to inert conservative, forces in American civilization.

Inert conservative forces provided the chief strength of isolationism during the Roosevelt era. To these were annexed, on one side, extreme nationalist elements and those sympathetic to the

Axis, and on the other those who raised pacifism to the status of an absolute principle destructive of all other principles of law, order, and self-defense. But these two wings did not include those nationalists who understood that internationalism was the best guaranty of national interest or those pacifists who understood that collective security was the best guaranty of peace, and they were correspondingly weak. The great mass of isolationists was simply conservative, and the main body of isolationist propaganda was designed to fortify the conservative temper. Like most conservative political doctrines, isolationism appealed for loyalty to a past that never existed.

The United States has never been isolated. Throughout its history it has played an active part in international economic, cultural, and political life. The Founding Fathers, whose example the isolationists so ardently and mistakenly invoked, organized in 1778 the French Alliance containing a grand array of economic, political, and military prior commitments and entanglements of decisive value in securing the independence of the United States. This was a permanent alliance. Isolationists of the nineteen-thirties daily libeled President George Washington as the author, in his Farewell Address, of the dictum "no entangling alliances." This was actually Thomas Jefferson's phrase. Washington could not completely repudiate the instrument which had saved his victory as Commander-in-Chief of the Continental Army. In his Farewell Address he wisely condemned *permanent* alliances because the existing government of the French Revolution was using the American Alliance to make the United States a vassal of France in its war against Great Britain. Washington at the same time specifically approved *temporary* alliances for the United States. Jefferson, the chief architect of theoretical isolationism, was also readiest to abandon it when need arose, as when he gave orders to Monroe to make an alliance with Britain if Napoleon persisted in his design to occupy Louisiana and, when Monroe was President, advised acceptance of Canning's 1823 proposal for an Anglo-American entente against the Holy Alliance.

It happened that no full-fledged alliance was ever again signed by the United States after the French Alliance was terminated in 1800. President Monroe and Secretary of State John Quincy Adams formulated the unilateral Monroe Doctrine, contrary to Jefferson's advice, because they understood that Britain would defend the independence of the Western Hemisphere against the Continental powers out of self-interest, without a pledge to the United States, and they wanted to be free to combat British ambitions within the Hemisphere and make annexations of territory against which Canning demanded a pact of mutual self-denial.

But the Clayton-Bulwer Treaty of 1850, providing joint Anglo-American guaranties regarding an isthmian canal, certainly constituted a prior commitment by the United States and not only entangled it in British designs but also entangled Britain in American affairs so deeply that the Taylor administration was accused of signing away the Monroe Doctrine. The Monroe Doctrine was, of course, a prior commitment to support some twenty foreign nations against aggression, but it enjoyed exemption from the rules of isolationism. The United States from time to time made similar commitments regarding territory outside the Western Hemisphere, such as the Hawaiian and Samoan Islands, and these also were ignored in public professions of isolationist purity.

At the turn of the century, commitments to the Open Door in China and Morocco entangled the United States in the power politics of Asia and Europe. The "unwritten alliance" between the United States and Britain after 1896 developed ties stronger, if anything, than those ordinarily created by paper alliances. During the nineteen-twenties, Republican administrations, while claiming credit among isolationists for violating their 1920 campaign pledge to join, if not the League of Nations, "an association of nations," entered into multilateral engagements in the Washington Treaties regarding the Open Door in China, the territorial status of Asia, and the size of the United States Navy. In the Kellogg-Briand Pact the United States made a prior commitment to the powers not to use offensively its highest instrument of national policy: war.

Beyond these and other fixed international political engagements, the United States throughout the course of its history continually and, following the formulations of Jefferson, with entire deliberation, played an active part in support of that *bête noir* of isolationists, the balance of power, first of Europe, then also of Asia, and finally on a world scale. Jefferson preached isolation but practiced involvement. It was only by an extraordinarily skillful manipulation of the weight of the United States in the scales of European power politics that such master diplomatists as Benjamin

Franklin, John Jay, Thomas Jefferson, and John Quincy Adams secured the independence and expanded the territory and power of the United States. They promised friendship for, or threatened enmity against, the shifting sides in the European balance and wrung concessions to the United States in return for promises and threats. No other technique could, in the face of predatory empires, secure the growth of the United States from a weak to a great power. The rivalries of those empires opened the road to American success, but American diplomacy did not wait passively for chances to make gains: it intervened aggressively to widen divisions among them, resorting even to war in 1775, 1798, 1803, 1812, 1846, 1898, and 1917.

In the face of this history of American foreign commitments, diplomacy and wars, isolationists appealed to the authority of the past to consecrate a policy of nonparticipation in international affairs. They failed to understand the value to the United States of its commercial, political, and cultural ties with the world, and their dependence on the continued existence of civilizations abroad with which the United States could maintain such ties. Isolationists ordinarily ignored the very existence of those ties; they were the most embarrassing of all the contradictions of the isolationist image of an arcadian, isolated, American past. Fear of the present and nostalgia for a fantasy of the past were the sources of isolationists' opposition to Rooseveltian internationalism.

Opposition to war was a more praiseworthy sentiment, and it was the chief public argument for isolation in foreign policy during the nineteen-thirties. So the debate revolved around the charge that the United States was more likely to become involved in war if it participated in measures of collective security. Beard has Roosevelt's advocacy of collective security and United States participation in the Second World War as his chief facts in evidence that the isolationists were right. It is the thesis of this book that his fallacy is the ancient one, *post hoc ergo propter hoc,* and that he has maintained it by distorting and excising the record.

# 2.

## *Roosevelt and the "New Neutrality"*

STATESMANSHIP HAS BEEN SAID TO BE THE ART OF RECON-
ciling the ideal and the possible. Franklin D. Roosevelt held
internationalism as an ideal throughout his career. As Assistant
Secretary of the Navy under President Wilson, and then as candidate for Vice President in 1920, he worked to carry out the ideal
by advocating United States entry into the League of Nations.
When that failed, he did not again advocate achievement of the
ideal by United States membership in a world organization until
the fall of France made the American people and their Congress
ready to try forehandedness in preventing war by the method of
collective security.

In the years between 1920 and 1940, Roosevelt did not abandon internationalism as an ideal, but he worked to install it as
the policy of the United States by measures short of joining a
world organization. During the twenties the American people
showed in elections that they were unwilling to join the League,
and Roosevelt himself came to distrust it as a distortion of
Wilson's project. Advocates of collective security held the United
States partly responsible for this distortion because its absence
encouraged use of the League for narrowly nationalist purposes
by the other victorious Allies. In any case, isolationist sentiment
in the Democratic Party became so strong that, in 1932, it was
politically expedient for Roosevelt as a presidential candidate to
reject United States entry into the League, and this he did before
he was nominated.

## A Revolution in International Law

But measures of collective security short of joining the League or making prior commitments or alliances had been installed by Republican administrations in the Washington Treaties, the Kellogg-Briand Pact, and the Stimson Doctrine of nonrecognition of conquests made in violation of treaties, and these measures Roosevelt supported and promised to continue. They amounted to a revolution in international law for the United States by which it abandoned indifference to aggression abroad and adhered to the same code as that prescribed for its members by the League Covenant. The distinction remained that while the League powers were committed to moral, diplomatic, economic and military sanctions against aggression, the United States had committed itself only to the sanctions of moral condemnation of aggression, diplomatic nonrecognition of conquests, and the exceedingly cautious consultation clause of the Nine-Power Treaty of 1922.

Roosevelt, as early as 1928, had proposed abandonment of imperialism in Latin America and tentatively formulated what became his Good Neighbor policy in that area.[1] The Hoover administration in the Clark Memorandum abandoned the Theodore Roosevelt Corollary of the Monroe Doctrine, under which the United States had assumed international police power over Latin America. Thus it cleared the way for Franklin D. Roosevelt's nuclear system of collective security in the Western Hemisphere.

The most important step of the United States government towards collective security before 1933 was the Stimson Doctrine. By it the United States led the world in its first action against an aggression by a first-class power, Japan. It carried into practice the revolution in international law which had occurred since pre-First World War days, when the rule had been general consent by the other powers to conquests by one nation and demands for shares in the spoils as compensation. Even the United States had on occasion played that game. When it took the Philippine Islands for itself, it threw a few other Spanish Pacific islands to Germany to quiet its complaints. Japan was always ready to "compensate" the powers, and particularly the United States, for its own gains in Manchuria and China, but the Stimson Doctrine marked a new era in which an aggressor became a criminal who could not bribe the jury. Its ultimate importance may be gauged by the fact that Beard points to Roosevelt's pre-Inauguration agreement to maintain it as "a fateful step leading in the direction of Pearl Harbor." [2] A supporter of the policy would call it the first of the series of actions which led the United States into the United Nations.

That a Republican administration should abandon imperialism in Latin America and move towards collective security in Asia has puzzled observers and historians. The development of public opinion was basic. The personal pacifism of President Hoover was doubtless influential. The Hoover administration was divided between internationalists led by Stimson, who advocated the new policies as steps towards full cooperation with the League of Nations, and imperialists who wished to checkmate Japan as a trade rival and to sacrifice the small gains of direct intervention in the Caribbean republics for the sake of large gains in Latin American good will and trade.

Roosevelt and Hull, like Stimson, regarded the new policies as minimum steps. But these renovations of foreign policy passed almost unnoticed by the public at large as the depression caused painful absorption in domestic affairs. The Hoover administration, with its gift for boring the public, had failed to dramatize the issues. Roosevelt, after he was elected President and before he was inaugurated, found in the Stimson Doctrine the only area in which he could cooperate with the outgoing administration. He promised Stimson to maintain his policy and confirmed the promise in a public statement.[3] This connection was the only one Roosevelt was willing to establish with the Hoover administration after the bitter election campaign, and it is symbolic of continuity in favor of collective security between the old and new regimes. Roosevelt kept his promise and the Stimson Doctrine became the foundation of his political foreign policy. Appointment of Cordell Hull as Secretary of State indicated that lowered tariff rates would provide an internationalist economic foreign policy more likely to relax political tensions and create a material interest in political internationalism than the extreme nationalist assault on world trade precipitated by Hoover when he signed the Smoot-Hawley Tariff Act.

The Good Neighbor policy of President Roosevelt later became associated exclusively with Latin American policy, but he announced it in his first Inaugural Address as his *world* policy, with overtones of Stimsonism:

In the field of world policy I would dedicate this Nation to the policy of the good neighbor . . . the neighbor who respects his obligations and respects the sanctity of his agreements in and with a world of neighbors.[4]

## A Tragedy of Timing

An immediate test of the new administration's foreign policy occurred in a field prepared by Hoover, one so confused by concealed motives that the new President's retreat from Hoover's position has been interpreted as a retreat from internationalism. Hoover had planned that a bargain should be made with the European powers whereby the United States would extinguish war debts they owed it and they in return should make trade concessions to the United States and disarmament agreements. Internationalists tended to support this program because it promised to solve at one blow three problems that disrupted world pacification.

Cordell Hull believed the United States must reduce its own tariffs as well as obtain concessions from other nations. President Roosevelt turned against the program. He saw it as an expression of Hoover's conception that the American depression was caused by the economic disorders of Europe and could be cured only by relieving the Allied governments of the necessity to pay their debts to the United States government. This would enable those governments to relieve Germany of the necessity to pay reparations to them. It would restore the value of private American investments in Europe, and revive the market for new private American loans to finance European purchases of American surplus goods. But in Roosevelt's view, the Hoover scheme would only postpone the day of reckoning as new loans would service old ones, and recreate the big business technique of prosperity of the twenties, with all its dangers of another crash like that of 1929.[5]

Roosevelt's primary purpose in 1933 was domestic recovery by domestic measures. He believed that the depression was caused by the abuses of big business and could be overcome only by the restoration of American purchasing power as well as American prices. He refused to bargain away the European war debts in the interest of the Hoover formula for recovery. For a time after he came to office he hoped to put into effect immediately the Hull program of lower tariffs, international stabilization of currencies, and disarmament as foundations for world political pacification. Hull planned to make American tariff concessions at the London Economic Conference, which Hoover had called together to extort tariff concessions from other countries. But Roosevelt's domestic measures of recovery forced postponement of the Hull program. Devaluation of the gold content of the dollar was launched to raise domestic prices and at the same time to cheapen American currency to foreign buyers of American surpluses in order to offset higher American prices. The NRA worked to raise wages as well as prices in trade and industry, and the AAA worked to raise farm prices. These programs could not be endangered by premature reductions of American tariffs, which would have flooded the country with foreign goods sent to take advantage of rising American prices, or by premature stabilization of the American dollar, which would have held its price high to foreign buyers of American surpluses.

The London Economic Conference was a tragedy of timing. It came too late for the Hoover big business program of international economic cooperation and too soon for Roosevelt to risk the New Deal program of domestic recovery for the sake of Cordell Hull's program of liberal international economic cooperation. The President's Bombshell Message destroyed the Conference in July, 1933. It was a year and more before domestic recovery justified launching the Hull program. That it was launched then and was accepted by most of the countries of the world suggests that the Roosevelt administration liquidated its responsibility for the failure of the London Conference, and that the refusal of the Axis nations to join in the Hull program was their own responsibility.

## Collective Security: The First Attempt

Before Roosevelt's temporary policy of economic nationalism had been imposed by the New Deal measures of recovery, he had made his first attempt to achieve collective security and had been frustrated by the United States Senate. The occasion was the Geneva Disarmament Conference. United States entry into inter-

national agreements to limit armaments was considered a respect-
able sort of international commitment which did not compromise
isolation. But France, at Geneva, refused to disarm in the face of
Germany without prior guaranties against German aggression.
The disarmament program desired by the United States was
countered by a French demand that the United States join a pact
for collective security outside the League and for the particular
benefit of France.

The Hoover administration was willing to promise participation in economic sanctions if the United States found in any
particular case that aggression had occurred. On January 10, 1933,
President Hoover asked Congress for legislation to empower the
President to designate aggressor nations and embargo arms shipments to them, while making arms available to their victims and
to powers joining in sanctions. A day after the Hoover message,
President-elect Roosevelt publicly approved it. On April 17, a
resolution in conformity with Hoover's request passed the House
of Representatives.

France wanted a prior commitment by the United States that
the power granted in such a resolution, if it passed the Senate,
would be used when aggression occurred. The seizure of power
in Germany by Hitler made action more urgent than ever if the
United States was to join in a system of collective security. It also
increased isolationists' fear of involvement in a war that was "none
of our business," as the result of a prior commitment which would
abandon the right of the United States to decide on its course in
a particular case when it arose. Roosevelt solved the dilemma
in April by offering the powers, in return for a disarmament agreement, a consultative pact. In it the United States would promise
to confer with signatories when one of them claimed that an
aggression had occurred, but it would leave the United States
free to decide for itself whether aggression was a fact justifying
the application of economic sanctions. The Congressional resolution for a discriminatory arms embargo, plus such a consultative
pact, would build a special annex of the League of Nations for
the United States in which it could cooperate for collective security without prior commitment or loss of sovereignty.

In February, Roosevelt had publicly promised that he opposed
United States entry into the League and entanglement in the
power politics of Europe. Beard calls this a repudiation of his

January endorsement of Hoover's message to Congress asking for a discriminatory arms embargo. He calls the President's explanations in April of the difference between a consultative pact and entry into the League or an entangling alliance further assurance that he would not support "any kind of internationalism for enforcing collective security." Certainly a consultative pact was a most significant "kind of internationalism" which might have saved the Geneva Disarmament Conference and frustrated Hitler.

Beard entirely distorts the most dramatic and significant incident of this first testing of the issues. Hitler had not yet consolidated his power or rearmed Germany sufficiently to risk a strong policy in the face of united opposition by the powers, especially if the projected annex of the League brought the United States into the balance against him. His claim that he wished to arm only in order to achieve equality of arms with the other powers was being met at Geneva by the program to *disarm* all the powers to the German level. Cornered, Hitler called a meeting of the Reichstag to hear a statement of policy. It was feared that he would withdraw from the Geneva Conference. But President Roosevelt dropped the domestic emergency on May 16, the day before the Reichstag met, and sent an "Appeal to the Nations" to the heads of all foreign governments. He proposed "complete elimination of all offensive weapons" and warned that no nation should take responsibility for failure of the Conference.[6]

Beard points out that the British, French, and American delegates at Geneva had feared disruption of the Conference by Hitler and that only a firm declaration by Roosevelt could have checked him. But Beard does not mention the extraordinary result of the President's Appeal, which was precisely what had been hoped for: Hitler's speech to the Reichstag the next day was conciliatory and did not disrupt the Conference. Beard states that internationalists who had hoped the President would make a pledge of participation in collective guaranties were "disappointed" by the Appeal.[7]

Obviously, the President could make no definitive promises to the powers of American participation in collective guaranties until the Senate acted favorably on the discriminatory arms embargo. Equally obviously, his Appeal nevertheless acquired force from the movement towards American participation in collective guaranties, as evidenced in April by favorable House action and by the President's offer to join a consultative pact. And Beard's suppression of Hitler's conciliatory response suggests that he does not wish to admit that the President's policy could have helped the peaceful powers to frustrate Hitler and demonstrated that his policy was, in fact, designed not to place the United States on "the road to war" but to safeguard peace for the United States.

Beard's suppression of the record continues. He does not mention that on the day the Reichstag met, Secretary Hull sent his second strong message to the Senate Committee on Foreign Relations urging favorable action on the discriminatory arms embargo.[8] Thus by distortions and excisions of the facts, Beard projects his image of a President who had "repudiated" his approval of Hoover's January 10 message to Congress and who led the public to believe that he did not support internationalism.

It was not Roosevelt but the Senate Committee on Foreign Relations that prevented the United States from joining a system of collective security in 1933. Senators were evidently frightened by Roosevelt's Appeal as much as, or more than Hitler had been. They did not allow their fears of "loss of sovereignty" and "involvement in European power politics" to be allayed by the Roosevelt plan to commit the United States to no more than consultation while retaining full freedom of action whenever aggression occurred. The Senate Committee on Foreign Relations, which reported the measure to the Senate on May 27, amended the House resolution to take away the President's authority to discriminate between the victim and an aggressor, and substituted a requirement that the President might lay an embargo only against all parties to a dispute.

This was the "new neutrality." It abdicated the rights of a neutral for which the United States had three times waged war, against France in 1798, Britain in 1812, Germany in 1917. It served notice to the world that the United States would penalize the victims of aggressions as well as their attackers. Such a law would make impossible United States cooperation in economic sanctions against aggression and, therefore, make useless a consultative pact. Rather than risk its passage, the administration dropped the issue and the resolution was not voted on. Norman Davis, the United States delegate at Geneva, withdrew the United States offer to enter a consultative pact. The opportunity to satisfy French fears for the security of the German frontier, to face Hitler while he was still weak with a united front of the peaceful powers, and to achieve universal disarmament was lost.

Beard dismisses the question whether the Roosevelt program might have made the Disarmament Conference a success as a purely speculative matter. But it is not speculative that Hitler's unexpected moderation on May 17, 1933, did follow Roosevelt's Appeal of May 16, or that Germany did leave the Conference after the United States Senate broke the united front of the peaceful powers. Evading these facts, Beard adduces none to support his innuendo that even if the United States had joined a program of collective action, other nations, particularly Great Britain, would have defeated it.[9]

If one new element was likely to change all other elements in the world situation in the nineteen-thirties, it was the adherence of the United States to the policy of collective security. The moral authority and military potential of the United States were such that it could radically alter the policies of all the powers. More specific adumbrations of the effects of this greatest "if" of modern history serve no useful purpose, but it seems unduly perverse to suggest that United States adherence to collective security would have *weakened* efforts of other nations to prevent aggression. And it is quite impossible to disprove the contention of Prime Minister Neville Chamberlain that one influence leading him to abandon collective security and turn to appeasement of the dictators was the failure of the United States to help organize a united front. In January, 1938, the British Prime Minister wrote privately to a relative in the United States:

U.S.A. and U.K. in combination represent a force so overwhelming that the mere hint of the possibility of its use is sufficient to make the most powerful of dictators pause, and that is why I believe that co-operation between our two countries is the greatest instrument in the world for the preservation of peace. . . . Therefore our people see that in the absence of any powerful ally, and until our armaments are completed, we must adjust our foreign policy to our circumstances, and even bear with patience and good humor actions which we should like to treat in very different fashion.[10]

Still, the questions may fairly be asked why Roosevelt allowed the action of the Senate Committee on Foreign Relations to go unchallenged, why he did not bring his enormous influence during the "honeymoon" of his administration to bear on the Senate, or beyond the Senate on the public at large, to secure restoration of the original House resolution and its passage by the Senate. First, it must be noticed that by refusing to challenge the Senate he at least avoided risk that the Senate might pass the nondiscriminatory arms embargo two years before it actually did pass, and that it was precisely such a challenge that resulted in its passage in 1935.

Roosevelt did not fully commit his influence to the achievement of collective security as his primary goal until January, 1939. In 1933, all goals in the field of foreign affairs were subordinated to the drive for domestic reform. This was a political decision on the highest level and depends for a judgment as to its wisdom on views regarding the relative importance of domestic reform and collective security to the welfare of the American people and nation at that moment. The ideal of achieving both at the same time was regarded by administration leaders as politically impossible: too much emphasis on international goals would have risked defeat of the administration in both areas. Cordell Hull has defined these political quantities expertly in his *Memoirs:*

Our policy of international cooperation faced almost overwhelming isolationist opposition during the years 1933–1941. It is due to say that those Americans who believed in isolation were well-meaning, patriotic citizens and thought they were pursuing this country's more or less traditional policies. This attitude of good faith by most of the isolationists made it all the more difficult to prevail on them to take note of external danger, however imminent and inevitable it might be. They failed to realize that a policy of isolation would make us as lonely in the family of nations as a martin on a fodder pole.

Hence, while advocating international cooperation at all times, we were faced with the extremely delicate task of being careful not to present and urge measures in such numbers as to alarm the people and precipitate isolation as an acute political issue in the nation. Had we done so, the Roosevelt Administration would have been thrown out of power bodily as soon as the American public had a chance to go to the polls, and the nation would have been thrown back still farther to the extreme isolationist period following the Senate's rejection of Wilson's League of Nations.

Our only alternative, therefore, was constantly to urge upon the country a general policy of international cooperation in every way we could, and from time to time present for Congressional approval such proposals as an arms embargo applied against an aggressor, peace through disarmament, American participation in the World Court and in the International Labor Organization, the Trade Agreements policy, and more flexible Neutrality legislation. These on their very face contravened nationalistic policies.

This was the only course under which we could hope to convince Americans that the United States was an integral part of world cooperation. Wherever the matter before Congress seemed about to become a serious national isolation issue, we did not press it to the point of a national campaign.[11]

Probably the most far-reaching advantage of the administration's compromise between the ideal and the possible was the opportunity it gave to use the highest offices of the national government as rostrums from which to conduct, with a minimum of controversy, the education of the American people in fundamental internationalist principles of foreign affairs. Cordell Hull was the dean of this corps of teachers and, like many good teachers, he was rather repetitious. The public preferred the flashier lectures of the President, which were never dull. But isolationists probably learned more and were more often converted by Hull's patient and sober repetitions. He used each new stage in the degeneration of world security to demonstrate the errors of isolationists and drill Americans in the hypotheses of internationalism until, after many failures, the first results of majority conviction and Congressional agreement were registered in November, 1939.

### Another Attempt

The Chaco War between Bolivia and Paraguay provided in 1934 the next testing ground of the administration's policy. Formerly the United States had not favored participation of non-American governments in efforts to stop a war between two American nations. The Roosevelt administration could choose to support any of three separate agencies attempting to end the Chaco War: a League of Nations Commission, mediation by Uruguay, and a subcommittee of the Montevideo Inter-American Conference. Hull and Roosevelt took the position that chief support should go to the League Commission as a means of bolstering the authority of the world organization. In May, 1934, the League Council recommended an arms embargo against both

Bolivia and Paraguay. Hull urged Congress to authorize such an embargo. Congress promptly complied.

Thus the administration used a situation which did not require challenge of isolationist faith in the principle of nondiscrimination between aggressors and victims to establish a precedent of United States cooperation with the League of Nations. The United States became a member of the Neutral Supervisory Commission set up by the League to supervise its plan of settlement of the war. Paraguay refused to cooperate and withdrew from the League, which therefore recommended that the arms embargo be lifted for Bolivia but retained against Paraguay. The Roosevelt administration did not attempt to secure discriminatory authority from Congress. The efforts of the League were allowed to lapse. The United States joined five American neutrals and by mediation ended the war in June, 1935.[12]

The willingness of the administration to work with the League to end a war in the hemisphere formerly treated as the exclusive preserve of the United States had been clearly demonstrated. Beard suppresses this significant evidence of policy and gives the false impression that the President had no sympathy for the League's efforts to stop the Chaco War.[13]

## The "New Neutrality" Triumphant

The Italian attack on Abyssinia in 1935, the first major aggression by a European power since the First World War, forced a conclusion of the issue between the administration and Congress. Although Roosevelt and Hull had carefully avoided making isolation a national political issue, isolationists did so and won the struggle for public opinion. Their chief forum was the Nye Munitions Investigation. The administration was caught off guard when isolationist Democrats, Vice President Garner and Chairman Key Pittman of the Senate Foreign Relations Committee, contrary to custom, appointed a Republican minority Senator, Gerald P. Nye of North Dakota, an extreme isolationist, chairman of a committee to investigate the truth of reports that American armaments manufacturers fomented wars to create markets for their goods. The administration favored the ostensible purposes of the investigation and hoped for legislation to establish government supervision of the armaments trade as a foundation for entry into international agreement to regulate it.

But the Nye Committee distorted its mission and set out to prove that American bankers and munitions makers were solely responsible for United States entry into the First World War, and to preach that if the sale of munitions and extension of loans to belligerents could be prevented, the United States would be safe from involvement in another war. The Nye Committee was very successful in fixing its oversimplified premise and dangerous conclusion in the public mind. Furthermore it injured relations between this country and Britain and France, to the edification of Mussolini and Hitler, as it violated the chairman's pledge to avoid publicity for documents the State Department made available to it which the United States government was obligated to Britain and France to keep in confidence. As usual in isolationist propaganda, ancient sins of Britain and France were exhumed and exhibited to stir up animosity against them at a time when their policies were chiefly in danger of becoming too enfeebled even for vice. In a period when Japan, Italy and Germany had clearly become the only threats to the security of the United States, the American public was encouraged to wallow in atavistic nightmares that the Redcoats were coming.

While the Nye Committee by these methods waged its winning battle for public opinion, Mussolini prepared to attack Abyssinia. Hull conducted extensive studies of possible neutrality legislation and came to the conclusion that any enactment would be a mistake. He found authority for the newest doctrines of international law derived from the League Covenant and the Kellogg-Briand Pact in the teaching of the seventeenth century Dutch jurist, Hugo Grotius, called the Father of International Law, who laid down the principle that a neutral was obligated "to do nothing whereby he who supports a wicked cause may be rendered more powerful, or whereby the movements of him who wages a just war may be hampered."

Hull identified "a wicked cause" with aggression. He believed that strict neutrality could not be reconciled with the existence of the League of Nations. The United States, as a neutral, was neither obligated to, nor in self-interest should it, treat aggressors and their victims alike. The worst mistake would be to serve notice beforehand that it would nevertheless do so. Hull neither wanted the United States under outmoded conceptions of international law to hand the same-sized stick to aggressors and victims nor did he want it, under isolationists' conceptions of neutrality, to refuse to hand a stick to either victims or aggressors. He wanted to bring the United States abreast of the new, moral conception of international law—that victims had superior rights over aggressors. Since it was politically impossible to make a prior commitment to this effect, Hull wished to avoid any commitment at all, in hopes that the possibility of United States aid to victims would restrain aggressors and that, even if it did not, public opinion and Congress would be sufficiently aroused by an actual armed attack to support the administration in a policy of aid to the victim and embargo of the aggressor.

As the Italian designs on Abyssinia became plain early in 1935, the administration worked to prevent the Nye Committee from taking jurisdiction over neutrality legislation and to secure the cooperation of Senator Pittman and the Foreign Relations Committee to avoid legislation. But isolationist sentiment in the Foreign Relations Committee was so strong that legislation was inevitable, and the administration was forced to work for an arms embargo which would grant to the President discretion both as to whether it should be invoked at all and as to which party or parties to a dispute should be embargoed. At the end of July a bill prepared by the State Department was approved by Roosevelt and sent to the Senate Committee on Foreign Relations. It included provisions calculated to prevent incidents and pressure which might involve the United States in war. It gave the President discretionary power to prohibit the use of American vessels to carry arms and munitions to belligerents, to place an embargo on loans to belligerents, and to withdraw government protection from Americans traveling on belligerent vessels. But on August 7 a subcommittee of the Senate body, set up to work with the State Department, refused to approve the bill.

Passage of the bill was essential if the United States was to take part in or influence the efforts of the powers to prevent war. Britain and France worked through the League for mediation, and threatened sanctions against Italy if it refused. Emperor Haile Selassie asked the United States to invoke the Kellogg Pact and secure Mussolini's observance of Italy's obligation as a signatory of that pact not to resort to war. Hull preferred that no step should be taken that might interfere with the League attempts to settle the dispute. League efforts failed, and Britain and France alone attempted to talk Mussolini into observance of a treaty of 1906, in which all three countries had agreed to respect the independence of Abyssinia.

Hull asked Britain and France whether action by the United States on the basis of the Kellogg Pact would be helpful. They answered that it might reinforce their efforts. The President decided to send a personal message to Mussolini. On August 18 an exhortation to refrain from war was delivered to the dictator. Mussolini answered that it was too late to escape war because Italy had mobilized. He threatened that interference with his plans would lead to extension of the conflict.

This threat was cleverly designed to support the isolationist argument that collective security was the road to war. It covered up the fact that the rickety Italian war machine was dependent on oil from the League powers and the United States. Hull decided that Mussolini's threat should be met by a counterthreat of United States participation in economic sanctions against Italy. He prepared for the President a letter to Pittman urging authorization of a discretionary arms embargo. Hull wanted the letter made public for its full effect on Mussolini. Roosevelt signed the letter. But Pittman, always feeble in his support of the administration and likely to crumple in a crisis, warned Roosevelt that he would not sponsor a discretionary arms embargo, and the letter was never sent.

Thus the administration avoided a political struggle it seemed certain to lose, and the most promising effort to join in collective security measures against the first of the new series of aggressions broke on the rock of Senate isolationism. Pittman introduced in the Senate on August 20 a neutrality resolution that included a mandatory arms embargo against aggressors and victims alike. Hull in a press conference on August 22 warned against the dangers of such a policy, but he and the President had already consented to a compromise which limited the embargo clause to six months.

The Pittman Resolution passed both houses quickly and was signed by the President on August 31, 1935. When he signed it Roosevelt issued a statement urging that the mandatory arms

embargo be changed later to allow flexibility in meeting unfore-
seeable situations. Hull had prepared a mild version of the statement which the President strengthened most significantly by
adding the essence of the internationalist argument—that the inflexible embargo might have the opposite effect from that intended: "In other words, the inflexible provisions might drag us
into war instead of keeping us out." This was the strongest statement in favor of collective security the President made until the
Quarantine Address of October, 1937.

It disproves Beard's thesis that the President did not publicly
support that policy. Beard's handling of the incident makes Roosevelt seem dishonest:

He commented adversely on the inflexible provisions of that measure;
but he informed the public that "The policy of the Government is
definitely committed to the maintenance of peace and the avoidance
of any entanglements which would lead us into conflict." [14]

The "but" implies that the President contradicted himself. Beard
draws out of the President's statement his own doctrine that collective security meant war, as if the President meant to conceal
this from the public.[15]

### The Oil Embargo

The President's faith in collective security was not vitiated by
his signature of the Neutrality Act of August, 1935. Several aspects of the law provided compensation for the mandatory arms
embargo. The six-months clause restricted its application to the
Italo-Abyssinian War, and a mandatory arms embargo harmed
Italy, which had ships and money to obtain arms from the United
States, more than it did Abyssinia, which had neither. And isolationists' naive notion that arms and money were the only source
of United States interest in the Allied cause in the First World
War made them neglect to impose an embargo on raw materials
such as oil. This left the administration an opportunity to impose
a "moral embargo" on the commodity Mussolini needed most.

The League in September prepared to impose sanctions against
Italy. In his fear that isolationists would oppose United States
action parallel with or following after League action, Secretary

Hull sought ways for the United States to act prior to the League. This strategy resulted in the United States doing more than the League powers to dry up Mussolini's sources of oil. The Presidential proclamation imposing the arms embargo on Italy and Abyssinia on October 5 went beyond the letter of the Neutrality Act to warn that sales of American goods other than arms and munitions to belligerents, while legal, would not enjoy the ordinary diplomatic protection of the government but would be at the sellers' own risk. Also, Roosevelt overruled Hull in order to use the discretion the Act gave him to withdraw protection from Americans traveling on belligerent vessels, even though only Italy owned passenger vessels and Abyssinia had no navy to make travel on them dangerous. He did this precisely because such travel aided Italy.

The President's warning against exports did not prevent an increase in sales to Italy. Therefore the administration made two strong appeals to the public to impose a moral embargo. The second of these, by Hull on November 15, specifically named oil as included in the moral embargo. Three days later, the League's sanction list was published, but oil was not on it. The proposed Hoare-Laval Pact of December revealed the impulse to appeasement in British and French policy and suggested that the League sanction list was designed to prevent decisive injury to Mussolini.

Hull contemplated asking for legislation to enforce the American embargo on oil and other commodities, but the policies of Britain and France discouraged him. Those powers blamed the United States for their own failure to make their sanctions effective. But the Roosevelt administration seemed to have gone as far as American public opinion would allow, certainly as far as Congress would permit, while the outcry in Britain and France against the Hoare-Laval Pact showed that their governments were willing to violate the sentiments of their own people in order to conciliate Mussolini. The Soviet government imposed nothing comparable to the United States moral embargo on oil against Italy, but sold it freely.

British, French, and Soviet policies strengthened the position of American isolationists and weakened the foreign policy of the Roosevelt administration. Neville Chamberlain, Chancellor of the Exchequer in Baldwin's government, noted in his diary on November 29:

U.S.A. has already gone a good deal further than usual. . . . I replied that if anyone else would give the lead, well and good, but in the last resort, if necessary, we ought to give the lead ourselves rather than let the question [of an oil embargo] go by default. . . . If we backed out now because of Mussolini's threats, we should leave the Americans in the air, and they would be unable to resist the arguments of their oil producers. . . . It was inevitable that in such circumstances U.S.A. should decline in future to help us in any way. . . .[16]

The Baldwin government not only "backed out" of an oil embargo but allowed Sir Samuel Hoare to negotiate with Laval and Mussolini a pact which betrayed the United States as well as the League of Nations. Still Chamberlain's prediction that the United States would in such case decline further help to the peaceful powers of Europe was not borne out. Anthony Eden, a supporter of the League and sanctions, and an opponent of appeasement of the dictators, displaced Hoare as British Foreign Minister on December 22 as a result of public revulsion against Hoare's policy, and the American administration could take hope from this development that it would not be "left in the air" if it strengthened its stand against Mussolini.

Roosevelt and Hull therefore worked to secure from the next session of Congress authorization for an embargo on oil and other raw materials. Their plans were carefully designed to win the essential point while conceding all others to isolationists. Senator Pittman was persuaded to sponsor a bill prepared by the State Department to succeed the embargo section of the Neutrality Act when it expired in February, 1936. This bill made no change in the mandatory arms embargo against all belligerents, but it added to that feature of the Neutrality Act new authority for the President to forbid exports to belligerents of essential war materials, such as oil, beyond normal peacetime amounts. It did not give the President authority to forbid such exports only to the aggressor, thus conceding to isolationists their demand that aggressors and victims be treated alike. But it did give the President discretion as to when the restrictions should be invoked and also as to what materials should be placed on the restricted list. These two powers provided such flexibility that the President could, even while he treated aggressor and victim alike, produce maximum injury to the aggressor and minimum injury to the victim. Most particularly, it would permit him to injure Mussolini's war machine by preventing abnormal shipments of oil from the United States; the same restriction would not affect Abyssinian power to resist because that unhappy country had more oil than its ill-equipped army could use. Furthermore, the discretion as to time would permit the administration to relate its action to action by the other peaceful powers for maximum effect.

The bill was introduced as a party measure in both Houses on January 3, 1936, the day President Roosevelt delivered his Annual Message to Congress. The great significance of the Message was that the President now for the first time used this most influential of all occasions to urge a step towards the policy of collective security. His theme was that the chief concern of democratic peoples was "to prevent the continuance or the rise of autocratic institutions that beget slavery at home and aggression abroad." He placed main emphasis on domestic reform as the means of frustrating autocratic institutions in the United States. But he pointed out that, although he had devoted only one paragraph to foreign affairs in his 1933 inaugural address, were he to deliver a similar address now he would be compelled to devote the greater part of it to world affairs. He made a strong plea for an awakening by Americans to the mounting dangers of war and urged enactment of the administration bill.[17]

The administration was now publicly committed to a policy of ending oil shipments to Mussolini's war machine. But the League powers seemed no closer to taking that step. American pacifists and peace organizations, who had formerly supported the League and cooperation with it by the United States, were disillusioned by such incidents as the Hoare-Laval Pact and turned to isolationism as the best means of safeguarding American peace. Administration concessions to isolationists in the Senate brought no important concession in return. Attack was concentrated against the administration request for embargo of abnormal oil shipments.

The bill was never reported to the Senate by the Foreign Relations Committee. Instead, the existing Act was extended to May 1, 1937, with amendments which imposed new handicaps on the administration. The President was required to extend the arms embargo to any additional states that became involved in a war. This meant that Mussolini was encouraged and the League powers were handicapped by realization that if Italy retaliated against sanctions, United States munitions would not be available to the League powers. Any American Republic at war with a non-American power was exempted from the Act, provided the American Republic did not itself cooperate with an outside nation. This created the possibility that the United States would furnish arms to an American Republic found guilty of aggression by the League, and it destroyed Hull's principle that no conception based on the Monroe Doctrine should interfere with opposition to aggression everywhere and cooperation with the League in every part of the world. One concession to the administration was made in the new Act. The President was not required to invoke the Act "upon the outbreak or during the progress of war," as formerly, but instead "whenever the President shall find that there exists a state of war." This seemed to expand his discretion.

The President signed the new Act on February 29, 1936. He renewed the arms embargo and at the same time the moral embargo against shipments of oil and other materials to Italy and Abyssinia. The moral embargo was at best only partially effective. Yet it placed the United States in the forefront of the nations imposing sanctions against Italy because they made no attempt whatever to limit shipments of oil. The result was that the United States was not only "left in the air," as Chamberlain had feared, but League sanctions permitted Mussolini to inflame Italian sentiment without actually injuring his power to conquer Abyssinia.

The United States thus turned out to be the nation foremost in its action to prevent the aggression of Italy. The policy of the administration which carried the United States that far and attempted to carry it even farther was conducted entirely in public. These facts are entirely suppressed by Beard. His only remark on administration policy during this period of the Abyssinian War, the moral embargo, and the fight to liberalize the Neutrality Act which is not limited to Roosevelt's pledges to avoid entanglements abroad and involvement in war, refers to a private letter of the President to Bishop G. Ashton Oldham of Albany. The President described his policy of taking positive steps towards international cooperation while observing the restrictions placed on his power by isolationists. This letter Beard cites as a private admission by Roosevelt that his actual policy differed from his public policy, that the policy of international cooperation and the policy of peace were irreconcilable, that he played a "dual role—of attempting to smother fires and of keeping out of war." [18]

The President's actual policy was not only fully public but he publicly presented it as the only one which added up to a sound *single* role: attempting to smother fires *in order to* keep out of war. The chapter in which Beard passes over the remarkable events whereby Roosevelt carried the United States to the forefront of the nations opposing Mussolini's aggression is entitled: "Hewing to the Isolationist Line."

The Chautauqua Address of August 14, 1936, is a chief exhibit of Beard and others who accuse the President of deceptively assuring the public that his policy was nonentanglement and peace. It was his leading address on foreign affairs during his campaign for re-election and he undoubtedly intended to appeal to isolationists for confidence in his intentions and for votes. Yet a reading of the whole speech, rather than the excerpts usually offered, and a recollection of the actual steps towards international cooperation then at issue between the administration and isolationists, make clear that Roosevelt did not dissemble his support of the ideal of internationalism or his support of collective security, and he certainly did not propose isolation as the best means to secure peace for the United States. After stating: "We shun political commitments which might entangle us in foreign wars; we avoid connection with the political activities of the League of Nations; . . ." he made clear that this did not provide the safety from war that isolationists believed it would:

We are not isolationists except in so far as we seek to isolate ourselves completely from war. Yet we must remember that so long as war exists on earth there will be some danger that even the Nation which most ardently desires peace may be drawn into war.

Then he gave the description of the horrors of war, beginning with "I have seen war" and ending, "I hate war," which was to be frequently quoted out of context against him to imply that he spoke as a pacifist and isolationist. But he went on to explain that his position regarding the chief point at issue between internationalists and isolationists, the Neutrality Act, was in support of the former:

. . . we must remember that no laws can be provided to cover every contingency, for it is impossible to imagine how every future event may shape itself. In spite of every possible forethought, international relations involve of necessity a vast uncharted area. In that area safe sailing will depend on the knowledge and the experience and the wisdom of those who direct our foreign policy. Peace will depend on their day-to-day decisions.

The chief purpose of the Chautauqua speech was to convince advocates of peace that the President stood with them and that they would therefore do well to vote for him. His emphasis on peace as the object of his policy was not only natural in making such an appeal but it also legitimately sought to restore to internationalists the credit they felt rightly theirs as the owners of the correct prescription for peace: "Keep the United States out of war by keeping war out of the world." [19]

## Non-Nonintervention in Spain

The greatest concession Roosevelt ever made to isolationism came during the campaign of 1936. On July 17, Franco, supported by Mussolini and Hitler, revolted against the Republican government of Spain, with which the United States had treaty relations. The Neutrality Act applied only to international war and left the Roosevelt administration legally free to follow standard procedure under international law, including maintenance of the right of the Republic to buy arms in the United States. This right was specifically confirmed in the 1902 Spanish-United States Treaty of Friendship.

But in violation of this treaty with Spain, contrary to both the old and the new rules of international law and the historic precedent of the American Civil War, reversing its policy towards all other instances of aggression, and going beyond the requirements of the Neutrality Act, the Roosevelt administration adopted the policy of denying arms to both sides in the Spanish Civil War. It did not give way to isolationist pressure in this case but deliberately initiated the policy. Lacking legal authority before Congress convened, the administration on August 11 placed a moral embargo on the export of arms and munitions to both sides in Spain. Hull based it on the "well-established policy of noninterference in internal affairs in other countries, either in time of peace or in the event of civil strife. . . ." [20] But this term "noninterference," like the "nonintervention" of the international committee established in London, was stretched to cover the policy of denying arms to the recognized government suppressing internal revolt, and this expansion of its meaning was not at all "well-established" in precedents of the United States or any other government. On the contrary, noninterference ordinarily meant the *denial* of arms to an unrecognized rebel and the *granting* of arms to the recognized government.

This was the meaning of the term which the Roosevelt administration supported in the Latin American sphere. To aid a revolt against a legitimate government is the obvious and worst sort of interference in the internal affairs of another nation, and avoidance of such interference therefore required chief emphasis on measures which would not disturb the normal advantage of a legitimate government and normal disadvantage of a rebel. It was with considerable point that opponents called Hull's policy "non-noninterference." It aided Franco. Seventy-five per cent of his oil came from the United States.[21] Hull in his *Memoirs* writes approvingly of a declaration by Pittman that noninterference did not help Franco,[22] but he also states that the Republican Loyalists wanted the embargo lifted while the Rebels wanted it retained,[23] which is probably a better indication of its effect.

In December several American exporters applied for licenses required by the Munitions Control Board to sell airplanes to the Spanish Republic. They could not be legally denied, but the President asked Congress to extend the arms embargo of the Neutrality Act to Spain. Within a day Congress passed the administration's resolution with only one dissenting vote. The President signed it on January 8, 1937, and all export licenses for war materials were revoked. One load of planes had got away the day before, but Franco captured the vessel. Public opposition to the embargo against both sides in Spain grew strong during the following years as the relation of the Spanish conflict to the rise of Axis power became clear. But the administration never publicly wavered in its support of the embargo.

Years later both Roosevelt and Hull felt called upon to justify for history their policy towards the Spanish Civil War. The President in 1941 wrote that the people and Congress in 1937 were not prepared to risk involvement in a quarrel which might develop into a general European war.[24] This was doubtless true, although it was less true before all chance of the Republic defeating Franco was gone and, in any case, the President in no other instance allowed isolationists' views to lead him into advocacy of an embargo on aggressor and victim alike. The President also argued in 1941 that Franco had control over more shipping than the Republic and therefore would probably have received greater amounts of arms and munitions from the United States than the Republic.[25] This is beside the point because it assumes a lifting of the embargo for both sides. Roosevelt's own policy in all other situations was to embargo the aggressor while allowing exports to the victim; this was the demand of an increasing number of Americans, and it was the policy of Mexico and the Soviet Union.

Franco and his allies, Hitler and Mussolini, loosed an undeclared submarine war against shipping to the Republic, but the Nyon Conference of September, 1937, promptly stopped it. This Conference was remarkable as a demonstration of the efficacy of collective action. Britain, France, and Russia participated. Their energetic decisions to establish joint patrols of the Mediterranean and to reserve "the possibility of taking further collective measures" were the only instance, during the whole period, of uncompromising pursuit of peace through collective security. It brought such immediate results that a world conditioned to believe in appeasement of the dictators as the only road to peace was thoroughly bewildered. Winston Churchill drew this conclusion from the Nyon incident:

It is the fact that whereas "appeasement" in all its forms only encouraged their aggression and gave the Dictators more power with their own peoples, any sign of a positive counter-offensive by the Western Democracies immediately produced an abatement of tension.[26]

His term "Western Democracies" is, however, peculiar, in view of Russia's presence at Nyon and the absence of the United States.

Churchill, while in opposition to the Chamberlain government, approved not only the Nyon Conference but also the Chamberlain "nonintervention" policy towards Spain. He based his "neutrality" on dislike of the "Communist pestilence," declaring that this "sect" had "seized power" over the Republic.[27] This is an oversimplification: the government of the Republic was actually based on a coalition in the Parliament of all liberal and radical parties and no Communist held Cabinet office. This government was comparable to other Popular Front governments, including Premier Blum's in France. It was the tactic of Franco and all fascists to identify any liberal or radical movement with Communism, and the cause of democracy, peace, and collective security suffered whenever this tactic was successful. The value of Churchill's explanation of his Spanish policy lies in its frankness.

Secretary Hull in his *Memoirs* argues in favor of "noninterference" in Spain chiefly on the grounds that Britain and France had taken the lead in establishing the policy, that it was supported by even such advocates of collective security as Eden, Churchill, and Blum, and that it did prevent the war from spreading into a general conflict.[28] This is perhaps less revealing than Churchill's admission that anti-Communism inspired his support of nonintervention in Spain and his conviction that not that policy but the Nyon Conference prevented the war from spreading. Furthermore, the supremacy of neutrality and appeasement in the governments of Britain and France did not in any other situation lead the Roosevelt administration to initiate "new neutrality" as the policy of the United States.

As sentiment in favor of the Republic increased in the United States, President Roosevelt considered changing administration policy. When the Basque shrine city of Guernica was bombed by Italian and German planes in a boldly publicized practice demonstration of civilian terrorization and slaughter, the President contemplated extending the arms embargo to Germany and Italy, and made the significant comment to Hull: "I am thinking about precedents and the future. It has been our contention that war exists if the government armed forces of any nation upon the territory of another nation are engaged in fighting." He added that he did not think the United States could "compound a ridiculous situation" in which Britain and France continued to assert solemnly that they had "no proof" of Italian or German participation.[29] But Hull obtained from Eden a statement that war could not be considered to exist between Spain and Germany and Italy so long as the latter two governments continued to participate in the Nonintervention Committee in London.[30]

This offered Hitler and Mussolini rewards for the cynical lies

of their agents on the Committee and explains their motive in
joining it. It guaranteed that they could with impunity intervene
in Spain and assure the victory of Franco. From Mussolini, Hull
received a threat that if the United States embargoed Italy it
might force him and Hitler to "spread the conflict beyond the
Spanish frontier." [31] The hollowness of this bluff was exposed by
the Nyon Conference, but Hull accepted it and used it to dissuade the President.

Hull in his *Memoirs* makes the curious point that the United
States might view Italian and German aid to Franco in the light
of their recognition of the Rebels as the government of Spain.[32]
He does not mention that United States aid to the Republic,
merely selling arms to it, and falling far short of the gifts by Hitler
and Mussolini of arms and troops to Franco, might even more
justifiably be viewed in the light of United States recognition,
long before the war began, of the Republic as the government of
Spain. He was willing to concede to the dictators more extensive
rights than he claimed for the United States. He secured Roosevelt's agreement to drop the plan of embargoing Italy and Germany.[33]

The growth of public sentiment in favor of the Republic is
indicated by a Senate Resolution of May, 1938, introduced by the
Republican and outstanding isolationist, Senator Nye, to lift the
embargo for the Republic while retaining it against Franco. Better evidence that Congressional opinion had changed could not be
expected. Hull advised Senator Pittman to oppose this resolution.
The President, more sensitive to the change in opinion, continued
to ponder a change in policy, but Hull gave him no support.[34]

The chief argument of Loyalists was that by granting the right
to purchase arms to the Republic the United States could help
secure a victory which would discredit Hitler and Mussolini,
whose regimes could be maintained only by an unbroken series
of successful aggressions, and thereby, in accepting the risks of
collective security regarding a small war, diminish the risks of attempting to prevent a great one. Hull answers this argument, a
standard one of his own in all other situations, by stating that
"Spain was not the cause of the European War when that conflict came." [35] But supporters of the Loyalists did not contend that
Spain *caused* the Second World War; rather they believed that

Germany and Italy caused both the Spanish conflict and the greater war and that the best way to prevent the Second World War was to prevent their victory in the earlier conflict. Hull, in short, does not answer the argument. It would be hard to imagine an answer that did not contradict his principles and his policy towards all other cases of Axis aggression.

The question why the Roosevelt administration reversed its otherwise consistent advocacy of collective security by initiating the embargo of the Spanish Republic and clinging to it even after public opinion and Congress became favorable to the Republic cannot be answered satisfactorily. Many observers believed the influence of the Catholic Church, which was concentrated in the Democratic Party and was aggressively pro-Franco in its propaganda, was the most important factor. Anarchists, Syndicalists, Communists, and Trotzkyites, who supported the Spanish Republic, committed atrocities against the Catholic clergy, and these received much more publicity in the United States than did the ancient abuses which provoked them, or the constructive program of the Republic—which included reduction of the economic and political power of the Church. Students of history knew that this Spanish pattern hardly varied from that of, for example, the French Revolution, and was probably inevitable without the participation of Communists. As in most such situations, the centuries-long atrocities of the old regime, and the more severe ones of a reactionary government determined to re-establish all of the old regime that could be salvaged, far outweighed the crimes incident to a revolution. But these commonplace articles of American faith were obscured by the strategy of identifying the Spanish Republic with Communism.

The change in American opinion probably grew out of a realization that American national interest was not served by installing a friend of Hitler in Spain. Hull admits that Franco aided Hitler and Mussolini in the Second World War "to some extent," but claims as a success for his policy, or perhaps as a mitigation, the fact that Spain did not enter the War.[36] It was only because Franco's demands on Hitler were too high that he did not formally join him in the Second World War.[37] As it was, the aid he gave Hitler and the difficulties, dangers, and loss of prestige to which he subjected United States diplomatic and military policy during the war make his refusal to enter it small consolation for the loss of the opportunity to stop Hitler in Spain and possibly prevent the Second World War.

It is worth recording that no one accused Roosevelt of desiring a victory for Franco. This charge, and the additional one that he was pro-fascist, was commonly directed at Neville Chamberlain. The British leader was merely overly hopeful that he could make the dictators pro-British. In his diary he wrote: "I think we ought to be able to establish excellent relations with Franco, who seems well disposed to us. . . ." [38] There is no evidence that this mistaken notion influenced the policy of the American administration.

Nevertheless Roosevelt's Spanish policy destroyed much of the cumulative effect of his pursuit of collective security in other situations and this is probably the heaviest charge that may be laid against it. That the Roosevelt administration for three critical years stood officially indifferent to the slow agony of the Spanish Republic and the heroic and tragic struggle of the Spanish people, who were the first to take arms against Hitler, weakened measurably the effect of the President's appeals for a stronger policy against the Axis.

Beard recognized the exceptional nature of Roosevelt's Spanish policy in peculiar fashion. In the Spanish situation alone he accepts the argument of internationalists that the "new neutrality" policy of embargoing the aggressor and the victim alike actually aided the aggressor. Having shifted his premise, Beard finds Roosevelt's Spanish policy of embargoing both sides not isolationist but "interventionist" in meaning. This rounds out the difficulty of understanding Beard's use of terms. The Spanish embargo, in Beard's book, becomes one more action indicating Roosevelt's determination to abandon neutrality in favor of intervention in foreign conflicts and in violation of his public pledges of nonentanglement. It helps explain "the growing fear that the President's measures, as distinguished from his published statements of policy, were carrying the United States along 'the road to war.'" [39] A further warp in this judgment is the distinction Beard makes between the President's "measures" and his "published statements of policy." Beard insists on this distinction in order to support his charge of duplicity against Roosevelt. In actuality Roosevelt gave, if anything, more publicity to his "measure" of an embargo against both sides in Spain than he did to his "policy" of nonentanglement and peace. The occasion was doubtless tempting because with his Spanish embargo he could for once satisfy the isolationist majority in Congress and the country. Beard does not explain or even mention that the isolationists in Congress voted unanimously for the "interventionist" Spanish embargo.

## A Loophole: Cash-and-Carry

The next problem facing the administration was to obtain revision of the Neutrality Act in 1937. The approaching expiration of the 1936 law renewed debate on the central issues of foreign policy and gave the administration opportunity to work for a law more favorable to the aims of internationalism. But the administration placed major emphasis on passage of the Judiciary Reorganization Bill, whose Supreme Court "packing" feature aroused the greatest opposition Roosevelt had yet experienced.

In the Court fight, Roosevelt weakened his influence in Congress, split the great Democratic majority, offended many liberals, and created distrust among the people at large so that the position he had won in the landslide vote of 1936 was partially lost. The fact that, in spite of only minor emphasis on revision of the Neutrality Act, the administration made significant gains in the form of "compromises" with the isolationists, indicates what might have been won if this struggle had received major attention. In the perspective of the Second World War, the Court "packing" fight may be called the most serious mistake the President made in his twelve years in office.

But in the perspective of 1937, the strategy of the administration was justifiable because the basic reform laws of the New Deal would very likely have been declared unconstitutional by the Supreme Court if, after the "packing" plan was proposed by Roosevelt, the two "roving Justices"—Hughes and Roberts—had not come to rest on the side of the liberal minority. The new majority found in favor of the constitutionality of the Wagner Labor Relations Act, the Social Security Act, and other reform measures. The President always asserted that this meant victory for his Court fight even though the "packing" features of the Judiciary Reorganization Bill were defeated. It did assure the permanence of the New Deal reforms. Even from a later perspective it is a matter of opinion, incapable of proof, that the success of the New Deal in renovating American institutions and restoring faith in the capacity of a democracy to solve modern social and economic problems was less important to the American people than securing a foreign policy more likely to prevent the Second World War than the Neutrality Act of 1937. It can be argued that foreign policy is a function of domestic policy, that internationalism in foreign relations is a function of liberal reform in internal relations, and that the President correctly gave priority to domestic reform.

However these matters are viewed, the record proves what Beard in his anxiety to demonstrate the "duplicity" of Roosevelt ignores: that the administration did work in 1937 to secure revision of the Neutrality Act in the direction of collective security and did win a partial victory. Secretary Hull correctly judged that by minimizing direct pressure on Congress the administration was likely to obtain maximum concessions. He did not prepare a bill for Congress. The chief hope was that Congress would convert mandatory actions imposed on the President into discretionary powers. Hull made this plain, in a manner as little "coercive" as possible, by announcing to a press conference:

"Generally speaking, the attitude of the Department the last two or three years has been more in the direction of permissive legislation as a policy than Congress has been disposed to follow. In those circumstances it is natural that the Department would not send over a bill of its own, but would be disposed to look with more favor on proposed legislation in either House that might contain the smallest amount of purely mandatory and inflexible legislation." [40]

This approach was fairly successful. In the new Act, Congress renewed the President's discretion to impose an arms embargo only when he found that a state of war existed. It added the famous "cash-and-carry" provision the President had asked for in 1936, but qualified in some respects this legalization of the moral embargo on oil and other commodities. Isolationists were widely believed to be unwilling to allow an embargo on commodities without a loophole, because it would injure exports. The President was granted discretion as to what commodities should be placed on a "cash-and-carry" basis. He was allowed no discretion over the requirement of the Act that commodities on his list might not be carried from the United States to a belligerent in an American-owned vessel, but it was left to his discretion whether they had to be paid for before they left the United States. The "carry" provision made available American oil and other materials to whichever belligerent controlled the sea routes to the United States. This meant Britain and France in a European war but Japan in an Asiatic war. Still the Act gave the President room to avoid this absurdity by refusing to "find" that a state of war existed in Asia when Japan, without a declaration of war, attacked China a few months later. The cash-and-carry provision would expire after two years, while the remainder of the law was permanent. Satisfied that gains had been made, Roosevelt signed the Act on May 1, 1937.

The President was allowed by the new law to impose an arms embargo without embargoing any of the commodities to which the cash-and-carry loophole applied, but he was not allowed to apply cash-and-carry to commodities without also imposing an arms embargo. From this rigidity stemmed the difficulty of the President's problem when the next assault on the world's peace occurred, not in Europe, but in Asia. Japan possessed a navy, a merchant marine, and war industries. China lacked all three. Japan's requirements from the United States were oil, scrap metal, and other materials to which cash-and-carry could be applied if an arms embargo was imposed. By selling silk and other products to the United States, Japan could obtain cash to pay for materials to feed its war industries, and it had the ships to carry them back to Japan and the navy to protect the ships. Therefore, invocation of the Neutrality Act, with or without inclusion in the embargo of materials to which the cash-and-carry loophole applied, could not seriously affect Japan's war-making power. China, on the other hand, would receive some benefit if the Act were not invoked. It would be able to borrow money in the United States and buy munitions, which American-owned ships would be allowed to carry to China.

For this reason the President took advantage of the discretion granted him in the law, and of the failure of Japan or China to declare war, to avoid invocation of the Neutrality Act during the war that Japan had launched in China on July 7, 1937. His failure to act was understood to favor China and was vigorously opposed by isolationists. On the other hand, internationalists were not content to see unlimited exports go to Japan to nourish its war machine in order that China might obtain the pitifully small amount of arms it could afford to buy.

## *"Quarantine the Aggressor"*

Non-invocation of the Neutrality Act was too ironic a solution to satisfy the administration's desire to halt Japanese aggression. It made a series of new attempts to move towards collective security within the limits imposed by isolationists. Shortly before Japan's attack, an important exchange of views occurred with the new Chamberlain government of Great Britain. Chamberlain advocated rearmament of Britain at the same time that he sought a "settlement" with the aggressor nations. He believed the most important possible contribution of the United States was amendment of the Neutrality Act to permit embargo of an aggressor while allowing arms to go to the victim. He proposed collaboration between Britain and the United States. He particularly feared simultaneous war in Europe and Asia.

Hull pointed out in his answer that the new Neutrality Act did give some discretion to the President, including exceptions in favor of trade with Canada. The United States advocated increase of international trade as the means of relaxing political tensions. As for collaboration against Japan, Hull proposed consultation and concurrent, parallel action by the peaceful powers. Such procedure was provided for in the Nine-Power Treaty, which, Hull assured Chamberlain, the United States considered to be still in effect. He warned Chamberlain that current discussions between Britain and Japan might call for new agreements but that the United States could not abandon the principles of the Open Door incorporated in the Nine-Power Treaty. Chamberlain answered that he was in full agreement with Hull.[41]

On July 16, 1937, Hull issued a public statement of the position of the United States and sent it to all the governments of the world with a request that they state their views on it. He asserted that armed hostilities anywhere affected the rights and interests of all nations and that the United States advocated self-restraint, abstinence from the use of force and from interference in the internal affairs of other nations, peaceful methods of solving international problems, performance of obligations, observance of international law, economic cooperation, and disarmament. He warned that the United States would increase rather than reduce its armaments in proportion to increases by other countries, and promised that, although the United States avoided alliances or entangling commitments, it believed in practicable methods of cooperation in support of its fundamental principles.[42]

This was a masterly statement of international morality and the United States position in support of it. Its value was not negated by the adherence to it, among all the other countries, of Japan, Germany, and Italy, or by Portugal's objection to "the habit of entrusting the solution of grave external problems to vague formulae." Hull states in his memoirs:

> I had several purposes in mind in constantly reiterating these principles. One was to edge our own people gradually away from the slough of isolation into which so many had sunk. Another was to induce other nations to adopt them and make them the cornerstone of their foreign policies. Still another was to get peoples everywhere to believe in them so that, if aggressor governments sought war, their peoples might object or resist; and, if war did come, such peoples, having these principles at heart, would eventually swing back to the right international road.[43]

The sharp limits of what were practicable methods of cooperation for the United States were exposed immediately after Hull's July 16 statement. Britain proposed joint action with the United States and France to bring about an armistice in China and made proposals to end the conflict. Hull feared that joint action would only strengthen the military party in Japan, disliked confinement of peace efforts to three nations, and did not want to arouse American isolationists, so he rejected the proposal. The British and Chinese governments blamed the United States for the failure of the British project.

But Hull did advocate to Britain parallel action and he did initiate a peace effort. On August 10, Ambassador Grew offered to Japan the good offices of the United States to end the conflict with China. The Japanese Foreign Minister, Hirota, rejected the offer and replied that the United States should persuade General Chiang Kai-shek promptly to make an offer to Japan. It was clear that Japan would not end the war without substantial gains. The United States was in much the same position as the British govern-

ment was to be when Germany, in 1938, demanded of Czechoslovakia the Sudetenland as the price of peace. Britain brought
pressure on Czechoslovakia to pay that price, but the United
States refused to press China to make an offer acceptable to Japan.
This defines the great and significant difference between the
Roosevelt administration's adherence to the principles of international morality and the Chamberlain government's futile pursuit of "peace at any price."

Instead, the Roosevelt administration reinforced the United
States Marines at Shanghai as a warning to Japan that the United
States would defend its rights and its nationals in China. It repeatedly protested Japanese bombing of civilians and appealed for
an end to the war. Isolationists called for a complete withdrawal
from China in order to avoid antagonizing Japan, but Hull struck
back with a statement of contempt for such a "cowardly" retreat.[44]

Britain, France, and China next attempted to obtain from the
Roosevelt administration a commitment as to its attitude if the
League took action against Japan. Hull insisted that the League
powers must decide the League program first, after which the
United States would consider cooperation with it. Nevertheless,
the American Minister to Switzerland, Leland Harrison, was authorized on September 23 to sit with a League subcommittee on
the Far Eastern conflict. To secure public support for parallel
action with the League, Hull urged Roosevelt to make a strong
address on international cooperation in Chicago, the heart of the
isolationist Middle West. This was the origin of the famous
"Quarantine the Aggressor" Address. The State Department prepared a first draft but the President himself strengthened it and
created one of his most important slogans by inserting the quarantine passage.[45]

The Quarantine Address marked a new stage in the development of Roosevelt's foreign policy. For the first time he appealed
directly to the American people to support collective security
without limitation and as a general principle. In his speech he
denied the basic premise of isolationists, that avoidance of participation in the efforts of other nations to stop aggression would
safeguard the peace of the United States. He declared that if aggression were allowed to succeed in other parts of the world, no
one should imagine America would not be attacked. The peace of
the Western Hemisphere could be secured only by a "concerted

effort" of the peace-loving nations. "There is no escape through mere isolation or neutrality." The technical and moral solidarity and interdependence of the modern world made it impossible for any nation to isolate itself from the spreading political and economic upheavals elsewhere. The peace, freedom, and security of ninety percent of the population of the world were jeopardized by the remaining ten percent who threatened a breakdown of all international order and law. The ninety percent "can and must find some way to make their will prevail." The situation was of universal concern because not only were violations of definite agreements involved, but also questions of war and peace, international law, world economy, world security, and world humanity.

It seems to be unfortunately true that the epidemic of world lawlessness is spreading.

When an epidemic of physical disease starts to spread, the community approves and joins in a quarantine of the patients in order to protect the health of the community against the spread of the disease.

It is my determination to pursue a policy of peace. It is my determination to adopt every practicable measure to avoid involvement in war. . . .

War is a contagion, whether it be declared or undeclared. It can engulf states and peoples remote from the original scene of hostilities. We are determined to keep out of war, yet we cannot insure ourselves against the disastrous effects of war and the dangers of involvement. We are adopting such measures as will minimize our risk of involvement, but we cannot have complete protection in a world of disorder in which confidence and security have broken down.

If civilization is to survive the principles of the Prince of Peace must be restored. Trust between nations must be revived.

Most important of all, the will for peace on the part of peace-loving nations must express itself to the end that nations that may be tempted to violate their agreements and the rights of others will desist from such a course. There must be positive endeavors to preserve peace.

America hates war. America hopes for peace. Therefore, America actively engages in the search for peace.[46]

The public reaction to the Quarantine Address was unfavorable. Secretary Hull believed it set back the educational campaign for international cooperation at least six months. In his *Memoirs* he implied criticism of the President's addition of the "quarantine" metaphor to the State Department's draft:

If we proceeded gradually and did not excite undue opposition, our words and actions, although not so dynamic or far-reaching as we might wish, had more effect on the world at large than if we made startling statements or took precipitate action and then, because of the bitter reaction we aroused, presented the world with the spectacle of a nation divided against itself.[47]

Roosevelt had sought to win public support for the principle and policy of collective security. He had exercised his talent for coining slogans in hope that "Quarantine the Aggressor" would match his "New Deal" and "Good Neighbor" slogans in power to cleave through opposition arguments, appeal to common sense and arouse enthusiasm.

But the new slogan died stillborn. It left too much room for isolationist charges that Roosevelt planned entangling alliances and involvement in war. His coinage of January, 1939, "measures short of war," was better guarded against misconstruction and more successful. Roosevelt evidently felt that description of methods whereby the United States could help quarantine aggressors without involving prior commitments or alliances would confuse the issue. It is likely that plans which he attempted in following months had not yet been formulated. In any case they required preparations which had to be secret and successful before they could be described to the public.

In the meantime proposal of an experimental approach—"America actively engages in the search for peace"—matching his experimental approach in domestic policy was not only frank but, once support was had for the principle of collective security, necessary. This interpretation the President gave to reporters who attempted to smoke out his plans for establishing the quarantine.[48] But his hope that the debate might remain on the high ground of principles was too optimistic, and isolationists won the debate with a hue and cry against United States "involvement in European and Asiatic wars."

### Fiasco at Brussels

The actions of Secretary Hull and the State Department provide insight into the President's policies and clues to a technique of "quarantine" the President may have contemplated. Beard neglects to make use of such evidence and is therefore able to speak of the Quarantine speech as announcing a new departure which was not instrumented. After the United States offers of good offices to Japan and China, Leland Harrison, American Minister to Switzerland, was instructed on September 20 to attend meetings of the Far Eastern Advisory Committee of the League of Nations. The Department of State announced that the United States thus acted on its belief in "the principle of collaboration among States of the world seeking to bring about peaceful solutions in international conflicts," and that it would "give careful consideration to definite proposals which the League may address to it," but would not "state its position in regard to policies or plans submitted to it in terms of hypothetical inquiry." [49] On September 28, after Germany and Japan refused to participate on the Far Eastern Advisory Commission, and the League Assembly had condemned Japanese air raids in China, the position of the United States was clarified by a statement that "while we believe in and wish to practice cooperation, we are not prepared to take part in joint action, though we will consider the possible taking of parallel action." It was also pointed out that spontaneous parallel action by governments indicated serious feeling more strongly and was more likely to succeed than joint action. Furthermore, the United States had now gone farther than other governments in efforts calculated to strengthen world peace, and others might well now direct their efforts to go as far or farther than the United States.[50]

The timing of the President's Quarantine speech of October 5 was related to publication of League of Nations reports in which Japan was found guilty of violating its obligations under the Nine-Power Treaty and the Kellogg Pact. The reports proposed that League members who were signatories of the Nine-Power Treaty should initiate consultation according to its terms and invite other nations interested in the Far East to participate. Britain informed the United States that it approved the conference proposal. On the same day, the United States announced its agreement with the League reports and suggested Brussels as the seat of a conference.

Here was a beginning of parallel action with the League and instrumentation of the strongest commitment of the United States. The reason for its failure deserves closest study. In the background was the large fact that the League had not used its own authority to impose sanctions against Japan but turned over the responsibility to the Nine Powers, ultimately the United States. The President seemed uninterested in the plans for a Nine-Power conference as a step towards a quarantine of Japan. He told reporters on October 6: "Conferences are out of the window. You never get anywhere with a conference . . . we are looking for a program." [51] But this remark was "off the record" and "not for background." Prime Minister Chamberlain on October 8 publicly endorsed the President's Quarantine Address and stated that in his call for a concerted effort for peace, "he will have this Government whole-heartedly with him." [52]

The first public indication that the coming conference would not quarantine Japan was made by Roosevelt. In a radio address on October 12, which he devoted chiefly to domestic affairs, the President ruled out sanctions against Japan. He declared that the purpose of the Brussels Conference would be to seek a solution of the war by agreement between Japan and China.[53] Britain thereupon worked to place responsibility for the prospective failure of the conference on the United States. On October 15, Foreign Secretary Eden specified that Britain would cooperate at the conference in the spirit of the Quarantine Address.[54] Belgium sent out invitations to signatories the next day and also to Germany and Russia. Japan and Germany refused to take part. Behind the scenes, Eden on October 19 sent a memorandum to the United States which made American participation in sanctions against Japan impossible. Without committing Britain to sanctions, he declared they would have to be preceded by political and military commitments. Sanctions might induce Japan to make peace, in his view, only if mutual assurances of military support and guaranties of territorial integrity were entered into among the powers before they applied sanctions. Britain and France made it known to other governments that at the conference they would go as far as the United States and no farther.[55]

Hull had often made it clear that the United States could not make political commitments of a general nature prior to action by other nations and prior to the development of an actual situation which required their application. Roosevelt and Hull did not take kindly to the maneuver of Britain and France. The President instructed the American delegate to Brussels, Norman Davis, to mobilize moral force to induce Japan to enter the conference and submit its differences with China to settlement by negotiation. Davis was told to take full account of public opinion in the United States—which was clearly opposed to a quarantine.

Davis thereupon warned Eden in Brussels on November 2, the day before the conference opened, that the United States would not take the lead and that a large body of opinion in the United States feared that Britain, holding larger interests in the Far East than the United States and unable to protect them, was maneuvering the United States into "pulling British chestnuts out of the fire." Eden replied that Britain would base its policy on American policy. Davis proposed to the conference plans to bring Japan to a settlement by negotiation with China. Japan consistently refused. The other governments placed the responsibility for stronger measures on the United States. Hull instructed Davis to counteract their charge by pointing out that primary responsibility had been in the hands of the League powers. Hull himself admits in his *Memoirs* that other nations would perhaps have followed a United States lead in stronger action but that American public opinion would not allow it. Furthermore, he believed that such action would have strengthened the Japanese military and might have led to a war in which the United States would have borne the brunt and for which it was not prepared.

Britain turned to propose a joint offer with the United States of good offices to Japan and China. As intermediaries, they would pass armistice and peace terms between the belligerents until a basis was formed for direct negotiations. Hull turned this proposal down because he believed it would involve transmission of terms which would be in violation of the Nine-Power Treaty and would make the United States appear to bring pressure on China.[56] This reasoning was significant because it placed the United States on record against appeasement of Japan. Since the United States had already offered its good offices unilaterally, Hull evidently believed that British policy would involve appeasement. With the failure of this plan, the Brussels Conference came to an end.

This set the seal on the failure of the League and the Nine Powers to take collective action against Japan. Japan celebrated its impunity by bombing the United States gunboat *Panay* on December 12. The reaction of Americans was led by isolationists who demanded that the United States withdraw its forces stationed in China. The administration allowed Japan to call the bombing a "mistake" and obtained indemnities.

Any attempt to assign prior responsibility for the failure of the Brussels Conference is futile. The conjunction of American isolationism and the unwillingness of the League powers to take the initiative produced the result. The part of the United States in the Brussels Conference hardly represented the quarantine policy the President had so vigorously announced. In his press conference of October 6 the President had said in answer to prodding as to the nature of his quarantine plan: "There are a lot of methods in the world that have never been tried yet," and that, although he could not give reporters any clue to it, he did have a plan.[57]

## The Welles Plan

What was the President's plan? If it was to secure repeal of the Neutrality Act, as Norman Davis recommended, that was ruled out after Hull canvassed Congressional leaders and found there was no prospect of repeal, suspension, or modification of the law.[58] Beard makes much of the "confusion" caused by the President's course after the Quarantine Address and describes him as seeming to return by the end of the year to "his long proclaimed isolationist position." [59] This reiterates the false thesis that refusal to make prior commitments or to enter entangling alliances constituted isolationism, and it also ignores the President's chief plan to implement the Quarantine doctrine. This plan was necessarily secret at the time because, as always in international diplomacy, premature publicity would force governments to assume positions before they could explore possibilities of new departures in their policies.*

The plan originated with Under Secretary of State Sumner Welles and constitutes a poignant "might have been" of world history during the years prior to the Second World War. Welles proposed that the President call a meeting in the White House of the diplomatic representatives of all nations on Armistice Day, November 11, 1937. Before this audience the President should de-

* The plan was made public by Sumner Welles in his book *The Time for Decision*, published in 1944, two years before Beard's *American Foreign Policy* was published.

liver a message to the governments of the world. Sumner Welles
later described the proposed message:

He would state that he had reached the final conclusion that, unless
the nations of the earth speedily resumed their observance of those
fundamental rules of conduct which the judgment of nineteen centuries and the experience of recent years had demonstrated as being
necessary in relations between states, world peace could not much
longer be maintained. He would continue by saying that doubtless
some would predict that, because many efforts to better the chances
of preserving world peace had failed, this new effort would also fail.
He was unwilling to accept any such prediction as an excuse for a
failure on his part to make one more fervent appeal.

He should then propose that all governments work to reach
unanimous agreement on: 1) principles of international conduct;
2) limitation and reduction of armaments; 3) methods of promoting economic pacification through equality of treatment and
opportunity; and 4) outlawing of inhuman methods of warfare.
The President would end his appeal by proposing that the United
States and nine other nations representative of all regions of the
world should meet as an "executive committee" to draw up proposals for submission to all governments as a basis for universal
agreement. He would not propose a general conference.

President Roosevelt adopted the Welles plan. He believed that
even if it did not succeed it would have beneficial effects in asserting the initiative and leadership of the democracies, uniting
peaceful nations, and exposing aggressor governments to unfavorable opinion among their own peoples.[60] But Secretary Hull opposed the plan as being "illogical and impossible." He believed
the Axis nations had already gone so far in preparations for aggression that the democracies should not be lulled by a peace
effort but aroused to arm themselves for self-defense. He felt that
principles of international conduct were already "taken care of"
in his July 16 statement to which sixty nations adhered and that
economic stability was provided for by the trade agreements program. He feared that the plan would lead to further appeasement
of the dictators by Chamberlain. Even if an agreement were reached,
a commitment by the Axis powers would be valueless.[61]

It is difficult to agree with Hull that the Welles plan would
actually have lulled the democratic peoples. Rather its effect

would very likely have been to arouse them to a new realization of their danger. The proposal by no means looked to disarmament without satisfactory assurance of disarmament by the aggressor nations, and if the latter were not forthcoming, the upshot would be an excellent preparation of democratic opinion in favor of rearmament. The adherence of sixty nations to the July 16 statement by Hull was of minor value, precisely because the sixty nations had not been required to take action on the basis of the principles, whereas the Welles proposal would require them to show in action the good or bad faith in which they professed pious principles. And universal economic agreements would transcend the scope of the American trade agreements program and accelerate the tempo of economic pacification. Most importantly, universal economic agreement, even if it did not secure the adherence of Germany itself, would create an alternative for the small nations that were being drawn into the economic orbits of the Axis powers.

Secretary Hull was jealous of his prerogative as the President's chief adviser on foreign policy and resented initiatives towards the President by his subordinates or by members of other departments. Welles stated later that his project was "almost hysterically opposed" by certain of the President's "closest advisers." [62] Certainly Hull's treatment of the episode in his *Memoirs* is scornful beyond ordinary measure. He was particularly distrustful of any scheme involving the President's personal leadership in foreign relations. The reasons Welles gives for opposition to his plan differ from those of Hull:

They insisted that it involved great dangers to the prestige of the United States. They argued that any such dramatic appeal . . . would be highly unwise unless the President had earlier received, at least confidentially, the assurance that the British or the French government would not regard it as running counter to negotiations which they already had in hand or to policies upon which they had previously determined.

Consequently, Welles adds, the President temporarily postponed action.[63]

This suggests that the President's advisers who opposed the Welles plan, among whom Hull must be presumed to be one, feared that it would interfere with current attempts by Chamberlain to appease Hitler and Mussolini and make a settlement for western Europe. Chamberlain had no faith in collective security. His hope for peace for Britain rested on the possibility of satisfying the ambitions of Hitler and Mussolini short of their supremacy in the Mediterranean or western Europe. His policy bore fruit in the Munich Agreement of September, 1938, although he was never able to secure a general four-power pact. Welles's analysis suggests that the same chasm which separated the Chamberlain appeasement policy from collective security separated the policy of Hull from the Welles plan.

This does not require a conclusion that Hull supported appeasement. He never initiated any compromise with an Axis government. But he believed that the United States government, limited by public and Congressional isolationism, could not take the initiative to organize a united front of peaceful nations against aggressors. That role was Britain's. Faced by the facts of British refusal of the role and turn to appeasement, Hull believed the United States had no right to endanger the success of the British policy. The Welles plan, to be sure, did not on its surface signify a united front of peaceful powers organizing measures of collective security against aggressors. But it could hardly be expected that the Axis powers would actually enter into, and carry out, a universal agreement for disarmament, and it was precisely the expected effect of their refusal, the awakening and uniting of democratic peoples and governments, that Welles foresaw and wanted. The Chamberlain policy, on the contrary, was to avoid facing Hitler with coercive demonstrations of unity against him and to offer him instead the cooperation of Britain and France in securing "reasonable" objectives by peaceful means. Among these objectives were not only territorial acquisitions but military and naval establishments incompatible with the Welles proposal of universal disarmament.

The Welles plan implied that disarmament was a necessary condition without which concessions to the dictators in return for promises to maintain the peace were naive and dangerous. The Chamberlain policy was to rearm Britain as a safeguard against the failure of appeasement. Hull correctly saw that the two programs were irreconcilable and he felt constrained to subordinate American to British policy.

Hull may be charged with timidity. If he had no faith in appeasement, the best way to scotch it was by some such initiative in
favor of a contrary program as Welles proposed. The genius of
the Welles plan was that it appealed to peoples, including the
British, as well as their governments, with the hardly resistible
prospect that the United States would take the lead in dealing
with the Axis without appeasing it, and in ways well known to be
acceptable to American isolationists. The Chamberlain government could not easily refuse to accept such an initiative from the
United States. But the plan, like any that was likely to succeed
in coercing the Axis nations, was bold, and Hull was unwilling to
attempt it.

The President allowed his first enthusiasm for the Welles plan
to be tempered by Hull's precaution that prior approval must be
obtained from the British government. This gave Chamberlain a
choice, uninfluenced by public opinion, between appeasement and
an attempt to contain the Axis without concessions to its aggressive ambitions. On January 11, 1938, Welles delivered to the British Ambassador in Washington, Sir Ronald Lindsay, a secret message from the President to Chamberlain. In it he outlined the
Welles plan and said that before taking the initiative he wanted
to obtain the British view of it. Winston Churchill later called
this "a formidable and measureless step." [64]

Lindsay forwarded the message with his own advice that the
plan be approved. It brought the Prime Minister back from the
country to London the next day. Anthony Eden was abroad and
was not consulted. Therefore Chamberlain's first answer was un-
tempered even by the opposition to appeasement within his own
Cabinet. Chamberlain rejected the President's proposal because
it would interfere with his plans to appease Hitler and Mussolini.
He told Roosevelt that he was in process of offering Mussolini
recognition of Italian conquest of Abyssinia in return for unspecified "evidence" of his "desire to contribute to the restoration
of confidence and friendly relations." [65] This served notice that
Chamberlain would violate the American Stimson Doctrine and
give approval to aggression in return for promises of future good
behavior. It set the pattern for Munich and frustrated the most
promising plan of the Roosevelt administration to find a way for
the United States to help prevent the Second World War. It
made the Chamberlain government equally responsible with

American isolationists for the defeat of Rooseveltian internationalism prior to that war.

The crucial significance of Chamberlain's rebuff to Roosevelt is revealed by the fact that it precipitated the Cabinet crisis which ended in the resignation of Eden as Foreign Secretary. Eden hurried back to London and sent a telegram to Lindsay asking him to moderate the impact of Chamberlain's refusal on the American government. Chamberlain argued that the dictators would use Roosevelt's "line up of the democracies" as an excuse for a break. Eden declared he would rather risk that than risk loss of American good will.[66]

The President replied to Chamberlain in a letter on January 17, 1938. He felt he had no alternative but to postpone the Welles plan "for a short while." And he added that he was gravely concerned over the Chamberlain plan to grant recognition to Italy of its rule in Abyssinia. He believed it would encourage Japan and offend American public opinion. Japan's adherence to the Axis Pact during the Brussels Conference had shown unmistakably the connection between European and Far Eastern aggressions. Cordell Hull, in delivering the letter to Lindsay, was even more positive. He said such recognition would "rouse a feeling of disgust, would revive and multiply all fears of pulling the chestnuts out of the fire; it would be represented as a corrupt bargain completed in Europe at the expense of interests in the Far East in which America was intimately concerned." [67]

Hull thus compensated for his timidity in refusing to coerce Chamberlain with a public challenge to abandon appeasement, by privately announcing American opposition to that policy. Pressed by Roosevelt, Hull, and Eden, Chamberlain consented to "compromise." He sent two letters to Roosevelt on January 21. One declared he welcomed the President's proposal but he would not take any responsibility if it failed and he criticized the procedure as bound to "irritate" the Axis governments. The other letter "explained" that he intended to recognize the conquest of Abyssinia only as part of a "general settlement" with Italy. Chamberlain said he believed economic concessions alone, as envisaged by the Welles plan, would not interest the dictators, but that an offer of political concessions had a chance of bringing them around to a "cooperative" frame of mind.[68] This was the nub of the difference between the Roosevelt and the Chamberlain policies and it was enough to prevent Chamberlain's "compromise" from opening a way to instrumentation of the Welles plan.

Roosevelt and Welles presently lost interest in opposing the Chamberlain policy of political appeasement. They did not attempt to discover in the "compromise" an opening to launch the plan. That they did not give up the plan *because* Chamberlain asked for political appeasement is suggested by Winston Churchill's account that Welles on January 22 told Lindsay "the President regarded recognition as as unpleasant pill which we should both have to swallow, and he wished that we should both swallow it together." [69] Welles in his account makes the explanation: "By this time, of course, many invaluable weeks had passed." He does not give the date of the January 21 Chamberlain replies, nor does he mention his own astonishing remark to Lindsay of January 22. He continues:

The situation within Germany was reaching a boiling point. In an interview which the British Ambassador in Berlin had with Hitler on March 3, Hitler . . . insisted upon the need for an immediate solution . . . of the problems of Austria and Czechoslovakia. Hitler stated that, in so far as the limitation of armaments was concerned, Germany would refuse to deal with Great Britain . . . unless Great Britain had previously begun satisfactory discussions with the Soviet Union.[70]

This is unconvincing. The "invaluable weeks" passed not before Chamberlain's "compromise" letters were received on January 22, but after that date and before the Hitlerian "boiling point" was reached on March 3. During these truly invaluable weeks, Welles —having suggested to Lindsay joint Anglo-American recognition of Italian rule in Abyssinia, that is, political appeasement—and Roosevelt both did nothing to exploit the Chamberlain "compromise." Even as late at March 3, Hitler's remarks left an opening for a disarmament initiative by the United States because the Soviet Union was not obstructionist during this period on this issue.

A judgment may be that Welles and Roosevelt were unwilling to risk political appeasement as a product of an American initiative, although they were willing to "swallow the pill together" with Britain, at least as regards Italy. But if this was the reason for abandonment of the Welles plan, it suggests that timidity had come to govern Welles himself, because the Chamberlain "compromise" letters only recorded the *opinion* of the British Prime Minister that political appeasement would be necessary and by no means bound the United States to act on that opinion. It is difficult to understand why a bold public initiative in favor of the Welles plan, even after January 22, would not have had a fair chance of achieving the results for which Welles originally hoped.

## Rearmament: The Best Remaining Means

A more plausible judgment is that Roosevelt, having abandoned hope of turning Britain away from appeasement, and at the same time lacking faith in the efficacy of that policy, turned to rearmament of the United States as the best remaining source of national security. In his Annual Message of January 3, 1938, he pointed to growing danger from aggression abroad, but proposed no unusual measures to meet it. On January 28, he sent a special message to Congress asking for a broad array of defense legislation, chiefly a heavy naval building program. Why the President should not have made his requests in his Annual Message aroused much speculation at the time. It now seems clear that the January 28 message marked a new policy undertaken as a result of Chamberlain's rebuff, the abandonment of the Welles plan, and the convictions that Chamberlain could not be turned away from appeasement and that appeasement held danger for the peace of the world, including the United States.

Doubtless the willingness of a large section of isolationists in and out of Congress to support a rearmament program was one of its attractions as an alternative to the politically risky Welles plan. Rearmament tended to split isolationists into two groups, nationalists and pacifists. Nationalist isolationists insisted that the building up of American defenses should not include any plan of naval or military cooperation with Britain, France, or any nation outside the Western Hemisphere. But Roosevelt retrieved from the failures of collective security the conception that the defense of the United States was bound up with the defense of the western European democracies. He did not conceal from Congress the fact that he regarded the armament program from an internationalist point of view; he stated that it was necessitated not merely by a threat to the security and peace of the United States but:

*Specifically* and *solely* because of the piling up of additional land and sea armaments in other countries, in such manner as to involve a threat to *world* peace and security. . . .[71]

Beard declares that "on its face," the January 28 message "seemed to have no particular significance," [72] and thus dismisses the portentous words quoted. But a few paragraphs later he describes the extreme significance isolationists discovered in the President's statement that his recommendations were made *specifically* and *solely* because of a threat to *world* peace and security.[73]

The nature of the President's proposed naval building program also emphasized that he had no narrowly "nationalist" conception of defense. He asked for new authorizations and appropriations to bring the total number of battleships under construction to six and of battleships authorized to eighteen. With them, for the first time, the United States would be able to operate offensively in both the Atlantic and Pacific Oceans at the same time. Such a program had obvious bearing on the capacity of the government to exercise diplomatic influence in favor of world peace and security in the only terms the aggressor nations respected. The President also proposed a plan of universal mobilization of American manpower, capital, and manufactures for use in case of war. "Total" mobilization was refused by Congress even after Pearl Harbor, but if it had been adopted in 1938 it would have reinforced the diplomatic weight of the naval program.

The naval building program was geared to British and French programs. It became known that the Chief of the Navy War Plans Division had conferred in London with British naval officials before the details of the President's message were worked out. Isolationists cried that the administration had made secret commitments to Britain, but probably in this, as certainly in later instances, they were confounded by the fact that the United States and British governments had enough confidence in each other to ignore the ordinary procedure of making formal agreements, and to reach understandings that were obviously dependent on the President's ability to obtain Congressional consent when the time arrived for any action which was constitutionally outside his ex-

clusive authority. In any case, public events made the synchronization of American and British naval policy apparent to the whole
world. In 1936 Japan had denounced treaties limiting naval armaments. It became a question whether Britain and the United States
would continue to observe treaty limitations. The London Naval
Treaty was drawn up later in 1936 by Britain, France, and the
United States with an escalator clause permitting new building to
match any new building by other nations. On November 6, 1937,
the day of the signing of the Anti-Comintern Pact by Germany,
Italy, and Japan, Virginio Gayda, spokesman of the Italian Foreign Office, published that Mussolini's valuable new ally, Japan,
was building battleships of 46,000 tons as compared with the
35,000-ton limitation in treaties. Japan also refused to limit the
calibre of guns to fourteen inches.

The Chamberlain government regarded rearmament as a "sanction" supporting its appeasement policy. It launched new air and
naval building programs. Chamberlain was determined to avoid
any cooperation with other governments which the dictators could
call a menace against them. But in the single matter of naval armaments Chamberlain's "isolationism" was violated, apparently as a
result of Roosevelt's private initiative. The Anglo-American naval
conference in London on war plans signified the cooperation of
the two powers on plans to control the seas in case of war. Their
cooperation was symbolized by the visit of three United States
cruisers to attend the opening of a new British naval base at
Singapore. Delegates of Britain, France and the United States met
as required by their 1936 treaty to consult on new naval building
programs.

Even this degree of cooperation was threatened in March when
Hitler's Austrian *Anschluss* and his demands on Czechoslovakia
threw Chamberlain into new paroxysms of fear. Anthony Eden
had resigned in February as a result of Chamberlain's rejection of
the Welles plan,[74] and left the British government without an important supporter of collective security. Chamberlain hesitated to
invoke the escalator clause. Roosevelt acted vigorously to save a
fragment of cooperation from the shambles and to instill vigor
into at least the defense arrangements of the democracies. The
United States threatened to invoke the escalator clause unilaterally, as the treaty permitted, if Britain and France did not agree to
build beyond the old treaty limitations.

By the end of March this pressure brought agreement. The three powers united in ending limitations and in facing the Axis governments with naval armaments which, in spite of their treaty violations, they could not match. In the light of the disasters which the British, French, and American navies met in the early years of the Second World War, it is easy to believe that, but for the decisions of 1938, the democracies would have suffered the absolute disaster of loss of control of the seas to the Axis with consequences conceivably fatal to their cause. For the decisions of 1938, the chief responsibility was Roosevelt's.

During these months, the various evidences that Roosevelt looked upon his rearmament program as a step towards collective security were used in Congress and the press as arguments against granting him his requests. Nevertheless, the votes in Congress were overwhelmingly favorable to the naval program and also to increased army and air programs which the President had proposed, and in some details appropriations exceeded his requests. Thus it was demonstrated that he had found minimum common ground for cooperation not only with Chamberlain but with nationalist-isolationists at home. This was an achievement in the realm of reconciling the ideal and the possible at a time when any action at all for collective security seemed impossible.

Opponents of the President's program forced an amendment of the Naval Expansion or Two-Ocean Navy Act which the President accepted when he signed the law on May 17. The amendment failed to frustrate the President's intent only because isolationists had so obfuscated terminology that they regarded "aggression" as a synonym for "collective security." They achieved this by an intermediate identification of collective security with defense of the British Empire and defense of the British Empire with aggression. It is possible that Roosevelt himself turned this monstrosity of political thought to a useful purpose: the amendment was drawn up by the House Committee on Naval Affairs after Chairman Vinson had conferred with the President. It forbade use of the new navy not for collective security but for "aggression."

It satisfied isolationists who cried against a "secret alliance" with Britain, and any believer in collective security could accept it in good conscience. The amendment in its positive authorizations was sufficiently broad. The new navy could be used "to guard the continental United States by affording naval protection to the coast line, in both oceans at one and the same time; to protect the Panama Canal, Alaska, Hawaii, and our Insular possessions; to protect our commerce and citizens abroad; to insure our national integrity; and to support our national policies." [75]

Imperialists were accustomed to regard citizens and their property abroad as part of the national domain, and nationalist-isolationists were satisfied by the terminology of the amendment, while supporters of collective security wished to be equally vigorous in protecting national interests abroad, but by different methods and for different purposes. The three factions also undoubtedly understood "our national policies" in different ways. It was reasonable to regard national security as strengthened by co-operation—short of "aggression"—with other nations against the Axis menace. In any case, on June 30 the United States signed a protocol with Britain and France, providing an increase of battleship size from 35,000 to 45,000 tons, without particular protest from American isolationists.

Secretary Hull cut through the ambiguities of words in the two-ocean navy debate in response to a request from Representative Ludlow. The proposed Ludlow Amendment to the Constitution called for a popular referendum before war could be declared, except in case of invasion. It would have violated the representative character of the United States government, weakened the influence of the Executive in foreign relations, and reduced American defense to a narrow and dangerous strategy of waiting for invasion. The administration strongly opposed it. The House voted it down in January by the narrow margin of 209 to 188. Ludlow's attacks on the naval program therefore expressed the attitude of extreme isolationists. Hull answered him in February that the program did not envisage use of the navy in cooperation with any other nation in any part of the world. Nevertheless, he continued:

This Government carefully avoids, on the one hand, extreme internationalism with its political entanglements, and, on the other hand, extreme isolation, with its tendency to cause other nations to believe that this nation is more or less afraid; that while avoiding any alliances or entangling commitments, it is appropriate and advisable, when this and other countries have common interests and common objectives, for this Government to *exchange information* with Governments of such other countries, to *confer* with those Governments, and, where practicable, to *proceed on parallel lines,* but reserving always the fullest freedom of judgment and right of independence of action.[76]

This was a valuable exegesis of the administration's policy of limited internationalism. It cut through the charges of isolationists and demolishes the image Beard creates of an administration pursuing isolation publicly and internationalism secretly. The facts do not permit Beard's reduction of the two terms to extreme and narrow definitions: Hull correctly described the administration's public and private pursuit of *limited* internationalism.

## The Pattern of Disunity

During the spring of 1938, new tests of the administration's policy were precipitated by Hitler's assaults on Austria and Czechoslovakia. On March 17, the day after Mussolini gave his consent to *Anschluss,* the Soviet Union proposed a conference with Great Britain, France, and the United States to organize measures of collective security. Chamberlain, on March 24, refused the Soviet proposal. United States willingness to join was therefore not tested. Roosevelt evidently could not have joined in measures of full collective security. But in the Welles plan incident Roosevelt had shown that he did not exclude the Soviet Union from his conception of limited United States cooperation against aggression.[77]

Chamberlain signed a pact with Mussolini on April 16 promising recognition of the King of Italy as "Emperor of Ethiopia" in return for "assurances" regarding the Mediterranean area. This was by no means the "general settlement" Chamberlain had promised Roosevelt in January he would require in exchange for recognition, because it left Mussolini's Axis connection in full force. If Welles had spoken truly when he told Lindsay that Roosevelt wanted to "swallow the pill" of recognition jointly with Britain, Chamberlain's reckless pact relieved the United States of any obligation or sympathetic interest. Chamberlain does not appear even to have consulted the United States before he made the pact. He proceeded to secure League approval for its other members to follow suit. Roosevelt and Hull issued statements which refrained from criticizing the British actions but refused to join in appeasement of Mussolini.[78] The United States never recognized Italian conquest of Abyssinia. It was left thoroughly "isolated" in adherence to its most important internationalist policy, the Stimson Doctrine. In the new period of Munich, the United States found itself in some degree in the position of the Soviet Union, that is, more *willing* to cooperate with Britain and France than the latter governments would *allow*.

The portentous question whether the United States could not have found common ground with the Soviet Union to oppose the Chamberlain appeasement program is answered by the unsatisfactory course of American-Soviet relations after Roosevelt recognized the Soviet government in 1933. Litvinov at that time had indicated that the Soviet government was willing to pay $100,000,000 in settlement of Tsarist debts to the United States. Interest also was expected, but the Soviet government never paid capital or interest. The United States consequently refused to make available Export-Import Bank credits for Soviet purchases and found the Soviet Union in default under the terms of the Johnson Act of 1934, which forbade loans to governments in default on their debts to the United States.

Soviet-American trade did not develop as promised. Hull conceded to the Soviet Union in July, 1935, unconditional most-favored-nation status so that it would receive benefits under the Reciprocity Trade Agreements Act, and the Soviet Union agreed to increase its purchases of American goods. This improvement in relations was nullified by the attendance of American Communists at the August, 1935, meeting of the Communist International in Moscow. Hull publicly denounced this as a violation of Litvinov's pledge that the Soviet government would prevent activity in Russia which aimed to overthrow the United States government. The Soviet government rejected the protest because it "cannot take upon itself and has not taken upon itself obligations of any kind with regard to the Communist International." Hull warned that this attitude could not fail to impair friendly and official relations.

The indecision of Soviet leaders as to whether they stood to gain more by cultivating Communist movements in democratic capitalist nations or by cultivating friendly relations with their governments ended in failure in both efforts and was disastrous to the cause of collective security. According to Hull:

The beneficial influence I had expected Russo-American cooperation to have on the political situation both in Europe and Asia did not materialize. I argued again and again with Soviet ambassadors that it was disastrous to let the comparatively small sum of Soviet indebtedness and other modest differences stand in the way of our thoroughgoing political relations. I pleaded with them again and again that if only the United States, Russia, Britain, and France could present a common moral front to the aggressor nations, Germany, Japan, and Italy, war might be prevented. I warned them again and again of the dangers threatening us all. But a common front did not come until long after war had begun.[80]

It follows from the refusal of the Roosevelt administration to support Chamberlain's policy of appeasing Hitler and Mussolini that it had no part in the responsibility for divorcing the Soviet Union from the western democracies. And when the common front was finally organized it was, as will appear, partly a product of the forbearance of the Roosevelt administration and its friendly advances toward the Soviet government even during the period of the Nazi-Soviet Pact.

By the summer of 1938 the pattern of disunity among the nations threatened by the Axis was complete and Chamberlain was free to offer the Sudetenland to Hitler in return for a Four-Power Pact. Preparations for this immoral deal deeply discouraged American internationalists and strengthened the position of isolationists. They argued that the United States must avoid the sinister power politics of the Old World. Nevertheless, the principle of isolation was not embraced by the Roosevelt administration. Instead, Secretary Hull increased the fervor of his denunciations of that principle, as, for example, in a speech on June 3:

Attempts to achieve national isolation would not merely deprive us of any influence in the councils of nations, but would impair our ability to control our own affairs. . . . There is desperate need in our country, and in every country, of a strong and united public opinion in support of a renewal and demonstration of faith in the possibility of a world order based on law and international co-operative effort.[81]

The Nazi Henlein rejected one set after another of Czech concessions to the Sudeten population. The British Runciman Mission weakened Czech resistance. Hitler whipped up a war crisis and it only became known years later that his generals were prepared to revolt rather than carry out his threats.[82]

Chamberlain accepted Hitler's threats at full inflated value and placed a peaceful solution above all other considerations. Hull on August 16 made a radio address in which he prayerfully pleaded for a return to international morality. He repeated the proposals of his July, 1937, message to the nations. He attempted to save Americans from the cynicism and isolationism events in Europe inspired:

Whatever may be our own wishes and our hopes, we cannot when there is trouble elsewhere expect to remain unaffected. When destruction, impoverishment, and starvation afflict other areas, we cannot, no matter how hard we may try, escape impairment of our own economic well-being. When freedom is destroyed over increasing areas elsewhere, our ideals of individual liberty, our most cherished political and social institutions are jeopardized. . . .

Hence it is necessary that as a nation we become increasingly resolute in our desire and increasingly effective in our efforts to contribute along with other peoples—always within the range of our traditional policies of nonentanglement—to the support of the only program which can turn the tide of lawlessness and place the world firmly upon the one and only roadway that can lead to enduring peace and security.[83]

It was left for the President himself, two days later, to implement these words with a concrete action which was the only step by any government during the Munich debacle towards unity of peaceful nations against aggression.

# 3.

# Munich: The Turning Point

AFTER THE MUNICH CRISIS, PRESIDENT ROOSEVELT TOLD AN interviewer * that his relation to it was to be found in his Kingston Address in Canada on August 18, 1938. On that day he took the occasion of receiving a degree from Queens University to create a new link in the chain of American nations united against aggression. He spoke of the international nature of civilization and said "we in the Americas" were charged with maintenance of that tradition. He noted that the effects of the Czech crisis were felt alike in Canada and the United States and asserted that the power of the American Hemisphere played a part in the calculations of aggressors. Then he made the historic pronouncement:

> The dominion of Canada is part of the sisterhood of the British Empire. I give to you assurance that the people of the United States will not stand idly by if domination of Canadian soil is threatened by any other empire.[1]

### A Great Link and a Small One

A narrow interpretation of the President's promise is that it extended the Monroe Doctrine to Canada. This only applied specifically to Canada what the "no-transfer corollary" of the Monroe Doctrine, which forbade transfer of a dependent American territory from one non-American nation to another, had meant ever since its formulation early in the nineteenth century. But the

* See below, p. 85.

method of enforcing the Monroe Doctrine had already been revolutionized by Roosevelt from unilateral action by the United States to multilateral action by all the American Republics, that is, by the methods of collective security.*

The multilateral method of enforcing the no-transfer corollary was to be implemented by the Act of Havana in August, 1940; and in that same month the Hyde Park Agreement established the Permanent Joint Board of Defense for Canada and the United States, which was the first institution for cooperation between the United States and a government fighting Germany. Defense of Canada strengthened the defenses of Great Britain. Therefore a broad interpretation of the Kingston Address of 1938 is that it created a link between the collective security system of Pan America and Great Britain. The Neutrality Act exempted Canada from cash-and-carry restrictions on trade with the United States. To the fullest extent possible under the terms of that law, the Kingston Address attached the United States to the coalition of powers which Chamberlain could assemble against Hitler. Chamberlain chose to use his resources of power not to prevent Hitler's conquest of Czechoslovakia but only to discourage him from launching an unnecessary war to take it. This betrayal of collective security did not detract from the significance of Roosevelt's promise to Canada as a step towards that policy, although it could be argued that the Kingston Address was too small a step to justify Chamberlain in refusing concessions to Hitler with the expectation of American support.

Politically, the narrow meaning of Roosevelt's Kingston Address made it acceptable to American isolationists even though its broad meaning was internationalist. It illustrated the President's ability to find common ground with his opponents and to lead them in practical matters towards understanding and acceptance of his policy. Beard ignores the Kingston Address. It was sufficiently public and sufficiently clear as a step towards collective security to refute his theses.

A trivial but symbolic act of direct cooperation between the United States and Britain had occurred a few days before the Kingston Address and added its measure of meaning to the development of Roosevelt's policy. The islands of Canton and Enderbury in the South Pacific Phoenix Group were uninhabited and

* See below, pp. 95-8.

valueless until they were found useful as stopping points for trans-Pacific planes. Both Britain and the United States dusted off old claims to them. But the conflict was dissolved by an Executive Agreement of August 11, 1938, which established a remarkable degree of Anglo-American cooperation. A condominium of joint ownership and common use was provided for fifty years. Both nations received access to the islands for purposes of civil aviation and arrangements for military aviation were designated for future agreement.[2]

The islands became an important link between the United States and Australia during the critical months after Pearl Harbor. A matter of small dimensions, the Agreement of August, 1938, was nevertheless of such symbolic import that President Roosevelt used it in a toast to the King of England when he entertained him in the White House less than a year later: "May this kind of understanding between our countries grow ever closer, and may our friendship prosper." [3] An isolationist administration would have found it easy and, from the narrowly nationalist point of view, advantageous to exploit the weak position of Britain in 1938 and obtain exclusive United States ownership of Canton and Enderbury.

Such was not the Roosevelt policy. When the Czechoslovakian crisis reached its climax in September, he could point to condominium in Canton and Enderbury, the Good Neighbor policy in Latin America, concert with Britain and France in his naval building program, uncompromising adherence to the Stimson Doctrine, and his Kingston Address as positive evidences that he stood for cooperation among peaceful nations against aggression. They failed to affect the crisis measurably because they could not overcome the effect of the Neutrality Act in removing the United States from the forces Hitler faced. Besides this, domestic problems, difficult of solution, weakened the international position of the United States and they must be examined for a fuller understanding of Roosevelt's policy during and after the crisis.

## Domestic Distractions

The chief domestic concern of the moment was recovery from the economic "recession" of 1937. That lapse in the prosperity achieved under the New Deal severely injured the prestige of the administration and public confidence in its economic policies. It discouraged initiatives in foreign policy and reduced the influence abroad of those that were attempted. In the spring of 1938, the President was forced to expand the rolls of the Works Progress Administration to give work to new millions of unemployed and to revive "pump-priming" with large-scale appropriations for deficit spending. Credit inflation was resorted to once more. These measures ended the recession during the summer, but the upturn was slow, and earlier hopes that the Roosevelt administration had found a permanent solution for economic depression had been discouraged. Signs multiplied that the administration was losing support even for the domestic policies which had been its chief attraction to voters.

Roosevelt's failure to win the Court fight in 1937 was matched in 1938 when Congress refused to enact the Executive Reorganization Bill on the grounds that it would make him a "dictator." His third great defeat on domestic issues came during the very days when the Czechoslovakian crisis mounted to its dangerous climax. His answer to the Democratic Congressmen who had combined with Republicans to defeat the Court and Executive bills was a campaign to persuade voters in the primary elections to nominate Democrats who supported his policies. This "purge" took the President chiefly into Southern constituencies whose representatives supported his foreign policy and it embittered them sufficiently to risk a party split that would add Southern Democrats to Western Democrats and Republicans in opposition to collective security.

Hitler's assault on Czechoslovakia and Roosevelt's "purge" campaign were identified by the latter's opponents as cut from one dictatorial pattern. Roosevelt raised fundamental issues in his designation of the South as the nation's "economic problem number one," requiring thoroughgoing application of reforms, and in his declaration that he preferred liberal Republicans in Congress as against conservative Democrats. Thus he invited simultaneously a revolution in the social structure of the South and a revolution in the party affiliations of voters in every section. In January, 1936, the President had declared that the forces which produced fascism and aggression abroad were the same forces which produced reaction against the New Deal at home.[4]

But this simple formula was contradicted by the complexities of factionalism in American politics. Conservative southern Democrats and northeastern Republicans supported a strong foreign policy against Axis aggression, while liberal western Democrats and Republicans were isolationists. The "purge" threatened to weaken rather than strengthen the administration's drive for a renovated foreign policy. A great fact became clear: the President could not win both further liberal domestic reforms and a new foreign policy. He had to choose.

The failure of the "purge" made the choice easier. The campaign was mismanaged by members of the Brains Trust, who were political amateurs to whom the President entrusted its strategy while Postmaster General James A. Farley, the genius of party regularity, was removed to the background. The failure to work consistently against all conservative Democratic candidates for office and lapses into hesitancy which political experts found inexplicable and which gave the "purge" campaign a strangely erratic quality, may be explained by a growing realization ón the part of the President in the days of Munich that he could not achieve both his domestic and his foreign purposes. The position of Senator Carter Glass on the two issues must have been educative. Glass opposed the "purge" and made a bitter retort when the President condemned the poll tax in southern states. A week later he announced that, as Chairman of the Senate Appropriations Committee, although he had formerly opposed the President's naval building program, in view of the European crisis he would now support it.[5]

Early in September, Roosevelt made his first response since the Kingston Address to the mounting crisis abroad. He directed a "quiet mobilization" of resources, including such measures as elimination of bottlenecks in electric power distribution which made eastern cities vulnerable. But this news was overshadowed by his announcement on the same day that he advocated a party revolution to make his own a party exclusively of liberalism and the Republican Party one exclusively of conservatism. Direct intervention in the European crisis was not contemplated. According to Anne O'Hare McCormick, *New York Times* political writer, the administration rested on the conviction that its actions during the past year served notice that "nobody can start anything without weighing the possible reactions in this country." She quoted administration officials: "We have traced a question mark in the

international sky, which must cast a long shadow over the calculations now in progress." [6]

Roosevelt during the next week carried the "purge" campaign
to sensational lengths by "invading" the eastern shore of Maryland to invite voters to defeat Senator Millard Tydings. He was
met by unfriendly demonstrations and banners: "Keep the Free
State Free!" At the same time, Europe mobilized and placed more
men under arms than at any time since 1914. Hitler rejected a
fourth set of Czech concessions to the Sudeten Germans. The dictator dilated to the music of *Parsifal* while Storm Troopers pa-
raded at the Nuremberg *Parteitag,* and then he bemoaned the
absence of the Bohemian crown from the Hapsburg imperial re-
galia he had captured in Vienna. A revolt in Chile gave evidence
of Nazi-Fascist inspiration. Hitler's closing speech at Nuremberg
was feared as a pronouncement of war. He declared Czech behavior to be "unbearable."

Chamberlain on September 15 made his first flight with um-
brella to confer with Hitler at Berchtesgaden. When he returned
to London to consult his Cabinet, the Czech government stiffened.
It drew up a warrant for the arrest of Henlein, and President
Beneš told Runciman that no settlement dismembering the Republic would be considered. The French government seemed to
support the Czechs; if France's support materialized, it would
bring France's Soviet alliance into effect.

At this moment Roosevelt's domestic campaign collapsed with
the victories in the primaries of the two men whom he had marked
most clearly for defeat—Senators Tydings, of Maryland, and
George, of Georgia. He canceled further speaking plans and un-
expectedly went to Washington to confer with his Cabinet on the
European crisis. This was perhaps the most momentous meeting
in the history of the Roosevelt administration. From this moment
forward, the struggle for domestic reform was subordinated to the
struggle for collective security.

## That Reason and Equity Might Prevail

The British Cabinet in conjunction with the French government announced to an astounded world that Czechoslovakia must
surrender territory of predominantly German population to Hitler and must neutralize its foreign policy for the future. Popular

opposition to this betrayal was instantaneous in Britain and France as well as in the United States, where the press was almost unanimous in condemnation. It was best expressed by Winston Churchill who said: "The belief that security can be obtained by throwing a small state to the wolves is a fatal delusion." He used the weight of his knowledge to combat any delusion that time was on the side of the democracies by adding: "The war potential of Germany will increase in a short time more rapidly than it will be possible for France and Great Britain to complete the measures necessary for their defense." [7] Tension mounted as the Czech Cabinet, although it agreed to Sudeten cessions, opposed any further retreat, inaugurated general mobilization, and installed General Syrovy as Premier of a government of national defense.

At this point, Roosevelt's decision to abandon the domestic "purge" and, beyond that, to abandon unfulfilled plans for domestic reform, was made implicit in a speech of Postmaster General Farley on September 22. It signified Farley's return to leadership of administration political strategy. He closed the "purge" episode, indicated that no reprisals would be made against the President's conservative Democratic opponents, and called upon all Democrats to close their ranks in a new demonstration of unity.[8]

The unity of the Democratic Party could not be restored merely by a word even from Farley, but the strategy had been fixed and it would be pursued now until it was successful a year later. In immediate terms, the Farley speech came in time to help turn the country from domestic squabbles to consolidated support of a presidential intervention in the European crisis at its most critical moment.

Chamberlain flew to Godesberg on September 22 to offer the Sudetenland to Hitler in return for an assurance that he would not take it by force. At the same time Britain worked at Geneva to give Hitler a guaranty that collective security was abolished as the policy of the League in return for a four-power pact which should end all conflicts among Germany, Italy, France and Britain. Hitler promptly raised his demands on September 23 to include plebiscites in Czech districts where Germans were in minority and delivered them to Chamberlain in an ultimatum with date of October 1. Chamberlain ordered air raid shelters to be dug in London parks and mobilized the Royal Navy. A British government spokesman announced that if Germany attacked Czechoslovakia, France would assist its ally, which would bring the Franco-Soviet Alliance into operation, and that Britain would stand by France. Chamberlain wrote to Hitler that his new demands were unacceptable and urged a renewal of negotiations.

United States diplomats cabled to the President urging that he intervene. Secretary Hull saw dangers in such a course and did not believe any feasible action would be effective. Welles urged action. The President saw no danger if he avoided involvement in such schemes as the one proposed by Ambassador to France William Bullitt, that Roosevelt should offer himself as arbitrator. The moment for intervention was carefully chosen. Hull warned the President not to allow himself to be associated with appeasement of Hitler.[9]

On the morning of September 26, *after Chamberlain had rejected Hitler's September 23 demands,* Roosevelt seconded Chamberlain's request for a renewal of negotiations in a letter addressed to Hitler and Beneš. Copies were sent to other governments. The Munich Agreement of September 30, in which Chamberlain and Daladier gave in to Hitler's demands of September 23 and more, has been used as Hull had feared it would be—to support the argument that Roosevelt's letter of September 26 supported Chamberlain's appeasement of Hitler at the expense of the Czechoslovakian Republic. But the date of the letter refutes this argument. On September 26 the public position of the British and French governments was one of rejection of further appeasement of Hitler; they promised to make a stand against the September 23 demands and to join in a united front with the Soviet Union in defiance of the ultimatum. Chamberlain's request for further negotiations in these circumstances did not foreshadow acceptance but rather rejection of Hitler's September 23 demands. Roosevelt's letter seconded the strongest stand against Hitler that Chamberlain made during the crisis, one which faced Hitler with an end to appeasement and the prospect of a two-front war.

Roosevelt's letter added the moral weight of the United States to the potential coalition against aggression. It asked Hitler to continue negotiations, which, the British government had publicly indicated, would take place on the basis of British and French rejection of the September 23 demands and of cooperation with the Soviet Union in defense of the Czech Republic against those demands. Roosevelt expressed hope that in the negotiations *"reason* and the spirit of *equity* may prevail." [10] These words cannot be interpreted to signify a desire for the capitulation to Hitler registered by the Munich Agreement. Roosevelt's letter of September 26 was an initiative in support of collective security.

Hitler's demands, prior to September 23, could be justified by an appeal to a narrow view of the principle of self-determination. His answer to Roosevelt exploited that view. But Hitler also attempted to deny that Roosevelt's hope for "reason and equity" in the solution would be violated if he further insisted on his September 23 demands for plebiscites in areas where Germans were in minority:

Since the Czechoslovak Government had previously declared itself already to be in agreement with the British and French Governments that the Sudeten German settlement area would be separated from the Czechoslovak state and joined to the German Reich, the proposals of the German memorandum [of September 23] contemplate nothing else than to bring about a prompt and equitable fulfillment of that Czechoslovak promise.[11]

Fair plebiscites in Sudeten-minority areas probably would not result in cessions to Germany beyond those already consented to by Czechoslovakia. Roosevelt in a second letter to Hitler, on September 27, did not reject the latter's strained interpretation of what "equity" required, but placed all emphasis on the continuance of negotiations and a peaceful solution.[12]

The answer of President Beneš to Roosevelt's September 26 letter expressed gratitude for the President's intervention not merely because it asked for a peaceful solution but because it asked for a just and equitable solution:

Czechoslovakia is grateful to you, Mr. President, for your message, a message which in these grave moments can contribute toward a just solution of the dispute. I believe that even today the dispute could be settled in a spirit of equity without resort to force and the whole Czechoslovak nation still hopes this will be the case.[13]

But Chamberlain in his reply ignored Roosevelt's appeal for "reason and equity" in the solution. He placed exclusive emphasis on a peaceful solution:

His Majesty's Government have done and are doing their very utmost to secure a peaceful solution of the present difficulties, and they will relax no effort so long as there remains any prospect of achieving that object.

He said he was making an appeal to Hitler to resume negotiations and thanked Roosevelt fulsomely for his "encouragement." [14] Chamberlain had decided to dissociate the Soviet government from the situation, which removed a chief element of strength in curbing Hitler, and instead to invite Mussolini to join in a settlement which should pave the way for a four-power pact. Behind the scenes, Chamberlain evidently enlisted Roosevelt's aid to secure Mussolini's participation. Roosevelt sent a personal telephone message to the Italian dictator urging him to help settle the conflict by negotiation.[15]

## Roosevelt an Appeaser of Hitler?

In this way Chamberlain made Roosevelt appear to support his own turn from collective security to appeasement. He informed Hitler he was ready to go to Germany to renew negotiations on a four-power basis and that he felt certain Hitler could "get all the essentials without war and without delay." [16] These words foreshadowed Chamberlain's capitulation to Hitler not only on the September 23 demands but on new territorial demands totally unjustifiable by any appeal to the principle of self-determination. They were sent on September 27, the same day Roosevelt sent his appeal to Mussolini. Even if the President knew of them, it would be difficult to regard them as committing him in any degree to the capitulation at Munich. Better evidence of Chamberlain's policy seemed to be his statements in a radio address on the same day that Hitler's demands were unreasonable and that Britain would fight if any nation decided to dominate the world by force.[17] And the best evidence for administration leaders was a telephone message from Ambassador Joseph P. Kennedy in London late on September 26 "that the British government had assured the French of its support in the event of war. Also, that Chamberlain had informed Hitler that his demands . . . could not be accepted, but asked him to continue negotiations." [18]

The only connection between the President and the Munich

Agreement was the indirect one of his support of Chamberlain's invitation to Mussolini. The absence of France's allies, Czechoslovakia and the Soviet Union, from the Munich Conference and the presence of Italy signified Chamberlain's abandonment of collective security and return to appeasement, but Chamberlain's and Kennedy's statements misled Roosevelt.

A clear indication that the administration intended to strengthen resistance by Chamberlain to Hitler was Hull's private assurance to Ambassador Lindsay, which "much moved" the latter, that, in the event of war,

I want your Government to know that our Government and nation will have no policy or purpose to supplant existing, established British trade in various parts of the world. Whatever we might do in the way of securing the trade of numerous other countries I might mention, we would have no intention to displace British trade by taking advantage of its disadvantages due to the war and Great Britain's participation in it.[19]

This assurance should have meant something to Chamberlain's government of businessmen, but in larger matters than trade they had lost their grip on political requirements of even the narrowest self-interest.

This was tragically demonstrated by the Munich Agreement of September 30. By it Hitler obtained his demands of September 23. But even this did not define the full extent of Chamberlain's appeasement. Plebiscites in German-minority areas of Czechoslovakia, which the agreement required, were never held and Hitler added those areas to his winnings a few days later without objection by Britain or France. Still further areas not even mentioned in the agreement were also taken by Hitler, equally without objection by the "friends" of the Czech government. The significance of these acquisitions was that they gave Hitler total control of the strategic areas vital to defense of the Czechoslovak nation and total control of transportation routes and economic spheres which were only partially within areas of majority Sudeten German population. Even Poland and Hungary were allowed to take slices of territory from the abandoned Republic. What was left of Czechoslovakia was militarily untenable, an open road for Hitler to the East. All this Chamberlain gave Hitler in return for promises to respect the integrity of the rump Republic, to make no more territorial demands in Europe, to refrain from war, and to consider a general settlement of all issues in a four-power pact. The first and second promises were violated in March, 1939, the third in September, 1939, and negotiations for a four-power pact quickly broke down when Hitler made impossible demands.

Roosevelt's message to Mussolini of September 27, sent at a moment when Chamberlain had publicly rejected Hitler's demands of September 23 and announced Britain's readiness to go to war, cannot be interpreted to associate him with Chamberlain's extreme appeasement of Hitler in the Munich Agreement and subsequent failure to hold Hitler to its terms. Rather the President's interventions, on September 27 and the day before, represent attempts to strengthen British policy at moments when it seemed oriented against appeasement and towards resistance to Hitler. This conclusion is strengthened by the fact that Roosevelt and Hull carefully and pointedly refused to approve the terms of the Munich Agreement.[20] On October 26, the President in a radio address made clear that he did not even share Chamberlain's faith that peace, if not with honor, at least peace "in our time," had been secured.*

The false charge that the President had implicated himself in Chamberlain's appeasement of Hitler at Munich was commonly made in highly colored political circumstances, especially the election campaign of 1944. Beard makes a somewhat different but equally false interpretation of Roosevelt's role in the crisis. He ignores the circumstances and facts which support the conclusion in the paragraph above and cites only those parts of Roosevelt's September 26 letter which stated the standard limitations of United States participation in international affairs—"the United States has no political entanglements"—thus enabling him to draw the conclusion: "It was far removed from any advocacy of collective security, sanctions, or coercion." [21] Examination of Roosevelt's actions during the months following Munich will make doubly clear that the author of the Kingston Address and of the appeal for "reason and equity" in the solution of the Czechoslovakian crisis was no isolationist in his public conduct of policy any more than in his private faith.

* See below, p. 86.

# 4.

# *The Primacy of Foreign Danger*

Within the three months after Munich, President Roosevelt completed the change-over from a political strategy whose primary emphasis was on the achievement of domestic reforms to one whose primary emphasis was on the achievement of a foreign policy of collective security. Farley's speech of September 22, 1938, closing the "purge" episode, was the first indication of the new orientation. But it did not suggest the full scope of the President's change of strategy. Nor did the blows suffered by the administration in Congressional elections make impossible continuance under full pressure of the struggle to wipe out the domestic evils against which the President had declared war in his statements that one third of the nation was ill-fed, ill-clothed, and ill-housed, and that the South was the nation's economic problem number one.

## *The Great Decision*

Relegation of that struggle to a secondary position was the result of a decision that Axis aggression presented greater dangers to the American people than did domestic evils. The "illogical" alignments of party factions on domestic and foreign issues made it impossible to pursue strong new measures in both fields at the same time. Roosevelt chose to conciliate southern Democrats and northern Republican business groups, who supported a stronger foreign policy, by conceding to their hatred of the New Deal.

The President's decision was based on his judgment that the Munich Agreement meant not peace but war. In his press conference on September 30 his only comments on the agreement were philosophic observations on the effects of modern communications on international crises, remarks so cool that they seemed to satirize enthusiasm for "peace in our time." Only minor officials, who refused to allow their names to be used, praised the agreement as a victory after twenty years for "a balance of power . . . in Europe." [1] The Soviet government was the first in the world to announce its convictions that peace was not assured by Munich and that Germany had been made more formidable for war.[2] American newspaper correspondents abroad during the days after Munich were undecided whether Europe had entered a new era of peace or a short interlude before war.[3]

Under Secretary of State Sumner Welles on October 3 sent up a trial balloon to discover whether "peace in our time" could indeed be made a reality. In a radio address he claimed that Roosevelt's messages had tipped the scales in favor of peace and asserted that the United States would welcome an international conference for arms reduction and economic peace.[4] This in a guarded way revived the Welles plan of the year before, but Roosevelt the next day refused to support Welles, and the State Department labeled conjecture on such a development "premature." [5]

A day later Roosevelt gave further indications that his policy would not be based on Chamberlain's assumption that Hitler had been pacified. He rejected requests to continue his "purge" campaign by helping Governor Earle and Senator Guffey of Pennsylvania win renominations, and he announced that the administration was concerned about foreign espionage in the United States, against which the Department of Justice would act. Another straw in the wind was the demand of the United States government on October 7 that Mussolini stop discrimination against American Jews in Italy.[6]

Secretary Hull announced that he would push the writing of reciprocal trade agreements, especially with Great Britain, but that Germany could not receive benefits from the American policy because it practiced discriminations against American trade. Hull appeared to be seconding Britain's efforts to pull Italy out of the Axis orbit when he declared that a *modus vivendi* for trade with that nation had been signed and that the cooperation of Roosevelt and Mussolini for peace at Munich created sentiments favorable to a reciprocal trade agreement.[7]

Hitler quickly gave proof that skepticism of "peace in our time" was justified. On October 9 he returned to the attitude of menace. He announced expansion of German armaments and said he could not rely on Chamberlain's promises because he might be replaced at any moment by Duff Cooper, who had resigned as First Lord of the Admiralty in protest against the Munich Agreement, by Churchill or by Eden, all of whom were "agents of Jewish internationalism and Bolshevism." Hitler had evidently not enjoyed his role of runner-up to Chamberlain as champion of peace. He said: "We just cannot stand for a governess-like guardianship of Germany." [8] At the same time he made farcical Chamberlain's efforts for a definitive four-power pact by demanding that Britain accept a limitation of air strength to 35 per cent of Germany's and threatening that otherwise Germany would scrap the Anglo-German Naval Agreement of 1935, which had granted Germany unlimited submarines and 35 per cent of Britain's strength in surface warships. The revival of menace by Hitler was matched in the Far East, where Japanese military extremists took advantage of the European crisis to get rid of the moderate Foreign Minister Ugaki and to launch an assault on Hankow in the Yangtze Valley.

Roosevelt's response was prompt. Two days after Hitler's return to menace, the President announced an expansion of United States armaments, naval and military, amounting to $300,000,000. He declared it was made necessary by the state of world affairs.[9] Secretary Hull urged the importation and stockpiling of strategic raw materials. On October 21 he wrote to the President that "events of the past few weeks" had shown the wisdom of action "with all possible despatch." Congress was unwilling to appropriate sufficient funds, so Hull in April, 1939, attempted barter trades of surplus wheat and cotton for British, Dutch and Belgian rubber and tin.[10]

The Chamberlain government struggled for many months to retain its prestige as the architect of "peace in our time," but at the same time accelerated rearmament. Roosevelt's policy did not contain the contradiction. His campaign against foreign spies filled headlines and was directed against Germany, Italy, and Japan. But its public effect, if not its actual operation, was nullified by the Dies Committee of Congress, which was authorized to investigate un-American activities. After a few days of concern over Nazi and Fascist subversion, it returned to its normal concentration on publicity for unsupported evidence that Communists caused sit-down strikes, that Red Russians were flooding immigration channels, and so forth in a continual stream of propaganda calculated to discredit the New Deal as "Communist." Representative J. Parnell Thomas of New Jersey announced that the New Deal was one of the "four horsemen of autocracy," along with Nazism, Fascism and Bolshevism. But this parity was too kind to the administration for Thomas to sustain and he explained that Bolsheviks had gained most under Roosevelt, who carried out Communist plans to sabotage capitalism by placing restrictive legislation and staggering taxes on American business.[11] This argument was the chief weapon of anti-New Dealers. It was calculated to distract public attention from Hitler and Mussolini and fix it on Stalin and Roosevelt as the chief enemies of American institutions. This was particularly necessary because the Gallup Poll showed that Roosevelt's intervention in the European crisis, his refusal to support its outcome, and his liquidation of the "purge" campaign were accompanied by the sharpest rise in his popularity of his career—from 53.3 per cent of the major party vote to 59.6 per cent in two weeks.[12]

Anne O'Hare McCormick, after conversations with the President, revealed in the *New York Times Magazine* of October 16 his analysis of the current domestic and foreign situations and his new determinations of policy. He had pondered the interrelations of domestic and foreign problems and decided that since Munich had made war more likely, with consequent danger to the security of the United States, it was mandatory to reorient his political strategy. The phrase "a little left of center" no longer described the direction of his domestic policy. He still thought of himself as a "fighting liberal." But he had now dropped the purge campaign to break traditional groupings in the two major parties and realign them to make his own a party exclusively of liberals and the Republican a party exclusively of conservatives. He told Mrs. McCormick he saw no good reason to establish a new party. The term "fighting liberal" seemed inappropriate as he told her that he contemplated nothing new in domestic policy. He now regarded the framework of New Deal reforms already laid down to be complete. No future "surprises" were in store. Henceforth, corrections, amendments, extensions and developments of existing legislation, but no "new departures" might be expected. He admitted that as "a good bargainer" he often asked for more than he expected to get. He had been defeated in the purge and would not be cast down if the coming Congressional elections gave him a further setback.

As for the fundamental issues he had raised in the purge, his mood seemed one of disillusionment with the advice he had received. He confessed to his interviewer that he himself did not know how to do what he thought ought to be done to strike a balance between the submerged one-third of the nation and the upper two-thirds, and he doubted whether anyone really knew enough about economics to guarantee results or could know enough in the face of continual and incalculable economic changes.

If these were moods hardly suited to a liberal fighting domestic conservatism, they were well suited to the strategy of a believer in collective security who had decided that the Axis had replaced domestic conservatism as the main threat to American democracy. Mrs. McCormick wrote that "the tense weeks of crisis convinced Mr. Roosevelt not only that the first defense of democracy is strength on the home front but also that if a new synthesis of interest and energies is required to save representative government it must be worked out in this country." This was a confession that the purge weakened the defense of democracy on the home front and that the President had learned a lesson from it and the European crisis which he would apply by refraining from any further "surprises" or "new departures" in domestic affairs. In the new period, danger from abroad necessitated internal unity and consolidation of forces. Munich was a setback to collective security but it was not a reason to abandon the conception that the United States had an interest in the preservation of free institutions in the world; rather a heavier responsibility had been placed on the United States precisely because Britain and France had not discharged their responsibility. Roosevelt would turn to consolidate the nation's unity and strengthen its defenses not in the spirit of isolationism but in order to create a bastion of world import.

As for future moves on the international stage, the President, as reported by Mrs. McCormick, was torn between a desire to play a role as a world leader of democracy and hard-headed suspicion of the "power politics" of other democracies. One may surmise that examples of "power politics" which caused the President's frustration and suspicion were Chamberlain's rejection of Roosevelt's proposal in January of the Welles plan, his subsequent betrayal of the Stimson Doctrine in return for narrow "assurances" from Mussolini of British Mediterranean interests, and most of all Chamberlain's betrayal of Roosevelt's expectation that he would keep his promises of September 24-27 to reject Hitler's September 23 demands and face him with a united front of powers including the Soviet Union—expectations on which the President had predicated his messages to the dictators. Perhaps he regretted his messages because they made him seem, however falsely, a party to the Munich Agreement. He told Mrs. McCormick the clue to his relation to the crisis was not to be found in those messages but in his Kingston Address. He claimed it had the direct effect in Europe of giving notice that the Western Hemisphere was a cooperative self-defense system. The major tendency of administration foreign policy would now be to build up that system. The idea of a round-table parley of world leaders had always appealed to the President, but for the present he was cautious and all signs pointed "Home!" [13]

Rearmament was one of the most important contributions of the United States to the cooperative system of the Western Hemisphere. Roosevelt also maintained a minimum cooperation along parallel tracks with Great Britain. Winston Churchill wanted to develop it into fuller cooperation. He appealed publicly to the United States to join Britain and France in curbing aggression in Europe.[14]

His was a voice in the wilderness. His own government misused and rejected such cooperation. American isolationists were infuriated by Churchill's invitation. William Randolph Hearst decided his answer to Churchill must be addressed to an audience wider than even his chain of newspapers provided. In a radio speech he ignored the Axis powers but condemned France as "communistic" and Britain as "monarchical." Both nations therefore lacked any basis for cooperation with the United States. Britain and the United States cooperating, Hearst said, would be "one hog, one guinea-pig." [15]

As it became clear that Roosevelt supported Churchill's view of Chamberlain's policy, opposition developed not only from expected sources like Hearst, but from sources inside the administration itself. Concurrence in the Chamberlain view of Munich, which had been announced anonymously by minor officials of the administration, was now expressed by the Ambassador to Great Britain, Joseph P. Kennedy, an intimate friend of Hearst. In a Trafalgar Day speech in London, he advised the democracies and dictatorships to stop emphasizing their differences and work together. Arthur Krock, whose information was generally authoritative, wrote that the State Department had seen and approved Kennedy's manuscript.[16]

The Kennedy view was summarized in a new slogan, "We can do business with Hitler," which represented the most blind and the most dangerous tendency of isolationist thought. It appealed to businessmen who controlled many of the nation's largest industrial corporations. It only became generally known after war began that their chief mode of doing business with Hitler was by no means the hard-headed, profitable arrangement the sloganeers implied. They continued to obey the terms of their cartel agreements with I.G. Farben and other German, Italian, and Japanese corporations long after the Axis industrialists had ceased to obey them and had turned the agreements into channels through which American corporations unprofitably served the interests of the Axis war machines, particularly by providing them with valuable new patents.[17]

### "Peace by Fear"

The Hearst and Kennedy speeches suggested that American isolationists would enlist powerful economic interests to support Chamberlain's appeasement of Hitler. Roosevelt answered the challenge in a radio address to the *Herald Tribune* Forum on October 26. It left no doubt that the President stood with Churchill as against Chamberlain and Kennedy. His purpose was to make Americans understand why they could not rely on Chamberlain's promise of "peace in our time":

It is becoming increasingly clear that peace by fear has no higher or more enduring quality than peace by the sword.
There can be no peace if the reign of law is to be replaced by a recurrent sanctification of sheer force.
There can be no peace if national policy adopts as a deliberate instrument the threat of war.

He made it unmistakable that he was speaking of Hitlerism:

There can be no peace if national policy adopts as a deliberate instrument the dispersion all over the world of millions of helpless and persecuted wanderers with no place to lay their heads.

There can be no peace if humble men and women are not free to think their own thoughts, to express their own feelings, to worship God.

Once more Roosevelt offered disarmament as a concrete measure in which the United States was willing to join to meliorate the world situation. But he coupled the offer with a warning that the United States, lacking "greater reassurance than can be given by words: the kind of proof which can be given, for example, by actual discussions, leading to actual disarmament," would increase its own military and naval establishments. He emphasized the threat more heavily than the offer. His peroration was an appeal for American support of international cooperation on the basis of the new drive for national unity:

Let us work with greater unity for peace among the nations of the world, for restraint, for negotiations and for community of effort. Let us work for the same ideals within our own borders in our relations with each other, so that we may, if the test ever comes, have that unity of will with which alone a democracy can successfully meet its enemies.[18]

This address was a preliminary announcement of the administration's new orientation. The new direction was not pursued without deviation. Vast movements of domestic liberal political import, however disunifying in their effect, could not be abandoned faster than their leaders, many of them internationalists as well as liberals, came to understand the harsh necessity. On November 4, 1938, the eve of Election Day, the President made a radio address in which he placed all emphasis on the need for domestic reform and the importance of electing liberals to Congress and to state offices. But the divisive issues and rancors of the purge campaign were not revived. The President had been accused of pursuing simple revenge against anyone who had opposed his Supreme Court "packing" plan. Governor Herbert H. Lehman had opposed it and Roosevelt in August, 1938, had urged Farley to run for Governor of New York, but on November 4 he strongly advocated Lehman's re-election. He made a strong plea that considerations of race, color or creed should not determine choice of candidates, and then wove it into his new theme:

Remember that the Fathers of the American Revolution represented many religions and came from many foreign lands.

Remember that no matter what their origin they all agreed with Benjamin Franklin in that crisis: "We must indeed all hang together or most assuredly we shall all hang separately."

Remember that in these grave days in the affairs of the world we need internal unity—national unity. For the sake of the Nation that is good advice—and it never grows old.[19]

The administration was dealt a double blow in the 1938 elections. Within the Democratic Party, conservatives won over liberals in the primaries in all contests which the President had entered except one. And in the elections on November 5, Republicans increased their strength in Congress for the first time since 1928. Democrats were still in majority in both houses, but the coalition of conservatives of both parties which had already defeated key administration domestic measures was greatly strengthened.

Roosevelt told his intimates that the defeats were the result in every case of local conditions. Farley collected opinions of Democratic leaders throughout the nation and found them agreed that the defeats were caused by opposition to the "radicalism" of New Deal domestic policies. Newspaper campaigns against the President's "left-wing" advisers, led off by Arthur Krock's report that Harry Hopkins had declared: "We will spend and spend, and tax and tax, and elect and elect," discredited the administration in the opinions of many voters. Farley asked Roosevelt to conciliate Democratic Representatives and Senators who had opposed him, and even to grant them patronage, but the President would not easily abandon his feuds with such men as Senators Carter Glass and Walter George.

The President was suspected of ambition for a third term. A loose association of conservative administration leaders was formed by Farley, Vice President John Nance Garner, Secretary Hull and others. They opposed the nomination of Roosevelt or any liberal such as Hopkins or Henry Wallace. Garner, Hull, and Farley were the leading candidates, according to polls. Farley later wrote that he had reason to believe the President favored him at the end of 1938.

As early as August, 1938, the President had advised Farley to run for Governor of New York to acquire a background of statesmanship in preparation for presidential candidacy in 1940. Farley

refused. Lacking such a background, he nevertheless led a conservative cabal against the President and in favor of his own candidacy during the next two years.[20] Thus presidential ambitions,
the classical disrupter of Cabinet harmony in American administrations, intensified opposition to the President's domestic policies and widened fissures between the President and conservatives
among voters, among members of both parties in Congress, and in
the administration itself. If Roosevelt had launched new campaigns
for domestic reform when the new Congress met, defeat and an
irrevocable split in his party would have been very likely.

He did not launch such campaigns. Farley and his circle, echoed
widely in the press, saw only the "damned Dutch stubbornness" [21]
of Roosevelt in refusing to surrender completely to his opponents
in Congress and slake their thirst for patronage to lubricate party
unity. But on larger issues of policy the President effectively checked
the growth of opposition by reducing domestic affairs to secondary position and working for party and national unity on a program of foreign policy.

External events created reason enough for this strategy without
making it necessary to impute it to *ad hoc* political considerations.
The external danger did not require artificial stimulation to make
it the leading issue in American politics. The isolationists who
abandoned their position within the following year and supported
the President's foreign policy consistently thereafter were obviously more influenced in their reversal by the rise of the Axis than
by Roosevelt's new strategy. But Roosevelt by that strategy reduced the bitterness over domestic issues which threatened to
interfere with his opponents' view of the Axis danger and to drive
them into blind opposition to anything he advocated. That the
menace became clear at a time when it provided a means for him
to restore his leadership was fortuitous but that did not make it
either more or less minatory. Besides, Roosevelt had made it clear
from the beginning of his administration that the danger was real
to him. And in the realm of human frailty and personal stubbornness, it was doubtless as difficult for him to concede to conservatives on domestic issues as it was for isolationists to concede to him
on foreign issues.

As if to verify the necessity for the President's decisions, Hitler
a few days after the November elections launched a brutal pogrom
against the Jews of Germany. No event did more to awaken Amer-

icans to the nature of Nazism. Prior to it, persecutions of religious and political minorities had been conducted with some privacy and verification of horrendous facts had been difficult. Hitler seemed oppressed by his promises of good behavior to Chamberlain at Munich, and fearful that the peaceful conquest of Sudetenland had frustrated the blood-lust of his followers. He seized the excuse of an obscure assassination to release upon thousands of innocent persons the bestiality his regime cultivated as a German virtue. Sadism was avowed as the policy of the regime. Dr. Joseph Goebbels pronounced the pogrom a proof of the "healthy instincts" of Germans. Scenes of torture in daylight on public streets, not by mobs but by trained and disciplined technicians, created fear and loathing of the Hitler regime such as no government had earned since the Middle Ages. President Roosevelt led the expression of American reaction in a statement to the press: "I myself could scarcely believe that such things could happen in a twentieth century civilization." He ordered Ambassador Hugh Wilson to return home, for "report and consultation." [22]

The unifying effect of Nazism on American opinion was demonstrated in a national radio protest by such diverse leaders as former President Hoover, Secretary of the Interior Harold L. Ickes, and Governor Alfred M. Landon. The administration studied the possibility of international action to help refugees get out of Germany, but the Nazi government used such efforts to blackmail the world into buying German exports to strengthen its war machine and they failed. President Roosevelt secured a ruling by the Attorney General extending the visitors' permits of refugees in the United States to avoid thrusting victims into Hitler's grasp. Official relations between the United States and Germany deteriorated rapidly. Hitler withdrew his Ambassador from Washington. Secretary Ickes prevented Germany from obtaining helium in the United States when its zeppelins stopped using hydrogen. In December he publicly attacked Henry Ford and Colonel Lindbergh for accepting German Eagle decorations from Hitler.

The German government made a formal protest against Ickes' speech and demanded an official expression of regret. Under Secretary Welles bluntly rejected the protest and the demand. He said Nazi policies "had shocked and confounded public opinion in the United States more profoundly than anything that had taken place in many decades." The President expressed his own view of Ickes' behavior by breaking precedent to drive out to his Secretary's country home, where he dined with him.[23]

Prime Minister Chamberlain confined his opinion of German barbarity to private expressions. He clung to the policy of appeasement. In November he obtained approval from the House of Commons for his April agreement with Mussolini and granted the Italian dictator *de jure* recognition of his conquest of Abyssinia.[24] France followed suit and signed a "good neighbor pact" with Germany on December 6. This was in the face of Hitler's preparations to violate his guaranty of Czechoslovakian independence. He placed the Catholic priest and Slovak Nazi Father Joseph Tiso in charge of a separate Slovakian government on December 1. Mussolini's Deputies on November 30 raised outlandish cries for "Tunisia, Corsica, Nice, Savoy!" At the same moment the Japanese Emperor, Advisory Council, Army, Navy and Privy Council announced the policy of a "new order in East Asia," which directly challenged not only China but all the powers with interests in that part of the world.[25]

The Roosevelt administration pursued an opposite course from that of Britain and France. It sought and found, in November and December, ways open to it before Congress met to strengthen United States policy against the Axis which would prepare for the crucial request to the new Congress to repeal the arms embargo.

## The Anglo-American Entente

The first of these was a reciprocal trade agreement with Great Britain. It was by far the most important agreement ever made under the Act of 1934. Secretary Hull had worked persistently since the London Economic Conference to induce Britain to modify its discriminatory and restrictive trading system of imperial preference tariffs and bilateral agreements. He bluntly told Ambassador Lindsay in 1936 that Britain's trade policy encouraged aggression by the Axis powers. In October of that year, the agreement among the United States, Britain, and France to stabilize their currencies and base them externally on gold established a foundation for trade agreements. Hull intensified his efforts.

But the British government was dominated by businessmen of

the Conservative Party who, like most American businessmen, saw nothing but the short-term economic interest of their own class in tariff protection. Secretary Hull delivered a remarkable series of lectures to the British government on the long-range economic and political effects of trade policy. He warned that if great industrial and trading countries like Britain and the United States did not liberalize their trade policies, countries that produced raw materials would be driven to establish their own industries and the Axis powers would presently "dominate nearly every square foot of trade territory other than that under the immediate control of Great Britain and the United States." He expressed "disappointment" that the statesmanship of Great Britain did not construct any policy alternative to that of rearmament in the passive expectation of war. It might be that war would come no matter what policy was pursued by the important nations, but the possibility of avoiding it by re-establishing sound trade on the basis of equal treatment for all nations must be grasped.

Hull placed the United States in the position of urging Great Britain to undertake economic internationalism as a peace offensive. It was a supreme test of the Secretary's talent for patience. Walter Runciman, President of the British Board of Trade, visited Washington in January, 1937, and tested Hull's patience too far when he indicated that Britain's economic policy towards Germany was as passive as its political policy. He said Britain was "waiting to see what Germany was going to do." Hull in his *Memoirs* states: "I jumped him." After this Tennessee operation, Hull proposed to Runciman that if Britain would take the lead in proclaiming a program of liberal economic relations, at least forty nations of the world would join and this would weaken the economic and political position of the Axis. Later in January, Lindsay delivered a memorandum in which his government cautiously indicated it was "approaching" the question of trade agreement negotiations with the United States.

Hull turned to Canada and secured the support of Prime Minister Mackenzie King as leverage on the British government. The British Imperial Conference of May, 1937, concluded that every practicable step to increase international trade should be taken. France and Belgium became interested. At last, in November, 1937, Hull could give formal notice that a trade agreement with Britain was to be negotiated. The effects were interesting. The

Nazi government studied whether American raw materials would supply Britain in case of war. Italy wanted to improve trade relations with the United States. The British Dominions favored Britain's action. But the full effect of the new departure could not be emphasized by the United States government. Hull writes:

On this side we had to minimize the political nuances of the prospective agreement, in deference to the widespread isolationist sentiment here. We could stress our belief that liberal commercial policy, epitomized by the trade agreements, tended to promote peace, but we had to be careful to emphasize that an agreement with Britain on trade comported no agreement whatever in the nature of a mutual political or defense policy.

Yet even without any such political or defense agreement, the effect of the action was to strengthen the ties between Britain and the United States in those two spheres.

Negotiations with Britain and Canada were carried on simultaneously. This helped break down British Conservative fears for the imperial preference system, which nevertheless impeded negotiations, as did the difficulties of finding items for concessions between two nations with similar industries. Several times negotiations almost broke down and were saved by Hull's direct appeals to Chamberlain. After Munich, Hull hurried negotiations to a conclusion and had the satisfaction of signing, on November 17, 1938, agreements with Britain and Canada which reversed the protectionist tendency of British policy and made large holes in the wall of imperial preference tariffs.

Hull in his *Memoirs* stresses the failure through tardiness of the agreement to achieve the highest result he had in view:

Again, the political effect of the accord was weighed throughout the world as much as its economic effect. But unfortunately it had come too late. Europe was already living in turmoil and fear. Had the British agreement been among our first instead of among our last, had it been negotiated in 1934, 1935, or 1936, its results would have been far greater. As it was, the agreement scarcely had a chance to operate. It came into effect [January 1, 1939] when war had been raging in Spain nearly two years and a half, in China nearly a year and a half; and only eight months after it began to operate Hitler marched into Poland.[26]

It was nevertheless true that the agreement marked a turn towards cooperation between the two great democracies whose significance transcended its economic terms. After lapses into extreme economic nationalism during the preceding two decades, the two nations established more intimate economic relations than ever in their history and also relations more intimate than those between any other two great powers. It was a demonstration of internationalism grafted on at the roots of world relations.

## Aid to China

Steps in the same direction were taken in the Far East before Congress met. In June, 1938, Hull had placed a moral embargo on airplane sales to Japan. That nation's exploitation of the European crisis to launch new military and political assaults was answered by the strongest demonstrations to date of support of China and opposition to its enemy. A stream of notes had been sent to the Japanese government by the United States since 1937 protesting persecutions of American citizens in China, seizure of their properties, and violations of American economic rights by Japanese monopolies. On November 3, 1938, the Japanese government justified its conduct in its proclamation of a "new order in East Asia," which baldly admitted that it was Japanese policy to destroy the Open Door and violate the Nine-Power Treaty in order to annex China to Japan. Foreign Minister Arita on November 16, 1938, told E. H. Dooman, United States Counselor of Embassy, that the Japanese government wanted "a new definition" of the Open Door in China.[27]

The United States reaction was not confined to words. A loan of $25,000,000 was made to the Chinese government early in December by the Export-Import Bank, and the Treasury arranged credits for the purchase of war materials. This aid flowed through a chink in the isolationist wall between the Johnson Act, from which China alone among larger peaceful nations was exempt, and the Neutrality Act, which the President had not invoked. It was an initial application of "aid to the victim of aggression."

At the end of the month, Secretary Hull sent a definitive answer to Japan. He stated that Japan's actions were not only "unjust and unwarranted" but counter to treaties voluntarily entered into by Japan with the United States and other powers. The attempt to make American enjoyment of rights in China dependent on American recognition of the Japanese "new order" which destroyed those rights, Hull labeled "highly paradoxical." The people and government of the United States "could not assent" to the establishment of the "new order." Hull denied that the United States "clung tenaciously" to any special rights and privileges in China; on the contrary, it steadily surrendered them in favor of China while encouraging the development of self-government and sovereignty in that country. Japan was invited to put forward proposals for peaceful negotiation of treaty revisions "based on justice and reason." [28]

Recognition of Japan's "new order" would have meant recognition of Japan's puppet government in China and violation of the Stimson Doctrine. The events of December showed that the United States government would not only adhere to that Doctrine but go beyond it to support China's war of defense. The European crisis had precipitated this development of American policy. Timidity would have dictated that the United States should retreat in Asia when danger loomed in Europe and the Japanese government synchronized its advances with preoccupation of the powers in Europe. But the Roosevelt administration was not intimidated. It countered the global scale of Axis advances with a global strategy of opposition.

## The Declaration of Lima

The third area in which the administration found it possible to move was Latin America. Isolationists supported policies in Latin America which, if applied to countries outside the hemisphere, they would not have tolerated. The administration was consequently allowed to implement in detail in Latin America the Good Neighbor policy, which had been originally announced as its world policy. That area was made a laboratory offering a preview of the policy for Europe and Asia which isolationists prevented the administration from carrying out until after the Second World War began. Latin America even offered a test in miniature of the effects of collective security on a potential aggressor nation. An analogy between the role of Argentina in American relations and the role of the Axis powers in world relations is not unduly strained because, what is usually forgotten, the Axis powers commanded approximately the same small percentage of world resources and military power that Argentina commanded in relation to the American Hemisphere.

Roosevelt's first task in Latin America was to liquidate American imperialist positions. He understood what President Wilson had failed to understand when he attempted in 1916 to combine the Latin American Pact for collective security with American imperialist encroachments on neighboring Republics—that the two policies were incompatible. A long and arduous process of demonstrating this in action began in 1933. All United States Marines and administrative agents were withdrawn from the Caribbean and Central American Republics, all rights of intervention and "protection" were abandoned, and new treaties were written with Cuba, Haiti, and Panama in which their absolute sovereignty was recognized. The Hoover administration had initiated this development and it met with no opposition in Congress.

The expropriation by the revolutionary Mexican government of President Cardenas of agricultural lands and oil properties owned by powerful American individuals, such as Hearst, and by such corporations as the Standard Oil Company, presented the most profound test of the Roosevelt administration's good faith in abandoning imperialism. Mexican action might establish a precedent for the expulsion of American economic interests from all Latin America as a corollary of the end of political imperialism. It provoked pressure in the United States in favor of strong measures. This pressure became formidable as American Roman Catholics demanded military intervention to suppress anti-clerical outbreaks in Mexico.

After many minor skirmishes, the climax of the Mexican attack on foreign property occurred on March 18, 1938, when holdings of British and American oil companies valued at several billions of dollars were expropriated. This was Mexico's declaration of economic independence and the date became a national holiday. All Latin America watched the response of the United States, and Axis agents worked to exploit the collapse of hemispheric unity. The Roosevelt administration resisted pressure to intervene with force, but it did make certain economic reprisals. For a time, it boycotted Mexican oil and suspended purchases of Mexican silver by the Treasury. Mexico broke off relations with

Britain, raised its tariff rates against imports from the United States, and made barter agreements to ship oil to Germany. It offered to pay owners for their actual investments, but American and British corporations insisted on payment also for unexploited oil reserves. They regarded the matter as involving the principle of property rights which, they maintained, the United States government dared not sacrifice without endangering such rights everywhere.

The Roosevelt administration saw the issue as involving the even more valuable principle of the Good Neighbor. Great powers like Britain had defaulted on their debts to the United States government and the essence of the Good Neighbor policy was that small nations should be allowed to exercise juridical equality with great powers. For three years Hull struggled without success to bring the American oil owners to agreement on Mexico's terms for payment, and then, a few days before Pearl Harbor, fearing war and desiring to cement relations with Mexico, he settled on Mexico's terms without the American owners' consent.[29] But in November, 1938, he had already laid out this pattern for settlement by accepting Mexico's terms of payment for expropriated agricultural lands owned by Americans.[30] This demonstrated that the American administration respected Mexican sovereignty as superior to extreme versions of private property rights, and it relaxed tension.

The timing of this preliminary settlement was obviously related to the new orientation of administration policy and the determination to erect a structure of collective security for the Western Hemisphere at the Inter-American Congress scheduled for the following month in Lima. It meant that the United States abandoned economic as well as political imperialism, as warranty of its good faith in proposing measures of collective security. Its success was registered in a private assurance from President Cardenas to Hull that the Mexican delegation to the forthcoming Conference was instructed to cooperate with the United States.[31]

The record of the United States at the Pan-American Conferences of 1933, 1936, and 1938 was one of steady and logical movement away from imperialism and towards collective security. In Montevideo, in 1933, the United States accepted a treaty with all the Republics which declared that no government had the right to intervene in the internal or external affairs of another state.

In Buenos Aires in 1936, Argentina, ruled by a dictator and threatening in its attitude towards neighbor republics, was recalcitrant. Hull obtained a convention in which all the Republics agreed to consult and collaborate in case of any menace to their peace from any source. The American Secretary favored compulsory consultation and collaboration, but Argentina inserted the weakening words: "if they so desire." [32]

The Conference at Lima in December, 1938, faced a dangerous increase of Axis economic and political activity in Latin America. Nazi agents took the lead in efforts aimed at destroying friendship for the United States and achieving hegemony for Germany in the region. They were so bold as to work openly at Lima to prevent cooperation with the United States by threatening reprisals against any republic that failed to take account of "new forces" in Europe and Asia. The methods of Hitler in Latin America were ominously similar to those he used to destroy his small neighbors in Europe. Americans who believed that events in Europe and Asia were "none of our business" and represented no threat to the security of the United States were less blind to the significance of Axis policy in Latin America. Argentina's policy most closely represented Axis desires and Hull had a difficult task to overcome its influence.

In his favor was the cumulative effect of the Roosevelt record of anti-imperialism. Hull chose the personnel of his delegation with an eye to counteracting Axis propaganda. Its co-chairman was Alfred M. Landon, the titular head of the Republican Party, who symbolized the conversion of his formerly imperialist party to the Good Neighbor policy. The Reverend John F. O'Hara, President of the University of Notre Dame, appealed to the Catholics of the Latin American Republics to avoid the error of condemning the United States as a "Protestant power." Representatives of the AFL and CIO made contact with labor groups in Latin America which were leading sources of anti-Axis influence on their governments' policies. These and other delegates made up an assemblage broadly representative of the unity of diverse segments of American society in support of the Roosevelt program.

The Argentine government sent a weak delegation aboard a cruiser, and the Foreign Minister Cantilo, after declaring that no action was necessary, retired incommunicado to the lakes of Chile, hoping to kill the Conference. Other governments were fearful that any action which seemed to be directed against the Axis would injure their trade with Germany.

Division into two blocs, with Argentina leading Chile and Uruguay, and the United States leading the others, was imminent. Argentinian delegates proposed a declaration which could be interpreted as directed against the United States. It caused joy in Axis circles. Hull worked vigorously to secure agreement by all the other Republics to a declaration of joint action against any threat from outside the Hemisphere and, after he succeeded, appealed over Cantilo's head to President Ortiz of Argentina. Ortiz and Cantilo were thus faced by twenty unified Republics and they were constrained to concede defeat. They agreed to all the essentials of the Hull declaration except permanent consultative machinery. It was a personal triumph for the diplomacy of the American Secretary of State and demonstrated the efficacy of cooperation among many governments in dealing with a disruptive government.[33]

The Declaration of Lima was adopted unanimously by the Conference on Christmas Eve. Besides reaffirming adherence to common principles of peace, international law, equal sovereignty of states, and individual liberty, and the purpose of defending them against all foreign intervention or other activities that might threaten them, the Declaration stated the determination of the twenty-one Republics in case of a threat against any one "to make effective their solidarity, coördinating their respective sovereign wills by means of the procedure of consultation . . . using measures that in each case circumstances may make advisable." [34]

Axis sources made much of the failure of Hull to achieve permanent consultative machinery, and Hull could not reveal that he had approached President Ortiz directly and won a victory over Cantilo. But the Declaration clearly marked a large step beyond the Buenos Aires Convention of 1936 because it bound the Republics to help each other not only in case of military attack but also against the indirect methods of assault used by the Axis. Much was also made of the fact that this was a declaration rather than a treaty. Argentina had refused to ratify all but one of the many important Pan-American treaties. It particularly ignored those sponsored by the United States, and the Declaration of Lima, which came into effect immediately without requiring ratifications, actually represented another success in overcoming Argentinian recalcitrance.

Lesser resolutions and conventions by the Conference strengthened hemispheric solidarity on many fronts and condemned Axis policies and activities. The explosive issue of Latin American governments' expropriations of United States-owned properties was postponed in recognition of Hull's November concession to Mexico. The American Secretary's closing address to the Conference on Christmas Eve nobly expressed the meaning of his own work:

> There are those who think the world is based on force. Here within this continent, we can confidently deny this. And the course of history shows that noble ideas and spiritual forces in the end have a greater triumph. Tonight especially we can say this, for on this night nearly two thousand years ago there was born a Son of God who declined force and kingdoms and proclaimed the great lesson of universal love. Without force His Kingdom lives today after a lapse of nineteen centuries. It is the principality of peace; the peace which we here hope in a humble measure to help to give by His grace to the continent of Americas.

And Hull did not conceal that in his view the methods of collective security were not limited in applicability to the Americas: "The principles of conduct upon which the countries of this hemisphere have chosen to stand firm are so broad and essential that all the world may also stand upon them." [35]

## A Formidable Record

On this last Christmas of relative peace before the Second World War, the record of President Roosevelt in attempting to carry forward his policy of internationalism was formidable. He had liquidated United States imperialism because it contradicted that policy. He had secured the support of the great majority of peaceful nations of the world in broad programs of liberal economic cooperation. Since the beginning of the year and after Chamberlain's rejection of the Welles plan, he had launched a rearmament program, placed a moral embargo against airplane sales to Japan, promised to defend Canada against attack, and intervened in the

European crisis to obtain a settlement far more favorable to Czechoslovakia than the one Chamberlain signed at Munich. He had
abandoned the pursuit of new domestic reforms in order to consolidate national unity and concentrate on measures against Axis
aggression. He had provided China with aid against Japan, rejected Japan's "new order" in East Asia, created new bonds with
Great Britain in the small matter of Canton and Enderbury and
in the great one of the Trade Agreement, and laid the cornerstone of hemispheric collective security in the Declaration of Lima.
In the face of all this Beard writes: "From the point of view of
internationalists, the pronouncements and actions of the Roosevelt Admistration in respect of American foreign policy during
the year 1938 were for practical purposes a total loss." In support
of this judgment he cites the opinion of the Geneva Associates of
the League of Nations that the Roosevelt administration had made
no gesture "in the direction of the internationalism *they* cham-
pioned," that is, in the direction of joining the League or "entangling alliances." Beard ignores the record and its momentous
meanings.[36]

He searched for signs of Roosevelt's internationalism in unlikely places. Long before the United States could possibly join
a league of nations or an entangling alliance for collective security, the arms embargo of the Neutrality Act had to be repealed.
Secretary Hull as he returned from the Lima Conference on January 4, 1939, heard aboard ship the President's broadcast address
to Congress which launched the struggle for that objective as the
major purpose of the administration in the new year. The actual
record as it was being compiled by the administration denoted
not only sound and logical step-by-step procedure but remarkable
speed considering hindrances from appeasement abroad and isolationism at home in constructing the new foreign policy of the
United States.

# 5.

## The Fight Against the Arms Embargo: Failure

THE HYPOTHESIS OF NUCLEAR FISSION WAS EXPERIMEN-
tally confirmed in January, 1939. A strange reflection of the isolationist temper of Americans at this moment was that American-
born physicists did not perceive the military implications of their
work or the danger to the United States if Axis scientists were
allowed to add an atomic bomb to their arsenal for world conquest. But underlying advantages of a free society nevertheless
rescued the United States from the danger. Hitler expelled scientists of "impure" race or dissident ideology, and their contribution
to the fight against the Axis was of stupendous value to the free
nations that welcomed them. Hitler regimented his scientists of
"pure" race into projects which seemed to him to be of more
practical value to the Nazi war machine than theoretical physics.

Foreign-born physicists in the United States, such as Szilard,
Wigner, Teller, Weisskopf, and Fermi, who were more aware of
the realities of the world political situation than their American-
born colleagues, insisted that publication of information regarding nuclear fission be restricted to prevent it from falling into
Axis hands. Foreign-born scientists worked to obtain United States
government support for further experimentation. Leading American and British physicists joined their efforts. Publication, except
for results voluntarily withheld by individuals, continued for another year. Dean George B. Pegram, of Columbia University, in
March, 1939, arranged a conference between officials of the Navy
Department and Enrico Fermi. The officials merely expressed interest and a desire to be kept informed.[1]

In this way a "united front" of scientists in the free nations offered a weapon of new dimensions to strengthen the foreign policy President Roosevelt offered to his own and the other free nations of the world.

## Intractable Materials

The materials with which Roosevelt had to work were more intractable even than uranium. The Chamberlain government through the winter of 1938–9 clung to "peace in our time" through appeasement, although its policy gradually stiffened. Roosevelt could not divorce the United States from its greatest potential ally but had to seek areas of common action upon which to build a joint policy of resistance to the Axis. Isolationism was stronger than ever in the new Congress which met in January, and there, too, the President could not risk a definitive split but had to reduce antagonism against his domestic policies and find grounds of common understanding on which to build his foreign policy.

In December, 1938, and January, 1939, the President supported Chamberlain in negotiations with Mussolini. His action provoked charges by isolationists that he had taken a hand in the "colossal poker game" of European politics, and by internationalists that he had joined in appeasement of Mussolini. Britain feared that Italy would maintain its military forces in Spain after Franco's victory and threaten the British position in Gibraltar. Chamberlain nourished hopes of drawing Mussolini away from Hitler. He and Halifax visited the Italian dictator in January. Prior to this, United States Ambassador William Phillips held conversations with Mussolini. Under Secretary Welles announced that their talks had been cordial and that Il Duce had been helpful and cooperative. Chamberlain obtained confirmation from Mussolini that he would withdraw his troops from Spain. Early in February a British cruiser helped Franco obtain the surrender of Republicans in Minorca, and it evacuated Republican troops to safety in France, in return for a Franco promise that Italian troops be kept out of the island.[2]

Perhaps United States influence helped to remove Italy from Spain and to postpone Italian entry into the Second World War. Roosevelt showed later that he was willing to make economic concessions in order to encourage Franco to resist use of his territory by Axis troops and to keep open the Straits of Gibraltar for Anglo-American strategic purposes. If he supported "deals" with the dictators, they were carefully calculated to gain military advantage for Britain and the United States, and therefore cannot be regarded as in any sense appeasement like Chamberlain's at Munich, which was predicated on the possibility of achieving peace by yielding military advantage to Hitler. In January, 1939, as on September 26 and 27, 1938, Roosevelt supported Chamberlain at a moment when he resisted Axis aggression, and, unlike his conduct at Munich, Chamberlain, in January and February, did not yield in his demand that Italy evacuate its forces from Spain. Chamberlain early in February also countered Axis attempts to isolate France by publicly announcing that any threat to the vital interests of France from any quarter would evoke the immediate cooperation of Britain.[3] This thwarted Mussolini's hopes of obtaining French territory without British interference.

Chamberlain himself felt encouraged to resist the Axis by President Roosevelt's drive to strengthen the foreign policy of the United States.[4] Far from encouraging appeasement, Roosevelt made the United States a factor in Chamberlain's decision in March, 1939, to abandon that policy.

## Methods Short of War

The central event in the history of Roosevelt's new orientation was his Annual Message to Congress on January 4, 1939. In it he announced that the period when his administration placed chief emphasis on the achievement of new domestic reforms had come to an end. The question, often posed, at what time, if ever, did Roosevelt abandon the New Deal, is easily answered by reference to the statement in this Message to which administration policy thenceforth strictly conformed. He said that with minor exceptions

the past three Congresses have met in part or in whole the pressing needs of the new [domestic] order of things.

We have now passed the period of internal conflict in the launching of our program of social reform. Our full energies may now be released to invigorate the processes of recovery in order to *preserve our reforms,* and to give every man and woman who wants to work a real job at a living wage.

Here, and in other parts of his Message, the President announced that he would not again launch massive programs of new reforms or commit his influence without limit in battles for the New Deal as he had done in every preceding year. But this did not mean he would abandon the New Deal. On the contrary, he would work to achieve certain minor additions to its structure and, more important, he would work to preserve and extend existing measures. He would, in short, go over from the offensive to the defensive in his strategy.

Bitter enemies of the New Deal would not be satisfied with anything short of repeal of all New Deal laws and dissolution of the executive agencies which enforced them. Roosevelt would never consent to pay this price for the objects he had in view, because he regarded the New Deal, incomplete as it was, as an essential element of American strength in foreign relations. It gave the great majority of Americans who supported it and benefited by it a stake in democracy without which the defense of democracy against the Axis would be futile. He said:

The deadline of danger from within and from without is not within our control. The hour-glass may be in the hands of other nations. Our own hour-glass tells us that we are off on a race to *make democracy work,* so that we may be efficient in peace and *therefore* secure in national defense.

While continuing the New Deal effort to "make democracy work," Roosevelt hoped by defensive rather than offensive strategy to conciliate all but the most bitter opposition and to achieve effective national unity.

He not only had to offer compromise to his opponents but he had to justify it to his supporters:

Events abroad have made it increasingly clear to the American people that dangers within are less to be feared than dangers from without.

The most specific concession he made to opponents of the New Deal was a virtual admission that it had discouraged new investments of private capital necessary for economic recovery and a conciliatory invitation to businessmen to put idle capital to work. But even here he did not concede what extreme opponents demanded—that public investment to prime the pump should be abandoned. Rather he offered cooperation between government and business in achieving increased employment and national income. He argued that the social and economic reforms of the last six years were as important as armaments in preparing the nation for defense:

We are conserving and developing national resources—land, water power, forests.

We are trying to provide necessary food, shelter and medical care for the health of our population.

We are putting agriculture—our system of food and fibre supply—on a sounder basis.

We are strengthening the weakest spot in our system of industrial supply—its long smouldering labor difficulties.

We have cleaned up our credit system so that depositor and investor alike may more readily and willingly make their capital available for peace or war.

We are giving to our youth new opportunities for work and education.

We have sustained the morale of all the population by the dignified recognition of our obligations to the aged, the helpless and the needy.

Above all, we have made the American people conscious of their interrelationship and their interdependence. They sense a common destiny and a common need of each other. Differences of occupation, geography, race and religion no longer obscure the nation's fundamental unity in thought and in action.

This registered the President's changed perspective since the months before Munich when he had launched new drives to raise the status of the poorest one-third of the nation and to solve the problem of the South. Now he regarded the New Deal as a completed structure requiring no new and disruptive struggles against its domestic enemies but, on the contrary, as a source of social and economic healing which strengthened national preparedness and unity.

A strong plea for national unity was the chief domestic theme of the Message. Military defense, the President said, was not enough to prepare the nation against attack, because a well-armed nation may be defeated if it is unnerved by internal dissensions.

In meeting the troubles of the world we must meet them as one people—with a unity born of the fact that for generations those who have come to our shores, representing many kindreds and tongues, have been welded by common opportunity into a united patriotism. If another form of government can present a united front in its attack on a democracy, the attack must and will be met by a united democracy. Such a democracy can and must exist in the United States.

The Message contained direct warnings that the United States was in danger of attack and must get ready for war. The charge which isolationists reiterated without end in the following years, that the President "wanted" war, was first answered on this occasion: he wanted peace, but he feared attack; he was determined to prepare to fight a victorious war if it came, and believed such preparation was the best method of discouraging attack.

The word "attack" was crucial in the debate that followed. Isolationists defined it as an assault with armed force on the United States or its possessions, or, as a concession, on other parts of the Western Hemisphere. The President proposed a broader definition based on an internationalist conception of the indivisibility of world peace, on the range and speed of modern weapons of offense, and on the organic unity between Axis programs of preliminary subversion of potential enemies' capacity to resist and ultimate military conquest. After repeating his earlier offers to "take counsel" with all other nations to end aggression and the armaments race, and to renew commerce, Roosevelt said:

But the world has grown so small and weapons of attack so swift that no nation can be safe in its will to peace so long as any other powerful nation refuses to settle its grievances at the council table. . . .

We have learned that survival cannot be guaranteed by arming after the attack begins—for there is new range and speed to offense.

We have learned that long before any overt military act, aggression begins with preliminaries of propaganda, subsidized penetration, the loosening of ties of good will, the stirring of prejudice and the incitement to disunion.

We have learned that God-fearing democracies of the world which observe the sanctity of treaties and good faith in their dealings with other nations cannot safely be indifferent to international lawlessness anywhere. They cannot forever let pass, without effective protest, acts of aggression against sister nations—acts which automatically undermine all of us.

The President paid tribute to the growing structure of hemispheric solidarity, but added:

This by no means implies that the American Republics dissociate themselves from the nations of other continents. It does not mean the Americas against the rest of the world.

The principle of collective security which Hull had instrumented at Lima a few days before was not regarded by the President as limited in its application to the Western Hemisphere. He proposed agreements with all nations of the world to end aggression and the armaments race, but obviously had no expectation that the Axis nations would accept. He stated his lack of faith in the Munich Agreement more strongly than he had in October:

A war which threatened to envelop the world in flames has been averted; but it has become increasingly clear that world peace is not assured.
All about us rage undeclared wars—military and economic. All about us grow more deadly armaments—military and economic. All about us are threats of new aggression—military and economic.

To meet the threat, he proposed "methods short of war" in three areas: in the military field—expansion of the armed forces and armaments, and organization and location of key industrial facilities against attack; in the domestic field—consolidation of national unity; and in the field of foreign policy he proposed "at the very least" the next logical step towards collective security, which was repeal of the arms embargo:

We have learned that when we deliberately try to legislate neutrality, our neutrality laws may operate unevenly and unfairly—may actually give aid to an aggressor and deny it to the victim. The instinct of self-preservation should warn us that we ought not to let that happen any more.

These he offered as some of many "methods short of war, but stronger and more effective than mere words," which should be used to stop aggression.[5]
The phrase, "methods short of war," acquired a famous history,

as it covered all future acts of defense and cooperation with the victims of Axis aggression until the United States was overtly attacked. It did not satisfy extreme internationalists, because it ruled out the ultimate sanction of collective security, the threat of armed force. It was a compromise between such internationalists and those isolationists who objected to any method of attempting to stop aggression until the United States or the Western Hemisphere should be assaulted with armed force. As a compromise between the ideal of full-fledged collective security and the realities of isolationism, it represented a high order of statesmanship.

## Congress Disposes

Having charted his new domestic and foreign courses, the President gave over to Congress and the people the task of deciding whether and when he would be authorized to begin the new voyage. In his anxiety to reduce internal dissension he did not for several months press Congress for action on the Neutrality Act. Such pressure in the recent past had raised the cry against him of "dictator." In his Message he had pointedly analyzed the methods an actual dictator would use to achieve national unity and a stronger foreign policy. Now he refrained, equally pointedly, not only from those methods but from using the legitimate influence of his office which obfuscators had equated with dictatorship. Apart from semantic problems of the word "dictator," the President was fearful that strong leadership would antagonize the strengthened opposition in Congress and result in a defeat which would have the disastrous effects of encouraging the Axis and discouraging Britain and France. Seven bills were introduced in the House and four in the Senate to modify or repeal the Neutrality Act. Outwardly, the administration supported none of them and offered no alternatives.

Privately, however, Secretary Hull told Senator Pittman that the State Department desired outright repeal because the arms embargo was "an incitement to Hitler to go to war." Failing repeal, Hull urged that the President be granted discretionary authority to place an arms embargo on an aggressor without embargoing his victim. Hull wanted the State Department to prepare the legislation. Pittman told Hull the Foreign Relations Committee should be allowed to prepare the legislation but that there was not the slightest chance of obtaining either one of his changes. The administration deferred to his judgment. On January 19, the Senate Committee indefinitely postponed action on neutrality.

Beard deduces from the public record that the President had failed to "urge a repeal of the neutrality legislation or any other measure pointed in the direction of action on the part of the United States against aggressors." [6] This slurs over—as though he had not delivered it—the passage in the President's Message of January 4 in which he criticized the existing law precisely because it might give aid to aggressors and deny it to their victims, and stated: "we ought not to let that happen any more." Beard could not know what Hull subsequently revealed in his *Memoirs*—that the President through his Secretary of State had made his wishes fully known to the Senate, as has been described.[7] The latter procedure can hardly be called deceitful in the light of the President's Message; rather it was dictated by a nice regard for the independence of Congress, a regard for which the administration seldom received credit.

## *The Guam Predicament*

Publicly, the President concentrated during these weeks on his rearmament program. The budget for national defense had already passed a billion dollars. On January 5, he asked Congress for an increase of over a half billion dollars to be spent chiefly on air power. On January 12, he sent a special message explaining his purposes. He had in view defenses capable of holding an attack in an emergency, while, by means of "educational orders," industry would have been prepared for immediate expansion of war production. Strengthening of air forces and military and naval bases was an important feature. Chiefly the President asked for development of modern weapons, for the sake of the young men of the nation who might be called on to use them.[8]

Congress was ready to go farther than the President requested. When the session ended in July, Congress had raised the appropriations of the previous year by almost two-thirds to a total of $1,645,000,000. The increase was obviously made in anticipation of war in Europe and in the belief that it and the Japanese war, already in progress, were very real dangers to the United States. Isolationists voted for the increase, at the same time that they voted against revision of the Neutrality Act on the grounds that war in Europe was not imminent and the United States was not in danger.

The most serious controversy arose over the proposal to fortify Guam. It became a source of false charges against isolationists by internationalists. The President had not named Guam among the bases he wished strengthened, because the United States was committed in the Five-Power Treaty of 1922 with Japan, Britain, Italy, and France not to increase fortifications in its Pacific possessions. Japan had violated the Treaty but the United States insisted it was still in force and must be obeyed.

Many internationalists who had not the official responsibility of the President and Secretary of State advocated fortification of Guam. The Navy Department drafted a bill for a submarine and an air base. President Roosevelt made it clear that he had not seen the bill and that he opposed unilateral denunciation of the Five-Power Treaty. Debate on the bill was heated. It was defeated by a close vote. This was not, as internationalists later claimed, an instance of isolationists' refusal to support the administration in a measure which might have mitigated the disaster at Pearl Harbor. Rather it was a victory for the President's policy of sacrificing military advantage for the sake of maintaining the principle of the sanctity of treaties. Still, it is highly doubtful whether isolationists voted against the bill for the same reason.[9] President Truman in August, 1945, fell into the common error of internationalists and charged that isolationists in Congress had "stifled" Roosevelt's preparedness programs. Later he retracted. Beard correctly points out that Congress never seriously reduced, and during three of the years before Pearl Harbor it actually increased, the President's requests for defense appropriations.[10]

Besides regular defense appropriations, the administration undertook many supplementary measures. The United States Maritime Commission began work on a program to build five hundred merchant vessels designed to serve as naval auxiliaries in time of war. The Civil Aeronautics Authority organized college training for fifteen thousand air pilots. A third set of locks was authorized for the Panama Canal, widely separated from the other two in order to reduce its vulnerability and large enough to accommodate the new battleships. Surveys for an alternative canal through Nicaragua began in August.

The administration's long campaign to stockpile strategic raw materials finally bore fruit in June, when Congress authorized purchases of rubber, tin, and other materials. The amount of money appropriated was so small that Hull negotiated barters of surplus cotton and wheat with Britain, Belgium, and the Netherlands. He had difficulty in allaying fears of those governments that their normal markets would be injured, but Britain agreed before the end of June to trade rubber for cotton.[11]

Defense programs of 1938 and 1939 were fundamental in placing the United States in an elementary state of readiness for war. They launched long-range preparations which could not be completed swiftly no matter how large the appropriations. Without them, the holding operations after Pearl Harbor and the rapid shift over to the offensive in both the Mediterranean and the Pacific within a year could not have been achieved.

## "The Frontier of America Is on the Rhine"

It remained true that in the field of defense the administration found common ground with isolationists even while they held opposing views on the best way to avoid the necessity of using the armed force they created. For Roosevelt, the time had come to work closely with Britain and France to strengthen their armaments. Britain was rapidly developing a powerful air force, but French equipment was obsolete and its production lagged. In 1938, Britain and France publicly bought respectively 650 and 100 planes in the United States. France was in the greater need, and the President instructed various government departments to place every facility at the disposal of a second French purchasing mission which arrived in December. This mission was not made public until an official of the French Air Ministry crashed in an American bomber in California on January 23. This seemed to isolationists to be a sensational revelation of the President's "secret methods." But all sales of planes had to be licensed and published in the monthly report of the National Munitions Control Board. Secrecy was observed only in the matter of cooperation between United States government departments and officials of a friendly government, which was within the discretion of the President. The administration announced, and no later evidence contradicted it, that secret equipment such as the new American bombsight had not been made available to foreign governments. The French mission proceeded publicly to buy 615 planes in a transaction which, because France paid cash as required of governments in default under the Johnson Act, was entirely legal.[12]

The sensation caused by the French official's death was surpassed within a few days by a rumor of what passed at an executive session of the Senate Committee on Military Affairs which the President invited to meet with him on January 31. Some member or members were reported to say afterwards that the President had given them a "truly alarming" picture of world conditions and had said the "frontier of America is on the Rhine." This report inflamed isolationists in the United States and Axis propagandists abroad. They raged in chorus against the President. The British and French took courage from it.[13] On February 3, the President told a press conference the report was a "deliberate lie." He seized the occasion to assure the public that his foreign policy had not changed and was not going to change, and to make a "comparatively simple" statement of it:

Number 1: We are against any entangling alliances, obviously.
Number 2: We are in favor of the maintenance of world trade for everybody—all nations—including ourselves.
Number 3: We are in complete sympathy with any and every effort made to reduce or limit armaments.
Number 4: As a Nation—as American people—we are sympathetic with the peaceful maintenance of political, economic and social independence of all nations in the world.[14]

The President's denial of the "frontier on the Rhine" report did not destroy its resounding political effect, because the phrase did express the point of view of internationalists and Roosevelt had made amply clear that he was working for an internationalist foreign policy. The fourth item of his statement of policy could not be construed otherwise than as sympathy for France and any other nations threatened by the Axis. But the President still held back from "dictation" to Congress of the most important step necessary to instrument such sympathy—revision of the Neutrality Act.

On March 7, he was challenged by a reporter to state his opinion of that law. He said it had not contributed to the cause of peace and that during the past three years the United States might have been stronger without it. He also spoke vigorously against the proposed Ludlow amendment to the Constitution.[15]

## Hull and Pittman Try Again

On March 20, Senator Pittman reopened debate on the neutrality issue by introducing a bill to whose terms Secretary Hull had agreed. The administration had paid a high price to obtain Pittman's cooperation. The bill did not repeal the Act of 1937 or authorize a discriminatory embargo against an aggressor while furnishing arms to a victim. It merely renewed the cash-and-carry section applying to unfinished materials useful in war which, in the existing Act, was due to expire on May 1, and it extended cash-and-carry to apply also to arms, ammunition, and implements of war.[16] This would at least permit Britain and France, so long as they controlled the sea, to obtain what arms and materials they could pay cash for and carry home in their own ships. It would not remedy the absurdities of the law's effects in Asia. The date perhaps explains why the administration agreed to accept this absolute minimum: on March 15, Hitler had marched into Prague.

This made farcical Hitler's claims that he wished only to wipe out the injustices of Versailles and incorporate German peoples in the Reich. He casually destroyed the Munich Agreement and launched a further campaign to dismember Poland. For a moment, Chamberlain seemed unwilling to admit the bankruptcy of his policy. He told Commons he was willing to accept the Nazi interpretation that the Munich Agreement had been made invalid not by Hitler but by Czechoslovakia itself, that is, by the disruption of the nation engineered by Hitler's agent Father Tiso. Chamberlain spoke against any deflection from the policy of appeasement, any light setting aside of "all hope for the world."

But the British people forced Chamberlain to abandon appeasement and embark on the policy of collective security. The change was announced with astounding suddenness in a speech on March 17, which had been advertised as treating domestic questions. Chamberlain's biographer, Keith Feiling, states that "strong representations as to opinion in the House, the public, and the Dominions," caused the Prime Minister's abrupt reversal.[17]

The next day Britain, France, and the Soviet Union protested Hitler's invasion. The new course had been started which would lead in a few days to the first British military guaranties of the territorial integrity of countries east of Germany—Poland, Rumania, Greece, and Turkey—guaranties which the British people would fulfill even when they stood alone against a Hitler who had conquered them all except Turkey, had separated the Soviet Union from Britain, laid France low, and stood at the Channel with nothing but British courage between himself and victory.

Not quite alone: Roosevelt supported the British at that moment to the extent that he had been able to bring the American people and Congress to heed the danger. Repeal of the arms embargo was the chief concession he had won by that time. In March, 1939, the only remaining hope that collective security would not merely win the war, but might yet prevent it, was a united front by Britain, France, and the Soviet Union, with the United States contributing at least its industrial power to the coalition. The events of March 17 and 18 were hopeful for the unity of the three European powers. Hull's agreement to accept the Pittman Bill, and its introduction on March 20, inevitably had the effect of contributing, in however small measure, to the last hope of preventing by collective security the Second World War.

From March 20 until Congress could no longer be held in session in July, the administration fought to make its contribution. This was in extreme contrast to the course of the Soviet Union. During the same months, it worked publicly to organize the united front and secretly to join Hitler in the partition of Poland. That the Pittman Bill was directed solely at the European situation was clear from its provision that the President would no longer have discretion to find or refuse to find that a state of war existed. He would be forced to apply the law within thirty days after armed conflict began. The Chinese government expressed its concern on March 27 that the Pittman Bill would require the President to apply the embargo against Japan and China, whereupon the cash-and-carry loophole could and would be exploited only by Japan.

This consideration made Roosevelt take second thoughts on the bill. He felt the concessions extracted by Pittman were too extreme. For the first time he intervened personally, authorizing Hull to inform Pittman and legislative leaders that the President believed the cash-and-carry plan, while it worked all right in the Atlantic, "works all wrong in the Pacific," and that he was convinced the Neutrality Act "should be repealed *in toto* without any substitute."

Pittman refused to support repeal. As a compromise, he introduced a resolution to embargo any nation violating the Nine-Power Treaty. Committee hearings began in April. Hull wished to appear. The Gallup Poll showed that 57 per cent of persons asked, who had an opinion, favored amendment of the Neutrality Act to permit sale of munitions to Britain and France. But this development was not reflected in Congress. Pittman warned Hull that his appearance before the Committee would provide isolationist members with an opportunity to embarrass him with questions intended to divert attention from the administration's fundamental purpose of helping to prevent war and to raise specters of "involvement." Hull wrote in his *Memoirs:*

I was in a dilemma. Of course one of our purposes was to assist the British and French; but even more fundamentally it was to prevent the outbreak of war in Europe. We felt that, if Hitler knew that Britain and France could have full access to our war and essential products, he would be less likely to order his troops to march. Of course we had been in constant touch with the British and French Governments, though we had no agreement whatever for any common action with them.[18]

He decided not to testify. Pittman told Hull that he could put through the bill if the administration did not give it public endorsement.

Public sentiment for revision in the direction of collective security was strong but it was also divided among Pittman's bill and others calling for a variety of stronger measures, the strongest of which was one proposed by Senator Thomas, of Utah, to embargo all belligerents and then allow the President, with the advice of Congress, to determine the aggressor as a belligerent who violated a treaty to which the United States was a party, including the Kellogg Pact, and lift the embargo from his victim. This bill received wide public support.[19]

The President by a dramatic action on April 14 exposed more clearly to Americans and other peoples the intentions of Hitler and Mussolini. The Italian dictator had invaded Albania on April

7. Roosevelt asked the two dictators for a ten-year guaranty that their armed forces would not "attack or invade" the thirty-one remaining independent nations from Ireland and Great Britain to Russia and Iran. If the guaranty were forthcoming, he was "reasonably sure" he could obtain reciprocal assurances from the thirty-one. And in the "resulting peaceful surroundings" the United States would gladly take part in discussions relating to disarmament and international trade. The message very clearly implied that the Axis nations alone threatened war. It answered Hitler's propaganda that Britain created danger of war by its new policy of "encirclement" with an offer of a structure of mutual non-aggression to which no genuinely peaceful nation could object.[20]

Ambassador to France William C. Bullitt had suggested the action. The President had no thought that his initiative would be successful but he undertook it anyway because, as he told Hull, it would serve the good purpose of putting "Hitler and Mussolini on the spot for what they were—planners of the conquest of Europe." [21] The results justified that expectation. Hitler made no answer for two weeks and then only in a transparently evasive harangue to the Reichstag. He brazenly denounced the Anglo-German Naval Agreement and the German-Polish Non-Aggression Pact. Mussolini in a public speech answered that his planning of the Rome Universal Exposition for 1942 sufficiently proved that he was not "cherishing obscure aggressive designs." [22]

In spite of this demonstration and the administration's cautious tactics towards Congress, Pittman's promises and majority public opinion were unavailing. The Senate Committee hearings ended on May 8. Pittman admitted defeat and threw the problem back to the administration. On May 1 the cash-and-carry provision covering materials useful in war had expired. This made the Neutrality Act less satisfactory than ever to internationalists, because it meant that in case of war Britain and France could obtain no manufactured or unfinished war materials under embargo from the United States on any terms whatever.

## President Roosevelt Tries

Time was running out. Britain introduced conscription on April 27. The Soviet government on April 16 privately offered Britain and France a mutual assistance pact. But on April 17 the

Soviet Ambassador in Germany held out to the Nazi government the possibility of "normal" relations followed by "better and better" ties between their governments.[23] The German State Secretary Weizsaecker admitted that the Soviet press "lately was not fully participating in the anti-German tone of the American and some of the English papers." [24] The world was allowed to guess that a Soviet diplomatic revolution was in the making from a speech in which Stalin proposed "businesslike relations" with all countries as proper Soviet policy. And on May 3, Maxim Litvinov, Soviet Foreign Commissar and exponent of collective security, was abruptly displaced in office by Vyacheslav Molotov.

Chamberlain, unlike Churchill, Eden, Lloyd George, Attlee, and Sinclair, allowed suspicions of the Soviet Union to interfere with his desire for a united front.[25] The Soviet government, on its side, pursued a pact with Germany secretly while it publicly raised the terms it demanded for a military agreement with Britain and France each time they met an earlier condition. On May 22, Germany and Italy signed a "Pact of Steel." On May 30 the German government decided to begin "definite negotiations" with the Soviet government.[26] The Soviet leaders demanded that Britain and France join in guaranties of the integrity of all the states of Central and Eastern Europe. Finland, the Baltic States, Poland, and Rumania were unwilling to accept guaranties from the Soviet government, although they did accept nonaggression pacts from Hitler. The revolution in Nazi-Soviet relations and the deadlock in Anglo-Soviet relations had crystallized by the end of May.

These developments the Roosevelt administration was able to discern sufficiently from public sources, and doubtless more fully from private sources. The threat of United States support of Britain and France with armaments and war materials was· the last small chance of discouraging Hitler from attacking them. To some small extent the United States could offset the loss of the Soviet Union in the united front. Roosevelt did not accept Pittman's failure to obtain revision of the Neutrality Act. He decided to take the risks of a public campaign of pressure on Congress. He had not urged his leading domestic measure, the Executive Reorganization Bill, as strongly as in 1938, and he avoided a struggle with Congress when the Bill was passed shorn of features which conservatives had labeled "dictatorial." He had given Congress its head for over four months to revise the Neutrality Act as it saw fit. It had not only refused, but had allowed the cash-and-carry clause to expire. Public opinion favored aid to Britain and France. The European situation required an end to delay, an end to caution. The President would throw the whole weight of his office and personal influence into a major campaign to revise the Neutrality Act and place the industrial power of the United States in the scales against the Axis.

On May 19 the President called a meeting of House leaders. He told them every possible effort should be made to eliminate the arms embargo from the Neutrality Act. Thus he asked for more than the Pittman Bill. He said he was not seriously interested in other aspects of the law, but did not object to cash-and-carry and thought a war-zone prohibition against American shipping and travel might be useful. He gave primary and secondary reasons for wanting repeal of the arms embargo. According to Hull, who was present, Roosevelt "said he felt sure this would actually prevent the outbreak of war in Europe, or, if it did not, it would make less likely a victory for the powers unfriendly to the United States." This dual propose cut through the arguments of isolationists with the conviction that the triumph of the Axis was dangerous to the United States and with the faith of an internationalist that support of Axis victims would increase the likelihood of the defeat of the Axis, either by diplomacy or by force, which the security of the United States required.

The House leaders warned Roosevelt that repeal of the arms embargo was very likely to be defeated by Congress. He told them the fight should nevertheless be made. He had invited the King and Queen of England to visit the United States as a demonstration of Anglo-American friendship and he particularly wanted the House to repeal the embargo in time to strengthen the effect of the demonstration.

The State Department prepared a new bill, which would repeal the arms embargo, establish the cash-and-carry system for all trade with belligerents, bar American shipping and travel from combat zones, and continue the National Munitions Control Board. Hull sent the bill to Congress on May 27 with a strong letter. He gave as the chief reason for repeal of the arms embargo the President's statement when he signed the Act in 1935, that it might drag the United States into war instead of keeping it out.[27] Representative Sol Bloom, Chairman of the House Com-

mittee on Foreign Affairs, and Senator Pittman introduced the
bill on May 29. The administration placed chief reliance now on
the House to act.

That same day, isolationists launched a ferocious attack against
the administration measure. Hamilton Fish said it would make
the United States a "slaughterhouse" for the particular benefit of
Great Britain.[28] President Roosevelt met the attack aggressively.
He called the Democratic leaders of both houses to a meeting on
May 31 and insisted that Congress be kept in session until it acted
on the bill. They agreed, but they warned the President he was
risking destruction of the precarious party unity which had been
so recently retrieved from domestic dissension.

Isolationists threatened a filibuster. The visit of King George
VI and Queen Elizabeth, while it was an undoubted success with
the American public, gave isolationists in Congress an excuse for
sarcasms and charges that the visit "confirmed a military understanding." In the House, by margins sometimes as small as two
votes, the administration Bill was amended to continue the arms
embargo. Hull appealed to the House leaders to eliminate the
amendment. But on June 30, by a vote of 201 to 187, the Bill
passed with the arms embargo and other changes which made it
an isolationist measure. It went to the Senate. Hull issued a statement reaffirming his support of the original bill and expressing
"regret and disappointment from the standpoint of peace and the
best interests of this country." American representatives abroad
were cabling the State Department that a Nazi-Soviet pact was in
the making and that the House action encouraged Hitler to attack Poland, Britain, and France, because he calculated that without American supplies those nations could be easily defeated.[29]

The President evidently had such cables in mind when, a few
days after the amended Bill reached the Senate, he publicly stated
his opinion that the House action had "increased the danger of
another war by creating an impression in the dictator states that
the people of the United States were not wholeheartedly supporting his efforts to throw the country's influence on the side of the
democracies." [30] This was certainly an unequivocal statement of
the President's purpose in asking repeal of the arms embargo.
Coupled with statements that repeal would promote peace, it left
no possible doubt that the President advocated the international-

ist method of supporting Britain and France to protect the peace of the United States. Beard, in order to sustain his indictment of the President, is forced to avoid any mention whatever of this statement by the President. He brings into his account only the subsequent July 14 statement of Roosevelt and Hull, although it also contradicts his thesis, as will be shown.

The Senate Committee on Foreign Relations voted on July 11 to postpone all further consideration of neutrality legislation until the next session in January. The vote was 12 to 11. Two of the members voting against the administration—Gillette, of Iowa, and George, of Georgia—were not ordinarily isolationists; they had been reported as undecided on the issue; but they had been marked for "purge" by the President a year before. The *New York Herald Tribune* justified them "because they know better than most other Americans what happens when a President is tempted to ape the dictators." [31] This said too much because obviously one of the things Senators Gillette and George should have known was that the victims of a purge by a dictator are not able to frustrate him and take revenge against him with impunity.

Still the President did not give up. The French government had accurate information that the partition of Poland was to be the basis of a Nazi-Soviet nonaggression pact.[32] Ambassador Bullitt had the confidence of the French government and communicated directly to the President.[33]

Eden volunteered to go to Moscow, but Chamberlain sent a minor Foreign Office official, Mr. Strang. His talks failed to solve the problem of objections by Poland and the Baltic states to Soviet aid. A more transcendent reason for the failure to organize a coalition was later revealed when Stalin told Churchill that the Soviet leaders had no faith that an alliance of Britain, France, and the Soviet Union would discourage Hitler from going to war.[34] This meant that the Soviet government, after the resignation of Litvinov, abandoned collective security as the most effective way to protect its own peace. It turned to a method comparable to the policy of American isolationists, that is, neutrality towards conflicts between aggressors and their victims, and an attempt to "do business" with Hitler. The errors of this policy were that it not only encouraged Hitler to launch war but also did not prevent him from invading the Soviet Union when he was ready.

## A Prophecy by Senator Borah

The Roosevelt administration did not fall into these errors. Rather, the withdrawal of the Soviet Union into isolation intensified the Roosevelt campaign to obtain revision of the Neutrality Act. Hull makes clear in his *Memoirs* that he inclined to cautious tactics in attempting to influence Congress. Roosevelt's final actions in the fight bear the mark of his own aggressiveness. But this did not mean that the President "split" with his Secretary of State. The United Press published sensational "reports" that a split occurred over a note on neutrality the day after the Senate Committee voted for postponement. The President issued a public statement that this latest divisive report was a "falsification of the actual facts," and that it represented a culmination of other false news stories by the United Press which reached the "limit of any decent person's patience." [35] Tempers rose in the Washington heat. The President, as he brought his campaign to a climax, could at least say that Congress had refused to respond to temperate methods during the past six months.

On July 14 he sent a special message to Congress and enclosed a statement by Hull, which had his "full approval." Roosevelt solicited for it the "earnest attention" of Congress and added:

It has been abundantly clear to me for some time that for the cause of peace and in the interest of American neutrality and security, it is highly advisable that Congress at this session should take certain much needed action. In the light of present world conditions, I see no reason to change that opinion.

Hull's statement was a masterly argument for the administration's policy. His theme was that the people and government of the United States "must not fail to make their just and legitimate contribution to the preservation of peace." He refuted isolationist propaganda and clarified issues by pointing out that both sides agreed on four principles:

1. The first concern of the United States must be its own peace and security.
2. It should be the policy of this government to avoid being drawn into wars between other nations.

3. This nation should at all times avoid entangling alliances or involvements with other nations.

4. In the event of foreign wars this nation should maintain a status of strict neutrality, and that around the structure of neutrality we should so shape our policies as to keep this country from being drawn into war.

Beard quotes this part of Hull's statement in full, with italics added to emphasize innuendoes in his comments that the administration hypocritically pretended once more to support policies incompatible with its actual aims. Beard then cannot avoid admitting that Hull went on to explain that the difference between isolationists and the administration did not involve the four principles but the method of achieving them. This must come as a shock to readers of Beard's book because it is the first time Beard allows a hint to seep into his text that the stated aims and the proposed methods of the administration's foreign policy were not incompatible. Theretofore, Beard presented a melodramatic narrative of the administration publicly advocating peace, non-involvement, and neutrality while harboring internationalist intentions, or, when it did expose its internationalism and met opposition, swiftly denying it by giving reassurances of adherence to peace, non-involvement, and neutrality.

The Hull statement demolishes Beard's melodrama, because it associated in most intimate logical relationship the administration's limited collective security measures with their end purposes —the neutrality, peace, and security of the United States. But Beard dismisses Hull's remarkable and extensive explanation of the relationship between the administration's means and ends in two vague sentences which are not without innuendoes of Roosevelt's lust for power and Hull's logical inadequacy.[36]

Hull's argument, in fact, made an excellent case for the administration view that repeal of the arms embargo for the purpose of aiding Britain and France in war could be reconciled with the policy of neutrality. He said it was in reality the arms embargo itself that was "directly opposed to the idea of neutrality," and explained:

It is not humanly possible, by enacting an arms embargo, or by refraining from such enactment, to hold the scales exactly even between two belligerents. In either case and due to shifting circumstances one belligerent may find itself in a position of relative advantage or disadvantage. The important difference between the two cases is that when such a condition arises in the absence of an arms embargo on our part, no responsibility attaches to this country, whereas in the presence of an embargo, the responsibility of this country for the creation of the condition is inevitably direct and clear.

There is no theory or practice to be found in international law pertaining to neutrality to the effect that the advantages that any particular belligerent might procure through its geographic location, its superiority on land or at sea, or through other circumstances, should be offset by the establishment by neutral nations of embargoes.

It followed that supporters of the arms embargo were urging not neutrality but what might well result in unneutrality and so were misleading the American people into relying upon a "false and illogical delusion" as a means of avoiding war. The arms embargo was illogical because the law forbade export of finished armaments but allowed export of materials equally valuable to belligerents, such as high-octane gasoline for aircraft. It was false because export of finished armaments to belligerents was a clearly recognized right of neutrals, subject to effective blockade and the right of belligerents to seize as contraband such articles going to their enemies. The United States had never engaged in serious controversy solely because belligerents exercised their rights of blockade and seizure of contraband.

Hull did not confine his argument to the technical facts of international law. He frankly admitted that the administration opposed the arms embargo also because it "plays into the hands of those nations which have taken the lead in building up their fighting power," that is, the Axis nations. It penalized peace-loving nations, especially those without munitions plants, and it rewarded aggressive nations that prepared for conquest. It encouraged the latter to attack and discouraged the former from resisting attack. Since the embargo had the effect of encouraging a general state of war in Europe and Asia, it was "directly prejudicial to the highest interests and to the peace and to the security of the United States."

So far, Hull's statement was incontrovertible to a candid mind. But his third great argument proposed as his profound belief that the arms embargo should be repealed as a step towards collective

security, and here he attacked the fundamental conception of isolationism:

In the present grave conditions of international anarchy and of
danger to peace, in more than one part of the world, I profoundly
believe that the first great step towards safeguarding this nation from
being drawn into war is to use whatever influence it can, compatible
with the traditional policy of our country of noninvolvement, so as
to make less likely the outbreak of a major war. This is a duty placed
on our Government which some may fail to perceive or choose to
reject. But it must be clear to every one of us that the outbreak of a
general war increases the dangers confronting the United States. This
fact cannot be ignored.[37]

The best gauge of the effectiveness of Hull's statement is that
after it isolationist Senators felt obliged to make their last stand,
not on any of the stock arguments which they tacitly admitted had
been demolished, but on the prediction that war was not imminent and, therefore, action on the administration bill could
safely be postponed until January. They destroyed the last chance
of the United States to use its influence to prevent the outbreak
of the Second World War, but when events proved them to have
been wrong and the administration right, Congress repealed the
embargo in time to help prevent an Axis victory. A further
memorable aspect of the Hull statement is that it amply filled
out the administration's record of frankly avowing the internationalist character of its foreign policy before the Second World
War began.

The climax of the administration's fight to repeal the arms embargo was sensational. Thirty-four Senators organized under a
pledge to fight to the finish for retention of the embargo. Roosevelt called a meeting of the Senate leaders of both parties in the
White House on the evening of July 18. He and Hull intended
to make a final appeal for the administration bill, or, if that
failed, to force the isolationists to take public responsibility for
their refusal. Among those present were Garner, Pittman, Barkley,
Warren Austin, and William E. Borah. The meeting lasted three
hours.

The issue quickly narrowed down to the question whether Hull
or Borah possessed the better sources of information on the likeli-

hood of war in Europe. It was of supreme significance that when they had no public audience the isolationists did not attack the administration's position on any other point. In order to justify his prophecy that no war would occur in Europe, at least in the near future, Borah had to insult the efficiency and judgment of the State Department's corps of diplomatic and intelligence agents and assert that his own sources of information were superior to those of Hull and Roosevelt.

Hull vigorously repelled Borah's attack, but the case was hopeless because he had frequently invited the Senator to inspect dispatches arriving in the State Department and Borah had never exposed himself to the experience. He preferred to rely upon what was later reported as an obscure press service in London which fed his convictions and served the Axis.[38]

The Senate leaders declared that a favorable vote on the bill was impossible because their canvass showed the Republican Senators unanimously opposed and about a third of the Democrats ready to vote with the Republicans. At midnight Roosevelt and Hull gave up. They obtained a definite promise that the Senate would consider neutrality at the beginning of the next session. Responsibility was located for the public in a statement in which Barkley, for the Democrats, and McNary, for the Republicans, stated that the Senate refused to act, and the President and Secretary of State reaffirmed their position that "failure by the Senate to take action now would weaken the leadership of the United States in exercising its potent influence in the cause of preserving peace among other nations in the event of a new crisis in Europe between now and next January." [39]

Reporters obtained the story of Borah's prophecy and Roosevelt made it clear in a press conference that the only disagreement at the meeting was over the relative merits of Borah's and Hull's information.[40]

Congress adjourned. The administration had failed in its first campaign to strengthen the foreign policy of the United States and help to prevent the outbreak of the Second World War. But the final argument, which was only a prophecy, on which the isolationists had taken their stand was so quickly proved false that the episode was fruitful for the administration and disastrous to the isolationist cause. Undoubtedly Hitler's decision to attack Poland in September was influenced more by the assurance given him by the Soviet government that it would not force him into a two-front war than by the failure of the United States Congress to repeal the arms embargo. Nevertheless, that attack discredited American isolationists, and especially their historic leader, Senator Borah, as false prophets. Beard, although he has many pages to spare for the public arguments of the isolationists, ignores Borah's private and decisive statement of their position. So sensational and influential a mistake cannot be so easily expunged from the historical record.[41]

Roosevelt was never again defeated by the isolationists on a major issue in Congress. Beyond Congress, the American people came to support the administration's foreign policy so widely that the Republican Party itself did not again dare to appeal to them for votes on an isolationist platform, even while a majority of Republican leaders showed by their votes in Congress that they still clung to their discredited faith. Therein lay the evidence that Roosevelt had done well immediately after Munich to make his internationalism the leading issue of American politics and to make the fight for repeal of the arms embargo. He had not achieved his ideal purpose of helping to prevent the Second World War, but it was certainly his most temporary, and perhaps his most constructive and honorable, failure.

# 6.

## The Fight Against the Arms Embargo: Success

Rooseveth HAD PUSHED HIS FIRST AND UNSUCCESSFUL fight to repeal the arms embargo to the limit of his resources because he believed war was imminent in Europe. After Congress refused to act, the President sought and found ways which did not require Congressional authorization to make the position of the United States felt by the Axis. Early in August, 1939, he established the War Resources Board to develop and report on plans for industrial mobilization in case of war. This was the ancestor of the agencies which directed American industry during the Second World War. Its establishment was a warning to the Axis that the administration was not as indifferent as Congress to world events. Its personnel, led by Edward R. Stettinius, Jr., was a bid to businessmen to support the administration.

### Japan Is Warned

The President could do no more on the domestic front. In foreign relations he found means for a telling act of opposition to aggression. Prior to the Czechoslovakian crisis of September, 1938, he had made the promise to defend Canada. Now a strong conviction that war would break out in Europe turned administration attention to the danger that Japan would, as usual, exploit a crisis in the West by launching new aggressions in the Far East. In the spring, Japan had taken advantage of Hitler's aggression against Czechoslovakia to embark on conquests which revealed new extensions of its imperialist program and for the first time violated territory belonging to a Western power. In February Japanese troops occupied Hainan, an island claimed by France which lies off French Indo-China, between Hong Kong and Singapore. To parallel notes from Britain, France, and the United States requesting an explanation, Japan answered that it only wished to strengthen its blockade of China; but Hainan obviously gave Japan significant strategic advantages for a campaign against British and French positions in southeastern Asia. In March, Japan claimed sovereignty over hundreds of islands, including the Spratly group which France claimed. The area was adjacent to the Philippines, and the United States Navy had reported, after a survey, that the islands were useful for naval and air forces. The Japanese government thus boldly exposed ambitions that threatened the United States.

The United States government made an extraordinary gesture of courtesy towards Japan after the death of former Ambassador Saito in the United States, by sending home his ashes aboard an American warship. The visit of the warship produced friendly popular demonstrations in Japan which were interpreted as evidence that the Japanese people preferred the friendship of the United States rather than that of Germany. At the same time, the British government found itself unable to fulfill its promise to Australia to send a fleet to Singapore. France threatened that, if Britain sent its Mediterranean fleet to Singapore, it would not join in the British guaranties to Poland, Rumania, and Greece. The United States fleet had moved into the Atlantic for the opening of the New York World's Fair. Lord Halifax suggested that it be sent back into the Pacific immediately. This was to be done in any case, and Roosevelt gave orders accordingly on April 15. It was a significant example of the administration's cooperation with Britain and France which, while it fell far short of the "secret alliance" or "commitment" isolationists perpetually espied, yet expressed in a practical way the actual community of interests among the peaceful nations.

In June, the Japanese Foreign Minister proposed to Hull that Japan should bring Germany and Italy and that the United States bring Britain and France into a conference to prevent war in Europe. Hull and Roosevelt rejected the proposal because they detected in it a maneuver by Japan to obtain sanction for its conquests in China. The Japanese Army at the same moment was engaged in new indiscriminate bombing campaigns against Chung-king which destroyed American property. British subjects were publicly stripped by the Japanese military, forced to leave China, and otherwise persecuted. Hull made strong protests and pointed out that the United States would work in a friendly spirit with every peaceful nation to preserve peace, but that it drew a line between such nations and "those who are flouting law and order and officially threatening military conquest without limit in time or extent. . . ." [1]

Thus the administration again ruled out appeasement of Japan as a way of achieving peace in Asia. The British government of Chamberlain was not so obdurate. Even after the collapse of the Munich Agreement and the revolution in British European policy in March, Chamberlain and Halifax sought to appease Japan. They had the excuse that, as Hitler threatened Britain and France more immediately than the United States, they could less well afford a strong policy in Asia which might lead to a global war. Japan obviously aimed to exploit Britain's weakness and separate it from the United States. Persecutions in Tientsin were directed solely at British subjects. In subsequent negotiations, Japan demanded that Britain make concessions in return for settlement of the Tientsin incidents.

The United States made known its opposition to any British recognition of Japanese rights in China and its own adherence to its principles and its rights. But Great Britain, nevertheless, signed an agreement on July 24, 1939, recognizing the "special requirements" of the Japanese military forces in the regions of China under their control. This was greeted with joy in the Axis press and with condemnation by internationalists as a betrayal of Britain's own principles and rights, a "Far Eastern Munich" at China's expense, another victory for the Axis, another defeat for the peaceful nations. Regarded as its worst aspect was Britain's lapse from the policy of parallel action with the United States, which encouraged the Japanese in their hope that they could divide the Western powers and discouraged the Chinese. The American administration made no direct comment on the Tientsin Agreement.[2]

But it made a resounding indirect comment on it two days later in its strongest action to date against aggression. Hull in a note to the Japanese Ambassador gave notice that the commercial treaty of 1911 between the United States and Japan would be terminated on January 26, 1940. The treaty itself granted either government the right to terminate it after six months' notice, therefore the action was in no sense comparable to Japan's violations of its treaties with the United States. Hull gave Japan as the reason for the notice merely that the administration had been examining its commercial treaties to determine what changes would better safeguard and promote American interests "as new developments may require." Of course the action contained a heavy threat that the United States would embargo Japan.

Shortly after July 26, Secretary of the Treasury Morgenthau announced he was reconsidering the policy of Treasury purchases of Japanese gold and silver which helped finance Japanese purchases in the United States, and Secretary of Commerce Hopkins made public an analysis of Japanese trade discriminations which would justify United States countervailing tariffs on imports from Japan. Hull's inner purpose was to fill Japanese leaders with uncertainty as to future United States policy and shock them into realization that their present course was unwise without, however, giving them occasion to consolidate their own people in antagonism towards the United States or tempting them too severely to seek elsewhere by conquest the materials they bought in this country.[3]

The Japanese treaty termination notice had extensive domestic and foreign meanings. Beard avoids them all by the simple expedient of excising the action from his account. Senator Arthur H. Vandenberg, the Republican isolationist of Michigan, had introduced a resolution in favor of giving such notice, and this expressed the general fact that isolationists were much more willing to support action against Japan than action against Germany or Italy. The Senate Committee on Foreign Relations postponed action on this resolution, as it had on repeal of the arms embargo, but the President required no authorization for termination notice. His action was enthusiastically approved by large majorities of the people, the press, and Congress. The Gallup Poll reported 81 per cent of those questioned as approving, newspapers were almost unanimous, and even Senator Borah joined the chorus.[4]

The action recovered for the administration the prestige it had lost in the struggle against the arms embargo and, more important, had the effect, which the President had been seeking since Munich, of consolidating the nation in support of a strong policy against aggression. It was consequently with a high degree of unity that the American people and their government faced the coming of war in Europe, and the President's action against Japan thereby helped prepare the country for repeal of the arms embargo immediately after war began.

As a step in the evolution of the administration's foreign policy, the termination notice built unmistakably upon the earlier moral arms embargo against Japan and extension of credits to China. It was another and stronger "measure short of war" with intimations that full economic sanctions against aggression were in the offing. It also had repercussions in Europe, where the evidence of Roosevelt's support of collective security and his ability to move forward in that direction, in spite of isolationist opposition, could not be ignored in the calculations of the dictators. The people of Britain and France generally approved it, and it discredited Chamberlain's Tientsin Agreement. That the Roosevelt administration intended its action to have the latter effect is suggested by its failure to inform the British government ahead of time of its purpose.[5]

The Soviet government, currently fighting its undeclared war with Japan on the frontiers of Manchuria, was the chief provider of war materials for the Chinese government. Britain's Tientsin Agreement had the effect of dissociating it from the Soviet Union in the Orient, while Roosevelt's termination notice placed the United States in closer relation to Soviet policy. For a few weeks it seemed that the United States and the Soviet Union might rescue a fragment in Asia from the wreckage of collective security in Europe.

On August 19, 1939, negotiations between Britain and Japan on the basis of the Tientsin Agreement broke down because Britain would not meet the extreme demands of Japan. But the Nazi-Soviet Pact of August 23, although the Japanese feared it was a betrayal by Germany designed to give the Soviet government a free hand in the East, was actually followed by a truce in September on the Manchurian frontier, and there were other agreements which relaxed tension between Japan and the Soviet Union. Subsequently, both Britain and the Soviet Union in their Japanese policy wavered between resistance and "deals."

The United States alone never retreated, never bargained away any of its principles or acts of resistance, never "appeased" Japan. It moved steadily from stronger to still stronger actions against Japanese aggression. The only criticism by internationalists of the administration's Japanese policy was that it advanced with agonizing slowness.

## Disaster

The Nazi-Soviet Pact of August 23 was a disaster for the United States as well as free nations everywhere. It came as no surprise to the Roosevelt administration. As early as November 30, 1938, the United States legation in Bucharest sent information that Hitler had secretly offered the Soviet Union a nonaggression pact. Early in July, 1939, Washington seemed to have better information than Britain and France on the negotiations between the Nazi and Soviet governments, and this information increased Roosevelt's anxiety to repeal the arms embargo. Early in August he attempted to exert influence on the Soviet government to adhere to the western democracies, but the failure of his campaign to repeal the embargo inevitably reduced the value of Britain and France as allies for the Soviet Union. Roosevelt's attempt was, nevertheless, important because it unmistakably made known to the Soviet leaders that the American President viewed the world situation as an internationalist. He used the classical argument of peace by collective security against the Axis, and he warned the Soviet Union of the dangers to itself of a rapprochement with the Axis. According to Hull's account, Roosevelt told Ambassador Oumansky and Ambassador Steinhardt for communication to the Soviet government:

that if war were to break out in Europe and in the Far East and if the Axis Powers were to win, the position of both the United States and the Soviet Union would inevitably be affected thereby immediately and materially. The position of the Soviet Union, he said, would be affected more rapidly than the position of the United States. For these reasons, the President concluded that, while he was not in a position, of course, to accept any responsibility or to give any assurances as to the course Britain and France might undertake in their negotiations with the Soviet Union, *he could not help but feel that if a satisfactory agreement against aggression on the part of other*

*European powers were reached, it would prove to have a decidedly stabilizing effect in the interest of world peace.* And in the maintenance of world peace the United States, as well as the Soviet Union, had a fundamental concern.[6]

But the Soviet leaders had abandoned faith in collective security and were bargaining with both Britain and Germany for the best possible military frontiers in western Europe. They demanded of Britain and France guaranties not only against aggression by military force against Poland and the three Baltic States, but also guaranties against "indirect aggression," a term which seemed to cover so broad a range of political, economic, and propaganda activities as to open the door to extinction of the independence of the four countries by the Soviet Union on grounds of Nazi acts of "indirect aggression" already committed.

The British government was unwilling to be party to an arrangement that would contradict its public policy of protecting the independence of small nations, which it had extended to Poland, Rumania, Greece, and Turkey. It would have made Britain guilty of a new Anglo-Soviet "Munich," after having revolutionized its foreign policy to wipe out the stain of the Anglo-German Munich.

Germany, on the other hand, had no such scruples. It offered the Soviet Union a secret agreement allowing it to take outright military possession of Eastern Poland, Finland, and the two Baltic States nearest to it, in return for a Nazi advance eastward to the demarcation, raw materials, and a public nonaggression pact in which the Soviet Union agreed not to take part in a united front against Germany. Thus, for the sake of a better military frontier, the Soviet Union gave up the chance of avoiding invasion offered by a united front. Anglo-French-Soviet unity might have prevented the Second World War by facing Hitler with the certainty that he would have to fight on two fronts. The Nazi-Soviet Pact, on the other hand, made war a certainty.

Defenders of the Nazi-Soviet Pact claimed that it won time for the Soviet Union better to prepare to hold off a Nazi onslaught, but they do not allow the same argument to be used to justify Chamberlain's Munich Agreement. They argue that the governments of Chamberlain and Daladier could not be relied upon to fulfill their obligations to Poland any better than they had fulfilled their obligations to Czechoslovakia, but the record of Britain and France did not compare with Hitler's for blatant dishonesty and they could hardly have dishonored an agreement in the way Hitler dishonored the Nazi-Soviet Pact, by invading their ally. The fundamental reason for Chamberlain's abandonment of appeasement was the revulsion of British public opinion against that policy and in favor of a stand against Hitler. It was the supreme task of the Soviet government to understand the depth of this new current in British opinion and to appreciate that no government in a free country could withstand or betray it.

History proved Chamberlain's word, that Britain would defend Poland, to have been better than Hitler's word that Germany would not commit aggression against the Soviet Union. The Soviet government made a mistake when it preferred to accept Hitler's word rather than Chamberlain's, a mistake against which President Roosevelt had warned it. His warning was based on his faith in the policy of collective security. As in his dealings with the American Congress, his warning was not heeded in time to help prevent the Second World War, but, again as with Congress, when events bore out the validity of his view, Roosevelt found the Soviet Union, invaded by Hitler, willing at least temporarily to adopt the policy of collective security in time to help win the war.

Frustrated in his fundamental policy by both the Soviet government and the American Congress, President Roosevelt nevertheless made a last desperate effort to prevent war. The British government believed Hitler intended to invade Poland on August 25 in the hope that Britain and France, stunned by the Nazi-Soviet Pact, would dishonor their commitment to defend Poland. Instead, Chamberlain alerted British air and naval forces on the day the Pact was signed, August 23, and sent a letter to Hitler warning him that "no greater mistake could be made" than to assume Britain would not intervene on behalf of Poland. He offered to discuss all questions at issue between Germany and Poland if Hitler would first call a truce to polemics and create a "situation of confidence." [7]

Premier Daladier had appealed to President Roosevelt the day before to call upon all nations to send representatives to Washington for a peaceful settlement. This recalled the Welles Plan of 1938. The President was not willing to issue the call prior to a settlement of the Polish dispute. Ambassador Kennedy reported that the British government was not in a position to press Poland strongly to negotiate. Roosevelt decided to appeal to Italy, Germany, and Poland in support of Chamberlain's offer of direct negotiations, and to add to it a repetition of the earlier offer by the United States to take part in a subsequent general conference. He asked King Victor Emmanuel of Italy to formulate proposals for the solution of the immediate crisis, and asked Hitler and the President of Poland to make a truce during which their controversies should be settled by direct negotiations, or arbitration, or by conciliation at the hands of a neutral European or American national. He safeguarded the proposal against the possibility of another Munich by specifying that, upon resort to one of the three methods, "each nation will agree to accord complete respect to the independence and territorial integrity of the other."

The King of Italy merely transmitted the message to his master, Mussolini. Roosevelt had evidently hoped that through the King he could appeal to the anti-war sentiment of the Italian people if not to the caution, based on military weakness, of Mussolini himself. Caution led Mussolini to postpone entrance into the war until he felt certain Hitler would win, and perhaps Roosevelt's message as well as caution led Mussolini to propose on August 31 a conference of Britain, France, Italy, Germany, and Poland. But he wanted to give Danzig as a peace offering to Hitler, and this the British government refused to do.

President Moszicki immediately answered Roosevelt, accepting his proposals. He said Poland considered direct negotiation the most appropriate method but also considered "conciliation through a third party as disinterested and impartial as Your Excellency" to be a just and equitable method. Hitler did not answer.

Roosevelt on August 25 transmitted Moszicki's message to Hitler and appealed to him to agree to the direct negotiation or conciliation accepted by Poland. Hitler did not answer. The deadline of August 25 was passed while Hitler explored the possibility of a "Polish Munich." Nothing in the record supports a supposition that Roosevelt's interventions encouraged Hitler to expect such a solution. As in his interventions of September 26 and 27, 1938, Roosevelt in August, 1939, supported Chamberlain when the latter promised to stand firm against concessions to Hitler, and this time Roosevelt guarded against misunderstanding by making the independence of Poland a pre-condition of the peaceful settlement he proposed.

Britain strengthened its unilateral commitment to defend Poland by signing on August 25 a mutual assistance agreement with that nation. Britain and France rejected all of Hitler's promises of good behavior and his offer of "protection of the British Empire" if they would abandon Poland. Hitler thereupon consented to direct negotiations with Poland, but he demanded that the Soviet Union be included among the guarantors of a settlement—a sinister requirement in the light of the Nazi-Soviet secret agreement to partition Poland—and he also required that a Polish plenipotentiary come to Berlin within twenty-four hours to receive proposals. Britain agreed to Russian participation but said immediate arrival of a Polish plenipotentiary was impracticable. A moment before Hitler's deadline expired, Ribbentrop read off the German proposals to the British Ambassador, refused to give him a copy, and announced that Germany considered the proposals "out of date" because no Pole had arrived.

A day later Germany invaded Poland. Britain and France warned Hitler that if he did not withdraw his troops they would declare war. Hitler took up Mussolini's proposal for a five-power conference, but the British government required that withdrawal of German troops from Poland must precede a conference. After two- and five-hour ultimatums, which Hitler rejected, Britain and France on September 3 declared war on Germany.[8]

The significance in relation to President Roosevelt's foreign policy of the manner in which the Second World War began is that it was the turning point in the history of collective security as an international system. That system, bravely inaugurated by Woodrow Wilson in 1919, abandoned first by the United States and dealt destructive blows from one side by aggressor nations and from the other by the failure of peaceful nations led by Britain to instrument the system, received the *coup de grâce* in the transfer of the Soviet Union on August 23, 1939, from the peaceful to the aggressive coalition of nations. But within ten days Britain and France converted Hitler's invasion of Poland into a world war precisely because they had finally determined that their own safety could be secured only by action on the requirement of collective security that every nation must defend every victim of aggression. This inaugurated the redemption of collective security as an international system.

From the Anglo-French-Polish nucleus the coalition of nations devoted to collective security grew until it embraced the United Nations and destroyed the Axis. The conditions of American politics forbade the Roosevelt administration to take the initiative with Britain and France in rebuilding the collective security system. The British and French declarations of war on Germany, not because Hitler attacked them but because he attacked Poland, restored life to the idea of collective security and raised a banner to which President Roosevelt could bring Americans to rally. If Poland was Britain's and France's business, it became easier to understand that Britain and France and Poland were the business of the United States. The defection of the Soviet Union and Communist propaganda in the United States, which appealed to isolationists to shun the Anglo-French-Polish "imperialist" cause, were more than offset by the effect of the British and French demonstration that free nations, even more reluctant to fight than the Soviet Union, and even without being directly attacked, must make a stand against aggression.

## An American Stand

The stand Americans were now willing to make was not very bold. In normal times it could not be called a "stand" at all, because normally belligerents can buy arms and materials in neutral countries without hindrance. But the Neutrality Act was extremely abnormal. Isolationists' greatest fear was that the United States would aid the cause of Britain and France. Repeal of the arms embargo was an act of aid to those two nations and, therefore, the largest step towards collective security the Roosevelt administration had yet proposed.

The President in a fireside chat on September 3 told the American people that he trusted the Neutrality Act could be changed to establish "true neutrality." But he did not take undue advantage of the paradox that conversion of American policy to one of true neutrality would aid Britain and France and injure Germany. He did not repeat Wilson's admonition of neutrality in thought as well as action. He said:

This nation will remain a neutral nation, but I cannot ask that every American remain neutral in thought as well. Even a neutral has a right to take account of facts. Even a neutral cannot be asked to close his mind or his conscience.

Secretary Hull had advised him strongly against such an official statement of unneutrality. Roosevelt insisted on the more frank course.[9] He stated as facts that:

the unfortunate events of these recent years have, without question, been based on the use of force and the threat of force. And it seems to me clear, even at the outbreak of this great war, that the influence of America should be consistent in seeking for humanity a final peace which will eliminate, as far as it is possible to do so, the continued use of force between nations.

Also:

You must master at the outset a simple but unalterable fact in modern foreign relations between nations. When peace has been broken anywhere, the peace of all countries everywhere is in danger.

To this assertion of the fundamental doctrine of internationalism he added a refutation of the isolationists' fundamental preachment:

It is easy for you and for me to shrug our shoulders and to say that conflicts taking place thousands of miles from the continental United States, and, indeed, thousands of miles from the whole American Hemisphere, do not seriously affect the Americas—and that all the United States has to do is to ignore them and go about its own business. Passionately though we may desire detachment, we are forced to realize that every word that comes through the air, every ship that sails the sea, every battle that is fought, does affect the American future.

Besides these clear statements of his position as an internationalist, the President promised that the administration was determined to avoid United States entry into the war:

Let no man or woman thoughtlessly or falsely talk of America sending its armies to European fields. . . .

I have said not once, but many times, that I have seen war and that I hate war. I say that again and again.

I hope the United States will keep out of this war. I believe that it will. And I give you assurance and reassurance that every effort of your Government will be directed toward that end.

As long as it remains within my power to prevent, there will be no black-out of peace in the United States.[10]

The two themes of internationalism and avoidance of war set the pattern for Roosevelt's pronouncements until the fall of 1941. While the President made his fireside chat, the British steamer *Athenia* was torpedoed with a loss of over one hundred passengers, including twenty-eight Americans. Few believed the announcement of the German Foreign Office that the ship had been sunk by the British in order to arouse the United States, which Admiral Raeder admitted in 1946 to have been a lie.[11] The administration did not attempt to exploit the incident. It adhered to the policy of forbidding American citizens and ships to enter war zones. Roosevelt wished to leave the nation free to make its decisions calmly and on higher grounds than such incidents, affecting a few individuals, as had led to United States entry into the First World War.

The President issued the neutrality proclamations on September 5. He did not exercise his discretion under the 1937 Act to refuse to find that a state of war existed in Europe, although such a refusal would have benefited Britain and France. Besides the fact that in Europe declarations of war had ruled out the fiction maintained in Asia that no war but only an "incident" raged, the President perhaps wished to demonstrate to the country precisely what the Act meant. One of his proclamations applied rules of neutrality derived from traditional concepts of international law. It raised no controversy until some of the rules were later suspended. It forbade within the territory of the United States any aid to a belligerent, such as recruiting, fitting out or arming a war vessel, organizing an armed enterprise, or despatching a vessel built in the United States for use in hostilities by a belligerent. Use of the territorial waters and ports of the United States was forbidden to armed vessels of belligerents beyond a twenty-four hour stay, which might be extended only because of weather, delay in repairs necessary to make them seaworthy, need for food and fuel in limited quantities, or because an enemy vessel had left within the previous twenty-four hours. In any case no more than three vessels of any one belligerent might be in port at the same time. No agency of the United States government might directly or indirectly provide supplies or repairs for a belligerent vessel of war. No belligerent vessel might search others or take prizes within the territorial waters of the United States. No person in the United States might take part directly or indirectly in the war.

This left Americans free to sell and carry to belligerents munitions and other supplies subject to the traditional right of their enemies to intercept and confiscate contraband. The current definition of contraband was very broad. Most powers admitted that raw materials useful in war as well as finished war materials were contraband. The President's second proclamation imposed the arms embargo required by the 1937 Neutrality Act. It forbade export of arms, ammunition, or implements of war to belligerents, either directly or for transshipment to them. The list of "implements of war" included all aircraft and equipment for aircraft, guns of all kinds above .22 calibre, ammunition, vessels of war of all kinds and armor plate, armored vehicles, cartridge and shell cases, poison gases, and all propellent powders and high explosives.[12]

Oil was not embargoed, nor were raw materials or semi-manufactured articles like brass tubing for shell cases. Since cash-and-carry had expired on May 1, 1939, Americans were allowed to sell on credit, except as this was prohibited by the Johnson Act, and to transport to belligerents any items not embargoed. Congressional failure to pass the administration's neutrality bill left Americans free to travel and navigate American ships in war zones. One of the absurdities of the "new neutrality" was that it prohibited the arms traffic which the United States government did not defend against confiscation, and permitted traffic which it must defend, with consequent danger of incidents and involvement which would repeat the pattern of entry into the First World War.

The embargo immediately stopped delivery to Great Britain and France of arms, especially aircraft, amounting to $79,000,000 in value. Cancellations to Germany amounted to exactly $49.[13]

Therein lay what opponents called the one-sided penalties of the embargo and what isolationists called the one-sided consequences of repeal. But, from either point of view, the fact was that the United States by domestic legislation reduced the value to

Britain and France of their geographic position, to the exploitation of which they were fully entitled under international law.

The occupation of Eastern Poland by the Red Army raised new problems. The Soviet Union did not declare war on Poland, but neither did Germany. The United States did not admit the Soviet contention that the Polish government had ceased to exist: it recognized the Polish government in exile. The Soviet government was free to buy arms in the United States and had an open sea lane to transport them. It was impossible to determine whether such arms, or Soviet arms these purchases could replace, would be sent to Germany under the Soviet leaders' "business relations" policy, which had been actually instrumented by economic engagements in the Nazi-Soviet Pact. Many internationalists as well as isolationists demanded that the arms embargo be imposed on the Soviet Union. But the administration decided to "appease" that nation for the same reason it later "appeased" Franco Spain and Vichy France: to reduce the number of Hitler's allies—a very different thing from Chamberlain's appeasement at Munich, which strengthened Hitler and sacrificed to him an unoffending third nation. Hull and Roosevelt felt that Germany and the Soviet Union would not become full allies and wished to avoid any provocation of the latter which might prolong their unnatural alliance.[14]

Soviet policy actually strengthened the administration's campaign to repeal the arms embargo. Japan had protested to Germany that the Nazi-Soviet Pact freed Russia for stronger action against Japan, and had abandoned pending negotiations to strengthen the Anti-Comintern Pact by a military alliance. But Japan's fears were mitigated, on September 16, when the Soviet Union agreed to a truce ending the fighting on the frontier of Manchuria. Japan's admission that a battle in August had resulted in 18,000 Japanese casualties and a severe defeat made Soviet willingness to sign a truce even more startling. Americans feared that the truce freed Japan to extend its operations in China and the southwest Pacific, and that it would be followed by a nonaggression agreement matching the Nazi-Soviet Pact. They saw Britain, France, and the Western Hemisphere faced by a solid bloc of aggressive powers controlling territory from the Rhine to the Pacific. The Soviet Union was regarded as lost to the Peace Front on both sides of the world. The Axis had taken large steps towards world domination, while the United States had not merely stood aside from Britain and France but had penalized them by offsetting their sea power in the Atlantic with the arms embargo.

The role of the Communist Party in the United States also strengthened the administration. Prior to the Nazi-Soviet Pact, and under a directive of the Communist International, American Communists had joined liberals in support of the New Deal and collective security. The sudden shift in Soviet policy led Communists to abandon collective security, take up the slogans of isolationists, and label the British and French cause "imperialist." The United States role in Puerto Rico was assessed as on a par with Hitler's role in conquered countries. Roosevelt's program of aid to Britain and France made him a "warmonger." The League against War and Fascism changed its name to the League for Peace and Democracy. Roosevelt was the enemy of peace because he advocated collective security, and the enemy of democracy because he sacrificed further domestic reforms for the sake of imperialist adventures in the interests of big business. This awkward and ridiculous turnabout of American Communists was self-defeating. Those who had applied labels like "Bolshevik" to the administration were confronted by the fact that it pursued its foreign policy consistently, while Communists turned against it with even more virulence than the Soviet government and press. This served the useful purpose for the administration of shifting the burden of Communist approval to the isolationists' shoulders, and, already burdened by approval of their policy by Axis governments and agents in the United States, they staggered under it.

The about-face of the Soviet Union and of American Communists strengthened public fear that an Axis victory would imperil democracy everywhere more effectively than had their support of collective security. Immediately after the outbreak, Americans had attempted to hypnotize themselves with the slogan "This is not our war." According to Gallup polls, the majority of 57 per cent which had favored repeal of the arms embargo in April was reduced to 50 per cent on September 3. But the majority then increased to 62 per cent within a month.[15] This was in spite of an intensified campaign by isolationists to prevent repeal. They were not lacking in old and new spokesmen of wide public prestige. Perhaps Senator Borah had lost by his mistaken prophecy in July, but he spoke for the diehards of ancient fights against internationalism when, in a radio address, he called repeal of the arms embargo a virtual taking up of arms.[16] Former President Hoover asked in a radio address for an impossible "compromise." He wanted the arms embargo lifted for "defensive" and retained for "offensive" weapons. This distinction had been proposed by him, when he was President, to the Geneva Disarmament Conference. Experts had never been able to agree on where the line between offensive and defensive weapons should be drawn because so many weapons were actually both.[17]

These voices were less influential than Charles A. Lindbergh, who launched himself as the spokesman of a new generation of isolationists in a radio address on September 15, the first in a long series. He had emerged from the chrysalis of an airplane pilot astonishingly as an expert on international relations in 1938, when he played an ambiguous role behind the scenes in the Munich crisis and received a decoration from Hitler. Lindbergh expressed no sympathy for the cause of democracy or concern for the position of the United States should the Axis dominate Europe, Africa, and Asia. The war in Europe, he said, was merely another of "those age-old struggles." [18] His voice soon became louder and his views more extreme.

President Roosevelt did not yield the initiative to isolationists. On September 13 he called Congress to convene in special session on September 21. Management of the campaign in Congress was not again entrusted to Senator Pittman. Instead, the eminent negotiator, Senator James F. Byrnes of South Carolina, was given charge. Before Congressmen returned to Washington, and while they were still in contact with their constituents, Byrnes canvassed them by telephone and obtained commitments from large majorities of both houses to vote for repeal of the arms embargo. The tide had finally turned.[19]

On the day before the session opened, the President called to a conference in the White House the titular leaders of the Republican Party, Alfred M. Landon and Frank Knox. This action symbolized the consolidation of national unity in support of his foreign policy for which the President had been working since Munich. It also officially inaugurated the "bipartisan foreign policy" which was to be developed steadily during the following years. Roosevelt thereby carefully avoided the mistake of President Wilson, who had offended Republican leaders by asking the country to support collective security as a partisan Democratic policy. Roosevelt's broad and conciliatory strategy bore fruit. It was estimated that 80 per cent of the nation's newspapers, including many that opposed the New Deal, supported repeal of the arms embargo. The National Republican Club came out in favor of the Roosevelt program.[20]

The essential meaning of the situation was that a large proportion of business sentiment in the nation had been won over by the course of events outside the United States and by the President's strategy of subordinating domestic reforms in favor of a stronger foreign policy. This had been accomplished without loss of liberals' support. The nation which had been bogged down in isolationist indifference for twenty years was ready for the first step on a long journey.

## The Tide Turns

With each new sensation in international affairs, especially the speed and ferocity of Hitler's victory in Poland and the cooperation of the Soviet Union with the Axis in the Far East as well as Europe, confirming his judgment, and with the tide of public opinion running strongly in his direction, the President asked Congress on September 21 to ratify his program. He demanded that, just as he admitted the desire for peace of isolationists, they must admit his desire for it also, since they differed only on methods of achieving it: "Let no group assume the exclusive label of the 'peace bloc.'" He reviewed "in a spirit of understatement" the history of aggressions beginning with the Japanese invasion of Manchuria in 1931. He made a broad distinction between the First and Second World Wars in order to demolish the view that they were the "same war." He denied the conclusion, based on disillusionment with the Allies' motives in the First World War as revealed by their secret treaties, that the Second was "not our war":

I note in passing what you will all remember—the long debates of the past on the subject of what constitutes aggression, on the methods of determining who the aggressor might be and on who the aggressors in past wars had been. Academically this may have been instructive, as it may have been of interest to historians to discuss the pros and cons and the rights and wrongs of the World War during the decade that followed it.

But in the light of problems of today and tomorrow, responsibility for acts of aggression is not concealed. . . .

The President told Congress he regretted that it had passed the Neutrality Act and added: "I regret equally that I signed that Act." This was perhaps a unique instance of a President in office admitting publicly that he had been wrong. He quoted passages from former addresses in which he had warned of the danger to the United States if aggressions went unchecked. This made clear enough that he proposed repeal because it would help stem aggression, but he declared that putting the country "back on the solid footing of real and traditional neutrality" was the issue. He pointed out that the only time in the nation's history when it abandoned its rights under international law and embargoed belligerents, in the Napoleonic Wars, the policy was a disastrous failure because it brought the nation's economy close to ruin and because it was the major cause of the War of 1812, during which, as he said, the Capitol in which he spoke was burned. Historians dispute his interpretation of the embargo as the "major cause" of the War of 1812, but not that the embargo brought the nation close to economic ruin. And the historian would add that the embargo had political consequences of weakening not only President Jefferson's leadership but the Union itself, for it made secession a live issue in mercantile circles of New England.

Roosevelt offered a new and effective argument in favor of repeal. Processing raw materials into implements of war would give work to Americans and build up an American defense industry. Profiteering could be restricted by Congress. But he placed chief emphasis on the need to return to international law, at the same time advocating abandonment of those rights under it, such as the right of American citizens and ships to travel through war zones, which did create a danger of provocative incidents. He proposed cash-and-carry for all exports to belligerents. Such safeguards, rather than the arms embargo, would mean "less likelihood of incidents and controversies which tend to draw us into conflict, as they unhappily did in the last World War. There lies the road to peace!" This, coupled with his belief that "methods short of war" in aid of the Allies would make more probable the defeat of the Axis, was the sense in which the President meant that his program rather than the isolationists' would maintain the neutrality, security, and peace of the United States.

The President closed with a plea to Congress to end partisanship in the consideration of foreign policy. As evidence of his own intention to practice the precept, he announced that he was asking leaders of both parties to remain in Washington after the special session to consult with him on future executive as well as legislative actions. He said darker periods might lie ahead and the United States, through no act of its own, was "affected to the core" by the forces which assaulted the foundations of civilization. He combined his call for awareness of this with an appeal for national unity in a moving peroration:

In such circumstances our policy must be to appreciate in the deepest sense the true American interest. Rightly considered, this interest is not selfish. Destiny first made us, with our sister nations on this Hemisphere, joint heirs of European culture. Fate seems now to compel us to assume the task of helping to maintain in the Western world a citadel wherein that civilization may be kept alive. The peace, the integrity, and the safety of the Americas—these must be kept firm and serene.

In a period when it is sometimes said that free discussion is no longer compatible with national safety, may you by your deeds show the world that we of the United States are one people, of one mind, one spirit, one clear resolution, walking before God in the light of the living.[21]

Beard artfully excludes from his quotations of this speech everything except the President's affirmations of peace and neutrality. He hides from his readers the evidence that showed the President was not indifferent to the danger of Axis victory, that while he made the return to international law the chief issue, his speech left no doubt that he wished the nation to use its rights under international law to aid the Allies. Nor does Beard point out that the President had made the important distinction between what he proposed—selling arms and materials under cash-and-carry and prohibiting travel and shipping in war zones—which would reduce danger of incidents, and the existing law which exposed the country to the multifold dangers of incidents and involvement.[22]

It is true that Roosevelt and Hull considered aid to the allies their transcendent object. But it is a very exalted conception of a President's duty that requires him to make a primary issue of the argument against which his opponents can arouse the most prejudice when another valid argument is available. In Hull's words:

> With isolationism still powerful and militant in the United States, it would have been the peak of folly to make aid to the democracies an issue in connection with neutrality legislation. We were sincere in our belief that the new legislation would afford us a better chance of keeping out of the war than the old legislation because, if Britain and France won the war, we could remain at peace, whereas if Germany won there was every likelihood that we should soon have to fight.[23]

Besides this, no one in the debate that followed seemed confused as to which side in the war the administration hoped repeal would help to win.

The climax of public and Congressional debate followed the President's address. A new issue was whether repeal of the arms embargo would constitute an unneutral act if it was done after the beginning of a war. A large majority of authorities on international law declared that it would not.[24]

Isolationists injured their own cause. They flooded Congressmen with letters and telegrams opposing repeal, overwhelming the messages of advocates of repeal by five and ten to one. But the similarity of most anti-repeal letters in stationery, typing and language, which was taken from speeches of the priest Coughlin, was so glaring that their effect was destroyed.[25] On October 13, Lindbergh spoke again and unwisely revealed that imperialism was at the heart of his isolationist doctrine. He deplored that Canada was a member of the British Commonwealth and said that sooner or later the United States must demand the freedom of this continent and its surrounding islands "from the dictates of European power." [26] This, and the President's promise at Kingston to defend Canada from any empire *except* the British, defined extremes of difference between "isolationism" and internationalism.

Within a few hours of Lindbergh's speech, Senator Lundeen, of Minnesota, told the Senate that the United States should take advantage of the preoccupation of Britain and France with Hitler and send its armed forces to seize the British and French West Indies. This, he said, would prove that the United States was a "good, strong, red-blooded, affirmative democracy." [27] The public and Congressional reaction to these revelations of isolationists' conception of how the United States should "mind its own business" and "practice democracy at home first" was one of disgust.[28] Their frankness was refreshing but their strategy mistaken, and such admissions were not often repeated during the next two years. Beard fills fifteen pages of his book with the speeches of isolationist Congressmen but he avoids Senator Lundeen's remarkable proposal, nor in his six pages of internationalists' speeches does he give space to statements like that of Senator Pittman, who declared that Lindbergh encouraged the ideology of totalitarian governments and seemed to approve the brutal conquest of democratic countries.[29]

Otherwise the debate rang the changes on the most weary arguments of both sides. A dramatic recruit to the President's banner of national unity was Alfred E. Smith. His break with the President in 1933 and his bitter opposition had made him the leader of conservative Democrats who would not tolerate the New Deal. On October 1, 1939, he returned to support of the President in a magnanimous statement that the people should stand solidly behind him "because he is so clearly right, so obviously on the side of common sense and sound judgment of patriotism that only those who lack an understanding of the issue will oppose him." [30] Former Secretary of State Stimson endorsed the President's program and did not hesitate to oppose the views of his former chief, Hoover.[31] Thus the outlines of the bipartisan coalition which the President would lead to victory over the Axis and into the United Nations became visible before the war was a month old.

As the tide of opinion moved strongly toward repeal, the administration struggled with Pittman to avoid unnecessary concessions to the opposition. The administration bill which had passed the House during the summer was rewritten by the Senate Committee on Foreign Relations to include several favorite plans of isolationists. Congress as well as the President was given power to name belligerents and invoke the law. This pleased those who professed fear that the President wished to become a "dictator" by accumulating power and those who professed fear that he wished to "drag the country into war." The President had earlier expressed his willingness to accept the amendment, and it stood. But Hull opposed other concessions, such as restrictions on United States shipping to belligerent ports outside combat zones and the exclusion of armed belligerent merchant ships from American ports, and most of them were dropped.[32]

On the eve of the Senate vote on the bill, Roosevelt spoke over the radio to the *Herald Tribune* Forum. He took the occasion to call the final hysterical argument of isolationists, that he planned to "send the boys of American mothers to fight on the battlefields of Europe," "a shameless and dishonest fake." At the same time he justified his former distinction between neutrality in action and neutrality in thought because "the people of this country, thinking things through calmly and without prejudice, have been and are making up their minds about the relative merits of current events on other continents."[33] Beard quotes the former but not the latter passage.[34]

The bill was passed in the Senate on October 27 by a vote of 63 to 30. The greater strength of isolationism among Republicans was evidenced by the opposition to the bill of 65 per cent of Republicans voting compared with only 18 per cent of Democrats voting. The most significant political aspect of the vote was that Republican votes were not needed to pass the bill because the split in the Democratic ranks had healed sufficiently to give the President his first victory on a major issue since 1936. At the same time, support of the administration by 35 per cent of Republicans voting gave bipartisan color to the result.

A conference committee rapidly considered the bill and reported it to both houses without important change. They passed it with large majorities and the President signed the Neutrality Act of 1939 on November 4. On the same day he issued a new neutrality proclamation, which lifted the arms embargo and imposed the terms of the new law. Britain and France could now buy arms as well as any other goods in the United States, but all purchases were on a cash-and-carry basis. The President established combat areas prohibiting American citizens and ships from going into any European belligerent port, the North or Baltic Seas or Atlantic waters near France, Britain, Ireland, or Norway south of Bergen.

### Chamberlain Fumbles

An anticlimax occurred when Britain failed to take advantage of the new law. France placed large orders, but British orders were trifling in size. The Chamberlain government pursued a passive

strategy, was unwilling to disturb unduly British peacetime industry, and relied on French fortifications, the English Channel and
the blockade to win the war. Its neglect of the opportunity Roosevelt had made to draw upon the enormous resources and industry
of the United States revived the situation of pre-war years when
the American President actually stood in advance of Chamberlain
in relation to the Axis. But Roosevelt had already in September
entered into personal correspondence with the new First Lord of
the Admiralty, Winston Churchill,[35] who would not neglect opportunities to acquire weapons when he took power six months later.

Meanwhile, serious controversy between the United States and
Britain was avoided chiefly because of the extremely friendly atti-
tude of the Roosevelt administration. Secretary Hull took the
initiative and worked out plans to prevent petty affairs incident to
Britain's blockade of Germany from seriously troubling Anglo-
American relations as they did during the early years of the
First World War.

The day after Britain declared war, Secretary Hull called in
Ambassador Lothian and proposed that the two governments designate experts to work out a system of navicerts similar to that
used in the First World War, whereby the British certified American cargoes before they left port to make unnecessary diversion
of American ships to British ports for examination. Hull also accepted without controversy a British rationing system whereby neutrals bordering Germany were allowed to import from the United
States only peacetime quantities of goods so that they could not defeat the British blockade by sending surpluses into Germany. Cooperative procedure prevented repetition of the flaring disputes of the
earlier war. The administration did not make known at the time
that it had actually initiated the revival of navicerts. It announced
publicly that the United States government reserved all its rights
under international law. Officially, the State Department treated
the navicert system as an arrangement between American exporters and the British authorities with which it was not concerned so long as no interference with legitimate trade occurred.[36]

## The Declaration of Panama

In another sphere the United States with the other American
Republics made demands on British good will and, when it was

not forthcoming, nevertheless exercised forbearance and gave valuable assistance to Britain. When war began, the United States Navy was ordered to patrol waters adjacent to the United States to enforce the Neutrality Act. On September 5 the Republic of Panama invited representatives of the American Republics to meet and put into effect the procedure of consultation provided for at Buenos Aires and Lima. They accepted. Dominant sentiment everywhere, even in Argentina, favored the Allies and the creation of a collective system of neutrality which should depend on the sea power of Britain and France to avoid injury to their cause. Under Secretary Welles presented to the delegates, on September 26, six proposals intended to prevent subversive activities, preserve liberal trade policies, establish an advisory committee on monetary and commercial problems, declare the neutral policies of the Republics, keep belligerent submarines out of American ports, and create a "safety zone" extending beyond the territorial waters around the Republics from which belligerent activities should be excluded. All of these proposals were adopted. The last one was incorporated in the Declaration of Panama. It startled international lawyers because it asserted unprecedented jurisdiction over waters from three hundred to one thousand miles beyond shore lines. The American Republics would patrol this zone individually or collectively by agreement.

The idea of the Safety Zone originated with President Roosevelt [37] and it clearly favored Britain and France. German merchant shipping was virtually excluded from the oceans by the British Navy, and the chief effect of the Zone would be to prevent German submarines and raiders from hunting Allied merchant vessels. All the Latin American Republics favored the proposal, and were confirmed in their support by the sinking of a British merchantman by the *Graf von Spee* within the proposed Zone. The next day, October 3, they signed the Declaration and asked the belligerents to respect it.[38]

Unprecedented in international law though it was, the American Safety Zone might be justified as an experiment in creating new international law in the best way it can be created—by agreement among governments. The function of the Neutrality Patrol as publicly announced by the State Department on November 3, 1939, was solely "to enable the governments of the American nations to obtain the fullest information possible with regard to what is going on within the restricted area." [39]

In practice, the United States Navy carried the chief burden of the Patrol and concentrated on the Caribbean area. In fulfillment of their function of giving information, patrol ships radioed "in the clear" the location of any belligerent warship they encountered. Obviously the most likely victims of belligerent action in the Zone, Allied merchantmen, would profit by news of the location of the warships most likely to appear in the Zone, German submarines and raiders. Nevertheless, the British government hesitated to accept the precedent of extending the traditional three-mile limit.

The most spectacular violation of the Safety Zone was committed by Great Britain as well as Germany. Early in December, 1939, three British cruisers fought the *Graf von Spee* off Uruguay and forced it to run to Montevideo for shelter. Advised by the United States, the Uruguayan government ordered the *Spee* to depart or be interned. British warships waited outside. The German commander scuttled his ship and committed suicide.

The twenty-one American Republics protested to Britain, France, and Germany against this violation of the Safety Zone. But all three governments rejected the principle of the Zone on the ground that it favored the enemy.[40]

Which side the Neutrality Patrol actually favored became more clear as the war progressed. The fate of the German liner *Columbus* was suggestive as to the value of the Neutrality Patrol's information service to the Allies. The *Columbus* was on cruise in the Caribbean when war began. It dropped its passengers at Havana and ran to Vera Cruz. There the activities of its crew created suspicion that it served as a supply depot for German submarines. In December, 1939, it made a dash for home. It was sighted by the United States cruiser *Tuscaloosa* about four hundred miles off the coast of New Jersey. Presently a British destroyer appeared, doubtless attracted by the Tuscaloosa's radio service, and the commander of the *Columbus* scuttled his ship to avoid capture. The *Tuscaloosa* stood by to pick up the crew. The German government thanked the United States for its assistance. This and other incidents made clear that the Safety Zone was not safe for German ships.[41]

Similarly, the economic policy which the United States developed at the Panama Conference favored the Allies. The Nazi economic assault on the Americas, which imitated the pattern of penetration in the Balkans, belied German apologists and American isolationists who claimed the Axis had no designs on the Western Hemisphere. The Nazi Minister to Central America ostentatiously moved with a large staff to Panama for the Conference and set up a nest of activity to undermine the solidarity of the Republics. The Japanese government addressed to the government of Panama insulting notes regarding its treatment of Japanese nationals near the Canal. Public Axis propaganda was directed against "Yankee imperialism." More privately, Nazi agents threatened the Latin American delegates with economic reprisals if they cooperated with the United States.

The Latin American economies were seriously disrupted by loss of markets resulting from the British blockade of Germany. Freight congested ports because services of belligerent merchantmen had been suddenly withdrawn. Nazi agents made sensational boasts and promises that Germany, after a quick victory, would buy all surpluses. But anti-Communism had been the most effective drawing card of the Axis in Latin America, and this card was not in play during the period of the Nazi-Soviet Pact. Franco Spain had earlier converted the cultural movement of *Hispanidad* into a pro-Axis, anti-Communist instrument under control of the fascist *Falange* Party, but the Nazi-Soviet Pact seemed to place the Axis on the side of Communism and thus aided the cause of American continental solidarity against the Axis. Furthermore, the charge of "Yankee imperialism" was wearing thin under the abrasions of the Good Neighbor policy.

Under Secretary Welles offered the economic aid of the United States to the twenty Republics, not as a means of coercion but as a contribution to the common welfare. He declared the United States would expand shipping services to Latin America, and provide credits to tide the Republics over emergencies and to finance new industries to take the place of those which had lost their markets. The last offer was the most significant because it showed that the United States was willing to finance an industrial revolution in Latin America in a manner quite different from both private capitalists and Axis governments. It would not restrict Latin America to "feeder" economies producing raw materials for the profit of advanced industrial nations. Instead, it would encourage industrialization, despite the fact that this would encourage competition with American exports. The United States allowed Latin American governments, as demonstrated by Mexico, to eradicate the "finance imperialism" of private American capitalists, helped them avoid falling into the even more exploitative pattern of Axis neo-mercantilism, and aided them to build up their economic as well as political independence.

Welles's plan was carried out, and it resulted in the construction of the first steel mills in Latin America. The best evidence of the meaning of this program was that it was advocated by the same Latin Americans who led the struggle against imperialism. This expansion and deepening of the meaning of the Good Neighbor policy revealed the creativity of Rooseveltian internationalism.

It also won the day at Panama. In practical respects it overcame the Axis and attracted even conservative Latin Americans with a penchant for fascism to the program of the United States. The chief formal agreement was the Resolution on Economic Cooperation, which established in Washington the Inter-American Financial and Economic Advisory Committee made up of experts from the twenty-one Republics. The Committee began on November 15, 1939, its important work of drafting recommendations to stabilize monetary and commercial relations among the Republics, promoting lower tariffs among them, establishing one centralized financial institution, promoting new industries and exchange of raw materials, and finding new markets within the hemisphere for its own productions.[42]

Besides the Safety Zone and the Economic Resolution, the Republics adopted resolutions incorporating United States proposals to coordinate police work against agents of belligerents, establish continental solidarity in policies of neutrality, provide for future meetings—particularly in case of danger that the no-transfer corollary of the Monroe Doctrine would be violated—, concert measures against subversive ideologies, and humanize warfare. The only resolution which could be interpreted as directed against the Allies rather than the Axis was one which asserted that food, clothing, and raw materials for peacetime industries of neutrals should not be considered contraband.[43]

At Panama the policy of collective security for the Western Hemisphere, which was the ultimate goal for America of Roosevelt's Good Neighbor policy, first was manifested not merely in promises and on political levels, but in economic and military as well as political actions.

## The Third-Term Question

The victory of the Roosevelt administration at Panama complemented and extended its victory in repealing the arms embargo. Together they made President Roosevelt undisputed moral leader of the Western Hemisphere. Within ten weeks after the outbreak of war, he had created a bloc of nations technically neutral but clearly determined to make its neutrality serve the Allies and give no comfort to the Axis. The President's two victories established policy for the first stage of the war. That this stage turned out to be, after the conquest of Poland, one of "phony" war or *"sitzkrieg,"* encouraged Americans to return to domestic affairs as their chief preoccupation. Politically, the question of Roosevelt's intention to run for a third term was uppermost. Conventional statements that he would not run were not taken seriously. It could be expected that he, like most Presidents, would postpone as long as possible a definitive announcement that he would not run, because to make it would diminish his influence in the party and disrupt his administration with a scramble of contenders for the nomination.

At the beginning of 1939, Postmaster General Farley believed the President would not be a "voluntary" candidate but might be persuaded. He thought the President would prefer a New Dealer like Harry Hopkins, but would probably be placed in a position to support one of the more popular conservatives, in which case he would choose Hull.[44] Farley himself, as the chief party organizer, was in a strong position to secure the nomination. He believed himself to be the victim of personal slights by the President, especially of ingratitude for his political services; in addition, he opposed the third term on principle. A break between Roosevelt and Farley was widely reported.[45]

Such a break would reopen the gulf within the party between New Dealers and conservatives which it had been the purpose of the President, since Munich, to close. Farley's candidacy would appeal to all conservatives in the party except the southerners, who were the particular objects of the President's solicitude for the sake of their support on foreign policy. Defeat of the administration bill to repeal the arms embargo in July emphasized the danger of such a break. On July 23 the President called Farley to Hyde Park for a conference. Farley spoke sharply against the New Dealers. The President mollified Farley by confiding in him that he would not run for a third term and that he would postpone public announcement until early 1940 in order to avoid making his role difficult. After war began, Roosevelt told Farley he would postpone his announcement until March or April, 1940. And he promised the Democratic Chairman that he would consider him for chairmanship of a new industrial mobilization agency.[46]

The "palace guard" of presidential advisers, chief of whom was Harry Hopkins, and many labor leaders and liberals believed that the President should run for a third term to ensure continuity of his domestic policies as well as strong leadership against the Axis. According to Secretary of Labor Frances Perkins, Roosevelt probably did not make up his mind earlier than March, 1940, to run for a third term, and then he allowed only a few intimates to know that he would run if the demand was sufficiently widespread.[47]

## War to the Rescue?

Second to the third-term issue in domestic politics was the problem of economic recovery. The constellation of New Deal agencies which aimed to achieve recovery and at the same time establish a greater degree of social justice was under heavy fire when the war began. Recovery from the recession of 1937–8 was slow and spotty. For this reason it has been remarked that the war in Europe "rescued" the administration by creating American prosperity based on foreign and domestic war orders.[48]

Analysis of the economic situation as it was developing prior to Hitler's attack on Poland suggests that opponents of the New Deal found much to object to in the distribution of the benefits of recovery as well as in its slowness. Laborers gained more than did farmers and the owners of industry. Between the lowest stage of the recession in May, 1938, and July, 1939, the index of industrial production rose from 76 to 98. Employment and the income of laborers rose while prices remained approximately stable.[49] Such a development was unknown in previous periods of recovery. It represented the success of the administration in its major goal of achieving recovery by an increase in the purchasing power of the lower income groups. Farmers also benefited from the recovery of 1938–39.[50]

The Roosevelt administration in August, 1939, was in process of achieving the *kind* of economic recovery it sought even though the *degree* of prosperity was uninspiring. Insofar as organized labor, the unemployed, and farmers continued to support the administration which had given them a taste of a prosperity whose chief benefits did not accrue to the wealthy, the administration can hardly be said to have stood in need of "rescue" by the European war.

It remains true that unemployment and federal deficits were eloquent of the failure of the New Deal to achieve general recovery; the European war did "rescue" the administration from the predicament of unemployment, and also from any strong political opposition to expansion of the federal debt. But the prosperity which came with war did not alter the administration's conviction that the kind of prosperity was primary and the degree a secondary consideration. Nor did the war interrupt its efforts to devise ways to distribute the benefits of prosperity in accordance with its conviction.

War prosperity is the classical arena for profiteering by business through inflation of prices, which lowers the real incomes of laborers and farmers even while their money incomes rise. The First World War had produced those results in the United States. President Roosevelt's desire to conciliate business opponents of the New Deal, for the sake of national unity and support of his foreign policy, created a temptation to allow business to resume control of the American economy. The appointment of representatives of big business to the War Resources Board in August, 1939, seemed a first move by Roosevelt to "rescue" his administration from the New Deal itself. The behavior of businessmen immediately after the outbreak of war gave warning of what such a "rescue" would involve. They promoted a speculative boom to discount the profits of war prosperity before it got underway. The stock market revived suddenly. Wholesale prices jumped from 75 in August to 79 in September, and held steady at that point through the winter. Retail food prices jumped from 93 in August to 98 in September.[51] Most significantly, prices of basic commodities and raw materials jumped about 25 per cent in September.[52]

President Roosevelt decided that he had gone too far in turning over the War Resources Board to big business. The Chairman, Edward R. Stettinius, Jr., was closely associated with the J. P. Morgan group of financial and industrial leaders. Roosevelt in September told Farley confidentially:

"Of course, if the war industries are dominated by the Morgan crowd, they would do all the business and make all the money. The Morgan crowd have been bitterly opposed to me and all I have advocated. I'll take the necessary steps. Henry Morgenthau made a mistake in naming one of an associated crowd and there's someone else definitely of Morgan influence. . . ."

In November the Board made its report. Roosevelt sent Stettinius a letter of thanks and put the Board "on the shelf." [53]

However much the "Morgan crowd" had opposed the President on domestic policy, it was well known that it supported a strong stand against the Axis in foreign policy. Roosevelt's action in shelving the Board denoted his decision to limit strictly the concessions to big business and avoid returning to it control over the economy in the name of national emergency and national unity. The agencies which succeeded the War Resources Board gave an equal voice to labor with business. The later course of prices and wages showed that farmers and laborers were the chief beneficiaries of the prosperity brought about by the Second World War.

The President in 1944 announced publicly that the New Deal was "dead," but that was an election year and anti-New Dealers did not believe him. They had only to notice the course of wages, the work of the OPA and the FEPC, the excess profits tax, and numerous other manifestations to conclude correctly that the New Deal was still in the forefront of Roosevelt's domestic policy.

# 7.

## The "Phony" War

By the end of 1939, Roosevelt's domestic and foreign courses in the Second World War were charted. Dismissal of the big-business War Resources Board and repeal of the arms embargo were the most revealing guides to his future programs in domestic and foreign affairs.

### Measures No Stronger than Mere Words

During the months of "phony" war on the Western Front, a perplexing challenge to the peaceful nations came from the Soviet attack upon Finland. To the majority of publicists, the Winter War signified the military weakness of the Soviet Union, and the permanent loss of that nation to the coalition of nations opposing the Axis. Conviction on the first "fact" made easier a conviction that the peaceful nations would lose little or nothing by treating the Soviet Union as an inevitable enemy. President Roosevelt's view on Soviet military strength does not appear, but his refusal to treat the Soviet Government as Hitler's ally argues that he did not underestimate Soviet military power.

Those who saw only the ideological struggle between capitalist democracy and socialist dictatorship, or only the similarity of forms of government in the Axis nations and the Soviet Union, placed the Soviet Union high on their list of enemies of the United States. Roosevelt and Hull were convinced that, however mistaken the Soviet leaders might be in trading off the moral prestige of their nation for the sake of narrow military advantages, fundamental conflicts of interest would prevent any profound or lasting cooperation between the Axis and the Soviet Union. Hitler controlled the Baltic, and expansion of Soviet frontiers in that region was obviously directed against Germany.[1]

In late September and October, 1939, the Soviet government pressed Estonia, Latvia, and Lithuania to accept "mutual assistance" pacts under which they became strategic outposts of Soviet power, with land and naval bases occupied by Red forces. These actions were explained by Molotov and others as designed to remove threats of unnamed imperialist powers to bring the Baltic States into their orbits for use in a struggle against the Soviet Union. Since the Baltic States remained technically independent, the United States government was not expected to take any action.

Finland was subjected to the same pressure but refused to accept a "mutual assistance" pact. Its government appealed to the United States for support. American admiration for "little Finland," the only nation that paid its war debts, was very strong. The Scandinavian countries seconded Finland's request for support. Crown Prince Gustav Adolf of Sweden, as well as the President of Finland, appealed directly to President Roosevelt. Hull opposed any appeal to the Soviet Government because it would only push it closer to Hitler. But he was absent from Washington, and the President consented to make an appeal. Hull, when informed, insisted on strict secrecy and altered the message Roosevelt proposed. The message was sent to President Kalinin on October 11, 1939, the day before Soviet-Finnish negotiations began in Moscow. In it Roosevelt stated his "earnest hope that the Soviet Union will make no demands on Finland which are inconsistent with the maintenance and development of amicable and peaceful relations between the two countries, and the independence of each." A leak to the press occurred and reduced whatever effectiveness the message might have had. President Kalinin answered, on October 16, with an acid reminder that the Soviet government had recognized and guaranteed the independence of Finland in 1920, and an assurance that the sole aim of the negotiations was reciprocity and cooperation "in the cause of guaranteeing the security of the Soviet Union and Finland." [2]

Finland refused to grant the Soviet government frontier changes and island bases on the ground that they would compromise its independence. It met with the other three northern neutrals in Stockholm and, on the initiative of Argentina, in concert with the other American republics, President Roosevelt addressed to the conference on October 18 a message supporting Scandinavian and Finnish "neutrality and order under law." [3]

The effectiveness of Roosevelt's attempts to moderate Soviet policy was further reduced by the *City of Flint* affair. As so often happened in Soviet-American relations, a minor dispute created rancors which destroyed possibilities of cooperation in major affairs. The *City of Flint,* an American merchantman, was captured on October 9 by the battleship *Deutschland.* A German prize crew, unwilling to risk running the British blockade to Germany, took the *Flint* to Norway. That country's government observed the requirements of international law and forced the prize to leave within two hours. The German crew took it into the Soviet port of Murmansk on October 23. The Soviet government allowed the *Flint* to stay in port, although the only proper neutral course was to intern the German crew, turn the ship over to its American crew and release it. This it refused to do in spite of strong representations from Hull. Instead, it allowed the ship to leave under the German crew. When the *Flint* again entered a Norwegian port, the government of Norway performed its duty of interning the German crew and allowing the Americans to take over their ship. This highlighted Soviet disregard for its obligations as a neutral and strengthened the opinion of many that its policy was one of collusion with Germany. Hull sent a strong note to the Soviet government declaring its action had caused "astonishment to both the American Government and the American people." He asked for an explanation. The Soviet government's reply contained inaccuracies and its explanation was unconvincing. The United States, nevertheless, dropped the controversy.[4]

The affair served the useful purpose of convincing Congressmen during the debate on neutrality of the wisdom of administration proposals to keep American ships and citizens out of combat zones. But it also irritated Soviet-American relations at a critical moment. Worse consequences were avoided by the exercise of forbearance on the American side.

On November 13, Soviet-Finnish negotiations broke down. Two weeks later the Soviet government denounced its nonaggression treaty with Finland and broke off relations. Roosevelt and Hull decided to attempt to capitalize on the clearly friendly attitude which the United States had demonstrated towards the Soviet

Union under provocation in the *Flint* affair. They sent a message to Moscow and Helsinki offering the good offices of the United States to solve the dispute by peaceful means. Finland accepted the offer but Stalin rejected it. Within hours he sent troops into Finland, planes to bomb its cities, and ships to bombard its shores.

The Soviet attack on Finland placed the Roosevelt administration in a dilemma. Roosevelt and Hull understood that the attack was directed ultimately at Germany, but they could not condone violation of their principle of opposition to aggression. The dilemma was solved by public condemnation of Soviet aggression, while at the same time avoiding any unnecessary act that might influence the Soviet government to adhere more closely to Germany. On December 1 the President issued a statement which maintained the principle of anti-aggression:

The news of the Soviet naval and military bombings within Finnish territory has come as a profound shock to the Government and people of the United States. Despite efforts made to solve the dispute by peaceful methods to which no reasonable objection could be offered, one power has chosen to resort to force of arms. It is tragic to see the policy of force spreading, and to realize that wanton disregard for law is still on the march. . . .

The people and Government of Finland have a long, honorable and wholly peaceful record which has won for them the respect and warm regard of the people and Government of the United States.[5]

Minister H. F. Arthur Schoenfeld reported from Helsinki that Soviet planes bombed civilians and set fires within a few blocks of the American Legation.[6] Roosevelt therefore applied the same moral embargo against export of planes to Russia that had been applied against other governments guilty of bombing civilians. He did this only after addressing appeals to the Finnish as well as the Soviet governments to desist from such bombing, which he called "inhuman barbarism," and after he had received an assurance of compliance from Finland but no reply whatever from the Soviet Union.[7]

The Soviet government's diplomatic behavior towards the United States and the methods it employed to secure better defenses against Germany could not be ignored. The administration asked American companies whose engineers were on loan to the Soviet airplane industry to call them home. It extended the moral embargo to materials, such as aluminum and molybdenum, used in manufacturing airplanes. It placed Finland's latest payment on its debt in a separate Treasury account, pending Congressional approval of its return. On December 10, the Export-Import Bank made available to Finland ten million dollars in credits for purchases of agricultural products. The administration engaged in reprisals against Soviet restrictions on United States consuls by applying reciprocal restrictions on Soviet consuls in the United States. Finland was allowed to buy forty-four airplanes the Navy Department had on order although they were nearly ready for delivery to the Navy. The War Department took a Finnish military mission on a tour of American armament plants and in other minor ways helped Finland.

Federal prosecution of the American Communist leader, Earl Browder, for obtaining a passport on a false statement resulted in his sentence to four years in prison on January 22, 1940. Fritz Kuhn, the leader of Nazis in the United States, was already in prison as a petty forger and thief. These incarcerations were political only insofar as they implied that even political leaders must obey the laws. But they satisfied public disgust with both "isms."

Public pressure was heavy on the administration to take stronger measures against the Soviet Union and in support of Finland. The remarkable success of the Finns' defense during December and January—so long as the Soviet leaders persisted in sending inferior divisions against the northern frontier where they lacked adequate supply services—raised the pitch of American enthusiasm to remarkable heights. Congress, when it met in January, seemed ready to violate traditional rules of neutrality in order to help Finland. Cancellation of the Finnish debt was the most moderate proposal. The most "unneutral" proposals were to loan Finland sixty million dollars without restrictions against buying arms in the United States and to authorize the War Department to sell Finland ten thousand of the Army's new semi-automatic Garand rifles "for experimental purposes." The administration, Congress, and the public seemed united in favor of new "methods short of war" to help stop aggression.

Furthermore, Britain and France planned action in favor of Finland, and the likelihood emerged that concerted action by peaceful nations against aggression would include closer cooperation by the United States than in any previous situation. Britain and France sent volunteers and arms to Finland. In mid-December Churchill advocated in the British Cabinet a plan to secure control of the port of Narvik in Norway to open a supply line to Finland and prevent Swedish ore from going to Hitler. He reported that in spite of a British violation of Norway's neutrality, "No evil effect will be produced upon the greatest of all neutrals, the United States. We have reason to believe that they will handle the matter in the way most calculated to help us. And they are very resourceful." [8]

The British Cabinet refused to authorize immediate action, but aid was stepped up and early in February, when the Finnish cause became desperate, the Allied Supreme War Council decided to send regular British and French troops to Finland according to the Churchill plan. On February 12, 100,000 men were ready to embark at British and French ports. The consent of Norway and Sweden were to be obtained first. Their governments were pressed by Germany as well as the Soviet Union and refused. Further plans were on foot when the Finns capitulated in March. [9]

President Roosevelt's strong words in December were expected to be instrumented by substantial "measures short of war" in aid of Finland and in support of Allied plans. Hatred of Communism was such that aid to Finland was supported by many who were otherwise isolationist. Former President Hoover, Chairman of the Finnish Relief Fund, collected funds for arms for Finland. [10] Finland needed and wanted arms from the United States on a scale which only the government could provide, and such a measure would have been more popular than any previous proposal for action against aggression.

But the Roosevelt administration drew a sharp line against any action which would tend to push the Soviet Union further into the Axis camp. Roosevelt and Hull decided not to invoke the Neutrality Act because they did not wish to make the Soviet Union a legal belligerent. [11]

Ambassador Bullitt in Paris asked the administration to urge Britain and France to take strong action against the Soviet Union in the League of Nations. Roosevelt and Hull refused. [12] The Soviet Union was expelled from the League on December 14, 1939—in strange contrast to Germany, Italy, and Japan, who had been allowed to resign—but the Roosevelt administration had no part in this action which could have the effect of pushing the Soviet Union "closer into Hitler's arms."

In his Annual Message of January, 1940, Roosevelt made no reference to the Soviet-Finnish War. He told a questioner that he had not even heard of some of the proposals in Congress for aid to Finland, and he refused to support any of them. He thought leaders in Congress might well agree on a bipartisan program. This dropped the problem squarely into the hands of Congress but, as often happened when Roosevelt failed to exert it, Congress demanded leadership by the Executive. Senator McNary, Republican floor leader, led the demand.[13]

Roosevelt responded with a letter, on January 16, to the President of the Senate and the Speaker of the House. He merely gave his opinion that "the most reasonable approach" would be to authorize an increase in the credit fund of the Export-Import Bank to finance exports of farm and factory productions "not including implements of war" to Finland and to the other Scandinavian countries and to South America as well. He emphasized that the matter was "wholly within the discretion of Congress."[14]

This was an anticlimax and a bitter disappointment to the friends of Finland. It seemed hypocritical because Finland did not need anything but arms, and had used only a fraction of its existing credit in the United States to obtain other materials. It had asked for about $30,000,000 for arms. A bill to provide the money for arms was now rewritten to increase the capital of the Export-Import Bank by $100,000,000 with the understanding that Finland might borrow a part of it for nonmilitary purchases. The President's proposal contradicted the administration position during the debate on repeal of the arms embargo, that no valid distinction existed or should be made between arms and other materials useful in war. It caused dismay among staunch supporters of the President's internationalist policy and led to confused debate, ending on March 2, after the Red Army had broken the Mannerheim Line. The President signed the amended bill.

The fiasco caused speculation as to the reason for the President's lapse into indifference regarding the Soviet aggression against Finland. Some were certain the President executed a strategic retreat from his foreign policy in order to obtain the support of isolationists in a campaign for a third term. But the President's policy after the Fall of France was one of strengthening his foreign policy, even at the risk of intensifying the opposition of isolationists, at the same time that he campaigned for a third term.

A better explanation is found in Hull's *Memoirs:* that the administration was unwilling to antagonize the Soviet Union. This explanation was implied publicly when Congress attempted to force the administration to break relations with the Soviet Union early in February. A House Resolution proposed to eliminate appropriations to pay the salaries of United States diplomatic employees in that country. Senator Pittman inquired of Secretary Hull whether the Soviet government had fulfilled the 1933 Roosevelt-Litvinov agreements with the United States. Hull in his answer, on January 30, stated very midly that on several occasions the administration had reason to believe the Soviet government had not lived up to its obligations. The United States had sometimes obtained results by making representations. On other occasions, "divergencies in the interpretation of the agreements" developed. Hull emphasized that breaking relations would prevent the possibility of making representations in the future. The House resolution to strike out appropriations failed by three votes to pass.[15]

In his *Memoirs* Hull wrote more clearly: "Our relations with Russia in 1940 were influenced by the desire to do nothing that would drive her further into the arms of Germany, but at the same time to keep our exports to her within such limits as not to afford her surpluses of strategic materials that could go on through to Germany." [16]

By February the administration had effectively prevented any significant "methods short of war but stronger and more effective than mere words" from being taken against Soviet aggression in Finland. In fact, Roosevelt's words became stronger in proportion as he avoided other methods of protesting Soviet action. In an address on the White House lawn to the American Youth Congress in the rain of February 10, he made a sensational denunciation of the Soviet government. He claimed consideration for his views because he had early recognized the social and economic idealism of the Soviet Revolution. But he abhorred Soviet regimentation, indiscriminate killings, and banishment of religion. He had hoped the Soviet government would gradually develop democratic institutions, but:

That hope is today either shattered or put away in storage against some better day. The Soviet Union, as everybody who has the courage to face the facts knows, is run by a dictatorship as absolute as any other dictatorship in the world. It has allied itself with another dictatorship, and it has invaded a neighbor so infinitesimally small that it could do no conceivable possible harm to the Soviet Union, a neighbor which seeks only to live at peace as a democracy, and a liberal, forward-looking democracy at that.

It has been said that some of you are Communists. That is a very unpopular term these days. As Americans you have a legal and constitutional right to call yourselves Communists, those of you who do. You have a right peacefully and openly to advocate certain ideals of theoretical Communism; but as Americans you have not only a right but a sacred duty to confine your advocacy of changes in law to the methods prescribed by the Constitution of the United States—and you have no American right, by act or deed of any kind, to subvert the Government and the Constitution of this Nation.[17]

This was the creed of a liberal democrat and an internationalist; the President was booed for it by some of his audience. Communists seemed stupidly unware that the President's actual policy was based on the proposition that the Axis represented a greater threat to the United States than the Soviet Union, and that the administration drew a sharp line against any action which ignored the anti-Axis potentialities of Soviet policy.

Roosevelt revealed in his Soviet policy, under most difficult circumstances, that his adherence to internationalism was not devotion to an abstraction and did not blind him to the practical necessities of power relationships. He compromised the theoretical requirements of his foreign policy for the sake of reducing potential enemies to the minimum number. The position of the Soviet Union was ultimately defensive in relation to the Axis. Holding to this fact as the fundamental one, the President subordinated abstract theory to the advantage of adding the Soviet Union to the coalition of powers opposing the Axis.

The Soviet government did little to win consideration from the administration. It was anxious to build up imports from the United States. It demanded brusquely, as matters of right, what Roosevelt and Hull could grant only if they disregarded the defenses of the United States and the possibility of Soviet re-exports to Germany. It wanted to buy a complete battleship from American builders, and Roosevelt and Hull were willing that it be bought. The Soviet government insisted that the warship contain not only equipment found on the latest United States battleships but new inventions which were not yet installed even on a United States vessel. Roosevelt and Hull refused.

The Soviet Ambassador, Constantine Oumansky, presented to Hull Soviet views on questions at issue by means of insults and demands. After the Winter War it was Hull's purpose to keep the Soviet government in a state of doubt as to the administration's intentions. For this reason the moral embargo was maintained. He hoped it would teach the Soviet government the disadvantages of alliance with Hitler. Early in April, 1940, Hull obtained from Oumansky assurances that his government would not take Bessarabia or territories in the Near East.[18]

On June 28 the Red Army occupied Bessarabia and Northern Bukovina. By that time, the Fall of France had produced a geological shift in world power relations, which did not alter the methods of the Soviet government but considerably changed its necessities, and Hull intensified his campaign to divorce the Soviet Union from the Axis.

### Difficulties with Chamberlain

During the winter 1939–40, while Soviet-American relations deteriorated in spite of the administration's remarkable forbearance, difficulties also arose between the United States and Great Britain. Hull's friendly initiative in favor of a navicert system to prevent petty quarrels over neutral rights was not reciprocated by the Chamberlain government. After Roosevelt established combat areas, the British Navy forced American ships to violate them by taking ships into ports within the zones for examination, which delayed them for weeks. The United States protested. The direct correspondence between Roosevelt and Churchill served a useful purpose, as Churchill intervened with orders to end diversions of American ships into combat areas and notified Roosevelt of his action.[19] More galling to Americans was the British practice of censoring American mail, including letters and parcels which did not pass through the United Kingdom but were intercepted on the high seas. It was suspected that the business-minded

Chamberlain government found it advantageous to abstract from the correspondence of American businessmen "trade secrets" having no contraband character. It rejected a protest by Hull.[20]

British policy fed the isolationist and Communist opposition in the United States. Hull exercised forbearance to avoid arousing anti-British feeling. He pleaded privately with the British Ambassador to understand the importance of strict regard for United States neutral rights. He felt that Britain's day of trial against Hitler lay ahead, and in February he warned Lord Lothian against the possibility of bad relations when that day should arrive. This protest was fairly effective, for Hull and Lothian worked out a gradual modification of British practices. Censorship of United States mails was relaxed, examination of American ships was made less irksome, and Hull's conditions for operation of the navicert system were accepted. When Hitler launched his attack on the West, Hull's patience and determination had largely eliminated the danger of a narrow British policy preventing American public understanding of Anglo-American community of interests.[21]

One of Hull's objects was to strengthen Anglo-American opposition to Japan. The Chamberlain government was inclined to appease Japan by withdrawing from China in order to reduce the danger of simultaneous war on both sides of the world. But Hull believed the Soviet-Japanese armistice of September 16, 1939, would not be followed by stronger ties between Japan and the Soviet Union. He believed, on the contrary, that the Nazi-Soviet Pact freed the Soviet Union in Europe to give attention to the Far East and checkmate Japan. Therefore, he reasoned, Britain, France, and the United States were in a stronger position in Asia than before.

In frank talks with Ambassador Horinouchi, Hull informally rejected a Japanese request to withdraw American forces from China, and he told the British and French governments he opposed capitulation in the face of Japanese threats. Ambassador Lothian answered that Britain wished to withdraw garrisons from China but would reconsider if the United States would contribute to the common cause. In late September and October, 1939, the two governments exchanged notes. Hull argued the unwisdom of appeasement of Japan, gave assurance that the United States would not withdraw its forces from China, and offered to increase

United States economic aid to China and impose greater restrictions on trade with Japan. Lothian promised that Britain would keep open the Burma Road to supply China. Britain and France, nevertheless, in November announced withdrawals of troops from North China.[22]

## Cultivating Japanese Doubts

This left the United States to maintain a stand alone against Japan. Shortly after the Soviet-Japanese truce, the Japanese press singled out the United States for a campaign of warning. Tokyo newspapers impertinently told the United States not to provoke Japan by building warships and not to take over Britain's role as watchdog of the Far East.[23]

The American administration stood firm. Besides refusing to join in the retreat of the British and French from China, Hull decided that a new effort should be made to dispel illusions and make the United States position plain to the Japanese people, in the hope that "moderates" could be strengthened against the Japanese military. The State Department prepared an address for delivery by Ambassador Joseph C. Grew to the America-Japan Society in Tokyo on October 19. Grew stated that on a visit to the United States he had familiarized himself with American public opinion and could assure his listeners that American disapproval of Japanese policy was not based on "propaganda" in the American press but on accurate knowledge of the facts. The facts, he said, were sufficiently damning to explain the hardening of American opinion and policy towards Japan. He suggested that the Japanese people were the victims of propaganda, insofar as the professed aims of the "new order in East Asia" and the actions of the Japanese military in China were poles apart. Real security and stability in the Far East could be achieved without any impairment of American rights.[24]

Even the Chinese government of Chiang Kai-shek was made to feel the opposition of the United States when it seemed to invite appeasement of Japan. A letter of the Generalissimo to President Roosevelt, delivered on November 2, 1939, proposed a conference for a settlement of the Far Eastern situation. The State Department prepared an answer which stated that a conference would be "inopportune" until Japanese military leaders changed their methods and objectives, because otherwise an adjustment could be made only by recognizing Japan's legal title to spoils in China. Hull's account of this episode is not entirely satisfying. Chiang proposed that if Japan refused to agree to a settlement, economic measures should be taken against it. This implied that not appeasement but measures of collective security as an alternative to a retreat by Japan were in Chiang's mind. If so, the administration perhaps believed that, since it could not fully participate in collective measures against Japan, and the Japanese government knew this, the conference could not carry out Chiang's strong program. Limitations on United States policy made futility or appeasement the only alternatives in such a conference.

Although the administration could not join in collective action against Japan and would not appease that nation, its position was saved from unreality by unilateral action against Japan in which other peaceful nations were encouraged to join. The Japanese feared that an American embargo would follow expiration of the commercial treaty in January, 1940. The American administration cultivated this fear as a means of imposing caution on the Japanese government. It warned Japan that it would not recognize the puppet regime of Wang Ching-wei, which Japan planned to establish in Nanking as the "independent" government of China. On November 24, Hull told Hironouchi that the United States did not feel called upon to take the initiative in improving United States relations with Japan. This, and Grew's address in October, seemed to bring about a slight improvement in Japanese policy. Grew found the government conciliatory regarding infringements of American rights in China. On the other hand, the Foreign Minister, Admiral Nomura, threatened Grew that if trade with the United States became impossible, Japan would seek other commercial channels. This was a threat to invade Southeast Asia and the Netherlands East Indies.

Hull and Roosevelt strove for a balance between acts of weakness, which would invite contempt for the United States, and acts of strength, which would invite defiance of it. Fearing that either simple alternative would encourage aggression, they fixed on a policy of keeping the Japanese government in a state of doubt, designed to inhibit new aggressions. On December 11, Hull advised the President to allow Japanese-American trade to continue unchanged on a day-to-day basis after the commercial treaty expired, and to reserve the weapons of discriminatory duties against imports of Japanese goods, and of embargo. The President agreed.

The Japanese government showed its anxiety. Nomura, on December 18, proposed that a *modus vivendi* be worked out to continue trade relations and that a new treaty be negotiated immediately to supersede the *modus vivendi*. The Roosevelt administration tightened the screw. Japan was negotiating with an American oil company to purchase plans and specifications for a high-octane gasoline plant. On December 20 a moral embargo was placed against such exports to any country that bombed civilians. To a Japanese protest, Hull responded with a note that cited a long list of Japanese bombings of civilians in China.

Ambassador Grew supported the proposal for a *modus vivendi* on the grounds that Japan was striving to meet United States demands and that it would strengthen "moderates" in the Japanese government. Lothian added his voice in favor of making terms with Japan. Hull decided to refine his "state of doubt" technique by refusing either to enter negotiations with Japan at that time, or to reject its proposal for negotiations.[25]

Japan's failure to form closer ties with the Soviet Union or Germany, its failure to carry out threats to move southward in search of raw materials, and its more conciliatory attitude towards the United States, all seemed to represent successes for the delicately balanced policy of the Roosevelt administration. On January 14, 1940, the Cabinet of Premier Abe fell and Admiral Yonai took power. American observers regarded the change as a success for the "moderate" party, but this ignored the facts that no changes occurred in the War and Navy ministries, and that the new Foreign Minister, Hachiro Arita, was author of the Anti-Comintern Pact and an outspoken admirer of Nazism and Fascism. But economic depression in Japan, many signs of popular discontent, and an extraordinary announcement that henceforth the Japanese Army in China would remain on the defensive, fed American hopes that the "new order in East Asia" would presently collapse of its own weakness.

When the commercial treaty expired on January 26, 1940, chauvinists in Japan called the day-to-day policy an affront, a "sword of Damocles," and reason to blame Roosevelt if "trouble in the future" occurred. But the Japanese Foreign Office accepted the situation resignedly and made a conciliatory statement that

Japan did not intend to eliminate the "just and reasonable interests of third powers in China." On January 31, Soviet-Japanese
negotiations to settle the boundary between Manchuria and Outer
Mongolia collapsed, and this provided a further source of satisfaction for the Roosevelt administration.

In the United States only Hamilton Fish objected to abrogation of the commercial treaty, which he called "just another blow
at King Cotton." Sentiment was strong for a legislative embargo
to stop the sales to Japan of oil, scrap steel and iron, and other
metals and machinery. Senator Pittman wanted to take action on
his resolution to embargo Japan by name. No encouragement
came from either the President or the Secretary of State.[26]

This situation caused wide complaint against the administration and charges by internationalists that it "appeased" Japan.
But, as has been shown, Roosevelt and Hull had firmly opposed
any move which might correctly be labeled appeasement, that is,
approval of conquest and recognition of "rights" won by force or
the threat of force. If they did not, on the other hand, take the
positive step of embargoing Japan to stop its aggression, they
could point to the unwillingness of Britain and France to make
a stand in Asia, and to the unpreparedness of the United States
and the obvious unwillingness of Congress to back up an embargo
with force. These conditions had largely changed when the administration finally in August, 1941, embargoed Japan.

In the meantime, hopes that Japan had genuinely moderated
its policy under United States pressure were partially disappointed
by the installation of the Wang Ching-Wei puppet regime at
Nanking in March, 1940. It was used to give legal plausibility to Japanese measures in violation of United States treaty rights in China.
This new assault against the United States was launched even before Hitler's invasions of northern and western Europe gave Japan
another opportunity to advance its imperialist program in Asia
while the rest of the world was preoccupied in Europe. For the
Roosevelt administration it posed a question of world strategy of
the highest order: on which of the two fronts in the Second World
War should the United States concentrate its diplomatic efforts,
and, ultimately, its military forces? The decision was to defeat
Hitler first, but without retreat on principle in Asia, and without
voluntary retreat from military positions. This decision was based
on the conviction that Hitler presented the more immediate dan-

ger of world conquest, and the greater danger to the United States of isolation from its friends and consequent defeat.

Japan, evidently anticipating Hitler's attacks on the Netherlands and France, announced itself "protector" of the Far Eastern possessions of those nations. The Japanese Foreign Minister claimed that the Monroe Doctrine was a precedent for Japanese opposition to any change in the *status quo* of the Netherlands East Indies. Two days later, Secretary Hull pointed out the importance of the NEI to the United States as a source of raw materials and insisted that *all* parties must observe the *status quo*.[27] Popular report had it that privately the Secretary responded to the slogan "Asia for the Asiatics" with the remark: "Yes, and Japan for the Japanese."

## The Welles Mission

On the European side, Roosevelt's last important act before the "real" war began was to send Under Secretary Welles to obtain information regarding the war aims of the belligerent governments and to explore the possibility of a just and stable peace. The Welles mission gave rise to charges that the President contemplated appeasement of Hitler. Waverley Root, in his *Secret History of the War,* relates the Welles mission to a "peace offensive" launched by Hitler to lull his next victims and their neutral friends.

According to Root's account, late in January, 1940, a German "peace plan" was submitted to the Pope. At the same time, businessmen with German connections and sympathies worked to convince Roosevelt that he could advance the peace offensive. The President had appointed Myron C. Taylor, former President of the United States Steel Corporation, to be his personal representative at the Vatican, and Taylor was reported to be sympathetic to a public proposal of ex-Kaiser Wilhelm II that Europe should immediately organize a league against Bolshevism. Close economic collaboration with Germany was the bait held out to the United States to act as mediator in the peace offensive.[28]

Mr. Root offers no supporting evidence for this account of the origin of the Welles mission other than his general acknowledgment of indebtedness to his journalistic colleagues for knowledge of "political secrets." [29] Facts which can be authenticated, partic-

ularly the dates of certain events, suggest that the "peace offensive" had origins and purposes very different from those suggested
by Mr. Root. The latter dates the beginning of Hitler's "peace
offensive" in late January, 1940. Long before this Roosevelt and
Hull had begun to work for peace in a sense quite different from
the Hitler offensive.

As early as September, 1939, Secretary Hull had initiated preliminary work in the State Department to organize a committee
which should engage in postwar planning with a view to United
States entry into a world organization for collective security.[30]
Hull understood that the first task was to educate the American
people "well in advance" for entry into a world organization. The
program instrumented the unneutral "thought" of the administration from the onset of the Second World War.

On December 23, 1939, President Roosevelt publicly launched
the "peace offensive" which culminated in the Welles mission.
It was a first effort to explore the grounds for a constructive postwar settlement and to mobilize American and world opinion for
such a settlement. Roosevelt selected the main religious organizations as initial collaborators. He sent identical messages to George
A. Buttrick, President of the Federal Council of Churches of
Christ in America, Pope Pius XII, and Cyrus Adler, President of
the Jewish Theological Seminary of America. He asserted that,
since the time of the prophet Isaiah, the hope of spiritual rebirth
had sustained mankind in eras of destruction. He believed that
such a rebirth was even now being built "silently but inevitably,
in the hearts of masses whose voices are not heard, but whose
common faith will write the final history of our time." Then he
cast the program for collective security into moral terms and affirmed that Americans accepted it in this form:

Because the people of this nation have come to a realization that
time and distance no longer exist in the older sense, they understand
that that which harms one segment of humanity harms all the rest.
They know that only by friendly association among the seekers of
light and the seekers of peace everywhere can the forces of evil be
overcome.

No leader could at the moment "move forward on a specific plan
to terminate destruction and build anew. Yet the time for that

will surely come." Roosevelt therefore suggested that he should send a personal representative to the Pope and that Dr. Buttrick and Rabbi Adler should confer with him in Washington from time to time.[31]

On Christmas Eve the President offered over the radio as a message not only to Americans, but to the peoples of the nations at war, the Sermon on the Mount, and indeed its invocations were appropriate to the moment beyond the ordinary:

"Blessed are the peacemakers: for they shall be called the children of God.
"Blessed are they which are persecuted for righteousness' sake: for theirs is the kingdom of heaven." [32]

It is probable that the moods generated by stalemate on the Western European Front, labeled "phony" war, leading to hopeful doubt as to Hitler's intentions, influenced the rapid development of Roosevelt's "peace offensive." But this is far different from the charge that Roosevelt intended to support a compromise peace instigated by those who wanted to "do business" with Hitler, and amounting to a climactic appeasement. As a result of delays, Myron Taylor did not enter upon his duties as the President's representative to the Pope until February 27. If there was discernible in the stately phrases of the messages exchanged between Roosevelt and the Pope little qualification in the Pope's words of the nature of the peace which should be procured, the President made it clear that it was not peace at any price which he sought. The Pope in his answer on January 7, 1940, accepting the Taylor mission, spoke of the moral qualifications necessary to peacemakers. The President in a letter of February 14, which Taylor carried to Rome, specified political terms that clearly ruled out a new Munich: "the re-establishment of a more permanent peace on the foundations of freedom and an assurance of life and integrity of all nations under God." [33]

Clearer and more public evidence of Roosevelt's and Hull's intentions appeared during the first week of January, 1940. In a statement on New Year's Day, Hull expressed his lack of hope for peace until after a period of intensified warfare. Then he stated the administration's long-range program:

If peace should come, we shall be confronted, in our own best interest, with the vital need of throwing the weight of our country's moral and material influence in the direction of creating a stable and enduring world order under law, lest the relations among nations again assume such a character as to make of them a breeding ground of economic conflict, social insecurity, and, again, war.

Hull interpreted this statement in his *Memoirs* as an insistence that the United States would take part in the postwar settlement, while trying to keep out of the war; and as an obvious statement of the administration's policy of United States participation in a new world organization. Furthermore, he intended to give full weight to his statement that the United States would help create the world organization, and not simply wait to join after other nations had founded it.

Within a week, Hull announced establishment of a committee in the State Department, with Under Secretary Welles as Chairman, to study the policies of foreign governments which might affect United States foreign relations after the war. The work of this committee, in spite of its rather tangential directive and its veiled title of "Advisory Committee on Problems of Foreign Relations," quickly, as Hull states, "expanded until it embraced active planning for a postwar organization." [34]

Meanwhile Roosevelt, as so often happened, became impatient with his Secretary's cautious procedure. The Pope delayed his answer to the President's letter suggesting the Taylor mission for over two weeks, until January 7. The President decided to send Welles on a mission to the belligerent governments. Welles dates the President's proposal to him as occurring "in the first days of January, 1940." [35] This shows that the President proposed the Welles mission two or more weeks prior to the launching of the Hitler "peace offensive." Hull declares the President later told him that Welles "secretly" on several occasions pleaded with him to be sent abroad on special missions. Roosevelt did not even consult Hull at the outset, so that Hull's subsequent naming of Welles as Chairman of his new postwar planning committee seems to have been an effort to "stake down" in the State Department the activities of the Under Secretary, whose close connection with the President in sensational schemes Hull did not approve.

Hull seemed more aware than Roosevelt that the Welles mission was subject to misinterpretation and even misuse in favor of Hitler. He warned the President to avoid raising false hopes of peace.[36]

His advice was followed, and this was useful when, late in January and during Welles's subsequent weeks abroad, dangerous rumors and Axis efforts to distort the purpose of the mission threatened to make it a disaster. But that Roosevelt's purpose was in direct opposition to a pro-Axis peace was made clear by the President himself, publicly, as well as privately to Welles.

In his State of the Union Message on January 3, 1940, the President repeatedly condemned dictatorship, its threat of world rule by force and, most significantly, he warned of danger to America

if all the small nations of the world have their independence snatched from them or become mere appendages to relatively vast and powerful military systems.

We must look ahead and see the kinds of lives our children would have to lead if a large part of the rest of the world were compelled to worship a god imposed by a military ruler, or were forbidden to worship God at all; if the rest of the world were forbidden to read and hear the facts—the daily news of their own and other nations—if they were deprived of the truth that makes men free.

We must look ahead and see the effect on our future generations if world trade is controlled by any nation or group of nations which sets up that control through military force.

Here was no comfort for proponents of a compromise peace with Hitler which would leave him dominant in central Europe. It was in this context that the President not only rejected scornfully the conception that the United States might live secure inside a high wall of isolation—"It is not good for the ultimate health of ostriches to bury their heads in the sand"—but he asserted that the United States had been and would continue to be *"a potent and active factor in seeking the reestablishment of world peace."* He called the pending renewal of the Reciprocity Trade Agreements Act an indispensable American contribution to a stable peace and emphasized that on such a foundation the United States could take *"leadership"* when the time came for the renewal of world peace.[37]

In these same first days of January, 1940, the President revealed privately to Under Secretary Welles the action which he hoped might contribute to the kind of peace he outlined in his Message to Congress. He told Welles the chances of success seemed to him only about one in a thousand. But if the all-out assault by Germany on the West occurred, the United States would be in danger of becoming involved. Even if that were avoided, a Hitler victory "would immediately imperil the vital interests of the United States." If the Allies won, it could be only after a desperate contest which would bring them to economic and social ruin, "with disastrous effects upon the American people." Therefore, Roosevelt said, he believed his duty required that he explore the remote possibility that peace might be possible now.

Welles should go to Germany, Italy, France, and England to learn the views of their governments as to the possibility of concluding a peace. The United States would "offer no proposals and no suggestions." On the other hand, Roosevelt made plain to Welles that he had no interest in any "temporary or tentative armed truce." [38]

The terms of the President's instructions to Welles ruled out any peace except one in which Hitler agreed to surrender his gains. Only the certain knowledge by Hitler that the United States would come into the coalition against him could have any effect on his plans. Obviously, the administration could not even attempt to bluff Hitler into a surrender. But it was just possible that American influence in Italy could be used to prevent Mussolini from declaring war against Britain and France and, in any case, the mission would yield valuable information for the President in the conduct of foreign relations.

The Welles mission might be criticized because it was, as Welles later wrote, "a forlorn hope," [39] but not because it was inspired by willingness to support a compromise peace favored by business or other groups friendly to Hitler. In England and France fears were expressed that the American government might throw its influence behind "peace at any price," and that if the Western powers refused, the effect on American opinion would be harmful to them.[40] Secretary Hull did not fear that the President intended appeasement of Hitler, but that the mission would hold out false hopes of peace to the people of England and France at a time when they should be preparing themselves against an onslaught from Germany.[41]

The President announced the Welles mission on February 9,

1940, in words which emphasized that the Under Secretary was not authorized to propose terms of peace or to transmit any proposals from one belligerent government to another.[42] The announcement provoked a rich assortment of outbursts. Isolationists cried "involvement." Reporters of "inside" news told of quarrels between Roosevelt and Hull. Most serious, the Allies and their friends accused the administration of promoting a peace at any price.

Hull, in spite of his disapproval of the mission, cooperated faithfully with the President. He made a public announcement denying that they had quarreled. He began a series of conversations with neutral governments on trade and disarmament to parallel the work of the Welles mission.[43] As rumors of appeasement multiplied, Hull advised the President to include in a public address to the Christian Foreign Service Convocation on March 16, 1940, the following clear-cut statement of the administration's conception of a supportable peace:

Today we seek a moral basis for peace. It cannot be a real peace if it fails to recognize brotherhood. It cannot be a lasting peace if the fruit of it is oppression, or starvation, or cruelty, or human life dominated by armed camps. It cannot be a sound peace if small nations must live in fear of powerful neighbors. *It cannot be a moral peace if freedom from invasion is sold for tribute.*[44]

The last sentence could not be construed as an abandonment of Britain, France, Belgium, the Netherlands, the Scandinavian nations, or others threatened by Hitler.

To make doubly sure, Hull cabled Welles a strict definition of the scope of his mission. Welles thereupon made a public statement that he had not received or conveyed any peace proposals and that he had only gathered information. British Ambassador Lothian thanked the President and Hull for their efforts to suppress the rumors of "peace at any price."[45]

The Nazi government attempted to exploit the Welles mission. It played a deadly game of rousing hopes for peace while planning the attack against Scandinavia and the West. Captured documents show that, by the end of January, 1940, Hitler's lieutenants had convinced him that Norway and Denmark should be invaded, and detailed planning had begun. Six weeks later, when Welles was about to return to America, Hitler hesitated to launch the attacks only because he could not find an "excuse," and he felt constrained to continue diplomatic negotiations with the victims until the attacks began, for fear that otherwise calls for help would go out to England and America.[46] Evidently the Nazi leaders had not allowed themselves to be deluded regarding the purpose of the Welles mission.

Nevertheless, the mission gave them an opportunity to try to delude the world regarding their own purposes. The Under Secretary arrived in Rome on February 25. He worked to convince the Fascist Foreign Minister, Count Ciano, that Italy's best interests required her to remain neutral. Ciano expressed contempt for the Nazi leaders and fears that Italy's interests were not respected by them. He mentioned Nazi terms for a compromise peace which he had learned in conversations with Hitler after the conquest of Poland, but he doubted that Germany would any longer be willing to accept those terms. Mussolini, on the other hand, told Welles he was optimistic that Germany might still accept such terms. He spoke in favor of the economic and disarmament policies of the United States and said he believed that the influence of the United States could be decisive after peace came. All this was meaningless, because Mussolini also declared that the basis for "a just political peace" would have to be found before anything else could be done.

In Berlin, on March 1, Welles emphasized to Foreign Minister Ribbentrop, as he had to the Italians, that his government was solely interested in a permanent peace and not in any temporary truce. Ribbentrop delivered a two-hour Nazi propaganda harangue. He said Germany wished for "nothing more in Europe than" a Monroe Doctrine, and that "propaganda" was responsible for the deterioration of German-American relations. Welles replied that Nazi persecution of minorities and use of force in international relations were the actual causes of that deterioration. Germany's autarchic trade policies and discriminations against United States goods prevented improvement of economic relations. As for the Monroe Doctrine, Welles pointed out certain differences between it and German policy in Europe. Ribbentrop did not discuss the possibility of a permanent peace in Europe.

From State Secretary Weizsaecker, Welles received hints that Italy might best approach Hitler himself with peace proposals.

On March 2, Welles saw Hitler in the hideous new Reich Chancellery. He made no proposals to Hitler. He spoke of President Roosevelt's hope for a stable, just, and lasting peace, and made clear that this would require Germany to abandon Hitler's foreign objectives. The United States would be willing to take part in trade and disarmament negotiations but not in political settlements. Hitler showed ignorance of trade problems. He merely repeated the standardized harangue justifying Nazi policy.

Welles became aware that decisions to expand the war had already been made. Hitler declared that German victory was the only way to peace and exposed the sinister irresponsibility of the Nazi leadership by agreeing with Welles's warning that even the victors would be losers. He said that, if Germany did not win, "we will all go down together. Whether that be for better or for worse." Hitler's deputy Rudolf Hess, sitting in front of a group of party thugs, repeated to Welles the same harangue. Field Marshal Hermann Goering, bedecked in jewels and decorations, received Welles in his hunting palace. He was more frank than the others but not less adamant.

Welles left Germany convinced that Italy had no influence on Axis policy and that nothing short of United States action in support of the Allies would make Hitler pause. In Paris, Welles found officials grateful for the repeal of the arms embargo and for other evidences of understanding on the part of President Roosevelt, but discouraged by the difficulties facing France. In Britain more determination was in evidence.

Welles returned to Rome on March 16. He conferred again with Ciano and Mussolini. Rumors spread that he carried peace proposals from France and Britain. Welles's actual report was that Britain and France would fight to the end unless they could obtain "practical and complete assurance that they would not again be plunged into a war of this kind." Ciano spoke of a four-power pact among Italy, Germany, France, and Britain, under which an aggressor would be countered with action by the other three. Welles declared that to this should be added international control over all offensive armaments, particularly airplanes, and over armament industries. Ciano agreed. Mussolini affirmed that he still believed in the possibility of a "good" peace.

Hitler had asked Mussolini, twelve hours before Welles returned to Rome, for a meeting at the Brenner Pass. Ribbentrop had visited Rome in the meantime to inform Mussolini of Germany's intention of launching a military offensive immediately and its confidence and insistence that the only solution was a German victory. Mussolini struck at the heart of the situation: he told Welles that when he met Hitler at the Brenner a day hence, he must offer him assurance that the Allies would provide Germany with *"lebensraum"* if he was to have any success in diverting Hitler from the imminent offensive. He asked for authority to communicate to Hitler the information Welles had obtained in Paris and London regarding the possibility of a negotiated peace. Welles answered that he had no such authority, but offered to telephone Roosevelt for instructions. In his account, Welles does not state whether Mussolini answered this proposal, nor does he make any further reference to it. Mussolini seemed to withdraw from his forward position by asserting that Allied recognition of a large German sphere of influence and satisfaction of all Italian claims must precede organization of a four-power security system and disarmament.

After the dictators met, Ciano in a secret conference told Welles that no peace proposals had been discussed. Welles, on March 19, made his public statement that he had not received or conveyed any peace proposals, and left for home. The mission was a failure except insofar as it provided the American leaders with fresh and comprehensive views of the European situation. The Axis propaganda machine had used the mission to sow confusion, but the governments of France and Britain were satisfied that the President's purposes were not contrary to their interest.[47]

The broadest significance of the Welles mission is that it showed Roosevelt's determination to exhaust every possibility of using the influence of the United States, within the limits imposed by his internal position, in favor of negotiation rather than force, in favor of peace, and to prevent the outbreak of the "real" war, which began within a month after Welles's return.

Welles had obtained a distinct impression that the weakness of Italy's material and spiritual commitment to Hitler could be played upon to encourage its neutrality and to limit the scope of the tragedy facing the Allies and the small neutral nations. This was the basis of President Roosevelt's next effort to change the course of European events. Administration policy towards the first stage of Hitler's offensive—the invasion of Norway and Denmark—

was confined to a public protest and an expression of concern for the fate of Iceland and Greenland.

## The Fight for Economic Internationalism

Meanwhile, during the few weeks remaining before the storm broke, Roosevelt and Hull fought to win a domestic political struggle which contained profound meanings for their foreign policy. The Reciprocity Trade Agreements Act was due to expire on June 12, 1940. Standard arguments of economic nationalists and protectionists against renewal were reinforced by the wartime dislocation of trade which, they claimed, made the program useless. But it was precisely the war that made Roosevelt and Hull more determined than ever to continue the program. They believed it was a fundamental component of an improved international order, and that without it the influence of the United States in favor of a stable peace, even following an Allied victory, would be nullified.

It was this meaning of the program that led Roosevelt to support it more strongly than ever before. He devoted a large part of his January Message to it. Hull had already opened his campaign of speeches in December, and he made effective statements to Congressional committees. Thorough investigation of the operation of the Act by hostile critics failed to discover the evils they had predicted. Behind the scenes, Hull convinced the British government that it did itself more harm than good by stopping its purchases of American products at this critical time, and he secured a partial reversal of its policy.[48]

On April 5, a few days before Hitler invaded Scandinavia, the bill finally passed, by the narrow margin of three votes in the Senate. When the President signed it, he condemned the tactics of critics of "this powerful instrument for promoting our national economic well-being and for strengthening the foundations of stable peace":

There is nothing more destructive of public welfare than the conjuring up of groundless fears for the sole purpose of discrediting a constructive policy which is invulnerable to attack on any legitimate basis.[49]

## The Atomic Race

An important indication that the Roosevelt administration during the winter 1939–40 did not subscribe to Senator Borah's definition of the "phony" war as containing no threat to the United States is that during this period important government actions placed the United States in the lead in the race to exploit the military values of nuclear fission. Shortly after the war began, Albert Einstein wrote to President Roosevelt a letter which gave the authority of his name to the effort to interest the government in the importance of physicists' hopes—and fears. The President immediately took the first of the daring series of actions which led to manufacture of the atomic bomb. He appointed an "Advisory Committee on Uranium," made up of the Director of the Bureau of Standards and representatives of the Army and Navy, and requested them to look into the military possibilities of fission. In this way the President overcame the inertia of the Navy, which had neglected to act upon the urgings of Pegram and Fermi.

The Uranium Committee met with scientists in October, 1939. Their recommendation to General E. M. Watson, the President's aide, that graphite and uranium should be procured with Army and Navy funds was acted upon early in 1940. By April, reports had come that a large section of the Kaiser Wilhelm Institute in Berlin was investigating uranium. But the Americans had by that time discovered the unique character of isotope U-235.[50]

## Congress Loses Interest

Final evidence of the President's estimate of the world situation appears in his development of armament and recovery policies. Congressmen in the new session showed no desire to build up further the nation's military defenses. But the President proposed for the fiscal year 1941 a 26 per cent increase over the estimated current expenditure, and a 62 per cent increase over the actual sum that was currently spent. Authorizations of amounts which would not be spent until later were also requested in increased measure. The total now hovered around two billions of dollars. The President's conception of the proper relation between foreign and domestic problems was made clear by the fact that the only important increases he asked for were in the field of armaments, while he proposed reduced appropriations for work relief and agricultural programs.[51] This instrumented his general policy since Munich, and in his Annual Message he again proposed no new domestic reforms but only a carrying on of the process of recovery, "so as to *preserve our gains. . . .*" Once more the peroration of his address was devoted to national unity.[52]

Congress noted that it was an election year, that the budget was still unbalanced and, most important, that "experts" had called the European war "phony." It proceeded to pare down the President's budget for defense. It had measurably reduced appropriations and drastically reduced authorizations for the future when Hitler invaded Scandinavia and the West. Even then Congress continued to dally with defense cuts, until the President, on May 16, summarily recalled its attention to realities with new requests.

## The Farley-Garner Cabal

The third-term issue came to a boil during the period of "phony" war. Secretary of Agriculture Wallace in October, 1939, told an audience that the war situation made it clear the President's talents were needed for another term.[53] Secretary Ickes had been urging a third term since the summer of 1938. He, too, believed dangers from abroad made continuation of Roosevelt's leadership necessary. Harry Hopkins, having abandoned his own ambitions for the office, which Roosevelt had encouraged, publicly advocated a third term in June, 1939.[54] Thus the most important leaders of the "left-wing" or pro-New Deal group around the President were united in favor of another term.

The "right wing" was equally united in plans to "stop Roosevelt." Farley has written an explanation of the strategy they developed in the winter of 1939–40. He urged Secretary Hull, on December 8, 1939, to work to win over delegates in favor of his own candidacy at the Democratic National Convention. Farley said he and Garner would do the same. "Then," he told Hull, "the three of us can sit down and determine what is best for the country and the party." Hull thought he would act shortly after the New Year.[55]

Within a week, Garner publicly announced his candidacy. Roosevelt was amused by the spectacle of Garner's decision to give up his opposition to an anti-lynching bill because such legislation would win Negro votes in the border states and in the North.[56]

Farley proposed to the President in January to throw his hat in the ring if his chief had no objection. Roosevelt told him, "Go ahead, Jim. The water's fine. I haven't an objection in the world," but Farley understood that this was not an approval of his candidacy. He announced his candidacy nevertheless, and his act was widely interpreted as a break with Roosevelt. A subsequent report by sources close to the President, that Roosevelt opposed Farley's candidacy because of his Catholic religion, embittered the Party Chairman.[57]

The same report declared that Roosevelt favored Hull for the Presidency. Hull, Farley later wrote, felt certain that the President was not sincere. Farley has written that Hull was embittered by the President's lack of gratitude for his services as Secretary of State, but this is contradicted time and again by Hull's own words in his *Memoirs*.[58]

It became clear to Roosevelt, as to any observer in the spring of 1940, that the struggle for the Democratic nomination involved not merely personal ambitions but supreme issues of domestic and foreign policy, and that if Roosevelt did not run for a third term, the nomination would in all likelihood go to Hull, who was conservative on domestic issues, or to Garner or Farley, who were conservative on domestic issues and also isolationists. And Hull seemed to Roosevelt, even on foreign issues, to be unimaginative and unduly cautious. Still, on the evidence of his intimates, it appears certain that the newspapers' epithet for the President during these months—"The Sphinx"—was not accurate, because he had no secret. As late as April 23, after the Hitler invasions of Denmark and Norway, Roosevelt seemed to Harry Hopkins to be undisposed to run again.[59] That he did not make his state of mind known publicly is sufficiently explained by the political fact that his influence in domestic and world affairs would end at that moment and his administration would be torn apart by candidates' quarrels. Doubtless, he had also long held a corner of his mind open to the possibility of a third term.

Hopkins and others became worried that the President would allow the succession to fall by default into the hands of the conservative-isolationist faction of Democratic leaders. They began to work to convince Roosevelt that it was his duty to run again. On the day Hitler invaded the Netherlands, Hopkins went to dinner in the White House. He stayed the night—and three and a half years more. Presently, without authorization from the President, Hopkins organized a campaign to secure the third-term nomination. Roosevelt did not object.[60] A strange feature of the situation was that the conservatives of the Garner-Farley faction, whose loyalty the President had managed to retain during the great 1935–38 fight for the New Deal, now abandoned him.

The decisive test occurred in the party primaries to elect delegates to the convention. Hull decided against allowing his name to be put forward in the primaries. Farley later wrote that Hull told him "in view of the world situation I do not feel I should use my position to seek office." [61] Farley himself was considered to be hoping for the vice-presidential nomination on a ticket with Garner. Other candidates made it clear that they would withdraw if Roosevelt would accept nomination. Only Garner remained as a serious contender. John L. Lewis exaggerated the general view when he lashed out at the Vice President in July, 1939, as a "labor-baiting, poker-playing, whisky-drinking, evil old man," but Garner's public reputation was hardly that of a statesman.

Roosevelt did not encourage or discourage the election of delegates committed to vote for his nomination. Nevertheless, in March such delegates easily won the contests in the important states of Illinois, Wisconsin and California. Such victories indicated that the rank and file of the Party heavily favored a third term. The city machine leaders wanted a winner and supported Roosevelt.

Garner explained to an intimate friend that in his view the chief reason the third-term campaign succeeded was the support of the army of office-holders to whom Roosevelt was a "meal ticket." [62] Garner had supported the Hatch Act of August, 1939, because he thought it "might prevent an officeholders' oligarchy controlling Presidential succession." [63] The President himself in January, 1939, had urged Congress to pass a bill to eliminate "improper political practices," especially among WPA personnel, by "rigid statutory regulations and penalties." Such a bill had been expanded in Congress by opponents of the administration to prohibit participation in political campaigns by all federal officeholders except highest-ranking policy-making officials. The

President had signed the bill and at the same time stated the view of the Attorney General that it could not "preclude Government employees from the exercise of the right of free speech or from their right to exercise the franchise." These rights he interpreted to include their right to attend political meetings, to contribute without solicitation to campaign funds, to express their opinions publicly without doing so as part of an organized campaign, and otherwise to take part in political activities as citizens but not as organizers or party agents. Furthermore, he declared that private citizens who were recipients of farm benefits, veterans' pensions, and other government funds were not subject to the law.[64] Any other interpretation of the law would have made second-class citizens of federal employees, veterans, and other large groups, and Garner admitted that the Hatch Act as a "stop Roosevelt" device was a failure.[65]

Another explanation by Garner to the same friend, although it was even more bitter, began with an interesting admission. The primaries provided Roosevelt in effect, he said, with

*"a plebiscite on his record* conducted in his own party instead of a vote on an open candidacy. There is no risk to him. The country is kept guessing. It scuttles all democratic processes. He can work this so the nomination will be worthless to anyone else but himself." [66]

The Democratic primaries were certainly a plebiscite on the President's record and the distinction between that and "a vote on an open candidacy" was perhaps not very great. That it "scuttled all democratic processes" was the reverse of the truth.

By April it was clear to observers that the President could have the nomination if he wanted it. It was equally clear that he could not have it and continue to hold the support of such influential party leaders as Farley and Garner. But the President, as early as December, 1939, had contemplated inviting Republican internationalists like Colonel Frank Knox—the Republican candidate for Vice President in 1936—to join his Cabinet in order to emphasize bipartisanship in foreign relations.[67] Adherence of such Republicans to the administration would more than compensate for the loss of isolationists like Farley and Garner. This transformation of the Cabinet, as well as the decision to run for a third term, came during the May and June days of catastrophe in Europe.

## Roosevelt's Faith

The period of "phony" war ended on April 9, 1940. Within the peaceful nations, the winter months had produced the climax of the confusions and indecisions of the pre-war years rather than the simplification of issues typical of war. That this was less true in the United States than in France and Britain was due to the clarity of President Roosevelt's formulations of policy, based, as subsequent history proved, on more accurate judgments of the realities of the world situation. The indecision and defeatism of French policy were notorious. Chamberlain as late as April 5 publicly declared that Britain and France had grown relatively stronger than Germany since September—that Hitler, in short, had "missed the bus."

American isolationists misread the situation as expertly as did Chamberlain, but Roosevelt during the whole period made no utterance which matched their optimism; he never underestimated the Axis danger, nor did he propose to the American people any easy or compromising avoidance of that danger. Convinced that American freedom would suffocate in a world dominated by the Axis, he conceived and installed policies designed to counter the aggressors to the maximum extent people and Congress would allow. He prepared, in a dark hour of disunity and confusion among the friends of freedom, for American leadership in a moral international order with faith that freedom could, and with determination that it must, win the victory. Perhaps the best statement of his faith, and one of the simplest, he delivered to a Pan American group a few days after the Nazi invasion of Norway:

In my conception, the whole world now is struggling to find the basis of its life in the centuries that lie ahead.

I affirm that that life must be based on positive and permanent values.

The value of love will always be stronger than the value of hate; since any nation or group of nations which employs hatred eventually is torn to pieces by hatred within itself.

The value of a belief in humanity and justice is always stronger in any land than the value of belief in force, because force at last turns inward and if that occurs each man or group of men is finally compelled to measure his strength against his own brother.

The value of truth and sincerity is always stronger than the value of lies and cynicism. No process has yet been invented which can permanently separate men from their own hearts and consciences or prevent them from seeing the results of their own false ideas as time rolls by. You cannot make men believe that a way of life is good when it spreads poverty, misery, disease and death. Men cannot be everlastingly loyal unless they are free.[68]

# 8.

## *"Behind Walls of Sand"*

THE FALL OF FRANCE IN JUNE, 1940, CAUSED A DECISIVE
turn in the history of American foreign policy. The worst proph-
ecies made by the Wilsonian generation of internationalists concerning the consequences of a failure of collective security had
to come true before Americans would believe them. When the
powerful and savage Nazi war machine stood on the Atlantic
shore and promised to satisfy fully the American appetite for isolation, Americans in majority finally understood that isolation
was not a cure-all but a deadly danger. They decided that their
institutions and their liberties could not thrive in isolation.

### Greenland and Iceland Threatened

On April 2, Hitler secretly ordered the invasion of Norway and
Denmark for a week later. The Department of State received on
the same day reports of the Nazi preparations. The Norwegian
Minister to the United States, Wilhelm Morgenstierne, suggested
that American representations be made to support his country's
neutrality. This was forestalled by the surprise attack on Norwegian ports at dawn on April 9 by Nazi troops hidden in freight-
ers flying the British flag. Denmark was occupied at the same
moment without fighting. Hull satisfied himself that the invaders
had set out before April 8, when the British decision to prevent
violation of Norwegian neutral waters by German ore boats provided Hitler with his official "excuse." President Roosevelt ordered
the freezing of Norwegian and Danish credits in the United

States to prevent them falling into German hands. He also extended the combat zone and applied the provisions of the Neutrality Act to Norway.

The brazen deceit of the Nazis, their brutality in visiting murder and torture upon two weak but courageous peoples who were held in affection by free humanity everywhere, deeply stirred Americans. The President issued a statement on April 13 expressing without qualification an "unneutral" attitude:

Force and military aggression are once more on the march against small nations, in this instance through the invasion of Denmark and Norway. . . .

The Government of the United States has on the occasion of recent invasions strongly expressed its disapprobation of such unlawful exercise of force. It here reiterates, with undiminished emphasis, its point of view as expressed on those occasions. If civilization is to survive, the rights of the smaller nations to independence, to their territorial integrity, and to the unimpeded opportunity for self-government must be respected by their more powerful neighbors.[1]

Hitler's invasion of Denmark brought the danger of aggression geographically and strategically closer to the United States than any other Axis move to date. Denmark owned Iceland and Greenland, two islands that flank the North Atlantic approaches to America. Hitler's desire to control them was urgent because from them could be observed the weather conditions that governed Western Europe and dictated tactics in the air battle of Britain. The German Admiral Walter Canaris as early as 1937 had sent a scientific expedition to Iceland. It made maps of airfield sites and plans for weather stations. Presently the Nazis established an "Arctic Office" in Berlin. Beyond the immediate war situation lay the possibility that these strategic positions, from which America could easily be attacked by air, would fall into the hands of an aggressive European power.

Officials of the State Department showed Secretary Hull maps which made clear that Greenland wholly and Iceland "largely" belonged by geography to the Western Hemisphere. The Monroe Doctrine therefore applied to them, particularly its provision that no Western Hemisphere territory belonging to one European power might be transferred to another. It was also clear that Iceland possessed the constitutional power to take the initiative in its foreign relations if the Danish government was unable to act in an emergency.

Immediately after the invasions, Hull informed Morgenstierne that the United States would continue to recognize him as the representative of King Haakon's government so long as he refused to take orders from the Nazi puppet government of Quisling. This was ordinary procedure under the Stimson Doctrine. But the case of Denmark was the reverse. There the King and his government continued to rule in theory, while everyone knew they were prisoners of the Nazis. Hull told the Danish Minister to the United States, Henrik de Kauffmann, that the United States would continue to recognize him, even if he was recalled by his government, on the grounds that his government was no longer a free agent.[2]

If the Roosevelt administration had searched for them, it could have found reasons in traditional codes of international law why it should ignore events in Denmark and allow Hitler to determine the fate of the islands whose mother country he had conquered. Instead it found ways to serve the strategic interests of the United States—ways which did not violate international law but fully exploited justifications available in the League Covenant, the Kellogg-Briand Pact, and other recent formulations, for acts of common sense and self-preservation. The new rules revived the Grotian concept of the obligation of a neutral to avoid aiding an aggressor or injuring his victim. This procedure had the domestic political advantage in the case of Greenland of strengthening the Monroe Doctrine, which isolationists so greatly respected.

President Roosevelt accordingly made it clear, at a press conference on April 18, that Greenland was part of the Western Hemisphere and that its security was essential to all the American nations. Probably he rejected the State Department view that Iceland was "largely" also part of the Western Hemisphere because the strain on the public idea of geography would be too severe.

In any case, the sturdy legislators of the thousand-year-old Icelandic Althing, or Parliament, had already taken care of their own security to a remarkable extent, although not without encouragement from Washington, which gave their act force. As early as April, 1939, Secretary Hull decided to establish a consulate in

Iceland if war came. Trade alone was too small to justify it. On April 9, 1940, the Althing empowered the Icelandic Cabinet to exercise the authority of the Danish King and conduct the island's foreign relations. Prime Minister Hermann Jónasson promptly requested the United States to enter into direct diplomatic relations with Iceland. Hull replied that such relations were welcomed. Representatives were exchanged and Iceland was released from the freezing order which the United States had applied to Danish credits. On May 10, the day Winston Churchill became Prime Minister, Great Britain sent troops to occupy Iceland. The United States received assurances that the forces would be withdrawn after the war and that they would not interfere with the government of the island. The Roosevelt administration made no objection.

Greenland became the special concern of the United States. Hull made this clear to Ambassador Lothian on April 12. He denied the validity of Britain's old and vague claims to possession of the island and warned that any attempt by Britain to assert authority there would make trouble in the United States. The Canadian government then came forward with a proposal to send forces to Greenland. Hull objected. He believed such actions gave excuses to aggressors to distort them into justifications for their own policies. He particularly wished to avoid giving Japan a precedent for Japanese occupation of the Netherlands East Indies if their mother country fell to Hitler.

The local authorities in Greenland thereupon authorized de Kauffmann to sound out the Roosevelt administration regarding the possibility that the United States would accept a protectorate over the island. This was done on April 19, as a response by the Greenlanders to Roosevelt's public statement the day before that Greenland was under the Monroe Doctrine. But the Danes had forgotten that the Roosevelt administration had pledged abandonment of the United States policy of unilateral enforcement of the Monroe Doctrine. Hull answered de Kauffmann:

"This Government has been opposing protectorates generally, chiefly because nations engaged in military conquest are seizing smaller nations under the pretext that they are merely protecting them, whereas their real purpose is permanent domination. Naturally, nations bent on conquest are looking for precedents established by those nations that criticize and condemn their course. And by precedent I don't mean a bona fide precedent for seizure and occupation by force, but any kind of precedent that could be distorted into use for this purpose." [3]

Hull turned down the offer. After the passage of the Lend Lease Act in March, 1941, Congressional authority to aid countries whose defense was vital to the United States overcame Hull's scruples.

The Roosevelt administration found ways in 1940 to support the security of Greenland against the Nazis without laying itself open to the charge of imperialism. The multilateral technique of enforcing the Monroe Doctrine was soon to be worked out in relation to islands close to Latin American republics, but this technique seemed to Hull at the time inappropriate in the case of a European possession that was close to Canada, which was not a member of the Pan American organizations. Instead, the United States supported a temporary declaration of independence by the Greenlanders on May 3.

A high degree of voluntary cooperation followed between the Greenland government and the United States. An American consulate was established at Godthaab. A Coast Guard cutter with supplies for the inhabitants carried Consul James K. Penfield to his post. The Greenlanders wept for joy when they saw the vessel was not Nazi but American. A regular Greenland Patrol was carried out by the Coast Guard.

The Canadian government was worried for fear that important deposits in Greenland of cryolite, necessary for the aviation industry, would be sabotaged by Nazi raiders. Hull preferred that the United States rather than Canada should provide the Greenlanders with means of defense. On the Greenlanders' request, the United States government sold them a gun to protect the mines at Ivigtut. Penfield was instructed to offer United States aid in planning island defenses and necessary equipment, and the offer was accepted.

The Greenlanders feared a British or Canadian landing force. They opposed any belligerent occupation whatever. The governors of the island on June 3 handed Penfield a request that the United States should land troops at Ivigtut. Hull replied that he had assurances from Canada and Britain that they would not land a force, and that the United States would not do so unless under exceptional circumstances.[4]

The Nazis rapidly created such circumstances. They made a series of daring attempts to set up secret weather stations in the remote wastes of the island by expeditions disguised as "Norwegian hunters and trappers." The outcome of the Battle of Britain in the fall of 1940 depended in part on the outcome of the strange arctic war fought against these expeditions. Supplied by the United States, the Greenlanders defeated the Nazi expeditions one after another.

This was the first attack by the Axis on territory of the Western Hemisphere, and the Roosevelt administration accepted and fulfilled United States responsibility for repelling it. It was done with little publicity beyond the essential public statement of policy. In August and September, 1940, United States Army experts surveyed Greenland for air fields. The case of Greenland was an excellent example of Roosevelt's determination to find ways and means to counter the Axis with measures "short of war." It provided certain elementary experiences which became the pattern for Lend Lease and other policies in an enlarged arena.

Application of the Stimson Doctrine to Norway led directly to United States cooperation with the first of a new batch of anti-Axis governments-in-exile. The large Norwegian merchant marine was an important factor in this development. The King of Norway decreed the requisitioning of all Norwegian vessels and set up in London the Norwegian Shipping and Trade Mission to control them. Norwegian ships in American waters or chartered by Americans were governed by the Mission with the approval of the United States and they played an important part in strengthening Allied communications.

The case of Danish ships was more difficult. The British wanted them transferred to their flag. Hull rejected a British request to influence Minister de Kauffmann, but he allowed the latter to establish a Danish Shipping Committee in New York. With Hull neutral in the dispute, Danish ships that were tied up in American ports remained out of service for more than a year.[5]

Problems of Norway and Denmark became secondary for the administration on May 9 when the Nazis loosed blitzkrieg on the West. But the gallantry of the Norwegians and their sufferings continued to be important polarizers of American sentiment against Hitler. The strategic values of Greenland and Iceland increased as the war turned towards the Atlantic, and the administration's foresight in safeguarding Greenland was rewarded.

## Bewilderment and Dread

The fall of the Netherlands, Belgium, Luxemburg, and France was the most dangerous blow suffered by the free world in modern times. Beginning May 9, 1940, American bewilderment and dread mounted as the Maginot Line and the "greatest army in the world" were shown to be, in Premier Reynaud's words to the American Ambassador, "walls of sand that a child puts up against waves on the seashore." [6] Americans had lived securely behind those walls for so long that they were hardly aware of their dependence on them. When the Nazi hordes rolled over them as if they were indeed sand, Americans learned the meaning of the phrase Roosevelt had been reported as uttering early in 1939: America's frontier is on the Rhine.

For Roosevelt and Hull, the shock of the Fall of France was eased by realization that it required no change in their policies but only an intensification of determinations already made; no abandonment of mistaken policies, domestic or foreign, but only expansion of preparations already begun.

Statements by the President and Secretary of State were pitched to a higher note. The President told a Pan American Scientific Congress:

This very day, the tenth of May, 1940, three more independent nations have been cruelly invaded by force of arms.

In some kinds of human affairs the mind of man becomes accustomed to unusual actions if those actions are often repeated. But that is not so in the world happenings of today—and I am proud that it is not so. I am glad that we Americans of the three Americas are shocked and angered by the tragic news that has come to us from Belgium and The Netherlands and Luxembourg.

The overwhelmingly greater part of the population of the world abhors conquest and war and bloodshed—prays that the hand of neighbor shall not be lifted against neighbor. The whole world has seen attack follow threat on so many occasions and in so many places during these later years. We have come, therefore, to the reluctant conclusion that a continuance of these processes of arms presents a definite challenge to the continuance of the type of civilization to which all of us in the three Americas have been accustomed for so many generations.[7]

Three days later Secretary Hull told the American Society of International Law:

> The specter of a new descent into the conditions of international anarchy which characterized the Dark Ages looms on the horizon today. I am profoundly convinced that it menaces the civilized existence of mankind—of every nation and of every individual. . . .
> Our own nation . . . is not secure against that menace. . . .[8]

King Leopold of the Belgians asked the President for "moral support," and the President sent on May 11 a message which said in part:

> "The people of the United States hope, as do I, that policies which seek to dominate peaceful and independent peoples through force and military aggression may be arrested, and that the Government and people of Belgium may preserve their integrity and their freedom." [9]

It was a time for action as well as words, but the possibilities of effective action were heartbreakingly slight. The first climax of compulsion to act came on May 15 when the Nazi tanks and dive-bombers broke through the French line at Sedan. On the same day Winston Churchill sent his first letter as Prime Minister to President Roosevelt.

## The First Churchill Letter

The assumption of power by Churchill was the one ray of light in the darkness of Allied fortune. On May 13 he electrified Britons and all friends of freedom by his statement of the policy of his government to Commons. He had nothing to offer but "blood, toil, tears and sweat":

> You ask, what is our policy? I will say: It is to wage war, by sea, land, and air, with all our might and with all the strength that God can give us: to wage war against a monstrous tyranny, never surpassed in the dark, lamentable catalogue of human crime. That is our policy. You ask, What is our aim? I can answer in one word: Victory—victory at all costs, victory in spite of all terror; victory, however long and hard the road may be; for without victory, there is no survival.[10]

The Churchill leadership, with its promise of no surrender, and its visible galvanizing of the British people to make the first all-out stand against the Axis since the Spanish Republicans fought Mussolini, Hitler, and Franco, had incalculable influence on the American people and the Roosevelt administration. Without it, it is unlikely that the United States would have made so rapidly its own decision to stand against the Axis. Isolationism, which fed on contempt for allies abroad, would have destroyed American realization of the value of allies. That realization became the common-sense foundation of the American decision to turn to internationalism.

Besides this, the Churchill leadership made possible an intimate and vastly fruitful private correspondence on terms of friendship and utmost trust between the heads of the two great surviving democracies. Churchill has written of their exchange of almost two thousand letters: "I felt I was in contact with a very great man who was also a warm-hearted friend and the foremost champion of the high causes which we served." [11] This correspondence was the source and guardian of cooperation between Great Britain and the United States. It was one of the reasons why that cooperation became closer and more efficient than history records between any other great allies. Cooperation was achieved before Pearl Harbor and before Russia was attacked, while Britain stood alone, and Britons themselves gave numerous indications that without it they considered their cause doomed.

Churchill's letter of May 15 was coolly honest in its statement of the situation. He noted Hitler's marked superiority in the air. The small countries were being smashed like matchwood. Mussolini could be expected to come in for loot. The British expected to be attacked at home by plane, parachute, and air-borne troops. If necessary Britain would continue the war alone, "and we are not afraid of that."

But he warned the President that the United States might face a Nazified Europe alone if it withheld its force too long and Britain fell. He asked the President to proclaim nonbelligerency, which he defined as help with everything short of fighting troops. Immediately he asked for forty or fifty old American destroyers to bridge the gap until new construction was ready, several hundred of the latest types of airplanes, antiaircraft equipment and ammunition, steel and other materials. Britain would pay dollars as long as it could, but "I should like to feel reasonably sure that when we can pay no more, you will give us the stuff all the same." A visit of a United States naval squadron to Irish ports would be valuable in relation to possible German landings there. The Prime Minister showed the extent of his trust in Roosevelt by confiding in him the details of British armaments.[12]

## A Momentous Determination

Striking reports from the American Ambassadors to France and Britain arrived in Washington at the same time as Churchill's letter. Bullitt happened to be present with Daladier when General Gamelin telephoned that the Nazis had broken through at Sedan. Daladier said it was obvious that without a miracle the French Army would be destroyed. He claimed the British were holding back support.

At the same moment, Churchill told Kennedy he would not send more troops to France because he was convinced Britain would be attacked within a month. And he added that even if Britain were burned to the ground, the government would move to Canada with the fleet and fight on. Kennedy himself concluded that the United States could do nothing to aid Britain to fend off destruction; rather it would do better to write off Britain and France and fight if necessary only in its own back yard.

Roosevelt and Hull decided otherwise. The latter has recorded in quiet words their momentous determination, which was consistent with their policy since taking office:

It seemed to us we should do better to keep the fighting away from our own back yard. This we could do by helping Britain and France remain on their feet. . . .

Of one point the President and I had not the slightest doubt; namely, that an Allied victory was essential to the security of the United States.[13]

Considering the fact that isolationists, despite their stated confidence that the United States had nothing to fear from Axis conquest of Europe, Asia and Africa, supported rearmament on a scale that was foolish if war was not expected, the issue between them and internationalists like Roosevelt and Hull narrowed down to one of strategy: which was the wiser course, to work for defeat of the Axis before or after it conquered the rest of the world and attacked America? To win the war away from American soil had such obvious advantages that the majority of Americans needed no more than this consideration to reach the conclusion that the isolationists were wrong and the administration was right.

### 50,000 Planes

The failure of Congress to enact even the January requests for defense appropriations led to the President's decision to ask Congress in his Message on May 16 to speed and to increase armament. Churchill's May 15 letter did not initiate the President's action —he had already outlined the Message to a press conference on May 14 [14]—but it doubtless influenced the final form of his requests.

This Message Charles A. Beard offers as evidence that the President continued in the face of disaster abroad to give the American public no more insight into his policy than that his objective was still peace. Beard quotes the following elided passage and adds italics for emphasis of the words which he considers most misleading:

"Our task is plain. The road we must take is clearly indicated. Our defenses must be invulnerable, our security absolute. . . . *Our ideal, yours and mine, the ideal of every man, woman, and child in the country—our objective is still peace—peace at home and peace abroad.* Nevertheless, we stand ready not only to spend millions *for defense* but to give our service and even our lives *for the maintenance of our American liberties.*" [15]

The words Beard left out included the following:

But our defense as it was yesterday, or even as it is today, does not provide security against potential developments and dangers of the future.

This referred in summary to the most sensational passage in the Message, the passage which excited most attention and altered the meaning of the whole Message, from one which merely reaffirmed the President's continued "ideal" and "objective" of peace, as

Beard would have his readers believe, to one which made absolutely clear the President's conviction that continued peace for the United States was highly unlikely.

He began by calling for an examination of "the dangers which confront us," and reviewed the revelations of the last few days regarding the speed and deadliness of motorized armies, parachute troops, air-borne landings, and lightning attacks far behind fighting lines, aided by fifth columns. He stated that United States vital interests were widespread. The oceans were no longer adequate defensive barriers because the new element of air navigation stepped up the speed of attack to two or three hundred miles an hour. Then he brought home to many Americans the vulnerability of the United States to attack:

From the fiords of Greenland it is four hours by air to Newfoundland; five hours to Nova Scotia, New Brunswick and to the Province of Quebec; and only six hours to New England.

The Azores are only 2,000 miles from parts of our eastern seaboard and if Bermuda fell into hostile hands it would be a matter of less than three hours for modern bombers to reach our shores.

From a base in the outer West Indies, the coast of Florida could be reached in two hundred minutes.

The islands off the west coast of Africa are only 1,500 miles from Brazil. Modern planes starting from the Cape Verde Islands can be over Brazil in seven hours.

And Para, Brazil, near the mouth of the Amazon River, is but four flying-hours to Caracas, Venezuela; and Venezuela is but two and one-half hours to Cuba and the Canal Zone; and Cuba and the Canal Zone are two and one-quarter hours to Tampico, Mexico; and Tampico is two and one-quarter hours to St. Louis, Kansas City and Omaha.

On the other side of the continent, Alaska, with a white population of only 30,000 people, is within four or five hours of flying distance to Vancouver, Seattle, Tacoma, and Portland. The islands of the southern Pacific are not too far removed from the west coast of South America to prevent them from becoming bases of enormous strategic advantage to attacking forces.

Surely, the developments of the past few weeks have made it clear to all of our citizens that the possibility of attack on vital American zones ought to make it essential that we have the physical, the ready ability to meet those attacks and to prevent them from reaching their objectives.

This means military implements—not on paper—which are ready and available to meet any lightning offensive against our American interest.

Then followed plain indication that the administration rejected the isolationist strategic conception of waiting to fight in America's back yard:

A defense which allows an enemy to consolidate his approach without hindrance will lose. A defense which makes no effective effort to destroy the lines of supplies and communications of the enemy will lose.

An effective defense by its very nature requires the equipment to attack the aggressor on his route before he can establish strong bases within the territory of American vital interests.

In this vivid context, the President's later affirmation that the ideal and objective of the United States was still peace was no more than an affirmation that it would not commit aggression, that it would retain the ideal and objective of peace even if, as now seemed very likely, it was attacked. Beard's carefully restricted quotation makes the President's armament program seem based on the illogical isolationist premise that the United States had nothing to fear from the Axis, that peace was his only thought; whereas it was actually based on the contrary premise and no one could hear or read the President's dramatic words and imagine otherwise than that the President feared war.

His assertion that an effective defense required a strategy of attack on the aggressor, far from American shores, expressed Roosevelt's and Hull's decision to reject the defeatist advice of Ambassador Kennedy. It was reinforced by a strong statement on aid to Britain and France. Roosevelt referred to the air superiority of the Nazis and proposed a goal of "at least 50,000 planes a year." But American defense needs must not take priority over the needs of Britain and France even in the matter of new planes:

For the permanent record, I ask the Congress not to take any action which would in any way hamper or delay the delivery of American-made planes to foreign nations which have ordered them, or seek to purchase new planes. That, *from the point of view of our own national defense,* would be extremely shortsighted.[16]

During the next months a bitter fight against isolationists revolved around these words. Beard omits them entirely. The President had clearly stated that he would not seek either peace or to build up

American armaments at the expense of aid to Britain and France, that in his view both peace and defense were best served by aiding the Allies to victory. The startling suggestion of 50,000 planes yearly, ten times current production, had come to the President from Hull, who felt that the figure was quite possible and would have good effects in stimulating Americans, worrying the Axis, and comforting the Allies.[17] As it turned out, United States' plane production reached the rate of 90,000 per year in August, 1943.[18]

In the light of Churchill's May 15 letter and subsequent events, the President's request for vast quantities of planes and other armaments signified that he envisaged the program as providing arms for Britain as well as the United States. Others viewed this question as one of alternatives: *either* aid Britain *or* rearm the United States; the President proposed that both be achieved at the same time. It was his first answer to the Churchill letter. It was also a ringing answer to the Axis, to isolationists, and to defeatists like Kennedy, all of whom were agreed that the United States had best confine its attention to its own back yard. Roosevelt let the world know that, in his view, the American back yard did not fence out useful fighting neighbors.

To isolationists the May 16 Message by Roosevelt was proof that the "phony war" had not affected his policy, that he would meet real war with real measures of defense, including aid to the Allies. The America First Committee promptly joined the issue with the President and launched a bitter campaign. Lindbergh decried "hysterical chatter" and declared the danger of war came solely from Americans who invited it by meddling with affairs abroad: "If we desire peace, we need only stop asking for war. No one wishes to attack us. . . ."[19] The priest Coughlin in his journal, *Social Justice,* and over the radio, smeared with vicious epithets anyone who voiced concern for the fate of democracy abroad. But such leaders and organizations were effectively fought by supporters of the President. Most important was the Committee to Defend America by Aiding the Allies, which was organized in May, 1940, by William Allen White, the celebrated Kansas Republican editor. This organization was bipartisan in its leadership and support, and it was a manifestation of the bipartisanship in foreign policy the President had striven for since Munich. Its leadership commanded respect. Its methods were honorable and its arguments reasonable.

The pattern of the armament program was set in the May 16 Message but its scope was rapidly broadened. Each new disaster abroad was matched by a demand by the President that American arms production be shifted into higher gear. On May 16 he asked for over one billion dollars—almost double the appropriations and authorizations for the year.

## Parent of All Defense and War Agencies

Immediately he appointed a seven-member Advisory Commission to the Council of National Defense. The latter brought together the Secretaries of War, the Navy, Interior, Agriculture, Commerce, and Labor. The Advisory Commission was the successor to the War Resources Board which the President had "put on the shelf" in November, 1939, because it was dominated by the "Morgan crowd." The Chairman of that body, Edward R. Stettinius, Jr., a close associate of the Morgan group and President of the United States Steel Corporation, was given the task of allocating materials in the new National Defense Advisory Commission. But on at least equal planes of authority with Stettinius were William S. Knudsen, in charge of production, and Sidney Hillman, in charge of labor. Other members were Leon Henderson, price stabilization, Ralph Budd, transportation, Chester C. Davis, farm production, and Harriet Elliott, consumer production. No chairman was ever named for the NDAC. For this Roosevelt was bitterly criticized. Robert Sherwood, who had access to the President, Hopkins and, later, to the Hopkins papers, has recorded that he never knew the President's "real reason."

In the light of his experience with the War Resources Board, it seems probable that Roosevelt was determined to avoid giving sole responsibility again to a representative of business. He wanted Knudsen, President of General Motors Corporation, and Stettinius to work in team with Hillman, President of the Amalgamated Clothing Workers of America, as an expression of his hope that an even balance could be maintained between business and labor. This was a significant product of the balance the President sought for between "national unity" and the New Deal. Conservatives more than liberals cried out against the inefficiency of the arrangement. If the President had been forced to name a single head of defense production agencies it would have been a businessman.

Roosevelt was always overly optimistic that his associates would cooperate rather than quarrel. The NDAC was the outstanding example during his twelve years in office of his administrative technique of making representatives of conflicting groups in the population share responsibility. Opponents saw only that this invited inefficiency and left the President in the position of ultimate arbiter. His friend and associate, Secretary of Labor Frances Perkins, saw more:

I would say that he was the catalytic agent through whose efforts chaotic forces were brought to a point where they could be harnessed creatively. He was a creative and energizing agent rather than a careful, direct-line administrator. He trusted people to whom he gave a job to do it. If they couldn't or wouldn't or didn't, he appointed someone else or gave part of it to someone else.[20]

The NDAC turned out to be the parent body of all the defense and war agencies. The President, at the beginning, had decided that such agencies should remain independent of Cabinet departments and peacetime agencies, because Congress would be more willing to give authority and money to temporary agencies which it could easily abolish after the emergency, and because new and independent bodies would not be bound by the gelid methods and conventions of the established bureaucracy.[21]

The astonishing effectiveness of the new scientific agencies which produced the atomic bomb, the proximity fuse, and dozens of other sensational contributions to the defense and war effort, all without filling newspapers with bureaucratic wrangling or public disturbance over their efficiency, suggests that not the President's administrative methods so much as the practice by the press of "politics as usual" was responsible for public alarm at the inefficiency of the NDAC and other agencies. Scientists working in fields with military implications, even though not employed by the government, imposed on themselves in May, 1940, voluntary censorship so that publication of their findings would not aid the Axis. This self-imposed restraint injured the material and career interests of scientists at least as much as the interests of business and labor were injured by governmental restraints, but they consented to it without complaint or publicity.

## A Cycle of Influences

The scientists' organ of censorship was the Reference Committee of the National Research Council. Hitler's attack on the West and the President's defense program produced quick developments in the field of nuclear fission. On the day of the German break-through at Sedan and of Churchill's first letter as Prime Minister to Roosevelt, General Watson was informed that experiments at Columbia University showed the practicality of carbon as a moderator of chain reaction in uranium. This suggested that nuclear fission could be controlled for use as an explosive.[22]

At the same time, the Nazi campaign to terrorize Americans into passivity misfired in the case of a most important individual. Charles A. Lindbergh made a practice of supplementing his public campaign with private attempts to frighten leading Americans by explaining Nazi strength with detailed information which the Germans had placed at his disposal. His purpose was to lead them to convince President Roosevelt that he should give up his program and advise Churchill to surrender to avoid hopeless slaughter. Some of his hearers cooperated in this "strategy of terror." But Dr. Vannevar Bush, President of the Carnegie Institution of Washington, heard Lindbergh and drew different conclusions. He decided that American scientists could and must outperform Nazi science and place their genius at the disposal of the President and his program of defense of freedom, rather than influence him and Churchill in favor of craven surrender.

Bush was appointed spokesman of a like-minded group of scientists, which included Presidents James B. Conant of Harvard and Karl T. Compton of the Massachusetts Institute of Technology. He interested Harry Hopkins, who during these days became the President's unofficial general assistant. Bush proposed a daring program to enlist scientific talent for an all-out effort to overcome the Nazi lead in weapons. The uranium project would become one part of the new program. The President approved, and thus was completed the remarkable cycle of influences leading directly from Lindbergh's friends in Germany through Bush and Hopkins to Roosevelt, which Sherwood aptly calls "the chain reaction," and cites as proof that "there are some peoples whom it is dangerous to alarm. . . ."

On June 15, 1940, the day after Paris fell, Roosevelt sent a letter to Bush authorizing the establishment of the National Defense Research Council, and including the following words:

This country is singularly fitted, by reason of the ingenuity of its people, the knowledge and skill of its scientists, the flexibility of its industrial structure, to excel in the arts of peace, and to excel in the arts of war if that be necessary.[23]

This truth and the policy of the Roosevelt administration answered the strategists of Nazi terror.

## Defense Beyond the Borders

On May 26 the President delivered a Fireside Chat on the subject of national defense. He spoke of the sufferings of women, children, and the aged in the invaded countries:

Tonight over the once peaceful roads of Belgium and France millions are now moving, running from their homes to escape bombs and shells and fire and machine gunning, without shelter, and almost wholly without food. They stumble on, knowing not where the end of the road will be.

He pleaded for contributions to the Red Cross, which was rushing aid to civilians. Then he turned to American problems and heavily underlined the "shattering of many illusions" isolationists had experienced in recent days. He repeated what he had told Congress, that his defense policy was not limited to defense of the United States: "Obviously, a defense policy based on that is merely to invite future attack." Thus he made amply clear to the whole public his anti-isolationist definition of the purposes of the defense program. He spoke to allay the panic which threatened regarding the state of military defenses. He refuted the hysterical rumors that had gained currency, including the charge that the administration had wasted billions formerly appropriated for defense. He showed that the Army, Navy, and Air Forces were roughly twice as strong in personnel and equipment as when he came to office. At the same time he stressed the high rate of obsolescence in military equipment. He invited men in private industry to help carry out the program. He denied that anything in the present emergency justified relaxation of wage and hour standards or other social reform policies of the administration. Nor would the American people relish the idea of any American "growing rich and fat in an emergency of blood and slaughter and human suffering." He warned the people against the strategists of terror who worked to divide and discourage by appeals to racial and class prejudice, and hatred of the government. "These dividing forces are undiluted poison." His peroration struck a religious note, ending: "In common affection for all mankind, your prayers join with mine—that God will heal the wounds and the hearts of humanity." [24]

The response to this Fireside Chat was heartening. Letters and telegrams pledging support and offering services and property flooded into the White House. The President showed reporters offers of services by retired officers, and experts: "engineers, physicians, pilots, chemists, et cetera;" and offers of property: "shipbuilding plants, furniture companies, manganese mines, airplane plants, bedding companies, aviation mechanics training schools," and so on through a long list.[25] Now the NDAC was launched, and the trek to Washington began a folk saga of hideous living conditions and fantastic welters of red tape that somehow resolved themselves in victory in the Second World War.

Within a week the President went to Congress for new appropriations. Investigation had quickly shown that new production facilities were necessary for munitions and new training schools for industrial and military personnel. The amount was about a billion dollars. He also asked Congress for authority to call into active service the National Guard and Reserves. Congress responded to all his requests, although not without normal delays and bickerings.[26]

## Nonbelligerency

Roosevelt had geared his pace to match the speed of Hitler's blitzkrieg. Before the surrender of France by the Pétain government on June 18, the United States had launched the defense program which would in two and a half years permit the landing of American troops in French North Africa. Despite temptations arising from American fears, the near-panic of the moment, and political considerations just prior to the party nominating con-

ventions, Roosevelt had refused to orient American defense towards isolationist conceptions, he had rejected the defeatism of
his own Ambassador to Britain, and he had publicly reaffirmed
that the defense of the United States would include aid to victims
of aggression by "measures short of war but stronger than mere
words." The most striking statement of his determination came
in his June 10 address to the graduating class of the University of
Virginia at Charlottesville:

In our American unity, we will pursue two obvious and simultaneous courses; we will extend to the opponents of force the material resources of this nation; and, at the same time, we will harness and speed
up the use of those resources in order that we ourselves in the Americas may have equipment and training equal to the task of any emergency and every defense.

This was an answer not only to Churchill's private message but
also to the Prime Minister's public call to America at the end of
the great statement to Commons on June 4:

. . . we shall defend our island, whatever the cost may be, we shall fight
on the beaches, we shall fight on the landing-grounds, we shall fight in
the fields and in the streets, we shall fight in the hills; we shall never
surrender, and even if, which I do not for a moment believe, this island
or a large part of it were subjugated and starving, then our Empire
beyond the seas, armed and guarded by the British Fleet, would carry
on the struggle, until, in God's good time, the New World, with all its
power and might, steps forth to the rescue and the liberation of the
Old.[27]

*"We will extend to the opponents of force the material resources
of this nation":* this pronouncement by Roosevelt ended one era
and inaugurated another. It is ignored by Charles A. Beard. Repeal of the arms embargo had cleared obstructions; now the administration would go forward to provide arms to victims of aggression. This put an end to the status of the United States as a
neutral under former rules of international law and made it a
nonbelligerent supporting the nations fighting in defense of their
independence and of treaties to which, like the Kellogg-Briand
Pact, the United States was a party.

## The "Stab in the Back"

Beard also ignores the passage in the Charlottesville address which, although it aroused more public excitement than the one quoted above, only dramatized the same policy of unneutrality. These were words, spoken of Mussolini's invasion of France, that abandoned the forms of discourse as well as the essence of the old neutrality: "On this tenth day of June, 1940, the hand that held the dagger has struck it into the back of its neighbor." [28] The American public was shocked by the President's frankness, and then, in vast majority, content that he had spoken well.

The genesis of the "stab in the back" passage was significant. It had originally been used by Reynaud and was relayed several times to Washington in cables from Bullitt. The President's participation in the moods of Hitler's victims made him want to use their very expression in his own address. Welles thought it impolitic to antagonize Mussolini, and his purpose indicates he had not yet decided that peace with Mussolini was impossible: the "stab in the back" statement would make it impossible to obtain Mussolini's cooperation "when the time came to make peace." The President first removed the passage from a draft of his speech and then on the way to Charlottesville restored it.[29] This was symbolic of the President's decision that he was finished with dreams of peace in Europe short of destruction of the Axis dictators.

Mussolini had not dared to strike until his prey was beaten down by a stronger beast. Roosevelt himself had striven to the end to spare France the degraded final blow from Italy. He summarized his efforts in the Charlottesville address. The Churchill letter of May 16 had encouraged his attempt, which had already begun late in April, after the Pope, through Myron Taylor, had urged the President to dissuade Mussolini from entering the war.

Roosevelt sent a personal message to the dictator, on April 29, containing a warning that no man could predict what nations would ultimately enter if the war spread. Mussolini answered with complaints that Italy was a "prisoner within the Mediterranean" and peace must solve "the fundamental problems of Italian liberty." Furthermore, the "new geography" resulting from Hitler's conquests must be recognized. On May 14, Ciano told Ambassa-

dor Phillips that Hitler's victories in Belgium and Holland had
led Mussolini to decide to enter the war. This news brought
urgent appeals from Premier Reynaud as well as Churchill for
stronger presidential pressure.

The President sent a letter of warning to Mussolini that heads
of states would lose control of events if the war spread, and no
man, "no matter how omniscient," could foretell the results to
himself or his people. Mussolini answered ominously: "Italy is
and intends to remain allied with Germany, and Italy cannot remain absent at a moment in which the fate of Europe is at stake."

Proposals fantastic in their desperation now poured into Washington and were rejected by Roosevelt and Hull. On May 25,
Churchill and Reynaud asked the President to promise Mussolini
that Italy's territorial grievances against France and Britain would
be considered by their governments with a view to agreement on
"reasonable" claims at the peace conference, to which Italy would
be admitted "with a status equal to that of any belligerent." Furthermore, they wanted the President to promise Mussolini that
the United States would do its utmost to make sure any agreement would be carried out if Italy did not go to war.

The President agreed, although he changed the form of the
projected arrangement so that he would not give Italy any assurance regarding the enforcement of an agreement. Instead he would
merely receive such assurances from Britain and France. His role
would be confined to "good offices," the transmission of messages
between the parties. In this way Roosevelt avoided the sort of
"commitment" isolationists constantly accused him of making.
The incident recalled the negotiations during the First World
War when, in 1915, the Allies brought Italy out of its alliance
with the Central Powers and onto their side with territorial
bribes in a secret treaty. There was, however, a significant difference between the 1940 negotiation and both the earlier one and
appeasement as practiced by Chamberlain. In 1915 and in 1938
Britain and France gave away territory that did not belong to
them. In 1940 they proposed to satisfy "reasonable" claims of
Mussolini only against themselves. Mussolini had specified on
numerous occasions what they were: irredentist areas of France,
Italian populated areas of French North Africa, a share in control
of Gibraltar and Suez. This, and Roosevelt's avoidance of any possibility of a United States guaranty of an agreement, projected

the negotiations as the exclusive affair of Britain and France. The President carefully and fully told his audience at Charlottesville in detail of the offer to Mussolini.[30]

The hypocrisy and irresponsibility of a dictator were startlingly clear in Mussolini's answer. Not negotiations which might legitimately satisfy Italy's claims, but war and loot were his objects. He answered that negotiations would not be "in accordance with the spirit of Fascism," which was one of the few honest statements of any Axis leader. Also, "any attempt to prevent Italy from fulfilling her engagements is not well regarded."

Roosevelt decided that if Mussolini was deaf to an offer of negotiations, he might listen to a blunt threat. He wrote, on May 31, that Italian belligerency would

at once result in an increase in the rearmament program of the United States itself and in a redoubling of the efforts of the Government of the United States to facilitate in every practical way the securing within the United States by the Allied Powers of all the supplies and matériel which they may require.

This statement may be seen in the perspective of the evolution of United States foreign policy as adoption of the large element in the system of collective security which involves sanctions. And Roosevelt did not hesitate to back it up with a threat of force as strong as he could make it without Congressional action. He reminded Mussolini of the Mediterranean interests of the United States, which had been upheld for a century and a half, and once had involved war. If Italy now entered the war, "direct interests of the Government of the United States will be immediately and prejudicially affected. . . . The legitimate interests of the American people will be gravely curtailed and such a possibility cannot be viewed with equanimity by their Government."

This strenuous effort to stop Italy by threatening sanctions and force, in effect the joining up of the United States in a united front against the Axis, came too late. The successes of Hitler were too much for Mussolini's cupidity. The diary of Count Ciano has exposed the mood of despairing criminality in which Mussolini took the unwilling and unprepared Italians into the war.[31] Ciano informed Phillips that Mussolini was decided and it was only a matter of days. Mussolini's answer to Roosevelt was crude. He would fulfill his engagements with Germany and he wanted no further "pressure" because it would only "stiffen his attitude."

France now made a direct offer to Mussolini to settle territorial claims. Mussolini answered that he wanted nothing from France by negotiation; he would make war on France. Roosevelt wanted to support the French offer, but Hull dissuaded him because it would only bring further insult from the bandit.[32]

Beard fails to mention the momentous development of the administration's foreign policy in May and June, 1940, from neutrality to nonbelligerency. The fact that the development occurred under the full glare of public scrutiny, with full pronouncements of its purpose and meaning by the President himself in his May 16 Message to Congress, his May 26 Fireside Chat, and his sensational June 10 address at Charlottesville, makes it necessary for Beard to delete the record of its central core if his thesis that a deceitful President plotted entry into war while promising neutrality and peace is to be sustained.

Risk of United States involvement in the war was present in the President's policy. He contended that isolationism contained even greater risks. This was an argument which could not easily be proved or disproved; it was a matter of probabilities and anxious judgment. The President submitted his argument to the people and Congress for judgment. It is difficult to imagine a course which could more properly solve the problem of leadership in a democracy.

Congress, fully warned that the defense program was intended by the administration to include aid to Britain and France, and that it was based on a strategic plan of defending the United States as far away from its shores as possible, proceeded to enact the legislation the President asked for with remarkable speed and large majorities. Indeed Congress provided appropriations larger than the President had requested.[33] In the face of the political furore over impending party conventions and the third-term issue, this support was satisfactory evidence that the administration's policy was acceptable to Congress and people.

## The Fall of France

It also strengthened the President's hand in his last-minute efforts to save something from the disaster of France. On May 30

the British began evacuating Dunkirk and in an astonishing maneuver recovered their trained manpower. But their best equipment was left behind, and, as immediate invasion of the island
was feared, this emphasized the British need for help which Roosevelt and Hull were already trying desperately to send.

A 1917 statute was discovered which authorized the government to trade army and navy aircraft back to manufacturers. It
was exploited so that manufacturers could sell planes to Britain.
Metropolitan France was regarded as defeated, and the President
decided to send some of the rifles, French 75s, machine guns, and
planes intended for France to Britain. These were declared "surplus," so that under another statute they could be sold outright to
private manufacturers, who then sold them to Britain.

For a time Premier Reynaud's recriminations against Britain
for failing to send the planes Churchill reserved for home defense
won Roosevelt's sympathy and he backed the French demands to
Churchill. The Prime Minister refused to change his stand. Bullitt supported French accusations that the British reserved their
planes and navy to use for bargaining in negotiations with Hitler.
Once more Roosevelt and Hull had to decide whether Britain
could be trusted with American arms; they did not hesitate but
accepted Churchill's assurances.

The fate of the British and French fleets emerged as the prime
considerations for American security. On May 26, the President
informed Churchill and Reynaud that their navies must not be
surrendered even if the battle in Europe was lost. Both governments gave assurances. But Roosevelt did not readily accept the
French promise. The demands of the French government for action by the United States were impracticable. It asked that the
American Atlantic Fleet be sent to the Mediterranean in spite of
the fact that no bases were available for its support there. Reynaud and Bullitt feared a Communist uprising in Paris and asked
Roosevelt for sub-machine guns to put it down. Marshal Pétain
had become Vice Premier. Talk of surrender by groups pro-Hitler
in their orientation accompanied hysterical attempts to place the
blame for surrender on Britain and the United States.

On May 18, Reynaud wanted Roosevelt to ask Congress to declare war. Bullitt pointed out to the French that Congress would
reject such a request almost unanimously and he accused the
French of wanting only to make a record. He recommended more

frank dealings. Three weeks later, just before retreating from Paris, Reynaud made a more realistic appeal to President Roosevelt "to state publicly that the United States would support the Allies by all means short of an expeditionary force." The Charlottesville address was an answer to this appeal. Privately, Roosevelt and Hull encouraged Reynaud to carry on from North Africa and to preserve the French fleet.

But Reynaud and his government were unwilling to take responsibility, and they struggled to lay it elsewhere. The Premier told Roosevelt that Britain would fall if France fell, and France would fall unless, within hours, the United States gave certainty that it would come into the war very soon. On the radio he publicly demanded that "clouds of war planes" cross the Atlantic to crush Hitler. The impracticality of the French demands made them more heartbreaking. Reynaud told Roosevelt: "You will see France go under like a drowning man and disappear after having cast a last look towards the land of liberty from which she awaited salvation."

The President did his best. To ask Congress for a declaration of war would not only be useless but it would be an irrevocable act which might destroy the possibility of obtaining from Congress the aid program already on foot. Roosevelt, on June 15, in reply to Reynaud spoke of the American admiration for French courage, recounted the planes, artillery, and ammunition already sent by the United States, and promised redoubled efforts. Every week that went by would see additional aid on its way to the Allies. He promised that the Stimson Doctrine would be invoked against territorial conquests by Germany. At the end he could only repeat and, in a grim anticlimax, qualify:

In these hours which are so heart-rending for the French people and yourself, I send you the assurances of my utmost sympathy and I can further assure you that so long as the French people continue in defense of their liberty which constitutes the cause of popular institutions throughout the world, so long will they rest assured that matériel and supplies will be sent to them from the United States in ever-increasing quantities and kinds.

I know that you will understand that these statements carry with them no implication of military commitments. Only the Congress can make such commitments.[34]

The next day Pétain became Premier of France, and the day after that his government asked Germany for terms.

Roosevelt and Hull struggled desperately to prevent Pétain from giving Hitler the French fleet. State Department findings on the danger were clear. If Hitler obtained substantial portions of the Allied fleets, "our position in the Atlantic would be dangerous in the extreme, unless we moved the Pacific fleet into the Atlantic, in which event Japan would inevitably swallow the whole of Southeast Asia." [35]

French bitterness against the British was such that Churchill's influence, brought to bear in personal visits to the government chiefs, was probably less than that of Bullitt and the United States. Churchill offered British-French union in vain. But at the crucial moment Bullitt, against the advice of Hull and Roosevelt, chose to stay in Paris while the government retreated to Tours and Bordeaux. He was reported to fear a Communist uprising, in spite of the fact that the French Communists were obviously supporting the Moscow policy of interposing no organized obstacles to Nazi conquest. Nor were they cooperating with the Nazis sufficiently to justify expectation that they would actively help them take Paris. This ambivalence in Soviet policy was understood by Roosevelt and Hull. Bullitt's request for sub-machine guns for use against a Communist uprising indicated that he did not understand it.

The result was that at Tours and Bordeaux the United States was represented by Anthony J. Drexel Biddle, Ambassador to the Polish Government-in-Exile, whose contacts with French leaders were greatly inferior to those of Bullitt. Hull attributes to this the loss of a "reasonable chance" for the United States to induce the French to continue the fight with the fleet and the colonies.[36]

Biddle interposed himself in the councils of the French leaders time after time during the days of chaos. On the night of June 16, Pétain's Foreign Minister, Baudouin, assured Biddle the fleet would never be surrendered to Germany. Roosevelt and Churchill wanted action, not words. The President urged that the fleet be sent to West African or West Indian ports; the Prime Minister wanted it sent to British ports. In the Mediterranean it could be captured or surrendered.

At this crucial moment the President could be said to engage in "secret diplomacy" involving the United States in "European power politics." But even isolationists could understand that the French fleet in Nazi hands would affect the security of the United States, and the administration knew how to exercise influence without making "commitments." Immediately following news of Pétain's request to Hitler for terms on the 17th, the administration froze French assets in the United States to prevent them being turned over to Germany. Hull sent notes to the German and Italian governments that the United States would not allow any transfer of French-owned American territory to another non-American power. He called a meeting of the American Republics at Havana to organize multilateral action against any attempt to make such a transfer. And an "almost brutal" message was sent to Baudouin and to Admiral Darlan, Pétain's Minister of Marine:

In the opinion of this Government, should the French Government, before concluding any armistice with the Germans, fail to see that the fleet is kept out of the hands of her opponents, the French Government will fatally impair the preservation of the French Empire and the eventual restoration of French independence and autonomy. Furthermore, should the French Government fail to take these steps and permit the French fleet to be surrendered to Germany, the French Government will permanently lose the friendship and good will of the Government of the United States.

Biddle gave this note to Darlan as he entered a Cabinet meeting on June 18, and he called Baudouin out of the meeting to give him a copy. Although both men were irritated by its tone, they were led by this letter to influence the Cabinet, Biddle believed, to decide that Hitler's armistice terms would be rejected by France if they included surrender of the fleet. The Cabinet considered sinking the ships, but this too Biddle opposed.[37] Destruction of the French fleet by Pétain would alter the world balance of sea power as effectively as if Germany had destroyed it in battle.

Professor William L. Langer of Harvard, who was given more complete access to archives of the United States government than any other writer on the Fall of France, supports Biddle's contention that the American note of June 17 influenced the French Cabinet decision on the next day.[38]

Perhaps more important in the ultimate failure of Hitler to take the French fleet was the dictator's policy of temporizing with France while concentrating on an agreement with Britain which would leave him free to turn east. Hitler ignored Mussolini's desire to take the fleet and everything else available. On the other hand, Hitler told the Italians that one of his reasons for refusing to ask for the French fleet was precisely that "France will not agree to that. . . ." [39] Therefore it may be interpreted that the American note of June 17 leading to, or at least fortifying French determination to reject armistice terms that included surrender of the fleet, was of considerable importance.

Another factor in the tortured situation was that French officials who believed in continuing the fight consented to the request for terms only because they believed Hitler's terms would be unacceptable. They were concerned about the attitude of the United States, which Roosevelt had presented so vigorously. Edouard Herriot wrote to President Lebrun on June 18: "To make a separate peace is to tear up our solemn agreements with Great Britain and Poland, to compromise our relations with the United States and to dishonor France before the world." [40]

The patriots began to organize the flight of the government to Africa. At the critical moment, Pierre Laval exerted pressure on Pétain and President Lebrun, and the decision to leave was reversed. Hitler's terms were regarded as much better than expected: no territorial cessions, occupation of only part of France, and demobilization of the French fleet in ports under German or Italian control but with a "solemn declaration" that it would not be used by Germany for purposes of war. The French government signed on June 22.[41]

## A Gun Cocked at the United States

The armistice, while it did not provide for turning over any French warships to Hitler, left open definite chances for Hitler to take a great share of them. This was the situation that led the Roosevelt administration into the mazy reaches of its "Vichy gamble." The decision was made to maintain relations with the Pétain government at Vichy in the first instance because such relations would permit the United States to offset Nazi influence in that government. A few days after the armistice Hull made very plain to Pétain's Ambassador, Count St. Quentin, the interest of the United States:

My country is greatly interested in France's not permitting Germany to get control and possession of the French Fleet. We have made clear to the world our interest in and our aid to France in the war. After we have incurred the ill will of Germany by reason of this fact, it is naturally a matter of very great importance to us if France hands to Germany a cocked gun to shoot at us.[42]

The Churchill government served the interests of the United States as well as Britain when it used drastic means to keep French warships out of German control. Many ships of the French fleet were in British or Empire ports, and Britain took them over. A few ships had escaped to Dakar. But two battleships, two battle cruisers and several cruisers lay at Oran in Algeria, subject to return to France to be disarmed and placed under German supervision.

The British destroyed these warships at Oran, killing many Frenchmen, rather than allow them to go to France. In the ultimatum to the French commander, the British offered him alternatives which included entrusting his ships to the United States. When he refused, the British opened fire.

This action stirred up anti-British feeling among many who saw only the tragedy. To Roosevelt and others who were not ready to assume that the British enjoyed killing Frenchmen, it was proof of the depth of British determination to fight Hitler without backward glances or compromise.[43] Hull, on the other hand, regarded the Oran affair as a "tragic blunder" by the British. But Churchill later told Hull that Vichy could not be trusted and it was necessary to stop rumors that Britain would surrender. Britain had acted on the supreme ground of self-defense. Even Hull admitted that, after Oran, those who feared the French Navy would help Hitler invade Britain "could now sleep of nights with a little more assurance." [44]

## Scraping the Bottom of the Barrel

Roosevelt needed proof of British determination because he was basing American policy on it. He besought Churchill to tell him his plans and expectations. Churchill answered that he expected invasion immediately after the Fall of France, that the British Fleet would no longer be afloat if the invasion succeeded, and that plans for removal of the government from Britain were indefinite. The Churchill government, in short, would go down fighting, if invasion succeeded. Later Roosevelt learned that Churchill expected Washington to take over leadership of the Dominions in such event.[45]

Advisers around the President were certain that it would be "suicide" for him personally and for the nation to gamble on the British. But Roosevelt, in one of the supreme decisions of his career, committed himself to the British cause. He "scraped the bottom of the barrel" in American arsenals to find arms for the British Home Guards, who were organizing against invasion. They soon received half a million rifles, eighty thousand machine guns, a hundred and thirty million rounds of ammunition, nine hundred French 75s with a million shells, TNT, and other munitions. The British defenders exchanged pitchforks and clubs for these weapons.

## Stimson and Knox

Some of Roosevelt's most ardent supporters wanted him to go farther. Most important among them was the Republican elder statesman, Henry L. Stimson. The former Secretary of State, on June 18, told a radio audience that the Neutrality Act should be entirely repealed, American ports should be opened to the Allied navies for use as repair bases, aid to Britain and France should be carried in American ships with American naval convoys, and compulsory universal military service should be adopted at once.[46]

This went far beyond Roosevelt's public position, but the next day the President invited Stimson to join the government as Secretary of War, and Frank Knox, who held similar views, as Secretary of the Navy.

Stimson was astonished. He asked Roosevelt whether his radio speech would be embarrassing to him. The President replied he was in "full accord" with it. Stimson accepted. In the Senate hearing on his appointment, he qualified his views only by declaring that as Secretary of War he would be concerned with defense more than foreign policy, and that his particular proposals "might not fit precisely with the requirements of the moment as seen from an official position." He took a stronger position than the President on the literal issue of "sending our boys to fight in Europe," of which isolationists made a fetish: "No one wishes to send American troops beyond our borders unless the protection of the United States makes such action absolutely necessary." The President defined "absolutely necessary" more narrowly as an attack against the United States. Stimson affirmed that he did not believe in a "defensive defense," or that Americans would be safe if they sat down and waited for the enemy to attack their shores. He vigorously supported aid to the Allies. On these issues the President had already identically committed himself.

Stimson stated in answer to a question by Senator Arthur Vandenberg of Michigan that the Kellogg-Briand Pact had abolished the whole theory of neutrality towards an aggressor and made "unneutral" acts "fully legal under international law." This was a valuable summing up of the administration's policy in terms more specific than Roosevelt or Hull ordinarily used.

Senator Robert Taft of Ohio tried to trap his father's former Cabinet officer into saying things he did not mean. Stimson insisted that he could not foretell his future views without knowledge of future circumstances. Later he wrote of Taft and the isolationists:

This readiness, in a great national emergency, to seize every opportunity of embarrassing the administration seemed to him a fantastic distortion of partisan duty. He had been questioned for two hours, and not a word had been said about his competence to direct the Army. . . . This was to be the attitude of the isolationists for the next eighteen months whenever he went to the Capitol. . . . Hearings and debates . . . became a sounding board for the hopelessly twisted views of a small group of men who, in the name of peace, would have kept America from acting to delay or block the greatest aggression in history.[47]

Perhaps isolationists avoided the matter of Stimson's competence because it could not be questioned. The Senate confirmed his appointment July 9 by a two-thirds majority of the members voting.[48]

Knox also was confirmed after similar controversy.[49] These two men made the President seem cautious in his policy as he himself made Hull seem cautious. Others around him urged Roosevelt to issue a "clarion call" to Congress and people asking for approval of a maximum number of actions "short of war." But Roosevelt feared that hasty pressure on Congress would result in defeat and destroy his policy. He was determined to take only the most calculated risk in an irrevocable act. He used old legislation of the First World War as authorizations whenever possible and, in the case of the National Defense Research Council, a law dating from the Civil War.

This caution was balanced, and more than balanced after Stimson and Knox joined the administration, by the decision to ask Congress to approve a policy of sufficient moment to justify risk of an "irrevocable act." This was Selective Service, and Roosevelt approached it as a supreme test of his support, one which, unprecedented as Selective Service was in peacetime, would be necessary in order to place the nation in a position to back up with force his program of aid to the Allies and "offensive defense."

## The Republic Rescued

In the meantime he found that his program rallied popular and Congressional support to a surprising degree. Many of the severest critics of his domestic policies, like Secretary of the Navy Knox, ardently advocated his foreign policy. Foreign events and the President's reversal of emphasis from domestic to foreign affairs since Munich were working a revolution in American opinion.[50]

The ability of Americans led by Roosevelt, Stimson and Knox to transcend their domestic quarrels and political predilections in the face of foreign danger once more rescued the Republic from diseases which had helped kill such a great nation as France. From a world viewpoint, Roosevelt had assumed for the American people leadership of humanity by taking responsibility that the Axis should not destroy human freedom.

This was an irrevocable act that went beyond the niceties of Presidential strategy imposed by the ancient Constitutional arrangements whereby Congress and Executive are encouraged to quarrel their way to a policy.

Roosevelt had performed this act within a matter of days after Hitler's onslaught against the West. Reynaud movingly acknowledged it the day after he fell from power. As a private citizen he could admit what he had not admitted as Premier, and, for a very great share of humanity as well as France, voice a prophetic conviction:

I wish to say to you, Mr. President, that I feel that the reply which you made to my last message went to the extreme limit of what was permitted by existing circumstances. . . . France feels that, because America exists, the form of civilization which is hers will not die, and that the day will come when liberty will be reborn in old Europe.[51]

# 9.

## *"Because America Exists"*

From late june to november 6, 1940, the presidential campaign interposed in the development of Roosevelt's new policy of aid to the Allies. Ordinarily, politicians dread untried issues when they appeal to the electorate for another term in office. Such issues arouse fears which lend themselves temptingly to exploitation by the opposition, simply because they are new. It is safer to concentrate on ancient and universally accepted principles.

### *The Third-Term Decision*

Besides this tradition of passivity at election time that Roosevelt had to overthrow, he decided to challenge the deep-seated prejudice against a third term. Dozens of explanations have been offered for his final decision to make this challenge, most of them flattering or contemptuous in strict accordance with their authors' prior attitudes towards the President and his policies, but none of them separates out what may have been the most important specific factor. He had been led by the necessities of the hour to sketch, in May and June, a design for American rearmament and aid to the Allies which could not be filled out for months to come. If he refused nomination for a third term at the Democratic Convention early in July, his decision would throw into doubt the fulfillment of the design not merely after January, 1941, but instantaneously. This was inevitable because the Democratic Party was split into factions with varying attitudes towards foreign policy, and the struggle for power among them, no matter who was nominated, would postpone firm determinations regarding the continu-

ance of the Roosevelt program until well after the new administration was inaugurated. The Republican nomination on June 28
of Wendell Willkie, who broadly supported the President's foreign policy, was no assurance that that policy would be continued
if he won the election, because the majority of Republicans in
Congress were isolationists. Republicans would control at least the
House of Representatives, and they might well frustrate the policy
of such a maverick ex-Democrat and politically unseasoned President as Willkie. In the Democratic camp the choice was clearly
Roosevelt or one of the leaders identified with isolationism,
such as Farley and Garner, or Hull, who was supported by an anti-
New Deal group which was largely isolationist.

Weighing these chances, the President could not be sure that if
he did not run his policy would be repudiated after the inauguration, but he could be absolutely certain that it would at least be
in suspension between July and January. The immediate requirement of his program was that industry should rapidly go over to
armament production. In July the first contracts for the new program were let. Businessmen would naturally be very reluctant to
make commitments that risked their capital and their competitive
positions without assurance that the program would be followed
through. Still more, Congress, which showed encouraging signs of
supporting the President's program, still had to legislate in July
and August in favor of arms appropriations and Selective Service.
Relinquishment of the President's leadership would invite fac-
tional eruptions among which the legislation could very easily be
lost.

Great Britain expected invasion momentarily after the Fall of
France. Failure of Hitler actually to launch it is accounted one of
the mistakes which lost him the war. Churchill and Roosevelt
could not hope for a mistake. Roosevelt was arming the British
Home Guards with the surplus American guns and ammunition
of the First World War. The more difficult matter of reinforcing
the British squadrons of destroyers to hold the Channel against invasion with overage American ships hung fire because, as Roosevelt told Churchill on May 18, it would require the authorization
of Congress and the moment was not opportune.[1] The moment
became less opportune on June 28 when Congress inserted into
the Naval Appropriations Bill a constitutional monstrosity: an
amendment which gave the Army Chief of Staff and the Chief of

Naval Operations, the President's subordinates, vetoes over him. No item of military matériel could be turned over to a foreign government without their certification that it was not "essential" for the defense of the United States.

It was no time to quarrel with Congress over constitutional proprieties. Opinions could differ over what the word "essential" meant. Supporters of the administration in Congress had struck out of the amendment the original and more confining words that isolationist Senator David I. Walsh of Massachusetts had proposed. Following "essential to" he had written: "and cannot be used in" the defense of the United States. The intent of Congress in voting approval of the more lenient form was obvious. But the President did not care to ask the Chief of Naval Operations to certify that the destroyers, which were being recommissioned, were not "essential."

Hatching in the realm of Anglo-American collaboration, especially in the Roosevelt-Churchill correspondence, was the idea of a "horse-trade" whereby the United States would receive in exchange for the destroyers a string of naval bases obviously more "essential" to the defense of the United States than the destroyers, because they would immeasurably facilitate the Atlantic Patrol and the defense of North America. Churchill did not relish a trade in which Britain would be so ignominiously bested. It required extraordinary joint ingenuity and many messages to solve this impasse by September.

Beyond the questions of rearmament, arming the Home Guards, and destroyers to hold the Channel, the whole question of British payment for American equipment was thrown into doubt by Churchill in his May 15 letter. He warned Roosevelt that Britain was running out of cash with which to buy in the United States. The grand invention in international relations that provided the answer was the Lend Lease Act of March, 1941. Minds on both sides of the Atlantic were busy with the problem in June. If the will to solve it and the continuity and strength of influence necessary to carry the country and Congress along were subtracted from the White House in July, as it would be if Roosevelt gave away his leadership, the British cause seemed hopeless.

From the point of view of Democratic politicians, the great advantage of Roosevelt as a candidate was that he could win the election even against a formidable opponent like Willkie. It was the movement of public opinion in support of the President's foreign policy and leadership that brought the votes of delegates to him in the Convention. Certainly he had not played the patronage game effectively to win them; rather he had time and again offended politicians' standards of party regularity, most recently and grievously by appointing two Republicans to Cabinet offices.

Roosevelt regarded Willkie as the most effective opponent the Republicans could have named. Perhaps he had contributed to Willkie's success by the dismay his appointments of Stimson and Knox caused the isolationist majority of Republicans. Stimson believed the charge that Republican dismay had been calculated by Roosevelt was "true, in part." [2]

Announcement of the appointments was made on June 20, the eve of the Republican Convention, and it threw the Republican leaders into a futile rage. They read Stimson and Knox out of the Party, an absurd proceeding in the United States where party discipline is farcical anyway. The isolationist stalwarts were caught off guard, and their fuming increased their disadvantage. The younger and more international-minded men in the Party gained position and were able to stampede the Convention for Willkie. Roosevelt's well-timed action had helped capture the Republican Party itself for an advocate of his bipartisan foreign policy.

Willkie in a certain way reciprocated the favor. He ignored the third-term question until after the renomination, and challenged Roosevelt to beat him. He was widely reported as saying prior to the Democratic Convention, "Bring on The Champ!" Roosevelt did not like to evade a challenge.

During the process of making his final decision to accept nomination for a third term, the President consulted Secretary Hull. Farley has written that Hull was embittered because Roosevelt showed no appreciation of his work as Secretary of State, and because he told others he supported Hull for the Presidential nomination but failed to tell Hull himself. Farley pictures Hull as, nevertheless, anxious for the nomination early in May: " 'I can only put my trust in what the President is telling everyone, even if he does not see fit to confide that trust in me.' " This lends point to Farley's interpretation that Roosevelt deprived Hull of the Presidency.[3]

Hull's own account of his relations with Roosevelt, however, is quite different. He states again and again his gratification at the

President's many public and private expressions of appreciation for his work. He writes that prior to the Fall of France the President "in personal conversations with me and with some Democratic Party leaders, had indicated his expectation and wish that I should be his successor." Roosevelt made this statement to Hull "at repeated intervals" after October, 1938, when the primacy of foreign affairs made him turn against Hopkins as his choice for his successor. About June 20, 1940, the President again told Hull he wanted him to become the next President, and he gave Hull no indication he would accept nomination himself—"in fact, just the opposite." But, Hull writes, he did not desire the office and he had taken every step he could to make it clear he was not a candidate.[4]

Hull may be accepted as his own best witness. His *Memoirs* give no impression of any desire to write an encomium of Roosevelt. He is critical of many of the President's actions, but he agrees with all writers of reminiscences who remained loyal to Roosevelt that the President was candid and honorable in his dealings with his associates. Hull specifically denies the charge of Farley and others that Roosevelt used him as a buffer for his own candidacy. "I am sure . . . that he meant what he said to me. Not desiring the post [as Farley did desire it], I was in a better position to judge than otherwise."

Far from "depriving Hull of the Presidency," Roosevelt, according to longhand notes Hull made at the time, as late as July 3 in an intimate political conversation at luncheon, deferred to Hull by telling him his plan to announce publicly his retirement. "Thereupon, [Roosevelt] said, the convention would nominate me."

Hull told him such an announcement would not delay his nomination for a third term "by a split second," and in any case he did not want the nomination. Now, however, on July 3 for the first time Hull received the impression that Roosevelt would be a candidate for a third term. His "whole tone and language" were a "complete reversal" of what they had been ten days earlier.

This is the best obtainable evidence that Roosevelt decided to accept nomination for a third term sometime between the Fall of France and the early days of July. Hull takes it for granted that it was the war crisis that led the President to make his decision. He attributes to his own refusal to run the "not unnatural" efforts beginning in early 1940 of the President's strong partisans, especially the "extreme New Dealers," to make Roosevelt run for a third term.

Roosevelt then tried to win Hull over to accept the vice-presidential nomination. Hull declined to accept the "honorable and easy" office Jefferson had described as giving him "philosophical evenings in the winter, and rural days in the summer." Roosevelt pressed him again and again, but Hull would not budge.[5] Henry Wallace became the President's choice for Vice President because Hull refused.

The implications of Hull's account are clearly that Roosevelt was concerned first of all that an internationalist, rather than a Farley or a Garner, should be the Democratic candidate for President, and that he accepted nomination himself to prevent Hull's refusal from throwing the Convention over to the opponents of the administration and its policies. Roosevelt was often charged with so much egotism that he prevented any possible successor to himself as President from winning experience and prestige in the Democratic Party and the country. This was not true in the case of Hull. The Secretary of State had won public confidence in many areas of conservative opinion because he seemed a more "safe" conductor of foreign relations than his chief and in liberal circles because of his trade policy. There were definite differences between Roosevelt and Hull over methods of procedure in foreign relations. Roosevelt, nevertheless, not only retained Hull in the leading office in his administration but to the very end offered to support him for the Presidency in 1940.

Hull on his side endured stoically the many injuries to his function as Secretary of State which the President visited on him by dealing directly with Hull's subordinates, by giving to other departments and agencies authority over matters Hull regarded as within the proper sphere of the State Department, and by overruling Hull's cautioning advice in order to make bold excursions into foreign affairs. But both Roosevelt and Hull were, to use Hull's favorite expression, "broad-gauged" men—they knew how to subordinate minor differences in order to carry to success through collaboration the great enterprise of establishing internationalism as the foreign policy of the United States. They were statesmen, and, despite justified provocations from each other and rancorous attempts by small politicians to destroy their collaboration, they remained loyal to each other to the end.

## Conference with Farley

Hull represented the kind of Democrat that Roosevelt was willing to support for the Presidency. Farley and Garner did not. He had deferred to Hull, now he would have to thwart Farley and Garner.

Farley had sulked through the spring to let Roosevelt know that he disapproved his silence on the third-term issue. A few days after he saw Hull, the President, on July 7, called his political manager to Hyde Park. By that time all either one could hope for was to avoid an open quarrel. Both were frank. The President, according to Farley's account, was almost apologetic in his explanation that he could not issue a statement rejecting a third term on February 1, 1940, as they had agreed in July, 1939, that he would do, because it

"would have destroyed my effectiveness as the leader of the nation in the efforts of this country to cope with the terrible catastrophe raging in Europe. To have issued such a statement would have nullified my position in the world and would have handicapped the efforts of this country to be of constructive service in the war crisis."

Farley did not care for the explanation because, to him, the primary concern was the President's obligation to play the party game according to the traditional rules. As it was, he told the President

he had made it impossible for anyone else to be nominated, because by refusing to declare himself, he had prevented delegates from being elected for anyone except Garner and myself. Many states, I said, had declared for him because there was no other course open; that leaders were fearful they might be punished if they did not go along with him. Further, I added, I would not have waited until that late day to tell a person so intimately associated for twelve years, as I was with him. . . .

Even within his narrow world of party politics, Farley must have understood that the reason "there was no other course open" to state leaders than to declare for Roosevelt was because they knew the rank and file of Democratic voters wanted Roosevelt. Lacking that circumstance, they could not have feared "punishment" by a repudiated President—certainly not after Inauguration Day.

The President made it clear to Farley that he would formally free the delegates at the Convention, but that he would accept if he were nevertheless nominated. It is difficult to believe that he made no reference to the fate of his new policies should he do otherwise. Perhaps he did in words which Farley sums up with disparagement: "Now he reverted to his customary restless, rambling consideration of a problem, which so often reminded me of a pup worrying a slipper." Farley told him he would allow his own name to go before the Convention. In his own case he believed he was motivated by principle.

Roosevelt indicated he wished to avoid a break with his rivals for the nomination, that he hoped Farley would manage the campaign, and he asked whether Garner might not run again for Vice President. Farley replied that their opposition to a third term on principle forbade them.

They discussed the Party platform plank on foreign relations. Roosevelt suggested:

"We do not want to become involved in any foreign war.
"We are opposed to this country's participation in any wars, unless for the protection of the Western Hemisphere.
"We are in favor of extending aid to democracies in their struggle against totalitarian powers, within the law."

This plank was to be wrestled with at the Convention more than Roosevelt seemed to anticipate.

The two men parted with professions that nothing would be allowed to spoil their long friendship, and, remarkably enough, their break never produced public or private bitterness until Roosevelt had died and Farley wrote his memoirs with the aid of a *Chicago Tribune* reporter. In the meantime, Farley's sincere ideal of party loyalty forbade him to attempt to disrupt the Party.[6]

## Total Defense

Three days after this notable conference, the President sent a message to Congress asking additional Army and Navy appropriations of over two billion dollars and contract authorizations of over two and a half billions. This message, coming as it did a few days before the Democratic Convention opened in Chicago, contained passages obviously directed against critics of the President's armament and foreign policies. But unlike all such earlier statements, which had argued that he did *not* do *too much* to meet foreign danger, this one argued that he *had* done *enough*. This change was forced by the attempts of opponents to play upon public panic after the Fall of France with charges that the President had neglected the country's moral and military defenses. He reviewed the record to show that his warnings of increasing danger had unhappily been correct, whereas those who had called them mistaken had been, unhappily, wrong. He showed that his requests for rearmament measures had been closely related to the development of events.

In the contest, rapidly becoming heated, to win votes in the face of public panic over Hitler's arrival at the Atlantic, the President could not lose. Whether or not he had done *all* that might have been done, he had clearly done much *more* than had his chief opponents, the isolationists, who had always minimized the foreign danger and in Congress had most recently obstructed armament measures under the spell of "phony" war.

Roosevelt in this message of July 10 reaffirmed that, "We will not use our arms in a war of aggression; we will not send our men to take part in European wars." At the same time he declared that the threats to American security and institutions were increasing in number and gravity from week to week. He now demanded a program of "total defense." Charles A. Beard quotes the former passage and ignores the latter.[7] In the very paragraph which named the startling figure of almost five billion dollars, Roosevelt reiterated in even broader language the reason for its necessity: "It is because of the grave danger to democratic institutions." [8]

Only a voter unaware of the ambience of affairs could fail to know that these words related to the President's well-publicized sympathy for Britain and determination to extend aid to it. During the campaign that followed, many argued the question whether the Republican nominee was an internationalist, but it is not on record that anyone doubted Roosevelt's position.

## *The Battle Over the Platform*

At the same time, it is true that Roosevelt, from July to November, reduced to a minimum his statements of internationalist faith and purpose and maximized emphasis on the limits within which he proposed to pursue that faith. American political campaigns traditionally reduce policies and programs to the crudest possible verbiage, and the 1940 campaign revolved around the incantation, "Don't send our boys to fight in Europe." The Republicans were determined to make the public believe that Roosevelt plotted war, and he denied it flatly.

It would have been more statesmanlike to accompany each denial with a careful explanation that his policy of aid to Britain contained a risk of reprisals by the Axis. But an excellent justification for not emphasizing this was that the Axis obviously did not make war or refrain from making war according to old-fashioned rules, but purely and simply in pursuit of a reasoned series of steps designed to bring it control of the world without provoking too many victims to defense at once or too soon. Besides, Roosevelt loved a fight in the less rarefied arenas of politics too well to worry about refinements which his opponents were the first to violate. He was called a warmonger; he replied with flat denials.

The first battle in the Democratic Convention occurred in the deliberations of the Platform Committee. Roosevelt, according to Farley, wanted main emphasis on a denial of the "sending our boys" charge, coupled with affirmation of aid to the democracies. Harry Hopkins organized the Roosevelt forces. He installed a private telephone line from his bathroom in Chicago to the White House. Robert Sherwood is authority for the statement that Hopkins "assumed this job on his own initiative." He did it with "effrontery" and "ruthlessness" [9] that outdid the methods of the party bosses, who distrusted him as an amateur, and his behavior became a scandalous legend. It made him a political liability and he had to resign as Secretary of Commerce.

It does not appear that Hopkins busied himself with the problem of the foreign policy plank. Roosevelt told his friends that Senator James F. Byrnes of South Carolina, who had organized the Senate for repeal of the arms embargo in November, would again be in charge of strategy at Chicago, and this appears to have been the fact in the matter of foreign policy.[10]

The Democrats had the advantage of earlier action by the Republican Convention. The Republicans had adopted a platform that concentrated on criticism of the New Deal—not the laws that embodied it but administration inefficiency and waste in enforcing them. On foreign policy it declared against "involving this nation in foreign war." But the victory of the anti-isolationists was registered in a declaration in favor of the President's policy of aid to the Allies:

We favor the extension to all peoples fighting for liberty, or whose liberty is threatened, of such aid as shall not be in violation of international law or inconsistent with the requirements of our own national defense.

This was forthright in all but the phrase "international law," which failed to specify whether the Republicans adhered to pre- or post-Kellogg Pact conceptions of neutrality. Considering that Republican administrations were responsible for that Pact and other actions which, in the opinion of many competent authorities on international law, had repealed the old rules of neutrality, it might be expected that the Republican Platform of 1940 meant the phrase in terms of post-Kellogg. On the other hand, the isolationist majority of Republican leaders still clung to the older rules.

Besides those two declarations, the Republican Platform declared in favor of defense measures sufficient to guard the Americas and "uphold in war the Monroe Doctrine." The Roosevelt administration was blamed for unpreparedness and "consequent danger of involvement in war" with the implication that expenditures had been wasted on domestic boondoggling.[11]

With the Republicans on record as supporting the latest essentials of Roosevelt's policy, it would have been normal strategy for the Democrats to differentiate themselves before the voters by setting forth a stronger internationalist policy. Evidence as to the President's position is conflicting. Beard writes, on the basis of sources he was "not at liberty to disclose," that an unnamed Senator and an unnamed Cabinet member presented to the platform drafting subcommittee a plank which they asserted "came from the White House." It was strongly internationalist, opening with "a caustic denunciation of the Axis dictators" and closing with a call for universal mobilization of man power for defense. Isolationists, Beard writes, turned it down because it meant "nothing short of totalitarianism for the United States." [12] Senator Byrnes in his book *Speaking Frankly* has nothing to say of an "interventionist" plank coming from the White House.

Senator Burton K. Wheeler of Montana and others proposed a flat isolationist plank: "We will not participate in foreign wars and we will not send our armies, navies or air forces to fight in foreign lands outside the Americas." This was no more than the anti-war pledge the President had told Farley he favored if it was coupled with a promise of aid to the Allies.

The isolationist minority of the Democratic Party was heavily represented on the Convention's platform committee by Senators Burton K. Wheeler, David I. Walsh, and Pat McCarran. Senator Byrnes again worked to reconcile differences as he had in the arms embargo fight. The isolationists threatened to bolt the Convention unless their plank was adopted. Byrnes persuaded them to accept a proviso: "except in case of attack." He agreed with Hull that even with this proviso, the plank would encourage the Axis. But the alternative was a party split that would encourage the Axis governments even more. And, as Byrnes told Hull, everyone knew that, whether or not it was "attacked," the United States would not send armies abroad without a declaration of war by Congress. The President and Secretary Hull thereupon agreed.[13]

The Democratic Platform was more internationalist than the Republican. It did not hedge the promise of aid to the Allies with the ambiguous phrase "such as shall not be in violation of international law." It declared in favor of extension of "all the material aid at our command, consistent with law . . . to the end that peace and international good faith may yet emerge triumphant." Thus only domestic law would limit aid to the Allies, and obeisance was paid not to unspecified, contradictory codes of "international law," but rather to the ideal of "international good faith," that is, sanctity of treaties, including those which had revolutionized the obligations of neutrals.

Elsewhere the Platform specifically ruled out the "spirit of appeasement" of the Axis, and condemned "ruthless aggressors." No such disclaimer and condemnation appeared in the Republican Platform. Coupled with the proviso "except in case of attack" attached to the anti-war plank, these phrases shaded important distinctions between the two parties even after Willkie captured the Republican nomination.

Nevertheless the proviso "except in case of attack" seemed to pledge that Roosevelt would not ask Congress for a declaration of war short of some such attack as occurred at Pearl Harbor. That is the way in which Roosevelt interpreted it. It became not an "escape clause" which might free his hands, as Beard suggests, quoting Anne O'Hare McCormick that the word "attack" might "easily be extended to mean any assault on American interests," [14] but a straitjacket.

This was not merely because Roosevelt stuck at a narrow definition of "attack" but because, during the campaign, he was impelled by Willkie's horrendous accusations to deny them in oversimplified statements of his intentions. These denials haunted him during the months before Pearl Harbor.

## Formal Unanimity

When the Convention came to vote for nominees, the "unanimous draft" for which Hopkins and Byrnes had been working failed by a scattering of votes for Farley, Garner and Tydings of Maryland. But Farley, unlike Al Smith eight years earlier, pledged support of the party candidate and moved for nomination of Roosevelt by acclamation. The motion carried with a roar. Formally, at least, party unity was re-established by this gesture expressive of Farley's highest ideal, party loyalty.[15]

## The New Wallace

After Hull refused to accept nomination for vice president, Roosevelt turned to support Secretary of Agriculture Henry A. Wallace. His choice was determined by considerations intimately related to foreign policy. Only a few years earlier, Wallace's "availability" would have been fixed by his championship of the farmer. But in 1940 new turns in the intellectual position of the mercurial Secretary of Agriculture reduced his availability in the Farm Belt but increased it in other areas. With boom times in sight, the farmer remembered the irritations of bureaucratic operation of the Wallace programs for staple crop control and the ever-normal granary.

Wallace shifted his interest from the farmer to labor, urban groups, and racial minorities. He began to take leadership in the task of forging intellectual weapons against fascism abroad and at home. Whereas most internationalist leaders in positions of political responsibility, including Roosevelt, tended to lump fascism with traditional forms of tyranny, and appealed to traditional emotions to combat it, Wallace learned to understand the new elements that made fascism more dangerous to democracy than monarchy had ever been. He realized that these new elements were present in American society and he set out to combat them at home as well as abroad.

The result was a number of striking speeches that ranged far away from the normal preoccupations of a Secretary of Agriculture. A speech in February, 1939, called "The Genetic Basis of Democracy" drew upon the findings of the famous anthropologist, Dr. Franz Boas of Columbia University, and condemned not only Nazi racist doctrines but prevalent American attitudes towards Negroes, Jews, "poor whites," and the unemployed. Wallace said:

We must remember that down through the ages one of the most popular political devices has been to blame economic and other troubles on some minority group.

Superior ability is not the exclusive possession of any one race or any one class. It may arise anywhere, provided men are given the right opportunities.[16]

Such addresses made Wallace by 1940 the leading exponent of the urban radical and intellectual opposition to fascism abroad and reaction at home. They also made him a favorite target of haters of Roosevelt, the administration, the New Deal, and internationalism.

Roosevelt found the new Wallace refreshing and politically useful. He himself could not always speak out as bluntly as he wished against reactionaries and fascists. Wallace would help hold liberals, labor, and radicals in support of the administration during the new period when Roosevelt himself was sometimes required by the exigencies of foreign relations to offend them. The President thought also in terms of his successor if he should die. But he did not decide until after Cordell Hull refused the nomination and the situation in the Chicago Convention required drastic action.

After Roosevelt's nomination, the delegates became restless. The air was filled with charges of a "phony draft" because the methods of Hopkins were resented. Tension was high among supporters of the candidates for Vice President, most of whom were conservatives and isolationists. Secretary Perkins telephoned from Chicago to plead with the President to intervene. He decided for Wallace, saying:

"I like him. He is the kind of man I like to have around. He is good to work with and he knows a lot, you can trust his information. He digs to the bottom of things and gets the facts. He is honest as the day is long. He thinks right. He has the general ideas we have. He is the kind of man who can do something in politics. He can help the people with their political thinking. Yes, I think it had better be Wallace." [17]

Roosevelt telephoned Farley to ask support for Wallace. The Postmaster favored RFC Administrator Jesse Jones of Texas, the businessman's favorite official in the administration. Farley said Jones would strengthen business support. Roosevelt objected that Jones was "not in good health." Farley declared that Wallace would not help the ticket because "the people" looked upon him as a "mystic." Roosevelt answered: "He's not a mystic. He's a philosopher. He's got ideas. He thinks right. He'll help the people think." [18] It was evidently because Wallace would provide Americans with strong anti-fascist ideas, necessary for their understanding of the meaning of the war, that the President decided in favor of the new-fledged radical philosopher.

His choice angered many conservative, Southern, and isolationist delegates. They called Wallace a "Communist" and an "apostate Republican." They greeted his name with boos that filled millions of radio receivers. They shouted against "dictation from the White House." Roosevelt was angered and prepared a draft of a speech refusing the nomination.[19]

But the insurrection was short-lived. The possibility that Roosevelt would not run cowed party leaders, who knew the sentiment of voters. One after another, candidates withdrew until only Speaker of the House William Bankhead remained in the running against Wallace. The latter was nominated by a narrow margin. Hopkins roughly forbade Wallace to make an acceptance speech to the Convention for fear of the reception he would get. Hopkins bore the brunt of the delegates' resentment, and his resignation as Secretary of Commerce followed. Roosevelt rewarded him with higher opportunities for which he was better fitted.

The distortions of the situation were evidenced by prevalent opinion that the Convention was a victory for the "New Deal" faction of the Party. Actually it was a victory for the internationalist group, of which Hopkins and Wallace had become dynamic leaders so recently that they were understandably still identified with their earlier activities in domestic affairs. The isolationists Wheeler and Garner were roundly defeated.

The Convention was, however, a victory for the New Deal in a secondary sense because men like Wallace would not repudiate their progressive records, rather, following the President's lead, they placed reform second only to foreign affairs in importance. And the peculiar value of Wallace was that he would organize pressure to prevent the President from making compromises with conservatives. But like most doctrinaires, Wallace could also be a heavy liability because he did not know the moment for compromise or was too "idealistic" to listen when it struck.

## The Acceptance Speech

The President in his speech accepting the nomination recalled to the delegates and the country the primacy of foreign problems. He did not go out to Chicago but delivered to the Convention by radio an address which opened his campaign and gives evidence of how, prior to Willkie's violent attacks, he intended to conduct it. He ignored the Platform statements on foreign policy and showed he considered their subtleties insignificant compared with the positive determinations of his own developing policy.

This speech began with an explanation that he had refrained from making an earlier announcement of his opposition to a third term because it would have weakened efforts to prevent the spread of the war and to aid victims of aggression. Now he would regard it as his duty to serve if elected just as all other citizens would serve the nation if they were called. The world was dominated by the single fact of successful armed aggression aimed at the kind of society and government Americans had chosen and established for themselves. This aggression was a revolution not to set men free but to enslave them. In the face of this fact, every citizen's first obligation was to serve the defense of free institutions in whatever capacity the country found him useful.

He declared he would not be able to make an ordinary campaign. "But I shall never be loath to call the attention of the nation to deliberate or unwitting falsifications of fact, which are sometimes made by political candidates."

The task of safeguarding American institutions was twofold. It must be accomplished, "if it becomes necessary," by the armed forces and by making government "responsive to the growing requirements of modern democracy." In the latter effort, "we have covered much of the road." The Republican Platform did not call for the repeal of New Deal reforms, but for efficient administration of them by Republicans. Roosevelt did not think the people wanted the New Deal social gains "to be placed in the charge of those who would give them mere lip-service with no heart service." And voters would smile at charges of inefficiency against a government which had boldly met the enormous economic problems which "the great efficient bankers and industrialists of the Republican Party left in such hopeless chaos in the famous year 1933."

American social progress was also endangered from abroad by forms of government which some called " 'new and efficient.' " Roosevelt declared that these forms of government were not new but as old and tyrannical as the Pharaohs of Egypt, who also gave their slaves a type of security and efficiency. Americans would "never willingly descend to any form of this so-called security of efficiency which calls for the abandonment of other securities more vital to the dignity of man."

Roosevelt in these words related the efficiency promised by Republicans to the efficiency of Axis tyranny, but he did not identify them provocatively as he had in 1936.

On the side of foreign policy he made a more direct charge, declaring that if the government passed to other and inexperienced hands next January, "we can merely hope and pray that they will not substitute appeasement and compromise with those who seek to destroy all democracies everywhere, including here." Then he delivered a ringing affirmation of his policy without regard for the guarded terms of the Platform:

I would not undo, if I could, the efforts I made to prevent war from the moment it was threatened and to restrict the area of carnage, down to the last minute. I do not now soften the condemnation expressed by Secretary Hull and myself from time to time for acts of aggression that have wiped out ancient liberty-loving, peace-pursuing countries which had scrupulously maintained neutrality. I do not recant the sentiments of sympathy with all free peoples resisting such aggression, or begrudge the material aid that we have given to them. I do not regret my consistent endeavor to awaken this country to the menace for us and for all we hold dear.

I have pursued these efforts in the face of appeaser fifth columnists who charged me with hysteria and war-mongering. But I felt it my duty, my simple, plain, inescapable duty, to arouse my countrymen to the danger of the new forces let loose in the world.

So long as I am President, I will do all I can to insure that that foreign policy remain our foreign policy.

All that I have done to maintain the peace of this country and to prepare it morally, as well as physically, *for whatever contingencies may be in store,* I submit to the judgment of my countrymen.[20]

Charles A. Beard admits that in these striking words the President "manifested no inclination to make terms" with isolationists. This Beard regards as an exception to the President's usual assertions that his policy was peace. He writes that in this same speech the President also "manifested no inclination to . . . reaffirm his often-expressed resolve to keep the country out of war." [21] This apparently means that the President's words beginning "All that I have done to maintain the peace of this country. . . ." were elegiac, commemorative of a dead policy, and not to be construed as intended by Roosevelt to relate to the promise in the preceding paragraph that he would do all he could to insure that his past foreign policy would "remain our foreign policy." Beard would have the reader believe that Roosevelt intended to give notice that his policy was no longer peace but war.

This is another example of how Beard's contention that internationalism is a war policy leads him into weird violence against the plain record. When, as in the case of the 1940 acceptance speech, Beard does not butcher the record but admits that Roosevelt avowed an internationalist policy, he finds the President guilty of repudiating peace. He will not allow that Roosevelt at one and the same time worked for aid to the Allies, defeat of the Axis, and peace for the United States. Granted that if the future showed aid to the Allies to be insufficient for defeat of the Axis, the time might come when these objectives would be mutually contradictory, they were nevertheless embraced in 1940 by the majority of the American people and the Republican candidate, as well as by the Roosevelt administration, and, contradictory or not, they are in the record as Roosevelt's consistently announced aims. It is true, as Beard states, that later in the 1940 campaign Roosevelt was led by Willkie to appeal to the anti-war plank of his Party but, as will appear, even then he did not "categorically assure the country that the United States would stay out of the war." [22] All that Roosevelt could and did assure the country was that his administration would not *lead* the country into war, an entirely different matter.

During the summer and early fall, Roosevelt disavowed any direct participation in the campaign while he made short inspection tours of defense industries and activities. These public appearances were "non-political." This was a disingenuous way of giving the country an image of the Commander-in-Chief hard at work on levels high above the partisan battle. Wallace upheld the political cause more directly by lambasting the Republicans as the party of appeasement. He declared that the supporters of business appeasement of Germany were "the backbone, even though unwittingly, of the most dangerous of all fifth columns." [23] These charges stirred the administration's opponents, including Democratic isolationists, into angry denials and served the useful purpose of making appeasement and the slogan "We can do business with Hitler" political poison.

### Selective Service

The President himself had given Wallace his theme for the campaign. The defense tours dramatized his preoccupation with the world crisis, but his time was chiefly taken up with the Selective Service Bill and the Destroyers-Bases Deal. These, more meaningfully than the defense tours, demonstrated his refusal to suspend his national leadership for the sake of partisan victory.

It is a rule of American politics that an administration must not in the midst of a campaign for re-election propose controversial new actions in domestic or foreign affairs because they give too easy a chance for the opposition to appeal to fears with predictions that the untried new actions will bring dire disaster. Roosevelt's decision to make tests of his policy in Congress and in the country at large in the midst of his campaign for re-election was unprecedented. But he understood better than the politicians that the voters admired boldness in a sound cause, and his action made convincing his contention that strong and consistent leadership was necessary in the crisis. These were the weeks when the Nazis loosed blitzkrieg on Britain from the air, and Roosevelt chose Selective Service as the first long-range action, after rearmament and emergency aid to Britain, to fulfill Reynaud's prophecy that civilization would survive "because America exists."

A universal military draft in peacetime was unprecedented, and shocked instinctive American feeling that a standing army is undesirable. The idea had been proposed as early as the British disaster at Dunkirk. Grenville Clark, a Republican and an old friend of Roosevelt, wrote the first version of the Selective Service Bill and persuaded Senator Edward R. Burke, a conservative Democrat of Nebraska, and Representative James W. Wadsworth, a New York Republican, to sponsor it.

From Roosevelt's point of view, its bipartisan sponsorship made this Bill eminently satisfactory. He made an indirect commitment to it when he appointed Stimson Secretary of War. Indeed, Stimson attributed his appointment to Clark's initiative. Roosevelt avoided direct contact with Clark and his friends because he wished Congress to feel the weight of public rather than Executive demand. At the same time he avoided conflict with Congress on any other issue so that the air might remain clear for calm consideration and maximum influence in favor of Selective Service.

Wendell Willkie came out in favor of a draft law in his acceptance speech, calling it "the only democratic way in which to secure the trained and competent manpower we need for national defense." Public opinion polls showed a rapid increase in support of conscription. The President thereupon spoke in favor of the principle in his acceptance speech. He said that "some form of selection by draft is as necessary and fair today as it was in 1917 and 1918."

The public, particularly the section of it that was fond of calling Roosevelt a dictator, would have been surprised to know how carefully the President refrained from exerting pressure on Congress. Stimson and others knew that the President's influence was decisive and they urged him to exercise it. Roosevelt had learned that the very supremacy of his influence antagonized many politicians and conservatives, and he developed a special skill in waiting for the right moment and finding the right way to exercise it, which Stimson found "tantalizing" but extremely effective. On August 2 the President told reporters he would not lay himself open to charges of "ordering Congress," that since 1934 he avoided sending any "must" legislation to Congress, and that he would only recommend policies and objectives. He declared he favored Selective Service because training would save lives in case of war and the volunteer system led to enlistment of men needed in defense industry. The details were up to Congress.

The effect of this statement, Stimson later wrote, was immediate. It cut through the devices of isolationists in Congress who had given up attempting to block the Bill and were offering vitiating amendments. The House had approved Hamilton Fish's amendment to throw the entire responsibility for conscription during this election year on the President, by requiring him to call for volunteers, and empowering him to use the draft only if he failed to obtain volunteers. This amendment was defeated in conference.

A more difficult issue that became entangled with Selective Service was conscription of wealth. Roosevelt had often approved the principle of equal conscription of wealth and manpower in wartime. Proponents in Congress seemed most concerned to make a demagogic appeal to voters who might otherwise resent Selective Service. The Russell-Overton amendment gave the Secretaries of War and the Navy blanket powers to take over factories and other property they deemed necessary for defense. Insofar as it was needed, such power already existed along with safeguards against its arbitrary exercise.

This amendment supported charges that New Dealers lacked proper respect for property rights and were not to be trusted in the defense emergency. Wendell Willkie denounced it. He called on Roosevelt to state his position.

The issue was dangerous because in the fevered atmosphere of the campaign Roosevelt could not oppose the amendment without seeming to betray his own policy of treating men and property alike. But he knew that an ill-considered conscription of wealth would disrupt the defense program. He refused to commit himself on the amendment. This was consistent with his refusal to take sides on any question except the general principle of Selective Service. His position on the principle of equality of burdens he had made sufficiently clear in a special message to Congress on

July 1, which called for a "steeply graduated excess profits tax" on all individuals and corporations "so that a few do not gain from the sacrifices of the many." Such a tax was enacted in October. And the Russell-Overton amendment was amended in the House to prevent arbitrary seizures of property, whereupon the President accepted it with the Bill.

The President signed the Selective Service Act on September 16 after it passed Congress by substantial majorities. It called for registration of all males between the ages of twenty and thirty-six and selection by lottery for one year of training. Service was limited to the Western Hemisphere and possessions of the United States. The Act gave the President discretion in naming the day for registration. Fearful politicians, mindful of the hysteria in favor of "mothers" which was whipped up by isolationists, wanted the date postponed until after the election. In an act of great integrity, Roosevelt designated October 16.

Critics of Roosevelt "the dictator" found nothing to support them in his conduct of the Selective Service struggle. The law was plainly a bipartisan product. Adverse votes were more numerous among Republicans, but the measure was supported by the nationalist school of isolationism.

Selective Service was a victory for Roosevelt's policy which matched the repeal of the arms embargo. Bold leadership wisely exercised had encouraged the people and Congress to overcome panic and mobilize intelligently against dangers ahead. Roosevelt avoided some of his own earlier mistakes and the mistakes of President Wilson. In sharp contrast with the mob persecutions and vigilante activity whipped up by the spy scares and racial emotions of the First World War, the public temper in 1940 was sensible and restrained.

Roosevelt himself established this mood, for example, in a public letter to law enforcement officials on July 31. He pointed out that the chaotic hunt for subversives by many federal agencies in the First War was corrected by centralization of authority in the Federal Bureau of Investigation. Then he gave a warning that was remarkably well observed throughout the Second World War:

And the common defense should be through the normal channels of local, State and national law enforcement. The untrained policeman is as ineffective as the untrained soldier. The amateur detective soon becomes a fussy and malicious busybody. We must be vigilant, always on guard, and swift to act. But we must also be wise and cool-headed, and must not express our activities in the cruel stupidities of the vigilante. There is where the Fifth Columns form the line.[24]

The beginning of the blitz on London caused the President to set aside a day of national prayer. He channeled the horror and fear of Americans into moods of resolution and dedication in this proclamation which is one of the pieces of his prose that merits attention as literature:

The American heritage of individual freedom and of Government deriving its powers from the consent of the governed has from the time of the Fathers of our Republic been proudly transmitted to each succeeding generation, and to us of this generation has fallen the task of preserving it and transmitting it to the future. We are now engaged in a mighty effort to fortify that heritage.

Mindful of our duties in the family of nations, we have endeavored to prevent the outbreak and spread of war, and we have raised our voices against international injustice. As Americans and as lovers of freedom we are humbly sympathetic with those who are facing tribulation in lands across the seas.

When every succeeding day brings sad news of suffering and disaster abroad we are especially conscious of the Divine Power and of our dependence upon God's merciful guidance. . . .

NOW, THEREFORE, I, FRANKLIN D. ROOSEVELT, President of the United States of America, do hereby set aside Sunday, September 8, 1940, as a day of prayer; and I urge the people of the United States, of all creeds and denominations, to pray on that day, in their churches or at their homes, on the high seas or wherever they may be, beseeching the Ruler of the Universe to bless our Republic, to make us reverently grateful for our heritage and firm in its defense, and to grant to this land and to the troubled world a righteous, enduring peace.[25]

On the day before the appointed Sunday, the Selective Service Act passed Congress. On registration day the President spoke over the radio. He said sixteen million young Americans that day revived "the three-hundred-year-old American custom of the muster" proclaiming "the vitality of our history." They prepared once more for defense:

Calmly, without fear and without hysteria, but with clear determination. . . . To the sixteen million young men who register today, I

say that democracy is your cause—the cause of youth . . . the one form
of society which guarantees to every new generation of men the right
to imagine and to attempt to bring to pass a better world.[26]

These fortunate phrases set the tone for a successful mustering of
the nation's youth without need or desire for the mob action
against "draft dodgers," "slackers," and "yellow-bellies" that
marred proceedings in 1917.

## The Destroyers-Bases Deal

The President consistently declared the object of Selective Service to be defense. But he did not allow the country to forget that
his conception of defense was far broader than that of the isolationists. This was the largest part of the meaning of the Destroyers-
Bases Deal which he consummated on September 3, a few days before the passage of the Selective Service Act. In it the President
took a long step away from old conceptions of neutrality and made
the United States a "nonbelligerent" on the side of the victims of
aggression.

Aid to Britain prior to the Destroyers-Bases Deal was organized
with some respect for the old rules of neutrality which forbade a
"neutral" government to provide arms for a belligerent. The government traded with manufacturers old equipment, particularly
planes, for new equipment; or "surplus" guns were sold outright
to private companies. The private companies then sold planes,
guns and other material to Britain. But no such device was possible in the case of the destroyers Britain desperately needed, because the Chiefs of Staff could hardly call them "surplus" or not
"essential" to American defense.

Furthermore, the rules of international law which surrounded
the transfer of war vessels to a belligerent had been stricter than
the rules applied to any other matériel. The issue had been partially tested in June, 1940, when the Navy Department planned to
trade in to manufacturers, for sale to Britain, motor torpedo boats
and submarine chasers not yet completed in their yards. Isolationists criticized the deal as a sham. Roosevelt asked Attorney General Jackson for an opinion. Jackson found that a 1917 statute,
embodying international law of that period, expressly forbade
sending out of the United States any warship *built* with intent, or

under agreement, that it should be delivered to a belligerent.[27] The United States had required Britain to pay damages for violating this rule in the Civil War case of the *Alabama*. Roosevelt instructed the Navy Department to stop trade-in arrangements for the uncompleted warships.

Britain desperately needed naval reinforcement. Her losses increased during Hitler's tests of Channel defenses against invasion. Churchill added a peculiarly effective warning in various messages to Washington. He declared that the United States could not be certain of picking up the British fleet out of the debris of a successful invasion, that it was possible a Quisling British government would surrender the fleet to Germany, making the Axis powers masters of the seas. Furthermore, the Nazis would claim islands and naval bases. The strategic position of the United States would thus become extremely dangerous.[28]

Publicly, for fear of loss of morale at home and the effect on the enemy, Churchill could not hint of any remote possibility that Britain would ever be ruled by a Quisling or that the fleet might not fight to the end or escape to the New World. Privately, he warned the United States that unless its efforts joined with those of Britain were successful, the Nazis with the British fleet might defeat America before it began to fight. Nor could Roosevelt, for the same reasons, proclaim publicly this ultimate and strictly defensive justification for the urgency with which he sought methods to overcome obstacles in the way of giving Britain the destroyers.

During July the obstacles seemed to have prevailed. But American public opinion was awakening to the urgency of Britain's need for destroyers, and rapidly produced strong support. General Pershing, several retired Admirals, Senator Key Pittman, who had earlier opposed "futile encouragement" to Britain to fight on, and many other leaders came out in favor of giving her the destroyers. Petitions were sent to Washington, and the Gallup poll in August reported that 61 per cent of persons polled were favorable.[29] Churchill reopened the question in a letter to the President on July 31. He described Britain's need eloquently and specifically, and ended: "Mr. President, with great respect I must tell you that in the long history of the world this is a thing to do *now*." [30] Wendell Willkie was informed of the secret negotiations that followed and he agreed not to make a campaign issue of the deal.[31]

Early in August, Roosevelt and Hull proposed to Churchill and

Lord Lothian that the destroyers might be forthcoming in return for bases in British possessions around the United States. This scheme overcame obstacles in domestic American law because the bases were obviously more "essential" to American defense than the overage destroyers. Attorney General Jackson furthermore ruled that because the destroyers had not been *built* with intent to send them to a belligerent, the deal would be legal. While this might satisfy the American law, it did not overcome the objection in older rules of international law against a "neutral" government sending war vessels to a belligerent. Roosevelt's determination to send them anyway was a decisive act taking the United States beyond the old code and placing it under new rules derived from the doctrines of collective security.

Minor obstacles cropped up on both sides. Churchill wanted to give the United States the bases as a free gift because the deal, considered purely as a horse trade, was far too favorable to the United States for British taste. But this would prevent the American Chiefs of Staff from agreeing that the United States received at least as much "essential" defense value as it gave. Roosevelt solved this dilemma by proposing that Britain should give the United States the two most important bases, at Newfoundland and Bermuda, as gifts, and the other six, in the Bahamas, Jamaica, St. Lucia, Trinidad, Antigua and British Guiana, in exchange for the fifty destroyers.

Roosevelt, on his side, wished to dissipate so far as possible the nightmare Churchill had projected of the British fleet turned over by a British Quisling to the Nazis. Churchill at first refused any declaration because it would injure morale and, moreover, might permit the United States to state that a moment had arrived when the fleet should go to America. He wished the United States to realize it could have no part in British decisions without entry into a war alliance. But late in August Churchill offered Roosevelt a formula whereby he declared a statement of his own in Parliament on June 4, 1940, that Britain would never surrender or scuttle her fleet, to represent "the settled policy of His Majesty's Government," and added, "I must, however, observe that these hypothetical contingencies seem more likely to concern the German Fleet or what is left of it than our own." Thus Churchill used his public policy to wipe out the private warning he had delivered to Roosevelt.

The President announced on August 16 that negotiations were going forward for the acquisition of British air and naval bases.

Churchill confirmed this and uttered remarkable words to Commons on August 20:

> Undoubtedly this process means that these two great organisations of the English-speaking democracies, the British Empire and the United States, will have to be somewhat mixed up together in some of their affairs for mutual and general advantage. For my own part, looking out upon the future, I do not view the process with any misgivings. I could not stop it if I wished; no one can stop it. Like the Mississippi, it just keeps rolling along. Let it roll. Let it roll on—full flood, inexorable, irresistible, benignant, to broader lands and better days.[32]

American isolationists were certain Churchill presaged absorption of the United States into the British Empire. And any critic might raise a question about the rather narrow "English-speaking" setting in which Churchill placed Anglo-American cooperation. But the cause of internationalism in 1940 depended for its life on this cooperation; Churchill, a great traditionalist, exploited to the full Anglo-American cultural-ideological ties; and no one can be certain that it was merely coincidence when the two powers with common culture and traditions of liberty and democracy brought the cause of internationalism to life after all the other great powers had betrayed it.

For Roosevelt the final question was whether the agreement must or should be submitted to Congress for approval. Jackson ruled that the Constitution permitted the President as Commander-in-Chief to make the arrangement in an executive agreement without the approval of the Senate required for treaties, because the subject matter, maintenance of the nation's defenses at their highest efficiency, was one over which the Constitution gave the Executive exclusive authority. Furthermore, world conditions forbade the Executive to risk any delay that was constitutionally avoidable.

On September 2 the Destroyers-Bases Deal was completed by exchange of letters and the next day it was announced to the world. Criticism in America was directed chiefly at the failure to secure prior approval of the Senate or Congress. Willkie approved the bargain but seized on the method, which he declared "the most dictatorial action ever taken by any President." This was extreme; the Destroyers-Bases Deal hardly matched President Lincoln's suspension of the writ of habeas corpus without the consent of Congress which the Constitution expressly requires.

But Roosevelt's defense was feeble; in fact, it was mistaken. He told the press he acted as President Jefferson did when he bought Louisiana: "There was never any treaty, there was never any two-thirds vote in the Senate." This was perhaps the only case when Roosevelt's knowledge of history failed him. Jefferson had in fact submitted the Louisiana Purchase Treaty to the Senate and did obtain an almost unanimous vote of approval. What Jefferson did not do was ask for the constitutional amendment to empower Senate and Executive to purchase territory which, according to his own "strict construction" views, should have preceded such a treaty of annexation. Jackson's opinion, however, provided sound ground for Roosevelt's procedure, and it was available to the public.

The Deal was called by some "an act of war" and Hitler could have regarded it as such if he had been addicted to the niceties of the older international code he had done so much to destroy. But other considerations determined Hitler's policy, as Roosevelt well understood. On the whole, the American public approved the Deal and this, too, Roosevelt had carefully calculated before he acted.[33]

## Hemispheric Solidarity in Action

Besides Selective Service and the Destroyers-Bases Deal, the Roosevelt administration during the election campaign strengthened hemispheric solidarity in two striking acts. Shortly after the Fall of France, Hull had invited the Canadian government to send army and naval officers to Washington for discussions of joint defense problems. President Roosevelt met Prime Minister Mackenzie King near the Canadian border and they signed, on August 18, the Ogdensburg Agreement. This provided for establishment of the Permanent Joint Board on Defense to study problems of the defense of the northern half of the Western Hemisphere.[34] This organization in 1941 planned delivery of Lend Lease cargoes to Britain.

The problem of Latin America was more difficult. The danger that the Nazis would occupy the American possessions of nations Germany had conquered was pressing. Within hours after the French request for armistice terms, Hull invited the Latin American republics to a conference in Havana. He himself headed the United States delegation. The Conference opened on July 22 in a highly charged atmosphere. Hull feared that even if Hitler did not take American territory, against which the United States had warned him, the Nazis through subversive activity and dazzling promises would win control over one or more American governments and break the solidarity of the hemisphere.

Out of the need of the moment came a remarkable instrumentation of the Good Neighbor policy, which completed the multilateralization of the Monroe Doctrine. This was the idea and the method of collective trusteeship proposed by Hull and embodied in the Act of Havana. Under it the no-transfer corollary of the Monroe Doctrine would be enforced against aggression from outside the hemisphere, not by the United States alone, but by all the republics joining to take temporary possession of and defend a threatened colony. Argentina, as usual, led the opposition to the United States proposal. Hull appealed directly to President Ortiz of Argentina for cooperation and thereby won unanimous approval for his policy.

The Act of Havana established a committee authorized to assume the administration of any threatened colony. In case of emergency, any republic or group of republics could act. The latter procedure was used by the United States and Brazil late in 1941 when Nazi activities became dangerous in Dutch Guiana, whose bauxite was essential to American aluminum production. Thus the theory of the Good Neighbor became practice in one more significant area of action.[35] The Act of Havana was bolstered by two more inter-American agreements strengthening activities to counter Axis subversion and increasing United States purchases of Latin American export surpluses in order to remove temptations to cooperate with the Axis.[36]

The military defenses of Latin American republics were strengthened by the United States under the terms of the Pittman Resolution of June 15, 1940. It provided a scheme somewhat like that of the Lend Lease Act, and was an ancestor of that famous law.[37] The willingness of the United States to build up the military as well as economic strength of Latin America was helpful in overcoming old fears of the Yankee colossus. And the administration on these levels, as on the political level, worked out first for Latin America the policies Roosevelt would apply to the whole world.

A significant aspect of the Ogdensburg and Havana Agreements is that the Roosevelt administration did not need to reverse or invent policies to meet the emergency of the Fall of France. The Agreements were logical culminations of policies of international cooperation initiated by Roosevelt before the rise of the Axis and consistently developed during the years before the outbreak of war. That they could so readily be carried forward to meet the emergency that did occur, and provided the highest degree of hemispheric security the United States had ever enjoyed, was a measure of the value of internationalism as it was conceived and practiced by the Roosevelt administration. By the time that Britain entered the ordeal of September, 1940, the United States had established a working system of collective security among the governments of the Western Hemisphere, and the policy of aid to Britain linked this system to the Old World. In this way, the Roosevelt administration put into practice new formulas of international cooperation so necessary and sensible that isolationists could not object. They were driven to make a last ditch stand on the issue of "sending our boys to fight in European wars."

### Britain Closes the Burma Road

A curiosity of the isolationist position was that very little fear was expressed of Americans fighting in Asiatic wars. Perhaps this was because the United States position in Asia had some of the color of imperialism. American businessmen felt the competition of Japan for markets more keenly than that of the other Axis nations. Cartel agreements were more numerous between large American corporations and potential competitors in Germany than in Japan. Isolationists in general believed that if the United States had an enemy outside the Hemisphere, that enemy was not Germany but Japan.

Roosevelt and Hull, on the contrary, believing as they did that the Axis threat to American democracy was more significant than its threat to American markets, placed Germany first on the list of American enemies. At the same time they carefully avoided appeasement of Japan. They tried to piece out the weakness of United States policy in Asia by holding the fleet at Pearl Harbor and by keeping the Japanese government in a state of doubt regarding future American actions.

The Japanese government saw Hitler's attack on Western Europe as, in Hull's words, Japan's "golden chance" to make aggressive gains while Europe and America were preoccupied. Immediately after the invasion of Norway, Foreign Minister Arita stated that

Japan was bound in intimate economic relationships with the South Seas, especially the Netherlands East Indies, and that his government was deeply concerned over any development of hostilities in Europe which might affect their position. The French government suggested to the United States and Britain a joint representation to Japan calling attention to the 1921 Four-Power Treaty in which Japan together with the three democratic powers had promised to respect the *status quo* in the Pacific.

Hull objected. He feared a joint action would bring reprisals. Instead he proposed individual action. He sent a strong statement to Japan pointing out that not only Japan but many nations, including the United States, were interested in maintaining the *status quo* in the NEI. He told the Japanese Ambassador that Japan's so-called Monroe Doctrine for Asia and the American Monroe Doctrine resembled each other no more than black and white.

The rich Dutch islands were suddenly orphaned by Hitler's conquest of their mother country. Hull opposed Allied as well as Japanese occupation, unless it was at the request of the Dutch authorities. Hull obtained approval from Britain for a statement on May 11 in which he pointed again to the four governments' promises to respect the *status quo* of the NEI. His only weapon was words, and he valiantly declared that the promises "cannot be too often reiterated." Privately he repelled attempts by the Japanese Ambassador to make a pretext for occupation of the NEI out of the visit of a few French and British troops to Dutch Guiana.

As the situation in Europe moved towards disaster and the Roosevelt administration decided to support Britain, Hull tried to hold off the Japanese by a long round of discussions between Ambassador Grew and Arita in Tokyo. Arita wanted at least a fixed *modus vivendi* as a substitute for the abrogated Japanese-American commercial treaty. He asked the United States to cease aiding China and to recognize "new conditions" there. He held out as bait a chance for the United States to help Japan "reconstruct China." Hull, despite the European crisis, clung to the policy of refusing to appease Japan. He countered Arita with proposals to exchange notes guaranteeing the *status quo* of Asiatic possessions of European belligerents and to consult should any question arise regarding them. Arita rejected these proposals.

Japan was engaged in economic negotiations with the NEI authorities which might give her control over strategic materials and include the islands in her "co-prosperity sphere" without the necessity of military occupation. Hull brought direct pressure to bear on the NEI government to resist vassalage to Japan. This had some effect in making the economic concessions which Japan obtained very slight.

The United States failed completely in the case of French Indo-China. Like Mussolini in jackal instinct, the Japanese government demanded of France, on the very day Pétain asked Hitler for armistice terms, that the railroad from Indo-China to China be closed and Japanese "inspectors" be allowed to enforce the order. The Pétain government, unlike the Dutch, gave in to Japan without a struggle. It further broke the front of powers opposing Japan by signing the sort of agreement that Japan wanted with all the powers. It recognized Japan's "special rights" in China.

Alarming signs appeared that Britain might join France in appeasing Japan. British and French banks at Tientsin turned over to the Japanese silver belonging to the Chinese government. Japan eagerly demanded that Britain withdraw her troops from Shanghai and close the Hong Kong and Burma frontiers to stop supplies going to China. The British, hourly expecting invasion by Hitler, felt compelled, as Lothian told Hull, to "reconsider" their policy in the Far East. Lothian said that if the United States did not take up some of the burden by embargoing exports to Japan, or by sending warships to Singapore—steps that admittedly might result in war—Britain would have to negotiate a full settlement with Japan. The Australian Minister to the United States, Richard A. Casey, joined Lothian on June 27 in presenting these alternatives to Hull.

Hull consulted Roosevelt. Their precarious policy of avoiding both appeasement and acts which might lead to war was now challenged by the only remaining friendly great power in the Far East. Still they clung to it. Hull answered Lothian that, on the one hand, the United States would not take any actions which would involve serious risk of war with Japan, and, on the other, it had nothing tangible to offer Japan and refused to offer her concessions at the expense of other countries. Lothian asked whether the United States would object to Britain and Australia trying to bring peace between Japan and China. Hull answered that the United States would have no occasion to object; but he warned that Britain must not offer Japan properties or interests belonging to China. Appeasement in any case would be futile because it would not guarantee Japanese behavior in the future. "Acquiescence" in Japanese depredations might be necessary but not positive "assent" to them.

The British government believed, however, that even "acquiescence" would not prevent Japan from attacking Britain immediately and imposing a global war on her which she could not possibly sustain. This judgment is difficult to dispute because, perhaps, no other nation ever had so much to defend as Britain, and so little with which to defend it. Therefore, Britain turned towards appeasement of Japan. The United States persisted in its "neither-nor" policy, within which was barely discernible a process of strengthening, at glacier-like pace, measures of opposition to Japan. Thus, as Hull later wrote, the parallel lines on which Britain and the United States had been acting in relation to Japan began to diverge in the summer of 1940.

Lothian, on July 12, told Hull that Britain, to stave off a declaration of war by Japan, would close the Burma Road during the three monnths of rainy season either to all traffic to China, or to military supplies only, and in the latter case would attempt a settlement of the Sino-Japanese war. Hull expressed "real regret and disappointment" because closing the Burma Road would deal China a heavy blow and injure the "international commerce" of the United States. The latter complaint was the only one Hull made public on July 16, two days after Britain announced closing of the Burma Road and the Hong Kong frontier to war materials for three months during negotiations with Japan.

## The Futility of Appeasement

Lothian had asked Hull for a public statement showing sympathy for Britain's difficult situation and hope for a permanent settlement. Hull instead publicly objected to "unwarranted interpositions of obstacles to world trade." Public sentiment in both Britain and the United States was largely unfavorable to Churchill's strange assumption of the role of "appeaser." Hull's prediction of the futility of appeasement was immediately borne out. Within a few days after Japan's diplomatic victory over Britain, Prince Konoye returned to power as Prime Minister and proceeded to liquidate Japanese political parties, the sources, he said, of "the evils of liberty, democracy, and socialism." He proclaimed that Japan would henceforth "stabilize" not only Manchuria and China, but French Indo-China and the NEI. The new Foreign Minister was Yosuke Matsuoka. Hull considered him to be "as crooked as a basket of fishhooks." Matsuoka turned to "strengthen" Japan's foreign position by an alliance with Germany and Italy. This was Japan's answer to Churchill's hope for settlement.

At the time of the Anglo-Japanese Burma Road Agreement, Roosevelt and Hull already had in hand a device to strengthen the embargo against Japan without directly affronting that country. On July 2, Roosevelt had signed an act authorizing the President to regulate by license, or to prohibit, the export of any commodities essential to national defense. Immediately he prescribed license control for exports of some forty basic war materials and products. This did not touch the oil, scrap steel and iron, or tetraethyl lead for aviation gasoline which Japan most needed from the United States. But the possibility of stopping exports of these items to Japan, which would be incidental to an embargo against their going to any country, must have been present in the minds of British and American leaders when Lothian asked the United States for an embargo as an alternative to appeasement. Lothian, however, had asked for a "political" embargo against Japan of the sort which would be much more of an affront likely to provoke war than action under the law of July which would be directed against Japan only incidentally. A "political" embargo with risk of war was precisely what Roosevelt and Hull were determined to avoid. Churchill in his memoirs frankly writes that Britain at this time wished the United States to enter the war.

As it was, Roosevelt and Hull proceeded to strengthen their "nonpolitical" embargo of Japan after the Burma Road Agreement. On July 26, the President proclaimed licensing regulations of exports of oil, iron and steel scrap and tetraethyl lead, and on July 31, the Administrator of Export Control forbade the export of aviation gasoline to countries outside the Western Hemisphere. To this extent the moral embargo of December, 1939, against Japan was now legally enforced. The American public was gratified. But for another year the embargo was not strictly enforced.

The Japanese Ambassador had been informed that the new measures were taken solely in the interest of national defense. On August 3 he nevertheless protested them. But neither government issued any official statement. The procedure brilliantly illustrated the administration policy of strengthening opposition to Japan within the narrow framework of "neither provocation nor appeasement."

At the same time it was true that in the Far East, where the isolationists were more ready for strong measures than in Europe, the Roosevelt administration failed to organize a united front with Britain against the aggressions of Japan. In the summer of 1940, Britain could reasonably expect that the United States should take the lead in actions which principles of collective security required. Roosevelt and Hull clung to the policy of no provocation, strengthened the embargo against Japan unilaterally and "inoffensively," and scolded Britain for turning to appeasement. Their policy had no more effect than Britain's in restraining Japan. Their best justification was that they gained time both for rearmament and for concentration on aid to Britain. And it was of indisputable moral value that they did not break the American record of refusal to appease an aggressor.

With Britain and the United States acting on divergent policies, Japan proceeded to exploit Hitler's victory over France. Hull found himself in direct competition with Hitler in pressing the Vichy government to resist Japanese demands. Japan held the whip hand because it refused to sign the Axis military alliance until Hitler forced Vichy to turn over French Indo-China to Japan. Hitler in turn wanted this alliance as a club to threaten the United States with a Pacific war and thereby reduce the aid it would send to Britain. Beyond this consideration, Hitler himself had intended to take over possessions of the Netherlands and France in the Far East, but defeat in the Battle of Britain forced him to concede to Japan.

Vichy kept the United States in ignorance of its agreement to turn over Indo-China to Japan for almost a month, until September 22. Five days later Berlin, Rome, and Tokyo announced signature of a military alliance directed against the United States. Article three provided for mutual assistance by all means when any one should be "attacked" by a power at present not involved in the European or Asiatic wars. Translated from Axis verbiage, this meant mutual assistance if and when one of the Axis partners should attack the United States. Other clauses provided mutual recognition of Germany's and Italy's leadership in establishing the "new order" in Europe and Japan's in Asia. Hull made a public statement that the alliance merely admitted a relationship which had long existed. He told the British Ambassador it represented Hitler's anxiety to divert attention from his failure to invade Britain. Churchill in his memoirs names the night of September 15, 1940, as the turning point in the Battle of Britain. Two days later Hitler postponed the invasion indefinitely. Hitler's new policy was to destroy Russia and divert the United States into a Pacific war before dealing final blows against Britain.

American aid to Britain, Selective Service, and the Destroyers-Bases Deal led Hitler to foment a Pacific war against the United States as part of a new, long-range campaign against Britain. Hull in his memoirs declares that the American administration understood, at the time, Hitler's unwillingness to support Japan until he was checkmated in the Battle of Britain—that, in short, the Axis military alliance was a product of German weakness rather than strength. It was an admission by Germany and Japan that they expected long wars with Britain and China, in which United States aid to their enemies could be decisive. It was an attempt to frighten the United States into abandoning its policy.

Understanding this, Roosevelt and Hull in an important conference on October 5, far from being cowed by the alliance, decided to increase aid to Britain and China, increase the tempo of American armament, and increase the effectiveness of the embargo against Japan. Roosevelt told an audience on October 12 in Dayton, Ohio, that "the Americas will not be scared or threatened into the ways the dictators want us to follow. . . . No combination of dictator countries of Europe and Asia will stop the help we are giving to almost the last free people now fighting to hold them at bay." [38]

The administration strengthened the embargo against Japan on October 16 by restricting exports of iron and steel scrap to countries of the Western Hemisphere. A new loan to China of $25,000,000, to be repaid with tungsten, was announced on October 15. Hull did not specifically promise public support of Britain when it reopened the Burma Road, but he told Lothian the United States would design its policy in the Far East on the basis of most effective aid to Britain in winning the war. And he held conversations with Lothian and Casey to lay the basis for exchange of information by staff officers of the United States, Britain, Australia, New Zealand, and the NEI regarding forces available to resist a Japanese attack.

The Japanese protested the iron and steel scrap embargo. Hull answered with a blistering condemnation of Japan's course. This was reinforced by a State Department announcement advising all Americans to leave the Orient and by dispatch of three liners to evacuate them. But the administration refused the invitations of Britain (backed by a Churchill letter to Roosevelt) and Australia to base the American Asiatic fleet at Singapore and to send a naval good-will mission to Australia. Nevertheless, the American response to the Axis alliance seemed to Hull to cause Japan to pause temporarily, giving the United States and Britain more of their most precious defense commodity, time. Churchill believed Hitler's failure to invade Britain had more to do with Japan's hesitation.[39]

So matters stood during the American presidential election. Towards Japan, as in other spheres, the administration had strengthened its policy in the midst of the campaign. Isolationists hit upon the possibility of American naval cooperation with Britain at Singapore as their chief target in the administration's Far Eastern policy, but this possibility had been fended off by the administration.

## Down to the Hustings

During the presidential campaign, the administration's actions in the foreign sphere spoke louder than Roosevelt's campaign speeches, with one glaring exception. In spite of this exception, which will presently be discussed, no one doubted that Roosevelt stood for maximum measures against the Axis short of war, and that the Republican Party, if not Willkie himself, favored a less advanced position. The degeneration of the campaign into a competition for the anti-war vote did not lead Republican isolationists to vote for Roosevelt. But Willkie's vigorous championship of aid to Britain, repudiation of appeasement, and charge that Roosevelt took dangerous chances and uselessly antagonized the Axis did seem to bring some internationalist-minded voters to his side without loss of the isolationist vote.

Fear of this was one thing that led Roosevelt to suspend his elevated role of Commander-in-Chief touring defense projects and, during the last two weeks before Election Day, go down to the hustings. Another was that he feared Willkie more than any of his earlier rivals for office and found it difficult to cope with Willkie's fervent and confused attacks. Willkie, for example, accused him of planning to send troops abroad immediately and also of having neglected the country's defenses so shamelessly that it had no means to fight if attacked. Willkie's earnestness and colorful personality captured the public imagination. He later told a Senate Committee that his most hysterical charge against Roosevelt, that he was plotting to send American boys to the shambles of the European trenches by April, 1941, was a "bit of campaign oratory." Roosevelt could not similarly laugh off his statements once the campaign was past, and he did not attempt to match Willkie's tactics of terrorizing voters; but Willkie did lead him to oversimplify his foreign policy in order to throw off the charge of warmongering and to retain the support of the isolationist minority of the Democratic Party.

Still his first oversimplification was not so "equivocal" as Robert Sherwood in his book *Roosevelt and Hopkins* declares. Sherwood writes that in the Madison Square Garden Speech on October 28,

Roosevelt went to the length or depth of taking credit for the Neutrality Law and other measures which he had thoroughly disapproved and had fought to repel and had contrived by all possible means to circumvent.[40]

Actually Roosevelt only took credit for certain clauses of the Neutrality Act, but not for the arms embargo. The "other measures" Sherwood refers to were evidently the specified clauses of the Neutrality Act itself. Roosevelt said:

We made it possible [by the Neutrality Act] to prohibit American citizens from traveling on vessels belonging to countries at war. . . .

We made it clear that American investors, who put their money into enterprises in foreign nations, could not call on American warships or American soldiers to bail out their investments. . . .

We made it clear that ships flying the American flag could not carry munitions to a belligerent; and that they must stay out of war zones. . . .

In all these ways we made it clear to every American, and to every foreign nation that we would avoid becoming entangled *through some episode beyond our borders.*

It was a fact, as has been shown in this book, that Roosevelt and Hull had consistently proposed and supported these measures. What they *had* opposed was that other clause of the Neutrality Act which provided for an arms embargo on aggressors and victims alike. Neither in the Garden speech nor at any other time did Roosevelt "take credit" for the arms embargo. On the contrary, he took credit in the Garden speech for repeal of the embargo and belabored the Republicans for opposing repeal in Congress:

> The Republican campaign orators and leaders are all now yelling "me too" on help to Britain. But this fall they had their chance to vote to give aid to Britain and other democracies—and they turned it down.
> This chance came when I recommended that the Congress repeal the embargo on the shipment of armaments and munitions to nations at war, and permit such shipment on a "cash-and-carry basis." It is only because of the repeal of the embargo law that we have been able to sell planes and ships and guns and munitions to victims of aggression.
> But how did the Republicans vote on the repeal of that embargo?
> In the Senate the Republicans voted fourteen to six against it. In the House the Republicans voted one hundred and forty to nineteen against it. . . .
> Great Britain and a lot of other nations would never have received one ounce of help from us—if the decision had been left to Martin, Barton and Fish.[41]

The President did not stress that he had signed the 1935 and 1937 Neutrality Acts even though they included the arms embargo. But he had already publicly expressed regret for ever approving the arms embargo, and perhaps it was forgivable that he did not repeat that confession in a campaign speech.

In the Garden speech he was interested in contrasting examples of Republican "mistakes" with the administration record, a normal partisan procedure. The facts of Republican majority opposition to rearmament and support of the arms embargo contrasted fairly with the administration record, and Republican complaints after the Fall of France that the administration had not gone even farther in pursuit of the policies Republicans had tried to obstruct made the records of Congressmen "Martin, Barton and Fish" fair game for Roosevelt. He simplified, but did not "equivocate" on his own record. Willkie said later: "When I heard the President hang the isolationist votes of Martin, Barton and Fish on me, and get away with it, I knew I was licked." [42] The President "got away with it" for the same reason Republican orators got away with blaming Roosevelt for the acts of other members of his party and administration. If Willkie felt it was unfair to "hang isolationist votes" on him, voters were bound to be concerned over the certainty that if the Republicans won the election in 1940, Hamilton Fish of New York would, as the President warned in his Garden speech, become Chairman of the House Committee on Foreign Affairs. [43]

Roosevelt enjoyed a legitimate debater's triumph when he read to roaring crowds the Republican record of votes in Congress on policies they now claimed to support. The discrepancies he most stressed involved rearmament and aid to Britain. Although Willkie and the Party Platform proclaimed a Republican change of heart on these issues, isolationist Republican Congressmen did not do so. Roosevelt illustrated in his Boston speech the ability of Republican Congressmen to ignore the Party Platform:

> For listen to this: Last summer, only a few weeks after the Republican National Platform had been adopted endorsing commodity loans for the farmers, the Republican members of the House marched right back into the Halls of Congress and voted against commodity loans for the farmers, 106 to 37. [44]

To counterbalance such evidence of Republican equivocation, Willkie found the President guilty of violating his campaign promises of 1932 to balance the federal budget and provide "sound money." This was the main Republican indictment of the administration's record. Willkie linked it with his accusation that the President in 1940 plotted war:

> I ask you whether his pledge for peace is going to last any longer than his pledge for sound money.
> On the basis of his past performances with pledges to the people, you may expect we will be at war by April, 1941, if he is elected. [45]

Roosevelt in 1932 had been challenged to explain how he could balance the federal budget and provide the federal relief to the unemployed which he also promised. He had answered that he was "utterly unwilling that economy should be practiced at the expense of starving people." [46] Nor was the managed currency system he had installed synonymous with "unsound money." The Roosevelt record was not as vulnerable to this kind of attack as the record of the majority of Republican Congressmen and Senators.

Roosevelt's most famous "oversimplification" came on October 30 in Boston when he said to "the mothers and fathers":

> I have said this before, but I shall say it again and again and again:
> Your boys are not going to be sent into any foreign wars. . . .
> The purpose of our defense is defense.[47]

It could hardly be thought he lied regarding his intentions. But the whole truth required more complex formulations than those "plain" words. Defense of the United States as Roosevelt conceived it required a strategy of cooperation with one group of belligerents to prevent the other from winning the war. Such cooperation made the question of attack on the United States pertinent to discussion. The President often reaffirmed his determination to aid the Allies and China, but he did not always qualify his promises to the "fathers and mothers" with the Platform clause "except in case of attack." On this occasion he had been urged to include the clause once more, but he had refused, saying: "Of course we'll fight if we're attacked. If somebody attacks us, then it isn't a foreign war, is it? Or do they want me to guarantee that our troops will be sent into battle only in the event of another Civil War?" [48]

It was a fair assumption that the "unneutral" acts of the United States would not be the determining factor in an Axis decision to attack the United States, but such acts would be likely to determine an earlier date for an attack. Neither Willkie nor Roosevelt took up such delicate calculations.

Willkie promised to outdo Roosevelt in aid to Britain and equally ignored possible effects on Axis policy. Both Willkie and Roosevelt reflected the determination of the great majority of Americans to help defeat the Axis, short of participation in the war, while thinking as little as possible of the likelihood that the Axis would not acquiesce in defeat on America's terms.

Robert Sherwood has written from first-hand experience of the hysterical letters and telegrams that flooded the White House and Democratic Headquarters in response to Willkie's turn, late in October, from support of the bipartisan foreign policy to charges that Roosevelt plotted war. It seemed to the President's advisers that, after the failure of the Axis alliance to frighten Americans, Willkie was attempting to terrorize them into a "stampede along the road which led to Bordeaux and so to Vichy even before the Panzers arrived on our home soil. . . ." Sherwood confesses that it was he who, on the presidential train to Boston on October 30, the day Willkie in Baltimore made his prophecy of war by April if Roosevelt was elected, and to satisfy urgent pleas from the mothers and Democratic leaders, told Roosevelt to say "again and again and again" that the boys were not going to be sent into foreign wars.[49]

This is the most that can be said for the unfortunate passage: it did not originate with Roosevelt as a vote catcher but was imposed on him by others who demanded that he allay the public panic Willkie created. Still it was ridiculed and thrown up to him by the isolationist press and speakers so often in following months that it nullified to a great extent in the public mind all the more reasoned formulations of policy that preceded and followed it, and Roosevelt felt constrained in 1941 to regard it as his most binding commitment to the American people.

Besides competing defensively and perhaps unwisely for the anti-war vote, Roosevelt launched an offensive attack against his opponent as head of an "unholy alliance" between extreme reactionaries and extreme radicals which portended evil in foreign as well as domestic affairs. Republicans had the support of Communists, who preferred the defeat of Rooseveltian liberalism and internationalism to a defeat for Hitler in his war against "imperialist" Britain. Fascist and Nazi organizations and the priest Charles E. Coughlin did not hide their preference for a Republican victory in the election. The sinister possibilities of the "unholy alliance" were indicated by strikes in defense factories, such as the great Vultee Aircraft strike, which were promoted by Communists, and a series of explosions, the most serious of them in the Hercules Powder plant, which Secretary of War Stimson said might suggest "Teutonic efficiency."[50]

John L. Lewis, head of the United Mine Workers Union and the Congress of Industrial Organizations, completed the strange assortment of Willkie's supporters. Lewis had his revenge for Roosevelt's refusal of the "pay-off" Lewis had expected after the 1936 election, and for Roosevelt's lack of interest in Lewis' suggestion that voters' objections to a third term would disappear if Lewis was the vice-presidential candidate. Willkie's agents wooed him.[51] A week before the election Lewis made a bitter radio address against Roosevelt and appealed to labor to vote for Willkie. He said he would resign from leadership of the CIO if Roosevelt was re-elected.

On November 1, Roosevelt in his campaign speech in Brooklyn examined the Republicans' political allies. He attributed to them Willkie's hot-and-cold attitudes towards New Deal reforms and dangerous posibilities in foreign affairs if Willkie should be elected:

We all know the story of the unfortunate chameleon which turned brown [Nazi] when placed on a brown rug, and turned red [Communist] when placed on a red rug, but who died a tragic death when they put him on a Scotch plaid. . . .

There is something very ominous in this combination that has been forming within the Republican Party between the extreme reactionary and the extreme radical elements of this country. . . .

I do not think that some of the men, even some of the leaders, who have been drawn into this unholy alliance realize what a threat that sort of an alliance may bring to the future of democracy in this country. . . .

They should remember, and we must remember, what the collaborative understanding between Communism and Naziism has done to the processes of democracy abroad.

Something evil is happening in this country when a full page advertisement against this Administration, paid for by Republican supporters, appears—where, of all places?—in the *Daily Worker*, the newspaper of the Communist Party.

Something evil is happening in this country when vast quantities of Republican campaign literature are distributed by organizations that make no secret of their admiration for the dictatorship form of government.

Then the President struck out bluntly at his opponents as the actual enemies of all the social and economic reforms achieved since 1933. He ridiculed their pretense in their platform and in campaign speeches that they approved the New Deal objectives. A prominent Philadelphia Republican lawyer in a campaign speech had given Roosevelt a rare opportunity to expose "the true attitude of some leaders of the Republican party toward the common man . . . their true sentiments in all their naked unloveliness":

"The President's only supporters," he said, "are paupers, those who earn less than $1,200 a year and aren't worth *that,* and the Roosevelt family."

I think we might just as well forget the Roosevelt family, but these Americans whom this man calls "paupers," these Americans who, in his view, are not worth the income they receive, small though it is— who are they? They are only millions and millions of American families, constituting a very large part of the Nation! They are only the common men and women who have helped build this country, who have made it great, and who would defend it with their lives if the need arose.[52]


"The Champ" did not defeat Willkie so much as he defeated the party of isolationism and conservatism which Willkie had so recently embraced. Secretary Ickes aimed an effective blow at Willkie personally in his comment on a photograph of the former President of the Commonwealth and Southern electric power corporation patting cows in his native Indiana: "The Barefoot Boy from Wall Street." But Willkie after the election proved himself to be, on many issues, no more a conservative than he was an isolationist. He won a personal triumph in the campaign which was acknowledged by Roosevelt when he accepted him as a valuable collaborator.

Roosevelt won the election in spite of the grievances and irritations seven years in power had accumulated, in spite of the tradition against a third term, the bitterness of conservatives against his reforms, and of isolationists against his internationalism. He won it chiefly because so many voters agreed that the policies and experience of his administration were needed by the nation and the world after the Fall of France. He contributed greatly to his own victory by his brilliant management of the defection from his leadership of isolationists like Farley, Garner, Woodring and Wheeler. He prevented the Democratic Party from being split on foreign policy; in fact he strengthened the Party by the accession of Stimson, Knox and other supporters of the bipartisan foreign policy initiated in 1938.

The victory was not a landslide like that of 1936. Roosevelt received 57.4 per cent of the total vote cast, the smallest margin of any successful candidate since 1916, and Willkie received a larger popular vote than had ever been given to a candidate of his party. The electoral vote gave ten states to Willkie, eight more than Landon won in 1936. These states were all in the "isolationist Midwest" except Maine and Vermont.

## Moral Leadership of the World

The victory of Roosevelt had world meaning. Churchill wrote later that his "indescribable relief" was due not to apprehension over Willkie's attitude towards Britain's fight, but to fear of his inexperience and the prospect of losing the confidence and friendship between the President of the United States and himself.[53] Englishmen often fail to comprehend the power of the American Congress to frustrate Executive policy. Churchill might well have feared, more than anything else, the isolationist majority in Congress which would have come to power if Willkie had been elected. Official Axis sources proclaimed "indifference" towards the outcome of the American election, but this did not entirely obscure the fact that Axis leaders understood its threat to their plans.

Re-election of President Roosevelt in 1940 placed him at the moral headship of the great majority of humanity who were horrified by Axis tyranny and aggression. Churchill occupied humanity's fighting headship, but his conservatism and proud declamations in praise of traditional British imperialism repelled holders of the broader faith Roosevelt inspired. Stalin was the world leader of those who believed that socialism justified dictatorship, but this group was reduced by Stalin's appeasement of Hitler and by Russia's method of defending itself by sharing the spoils of Hitler's aggressions. Only Roosevelt raised a banner for all humanity, for Indians who suspected Churchill fought only for white men's liberties, for socialists who believed food without freedom was no bargain, for democrats and people of despised races and submerged classes everywhere. Only Roosevelt had used his power at home to fight for the economic and social benefit of the least fortunate Americans without impairing their exercise of full liberty. Only he had used his power to liquidate the imperialism of his own country as well as to oppose the imperialism of the aggressors. It was not enough in 1940 for America to exist. Roosevelt's leadership reflected the best impulses of the American tradition and people and he proposed to transmit these to the world. Roosevelt's victory made it more certain that civilization would not die "because America exists."

## 10.

## *The Vichy Policy*

ALL-OUT AID TO BRITAIN WAS THE MOST IMPORTANT specific mandate of the 1940 election. Invention and enactment of the Lend Lease Act consumed the winter months of 1940–1. In the meantime, the President developed his administration's internationalist foreign policy in another area, where no specific mandate helped him and, indeed, misunderstanding and criticism came chiefly from his most ardent internationalist supporters. His Vichy policy was fixed shortly after the election and prior to the formulation of Lend Lease.

### *Three Bold Objectives*

The most striking features of the Vichy policy were obscured at the time by loud and mistaken cries of "appeasement." The chief objects of Roosevelt and Hull in their French policy were to withhold the French navy from Hitler, to re-establish the united front between France and Britain against the Axis, and to organize centers of resistance to Hitler in France and in her possessions—centers which were used, when the moment arrived, to expel Hitler from Africa and France and defeat him in Germany. All three objectives were extremely bold. The first—to withhold the French fleet from Hitler—required constant diplomatic pressure. In pursuing the second, Roosevelt and Hull became the chief political architects of the coalition of nations which ultimately defeated the Axis and established the United Nations. Britain lost leadership in such an undertaking for the first time in modern history. In pursuing the third, the United States assumed leadership in the formulation of the military strategy which achieved victory for the coalition.

These goals were attained in the face of accusations by many Americans that the Roosevelt administration was "pro-Vichy," that it betrayed democracy while it strengthened Hitler's puppets. If treason to democracy by Roosevelt himself was too large a dose for Americans to swallow, they were told that stupidity, if nothing worse, in the State Department and Foreign Service perpetrated a policy favorable to Hitler while the President, evidently, slept.[1] Communists who had swallowed the Nazi-Soviet Pact in one mechanical gulp loudly condemned American "appeasement" of Pétain and Hitler.

For the many liberals and internationalists who objected to the Vichy policy there was the excuse that its broad objectives could not be made public without defeating them, and superficial appearances were damaging. Still it was strange that so many of Roosevelt's supporters imagined him so passive in the field of foreign relations as to be the victim of colossal "stupidity" among his subordinates.

The Pétain government was fascist and pro-Hitler. This was the first premise hurled against the administration, as if Roosevelt and Hull did not know it or ignored it when deciding on American policy. Roosevelt and Hull knew it very well. Ambassador Bullitt reported in detail the eagerness of the new French leaders to make France "a new *Gau*" acceptable to Hitler in a Nazified Europe after the victory the French leaders chose to regard as inevitable. Placing France at Hitler's disposal for exploitation, and foisting a fascist authoritarian regime of *Travail, Famille, Patrie* on the French people in place of *Liberté, Egalité, Fraternité,* Bullitt wrote, seemed to the Pétainists France's golden opportunity to become Hitler's "favorite province." French businessmen who looked for profits through collaboration with Hitler backed the sinister Pierre Laval in trying to sell the "national revolution" to the French people as Laval had sold himself to Hitler. All the new leaders believed their dictatorship in France would win better peace terms from Hitler.[2] While Bullitt could write thus frankly to his superiors in Washington, his statements to the American public when he came home in July, 1940, were necessarily more cautious. He refused to label the new French state "fascist," and spoke of Pétain sympathetically as "universally respected in France . . . doing his best . . . thoroughly honest and straightforward." [3]

The first impulse of the administration was to adopt the British policy of antagonism towards Vichy, but second thoughts, chiefly concerning the necessity to do everything possible to prevent the French fleet from being turned over to Hitler, led to the decision to maintain diplomatic representation at Vichy. Roosevelt and Hull had reason to believe the United States had had some influence on the armistice terms in their relation to the French fleet, and the ambiguous situation of the ships in French ports left open the possibility that United States influence would be useful either in fending off a voluntary surrender of the ships or in leading the French to scuttle the ships if Hitler violated the armistice terms.

On November 8, 1942, after the American landing in North Africa, Secretary Hull could at last explain to the public the ultimate purposes of the administration's Vichy policy. He declared it had been directed toward liberation of France from Germany, and that the American, British, and Canadian governments had wholeheartedly favored and supported the policy. Waverley Root has commented on this last assertion: "Definitely untrue. Although Winston Churchill was later won over to temporary approval, Britain and Canada long disagreed with American policy." [4] The absurdity of this comment is made apparent by Churchill himself. Not "later" but, as will be shown, from the beginning of American relations with Vichy, Churchill privately supported and utilized for Britain's benefit the American contacts with Pétain. Nor was his approval of American policy "temporary." In 1949, four years after Root's book was published, Churchill wrote in *Their Finest Hour* a careful restatement of his approval of the American Vichy policy, his reasons therefor, and the benefits Britain obtained from it. He also demonstrated in detail that Britain did not close all doors to Vichy or accept De Gaulle without reservations. Britain's policy was actually not the reverse of the American policy but only a modification of it, inevitably so because the British were at war, and therefore bore the brunt of the unhappy necessity to use force against Vichy, as they did at Oran and Dakar. Root, on the other hand, is certain that "complete harmony" existed between the British and the De Gaullists, and "nearly complete disharmony" between London and Vichy.[5]

Root's unnamed sources of information, however "secret," can hardly be regarded as more accurate on such matters than Churchill's. Root has sought to perpetuate as history the views of critics eager to find fascist sympathy in the American government although they were unable, at the time, to know the facts which explain and justify the Vichy policy of Roosevelt and Hull.

Several things were not understood by the public. Churchill had not wanted to disrupt British relations with Pétain except under the military necessity of preventing by force French warships from going to Hitler. He recognized, on August 7, the movement of General De Gaulle to organize new French resistance to Hitler, but he encouraged the United States and Canada to maintain recognition of the Pétain government in order to provide for Britain "a window upon a courtyard to which we had no other access." And he used the United States channel to Vichy and its influence on Vichy policy to keep French warships out of German hands.

Thus, when it appeared in the fall of 1940 that the great unfinished French battleships *Richelieu* and *Jean Bart* would be sent from North Africa to Toulon, where they could be completed and taken over by Hitler, Churchill worked through Roosevelt to prevent their return. He appealed to the President to speak in the "strongest terms" to the French Ambassador. Roosevelt did so, using as weapons the threat of American indignation against France, serious prejudice of official relations, and stoppage of all aid. These appeals, Churchill wrote in his memoirs, were "not in vain." Pétain gave assurances which were never violated.[6]

Another argument against Roosevelt's Vichy policy was that the "narrow" advantages which might be won thereby were more than nullified by the loss of moral prestige and consequent injury to the anti-Axis cause. But the narrowest stake for which Roosevelt and Hull played in their Vichy gamble was nothing less than naval control of the Atlantic Ocean. The whole American fleet in the Pacific could not be brought into the Atlantic without laying open the whole of southeast Asia and the south Pacific, the NEI, the Philippines and Australia to immediate Japanese attack. Reinforcement of the German Navy by the French fleet would give it mastery over the thin-spread British Navy. Such mastery meant defeat of Great Britain in the war. This reasoning, which seems as sound as calculations of probabilities in war can ever be, made Roosevelt and Hull decide that it was no "narrow" advantage for which they threw away the moral benefits of a rupture with Vichy, but nothing less than prevention of quick victory by Hitler.

Root in his *Secret History of the War* develops the further argument that after the Washington administration had learned from experience the futility of its Vichy policy, it nevertheless clung to it out of sheer stubbornness and unwillingness to admit error.[7] As early as September, 1940, Roosevelt and Hull had found ample reason, beyond the defensive question of the French fleet, for clinging to their contact with Vichy until the moment of the North African landing, and this reason did not require them to resort to stubbornness in the service of their "error."

In September, 1940, Pétain sent General Weygand to North Africa as Delegate-General. Weygand was reputed to enjoy the enmity of Pierre Laval, who engineered his removal from Pétain's Ministry. This was an important recommendation of Weygand to opponents of Hitler. Hull and Roosevelt decided that Weygand in North Africa "might become a cornerstone around which to build a policy of resistance to Germany," that, in other words, Weygand might retrieve the failure of the French government itself to continue the fight from North Africa. Hull worked to establish close contact with Weygand. He fed him evidence that the Vichy hope of a "soft peace" for France from Hitler was illusory and that Vichy betrayed France by giving in to the Germans' demands beyond the requirements of the armistice.

The administration decided that economic aid was the best lever with which to establish Weygand as a cornerstone of resistance to Hitler in North Africa. Accordingly Robert D. Murphy, former Consul General in Paris, was sent to Weygand in North Africa to discuss economic relations. Presently an extraordinary number of assistants joined Murphy and their espionage activity was an important factor in the success of the North African invasion of 1942.[8]

Murphy became a favorite exhibit in the chamber of fascist horrors many Americans professed to find in the American State Department and Foreign Service. This was because his program of economic collaboration with the French in North Africa was not understood to be merely the public aspect of his important secret duties. Hull himself in his *Memoirs* feels constrained, by the many years of bitter opprobrium he and his subordinates endured, to spread evidence on the record that he disapproved of the fascism and pro-Hitler orientation of the Vichy government. It is not necessary to labor this point, but his evidence on minor as well as major purposes of administration policy is invaluable.

## A Concession to Vichy

Major purposes of the Vichy policy were then, first, to prevent the French fleet falling into German hands; second, to prevent war between Britain and France; and third, to build up in North Africa resistance to Hitler. A minor purpose was to prevent French possessions in the American Hemisphere from being used to Hitler's advantage. But the major objectives were considered so important that the Roosevelt administration was unwilling to endanger them by pushing too hard for the minor objective. Critics, on the other hand, failing to understand or refusing to give credit to the administration for its primary interest in the French fleet, peace between Britain and France, and plans for North Africa, abused it for its "immorality" in compromising on such minor issues as Martinique and St. Pierre and Miquelon. They demanded a simon-pure attitude of no dealings with Vichy and refused to believe that American diplomacy was capable of extorting from Vichy more than it gave. In this they were victims of both the ancient legend that the diplomacy of the United States was naive and bound to be defeated by Old World guile, and the current one that the Axis governments were invincible in diplomacy as in war.

The Roosevelt administration punctured these legends. It achieved the major purposes of its Vichy policy, which profoundly affected the outcome of the war, by means of minor concessions to the government of Pétain. At Martinique the danger was naval war between Britain and France which might throw Vichy into active alliance with Hitler. The armistice caught several French warships at the little West Indian island, including the great aircraft carrier *Béarn* with 106 American-made planes. Also there was a quarter of a billion dollars of French gold. The Governor of the island, Admiral Robert, was aggressively pro-Vichy and he quickly established a dictatorship on the Pétain-Laval model. Great Britain sent warships to patrol the island on July 4, the day after it shelled French ships at Oran. Britain claimed title to the planes at Martinique under post-armistice arrangements whereby it took over French orders for war materials made in the United States.

Uppermost in Washington was the fear that British-French difficulties would increase until France actively re-entered the war on Hitler's side. Hull therefore warned Lord Lothian, on July 5, that if the British seized the war materials at Martinique or the island itself, it would involve "real trouble" between the United States and Britain. Lothian immediately denied that Britain had any such intentions. Hull then proposed an agreement between British and French authorities under which Britain would get the planes at Martinique and the ships would be interned in the United States.

Thus, to prevent a British clash with Vichy was the administration's main purpose at Martinique. That achieved, it would work for a solution, favorable to Britain, of the lesser problems. The President sent a heavy cruiser and six destroyers to Martinique to make certain that no naval battle occurred there.[9] This objective was achieved, but the administration could not explain publicly the appalling disaster to the anti-Axis cause it had helped to prevent.

Rear Admiral John W. Greenslade was sent on special mission to Admiral Robert. The Vichyite would do no more than give vague assurances that the French ships, planes, and gold would not be turned over to Germany. Early in October the First Marine Brigade went into training at Guantanamo, Cuba, for landing operations. Obviously this force could readily be used to occupy Martinique. A crisis occurred when Laval engineered the Montoire Conversations on October 24 between Pétain and Hitler. The two leaders arrived at an agreement on the principle of collaboration that went beyond the terms of the armistice between France and Germany. This opened wide the question of the French fleet and of France's entry into the war.

Roosevelt and Hull were ready to act in Martinique in case of necessity, but they refrained from any act that would at this critical moment give Pétain additional excuse to strengthen ties with Hitler. Instead, they used the American representative at Vichy to exert pressure on Pétain. On October 24, Roosevelt sent the strongest of his letters to Pétain, and the next day he transmitted a similar one from King George VI. Pétain answered with assurances that his government would retain its liberty of action and would never surrender the French fleet. He spoke bitterly of British encouragement of the Gaullist "rebels," but stated that in spite of provocation France would not unjustifiably attack Britain and wished to maintain its traditional friendship with the United States.[10]

To help hold Pétain to these commitments, Roosevelt wisely decided to concede the Vichy position in Martinique. But he demanded definite guaranties from Admiral Robert and backed up the demand by sending a United States aircraft carrier with patrol planes to the new United States base nearby at St. Lucia. Martinique was virtually blockaded. Robert thereupon made a "gentleman's agreement" with Admiral Greenslade under which the United States was allowed to station a naval observer in the island and maintain a naval and air patrol. Robert also promised to give the United States government ninety-six hours' notice of any ship movements. The United States agreed to supply the French islands with food paid for out of blocked French funds.[11]

In this way, the Roosevelt administration came to "support" or "appease" the Vichy regime in Martinique. The arrangement created the pattern for the larger problem of French North Africa. The fighter planes rusted away on the island while they might have served Britain well during the blitz, and the French warships were neutralized. But they did not fall into German hands; nor did Vichy implement the Montoire Conversations by turning over to Hitler the French fleet or by entry into the war. Such gains were nonetheless real for being negative. But, to many Americans, careless of alternatives and consequences, these were unsatisfactory compensations for seeming cooperation with the rule of Vichy.

But Roosevelt and Hull could take satisfaction from them and from a striking event as the year ended. On December 13, Pétain dismissed Laval from his government and had him arrested. Hull had conveyed to Pétain the American extreme distrust of Laval.[12] Dismissal of Laval indicated that the Montoire Agreement would not be enforced, that Pétain would attempt to find a balanced position between the demands of Hitler and those of the United States and Great Britain. It seemed to prove that Roosevelt and Hull could influence French policy and win further gains for the anti-Axis cause.

### The Leahy Mission

Roosevelt and Hull decided to strike for stronger influence in Vichy by sending an outstanding American as Ambassador. Their first choice was General John J. Pershing, but his ill-health prevented. They named Admiral William D. Leahy, whose eminence and varied experience as a naval diplomat would help him in relations with Admiral Jean François Darlan, who had taken Laval's place as Vice Premier. Furthermore, appointment of a sailor emphasized American primary interest in the French fleet.

Darlan was a defeatist, but he had a strong interest in maintaining for France the friendship of the United States. The position of the American government was summed up in instructions to Leahy on December 20, 1940. He was told to cultivate close relations with Pétain and bring to his attention acts inimical to the United States which his subordinates were said to conceal from him. Leahy should tell Pétain that the United States was determined the Axis must be defeated, and would give all assistance short of war to nations fighting aggression. He should express President Roosevelt's concern that France might cooperate with Hitler beyond what was required by the armistice. Detailed information of any such aid should be gathered. Pétain should be told that the United States government was convinced France would become a dismembered vassal of Germany if Hitler won. Preservation of the French fleet, out of German control, was vital to the defense of the American hemisphere and to the eventual redemption of France itself. Leahy should also warn French officials and high naval officers that to permit Germany to use the fleet or French bases would cause France to "forfeit the friendship and good will of the United States, and result in the destruction of the French fleet to the irreparable injury of France." This threat was coupled with promises that the American Red Cross would send medical supplies and milk for children to France and that, because the President was sympathetic to French efforts to maintain authority in North Africa, he would offer economic assistance for that purpose.[18]

## The Secret Halifax-Chevalier Agreement

The Roosevelt-Hull policy of piecing together the broken bits of the Anglo-French entente now produced remarkable results. While Leahy was en route to Vichy, a secret arrangement was made between the governments of Pétain and Churchill. As early as July 25, Churchill, while publicly arranging a military agreement with De Gaulle, decided on a policy towards Vichy quite different from the one held up to the public view. He wrote to his Foreign Secretary:

I want to promote a kind of collusive conspiracy in the Vichy Government whereby certain members of that Government, perhaps with the consent of those who remain, will levant to North Africa in order to make a better bargain for France from the North African shore and from a position of independence. For this purpose I would use both food and other inducements, as well as the obvious arguments.

This was the essence of Roosevelt's policy, and the British and American lines of action, which culminated in the liberation of North Africa, were differentiated not in conception or purpose but only by secrecy on the British side and a limited amount of publicity on the American. Churchill by October accepted a secret contact with Vichy in the person of "a certain M. Rougier," the personal representative of Pétain. Churchill writes that he was "very glad" when Roosevelt sent Leahy as Ambassador to Vichy, and that he repeatedly urged the Canadian government to maintain its relations also.[14]

On the basis of the same designs that led Roosevelt to appoint Leahy, Churchill in December allowed Lord Halifax, his Foreign Minister, to negotiate an agreement with M. Chevalier, a member of Pétain's government, who succeeded Rougier as secret representative in Britain. This agreement provided that a state of "artificial tension" between Britain and Vichy should be maintained to deceive the Germans while the two governments cooperated on the following program: France would not turn over to Hitler naval vessels or bases; Vichy would not attempt to reconquer De Gaullist colonies; Britain would permit food, oil, rubber and other commodities to pass through its blockade of France. Pétain approved these arrangements in principle and they were observed as a program of practical cooperation.[15]

This secret Halifax-Chevalier Agreement between Britain and Vichy must be taken to change the meaning of the public quarrels between the two governments which, during following months, made the Roosevelt policy towards Vichy inexplicable to many observers. Upon the "artificial tension" between Britain and Vichy depended the success of the Churchill-Roosevelt scheme to recover France for the anti-Axis cause. Thus, at the very time of the Halifax-Chevalier Agreement to relax the British blockade of France, the British government publicly, on December 10, stated that it could not allow food shipments to France because they would indirectly aid the Germans and thereby postpone liberation of the French. Nevertheless, Britain did allow shipments by the Red Cross of food and medical supplies from the United

States to unoccupied France. In view of the Halifax-Chevalier Agreement, the British statement of December 10 cannot be regarded otherwise than as dust in the eyes of Hitler to blind him to the organization of cooperation among Britain, Vichy, and the United States. The procedure left the United States and particularly Hull to bear the odium of publicly appearing to be "pro-Vichy," and Hull in his *Memoirs* suggests that he did not relish the burden.[16]

At first the British were so optimistic as to believe that the Pétain government might be led to move to North Africa and enter the war against Hitler. Immediately after the Halifax-Chevalier Agreement, Churchill used the American channel to Pétain to offer him strong military forces to help defend North Africa if he would move his government there. Twice in January, 1941, the offer was repeated, and the French warships held by the British at Alexandria were added to the bait. Pétain refused to move.[17]

Pétain was under severe pressure from Hitler to reinstate Laval. Hitler decided that the Montoire policy was too lenient to France because it promised a place for it in the "New Order" in return for collaboration. He would take what he pleased of France and force cooperation in the war. Pétain was fearful of this nightmare and sensitive to German use of French prisoners of war for bargaining purposes. Far from contemplating removal to North Africa and renewal of the war, Pétain and Darlan were on the defensive in the face of Hitler's extreme demands. They exhausted their small store of authority in avoiding reinstatement of Laval. The British were chasing the Italians out of Egypt and across Tripoli, but this success would very likely bring Germany to the rescue. A German campaign in North Africa was expected to involve use of Bizerte or other French North African ports in violation of the armistice. To fend this off was all Vichy dared attempt. Weygand refused to join De Gaulle, but he also defied Hitler, on February 7, by stating that France would refuse to allow Nazi occupation of Bizerte or any part of North Africa.

## The Franco Policy

Later it became known that Hitler during the winter of 1940–1 looked to Spain as his route to control of the Mediterranean and conquest of North Africa. But there too he found resistance, which Britain and the United States had tried to maximize in the face of more accusations of "appeasement." In the case of Spain, however, British and American policy synchronized in public as well as in private. Immediately after the Fall of France, the United States offered Franco food, cotton, and oil if he would remain neutral. He agreed, and consented to stipulations safeguarding American shipments against re-export to Germany. In October, 1940, a first shipment of wheat by the American Red Cross was held up because Franco's pro-Hitler brother-in-law, Serrano Suñer, had become Foreign Minister. The food was turned into a frank political weapon by a decision that United States government and not Red Cross funds would pay for it. Then Suñer was warned that collaboration with the Axis, cruelty towards refugees, and executions of Republican political prisoners would make impossible American aid.

Franco in November gave United States Ambassador Alexander W. Weddell assurances which practically satisfied American requirements. Famine threatened in Spain, and the British were fearful that if it were not prevented, it would force Franco into the war to obtain German relief. Hull and Roosevelt doled out relief in small quantities which were related on a day-by-day basis to the convolutions of Franco's policy.[18]

While Franco gave in to American demands for assurances in return for relief, he himself made fantastic demands on Hitler in return for collaboration. After the Fall of France he told Hitler he would enter the war in return for Gibraltar, French Morocco, Oran, and French territory at Rio de Oro, Africa, as well as supplies of food and munitions. These demands were too high. Hitler in October met Franco at Hendaye. Hitler refused to make promises regarding French territory because, he said, granting Franco's demands would cause revolts in the French colonies. Franco was fearful of the ultimate role of the United States even if Britain were defeated. He infuriated Hitler and the meeting was a failure.

During the winter Franco continued to resist. He rejected Hitler's plan for joint action in January, 1941. A break between Hitler and Franco came in February after American relief shipments to Spain had begun. Hitler wanted to move on Africa through Spain and Gibraltar. Franco told him that closing Gibraltar to the British would not be decisive unless Suez were also closed, and he refused to cooperate.

Franco would not have dared to pit weak and starving Spain against Hitler, unless he were to receive benefits from Britain and the United States in return for continued neutrality. At the time, few Americans would believe that the cooperation of the dictators was less than perfect, or that the United States could strengthen Franco's resistance against Hitler. That these notions were false has been proved by captured documents which reveal the correctness of calculations by the Roosevelt administration and successes of its policies.[19]

## "Like a Thousand Hawks"

By February, 1941, it was apparent that Pétain's cooperation with Hitler's enemies would be strictly limited to the terms of the Halifax-Chevalier Agreement. At the same time, he would do nothing avoidable to instrument the Montoire Agreement with Hitler. Churchill and Roosevelt had failed in the play for higher stakes, and once more they had the choice of accepting Pétain's minimum of cooperation, which protected the French fleet from Hitler, or pushing him into Hitler's arms. They chose the former as the lesser evil.

Simultaneously Roosevelt and Hull worked on the long-range plan to exploit relations with Vichy in order to create a "cornerstone of resistance" to Hitler in French North Africa. After a month there, Robert D. Murphy sent to Hull a remarkable report, dated January 17, 1941. He had obtained from General Weygand and other leaders assurances that while they would remain loyal to Pétain, they wanted a British victory and would oppose any German attempt to take over the French colonies. They would also take anti-Hitler military action if Pétain ordered it, or if the Germans occupied all of France, or if the United States entered the war. They felt that Africa was France's last trump, and that it "must be played only on a well-timed, carefully planned basis."

Murphy had followed Weygand to Dakar. A British and De Gaullist expedition had failed to capture this base on the West African coast where American interest was vital because Dakar was the danger spot closest to the American Hemisphere south of

Greenland. Weygand and the Governor-General of Dakar gave Murphy repeated assurances that with or without a British victory they were determined to oppose any German effort at domination. Back in Algiers, Weygand told Murphy that only United States economic aid could save French Africa from Germany if it attacked in the spring. He gave the American full details of the economic requirements of the colonies.[20]

Murphy established excellent personal relations with General Weygand. Even more than Pétain, Weygand struggled to find a position between German pressure administered by Armistice Commissions and his desire to cooperate with the United States. He was not ready to rebel, but he compromised himself sufficiently to merit removal by Pétain in November, 1941, and arrest by the Nazis a year later.[21]

The Roosevelt administration decided that major economic aid should be sent to the French colonies. It was realized that this would indirectly aid the Nazis, who plundered the colonies of food and raw materials. But it was believed that the alternative was worse: if the populations of the colonies were allowed to hunger, they would fall easy prey to Germany. American aid would not only prevent that but it would create among those populations a surge of faith in the United States and in the ultimate triumph of the anti-Hitler cause, and it would prepare the way for use of North Africa as a staging point on the route to Berlin. In the winter of 1940–1, the possibility of drawing in French North Africa a line of containment against the aggressions of Germany was uppermost in the minds of British and American leaders.

The Department of State in December, 1940, decided that Morocco, threatened by Spain as well as by Germany, should be helped to maintain its independence. Conversations were held with the British. After some delay, during which the Americans explained that their purpose was political, in February, 1941, the British agreed to open the blockade for American supplies of food and materials essential to the local population. The British suggested that United States officials supervise distribution in Morocco to make sure that supplies did not reach the enemy, and they were willing to permit the same procedure in Algeria and Tunisia. Britain also wanted the United States to obtain release of interned British vessels as a condition of aid. Hull rejected these

British "conditions," and told the new British Ambassador, Lord Halifax, that the United States was "going forward" with its plan.

Fear of a Hitler drive into French Africa, heralded by an influx of Nazi officials and "tourists," had already in late January caused Hull to instruct Murphy to work out an arrangement with Weygand. The French had prepared an agreement. They welcomed supervision of shipments by American officials on the spot. By March 10, Washington and Vichy had formally approved the Murphy-Weygand Agreement. Under it, American oil, tea, sugar, coal and other items were to be bought with French money frozen in the United States. The shipments would go in French vessels interned in the United States so that no shipping would be diverted from the North Atlantic run.

About the clause permitting United States officials to supervise distribution, Hull writes in his *Memoirs* that the administration immediately saw in it a great opportunity to go beyond economic matters into the *"political and military fields."* The officials, designated "vice consuls," were American Army and Navy personnel in civilian clothes. Murphy stayed in Algiers to supervise them in consulates scattered along the coast. He was told to report on everything of political, economic, and military interest. The result was an extraordinarily effective network of American agents "watching events like a thousand hawks," who provided information, countered Nazi influence and rallied the populations to support of the anti-Axis cause. They laid the groundwork for the successful Allied landing in November, 1942.[22]

But at the time, Americans saw only that the shipments to North Africa replaced what the Nazis took, and that these shipments seemed to defeat British blockade efforts. Many were quick to believe the administration was the victim of a pro-fascist plot or, at least, naive and stubborn in imagining it could concoct a policy to which Vichy would consent that did not help Hitler more than it injured him.

Nor was it easy to understand why the administration did not work with De Gaulle rather than with Vichy. The later record of De Gaulle, after 1945, was foreshadowed in information coming to the State Department in 1940 and 1941 that his leadership was not acceptable to the broad mass of Frenchmen and that the United States could build up more useful ties with the French people by dealing with Vichy.

## The Strongest Foreign Influence in Vichy

Churchill himself intervened when his subordinates failed to understand the value of American relations with Vichy. Early in March, 1941, Hull found Halifax had turned, since fall, inflexibly against allowing the relief supplies to be shipped to unoccupied France which he had promised to Chevalier. Hull warned the Ambassador that such supplies helped prevent Laval from pushing Darlan and Pétain closer to Hitler and served as a safeguard against an "explosion" between Vichy and Britain. Darlan bore this out in a public threat to use the French fleet to break the British blockade.

On March 13, Churchill sent a letter to Roosevelt appealing to him as the friend of both sides to work out a secret agreement between Britain and Vichy. He wanted, in effect, to strengthen and broaden the Halifax-Chevalier Agreement by using American aid as leverage to obtain important concessions from Vichy. Britain would allow a ration of wheat to pass through the blockade, in return for which Vichy should prevent German infiltration into French Africa and dispatch French warships from Toulon to West Africa.

The administration approved British requests to send large numbers of American observers to Africa to counteract Nazi infiltration, but it did not believe Pétain could be brought to take such bold actions as preventing that infiltration or sending the French Navy out of Nazi reach. Furthermore, Roosevelt and Hull had begun to discount the Nazi threat to North Africa, despite Rommel's successes in Libya during the spring, because they had obtained advance information that Hitler planned to attack the Soviet Union. Therefore, the Churchill proposal to ask Vichy for a formal agreement tying American aid to the anti-Hitler actions was rejected. Instead, Hull proposed, and the British agreed, that American wheat should go to unoccupied France, while the United States in separate representations attempted to influence Vichy favorably to British desires.

This program was carried out in April and May. In the latter month new concessions of Darlan to Hitler endangered the success of American policy. Passage of the Lend Lease Act in March was followed by broad reconsideration of policy in all fields. For a time, strong measures in the French area were studied in Washington. Under Secretary Welles obtained the approval of Roosevelt for a declaration that would place West Africa and the Atlantic islands near it under the guaranties of the Monroe Doctrine, but Hull convinced the President of its unwisdom because such a declaration would invite Germany to take over the area.

The policy of the administration bore new fruit in June. The United States served as intermediary to end fighting between the French and British in Syria and helped prevent that situation from exploding into a general Anglo-French war. The "Paris Protocols" between Darlan and the Nazis, giving the latter extensive concessions in Africa, including use of Dakar as a base, were rejected after Leahy, and Weygand and other French officials friendly to the United States brought pressure to bear privately on Pétain; and after Hull and Roosevelt protested publicly. The President, on May 22, had ordered the Navy to prepare an expedition to take the Azores. Pétain had been made to see that the Paris Protocols would lead to a break in relations with the United States and to war with Great Britain. Perhaps Hitler only meant the affair to cover his preparations against Russia, but Hull writes that Pétain's rejection of Darlan's Paris Protocols "provided ample justification for our policy toward Vichy France. . . . The United States came through the crisis as the strongest foreign influence in Vichy." [23]

Certainly United States policy from June, 1940, to June, 1941, had done much to help prevent the Vichy government from going to war against Britain when that country stood alone; it had created a pro-American influence among Vichy officials, including Pétain, which helped hold the French fleet out of German hands; and it had laid the foundations for the use of North Africa in the reconquest of Europe. These gains were of considerable weight in favor of the Roosevelt Vichy policy.

# 11.

## Lend Lease

THE LEND LEASE ACT TRANSFORMED SMALL BEGINNINGS into a stupendous counter-drive which promised victory in the war against the Axis. It pitted against the Axis the greatest single military potential in the world—the industrial power of the United States. It invited all governments attacked by the Axis to join a new united front for collective security. Resistance to aggression was the sole requirement for admission. Lend Lease held out assurance to humanity for the first time since the rise of the Axis powers that resistance would not be in vain, that the overwhelming superiority in power of the peaceful nations might yet be organized and thrown into the scales in time for victory.

Lend Lease was the Roosevelt administration's invention. It seemed even more original than it was because Roosevelt did not place it in the framework of theoretical debates on collective security. Rather, he placed it in a setting of practical necessity, pointing to an *ad hoc* solution, and in this he satisfied a profound American suspicion of theory. Nevertheless, he answered the isolationist charge that Lend Lease meant war with the reasoning of a believer in collective security—that aid to the victims of aggression was a duty which gave no legal justification for reprisals, and that helping to defeat aggressors offered a better chance of avoiding war than standing idly by while they conquered peaceful nations one by one.

*Ad hoc* considerations, however, were uppermost in Roosevelt's mind when he conceived Lend Lease. Robert Sherwood has written a revealing description of the process whereby the President addressed himself after the election to the immediate problem of

Britain's inability to continue paying cash for war supplies. Roosevelt went into a "mental retreat" aboard the *Tuscaloosa,* cruising in the Caribbean. He had no one aboard with whom he could discuss Britain's crisis and possible solutions for it. Harry Hopkins was aboard and later said:

"I didn't know for quite awhile, what he was thinking about, if anything. But then—I began to get the idea that he was refueling, the way he so often does when he seems to be resting and carefree. So I didn't ask him any questions. Then, one evening, he suddenly came out with it—the whole program." [1]

But, as will be shown, this view of the origins of the Lend Lease idea is exaggerated. "The whole program," and even the essential idea, were not worked out for several more weeks, or without reference to the Pittman Resolution of June, 1940, and intervening work of Treasury lawyers.

## Churchill's Division of Labor

Roosevelt received during the cruise on the *Tuscaloosa* a letter from Churchill describing the British financial problem in great detail, but Churchill had no solution to offer. This letter was important beyond the details of Britain's financial situation, which Roosevelt already knew and which Secretary of the Treasury Morgenthau made his particular province of study. Britain had carefully built up and carefully spent its supply of dollars. The government had requisitioned privately-held dollar investments and sold all but a fraction which were not easily marketable and were needed for reserve. Out of a total six and a half billion dollars, it had spent by November, 1940, four and a half billions. When Churchill came to power in May, the cautious policy of Chamberlain was dropped and orders were placed in the United States without regard for the dwindling supply of cash with which to pay for them. All French contracts in the United States were taken over. Six months later it was apparent that the cash would not be available. New contracting stopped. This, in brief, was the impasse Roosevelt had to break if the policy of aid to Britain was to be carried out.

Churchill wrote Roosevelt, on December 8, a letter of nineteen paragraphs. He had evidently studied American politics and the meaning of the election campaign so that he understood better than he had in May and June the limits within which Roosevelt could act. He now projected, strictly within those limits, a brilliant formula for Anglo-American cooperation. He wrote that the vast majority of Americans had recorded their conviction that the safety of the United States, as well as the future of the democracy and civilization for which Britain and America stood, was bound up with the survival and independence of the British Commonwealth. Only such survival could preserve control of the Atlantic and Indian Oceans in friendly hands. Control of the Pacific Ocean by the United States Navy and of the Atlantic by the British Navy was necessary to the security and trade of both countries, and was "the surest means of preventing war from reaching the shores of the United States."

It was Britain's duty, Churchill continued, to hold off the Nazi power during the next two years while the United States converted its industries to war production. Victory might come in that time but could not be counted on.

These considerations were the bases of "a solid identity of interest between the British Empire and the United States while these conditions last." It was "upon this footing," that Churchill addressed the President. Churchill placed Britain in the position not of a supplicant for aid but of a partner proposing a division of labor based on mutuality of interest. Americans might decide for themselves whether their task was so much the easier as to be almost ignoble. Churchill made the American role seem honorable and sufficient.

He wrote an incisive analysis of Britain's war strategy. Britain was not able to match the land power of Germany but it would use sea and air power in areas where the main German armies could not be brought to bear, and it aimed to prevent Nazi expansion into Africa and Southern Asia. Fifty or sixty divisions were being organized to defend the British Isles. Churchill's opposition to the strategy of large-scale land warfare was apparent in his statement that, even if the United States were Britain's ally, instead of its "friend and indispensable partner," Britain would not ask for a large American expeditionary army. Shipping, not men, was the limiting factor of Britain's efforts.

This notification to Roosevelt was important as a justification of his position before the American public that his policy did not involve "sending our boys into European trenches." Churchill's description of British strategy answered the question, how Nazi power on the continent of Europe was to be destroyed, by pointing to air power alone.

Britain's danger of being destroyed by a sudden blow, Churchill wrote, had receded, but an equally deadly danger of being slowly strangled by German submarines had to be faced in 1941. The "crunch of the whole war" would be found in the Atlantic Ocean. If the Atlantic were kept open, British air power and the rising anger of European populations might bring the war to a glorious end. Churchill gave Roosevelt statistics of shipping losses and needs. He stressed the necessity of further destroyer reinforcements. Even in battleships, Britain was pressed to maintain superiority in the face of a possible fleet action. Capitulation to Hitler by Vichy France would give Germans control of West Africa, threaten South America and communications between the North and South Atlantic. Britain had no forces available to counter a reported Japanese expeditionary force into Southeast Asia and the NEI.

Yet Britain must, nevertheless, in 1941 build up strength to "lay the foundations of victory." This audacious program, Churchill felt, entitled him to lay before Roosevelt "the various ways in which the United States could give supreme and decisive help to what is, in certain aspects, the common cause." He proposed two alternative sets of measures. First, reassertion by the United States of the freedom of the seas so that, with repeal of the limiting clause of the Neutrality Act, and in accordance with German agreement to the principle in 1935, United States ships would carry cargoes to Britain; protection of this shipping by warships and planes, which might lead to incidents but not to a declaration of war by Germany because Hitler followed the maxim "one at a time," feared making the mistake of the Kaiser in the First War, and wished to avoid war with the United States until Great Britain was reduced. Second, failing the above measures, Churchill proposed the "gift, loan, or supply" of American warships, extension of American sea control to the approaches of the new American bases on British territory, and American diplomatic aid to induce the government of Eire to give Britain use of Irish bases. To ensure victory, Britain needed three million additional tons

of shipping, which only the United States could supply, and reinforcement of her ability to manufacture aircraft as well as a
further quota of American planes of two thousand per month,
including maximum numbers of the heavy bombers on which
Churchill relied to shatter Nazi power in Europe. American machine tools for munitions were needed. He noted gratefully arrangements made for equipping Britain's new army and, foreseeing requests of countries trying to regain their freedom "when
the tide of dictatorship begins to recede," he urged expansion of
American productive capacity for arms, artillery, and tanks.

"Last of all," Churchill wrote, "I come to the question of Finance." He reviewed the position. The end of dollars was in sight
and Churchill believed it would be wrong to strip Britain to the
bone. Such a course would violate the "moral and economic interests" of both countries. Britain would be unable after victory
to buy its customary surplus of American imports above exports,
"agreeable to your tariffs and industrial economy." Britain would
suffer cruel privations, and unemployment in the United States
would follow a drop in exports to Britain. Having reached the
crux, Churchill concluded his letter with a statement of faith:

18. Moreover, I do not believe that the Government and people of
the United States would find it in accordance with the principles
which guide them to confine the help which they have so generously
promised only to such munitions of war and commodities as could be
immediately paid for. You may be certain that we shall prove ourselves
ready to suffer and sacrifice to the utmost for the Cause, and that we
glory in being its champions. The rest we leave with confidence to you
and to your people, being sure that ways and means will be found
which future generations on both sides of the Atlantic will approve
and admire.
19. If, as I believe, you are convinced, Mr. President, that the defeat of the Nazi and Fascist tyranny is a matter of high consequence
to the people of the United States and to the Western Hemisphere,
you will regard this letter not as an appeal for aid, but as a statement
of the minimum action necessary to achieve our common purpose.[2]

The largest political meaning of this letter was that it offered
the United States a reasoned strategy and hope for victory if
it contributed to Britain's fight with "measures short of war."
Churchill's faith in the capacity of air power to destroy Hitler in
Europe was not tailored for the occasion: it was his governing

thought much earlier, and even after the United States had entered the war. He did not present United States naval convoys in the North Atlantic as a requirement of victory, but only as a preferred alternative to measures less likely to provoke dangerous incidents. This letter specified details which Churchill could not make public, but for Roosevelt it thoroughly justified the Prime Minister's public cry, "Give us the tools, and we will finish the job!" Even to Roosevelt, this cry might have seemed optimistic, but Roosevelt was likely to be guilty of the same emotion. On the other hand, British air power had already won a quite unforeseen victory in the Battle of Britain, the prophets of victory through air power were plausible and influential, and in the winter of 1940–1 the conception of strategic bombing was untried. It promised miracles, and its scope and limitations are to this day a matter of dispute.

British victory through air power became the strategic foundation of Roosevelt's program in 1941 to carry out his campaign promises within the boundaries of no entry into the war.

### Eliminating the Dollar Sign

The Lend Lease Bill was Roosevelt's answer to Churchill's December 8 letter. Several components of the Bill were already familiar to Roosevelt when he read Churchill's letter aboard the *Tuscaloosa*. Late in the summer of 1940 he had told the Defense Advisory Commission it should not be necessary for the British to pay cash or to borrow dollars for merchant ships. Finished vessels should be leased to them for use during the emergency. Treasury lawyers had unearthed a law of 1892 under which the Secretary of War, "when in his discretion it will be for the public good," could lease Army property "not required for public use" for periods up to five years. The Pittman Resolution of June 15, 1940, had authorized assistance to the other American Republics in obtaining arms in the United States. Many officials and agencies of the government expored such possibilities after the Fall of France.[3]

An ordinary lease would not meet the whole British situation, however, because it would involve a fee and a definite term specified in the contract. Such stipulations might be useful in some cases; in others they would obstruct transfer of material. The

President looked for a formula that would eliminate all "artificial" hindrances and leave nothing but the policy of the United States as a control over aid. He found it in the words of the Act as approved on March 11, 1940: "To sell, transfer title to, exchange, lease, lend, or otherwise dispose of. . . ." Terms of repayment should be those which "the President deems satisfactory, and the benefit to the United States may be payment or repayment in kind or property, or any other direct or indirect benefit which the President deems satisfactory." He could consider a contribution to the defense of the United States satisfactory repayment. Contributions to a peaceful world order after the war also could be regarded as satisfactory payment, and reduction of trade barriers was one of the most interesting of these potentialities of Lend Lease.

These terms meant that high considerations of American policy and nothing else would determine every decision, and the question whether the form should be that of gift, barter for goods or in return for direct or indirect benefits, lease, loan or sale would be answered by reference to expediency. Formerly, the decision as to what material went to a country like Britain was made by Britain; henceforth it would be made by the United States. Formerly, possession of dollars was the ultimate factor limiting a government which wished to buy war material in the United States, and under the Neutrality Act any belligerent, even an aggressor, might buy. Henceforth, the United States would determine, on grounds of its own policy, what nation would obtain materials and in what amounts.

The new system shifted into the hands of the United States government authority formerly scattered among foreign nations. It made selected nations "clients" of the United States. Lend Lease made the economic power of the United States a stupendous weapon of its foreign policy. Because its industrial power surpassed that of any other nation, Lend Lease converted the potentiality of United States political leadership of the world into actuality.

The portentous conception of Lend Lease was presented by Roosevelt to a press conference immediately after his cruise in words so homely and convincing that the American public understood and in great majority quickly approved. The whole complicated purpose of subordinating all factors affecting aid to the single determinant of United States policy he summed up in elementary fashion:

Now, what I am trying to do is to eliminate the dollar sign. That is something brand new in the thoughts of practically everybody in this room, I think—get rid of the silly, foolish old dollar sign.

This was shocking to conventional notions of how wars should be financed. The President knew it and ridiculed such notions with a story of how, in 1914, on the Bar Harbor Express, he had won five-dollar bets against bankers who had sagely predicted that the war wouldn't last six months because there wasn't enough money in all the world to carry on a European war longer than that. This illustrated the President's statement, "in all history, no major war has ever been won or lost through lack of money." It was refreshing at a time when Americans were being told by "experts" that Dr. Schacht's unorthodox financial measures insured German defeat, and that the credit of the American government was in danger because of the excessive public debt.

Another illustration was vastly influential:

Well, let me give you an illustration: Suppose my neighbor's home catches fire, and I have a length of garden hose. . . . Now, what do I do? I don't say to him . . . "Neighbor, my garden hose cost me $15; you have to pay me $15 for it." What is the transaction that goes on? I don't want $15—I want my garden hose back after the fire is over.

Then the President described somewhat optimistically how the neighbor, before returning the hose, would repair it if it was damaged.[4]

After the election the American public had debated earnestly how the administration's commitment to aid Britain should be carried out. The Roosevelt solution of "lending the neighbor the garden hose" resolved the issue and satisfied all but last-ditch isolationists. Encouraging support was forthcoming from businessmen, who had been subjected to a campaign in which such leaders as Knudsen, Stettinius, and W. Averell Harriman, during November and December, told groups all over the country of the dangers the country faced.[5]

## *"The Great Arsenal of Democracy"*

On December 29, Roosevelt in a Fireside Chat on national security proposed that the United States should be "the great arsenal of democracy." This phrase defined for the new period the role of the United States and it became a slogan as well as a label. The President compared the moment to the banking crisis of March, 1933, and said he wanted to face the world crisis with the same courage and realism.

Never before since Jamestown and Plymouth Rock has our American civilization been in such danger as now.

For, on September 27, 1940, by an agreement signed in Berlin, three powerful nations, two in Europe and one in Asia, joined themselves together in the threat that if the United States of America interfered with or blocked the expansion program of these three nations—a program aimed at world control—they would unite in ultimate action against the United States.

He quoted a recent proclamation of Hitler that there could be no ultimate peace between the Axis and the rest of the world. On this ground Roosevelt declared the United States had no right or reason to encourage talk of peace until the aggressor nations gave up the policy of controlling the world.

So long as Britain stood, the Americas need not fear attack. If Britain fell, the Americas would live "at the point of a gun—a gun loaded with explosive bullets, economic as well as military."

The President said many people had written to him asking him to tell "the plain truth about the gravity of the situation." But one telegram, representing a small minority, begged him not to mention again the ease with which American cities could be bombed by a hostile power which had gained bases nearby; in short, "Please, Mr. President, don't frighten us by telling us the facts." Roosevelt answered:

Frankly and definitely there is danger ahead—danger against which we must prepare. But we well know that we cannot escape danger, or the fear of danger, by crawling into bed and pulling the covers over our heads.

Germany had used as an excuse for the invasion of Belgium the pious fraud that she was saving the Belgians from aggression by the British. Would she then hesitate to occupy a South American country to save it from aggression by the United States?

There are those who say that the Axis powers would never have any desire to attack the Western Hemisphere. That is the same dangerous form of wishful thinking which has destroyed the powers of resistance of so many conquered peoples. The plain facts are that the Nazis have proclaimed, time and again, that all other races are their inferiors and therefore subject to their orders. And most important of all, the vast resources and wealth of this American Hemisphere constitute the most tempting loot in all the round world.

Roosevelt said the government was ferreting out evil forces already within the gates, forces that had crushed and undermined and corrupted so many other nations. Foreign agents stirred up class strife, reawakened old racial and religious enmities which should have no place in the United States, and exploited Americans' natural abhorrence of war. And some American citizens, "many of them in high places," most of them unwittingly, aided and abetted these foreign agents. They went so far as to say that Americans could and should become the "friends and even the partners of the Axis powers."

Experience had proved beyond doubt that the Nazis could not be appeased. "No man can tame a tiger into a kitten by stroking it." American appeasers asked for what they called a "negotiated peace":

Nonsense! Is it a negotiated peace if a gang of outlaws surrounds your community and on threat of extermination makes you pay tribute to save your own skins?

What the Axis powers called their "new order" was nothing but a revival of the oldest and worst tyranny. "Shootings and chains and concentration camps are not simply the transient tools but the very altars of modern dictatorships."

The President declared that the future security of the United States was greatly dependent on the outcome of Britain's fight. "Our ability to 'keep out of war' is going to be affected by that outcome." Aid to nations defending themselves against attack offered far less chance of getting into war than acquiescing in their defeat and waiting to be attacked in another war later on. There was risk in any course:

But I deeply believe that the great majority of our people agree that the course that I advocate involves the least risk now and the greatest hope for world peace in the future.

Roosevelt then paraphrased Churchill's letter of December 8:

The people of Europe who are defending themselves do not ask us to do their fighting. They ask us for the implements of war. . . .
There is no demand for sending an American Expeditionary Force outside our own borders. There is no intention by any member of your Government to send such a force. You can, therefore, nail any talk about sending armies to Europe as deliberate untruth.
Our national policy is not directed toward war. Its sole purpose is to keep war away from our country and our people.

He asserted that it was no more unneutral for the United States to send war materials to defenders in the front lines than it was for "Sweden, Russia and other nations near Germany" to send it such materials.

The President closed with a powerful appeal to labor, management, and all citizens to abandon "business as usual," to unite in an all-out effort to make America "the great arsenal of democracy. For us this is an emergency as serious as war itself." He believed the Axis powers were not going to win the war. He was convinced the American people were now determined to put forth a mightier effort than they had ever yet made "to meet the threat to our democratic faith."

As President of the United States I call for that national effort. I call for it in the name of this nation which we love and honor and which we are privileged and proud to serve. I call upon our people with absolute confidence that our common cause will greatly succeed.[6]

## A New Note?

Charles A. Beard has detected in this address of December 29, 1940, a "new note," namely, a note of doubt by Roosevelt regarding his statement in a campaign address of November 2: "Your President says this country is not going to war." Beard ends his first book on Roosevelt's foreign policy by suggesting that once he was safely re-elected he "changed his line" and exposed a bit more frankly his inner purpose of leading the country into war.[6a]

It is doubtful whether the public was able to detect any such "change of line." Beard neglects to remind his readers that in the same Buffalo speech on November 2 in which Roosevelt said "This country is not going to war," he also said: "There is potential danger to America. . . ." [7] Roosevelt time and again—before, during, and after the campaign—coupled his statements that the country was not going to war with such warnings of danger to America. He made it clear that the decision for war or peace was not entirely in his hands. He meant his audience to believe, not that war was unlikely, but that war was not his policy. After all, any other meaning, an attempt, such as Beard implies, to make his audience believe he could predict *absolutely* that "this country is not going to war," would have been absurd.

A "new note" of a different kind was sounded by President Roosevelt in his December 29 address. He substituted a calmly considered long-range program for the desperate emergency measures of aid to Britain during the period after the Fall of France. The "change of line" reflected a change from fear of defeat to hope for victory. The election played its part in encouraging Roosevelt to sound this new note, because it authorized him to conduct foreign relations for four more years. Long-range planning, which might have done more harm than good if another person occupied the White House in 1941, was now in order. But more important than the American election in explaining this new note were the victory of Britain in the Blitz, the passing of the invasion season, partial success in the Vichy policy, the initiation of planning for the offensive, and first distant glimpses provided by Churchill of how victory might be won.

## The Four Freedoms

Action was rapid after the Fireside Chat. Harry Hopkins was sent to London to maintain personal contact with Churchill for the President after the resignation of the defeatist Ambassador Kennedy and the death of Lord Lothian. Treasury lawyers worked out the details of the Lend Lease Bill. The President, on January 6, 1941, in his Annual Message to Congress asked for authority and funds to manufacture war supplies "to be turned over to those nations which are now in actual war with aggressor nations." He said such action was not an act of war, and summarized the reason why the former code of international law was inapplicable: the aggressors had converted it into a "one-way international law, which lacks mutuality in its observance, and, therefore, becomes an instrument of oppression."

In this Message, Roosevelt announced foundations of a new moral order for the world in opposition to the aggressors' and appeasers' program: freedom of speech and expression; freedom of worship; freedom from want; freedom from fear. The last two the President related to his ancient premises of American internationalism, reduction of trade restrictions and disarmament. Then he approached very close to the terminology of collective security by declaring that reduction of armaments must be so thorough "that no nation will be in a position to commit an act of physical aggression against any neighbor—anywhere in the world," and: "The world order which we seek is the cooperation of free countries, working together in a friendly, civilized society." [8]

The Four Freedoms thus defined stopped just short of including American participation in a world organization for collective security. They brought that eventuality well into view as the ultimate aim of the United States. Churchill still clung to nationalist ideology suitable to Britain's defensive position. But with the Four Freedoms, Roosevelt took the offensive in formulation of war aims, proposed internationalism as the overarching purpose of United States nonbelligerency, and placed the United States in advance of Britain as the leading architect of the postwar world. The Four Freedoms statement was a long step forward in the development of Rooseveltian internationalism. The Atlantic Charter of August, 1941, represented Roosevelt's success in bringing Churchill to agree on these broader war aims.

An unusually intimate picture of the evolution of Roosevelt's thought is available in the case of the Four Freedoms. Shortly after the Fall of France, on July 5, 1940, a reporter challenged the President in a press conference to reassert his earlier hopes about "certain long-range peace objectives." The reporter said he found four objectives in statements of Roosevelt and Hull. The first, he said, was to "prevent aggression—." This was too bold. The President broke in and launched on a lengthy interpretation of the evolution of the American form of government and democracy which, he suggested, now pointed towards certain freedoms as American ideals essential for world peace: freedom of information, freedom of religion, freedom of expression, and freedom from fear of aggression. A reporter proposed a fifth, freedom from want. Roosevelt accepted it, and it became the fourth later, when he combined into one his original freedom of information and freedom of expression.[9]

Thus, in July, 1940, the President had shied away from the positive formulation of "preventing aggression" as an objective of the United States. But in January, 1941, he was ready to state it as the central link between the old American policy of disarmament and the ultimate goal of a world order of cooperation. This progress illustrates both the evolution of Roosevelt's thinking and his application of his famous "sense of timing"; six months after the Fall of France, and three months after the Blitz against Britain, he judged that Americans were ready for closer approaches to full-fledged internationalism.

Charles A. Beard in his treatment of the Annual Message of January 6, 1941, dwells at length on the President's statement that Lend Lease was not an act of war, "even if a dictator should unilaterally proclaim it so to be." Beard states that this meant, "in other words, a dictator might treat it as an act of war and meet it by an attack on the United States." This sleight-of-hand is too obvious: Roosevelt meant, "in other words," precisely the opposite: a dictator might *not justifiably* treat Lend Lease as an act of war and answer it with an attack on the United States.

Beard wishes his readers to be ignorant of the crucial argument of internationalists that the code of neutral obligations had been altered by the League Covenant, the Kellogg-Briand Pact, and other international agreements. He writes as if there were no such argument and as if the views of isolationists like Senator Wheeler were undisputed truths. He states: "Under international law, as long and generally recognized, it was an act of war for a neutral government to supply munitions, arms, and implements of war to one of the belligerents engaged in a war." Many leading authorities on international law in free countries, including the United

States, denied that the international law which **Beard describes** as "generally recognized" still prevailed.[10]

## The Distant Goal

Lend Lease and the Four Freedoms were complementary definitions of the new position of the United States as a nonbelligerent in the war. Lend Lease designated the action the United States would take to assure victory, and the Four Freedoms designated what the United States aimed to do with the victory after it was won. Coalition with Great Britain to defeat Hitler was the narrowest and most immediate significance of the dual policy, and a world organization for collective security was the broadest and most distant prospect it brought into view.

Lend Lease itself was intended by Roosevelt not merely to help Britain defeat Hitler but to help pave the way to that more distant goal, a world system of collective security. This was why the President insisted that the Bill, which originated in the Treasury Department, should be so broad in its authorization that it would permit him to aid an indefinite number of nations for victory against the Axis. The only check on this authority, besides Congressional control of appropriations, was the President's judgment of the requirements of national defense: "When he deems it in the interest of national defense. . . . For the government of any country whose defense the President deems vital to the defense of the United States."

## HR 1776: The Great Debate

When the Bill was entered in Congress on January 10, as House of Representatives 1776, isolationists immediately noted its vast grant of authority and they condemned the Bill as a "blank check." They meant that it was a "blank check" which would permit the President to take the United States not into a world coalition of opponents of aggression but into the war as a full-fledged belligerent.

The result was that the great debate on Lend Lease did not explore the meaning of the Bill as a step towards collective security or take up its relation to the President's proposal in his

Annual Message to work for a world in which "no nation will be in a position to commit an act of physical aggression against any neighbor." Instead, the isolationists took the offensive by charging that the Bill, a "blank check," meant war. Supporters of the Bill, among whom were all internationalists as well as many who saw it purely in terms of immediate national need, were placed on the defensive.

Senator Burton K. Wheeler was chiefly responsible for this turn of the debate into narrow channels. Shortly after the Bill was entered, he declared:

Never before has the Congress of the United States been asked by any President to violate international law. . . . Never before has the United States given to one man the power to strip this Nation of its defenses. Never before has a Congress coldly and flatly been asked to abdicate. . . . The lend-lease-give program is the New Deal's triple A foreign policy; it will plow under every fourth American boy. . . . [It] means war, open and complete warfare. . . .[11]

Wheeler's tirade distracted the President himself from discussion of the constructive purposes of the Bill. Reporters asked him whether he had a comment on the "blank check" label. He answered:

Yes, I suppose so; the easiest answer is: "Write me another that you would not put that label on but which would accomplish the same objective."

This might well have been pursued into discussion of his objective on the level of the Four Freedoms address, but instead Roosevelt felt constrained to answer Wheeler:

That is a perfectly good answer to all these people. That is not an answer at all, however, to those who talk about plowing under every fourth American child, which I regard as the most untruthful, as the most dastardly, unpatriotic thing that has ever been said. Quote me on that. That really is the rottenest thing that has been said in public life in my generation.[12]

This interchange set the tone for a debate that lasted two months. Once more Charles Lindbergh, Father Coughlin and the others filled the radio channels with charges of "warmonger," and pleas that the United States "do business" with Hitler. Once more isolationist Congressmen tried in hearings to trap administration leaders and other supporters of the Bill into admissions that their "real" purpose was war. Advocates stressed only the most narrow argument of internationalism, that aid to victims of attack, enabling them to win the victory, was the best available way of defending the United States, and of making American entry into the war as a result of Axis attack less likely.

Perhaps it was wise of supporters of Lend Lease to accept the isolationists' definition of the issue. If they could be defeated on their own ground, it would mean that a large percentage of the public and of Congress who were not internationalists would have been brought to see the error of the isolationists' proposition and to support the first premise of internationalism: that it was the most intelligent *nationalist* policy. If broader objectives and methods of collective security had been stressed, the process of education in world events, which was bringing many nationalists to abandon isolationism and accept piecemeal the arguments of internationalism, might have been frustrated. The administration needed more than bare majorities to vitalize its program, and it won them. An amendment to name in the Bill the countries which would receive aid was opposed by the administration and defeated.[13]

Isolationists made the hearings on the Lend Lease Bill prosecutions of its advocates. They sought to make even the drafting of the Bill appear a sinister plot, after Secretary Hull had told the House Committee on Foreign Relations that it was a Treasury product, and Secretary Morgenthau had denied it. Morgenthau insisted to the Senate Committee on Foreign Relations that officials of the Treasury Department, including himself, collaborated with members of Congress, officials and heads of many Departments and agencies, and the President to produce the Bill, that it was "a product of many brains." [14] This description of its origin is substantiated by the account later published by Edward R. Stettinius.[15]

Charles A. Beard, however, accuses Morgenthau of concealing from Congress that the Lend Lease Bill actually originated in Churchill's letter of December 8, 1940, to President Roosevelt. He attempts to prove the accusation by distorting a quotation from Churchill's letter, which Morgenthau included in an article he wrote for *Collier's* magazine, October 18, 1947. Beard declares Churchill's letter proposed "a form of American aid to Great Britain free from what President Roosevelt called 'the dollar sign.' " [16] Actually, as has been shown, Churchill did not suggest any "form" of aid. He merely described Britain's financial situation and proposed no solution whatever. Beard by this distortion intends his readers to believe as truth the isolationist charge that Lend Lease was a "British plot."

Morgenthau again and again in the hearings described accurately the British part in the affair as being one of stating Britain's financial situation and leaving the decision whether the United States would act, and, if so, what form aid should take, entirely in the hands of Americans. For example:

Senator Nye: Does Britain very definitely ask for the aid that is contemplated under this bill?

Secretary Morgenthau: No. What the British Treasury does is simply this—as a matter of fact, the late British Ambassador, Lord Lothian, was the man who made the first announcement as to their needs, and simply put at our disposal the cold, hard facts—they are not in any way hysterical about it. . . .

If this bill does not pass they cannot continue to fight. The decision rests with the Congress of the United States as to whether Great Britain, Greece, and China should or should not continue to fight.

Senator Nye: Have British spokesmen said as much?

Secretary Morgenthau: No; not in just those words. I do not go into those questions with them. The facts are that they will not place orders that they cannot pay for. Therefore, the ordering has practically ceased.

That is the situation, gentlemen. [17]

Morgenthau also accurately designated the most significant origin of the Lend Lease idea as the Pittman Resolution of June 15, 1940, which made war materials available to Latin American governments. [18] In short, Lend Lease originated as an American policy which the Roosevelt administration applied first to the Western Hemisphere and then to the world.

The question of naval convoys was also raised by opponents of the Bill. It would be foolish for the United States to manufacture war materials for Britain only to allow the ships carrying them to be sunk by German submarines. Therefore, isolationists argued, a necessary corollary of Lend Lease was United States naval escort of merchant ship convoys, which would be an "act of war." Senator Nye asked Secretary of the Navy Knox whether he thought the Bill permitted convoying of British merchantmen by the American Navy. Knox answered that the President had the power to use the Navy for escorts whether the Bill passed or not.[19] In this answer Knox was on solid ground. The authority of the President, without a declaration of war by Congress, to order the Navy to engage in all manner of "belligerent" action, including attack against warships and shore positions of a foreign country with which the United States was legally at peace, had often been exercised and had never been successfully challenged in the courts.

This view of Secretary Knox made quite reasonable his part in a subsequent interchange with Nye which Beard presents as something remarkable:

Nye: You stand very much opposed to the idea of convoying merchantmen across the Atlantic?
Knox: Yes.
Nye: Would you change your mind about it if the President were to order a convoy?
Knox: Certainly.[20]

Secretary of War Stimson in testimony before the same Committee argued for the post-Kellogg Pact view of international law and denied that convoying would put the United States "in the war." [21] Opponents of the Bill wanted an explicit prohibition of convoys incorporated in it, but supporters pointed out that such limitation on the President's authority over the Navy was contrary to the Constitution. They worked out instead a formula which provided that nothing in the Bill should be construed to authorize naval convoying or entry of an American vessel into a combat zone.

This was a defeat for the isolationists. The amendment did not reduce the general authority of the President as Commander-in-Chief in the slightest respect. Beard discusses this amendment, and another one declaring that existing laws relating to the use of the land and naval forces remained unchanged, in a manner calculated to prepare the way for his description of the President plotting entry into the war by means of convoying. He interprets the amendments as meaning "in other words" that Congress had declared that the President in executing the Lend Lease Act "could not order the armed forces to commit acts of war." [22] This is a gross misrepresentation of the amendments. The amendment prohibiting convoys had been defeated. The amendments that were adopted clearly left unchanged the President's well-established authority to order the naval and land forces to commit acts of war. They were a sop to the isolationists only insofar as they gave assurance that the Lend Lease Bill conferred on the President no *new* authority if he wished to order convoys or other "acts of war." Such authority came to him directly from the Constitution and could not be altered by Congress.

Representatives like Hamilton Fish of New York and George H. Tinkham of Massachusetts, Senators like Nye and La Follette, and publicists like Colonel Lindbergh and Norman Thomas argued that the Lend Lease Bill was a "war bill" which gave the President dictatorial powers to wage undeclared wars and at the same time give away the United States Navy and the other defenses of the country, leading inevitably to a full-fledged war which the United States would lose.

Dr. Charles A. Beard was the most eminent scholar among the isolationists who appeared before the Senate Committee, and he offered interesting prognostications which throw much light on his effort in later books to perpetuate his own views. He supported as an historian the standard isolationist view that the Old World was sunk beyond recovery in traditions of violence. He said the "exuberance" of Americans who "clamor" that it is the mission of the United States to "make over" Europe and Asia is "on a par with the childish exuberance of the Bolshevik internationalists who preach the gospel of one model for the whole world." His disillusionment with the history of the First World War put him "on guard" against another "crusade." He did not mean to say the present war was identical with the last war but, in the light of the long history of the Old World and the long conflicts of the great powers, "a discussion of their mere war aims shrivels into futility."

But, Beard continued, the Lend Lease Bill made it the solemn duty of Congressmen to discuss the aims of the United States government in the activities the Bill would "let loose." They could not escape these questions:

Does Congress intend to guarantee the present extent, economic resources, and economic methods of the British Empire forever to the Government of Great Britain by placing the unlimited resources of the United States forever at the disposal of the British Government, however constituted? [23]

But Beard ignored what the Lend Lease Bill itself and its supporters had made amply clear: that the decision as to whether a certain nation should receive aid would be determined not by the nature of its internal social, economic, or governmental structure but by its foreign policy in relation to American defense. Earlier in the Senate Hearings, Secretary Knox had been challenged on the crucial question of Russia:

Senator Nye: Assume, Mr. Secretary, that Russia were to take up arms or one of these days show an opposition to the forces of Germany; would the President have power under this bill to make its provisions applicable to Russia as well as any other nation?
Secretary Knox: If he regarded it as being for the benefit of or vital to the defense of the United States; yes. [24]

The administration clearly placed national defense through aid to any defenders against aggression first, and achievement of the expansion of American ideals of democracy second. Beard sought to frighten Congressmen away from achievement of the first goal by pointing out the difficulties in the way of the second:

And if European or Asiatic powers should propose to make settlements without providing democracy, a bill of rights, and economic security for everybody, everywhere, will Congress insist that they keep on fighting until the President of the United States is satisfied with the results?

Then Beard raised the usual question of throwing "millions of boys" after the "billions of dollars." He anticipated the need after the war for what was later called the European Recovery Program or Marshall Plan, and questioned whether it could succeed. He asked Congressmen whether they were "absolutely sure" that "the flames of war and civil commotion" would not spread to the United States itself. He stated as a certainty that "the war boom of fool's gold" would "burst with terrific force."

These formulations were derived from doctrinal faith in the adequacy of a past policy for the present and future—isolationism. Beard preferred to call it "continentalism," a conception, as Senator Johnson of California presently reminded him, which he had based on the policy of President George Washington and had described in a book entitled *A Foreign Policy for America.* Beard agreed with the Senator that he perceived no need for a change in foreign policy since Washington's time:

Here, on this continent, I believe we may be secure and should make ourselves secure from the kind of conflict and terrorism in which the old worlds have indulged for such long ages of time.

After these declarations, it was surprising, if not contradictory, that Beard proposed defeat of the Lend Lease Bill but nevertheless immediate aid to Britain by means of a generous extension of governmental credit. He even said a good word for America's mission to help reconstruct the world after the war. The United States should then, he said,

in keeping with its historic traditions, tender to the shattered nations of the earth those services which it can competently offer, in keeping with our peace and security on this continent.[25]

How aid to Britain, to an "amount generously above a careful estimate of British needs," as Beard proposed, would prevent "a war boom of fool's gold," which would "burst with terrific force;" how such aid differed from Lend Lease in compatibility with "continentalism;" why such support of one party in Europe's age-old quarrels was preferable to Lend Lease, which also extended credit but asked for repayment in the form of goods and services instead of dollars: these questions Beard did not discuss.

Lindbergh, too, said he favored aid to Britain to carry out "commitments that we have already made," after he had told the Committee he preferred "a negotiated peace" between Hitler and Churchill "to a complete victory by either side." This was a "moderate" position which Lindbergh had carefully worked out after his suggestion in August, 1940, that a victorious Nazi Germany would be as good a neighbor to the United States as Great

Britain had been, had produced a revulsion of public opinion against him.[26] Now, Lindbergh said he thought the possibility of British victory to be "extremely doubtful," and that the Lend Lease Bill endorsed a policy that would "lead to failure in war." He did not in fact want a British victory, yet he did not oppose continuing aid to Britain.[27]

These seeming contradictions may be resolved by consideration that, on the one hand, aid to Britain was so overwhelmingly popular it could hardly be opposed by a publicist who wished to be influential and, on the other, men like Beard and Lindbergh correctly understood that Lend Lease was for the Roosevelt administration a step forward in the evolution of American internationalism, a large step towards adoption by the American people of the policy of collective security; wherefore, as faithful isolationists or continentalists, they sought some more limited and "harmless" way of satisfying the nearly universal demand for aid to Britain. At the same time it was noticeable that isolationists seemed not to share the general American horror of Nazism and Fascism. They seldom expressed more than perfunctory opposition to them; they were quicker to point out the sins of democratic countries like Britain and France.

Opponents of Lend Lease predicted that, if the Bill passed, Congress and people would not again have an opportunity to prevent American entry into the war. Supporters answered that if Lend Lease failed to secure victory against the Axis, Congress and people would decide the next step, and many of them said they would oppose entry into the war under any circumstance except direct attack on the United States. Others were willing to say that if American interests in a later situation required, they would advocate war.

The main votes on the Bill gave it strong majorities: 260 to 165 in the House on February 8 and 60 to 31 in the Senate on March 8. The House on March 11 finally accepted the Bill, including minor Senate changes, by 317 to 71. More than one-third of the Republicans voted no, but only one-sixteenth of the Democrats. Almost all of the opponents were from the Middle West. Southerners were unanimously in favor of the Bill.[28]

The President signed the Bill on the same day, and declared the defense of Great Britain and Greece to be vital to the defense of the United States. Transfer of material up to $1,300,000,000 in value, which Congress had previously appropriated, began. Among the articles which went to Britain were twenty-eight of the motor torpedo boats for which Churchill had first asked ten months earlier. Mussolini's troops were being pushed out of Greece, but Bulgaria followed Rumania and Hungary into the Axis, and Hitler came to Mussolini's rescue through Yugoslavia and Bulgaria, so that Lend Lease aid was too late for the fighting Greeks. Roosevelt asked Congress on March 12 for $7,000,000,000 for expansion of defense production for the purposes of Lend Lease. Congress passed the appropriation in two weeks. On May 6 the President declared China eligible for Lend Lease aid.

## The Bipartisan Policy of the Nation

Immediately after the Congressional approval of Lend Lease, the House Minority Leader Joseph Martin and the Senate Minority Leader Arthur H. Vandenberg, both of them active isolationists, issued statements pledging full support of Lend Lease by their Party and adherence to it as the bipartisan policy of the nation. All but the most embittered isolationists followed suit. On March 15 the President said at the White House Correspondents Association dinner: "Let not the dictators of Europe and Asia doubt our unanimity now. . . . Yes, the decisions of our democracy may be slowly arrived at, but when that decision is made it is proclaimed not with the voice of one man, but with the voice of one hundred and thirty millions." [29]

And indeed the Lend Lease debate, for all its slowness, was a remarkable display of democracy in action. No one could deny that the opposition had its day—in fact, two months—or that free formulation of public opinion occurred. Leaders of public opinion were more evenly divided than the public or Congress. Labor leaders who subscribed to the Communist definition of the war as imperialist on both sides were not widely supported by union members. Businessmen grouped around General Robert E. Wood of Sears, Roebuck and Company and his America First Committee were not able to turn the business community as a whole against the Bill. Alfred E. Smith and Wendell Willkie supported the Bill, while Alfred Landon and Herbert Hoover opposed it. Thomas E. Dewey opposed it until it was clear that the country and Congress approved it; then he came out in its favor shortly before the votes were taken. At the Hearings, each side matched the other's distinguished witnesses from such fields as law, education, and religion. It helped the administration that the country's most unpopular small groups—Nazi Bundists, Fascists, and Communists, as well as discredited larger groups of the reactionary lunatic fringe led by Father Coughlin and Gerald L. K. Smith—were all united against its program. Most Americans inclined to regard any position they took as evidently wrong. The possibility, however, that the Axis governments had established working relations with some highly placed Americans in efforts to divide the country and subvert its defense began to be understood during this period as being ominously similar to the early stages of Axis activities in countries subsequently attacked. This led to the decision of the Roosevelt administration to prosecute suspects for sedition, and grand jury investigations began in September.

The Lend Lease debate contributed greatly to the orderly and constructive evolution of American foreign policy. If the debate failed to assess the long-range internationalist implications of the law, it nevertheless increased public understanding and support of the immediate necessity for a great, practical effort to oppose aggression and support its victims. Perhaps the broadest meaning of the event was that Americans now admitted in an unprecedented piece of legislation their dependence on foreign friends and fighters for their cause.

## 12.

# The Convoy Conundrum

After the passage of the lend lease act, the chief question facing Roosevelt was how to insure delivery of the cargoes of weapons and materials to Britain. Admiral Doenitz had begun to organize his increasing number of submarines in "wolf packs." As early as October 12, 1940, the President in a Columbus Day address on hemispheric defense had described the naval defenses of "this half of the world" and made what amounted to a campaign promise:

No combination of dictator countries of Europe and Asia will stop the help we are giving to almost the last free people now fighting to hold them at bay.[1]

In his address of December 29, 1940, Roosevelt had virtually promised that the United States would not permit the defeat of Great Britain.[2] Quite apart from such promises, it was obvious that Lend Lease required delivery as well as manufacture of the goods needed in Britain and elsewhere for victory.

The equally obvious way to insure delivery was to use United States naval escorts to protect convoys of merchantmen. "Wolf pack" tactics of the German submarines made larger naval escorts necessary, and the Royal Navy was inadequate. Britain was losing the Battle of the Atlantic in the spring of 1941. Its monthly losses of merchant ships were from two to three times greater than its ability to replace them. Turning over to the Royal Navy important portions of the American fleet was "legal" under the Lend

Lease Act, but during the debate it had been ruled out as absurd by Knox, Roosevelt and other administration leaders. They had also stated in various forms that the administration did not contemplate use of the American navy to escort convoys. On January 22, 1941, the press reported that "sources close to the White House said it was obvious that if the United States Navy convoyed ships . . . into a combat zone, shooting was pretty sure to result and shooting came awfully close to war." [3]

It is to be noticed that this did not rule out escort of convoys outside combat zones. But isolationists concentrated on the convoy issue after passage of Lend Lease and raised a fearful clamor of charges and rumors that the administration was already escorting convoys or would presently do so. Charles A. Beard claims to establish the truth of these charges as historical fact. He presents Roosevelt's solution of the conundrum as one of his chief exhibits in the case against the President. He finds Roosevelt guilty of ordering escorts in April, 1941, while he and other administration leaders continued to assure the public that convoys were not being escorted. Beard finds the administration guilty of lies in its plot to carry the country into war.

## "Appearances" and "Realities"

The truth is that Roosevelt, advised by Hull, solved the conundrum of how to make good the delivery of Lend Lease aid to Britain entirely without resort to escort of convoys until July 11, 1941, when United States Marines occupied Iceland, and after that date ordered escorts of convoys only on the route as far as the American-occupied island, that is, outside the combat zone surrounding the British Isles.

A curiosity of Beard's treatment of the convoy question is that his chapters contain adequate factual material for a reader to discover the truth if he will disentangle the facts from the mass of falsified comment and implication in which Beard imbeds them. He treats this subject, like every other one in his second volume, in two widely separated sections, the one labeled "Appearances," and the other "Realities." This device permits him to make implications under "Appearances" that do not square with the material under "Realities." For example, Beard quotes the President as stating to the press on April 25, 1941, that the United States Navy was engaged in patrolling, not convoying, in the Atlantic. In a footnote, Beard comments:

> As a matter of fact, the United States Navy was then and had been for some time secretly engaged in cooperating with the British in main-taining "escorts" to keep "convoys" moving in the Atlantic. . . . See below, Chap. XIV.[4]

This footnote is a masterpiece of distortion. The phrase "As a matter of fact," opens the reader's mind to expect a statement be-lying the President's words. Actually, the words "cooperating with the British in maintaining 'escorts' to keep 'convoys' moving in the Atlantic" do not belie the President's words at all, they merely minimize the distinction the President was making be-tween patrolling and convoying. And if the reader turns as sug-gested to Beard's Chapter XIV, he can find no evidence that the United States at this time was convoying or escorting convoys. In-deed, Beard quotes from a letter of Admiral Stark, dated July 31, 1941, in which the Admiral describes himself after the invasion of Russia as urging the President to *"start* escorting." [5]

The distinction between convoying and patrolling is the heart of the dispute. Beard fills many pages with the charges of isola-tionists that the President ordered convoying by the Navy after he signed the Lend Lease Act. The general conclusion one draws from his discussion is that although the administration denied them, the charges were true. Yet he quotes words of one of the chief initiators of the clamor, John O'Donnell, a bitter isolationist columnist in the *New York Daily News,* in which O'Donnell admits that his first statement, on April 16, that "the Navy and Coast Guard are now giving armed escort to munition-laden British merchantmen leaving Atlantic ports for the European bat-tlefront," might have been inaccurate, and that a "quibbling" de-scription was, "whatever the word for it, American naval vessels were in fact giving to British ships all assistance of information, patrol, and reconnaissance. . . ." Beard then quotes the Presi-dent's reply to O'Donnell, made through Stephen Early, his Press Secretary. Early stated that American naval vessels were operat-ing far out into the Atlantic on Neutrality Patrol and transmitting by radio news of the location of alien ships "in the clear," that is, without use of code. Then Early denied for the President the accusations of convoying:

The President of the United States, after reading a morning paper, said that he thought the author of the story had very closely woven the long-time and historic policy of the United States into a story which was a deliberate lie.[6]

This seems to be an accurate description of both O'Donnell's and Beard's methods. The Neutrality Patrol was "long-time" in the sense that it had been established at the very beginning of the war. It had been initiated to carry out the "historic" policy of the United States of protection of shipping. O'Donnell, like Beard later, made incidental admissions that the United States was not convoying but patrolling, but his account presented this as if it meant the same thing as convoying.

O'Donnell wrote in support of a resolution offered by Senator Charles W. Tobey, of New Hampshire, to forbid convoying. The resolution incidentally admitted what Beard denies—that the amendments of the Lend Lease Act did not forbid the President to order convoying. Beard, like Tobey in the debate, ignored the distinction, reiterated by the President and others, between convoying and patrolling. He comments on Early's statement for the President:

The nature of the relation between the historic policy of the United States and the policy of convoying the merchant ships of a foreign belligerent in April, 1941, the President did not indicate.

This is designed to make it seem to the reader that O'Donnell, Tobey, and Beard established it as a fact that convoying was being employed; otherwise the sentence is meaningless because the President through Early had once more made it thoroughly clear that in his view there was no necessary "relation between the historic policy of the United States and the policy of convoying." The President denied he was convoying; he showed only a relation between historic policy and patrolling. Beard continues:

Nor did he explain its connection with the charge that American naval vessels were convoying or otherwise giving protection to British ships on the high seas.

This redundancy is for the purpose of smuggling into the text the escape clause "or otherwise giving protection to British ships," as if patrolling were synonymous with convoying. Then Beard concludes portentously: "As reported the President's statement conveyed the idea that Mr. O'Donnell's story was false." [7] This is a heavy, ironic understatement that O'Donnell was right, Roosevelt wrong.

Secretary Hull in his *Memoirs* claims credit for the suggestion to Roosevelt that extension of the Neutrality Patrol would serve the purpose of protecting Lend Lease shipments to Britain without resort to escorting convoys. He points out that the definite limits of the Western Hemisphere Neutrality Zone adopted at Panama in 1939 had "fizzled out" because international law provided no definition of such limits and both belligerents refused to observe them. Hull argued for a "flexible" zone, and that the American nations had a right of self-defense to send naval patrols out to any distance from the coast they felt necessary to protect the Hemisphere.[8]

On April 2, 1941, Roosevelt considered the possibility of providing naval escorts for Atlantic convoys, but by the end of the month he had decided against it. Instead he decided to strengthen the Neutrality Patrol. The limits were extended to the line of longitude 25° West, which passes half way between Brazil and the west coast of Africa and slightly west of Iceland. Later the line was bent eastward in the north to include Iceland. Churchill was notified of this decision and synchronization of efforts was asked for by Roosevelt in the following words which reveal the import of the strengthened patrol: "We will want to be notified by you in great secrecy of movements of convoys so that our patrol units can seek out the ship of an aggressor nation operating west of the new line of the security zone." He also told Churchill of other measures to improve the shipping situation, and said that he would declare the Red Sea no longer a combat zone so that United States merchantmen could carry goods to nonbelligerent ports of the Middle East.[9]

Everyone knew, and the President and others made it quite

clear, that the Neutrality Patrol from beginning to end was based on the administration's conception of the United States obligation under international law as a neutral or "nonbelligerent" to favor the victims of aggression. The information service of the American patrol ships was described to the public time and again. It was obvious that the service aided Britain and injured Germany. Britain's interest in the Western Atlantic was to protect merchant shipping, while Germany's interest was to wage submarine warfare against it. If any doubt about these elementary "realities" of the situation remained after the Lend Lease Act was passed, the President dispelled it in a crescendo of public announcements. After Early's statement, the President himself in a press conference on April 25 explained matters at great length. He gave definitions of "convoy" and "patrol," and added an analogy which made very clear the kind of assistance the patrol ships gave to British convoys:

While wagon trains going westward in pioneer days had armed guards, they also had scouts. It was sensible to keep the trains more than two miles from where the Indians were. . . .

The *New York Times* account added:

The clear implication was that the neutrality patrol would do the same for ships crossing the Atlantic and operating elsewhere.

Roosevelt also made clear that the patrol had been extended, what its purpose was, and the way it functioned:

Because the danger to the Western Hemisphere was growing greater, the patrol was operating farther at sea and would operate still farther as need to do so developed.

The patrol, made up of warships and planes, will go as far in the waters of the seven seas as may be necessary for the protection of this hemisphere. . . .

This was a patrol, however, and not a convoy. A convoy meant escorting merchant ships traveling in a group and protecting the ships from attack by fighting off an assailant. A patrol is a reconnaissance in certain areas to detect any aggressor ships which might be coming to the Western Hemisphere. It was indicated that ships could avoid areas reported to be dangerous. The patrol would report the presence of any aggressor to the President, and he would decide what to do.

This government has no idea at this time of escorting convoys.[10]

On April 30 the Senate Committee on Foreign Relations defeated the resolution to forbid convoying by a vote of ten to thirteen.

## Unlimited National Emergency

Charges that the Navy was convoying continued to appear in the isolationist press and receive credence in Congress. On May 27, 1941, the President spoke on the subject to a national radio audience when he addressed a Pan American group. He reviewed the course of the war, pointed to the signs that Hitler's next move might be into Spain and Western Africa, emphasized the existing crisis of the Battle of the Atlantic, and revealed that Nazi sinkings totalled more than three times the British and twice the combined British and American capacities to build ships. Then he detailed with remarkable fullness his program to meet the crisis:

We can answer this peril by two simultaneous measures: First, by speeding up and increasing our great ship-building program; and second, by helping to cut down the losses on the high seas.

Attacks on shipping off the very shores of land which we are determined to protect present an actual military danger to the Americas. And that danger has recently been heavily underlined by the presence in Western Hemisphere waters of Nazi battleships of great striking power.

Most of the supplies for Britain go by a northerly route, which comes close to Greenland and the nearby island of Iceland. Germany's heaviest attack is on that route. Nazi occupation of Iceland or bases in Greenland would bring the war close to our continental shores; because they are stepping stones to Labrador, Newfoundland, Nova Scotia, and the northern United States, including the great industrial centers of the North, East, and the Middle West.

Equally the Azores and the Cape Verde Islands, if occupied or controlled by Germany, would directly endanger the freedom of the Atlantic and our own physical safety. Under German domination they would become bases for submarines, warships, and airplanes raiding the waters which lie immediately off our own coasts and attacking the shipping in the south Atlantic. They would provide a springboard for actual attack against the integrity and independence of Brazil and her neighboring republics.

I have said on many occasions that the United States is mustering its men and its resources only for purposes of defense—only to repel attack. I repeat that statement now. But we must be realistic when we use the word "attack"; we have to relate it to the lightning speed of modern warfare.

Some people seem to think that we are not attacked until bombs actually drop on New York or San Francisco or New Orleans or Chicago. But they are simply shutting their eyes to the lesson we must learn from the fate of every nation that the Nazis have conquered.

The attack on Czechoslovakia began with the conquest of Austria. The attack on Norway began with the occupation of Denmark. The attack on Greece began with the occupation of Albania and Bulgaria. The attack on the Suez Canal began with the invasion of the Balkans and North Africa. The attack on the United States can begin with the domination of any base which menaces our security—north or south.

Nobody can foretell tonight just when the acts of the dictators will ripen into attack on this hemisphere and us. But we know enough by now to realize that it would be suicide to wait until they are in our front yard.

When your enemy comes at you in a tank or a bombing plane, if you hold your fire until you see the whites of his eyes, you will never know what hit you. Our Bunker Hill of tomorrow may be several thousand miles from Boston.

Anyone with an atlas and a reasonable knowledge of the sudden striking force of a modern war knows that it is stupid to wait until a probable enemy has gained a foothold from which to attack. Old-fashioned common sense calls for the use of a strategy which will prevent such an enemy from gaining a foothold in the first place.

We have, accordingly, extended our patrol in North and South Atlantic waters. We are steadily adding more and more ships and planes to that patrol. It is well known that the strength of the Atlantic fleet has been greatly increased during the past year, and is constantly being built up.

These ships and planes warn of the presence of attacking raiders, on the sea, under the sea, and above the sea. The danger from these raiders is greatly lessened if their location is definitely known. We are thus being forewarned; and we shall be on our guard against efforts to establish Nazi bases closer to our hemisphere.

The deadly facts of war compel nations, for simple self-preservation, to make stern choices. It does not make sense, for instance, to say, "I believe in the defense of all the Western Hemisphere," and in the next breath to say, "I will not fight for that defense until the enemy has landed on our shores." And if we believe in the independence and integrity of the Americas, we must be willing to fight to defend them just as much as we would to fight for the safety of our own homes.

It is time for us to realize that the safety of American homes even in the center of our country has a definite relationship to the continued safety of homes in Nova Scotia or Trinidad or Brazil.

Our national policy today, therefore, is this:

First, we shall actively resist wherever necessary, and with all our resources, every attempt by Hitler to extend his Nazi domination to the Western Hemisphere, or to threaten it. We shall actively resist his every attempt to gain control of the seas. We insist upon the vital importance of keeping Hitlerism away from any point in the world which could be used and would be used as a base of attack against the Americas.

Second, from the point of view of strict naval and military necessity, we shall give every possible assistance to Britain and to all who, with Britain, are resisting Hitlerism or its equivalent with force of arms. Our patrols are helping now to insure delivery of the needed supplies to Britain. All additional measures necessary to deliver the goods will be taken. Any and all further methods or combination of methods, which can or should be utilized, are being devised by our military and naval technicians, who, with me, will work out and put into effect such new and additional safeguards as may be needed.

The delivery of needed supplies to Britain is imperative. This can be done; it must be done; it will be done.

Roosevelt concluded this address by declaring an unlimited national emergency and asserting that the armed forces would be used to repel attack:

We choose human freedom—which is the Christian ideal.

No one of us can waver for a moment in his courage or his faith.

We will not accept a Hitler-dominated world. And we will not accept a world, like the post-war world of the 1920's, in which the seeds of Hitlerism can again be planted and allowed to grow.

We will accept only a world consecrated to freedom of speech and expression—freedom of every person to worship God in his own way—freedom from want—and freedom from terrorism.

Is such a world impossible of attainment?

Magna Carta, the Declaration of Independence, the Constitution of the United States, the Emancipation Proclamation, and every other milestone in human progress—all were ideals which seemed impossible of attainment—yet they were attained.

As a military force, we were weak when we established our independence, but we successfully stood off tyrants, powerful in their day, who are now lost in the dust of history.

Odds meant nothing to us then. Shall we now, with all our potential strength, hesitate to take every single measure necessary to maintain our American liberties?

Our people and our Government will not hesitate to meet that challenge.

As the President of a united and determined people, I say solemnly:

We reassert the ancient American doctrine of freedom of the seas.

We reassert the solidarity of the 21 American Republics and the Dominion of Canada in the preservation of the independence of the hemisphere.

We have pledged material support to the other democracies of the world—and we will fulfill that pledge.

We in the Americas will decide for ourselves whether, and when, and where, our American interests are attacked or our security threatened.

We are placing our armed forces in strategic military position.

We will not hesitate to use our armed forces to repel attack.

We reassert our abiding faith in the vitality of our constitutional Republic as a perpetual home of freedom, of tolerance, and of devotion to the word of God.

Therefore, with profound consciousness of my responsibilities to my countrymen and to my country's cause, I have tonight issued a proclamation that an unlimited national emergency exists and requires the strengthening of our defense to the extreme limit of our national power and authority.

The Nation will expect all individuals and all groups to play their full parts without stint, and without selfishness, and without doubt that our democracy will triumphantly survive.

I repeat the words of the signers of the Declaration of Independence —that little band of patriots, fighting long ago against overwhelming odds, but certain, as are we, of ultimate victory: "With a firm reliance on the protection of divine providence, we mutually pledge to each other our lives, our fortunes, and our sacred honor." [11]

Beard is not satisfied that this address was informative. He gives his readers an incomplete account of what the President said and then complains that the President only informed the country that supplies would be delivered to Britain, "leaving undescribed the exact methods he intended to employ." The President, Beard writes, referred to the extension of the American patrol "as if" still clinging to the distinction which he had drawn before between patrol and convoy.[12]

### Stimson Dissents

The President's May 27 address settled the convoy controversy for all but willful distorters of the facts. Those who ran could read or hear and judge the President's solution of the conundrum. Many of his supporters objected that it compromised too weakly with the isolationists, that the United States should not only escort convoys under Presidential authority granted by the Constitution, but repeal the Neutrality Act to abolish the self-imposed combat zones and carry the goods all the way to Britain in American ships escorted by the American Navy.

Secretary of War Stimson was the leading exponent inside the administration of the thesis that the President unduly feared isolationist opinion, that he moved too slowly. Stimson has recorded in his memoirs that in the fall of 1940 he "gradually became convinced that war was inevitable." On December 16, after a meeting with Secretary Knox, General Marshall, and Admiral Stark, Stimson wrote in his diary that all were agreed the emergency "could hardly be passed over without this country being drawn into the war eventually." This was an estimate of probabilities by the four men who carried the direct burden of military responsibility for the nation's safety. Stimson recognized that this estimate did not require him to interfere with the President's decision to adhere to "measures short of war." Isolationists in Congress bedeviled Stimson to force him into admissions that he believed war necessary to prevent a Nazi triumph, but "he was bound to silence by the requirement of loyalty to his chief."

Until the passage of Lend Lease, Stimson was satisfied the President led the country "just as fast as it was willing to go." But beginning in April, 1941, he strongly believed the President wrongly conducted himself as the representative of public opinion rather than its leader. Stimson viewed the Presidency from the standpoint of an old-fashioned Republican with Federalist antecedents and he opposed those modern Republicans who quailed before an aggressive Chief Executive like Franklin D. Roosevelt or Woodrow Wilson. This eminent Republican's opinion of Roosevelt as too timid a leader is an interesting contrast to those who cried "Dictator!" whenever Roosevelt moved. Stimson wrote of himself: "Of the power of forthright leadership he had a higher opinion than the President."

Stimson believed the President should follow up his victory in the Lend Lease debate with forthright resort to convoying and statements to the people of the necessity to enter the war. He blamed Roosevelt for giving Americans an illusion that the Axis could be defeated without the United States throwing into the battle more than its material goods. He believed the President paved the way for specific steps "with unequaled political skill," but that in the process "he was likely to tie his own hands for the future, using honeyed and consoling words that would return to plague him later." Stimson admits that at times entire frankness about the future is impossible, but asserts: *"The essential difference between Stimson and the President was in the value they set on candor as a political weapon."*

These views of Secretary Stimson, who arrived at them in the course of a personal experience of American government unique in modern times, merit the highest consideration. The difference between him and the President, Stimson carefully states, "was one of degree, not of kind," and he declares that "nothing could be farther" from his position than the isolationists' "view that Franklin Roosevelt dishonestly pulled the American people into a war they never should have fought."

Furthermore, Stimson indicates to some extent the two chief considerations which made the President pursue the more cautious course after passage of Lend Lease: counterbalancing advice from the State Department, which made Roosevelt's course a middle one between two extreme opinions among his advisers; and fear of disaster to his whole program if a proposal were defeated in Congress or disapproved by the people.[13] A fuller understanding of the President's course requires amplification of Stimson's brief remarks on these vital deterrents.

In the first place, Roosevelt did not regard support by a mere majority of the people as sufficient to warrant the measures Stimson advocated. The Gallup Poll reported that 70 per cent of voters asked late in April, 1941, did support naval escorts for convoys to Britain if British defeat seemed certain without them.[14] But the *New York Times* reported on April 26 that Presidential aides "privately maintained" that Roosevelt "was reluctant to provide naval escorts for shipping unless public demand for such action was overwhelming." Two weighty reasons for the President's requirement of near-unanimity may be discerned. A virtual pledge had been given by administration leaders that Lend Lease did not require convoying, and this pledge could be broken only if those who had desired it, chiefly the isolationists, demanded that it be broken. Leaders like Stimson and organizations like the Committee to Defend America made amply clear to the public that naval escorts would provide excellent assurance of deliveries of Lend Lease aid to Great Britain, but a large minority of the public was unconvinced. Also, after Hitler's statement on January 30,

1941, that every ship that helped England would be torpedoed, and his extension on March 26 of the German war zone to within three miles of Greenland, little doubt could remain that escorts would produce dangerous incidents. Employment of escorts therefore required near-unanimity not merely to absolve the President from observance of his pledges but because no leader of a democracy dares to carry a divided people into war.

Stimson wanted Roosevelt to ask the people to support escorts and war, but the President regarded the request itself as a violation of his pledges because it was precisely against the adoption of a war policy that he had pledged himself. He decided to wait for events to lead the people as a whole to demand abandonment of his pledges. This, Stimson declares, involved the other risk that the Axis leaders would do nothing to unite the American people against them. Stimson was chiefly worried because policies "short of war" were no inspiration to his new Army of drafted soldiers. Roosevelt, however, could consider the possibility that the Axis could be defeated without using the American Army or even the Navy for more than patrol. Especially after Hitler invaded Russia on June 22, 1941, there was reason for Roosevelt to believe Churchill's declaration of December, 1940, that Hitler could be defeated with American aid short of war and without naval escorts. This was a promise of success Stimson does not consider. As for the risk that the Axis leaders would allow the American people to help win the victory over them without forcing them to fight, it was one which Roosevelt was evidently glad to assume.

Stimson believed that fighting with goods but not men was ignoble. The glorification of war as an ennobling enterprise which surrounded the American imperialist adventures of earlier Republican administrations still echoed persuasively in Stimson's mind. Roosevelt responded to the modern hatred of war as a debasing enterprise which could be justified only if all other means had been absolutely exhausted.

Roosevelt had to reckon not only with public opinion, but with a Congress that lagged behind the people in willingness to adopt strong measures against the Axis. The struggle to obtain extension of the Selective Service Act in July and August, 1941, and its passage in the House by one vote, is strong evidence that the President would have courted disaster if he had submitted Stimson's program to Congress for approval. Stimson's complaint against Roosevelt, that he used "honeyed and consoling words which would return to plague him later," applies to his dealings with Congress as well as the public. But it seems probable that the President would not have obtained from Congress repeal of the arms embargo, passage of the Selective Service Act and the Lend Lease Act, and extension of Selective Service if he had not used "honeyed and consoling words." Roosevelt had determined to avoid in the field of foreign policy the defeats which Congress had dealt him in the field of domestic policy.

Stimson himself seems to retract his complaint against the President in his description of an incident during the struggle to extend Selective Service. Many Congressmen, he writes, hoped by inaction on the subject

to force the President to do by trickery what they themselves refused to do openly. On August 7, Representative Walter G. Andrews, of New York, came to see Stimson. Andrews, "a very good man," and a supporter of the bill for extension, "fished out an opinion which he said the opponents were relying on which held that technically, although not morally, the President would have the power to extend the term of service of each man himself after his one year expired by passing him into the Reserve and then calling him out from the Reserve. This is one of those finespun technical interpretations which possibly is legally correct (I think I can say probably) and yet which is contrary to the intention of the Congress at the time when the statutes last summer were made and I am sure it would arouse great resentment against the President if he followed that. Yet that is just what these cowards in the Congress are trying to do. They want to avoid the responsibility themselves . . . and to throw it on the President and then, if he should take this interpretation, they would be the first ones to jump on him as violating the real purpose of the law." (Diary, August 7, 1941) Stimson himself had felt on several occasions that Mr. Roosevelt might well be more frank with Congress than he was, but *certainly in the face of this kind of pusillanimous hostility it was not easy for the President to be trustful.*[15]

If this was Stimson's judgment of Roosevelt's problem in obtaining from Congress such a minimum defense measure as extension of Selective Service, it seems fair to judge that the problem would have been much more difficult if naval escorts and war had been placed before the legislators. The cases were analogous to a degree: the President had technical Constitutional power to order escorts but morally he was committed to Congress and people to refrain from using it. He refused to do "by trickery" what Congress would in all probability refuse to sanction openly. Had he asked Congress to approve escorts, the likelihood seems very great that resentment against him would have resulted in the defeat of even such measures as Selective Service.

## War Plans

In the isolationist thesis, the question of naval escorts is entangled with the broader problem of the administration's war planning activities prior to Pearl Harbor. Stimson emphasizes what the President failed to do, and Beard accuses him of secretly doing too much. Therefore it is pertinent to review what he and his subordinates actually did. The reports of the investigations by the Joint Congressional Committee which, after the War, studied the documents relative to administration actions prior to Pearl Harbor, provide some assurance that the facts can be known. A minority of the Committee was patently hostile to the Roosevelt administration and determined to ferret out evidence to prove the isolationist thesis regarding the origins of American participation in the war. Beard's books, like George Morgenstern's *Pearl Harbor: The Story of the Secret War*,[16] which Beard relies upon to supplement his own work,[17] are arguments in support of the Minority Report of this Committee. Here it will be contended that the most "damaging" facts the minority could unearth do not substantiate the isolationist thesis or invalidate the Majority Report.

The Navy Department, prior to and after passage of Lend Lease, made plans for convoying, which Beard describes as thoroughly sinister. Beard sometimes treats the evidence showing that the Navy Department made such plans as evidence that it used them, and sometimes as evidence that the President did not tell the truth on occasions when he denied that the administration was "considering convoying." Elementary knowledge of the functions of war plans divisions in the military departments of the American and every other government is sufficient to repel these accusations. The War Plans Division of the Navy Department had the obvious duty of preparing plans for every conceivable emergency the Navy might face. Doubtless the Navy Department prepared plans for "war against Great Britain."

Early in 1941, the possibility that the United States Navy might be ordered to escort convoys was obvious; therefore the War Plans Division was under double compulsion to make plans for so complicated an operation. Work on convoy plans did not make it necessary for the President to describe it or even admit that it was going on in order to tell the truth about administration intentions. Military planning activities have no political meaning, whereas if the President had declared publicly that convoying was being considered in administration circles, the statement would have had a political meaning that the order to escort convoys was likely to be given soon.

## ABC-1

The Joint Committee also found evidence that American military officials a year or more before Pearl Harbor engaged in planning for military cooperation with Great Britain and other potential allies, and that reports were drawn up by several conferences in which American military officials took part with British and Dutch staff officers. These reports are used as chief exhibits in the case against Roosevelt. They are called proof that he did make commitments to go to war without Congressional consent, that he did plot to take the country into the war before Pearl Harbor.

The fact is that these reports without exception contained provisos which made their proposals inoperative and of no effect unless and until the United States should enter the war. This differentiated them absolutely from "commitments to war." They were no more than plans to concert military activities *if* the United States went to war. They did have the political meaning of demonstrating an *intention* to cooperate with other victims of Axis attack *if* and *when* the United States should be attacked, but such an intention cannot be distorted into a commitment to war.

The British and other foreign officials who drew up the reports with Americans worked frankly to make them unconditional. They failed. American isolationists have chosen to explain to these British and Dutch staff officers that they did not, after all, fail. But they and their home governments knew better, as proved by the fact that they continued to try to obtain an American commitment until the very moment when bombs fell on Pearl Harbor.

The staff conferences were the result of the Japanese invasion of Indo-China and the Axis military alliance of September, 1940. Britain had for years urged Anglo-American political and military cooperation in the Far East. Hull just as steadily had refused and adhered to the policy of "parallel action." During the Indo-China crisis in September, 1940, Ambassador Lothian and Australian Minister Casey suggested Anglo-American conferences regarding joint defenses against Japan to impress the Japanese Government. Hull answered that Japan already assumed such steps would be taken on short notice if it gave cause.[18] But Japan immediately extorted concessions in Indo-China from the Vichy government and signed the Axis alliance. Hull was alarmed. He addressed a pointed inquiry to the British Ambassador: whether the British and Dutch governments had conferred on pooling their defenses, and if so, what was the size of their combined forces and what size Japanese forces could overcome them? [19]

Britain's reopening of the Burma Road in October, 1940, reassured Hull. He and Roosevelt decided that the Axis alliance must not be allowed to divert the United States from its primary emphasis on aid to Britain. They would refuse to compromise with Japan on principles, allow its government to know that the United States was strong in the Pacific and gaining in strength, refrain from quarreling, and leave the door open for discussion and agreement on American principles. Most important of all, the administration now moved towards planning for military cooperation with potential allies in case the United States entered the war. The possibility of Axis attack against the United States had come into view with the signing of the Axis alliance.

Hull held conversations with Lothian and Casey early in October "to lay the basis for exchanges of information among the United States, Britain, Australia, New Zealand, and the Dutch East Indies concerning the forces available in the Far East to resist a Japanese attack." [20] In late November, Lothian returned from a trip to London with renewed and strengthened requests to base the American fleet at Singapore. This the administration refused to do, but restrictions on exports to Japan were increased, the Export-Import Bank made a new loan to China, and additional naval vessels were sent to the Philippines. Hull believed that the strengthened American policy and Anglo-American cooperation were responsible for a setback to the most aggressive Japanese leaders and postponement of war. More than a year's time was thus obtained to send help to Britain and Russia and to arm the United States.[21]

Admiral Stark at first was skeptical of British plans for the Far East. He was particularly suspicious because "we have no idea as to whether they would at once begin to fight were the Dutch alone, or were we alone, to be attacked by the Japanese." [22]

The British sent a staff committee to Washington which began in January, 1941, to meet informally with Admiral Stark and other American officers. It was made explicit by the Americans from the beginning that they could make for the United States no commitments whatever, either to go to war or to take any actions prior to war, and that they would discuss plans which could go into effect *only* if and when the United States entered the war. The report of the conference, known as "ABC-1," declared that the discussions were held with a view

to determine the best methods by which the armed forces of the United States and British Commonwealth, with its present allies, could defeat Germany and the powers allied with her, *should the United States be compelled to resort to war.*

It further declared that plans agreed on were subject to confirmation by the highest military authorities in the United States and Britain and also by the governments of both countries. It was on these bases alone that Stark and the other Americans agreed to confer, and Stark made a statement to the conference to this effect at its first meeting on January 27, 1941.[23]

The conduct of Admiral Stark underscores the totally nonpolitical character of his work. He did not ask the permission of President Roosevelt or of Secretary Knox to begin the conference. He later informed the President that he was going forward with it, and the President was noncommittal. Had the conference been intended to discuss political questions, Stark could not have proceeded without authorization and direction by the President and Knox. As a planning activity of the sort which the War Plans Division continually conducted, the conferences could properly be considered by Stark to be a matter within the authority of the Chief of Naval Operations.[24] The heads of the American Army and Navy War Plans Divisions, Brigadier General Leonard T.

Gerow and Rear Admiral Richmond K. Turner, both took part in the conferences. They ended on March 27, 1941. The report, ABC-1, was subsequently approved by Stark, Marshall, Knox, and Stimson. It was submitted to the President on June 2, 1941. On June 7 he returned it without official approval. The British government had not ratified it and therefore the proposal for ratification by both governments was not fulfilled. Roosevelt said the report should be returned to him for approval in case of war.[25]

If Roosevelt had signed ABC-1, a case might be made that it constituted an executive agreement. Even then, it could not be construed as an interference with the authority of Congress to declare war, because the content of ABC-1 so clearly and specifically left aside the question of United States entry into the war. Nor could it, as an executive agreement, have been construed as an alliance, because it did not *promise* military cooperation; it only brought together statements of the individual military plans of the individual governments' military planning authorities for use *if* the United States entered the war.

But Roosevelt did not sign ABC-1, therefore it was not even an executive agreement. It was merely a report of an exchange of planning information by the subordinate officials of both governments who were responsible for drawing up plans to meet a contingency their respective countries might face. They foresaw that if the United States became involved in war with Germany, it would also engage in war with Italy and in these circumstances, they reported, the possibility of war between Japan and an association of the United States, and the British Commonwealth and its allies, including the NEI, had to be taken into account. Nevertheless, the United States would concentrate its principal effort in the Atlantic and European area because Germany was the predominant Axis power. In the Pacific, Britain would aim to hold the positions essential to the security of the Commonwealth, and the United States would use its fleet to weaken Japan economically, divert it from the Malaysia barrier by raids into the Marshall islands, and defend the area from the American hemisphere to the International Date Line in the south and to the longitude of Japan in the north.[26]

Possessing these declarations of intention, the planning authorities of both governments could work out specifications for their own activities in case the "ifs" became realities. The ABC-1 report was no executive agreement and, all the more so, it was not a treaty, because a treaty requires not only the signature of the President but also the approval of two-thirds of the Senate. Lacking both, it was well understood by all parties to have no effect or meaning as representing a "policy" or a "promise" of the President or the United States government.

In the face of these facts, the Minority Report of the Pearl Harbor Investigating Committee refers to ABC-1 as "the President's commitment to Great Britain. . . ." Then it admits the President did not approve the report but in the same sentence accuses him of acting "just as if a binding pact had been made," and blames the armed forces for making "no separate over-all plan for the simple defense of American possessions against Japan. . . ."²⁷ Undoubtedly the War Plans Divisions of the Army and Navy had plans for use in case the United States alone fought Japan. Such plans, as General Gerow told the Committee, are the routine grist of such agencies.²⁸ But Stark and Marshall were guilty of foreseeing the possibility that allies might be available if the United States were compelled to fight, and that the country would prefer to fight with them rather than alone.

Morgenstern does not bother with the shadings employed in the Minority Report. He introduces the subject of the Anglo-American staff conferences as follows:

Among the most important of the President's decisions was to *consummate* secret *war alliances* with the British and the Canadians in the Atlantic and with the British and Dutch in the Pacific.²⁹

The material which proves the absurdity of such a statement is present in Morgenstern's text, but it is so deeply buried under assumptions which ignore and contradict it that the reader is obviously intended to believe absurdity to be truth. Again Morgenstern writes:

The defense of the Roosevelt administration later for entering a *war alliance* through the Washington and Singapore staff agreements was that the *commitments* assumed were not *binding*.³⁰

The Roosevelt administration did not defend itself "for entering a war alliance:" it denied that it had entered one. Morgenstern makes his only reference to the fact that the reports (they were not "agreements") of the conferences were not binding in a sentence which falsely implies that the administration admitted it entered into a "war alliance." This is his method of distracting his readers' attention from his own failure to present any evidence that the reports *were* binding commitments.

Beard, on the other hand, gives his readers a fair introductory statement of the meaning of the conferences. His knowledge of the machinery of government precludes the falsifications of Morgenstern. The conferences developed, Beard writes,

technical plans for joint action in war, when and if it came, or to use the American form of reservation "should the United States be compelled to resort to war." These plans did not bind the United States to enter the war on any given contingency or set of contingencies. Such an agreement would have been in the nature of an alliance, and hence under the provisions of the Constitution called for ratification by the Senate. In form they were, the majority of the Congressional Committee on Pearl Harbor stated, the result of "technical discussion on a staff level"—"nonpolitical" in nature; practically they served as the basis for collective action in diplomacy and war.[31]

Beard goes on to declare, more tendentiously, that the 1941 conferences were "continuations" of Anglo-American discussions for cooperation in the Far East which were carried out according to American "imperialist strategy" to "draw Great Britain into the American line of policy against Japan." Beard presently adumbrates not only "imperialists," but advocates of " 'peace' by 'collective security' " as working to obtain British aid against Japan. Roosevelt's pre-inauguration promise to uphold the Stimson Doctrine Beard fits into this history as "a fateful step leading in the direction of Pearl Harbor." [32] In this passage Beard restores by innuendo the image of Roosevelt plotting war which he had momentarily obliterated in his accurate statement of the meaning of the Anglo-American staff conferences. Although he admits that peace through collective security functioned as a motive of unnamed American leaders, "imperialism" is placed in the foreground and Roosevelt is pictured not as adopting collective security for his foreign policy but as taking "a fateful step leading" to war. The passage is also interesting because it pictures the United States as the instigator and Britain as its tool in the Far

East. This is contrary to the usual isolationist accusation, which Morgenstern maintains, that the United States under Roosevelt was victimized by the British. Voluminous and detailed evidence presented by Cordell Hull in his *Memoirs* suggests that the actual Anglo-American relationship was not one of victimizer and victim but of a slow movement through the way station of "parallel action" towards joint action for joint defense against Japan, and onwards to the ultimate goal of collective security.

On this journey Hull and Roosevelt tarried at "parallel action" longer than the British desired. Britain's temporary closing of the Burma Road in 1940 had perhaps taught the Roosevelt administration that, unless it moved on, the British would jump the track and head towards appeasement of Japan. The opening of staff conferences in January, 1941, marked American progress towards joint action for defense. For this reason one may accept Beard's dictum that the discussions served "practically" as the "basis for collective action in diplomacy and war," that is, diplomacy fairly soon and war, in Beard's words, "when and if." [33]

## ADB

The second conference in which American planning officers participated took place on April 21-27, 1941, in Singapore. Dutch as well as British and Commonwealth officers took part, and they met several more times prior to Pearl Harbor. These conferences were held under the same limiting American terms as the Washington conference of January to March. They were concerned with details subordinate to the considerations set forth in ABC-1.

Again the report of the conference, known as "ADB," contained explicit recognition that no political commitments were implied. But in this case General Marshall and Admiral Stark felt that some of the material of the report did have political implications and for this reason they refused to approve it. Beard and Morgenstern neglect to mention this proof that responsible leaders of the Roosevelt administration, including the two heads of the armed forces, observed scrupulous regard for the necessity to restrict the conferences to contingent technical problems, and that they refused to make a commitment to take political action involving prerogatives of Congress.

The Minority Report of the Congressional Committee is not so reticent as are Beard and Morgenstern. It lumps together ABC-1 and ADB in order to create the false impression that ADB was sent up the chain of command in Washington and, with its political content, received like ABC-1 approval falling short only of the official approval of the President. The Minority Report states:

Beginning in January, 1941, representatives of the American armed forces and representatives of British and Dutch armed forces on the suggestion of the United States started a series of conversations in respect of cooperation against Japan in the Far East. Out of these and *subsequent* conversations were developed American-British-*Dutch* war plans for combined operations against Japan if Japanese armed forces started hostile actions against British, Dutch, *or* American possessions in the Far East. President Roosevelt approved *these plans,* "except officially," as Adm. Stark testified.[34]

Contrary to the clear meaning of this passage, representing the "findings" of the isolationist minority of the Investigating Committee, President Roosevelt did *not* approve officially or unofficially the ADB report; it was not even approved by his military subordinates.

The reason why they did not approve the ADB report was that it *named* contingent circumstances in which the United States *would* enter the war. The list of contingencies included not only Japanese attack on American territory but also Japanese attack on territory of the British Commonwealth or the NEI, or Thailand west of 100° E. or south of 10° N., or Portuguese Timor, or New Caledonia, or the Loyalty Islands. If Stark and Marshall, or Knox and Stimson, or especially if the President had approved such a report, it could have been regarded as a commitment to some degree by the United States to go to war under circumstances other than attack upon United States territory, and therefore under circumstances in which the President did not have exclusive authority. Everyone knew that in the end only Congress could make such a commitment, but the President's unrestricted authority to direct the armed forces opened the possibility that he could, by exercising that authority, commit the country to war in such fashion that Congress would be virtually helpless to prevent him or veto him. Therefore Stark and Marshall refused to approve ADB, and their refusal had the effect of avoiding a commitment to war under circumstances other than direct aggression against territory of the United States. Even if they had signed it, the report would have lacked the binding quality of an executive agreement, but they scrupulously refrained from signing because such action might be interpreted as undertaken by the President's agents.

Morgenstern denies these facts in order to build up the case of Rooseveltian "provocation" of war:

Once the *United States* signed the Washington *and Singapore* staff agreements, the British, Australians, Dutch, and Chinese proceeded on the assumption that this country was an outright ally. . . .

Japanese diplomatic messages show that America's role as a partner of Britain, China, and Holland in a Pacific war alliance was not lost upon the Japanese. . . .

and he proceeds to justify accordingly Japan's attack upon the United States at Pearl Harbor.[35]

The political substance of ADB did reach the President a short while before Pearl Harbor. It reached him *not* as the report of the American-Dutch-British conferences at Singapore but as a *recommendation* which Stark and Marshall offered on their own motion in fulfillment of their duty as Presidential advisers. No commitment of any sort to a foreign government was involved in their recommendation. They simply offered as their own best opinion that the United States in its own interest should fight if the Japanese moved farther into the South Pacific area, even if the Japanese refrained from direct attack on American territory. Their recommendation contemplated the normal procedure whereby the United States goes to war: by Presidential recommendation to Congress followed by Congressional declaration of war. By artfully glossing over or distorting essential facts in the record, the Congressional Committee Minority Report, followed by Beard and Morgenstern, makes it appear that the *recommendation* of Stark and Marshall was part of the journey up the chain of command of the Singapore conference report.[36]

The staff conferences were not commitments to war. They were, nevertheless, steps towards collective security because they posited a united front among peaceful powers against aggressors, and this would involve military cooperation if the United States entered the war. Such a united front could serve as the nucleus and spring of action for a world organization, and Roosevelt set out to advance these broader potentialities of the united front in agreement with Churchill during the summer of 1941, even while the United States was still only a nonbelligerent in the war. It was not in pursuit of American imperialism but in furtherance of collective security that the United States and Great Britain in 1941 drew closer together. This development was an accomplishment of the Roosevelt administration which may absolve it to some extent of Stimson's charges of indecision and inaction during those months. It represented progress in the direction of the administration's primary aim of collective security, beside which the question of naval escorts and even the question of asking Congress for a declaration of war were of secondary significance.

If the Japanese had refrained from attacking American territory but had attacked one or more of the potential allies of the United States in the south Pacific area, Roosevelt would not have been compelled to enter the war in order to discharge any "commitments" to "allies." But he would have been placed in a severe dilemma between American interest and his antiwar pledge to the American people. The Japanese leaders were too irresponsible to pursue the more moderate course, but this does not prove, what isolationists imply, that Roosevelt engineered the tragic escape from his dilemma. The Japanese militarists engineered it.

In the event, the work of the American-British-Dutch staff conferences turned out to be invaluable. It laid the foundation for the military strategy and successes of 1942 which halted the Japanese advance at Midway Island and the Coral Sea, even while the main effort of the United States and Great Britain was concentrated against Japan's European partners. Furthermore, the staff conferences of early 1941 laid the groundwork for the diplomacy which culminated in the United Nations.

The staff conferences were cautionary actions to counter the global Axis alliance with global defense planning. They extended Anglo-American cooperation to the Pacific at the same time that Roosevelt and Hull overcame a serious obstacle to Anglo-American cooperation in the Atlantic. This was solution of the problem of Greenland, an accomplishment during the "weeks of indecision" after passage of Lend Lease which Stimson in his memoirs fails to mention.

## The Greenland Protectorate

Roosevelt and Hull, like the Greenland authorities, had objected to British or Canadian occupation of the vast island and they had also refused to accept an American protectorate over it. But Nazis were trying to set up secret weather stations in its remote wastes, Hitler on March 26 extended his war zone to Greenland's territorial waters, and the British were anxious to develop a base on the island for American Lend Lease bombers being flown to Britain. The Danish Minister de Kauffmann and the Greenland authorities urged the United States to act.

Immediately after Lend Lease passed, an American expedition was sent to the island to survey a site for an airfield. The administration decided to accept a temporary protectorate under the provisions of the Act of Havana. Thereby the delicate questions involving the no-transfer principle of the Monroe Doctrine which British occupation would have raised were avoided. The United States gave Denmark a guarantee that the American protectorate would be temporary, and an agreement to that effect was accepted by de Kauffmann on April 9. His Nazi-dominated home government repudiated him but the United States continued to recognize him as the representative of Denmark. The President authorized construction of aviation bases in the island. On April 10 he announced the agreement publicly.[37]

Occupation of Greenland, a leg beyond the new American base at Newfoundland, required protection of supplies from the mainland and thereby extended out over the North Atlantic United States naval protection to shipping.

## The Bridge of Ships

Many other actions were taken to strengthen Britain in the Battle of the Atlantic. On March 15 the President announced that upon American will depended "the survival of the vital bridge across the ocean; the bridge of ships which carry the arms and food for those who are fighting the good fight." [38] While the huge new shipbuilding program got underway, Roosevelt, on March 30, ordered the Coast Guard to seize Italian, German, and Danish ships in American ports because evidence had been found that they were being sabotaged by Axis agents. The considerable number of Danish vessels was requisitioned and used by the United States government to relieve the shortage. Protests from the three governments were rejected and Hull required Mussolini to recall his naval attaché to the United States because he had directed the sabotage.[39] On May 29, Roosevelt authorized training of British airmen in the United States.

During April and May about one-fourth of the fighting ships of the Pacific Fleet were ordered to the Atlantic to reinforce the Neutrality Patrol. Much has been made of this action as an item in the isolationist case against Roosevelt. It depended for its validity on the administration's judgment regarding the relative priority of the two main arenas. The Navy Department believed that even if Japan made war against the United States without German involvement, the United States should nevertheless, as Admiral Turner later expressed it, "launch our principal efforts against Germany first, and . . . conduct a limited offensive in the Central Pacific, and a strictly defensive effort in the Asiatic." [40]

Stark and Marshall in their November 5, 1941, memorandum to the President stated the reasoning on which this strategy was based:

The primary objective of the two nations [Britain and the United States] is the defeat of Germany. *If Japan be defeated and Germany remain undefeated, decision will still have not been reached.* In any case, an unlimited offensive war should not be undertaken against Japan, since such a war would greatly weaken the combined effort in the Atlantic against Germany, *the most dangerous enemy.*[41]

The Minority Report of the Joint Congressional Committee found the "high authorities in Washington" guilty of failure to allocate to the commanders at Hawaii sufficient matériel to repel attack by Japan. It declares that "no requirements of defense or war in the Atlantic did or could excuse these authorities for their failures in this respect." After such a flat statement, the Minority Report nevertheless remarks that "this conclusion may be arguable from the point of view of some high world strategy. . . ." The phrase, "some high world strategy," suggests isolationist reluctance to believe that a global danger from the Axis faced the United States and called for a concomitant global strategy in Washington. The possibility is now admitted to be "arguable" only in order to indict Roosevelt for a more serious delict than poor judgment. The sentence quoted continues:

but it is not arguable under the Constitution and laws of the United States. The President, it is true, had powers and obligations under the Lease-Lend Act of March 1941. But his first and inescapable duty under the Constitution and laws was to care for the defense and security of the United States against a Japanese attack, which he knew was imminent. . . .[42]

That the President knew a Japanese attack on American territory "was imminent" is an isolationist contention which has not been proved, as will be shown hereafter. And even isolationists do not claim that Roosevelt had such knowledge until a few days prior to December 7, 1941; therefore the argument that such knowledge should have influenced fleet dispositions between April and November, 1941, is doubly false.

Equally false and also ridiculous is the assumption of the minority that "the Constitution and laws" provide an answer to problems of defense strategy. Solution of such problems is, it need hardly be stated, within the discretion of the Commander-in-Chief. Roosevelt solved them according to the best judgment, including his own, of responsible authorities. Decision on the global problem was that the defense and security of the United States was best served by concentrating on aid to nations fighting Hitler.

Morgenstern finds especially significant an incident in which Harry Hopkins "as he lay in bed, nonchalantly smoking a cigaret," told Pacific commanders that certain bombers wanted in Hawaii were being sent to Britain.[43] Hopkins in this, as on all occasions, acted solely as the President's agent. Indeed, his biographer, Robert Sherwood, makes plain that a special service he performed for the President was to relieve him of some of the burden of dealing with officials who disapproved of policies which seemed to involve neglect of their local requirements. Hopkins became, for enemies of the administration, a weaver of dark webs, possessed of undefined but vast independent authority, the one man whom the "dictatorial" Roosevelt did not dominate. But they fail to specify an instance of Hopkins acting at variance with the policies and determinations of his chief.

Morgenstern next enlists Hitler and Admiral Doenitz to support his argument. He shows that the Nazi leaders wanted Japan to attack the United States in hope that "the natural sense of outrage in the United States would divert America's major effort to the Pacific, leaving [Hitler] free to complete his unfinished business." [44] This is intended to prove that Roosevelt was unwise in his determination that America's major effort should not be diverted to the Pacific. Hitler wanted the isolationist conception of proper strategy for the United States to overthrow the Rooseveltian conception. He incited the Japanese to attack the United States in hope that it would force repudiation of Roosevelt and an isolationist triumph.

It is doubtful whether historians should accept Hitler's conception of the proper strategy for the United States as the one which would have best served the country's defense and security. Rather it seems fairly obvious that Hitler's conception, although it did coincide with the conception of American isolationists, was the one which would most likely destroy the defense and security of the United States. That was certainly the end Hitler held in view. It seems strange to use it to discredit Roosevelt's strategy, because it is actually evidence that Roosevelt's strategy, the reverse of Hitler's desire, was sound.

The Japanese attack on Pearl Harbor did not lead the American people or administration to adopt the isolationists' strategy of primary concentration in the Pacific. One of the reasons was that this was not only the isolationists' desire but also, and too obviously, Hitler's. Axis contempt for the wisdom of a democracy was an essential ingredient of Axis strategy. American isolationists, a steadily dwindling faction, may have deserved contempt for playing Hitler's game but, as the event proved, Axis leaders made a great mistake in confusing American isolationists with the American people.

On April 24, 1941, Roosevelt ordered the ships of the Neutrality Patrol to "trail" Axis vessels and broadcast their locations at four-hour intervals.[45] Prior to this, American ships presumably navigated fixed patrol routes and lost sight of Axis vessels after crossing their paths. The change increased the efficiency of the Patrol in aiding delivery of Lend Lease material to Britain and it was evidently made possible by reinforcement of the Atlantic Fleet.

## The Island Outposts

On May 22, Roosevelt ordered Admiral Stark to prepare an expedition to seize the Azores from Portugal. It was intended to sail if the current threat of Hitler to move through Spain to Africa materialized. Occupation of Martinique was also contemplated in the expectation that relations with Vichy France would be altered by the same event. Roosevelt gave public warning of these plans in his address of May 27. The Nazis had the armed power, he said,

at any moment to occupy Spain and Portugal; and that threat extends not only to French North Africa and the western end of the Mediterranean, but also to the Atlantic fortress of Dakar, and to the island outposts of the New World—the Azores and Cape Verde Islands.

The Cape Verde Islands are only 7 hours' distance from Brazil by bomber or troop-carrying planes. They dominate shipping routes to and from the South Atlantic.

The war is approaching the brink of the Western Hemisphere itself. It is coming very close to home.

Control or occupation by Nazi forces of any of the islands of the Atlantic would jeopardize the immediate safety of portions of North and South America, and of the island possessions of the United States, and of the ultimate safety of the continental United States itself.

He declared that the Axis powers could win only if they first obtained control of the seas, that if they failed to obtain control of the seas, "they are certainly defeated." All freedom depended now as in the past on freedom of the seas.[46]

"Freedom of the seas" had in former epochs been defended by the United States in pursuit of its right as a neutral to ship noncontraband to European belligerents. But the United States under the Neutrality Act did not assert the right to send any American-owned goods or merchant ships into combat zones surrounding the belligerents. Roosevelt invoked a more fundamental meaning of "freedom of the seas," one derived from post-Kellogg Pact conceptions of international law, namely, the right to prevent an aggressor nation from using the seas to press its attacks against victims.

Congress opposed naval escorts for convoys to Britain, therefore the President refrained from exercising that degree of protection for shipments to Britain and of "provocation" of the Axis. But he explained in the May 27 address that the problem of defending the freedom of the seas had now become, in the face of long-range bombers and battleship raiders, more difficult than in the First World War when naval escorts sufficed to offset submarines. And he served warning that in this situation the United States could not allow the Axis to gain control of the seas by seizing the "island outposts of the Western Hemisphere."

In this light, American preventive action regarding the island outposts became a more important measure to ensure freedom of the seas and delivery of Lend Lease goods to Britain than naval escorts. Isolationists had made "convoying" a politically dangerous subject. Roosevelt, with prescience for which Stimson does not give him credit, had found that the dangerous subject was obsolete. His procedure may be called "devious" or "lacking in candor" only if it be denied that naval escorts had actually given way to bases as the more important protection for Lend Lease deliveries.

The American public in great majority accepted the President's view. Occupation of island outposts seemed to be more "defensive" than naval escorts. It satisfied the public hope that actions could be taken which would be sufficient to help Britain win the war but yet short of American entry into the war. It satisfied public desire for an offensive-defense policy which would somehow avoid an "act of war" of the traditional sort.

As it turned out, Hitler did not move through Spain and Gibraltar to French Africa and the American expeditions to occupy the Azores and Martinique never sailed. Instead, Hitler on June 22, 1941, launched the attack against Russia. This made Iceland doubly important as a position on the route to Murmansk as well as Britain. American occupation of Iceland in July fulfilled the design Roosevelt had outlined on May 27.

### Behind the Scenes

Sherwood in his book on Hopkins presents several glimpses of Roosevelt during the days when the May 27 address absorbed his attention. Hopkins told Judge Rosenman and Sherwood that he believed the President intended in the forthcoming speech to declare an "unlimited national emergency." Accordingly they incorporated it in a draft of the speech. But when the President read the draft to Sumner Welles and Adolph Berle of the State Department, he assumed an air of "artless innocence" when he came to the key phrase. Sherwood said Hopkins had told him and Rosenman that it was what the President wanted. The proclamation remained.[47] This account suggests that the proclamation was almost "accidental," or that Hopkins foisted it artfully on the President, or at least that the President wanted State Department officers to think he had. But Cordell Hull, who does not hesitate in his *Memoirs* to declare that he opposed many of the President's more dramatic actions, states that Roosevelt discussed the proclamation with him in days preceding the address and that he agreed the time had come to issue it.[48] This makes Sherwood's account less significant and the incident more reassuring as to the President's method of formulating policy.

In the address, Sherwood continues, the President refused to mention Russia or Japan as aggressors or even the word "dictatorships" as a synonym for "aggressors," because he wished to avoid antagonizing either government: Japan for fear it would enter the war on Hitler's side, Russia in hope that it would enter the war against Hitler. Also Sherwood makes clear that the White House circle believed Hitler was very concerned to offset and discredit Roosevelt's announcements of policy. He sent his greatest battleship, the *Bismarck,* into the Western Atlantic evidently to destroy a convoy coincidentally with Roosevelt's forthcoming address. At the same time a German submarine sank the merchant vessel *Robin Moor,* the first American ship sunk in the war. But on the day of Roosevelt's speech, the Royal Navy sank the *Bismarck,* and Americans rejoiced that it was a bomber the United States had sent to Britain that spotted the Nazi ship and directed the Royal Navy to the kill. The Nazi first experiment in ruthlessness directed against the United States also failed: the crew of the *Robin Moor* were left adrift in lifeboats in the open sea for four weeks, and the report of the sinking did not reach the American public until June 20. The news led Hopkins to advise the President to strengthen the Neutrality Patrol by ordering the Navy to take "what measures of security are required" to establish freedom of the seas and security for American flag ships outside the combat zones. Roosevelt refused. He only denounced the sinking, in a public statement, as an act of an "international outlaw" showing "total disregard for the most elementary principles of international law and of humanity."

Sherwood writes that this and Roosevelt's refusal to order convoying or to ask Congress to change the Neutrality Act, in spite of a highly favorable public response to the May 27 speech, was a reversal, unaccountable to the President's intimates, "from a position of strength to one of apparently insouciant weakness." [49] But to an observer of the public rather than private course of the President, occupation of Iceland seems to have been quite a "strong" action to fulfill the design of May 27. If his intimate advisers like Hopkins, as well as his Constitutional advisers like Stimson, had been chosen because they believed in moving towards his own goal, they, lacking his ultimate responsibility, were understandably impatient. But Roosevelt did have the responsibility; he could not forget that the isolationists had not yet finally lost the battle for public opinion and were a very strong minority in Congress. He was determined to take no avoidable risk of an "irrevocable act" that might destroy his policy.

# 13.

## America and Russia

Hitler's invasion of russia was no surprise to the Roosevelt administration. It had warned the Soviet government of the impending attack as early as January, 1941, as part of its effort to build up the united front of powers opposing the chief aggressor nations. This action is significant evidence of the administration's lack of prejudice regarding internal political regimes and willingness to work with any government that would oppose aggression. Few critics of the Roosevelt administration objected to its "appeasement" of *both* Communist and Fascist governments. The fact that the administration dealt with or gave support to Communist Russia as well as Falangist Spain, Vichy France as well as Communist China is evidence that it regarded the nature of a government's internal regime as a secondary consideration compared with the nature of its foreign policy; that it made the only distinction among governments which will serve the policy of collective security: the distinction between aggressors and their victims.

In the case of Russia, Roosevelt and Hull clung to this distinction as the decisive one in spite of grave tests of their conviction. The Soviet leaders, in the opinion of most observers in free countries, had helped to precipitate the war itself by failing to understand that the British and French people would not allow their governments to betray the pledges made to countries east of Hitler after he occupied Prague in March, 1939, and by opening the door to Hitler with the Nazi-Soviet Pact of August, 1939. This, together with seizure of East Poland, the Baltic states, and Bessarabia, and the war against Finland placed the Soviet Union in the same immoral category as the Axis governments. But Roosevelt and Hull understood that the fundamental interests of the Soviet Union were incompatible with those of the Axis governments; that Axis aggression was offensive and unlimited while Soviet aggression was, at least so long as the Axis existed, defensive and limited; and that Soviet adherence to the anti-Axis cause would serve the major moral cause challenging the world, not because the Soviet leaders preferred morality but because Hitler forced them to serve it. Hitler, as Roosevelt and Hull foresaw, would force the Soviet leaders into the united front against aggression and their nation's strength made them welcome. Then the distinction in professed goals between Communism and Fascism, a distinction between humanist and beastly ideals, made the hope seem tenable that the Soviet Union, after its leaders' dogma that a capitalist government was by definition imperialist was proved false, might adhere honestly and permanently to a system of collective security. Thus Roosevelt and Hull played for great stakes in their Russian policy, stakes that justified risk.

## Friendly Gestures to Russia

The diplomacy of the Soviet government was one of the chief obstacles Roosevelt and Hull had to surmount. Documents found in Germany show that even after Hitler had lost the Battle of Britain, as late as November, 1940, the Soviet government worked to reach an agreement with Germany going far beyond the secret protocol of the Nazi-Soviet Pact of 1939 and amounting to a division and sharing of the world through conquest.[1] This program was reflected in the Soviet attitude of antagonism towards the United States. Hull found it impossible to make the Soviet Ambassador, Oumansky, deal constructively with problems that hindered better relations.

But the State Department had information that Molotov's mission to Berlin in November, 1940, had antagonized Hitler for the same reason Franco had antagonized him: he had asked Hitler for too large a share of the spoils. Hull made the most of Molotov's failure. He possessed a powerful lever to encourage Stalin to distrust Hitler as much as Hitler, in November, showed he distrusted Stalin.

In his *Memoirs* the American Secretary of State tells a remarkable story. Sam E. Woods, the American commercial attaché in Berlin, developed a contact with a German highly placed in Nazi circles. As early as August, 1940, Wood's informant told him that Hitler was preparing for war with Russia. The evidence steadily became more detailed and weighty with such items as the printing of bales of ruble notes and the German strategic plan for attack along three fronts. Preparations were to be complete by the spring of 1941. Information of the coming German attack on Russia did not diminish the importance of other information pointing towards a German campaign through Spain into Africa. One report was that Hitler said privately he would have "only my soldiers from Vladivostok to Gibraltar."

After he learned of the failure of Molotov's mission to Berlin, Hull in January, 1941, directed Under Secretary Welles to strengthen his position in conversations with Ambassador Oumansky by conveying to him for the benefit of the Soviet Government the American intelligence of Hitler's plans. Further information was relayed to Oumansky as it arrived during the spring. The administration decided to make other gestures of friendliness towards the Soviet government. On January 21 the moral embargo against Russia initiated during the Soviet war against Finland was lifted. In February, Hull rejected a British request that American exports to Russia should be rationed. The British request corresponded to the desire of many Americans who objected to allowing American goods or their equivalent to be sent by Russia to Hitler under the trade clauses of the Nazi-Soviet Pact. But Hull told Lord Halifax that exports to Russia were not increasing to any "alarming" extent, and that the United States did not wish to give the Soviet leaders new reason for displeasure while the influence of Russia in the war, even if it were "standing asleep like a piece of statuary," might become so powerful.

At the same time Hull worked to improve relations between Britain and Russia, just as he did in the case of British relations with Vichy. He resented the British public announcement prior to discussions that Halifax would ask him to ration exports to Russia.

Hull believed that the stiffening attitude of the Soviet government towards Hitler during the spring of 1941 was perhaps a consequence of the intelligence provided by the United States. Shortly after a session between Oumansky and Welles in March,

Stalin suddenly concluded a Neutrality Pact with Japan which was obviously designed to avoid a two-front war if Hitler attacked. The treaty could also be contrasted with the refusal of the Roosevelt administration to make a "deal" with Japan so long as it continued its aggressive course, although the United States had an equal interest with Russia in avoiding a two-front war. In the Balkans, when Hitler invaded Greece and Yugoslavia, Soviet support of Hitler's victims was valuable to the anti-Axis cause.

## The Russian Diplomacy of Ill Will

American services to Russia were seldom regarded by the Russian leaders as sufficient to improve relations. Soviet diplomacy was handicapped by the xenophobia that followed the Moscow trials of 1936–8. Officials like Oumansky were not allowed to exercise discretion even in minor matters. They seemed to live in fear that anything but an absolutely uncompromising attitude would prove to their superiors and the Soviet secret police that they were tainted. Periodic demonstrations of ill will towards a foreign government seemed necessary for a Soviet diplomat to prove his loyalty. Willingness to show a spirit of accommodation towards another government in minor matters, the chief function of diplomatic agents if they are to serve their governments' major interests, seemed forbidden to Soviet agents. The Soviet government ordered Oumansky to obtain larger shipments of strategic raw materials from the United States, and he drove his demands to the point of disrupting the talks with Welles.

He went to Hull on May 14. Hull explained to him that the American defense program and commitments to Britain made unlimited shipments of strategic materials to Russia impossible. The American trade of many other governments had suffered as a result of American and British requirements, and they did not take offense. Russia was maintaining commercial relations with Germany but refused to recognize that fact when the United States sought to prevent military supplies from going to the Nazis. Oumansky handed Hull a note which accused the Roosevelt administration of a "hostile attitude" towards the Soviet Union and threatened that his government would "draw all necessary conclusions." Orally he accused the American administration of a personal act due to personal hostility. Hull rejected these accusations and the discussion became, in Hull's words, "a little animated." But Hull did not allow diplomatic blundering to distract him from the fundamental fact that the United States and the Soviet Union had a common interest in the defeat of the Axis. He continued to pass on to the Soviet leaders information regarding Nazi plans which proved to be highly accurate.[2]

A display of disruptive stupidity even more striking than Oumansky's diplomacy was the behavior of American Communists during the spring of 1941 and up to the very moment of the Nazi invasion. Clinging to the "line" that Hitler, Churchill, Mussolini, and Roosevelt were all "imperialist warmongers," American Communists promoted obviously political strikes in key defense plants of the United States, in the Vultee Aircraft strike in November, 1940, and most damagingly in the North American Aviation strike of June, 1941.[3]

The Communist-inspired "American Peace Mobilization," which succeeded pre-1939 groups that had opposed Fascism, conducted demonstrations, including picketing the White House, to arouse public opposition against the Roosevelt policy. Late at night on June 21 the White House pickets and a "Negro March on Washington" scheduled for the next day were suddenly called off. But Communist behavior during the period of the Nazi-Soviet Pact had served to discredit the isolationist as well as the Communist cause among Americans.

## Military Pessimism

Roosevelt and Hull had foreseen and prepared for the adherence of the Soviet Union to the anti-Axis cause. But their readiness to welcome the tardy recruit was not immediately shared by the American people or even by all the leaders of the administration. Military leaders were particularly influential in discouraging hopes that Russia would be a valuable member of the anti-Axis front. They predicted that the Red Army would be defeated in six weeks. Ribbentrop estimated that eight weeks would be necessary. And isolationists were able once more to admire Nazi Germany as a bulwark against Communism and add this theme to their arguments against the administration's policy.

Roosevelt and Hull regarded Hitler as the immediate menace and a worse one than Russia or Communism. In this they saw eye to eye with Churchill. The Englishman's greater conservatism and well-publicized hatred for Communism made his quick acceptance of the Soviet Union as an ally a valuable demonstration. On the same day that Hitler attacked, Churchill announced: "Any man or State who fights against Nazism will have our aid. Any man or State who marches with Hitler is our foe." [4] Britain quickly concluded a twenty-year military alliance with the Soviet Union and gave material aid out of its short supplies. This was the British answer to Hitler's hope to revive the spirit of Munich. The mysterious flight to Britain in May of Hitler's lieutenant, Rudolph Hess, had roused fears that a deal might be in the making whereby the spirit of Munich would be exhumed to make peace in the West and permit Hitler to fight only on the Eastern front. The secrecy which the British government imposed on the affair had left even President Roosevelt mystified.[5] But Churchill coupled his statement of support of Russia on June 22 with pointed words condeming the "vile race of Quislings." [6]

Churchill's clear-cut stand in support of Russia was followed by Roosevelt's statement on June 24 that American aid would be forthcoming. He too declared that any country fighting Germany merited the support of the United States. Credits were immediately released to Russia and the President refused to apply the provisions of the Neutrality Act to it. This had the important result that the port of Vladivostok remained open to American ships carrying supplies.[7]

Production machinery and raw materials which had been ordered earlier by the Soviet government and held up were immediately granted export licenses. But no arms were sent. Opinion was strong that Russia would collapse by August 1 and that any weapons it received would fall into Hitler's hands. Roosevelt, Hull, and Hopkins felt confident that Russia would hold out. The Soviet government was invited to make requests for supplies. But inertia seemed to grip many officials in Washington. Roosevelt insisted on speed. A first list of supplies amounting to $21,000,000 in value was approved by the President, Acting Secretary of State Welles, and Stimson on the same day it came to them. But almost six weeks passed and practically nothing was actually on the way. Roosevelt made it a matter of Cabinet discussion.[8]

In Congress the second appropriation under Lend Lease was due for debate. Strong opposition to the possibility of Lend Lease aid for Russia had developed during the original debates on the law. The administration feared that isolationists would win new strength among those whose hatred for Communism outran their opposition to Axis aggression and impose a restriction against use of the second appropriation to aid Russia. Roosevelt decided that he needed substantial evidence of Russia's willingness to fight in order to counter the views of his own military advisers.

The weight of this military opinion, which Roosevelt set out to change or override, may be judged from a careful report by Secretary Stimson on June 23 which he made after spending the day in conference with General Marshall and officers of the War Plans Division. The latter estimated, Stimson told the President, that Germany would defeat Russia within a maximum of three months. The military leaders saw the Russian invasion as giving the United States this short period of unforeseen respite which "should be used to push with the utmost vigor our movements in the Atlantic theater of operations." Stimson wrote that Marshall and he had been much worried that the United States might face premature trouble on the two flanks of the route to Britain, namely, Iceland and Brazil. Germany had relieved this anxiety and could not for the time being attack Iceland or prevent the United States from occupying it. Roosevelt also learned that British military authorities estimated the Ukraine and Moscow would be occupied within three to six weeks *"or more."* [9]

These opinions could not easily be overlooked by the President. He decided to exploit the minimum respite they guaranteed him by occupying Iceland. But on July 11, the day that operation was complete, he sent Harry Hopkins on the mission which paved the way for the Atlantic meeting with Churchill and Lend Lease aid to Russia.

## Occupation of Iceland

The occupation of Iceland was only in its timing a product of Hitler's invasion of Russia. It had been foreshadowed in Roosevelt's May 27 address and long before that negotiations with the Icelandic authorities had begun. In December, 1940, the American Consul in Reykjavik, Berbel E. Kuniholm, discussed with Iceland's Prime Minister the possibility of the United States placing the island under the Monroe Doctrine and providing American forces to defend it in place of the British troops. Hull put a stop to these negotiations in January, 1941. They were renewed in April after the passage of Lend Lease. Hull in his *Memoirs* writes that the Navy Department attended to the negotiations, but Sherwood states that Hopkins and Under Secretary Welles actually carried them out in utmost secrecy.[10]

On May 17 the Icelandic Althing declared independence of Denmark. Early in June the British stated willingness to give over defense of the island to American troops. On July 1 the Icelandic government agreed to entrust protection of the island to the United States and on that same day the President issued orders for a Marine detachment to sail.

The venom of isolationists was illustrated on July 3 when Senator Burton K. Wheeler told the press he had reliable information of the President's action. This report [11] amounted to military information valuable to Nazi submarine commanders who might attack the American expedition.

On July 7 the President received word that the expedition had landed safely and he sent a message to Congress giving it full information. Stimson, prior to this message, had made his last effort to convince the President he should assume a more warlike position. But Roosevelt decided to adhere to his theme of May 27, that Iceland was an outpost vital to the defense of the Western Hemisphere. Stimson in his memoirs does not mention the remainder of the July 7 message,[12] in which the President announced another forward step in the Battle of the Atlantic. He told Congress he had

issued orders to the Navy that all necessary steps be taken to insure the safety of communications in the approaches between Iceland and the United States, as well as on the seas between the United States and all other strategic points.

The sea lanes, Roosevelt declared, shall be "open and free from all hostile activity or threat thereof." [13]

This announcement was instrumented by Hemisphere Defense Plan 4, issued on July 11 for execution beginning July 26, 1941. General tasks of the Navy under this order included insurance of communications with strategic outposts of the United States, and defense of United States and Icelandic flag shipping against hostile attack or threat of attack. Before the order was executed this was made specific with orders (a) to protect United States and Icelandic flag shipping by "escorting, covering, and patrolling, as required by circumstances, and by destroying hostile forces which threaten such shipping;" and (b) 1) to escort convoys of United States and Icelandic flag shipping, 2) including ships of any nationality which might join such convoys between the United States and Iceland. But on the day before execution, Stark ordered the Navy to postpone execution of the second clause under (b). That part of Hemisphere Defense Plan 4 was not carried out until September 16, after a German submarine had attacked the United States Destroyer *Greer* on September 4 and the President had announced publicly the "shoot on sight" order on September 11.[14]

Therefore, between July 26 and September 16 the Navy did not engage in escorting to Iceland any ships not of United States or Icelandic flag. Patrolling, trailing and reporting in the clear remained the methods whereby the Navy helped protect British convoys. The Patrol was extended to Iceland insofar as warships were available. July 26 thus marked a new contribution of the United States to the winning of the Battle of the Atlantic, one which Stimson neglects to mention in his description of Roosevelt as moving "too slowly." Beard, on the other hand, exaggerates the affair to fit his thesis that the President moved "too fast" and "plotted" entry into the war. Beard calls Admiral Stark's testimony before the Congressional Joint Committee on the details of the Navy's orders a disclosure of "realities that offered a strange contrast to many statements made public by President Roosevelt earlier in the year. . . ."[15] This ignores the President's public announcements of new policy, first in the case of Iceland, and then in the case of the "shoot on sight" speech which preceded the order to escort convoys containing other than United States and Icelandic ships.

The German attack on the *Greer* in September was interpreted by Roosevelt as relieving him of his virtual pledge against naval escorts of convoys containing Allied merchant ships. This opened the period of limited and undeclared warfare for the United States.

In July, escorts for Allied merchantmen were postponed because this "act of war" seemed unjustified prior to the German attack on the *Greer*. Without such a justification, escorts would have given fuel to the isolationist campaign against extension of the Selective Service Act. Roosevelt decided that stronger political bonds between the United States and Great Britain should precede extension of United States cooperation with defenders against aggression by providing escorts and extending Lend Lease aid to Russia.

## The Hopkins Mission

The result was the meeting of Roosevelt and Churchill at sea early in August and their joint declaration known as the Atlantic Charter. On July 13, Harry Hopkins flew to Britain in a Lend Lease bomber to arrange the meeting. He told Churchill of the new limits of United States naval patrol activity, which included Iceland. Hopkins advised Roosevelt to bring leading staff officers to the conference for discussion of strategy in the Battle of the Atlantic as it related to British determination to defend the Middle East, a determination which many Americans believed unwise. Current Anglo-American policy towards Japan seemed successful. Roosevelt and Churchill were convinced Japan did not want to fight Britain and the United States at the same time. A conference with Stalin seemed to Hopkins necessary before the Atlantic Conference in order that the Russian factor could be added to the Middle Eastern, Asiatic and Atlantic situations for a discussion of global dimensions.

Roosevelt highly approved the Hopkins trip to Moscow. The findings of the American during his brief trip turned the opinions of leading American and British officials towards optimism. Stalin gave Hopkins more information about the Russian situation than any other outsider possessed. His requests for aid stressed raw materials such as aluminum and showed that he expected to fight a long war.

Churchill told Hopkins he hoped the United States would enter the war if Japan attacked Britain, and Stalin told him that the enormous world influence of the United States and its President, if it declared war, might bring about the defeat of Hitler without the United States firing a shot. But the President's instructions to his representative were clear. They read, in Hopkins' notes: "No talk about war." These instructions also made clear that only attack against the United States would be regarded by Roosevelt as grounds for United States entry into the war. In a reference to clause (2) in section (b) of War Plan 4, whose execution was presently postponed, Hopkins noted the President's attitude: "Convoy can join up with American flag or Icelandic flag ships. Must be an American ship if conflict comes." This emphasized that Roosevelt would not ask Congress for a declaration of war on the general grounds proposed by Churchill, Stalin, and American interventionists. And as it turned out, he did not even regard attacks on American ships as justification for more than limited and undeclared warfare.[16]

Harry Hopkins' mission to Moscow was a typical Rooseveltian initiative towards a united front of nations opposed to the Axis. It bridged over the normal channel of diplomacy, which seemed to be an obstacle rather than a route to improve relations between the Soviet Union and the western democracies. Time and again it would be demonstrated that personal contact with Stalin was the only way to overcome the work of his diplomats and agents. Such contact also overcame the barriers of caution which Hull erected in the State Department. For Roosevelt, the possibility of adding a powerful nation to the coalition forming against the Axis justified the risks that attended reliance upon the Soviet dictatorship. But he did not need to rely on Stalin so much as on Hitler to make the Soviet Union a useful ally, and the Nazi dictator never failed to encourage his victims to hang together as the only way they could avoid hanging separately.

## 14.

## The Atlantic Conference

Hopkins accompanied Churchill and his subordinates on the battleship *Prince of Wales* to the August 9, 1941, rendezvous off Argentia, Newfoundland, where it met the cruiser *Augusta* which carried Roosevelt, Under Secretary Welles, and staff officers. The fact that the leaders of the two great democracies met and became friends as well as collaborators in itself justified the meeting. It was a demonstration of incalculable value to the morale of humanity and an important defeat for the Axis, whose propaganda proclaimed that distrust prevailed between the Americans and the British.

Three main subjects were dealt with by the members of the Atlantic Conference: military and naval strategy against Hitler and Mussolini; a joint declaration of peace aims; and diplomatic strategy against Japan. They will be taken up in turn. Beard, Morgenstern, and the Minority Report of the Joint Congressional Committee all charge that Roosevelt made commitments to Churchill in all three fields which proved his intention to lead the United States into the war by means of "complicated maneuvers," a "secret alliance with Britain," "provocations" of the Axis governments, "deceit" towards the American people, and sundry other techniques.

The best authorities for what actually happened at the Atlantic Conference are Sumner Welles in his testimony before the Joint Committee and in his book, *Where Are We Heading?* [1] and Robert Sherwood, who was permitted to compare British records with Welles's material and Hopkins' private papers. Sherwood found nothing in the British records to support Beard's ominous refer-

ence to "personal understandings" between Roosevelt and Churchill; on the contrary, they agree "in point of fact" with Welles's
evidence.[2]

Beard's claim that one "personal understanding" was exposed by
Churchill in a speech on January 27, 1942, may be disposed of
merely by a reading of the passage from the speech to which Beard
refers his readers. Beard wishes to prove that the President made
a *commitment* to Churchill to enter a Pacific war even if the
United States was not attacked. But Churchill speaks only of the
*"probability"* after the Atlantic Conference that the United States
would do so. A "probability" is hardly a commitment. Besides,
Churchill obviously wished to maximize for a British audience his
own role in the events which ended in the United States entering
the war on December 7, 1941. This led him into the queer logic of
the paragraph Beard quotes, that somehow the event of December
7 fulfilled the "probability" that the United States would enter
the war even if it was *not* attacked. All contemporary evidence
agrees that Churchill and Roosevelt did not expect Japan to make
the colossal blunder of attacking *both* Britain and the United
States. Churchill uses extreme illogic to suggest that he did in fact
foresee the Japanese blunder, that it somehow did not make unnecessary his unsuccessful efforts to obtain a commitment from
Roosevelt that the United States would enter the war even if it
was *not* attacked.[3]

## The Azores

The British members of the staff conference at Argentia
wished to discuss problems of strategy which would go beyond the
scope of earlier Anglo-American staff meetings. The American
members refused. They confined the discussions to details of Lend
Lease planning, patrol and convoy operations, and problems of
the strategic outposts of the Western Hemisphere which Roosevelt had publicly brought within the scope of American defense.
Within these areas, important new determinations were achieved.
An American-British-Russian conference in Moscow was decided
upon to implement Hopkins' report and concert measures of aid
to the Soviet Union.

The question of the Azores and other islands was discussed in
detail by Roosevelt and Churchill. In effect, Roosevelt used the

occasion of the meeting to conduct negotiations with the British government regarding the Azores of the sort which had preceded American occupation of Greenland and Iceland. President Salazar of Portugal, like the authorities in Greenland and Iceland, had informed Roosevelt that occupation of the Azores would be permitted as a means of preventing their falling into the hands of Germany. Churchill told Roosevelt he planned to occupy the Canary Islands because of revived fears of a Hitler move through Spain to Gibraltar and North Africa. Therefore he would ask Salazar to request occupation of the Azores by the United States. Roosevelt agreed that if Salazar made the request, the United States would send the necessary forces.

Beard calls this a "commitment" and thinks it notable that no "official announcement" of the project was made to the public. Beard by this time uses the word "commitment" to cover any information Roosevelt gave another government of an intention to take any action under conditional circumstances. But as an isolationist epithet, the word "commitment" meant a promise to another government by the American President, or by a treaty such as the Covenant of the League, to go to war—a promise that ignored or circumvented the exclusive Constitutional authority of Congress to declare war. Since Roosevelt made no such commitment, he can be found guilty only by stretching the word to cover any acts of cooperation with other governments that involved opposition to the Axis. As for an "official announcement" of the Azores project, the President in his May 27, 1941, speech had made very clear the general intention of the United States to prevent those islands from falling into Hitler's hands. The announcement could be made more specific only by giving German submarine commanders information as to the date or destination of an expedition.

The British officers at Argentia proposed further staff conferences at Singapore but no decision was reached. Churchill thereupon took up the question directly with Roosevelt in connection with Far East diplomacy. At Argentia, as Sherwood makes clear, the United States staff officers insisted that they would discuss only problems of Hemisphere defense as publicly defined by Roosevelt to include strategic outposts.

The work of the staff officers at Argentia was made clear to the public, short only of giving out details of value to Hitler, in the joint statement issued at the end of the Conference. The statement declared that high ranking officers of the two governments' armed forces were present; that problems of Lend Lease aid had been examined; that the supply problems of the Soviet Union would receive continued attention; and that the President and Prime Minister had "made clear the steps which their countries are respectively taking for their safety" in the face of dangers arising from the policies of world domination upon which the Hitler and other associated governments had embarked.

A more definite reference to the exchange of intentions regarding the Azores would have defeated it, first because it would have exposed Salazar to Hitler's wrath, and second because if he had been directly challenged, Hitler could hardly have avoided using force to prevent American occupation. Also, the facts that the plan was still highly conditional, and was never actually carried out by the United States (Churchill received permission from Salazar in 1943 to establish British bases in the Azores), indicate that Beard and the isolationists really demand in the name of "frankness" that the President should have been foolhardy in the extreme and actually have made the "empty threats" against Hitler of which they accused him.

Roosevelt had originally wanted the joint announcement to contain a clear negative directed against isolationists, namely, that "these military and naval conversations had in no way involved any future commitments between the two Governments, except as authorized under the terms of the Lend-Lease Act." Churchill dissented, although not, as Beard states, because they had actually made commitments or agreements that deserved the name, or because Churchill had overlooked a fancied distinction in Roosevelt's proposal between commitments entered into by the staff officers and commitments entered into by the two leaders.[4]

As Welles states, Churchill dissented because he wanted a positive statement of accomplishments to encourage all opponents of Hitler rather than a discouraging emphasis on what was not done. Thereupon Churchill and Roosevelt agreed on positive phraseology which referred to such matters as the Azores not as an "agreement," because that word would be interpreted as a binding executive agreement, certainly not as a "future commitment," because "commitment" in current American isolationists' usage meant war, but as an exchange of information regarding inten-

tions ("made clear the steps their countries are respectively taking. . . ."), a locution positive enough to boost morale and yet free
of words American isolationists tortured into epithets.[5]

## A Cryptic Remark

Further indication that the Roosevelt-Churchill joint statement
of August 14 did not constitute in any sense an executive agreement came in a remark by Roosevelt in 1944. He then pointed out
that the Atlantic Charter had not been drawn up in a single document and duly signed by himself and Churchill. His purpose was
to show that it was not legally binding in the manner of an executive agreement.[6] This statement scandalized many persons and it
was cryptic enough to confuse anyone. Nevertheless it was correct.
The Atlantic Charter was issued, along with the preliminary statement on the meeting at Argentia, only in the form of a press release embodying a joint declaration. It was presented as a "statement signed by the President of the United States and the Prime
Minister of Great Britain" to indicate their agreement on the content of the press release and joint declaration. The text was radioed
to Washington and London before the President and Prime Minister left Argentia. Mimeographed copies were the only "official
version," and no signed "original copies" were prepared for
the archives of the two governments. As a "joint declaration" the
Atlantic Charter with its preliminary statement had none of the
legally binding quality of an executive agreement. A brief lecture
by the President on the differences between a joint declaration
and an executive agreement would have served public understanding better than his remark of 1944 that the Atlantic Charter had
not been "signed."

## "No Economic or Territorial Deals"

The name "Atlantic Charter" for the joint declaration is honor-
ific and was bestowed by others than the participants in the Conference. It made bilateral a part of the Four Freedoms declaration
Roosevelt had announced for the United States in January. Its
ideas were the common coin of democratic idealism. As such they
had no specific origin. But Roosevelt had issued some of them as
American aims in the international arena, and now his "Free-

doms" were expanded to form the ideological basis of Anglo-American cooperation.

Some confusion resulted from Welles's revelation that Churchill carried to Argentia a proposed draft for the joint declaration, but Sherwood makes clear that the impulse to make such a declaration came from Roosevelt. Hopkins carried the impulse from Roosevelt to Churchill. He kept no record of his conversations with Churchill on preparations for the meeting, but his notes on Roosevelt's instructions indicate that the President's chief concern was to obtain from Churchill a statement of anti-imperialism as the war aim of the British government. He was determined that his Four Freedoms should not be undermined like Wilson's Fourteen Points by British imperialist deals of the sort that were embodied in the Allies' secret treaties during the First World War. Hopkins' note on Roosevelt's purpose was succinct: "Economic or territorial deals—NO."[7]

Avoidance of the mistakes of Wilson was a very important compulsion in Roosevelt's determinations of policy. As Sherwood has written:

The tragedy of Wilson was always somewhere within the rim of his consciousness. Roosevelt could never forget Wilson's mistakes, which had been made with the noblest will in the world, impelled by the purest concept of the Christian ethic. Wilson had advocated "peace without victory," . . .[8]

## Political Anti-Imperialism

This preoccupation of Roosevelt's is the best clue to his part in the much-controverted discussion with Churchill on projected outlines of the peace to follow the Second World War. The proposed draft, which Sir Alexander Cadogan handed Sumner Welles, contained five points. The first four fully expressed Roosevelt's "Economic or territorial deals—NO." They amounted to probably the most sweeping statement of anti-imperialism a British Prime Minister had ever given to the world. The first three were political: "no aggrandizement, territorial or other;" "no territorial changes that do not accord with the freely expressed wishes of the peoples concerned;" and "the right of all peoples to choose the form of government under which they will live." A reference to "freedom of speech and of thought" without which the choice of government "must be illusory" was omitted in the final draft because it was inherent in the proposition in favor of the right of peoples to choose their form of government. Instead, Welles proposed and the British accepted a clause in favor of the restoration of rights of self-government "to those who have been forcibly deprived of them." Churchill coupled "sovereign rights" to the term "self-government." Otherwise the first three items embodying political anti-imperialism were left intact in the final draft.

## Economic Internationalism

The fourth item, embodying economic internationalism, caused a dispute. The British draft read:

. Fourth, they will strive to bring about a fair and equitable distribution of essential produce not only within their territorial boundaries but between the nations of the world.

Welles's redraft made this square better with the more advanced reciprocal trade agreement policy of the United States. It repudiated the imperial preference system of the British:

Fourth, they will endeavor to further the enjoyment by all peoples of access, without discrimination and on equal terms, to the markets and to the raw materials of the world which are needed for their economic prosperity.

Churchill objected that, although he had always opposed imperial preferences, he was powerless to commit the dominion governments to repudiation of the Ottawa agreements. Welles was adamant and the British largely gave way. A compromise was agreed upon as follows:

Fourth, they will endeavor, with due respect for their existing obligations, to further the enjoyment by all states, great or small, victor or vanquished, of access, on equal terms, to the trade and to the raw materials of the world which are needed for their economic prosperity.

Since Welles's redraft had only proposed that the two governments should "endeavor to further" nondiscrimination in trade, the final version merely made explicit what the redraft could be understood to imply, namely, "due respect for their existing obligations." That proviso brought criticism from Americans but this was essentially the result of a misunderstanding of the nature of the joint declaration. It could not overrule or repudiate existing laws of the two governments.

## Security and Freedom

The fifth item was suggested by Churchill. It combined ideas of the New Deal and of the British Labor Party:

Fifth, they desire to bring about the fullest collaboration between all nations in the economic field with the object of securing, for all, improved labor standards, economic advancement, and social security.

The sixth item came from the Welles redraft and embodied two of Roosevelt's Four Freedoms:

Sixth, after the final destruction of the Nazi tyranny, they hope to see established a peace which will afford to all nations the means of dwelling in safety within their own boundaries, and which will afford assurance that all the men in all the lands may live out their lives in freedom from fear and want.

The seventh item also came from the Welles redraft:

Seventh, such a peace should enable all men to traverse the high seas and oceans without hindrance.

This recalled Wilson's famous Point in favor of freedom of the seas, to which the British had objected during the peace negotiations after the First World War. Roosevelt had made it the chief theme of his May 27 speech. A less comprehensive statement of it had been proposed by the British in Cadogan's draft. No account of discussion of the item appears in Welles's memorandum.

## Collective Security

Other clauses in the British draft caused a major dispute which isolationists exploited when Welles made it public. They found in the dispute a scandalous exhibition of Roosevelt's secret purposes. The British proposal read:

Fifth, they seek a peace which will not only cast down forever the Nazi tyranny but by effective international organization will afford to all States and peoples the means of dwelling in security within their own bounds and of traversing the seas and oceans without fear of lawless assault or need of maintaining burdensome armaments.

After freedom of the seas was disposed of as item seven, the final version of the remainder of the fifth British point read as follows:

Eighth, they believe that all of the nations of the world, for realistic as well as spiritual reasons, must come to the abandonment of the use of force. Since no future peace can be maintained if land, sea, or air armaments continue to be employed by nations which threaten, or may threaten, aggression outside of their frontiers, they believe, pending the establishment of a wider and permanent system of general security, that the disarmament of such nations is essential. They will likewise aid and encourage all other practicable measures which will lighten for peace-loving peoples the crushing burden of armaments.

Roosevelt initiated the substitution of this version for the British draft. He told Churchill that he could not agree to the phrase "effective international organization" not only because it would create suspicion and opposition among isolationists in the United States, but because he personally was not in favor of creating an organization like the Assembly of the League until after a period of time had elapsed, during which time an international police force, composed of the United States and Great Britain, could function to create conditions in which an international organization would have a better chance of success than the League had. In the Welles redraft there was no reference to a system of general security. Churchill said he felt Roosevelt's program would create a great deal of opposition among "extreme internationalists."

The President agreed, but said he felt the time had come for "complete realism." [9]

Roosevelt in this momentous interchange showed that he believed one of Wilson's mistakes leading to the failure of collective security after the First World War to have been his insistence that the League of Nations Covenant be an integral part of the Treaty of Versailles. Many authorities agree with Roosevelt's view. They believe that the tasks of enforcing the treaties, disarming the aggressor nations, and policing the world placed an impossible burden on the newborn League because it had neither legal authority nor force equal to those tasks. As Roosevelt saw it, an international organization could function successfully only after the governments that defeated the aggressor nations had finished the job by establishing a stable peace. This would require not only military victory but such operations as disarmament of aggressor nations, reconstruction of devastated areas, re-education of peoples corrupted by militarism, revival of peaceful economies and international trade, organization of peaceful governments in former aggressor nations, and general settlements in peace treaties.

It seemed to Roosevelt that these huge tasks could be performed only by the national governments of the great powers that would defeat the Axis. Those governments would have available the necessary forces. Their authority should not be restricted by other governments which, lacking power, lacked responsibility. The responsibility of the great powers derived from their ability to enforce their will—a doctrine distasteful to Wilsonians and other idealists, but which the history of the League seemed to support. The interest of Great Britain and the United States was on the side of world peace, therefore humanity might wisely trust them.

During the interval in which the United States and Great Britain would exercise international police power, a new organization for collective security would have time to grow up to its ultimate task. Then the great powers would turn over to it a world in which the chaos and dangers of the war's aftermath had been overcome and peace was a going concern. In such a world, actually at peace, guardianship of that peace by the methods of collective security would have a fair chance to succeed.

This was Roosevelt's "realistic" approach in 1941 to the question of how collective security should be made the ultimate fruit of military defeat of the Axis. Before he died, President Roosevelt gave up his 1941 plan, and he worked during 1944 and early 1945 to establish the United Nations as a functioning organization for collective security even before the war ended. But in some respects he persisted in the 1941 plan: the Charter of the United Nations was not linked with peace treaties, the great powers were to exercise national authority over the defeated countries, and the veto power in the Security Council was reserved to the five great powers chiefly responsible for maintaining the peace.

Roosevelt in 1945 as well as in 1941 was willing to risk losing the support of extreme internationalists. He hoped to win the support of a broad sector of opinion, centered on moderate internationalists, to which he could attract moderate isolationists. This seemed politically wise especially in 1941 because the isolationists in Congress during the days of the Atlantic Conference were staging a strong revival. On August 12, the day the Atlantic Conference ended, news of passage of the extension of Selective Service in the House by a margin of one vote dropped, as Sherwood writes, "like enemy bombs" on the *Augusta* and the *Prince of Wales*.[10]

It was no time for Roosevelt to inform the country he proposed to revive Wilsonian internationalism in all its discredited idealism. And among those who were satisfied by the "realistic" program was Prime Minister Churchill. He evidently did not regret Roosevelt's summary disposal of extreme internationalism. He remarked that "of course he was wholeheartedly in favor" of the President's draft of item eight.

Subsequently Cadogan told Welles he thought it would be a tragic thing to omit all reference to the need to create an international organization after the transition period was concluded. Welles took up the question with Roosevelt, who said it seemed to him entirely desirable to propose a permanent international organization if it was made clear that a transition period would intervene. Thus it was that the phrase "pending the establishment of a wider and permanent system of general security" was inserted in the final draft. It made item eight a complete statement of the President's program.

## An Epochal New Foreign Policy

Beard, like other isolationists, made much of the evidence in the Welles memorandum that the President did not advocate the program of "extreme internationalism." Beard's readers must find his surprise itself surprising, because he ordinarily insists that not American entry into an international organization, but United States entry into the war was Roosevelt's purpose. Beard is disturbed by Roosevelt's lapses from internationalist virtue in proposing that the United States and Britain should "police the world," and in failing to invite Russia in August, 1941, to join them as police powers. Beard supplies the text of Welles's memorandum so that "readers may form their own judgments" as to whether the President was, in Beard's words and italics, *"at heart an isolationist."* [11] But his own discussion encourages his readers to form images of "Roosevelt the anti-Russian;" "Roosevelt the isolationist;" "Roosevelt the warmonger."

Morgenstern, on the other hand, finds it possible to solve the problems of the origins of the Atlantic Charter, the disagreements it caused between Churchill and Roosevelt, their compromises, and the significance of the document, all in less than a paragraph:

Churchill tackled the problem of getting Roosevelt to sign an acknowledgment of Anglo-American alliance in the Atlantic which could be waved in Hitler's face. Roosevelt assented without making difficulties. The Atlantic Charter was the product.[12]

Waverley Root might be expected to relate the Atlantic Charter to his voluminous interpretation of the "sad spectacle of American foreign policy." He indicts the State Department because it "weakened the Allied position and delayed the day of final victory" through "errors in diplomacy" which "would be measured in terms of human lives." The President, Root believes, allowed the following "distorting influences . . . to operate unchecked because of the *absence of any basic policy* to oppose to them:" anti-Russian prejudice; anti-British prejudice; American imperialism; and class and special interests.[13] Root evidently does not consider the Atlantic Conference between the American and British leaders a possible source of information on Roosevelt's "basic policy." He never mentions it and his sole and complete reference to the Atlantic Charter is the statement: "On August 14, President Roosevelt and Prime Minister Winston Churchill drew up the Atlantic Charter."[14] In extenuation it might be thought that Root wrote his book before Welles had made public his memorandum of the

Conference. Root was interested only in exposing the "Secret History of American Foreign Policy." But before he decided that the United States suffered from "the absence of any *basic* policy," he might well have considered the possibility that basic policy was not likely to have been kept a secret; that, indeed, an important formulation of it could be found in the Atlantic Charter.

The very fact of a meeting between Roosevelt and Churchill and their subordinates was a sensational demonstration that the basic policy of the United States was not anti-British. The public joint declaration made clear that important steps had been taken and that more would be taken by the United States and Britain in the future to overcome anti-Russian feeling for the sake of a united front against Hitler. The leading items of the Atlantic Charter expressed adherence to ideals of anti-imperialism. Other items projected, as American and British foreign policy, ideals associated with Roosevelt's New Deal, a program which was not ordinarily described as one designed to further "class and special interests," at least not within Root's meaning. "Isolationist" is evidently too mild a label for Root to attach to American foreign policy, but the Atlantic Charter named "a permanent system of general security" as Roosevelt's and Churchill's ultimate goal, and this quite "basic" policy of collective security was clearly opposed to Root's whole list of "unchecked distorting influences."

A strange journalistic phenomenon during the years when Roosevelt revolutionized the foreign policy of the United States from isolationism to collective security was the endless harping on the theme: "We have no foreign policy." Editorial writers, columnist-savants and plain journalists were, like Root in his *History*, preoccupied with the game of trying to expose "secrets" of Roosevelt's administration which usually remained largely imaginary. Their preoccupation with secrets seemed to blind them to the existence of the obvious public steps Roosevelt took to lead the country to adopt an epochal new foreign policy.

No imaginary or genuine "secrets" of the Atlantic Conference can alter the central meaning of the most important clause of the Atlantic Charter. In it Roosevelt for the first time since he took power did not stop with advocating "measures short of collective security," but proposed United States entry into a "permanent system of general security" as his ultimate goal.

## "No Talk of War"

Roosevelt did not regard American entry into the war as a necessary consequence of his joint declaration with Churchill of war aims. He had indefinitely postponed the "act of war" involved in providing naval escorts for convoys of Allied merchant vessels. He made a revealing explanation to Welles during the Conference of his conception of the relation between the Atlantic Charter and the United States entry into the war.

Welles had told him that he anticipated "considerable opposition on the part of extreme isolationists" to the clause in item eight which proposed disarmament of aggressor nations during the transition period after the war. Welles said that isolationists would take the President to mean that the United States would go to war to disarm aggressor nations. Roosevelt answered that the whole intent of item eight was "to make clear what the objective *would be if the war was won* and that he believed people in the United States would take that point of view." [15] The President's view was made clear in the words of the joint declaration which introduced the Charter. They pointed out that the Charter named principles on which the two leaders "base their hopes for a better future for the world." [16]

This meant that the Atlantic Charter was a statement of goals obviously attainable only if the Axis was defeated but requiring no further means than the supply of Lend Lease aid as the American contribution to Axis defeat. In short, Roosevelt adhered at Argentia to the instructions he had given Hopkins—"No talk of war"—and he did not look upon his participation in a joint declaration of war aims as implying closer participation in the war than Congress had authorized, or as a violation of his pledge against making participation in the war his policy.

## The Third Round: Japan

The Argentia discussions of the Azores and the Atlantic Charter did not provide Beard, Morgenstern and the Minority of the Congressional Committee with the chief exhibit in their case against Roosevelt. They found that in the third round of discussions at the Conference, which dealt with the question of Japan. After the British staff officers failed to obtain a promise from the American officers that the United States would go to war if Japan attacked the territory of a country other than the United States— a repetition of their failures in the earlier talks at Washington and Singapore—Prime Minister Churchill attempted to obtain such a promise from Roosevelt.

He proposed that the governments of the United States, Great Britain, and the Netherlands should make "parallel and simultaneous" declarations to Japan. The Soviet government should be informed and the question considered whether it should be asked to join in the parallel declaration. A draft of the declaration prepared by Cadogan read:

1. Any further encroachment by Japan in the Southwestern Pacific would produce a situation in which the United States [British, Netherlands] Government would be compelled to take counter measures even though these might lead to war between the United States [Great Britain, the Netherlands] and Japan.
2. If any third Power becomes the object of aggression by Japan in consequence of such counter measures or of their support of them, the President would have the intention to seek authority from Congress to give aid to such Power [His, Her Majesty's Government would give all possible aid to such Power].[17]

Since the President already had authority from Congress to give Lend Lease aid to such a third power, the last clause was a strong hint that the President would ask Congress for a declaration of war, and the phrase to be used in the declarations of the other two governments, "give *all possible* aid," meant the same thing. The most likely event foreseen was a Japanese attack against the NEI. Britain expected to join in the defense of the rich islands, and Churchill's proposal was that the United States should warn Japan that it would in such a situation enter the war.

Churchill proposed this three- or four-power parallel declaration because, as he told Welles, he believed it was the only hope of preventing Japan from embarking on new aggressions which, unless the United States entered the war, would destroy British shipping in the Pacific and Indian Oceans and cut the lifeline between the British Dominions and the British Isles. If Japan were not restrained, or the United States did not enter the war following a Japanese attack against Great Britain, directly or indirectly through the NEI, the blow to the British cause might be decisive.

What Churchill proposed was, therefore, a united front to prevent Japan from defeating new victims one by one. He wished to face Japan with the certainty that if it attacked any one of the members of the united front, it would have to fight them all. It was an important British initiative to use the technique of collective security to prevent the war from spreading in the Far East.

No one among the Anglo-American leaders believed that Japan itself would in the end force war upon the three powers by attacking them all at once. The foolhardiness of that procedure placed it outside the calculations of Roosevelt and Churchill. This was proved by the nature of the Churchill proposal and the discussion that followed. The United States was thought to be the last power Japan would attack directly. Such a calculation was inevitable because it was the only procedure that made sense from the point of view of Japanese military interests and because Japan, like the other Axis governments, had so obviously pursued the "sensible" one-by-one strategy in its aggressions. It was the disunity of the peaceful nations that had made it possible for aggressor nations possessing a minority of world power to succeed in their designs. No reasonable person could be expected to foresee, prior to December 7, 1941, that in one blow the Axis would destroy the condition which alone made its victory possible. This is of supreme importance in the refutation of the isolationist thesis that Roosevelt "planned" Pearl Harbor.

The only event for which Churchill asked Roosevelt to plan was a Japanese attack on territory other than that of the United States. Because he proposed a plan based on the central conceptions of the policy of collective security, that an aggression against one peaceful nation is an aggression against all peaceful nations, and that the best way to prevent aggression is to face the potential aggressor with the certainty that it cannot attack one without fighting them all, the parallel declaration was bound to win a sympathetic hearing by Roosevelt. It presented him with the same choices he had faced again and again since he came to power, this time in the ultimate form of the ultimate sanction: war. The diplomatic sanction of the Stimson Doctrine he had inherited and sustained. The intermediate sanction of a discriminatory arms embargo against an aggressor, which he had tried and failed to make the policy of the United States prior to 1939, he had accomplished by August, 1941, and had reinforced with the unprecedented policy of Lend Lease aid to victims of aggression. In the Atlantic Charter he proposed eventual entry of the United States into a full-fledged system of collective security. But Churchill asked him to join immediately a united front of peaceful nations to prevent further spread of the war by invoking the ultimate sanction of collective security. It called for one of the crucial decisions of Roosevelt's career. To understand his decision, review of United States relations with Japan during preceding months is necessary.

# 15.

## Roosevelt and Japan

Secretary Hull believed that in the fall of 1940 the United States caused Japan to postpone new aggressions. The Roosevelt administration advanced new economic sanctions against Japan when Japan joined the Axis military alliance, and carefully nourished the uncertainty of Japanese leaders regarding future American intentions. This, Hull believed, had kept Japan from seizing the greatest opportunity of its history when France and the Netherlands fell and Britain seemed about to fall.

During the winter, Foreign Minister Yosuke Matsuoka and other pro-Axis and militarist Japanese turned once more to belligerent assertions of Japanese ambitions. Hull on January 13, 1941, told the House Foreign Affairs Committee that the "new order" in Asia meant domination of nearly half the people of the world by one country and that such a program was of concern to every other nation. Matsuoka answered in a speech to the Japanese Diet a week later that he wanted the United States to agree to Japanese supremacy over the whole of the western Pacific and to end economic restrictions against Japan. Hull told the press next day:

We have threatened no one, invaded no one, and surrounded no one. We have freely offered and now freely offer cooperation in peaceful life to all who wish it. This devotion to peace and friendly processes naturally warrants no implication of a desire to extend frontiers or assume hegemony. Our strategic line must depend primarily on the policies and courses of other nations.[1]

## Japan's Secret Program

Matsuoka's statement afforded a public glimpse of the secret program of the Japanese government, which was fully exposed after the war by the International Military Tribunal for the Far East. It was adopted in October, 1940, and designated three objectives: early successful settlement of the China Incident; a non-aggression pact with Russia; and incorporation of the countries of southeast Asia and the southwest Pacific, including Malaya, India, Australia, and New Zealand, in the Greater East Asia Co-Prosperity Sphere. Singapore and the Philippines were regarded as the keys. If they were won, all the rest would fall easily to Japan.

Action to achieve the third objective was planned on two fronts: diplomatic and military. Britain would be offered Japanese mediation in the European war in return for recognition of the Co-Prosperity Sphere, including surrender of Singapore. In February, 1941, the Japanese leaders told the Germans that a military attack against Singapore was planned. Military bases were to be secured in Indo-China and Thailand. The United States was to be offered Japanese recognition of "Philippine independence" in return for American recognition of the Co-Prosperity Sphere. In January, 1941, the Japanese Commander of the Combined Fleets approved and transmitted to Imperial General Headquarters a plan for a surprise attack on Pearl Harbor while the two countries were at peace. In May, 1941, the Japanese Navy began training for the attack.[2]

Thus it is now clear that when Matsuoka told the Japanese Diet in January, 1941, that he wanted the United States to agree to Japanese supremacy in the western Pacific, he actually demanded American cooperation with Japan to achieve its conquests as the price of American immunity from Japanese attack against the United States.

In the innumerable American-Japanese conversations of 1941, the Roosevelt administration never refused to discuss a Japanese proposal, it never issued an ultimatum, and it never offered or agreed to proposals which signified appeasement, that is, which gave consent or support to Japanese conquests of territories of third countries. The administration gradually ended American economic support of the Japanese war machine, most decisively after Japan in July invaded southern Indo-China.

American isolationists argued that the Roosevelt administration should make an agreement with Japan, abandon economic sanctions, and "get out of Asia." They charged that the Roosevelt administration was responsible for the attack on Pearl Harbor because it did issue ultimatums to the Japanese government and encircled Japan with an alliance of the ABCD powers. The latter charge may be disposed of at the outset by reference to the fact that the first Anglo-American staff conference occurred no earlier than the formulation of the Japanese plan to attack Pearl Harbor. Besides, those conferences only considered defensive measures, while the Japanese planned aggression.

## A Proposal by Clergymen

After the Hull-Matsuoka exchange, the 1941 record begins with a proposal to Roosevelt by two Roman Catholic clergymen that the United States should pacify Japan. Bishop James Edward Walsh, Superior General of the Maryknoll Foreign Mission Society, and Father Drought returned from Japan in January and obtained through Postmaster General Frank C. Walker an interview with the President. They conveyed the opinion of leading Japanese moderates that they could overthrow the militarists if the United States would give Japan an agreement which would assure her "security." Matsuoka at the moment was engaged not only in verbal assaults but in operations to gain control of Thailand. Hull and Roosevelt believed that no new agreements were necessary, provided Japan observed those it had already signed, but they believed also that no opportunity to reach a peaceful settlement should be neglected. They asked Walker and the two clergymen to continue their conversations with the Japanese and to reduce to writing the Japanese proposals.

A new Japanese Ambassador, Admiral Kichisaburo Nomura, arrived in Washington in February. Hull found that he got on well with Nomura personally, and in his *Memoirs* gives him credit for sincerity in trying to avoid war. Perhaps Nomura lacked knowledge of the secret plans of his government. Roosevelt proposed a series of frank discussions between Nomura and Hull and other State Department officers to see whether relations could be improved. Nomura promised to do all he could. He made to Roosevelt an admission highly unusual for a diplomat: that the military group in control of his government would be the "chief obstacle" to better relations.

Because Nomura was so frank, Hull pointed out to him that he, Hull, would be wary, even while they conversed, of surprise moves by the Japanese militarists into southern Indo-China, Thailand, the NEI or Singapore. Rumors had reached Hull of the Japanese plan to attack Pearl Harbor. He turned over the information to the War and Navy Departments.

### Conversations Begin

Extended conversations between Hull and Nomura in the privacy of the former's apartment began early in March. On April 9 Bishop Walsh and Father Drought gave Hull a draft proposal for an agreement with Japan. In it the Japanese government would promise to go to war under the Axis alliance only if one of its members was "aggressively attacked" by a power not at present involved in the European war. This would leave the Japanese government free to determine what it would regard as an "aggressive attack." The draft proposed a "settlement" of the "China Incident" in ways seemingly respectful of Chinese independence and of the Open Door policy in principle, but vitiated by requirements that the Japanese puppet government of China must "coalesce" with the government of Chiang Kai-shek, and that the United States must abandon the Stimson Doctrine and recognize Japanese conquest of Manchuria. If Chiang Kai-shek did not agree to these peace terms, the proposal continued, the United States would be obligated to abandon aid to China. In either case, the United States would be required to abandon its restrictions against exports to Japan, give Japan a gold credit to finance such exports, and help Japan obtain raw materials from the NEI and other countries.

These provisions would clearly place the United States in the position of a diplomatic partner of Japan in imposing a peace upon China which would violate its independence. And if China refused to accept this peace, the United States would also become an economic and moral partner of Japan in waging war against China. In short, the proposal was not that the United States should "isolate" itself from the Far Eastern conflict, but that it should shift sides in it, abandon support of China and restrictions against Japan, and turn to support of the aggressor and a policy of pressure and punishments against his victim.

A "Far Eastern Munich" was clearly envisaged, with Manchuria in the position of the Sudetenland as the price of peace to be thrown to the aggressor, and the rest of China open to destruction in future by the aggressor's agents within its government in the manner of the Nazi reduction of Prague's "independence." Roosevelt was cast in the role of Chamberlain. It was proposed that he should meet Premier Konoye in the Pacific to seal the fate of China in a demonstration of "peace" through "cooperation" between the United States and Japan. As for Japanese troops poised in northern Indo-China, a piece of whose territory Japan "awarded" to the pro-Japanese government of Thailand at the very time Bishop Walsh and Father Drought offered Hull the proposed draft, nothing was said about them or what they might portend.

The United States position was weakened at this moment by the signature of the Neutrality Pact between Russia and Japan on April 13, 1941. This meant that Japan could feel more secure in its rear. Hull took the brighter view that it signified Stalin's growing concern over an attack by Hitler.

## Matsuoka Wins

Hull did not reject out of hand the Walsh-Drought-Walker draft proposal for a settlement with Japan. He saw in it, besides objectionable clauses, some proposals which were acceptable, and some which might become acceptable if modified. Therefore he discussed the document with Nomura, who told him he had participated in its preparation and that his government might favor it. Hull told Nomura he would accept the draft as a basis of negotiations if the Japanese government would first give definite assurance that it would abandon its doctrine of military conquest by force and adopt the principles which the United States government proclaimed as the foundation on which all relations between nations should rest. He summarized these principles as: (1) respect for the territorial integrity and sovereignty of all nations; (2) non-interference in the internal affairs of other countries; (3) equality, including equality of commercial opportunity; (4) no change in the *status quo* in the Pacific except by peaceful means. If the Japanese government would accept these principles, and instructed Nomura to propose the draft agreement, conversations would start, and the United States would offer counterproposals. Nomura agreed to report the proposition to his superiors.

Ominous Japanese troop concentrations pointing towards Malaya and Thailand led the British government to ask the United States to make a declaration with Britain and the Netherlands, jointly or separately, that any further Japanese move southward would affect their interest "jointly and individually." The British also wanted United States help in pulling Thailand away from Japan. Hull opposed a joint declaration and was afraid Thailand was already lost, but he promised to consider what might be done.

In Japan a struggle between Konoye and Matsuoka for the Emperor's support was won by Matsuoka, who sent an answer to Hull rejecting the draft proposals because "Japan could not injure the position of her allies," Germany and Italy. This meant that although the "moderates" led by Konoye wanted the United States to submit to a "Far Eastern Munich," Matsuoka and the pro-Nazi militarists, supported by the Emperor, preferred to proceed with plans for conquest without bothering to make the formal promises to the United States which appeasement ritual required.

Nomura told Hull, on May 7, that he would not transmit the Matsuoka message because many things in it were "wrong," but Hull already knew its contents. Army and Navy intelligence officers had broken the Japanese code, and intercepts bearing the name "Magic" came to the leading officials of the administration. Nomura proposed a nonaggression treaty. Hull rejected the idea because it would merely have given the Japanese government assurance the United States would refrain from war no matter what Japan might do. He told Nomura the United States government was not interested in anything except the broad principles which he had named as a basis for negotiations.

On May 6, aware of Matsuoka's rejection of the draft proposals, President Roosevelt declared China eligible for assistance under the Lend Lease Act. The timing signified that he had waited to explore the remote possibility that the draft proposal would bear fruit.

## Matsuoka Rewrites the Draft

Matsuoka now made a gesture in favor of negotiations. On May 12, Nomura handed Hull a new draft of the proposed agreement. It contained sharper phraseology regarding Japanese obligations under the Axis alliance. The original words defining Japan's purpose under the alliance were: "to prevent the extension of military grouping among nations not directly affected by the European War." This was rewritten to read: "to prevent the nations which are not at present directly affected by the European War from engaging in it." A further statement of the original draft, in which Japan declared that its military obligation under the alliance would come into force only when one of the parties of the alliance was "aggressively attacked," was left out of the new version. Thus Matsuoka made the clause a direct threat, which the United States should agree to as proper, that if it entered the European war, Japan would go to war against the United States. The clause was made even more specific in a correction of "error" Nomura handed Hull on May 23. This made the definition of Japanese purpose read: "to prevent the participation of nations in the European War not at present involved in it."

This definition of the conditions under which the Axis alliance would lead Japan to go to war against the United States had the merit of frankness. It made plain how the Japanese government interpreted the phrase in the alliance which required Japan to enter the war if Germany or Italy were "attacked" by the United States. If the administration had signed the revised draft agreement, it would have constituted approval of a Japanese declaration of war against the United States if the United States for *any reason whatever,* including direct military assault by Hitler, became involved in the European war. Isolationists opposed commitments by the Roosevelt administration, yet they blamed it for not reaching a settlement with Japan which would have involved a commitment fantastic beyond measure.

Another significant alteration by Matsuoka occurred in the statement of the attitude of the United States government towards the European war. The original draft had declared that the United States attitude would not be determined by any "aggressive alliance aimed to assist any one nation against another." This might be thought acceptable, because United States assistance to Britain certainly did not constitute an "aggressive alliance." The clause was rewritten to state that the United States attitude would not be directed by "such aggressive measures as to assist any one nation against another." This transparently referred to Lend Lease aid to Britain. Matsuoka asked the United States to abandon not only China to Japan, but also to abandon Europe and Great Britain to Hitler. To make this quite clear, the revised draft contained a new clause pledging the United States to work jointly with Japan "speedily to restore peace in Europe." A "speedy" peace in Europe for which Japan would work could only mean a Hitler peace.

In the section dealing with China, Matsuoka had deleted the specifications of peace terms, some of which had held out promise of Chinese independence. More favorable terms for China were held out by Nomura in an "oral explanation" to Hull of the revised draft. Certain basic principles of Premier Konoye were said by Nomura "to imply" favorable peace terms for China. In the revised draft itself, "basic principles" of the Japanese government were referred to, rather than Hull's list. The Japanese list contained phrases, like "neighborly friendship," which had become sufficiently sinister when Japan invoked them to justify and explain its conduct in China.

The government of the United States was asked in the new draft to acknowledge these Japanese principles and ask Chiang Kai-shek to negotiate peace "relying upon the policy of the Japanese Government to establish a relationship of neighborly friendship with China. . . ." With nothing more to rely upon in the way of peace terms than the "policy of the Japanese Government," the United States was further asked to sign a separate and secret agreement that it would discontinue aid to China if Chiang Kai-shek refused to negotiate with Japan. A demand to help Japan conquer China could hardly be more bald. All the clauses of the original draft pertaining to American economic assistance to Japan were retained in the new draft.[3]

Matsuoka's revision of the Walsh-Drought-Walker proposal extended its meaning beyond a "Far Eastern Munich" to include a new "Munich" for Hitler's benefit as well. The United States should not only support Japan in Asia but Hitler and Mussolini in Europe. It was asked to become an economic, political, diplomatic, and moral partner of the Axis.

Nevertheless, Hull, after consulting the President, did not refuse to begin conversations with Nomura on the basis of the revised draft. Such discussions would at least deal with the fundamental questions at issue. The Roosevelt administration was determined to adhere to its principle of peaceful negotiations. Japan had at least made an offer which Hull could endeavor to alter through negotiation on the remote chance that the basic principles of the United States could be satisfied. And any wedge that could be driven between Japan and Hitler would be a sharp blow to the Axis. On May 16, Hull handed to Nomura suggested redrafts of the critical points at issue.

## The American Redraft

These American suggestions left intact all the Japanese proposals except those which called for American approval of Japanese and German aggression. Hull made amply clear to Nomura that the United States in its policy of aid to the victims of Hitler acted on its inalienable right of self-defense, and could not repudiate that policy in an agreement with Japan. Clauses defining the attitudes of Japan and the United States towards the European war were rewritten to specify that Japan's military obligations under the Axis alliance would come into force only if one of its partners was "aggressively attacked" by a power not at present involved in the European war. The attitude of the United States government was expressed in terms which ruled out the possibility of Japan defining American policy as one of "aggressive attack" against Hitler:

The Government of the United States declares that its attitude toward the European hostilities is and will continue to be determined solely and exclusively by considerations of protection and self-defense: its national security and the defense thereof.

To clinch the matter, a disclaimer by Japan was suggested as follows:

The Government of Japan further declares that it is under no com-

mitment under its Axis Alliance or otherwise which is inconsistent
with the terms of the present declaration of policy and intention
agreed upon between the Government of Japan and the Government
of the United States.

The Axis alliance was in its formal terms defensive. Hull in these
suggested clauses challenged the Japanese to accept exact definitions of that alliance as genuinely defensive. The realities of the
Axis alliance were such that Japanese affirmation of genuinely defensive definitions of it would render it meaningless and signify
a major defeat for Hitler.

On the Chinese question, Hull's suggested redraft restored all
those terms for a Sino-Japanese peace proposed in the Walsh-
Drought-Walker draft which would leave China independent. The
clause which called for "coalescence" of the Japanese puppet government and the Chinese government was left out. Japanese claims
that it acted in China to prevent Russia from dominating that
country were met in a provision for "parallel measures of defense
[by Japan and China] against subversive activities from external
sources." Hull showed that he was primarily concerned to prevent
future aggressions and would not let the old question of Manchuria stand in the way of partial agreement by a clause which left
"the question of the future of Manchuria to be dealt with by
friendly negotiations" after the proposed agreement should have
been completed. The Japanese desire to commit the United
States, in a secret agreement, to punish the Chinese government
economically if it did not make peace with Japan, Hull refused to
satisfy. The United States would offer its good offices to both governments to initiate peace negotiations, but it would not coerce
one of them for the benefit of the other. But if Japan would
pledge itself, like the United States, to use only peaceful means in
the southwest Pacific area, the United States would cooperate towards ensuring for it equal access to natural resources in that
area.[4]

The Japanese government did not desire the neutrality of the
United States in the Far East sufficiently to accept Hull's proposed
disavowals of aggressive intentions. Matsuoka told Ambassador
Grew that British troop concentrations in Malaya might make it
impossible for Japan to carry out its southward advance by peaceful means. Such talk really admitted that peaceful access to raw

materials which Hull was ready to help Japan obtain was not what Matsuoka wanted. He wanted the kind of "access" which British troops were bound to oppose, in other words, conquest and Japanese monopoly. The embarrassment of this meaning was repelled by Matsuoka's contention that it was Britain that threatened Japan. The sophistry, as Hull writes in his *Memoirs*, was that of Hitler,[5] and, it might be added, of those American isolationists who believed that Roosevelt's and Hull's bellicosity were responsible for Japanese aggression.

If the Japanese government had accepted Hull's suggested revisions of the draft agreement, which cannot be called incompatible with legitimate and peaceful Japanese ambitions, there is no reason to believe that Roosevelt and Hull would not have signed the agreement and proceeded to carry out the American part in the pacification of the Orient, including suspension of those staff talks which the isolationists, distorting their meaning, damned as "commitments to war," explaining and justifying the Japanese attack on Pearl Harbor.

## "No Freedom from Anxiety"

It was the Japanese government that prevented agreement on terms entirely compatible with Japanese rights and interests. Nomura on May 20 sidestepped Hull's suggestions. He pleaded that his whole government, including the Emperor, approved the Japanese draft and that if the United States did not accept it as it stood, he would be placed in a very embarrassing position, evidently because he had assured his superiors that the United States would accept the Japanese draft. And it was made very plain to Hull that in no circumstances would Japan withdraw its troops from North China.

Rumors had reached the public that Hull was undertaking peace negotiations between China and Japan. Americans in great majority opposed such negotiations; the current view was that Japan was "bogged down" in China and that the United States should not by appeasement help Japan extricate itself with any of its loot. Particularly it was feared that Japan merely aimed to use forces and supplies, now absorbed by its struggle with China, in the southwest Pacific. Hull told Nomura he would inform the Chinese government of the attitude of the United States before he would enter into any official negotiations with Japan. He did so, and Ambassador Hu Shih expressed his appreciation of Hull's promise that he would not "take matters to a serious stage" without first consulting the Chinese government.

This action by Hull is valuable evidence that appeasement of Japan at China's expense was not the goal of the Roosevelt administration. Hull and Roosevelt were heavily criticized on the basis of rumors that they contemplated appeasement of Japan. They had difficulty adhering to the program of conversations with the Japanese. The pressure of public criticism is visible in Hull's assurance to China and in additional suggested changes of the draft agreement which he handed Nomura on May 31.

These changes plugged loopholes which Nomura had indicated his government intended to exploit. In the section on the Axis alliance, a further sentence was proposed: "Obviously, the provisions of the pact [requiring Japan to go to war] do not apply to involvement [by the United States in the European war] through acts of self-defense." In the section on China a sentence was added to require Japan to withdraw troops from China promptly and in accordance with an agreement to be concluded between Japan and China. The Japanese argument, that its troops in North China merely expressed the policy of parallel measures with China against subversive activity, was answered by ruling out the troops and by a further Hull suggestion that the question of defense against Communism be a subject for later discussion between Japan and China. The May 31 proposals were headed: "Unofficial, Exploratory and Without Commitment." This emphasized that negotiations had not begun, and the administration could correctly deny public rumors that negotiations were underway.[6]

Nomura objected to the "phraseology" of the American proposals. Hull agreed to conversations between subordinates for the purpose of ironing it out. But it turned out that the Japanese objected to substance as well as phraseology. They wanted to delete entirely the definition of their obligation under the Axis pact as not applying to "involvement [of the United States in the European war] through acts of self-defense." A Japanese Colonel, Iwakuro, who brought the views of the Japanese Army into the conversations, admitted to the Americans that the proposed agreement was not intended by Japan to "provide freedom from anxiety" that if the United States should become involved in the European war under circumstances such as would call for Japan to act under *its interpretation* of its obligations, Japan would feel obliged to discharge those obligations, much as Japan would regret taking up arms against the United States.[7]

Clearly, the Japanese did not want to be hampered in their interpretation even by the phraseology of self-defense in an agreement with the United States. They asked the Americans to agree to their own earlier proposal, that the United States should declare it "does not and will not resort to any aggression aimed to assist any one nation against another," that is, the United States should admit that Lend Lease aid to Britain was an "aggression" against Hitler under the terms of the Axis alliance.[8]

These and many other changes showed what Nomura meant by objecting to the "phraseology" of the American suggestions. On June 6, Hull told Nomura bluntly that Japanese procedure, far from bringing agreement closer, showed a desire to stress Japan's alignment with the Axis, to avoid indicating an intention to place Japan's relations with China on a peaceful basis, and to evade commitments to peace and nondiscrimination in the Pacific area. Nomura protested that his government did want peace and a speedy understanding with the United States. At the same time he asked whether President Roosevelt could not propose to the Chinese government that it negotiate for peace with Japan "on his own initiative," prior to any general agreement between the United States and Japan. The meaning of this weird suggestion was exposed by Colonel Iwakuro. He told Hull that it did not befit Japan's dignity to come to the United States "in a suppliant attitude" to help settle the China incident.[9]

Evidently the Japanese militarists were not happy over the rumors that they would be appeased by the United States, because even appeasement contained a suggestion that Japan would make promises of good behavior—the sort of promises Hitler had made in the Munich Agreement and had so much irritated him with the "English governesses" who took the promises seriously.

Nomura's request and Iwakuro's explanation dissolved Japanese pretensions of good faith in conducting conversations with the United States. Hull told Nomura that the President would have to have an agreement in unequivocal terms before he would ask China to make peace.

Still, drafts and counterdrafts were exchanged. Hull became impressed with the special significance of the Japanese avoidance of any admission by implication that American aid to Britain was not an act of "aggression" against Hitler. On June 21 he told Nomura it could not be ignored that the only kind of understanding Japan wanted was one in which the United States would endorse Japanese attack against the United States if it became involved in European hostilities as a result of its present policy of self-defense. Matsuoka currently justified Hull's suspicion publicly in a message to Mussolini, endorsing his statement that "Japan will not remain indifferent in the face of American aggression against the Axis." Furthermore, Hull told Nomura, the United States could not place itself in the position of supporting violation of the sovereignty of a third power, as Japan demanded in the matter of stationing troops in North China and Inner Mongolia.

## Roosevelt and Hull Call a Halt

The Japanese-American conversations had all but broken down when Hitler invaded the Soviet Union on June 22. The Roosevelt administration became concerned that the Japanese would attack Russia or take advantage of Russia's preoccupation to launch the long-expected southward movement. The President sent a message to Premier Konoye on July 6 stating the earnest hope of the United States government that reports of Japan's decision to enter the war against the Soviet Union were not based on fact, because it would destroy the possibility of strengthening the peace of the Pacific area. Konoye answered with a copy of an oral statement Matsuoka had made to the Soviet Ambassador on July 2, declaring that Japan, in its present "awkward" position, hoped to preserve the spirit of mutual trust among the Axis allies while maintaining good relations with the Soviet Union. And Konoye turned about to ask the United States whether reports were true that the United States intended to intervene in the European war. The American answer to this was that United States policy was based solely on self-defense against the Germans, who were the chief threat to the security of the Western Hemisphere, and that American aid to Russia would "in no manner threaten the security of nations which have not joined the conflict on Hitler's side." [10]

At the same time, the Roosevelt administration received alarming information of Japanese preparations for a major war. Ominous movements were made publicly, and Magic intercepts contained such signals as the following, in a message from Tokyo to Berlin on July 2, the day of an Imperial Conference:

The Imperial Government shall continue its endeavor to dispose of the China incident, and shall take measures with a view to advancing southward in order to establish firmly a basis for her self-existence and self-protection.

Other intercepts named French Indo-China and Thailand as immediate targets. Matsuoka instructed Nomura:

In the meantime, diplomatic negotiations shall be carried on with extreme care. Although every means available shall be resorted to in order to prevent the United States from joining the war, if need be Japan shall act in accordance with the three-Power pact and shall decide when and how force will be employed.[11]

Matsuoka was not quite frank with Nomura. The Far East Tribunal later learned that the Imperial Conference of July 2 had decided to continue conversations with the United States as a cover while final preparations for military action were completed. Troops that later landed in Malaya and the Philippines now began practicing.[12]

On July 18, Admiral Teijiro Toyoda replaced Matsuoka as Foreign Minister of Japan. This shift is called by Morgenstern proof that Japan was amenable to American criticisms of Matsuoka.[13] But promptly after the change, on July 21, Japanese troops invaded southern Indo-China, and it is doubtful whether Roosevelt and Hull could, in the light of that act, sensibly interpret the fall of Matsuoka as a sign of a Japanese turn against the policy of aggression. In southern Indo-China the Japanese occupied and built up bases which gave them a strategic position pointing inexorably towards the Philippines, Malaya, Singapore, and the NEI. In short, the new aggression was proof that the program of southward advance was underway.

It made a farce of Nomura's pretense that his government wished a "peaceful settlement," that Matsuoka's belligerence was a matter of "politics" only for "home consumption." The conversa-

tions were broken off by the United States on July 23. It was
Japan's new aggression, in contradiction of its professions in Washington, that led Roosevelt and Hull to call a halt. Morgenstern
distorts the incident by avoiding mention of the crucial sequence
of dates and by giving Japanese unwillingness to sign a blank
check for the United States in Europe as the reason why negotiations "stalled." The Japanese, in Morgenstern's account, gave
ample proof of good faith by dismissing Matsuoka from power.
The Roosevelt administration was unreasonable in its demands
and sought excuses to break off conversations in order to invoke
economic sanctions with "clear understanding" that they "might
easily precipitate war." [14]

The possibility that Japanese invasion of southern Indo-China
may have influenced the administration is carefully ignored by
Morgenstern. On July 23, two days after that invasion, Sumner
Welles told Nomura that Secretary Hull could see no basis for
continuation of their conversations. He asserted that agreement
with the United States would have given Japan an "infinitely
greater amount of security, both military and economic," than it
could obtain by conquest. He said the United States had to assume
that the Japanese government was taking "the last step" before
proceeding on a campaign of totalitarian expansion in the South
Seas. Nomura pleaded for "patience" and against "hasty conclusions." He said an embargo on oil exports to Japan would undoubtedly "inflame Japanese public opinion." Welles assured him
that Hull would wish to talk again with him.

## Roosevelt Makes an Offer

The next day President Roosevelt agreed to Nomura's request
for an "off-the-record conference" in the White House. Welles
and Admiral Stark were present. The President took up the question of oil shipments to Japan. In a remarkably plain way he explained that the United States had not shut off oil exports to
Japan during the past two years because that would have given an
"incentive or a pretext" for Japanese conquest of the NEI. But
Japan had given every indication of pursuing, nevertheless, a policy of conquest in conjunction with Hitler's plans for world domination. And the average American citizen could not understand
why, in the face of government curtailment of his own use of

gasoline, the government continued to furnish Japan with oil for use in carrying on aggressions. The President said he had followed the Ambassador's conversations with Hull in detail and that the invasion of southern Indo-China was "completely opposed to the principles and the letter of the proposed agreement."

Nomura stated that the move by Japan into Indo-China was something he "personally deplored." Roosevelt told Nomura that if Japan attempted to seize the oil supplies of the NEI, the Dutch would resist, the British would immediately assist the Dutch "and, in view of our own policy of assisting Great Britain, an exceedingly serious situation would immediately result." But no matter how late the hour might be, the President said, he still wished to seize every possible chance of preventing a situation which "could only give rise to serious misunderstandings" between the Japanese and American peoples. Therefore he proposed that if Japan would withdraw from Indo-China, he would do everything in his power to obtain a binding and solemn declaration by China, Britain, the Netherlands and the United States, provided that Japan would make the same commitment, to regard Indo-China as neutralized territory like Switzerland. The four powers would also guarantee that during the present emergency the French authorities in Indo-China would not be dislodged by the Gaullist Free French. Japan would, furthermore, be afforded fullest opportunity to obtain the food and other raw materials it sought in Indo-China.

Nomura was "impressed" by the President's proposal, but remarked that only a "very great statesman" would be willing to "lose face" by reversing his policy. Roosevelt referred to another aspect of Japanese policy in which it lost face by seeming to be subservient to Hitler. He told Nomura that Hitler, if he conquered Russia and then Europe and Africa, would turn to Asia as well as the Western Hemisphere, sooner or later. If this happened, he said, the laws of chance made it possible that the navies of Japan and the United States would cooperate against Hitler as their common enemy.

Roosevelt's striking proposal to neutralize Indo-China was designed to cut through Japanese pretexts for invasion. The Japanese government did not answer for two weeks. Meanwhile, its pretexts were thoroughly exposed in a public statement by the State Department, which denounced the Japanese invasion because it was undertaken to obtain bases for purposes of further movements of conquest in adjacent areas. The action was said to endanger peaceful use of the Pacific by peaceful nations, and to jeopardize United States procurement of essential materials such as rubber and tin.

## Economic Sanctions

On July 25 the administration froze Japanese assets in the United States to prevent their use in trade between the United States and Japan "in ways harmful to national defense and American interests." It also froze Chinese assets at the request of the Chinese government to prevent liquidation of those which were obtained by "duress or conquest." The purpose of the latter action was underlined in a statement of the President that the administration of the licensing system with respect to Chinese assets would be conducted with a view to strengthening the Chinese government and was "a continuation of this Government's policy of assisting China." [15] Synchronization of British policy was apparent the next day when Britain froze Japanese assets and denounced its commercial agreements with Japan. Also on July 26, President Roosevelt nationalized the armed forces of the Philippines.

On the day the United States froze Japanese assets, Colonel Iwakuro told Joseph W. Ballantine, of the State Department, that if the United States took such action, he believed Japan would have no alternative but to go south to Malaya and the NEI to obtain essential supplies. He said such action would also prevent another attempt to reach an "understanding," which his government otherwise urged. Iwakuro said Nomura was too "gentle" to express these views as he did. Ballantine received the impression that the Japanese had no real expectation that conversations would be resumed and that no reply was called for beyond the statements of Welles and Roosevelt to Nomura.

In Tokyo, Ambassador Grew asked Toyoda to consider well how the President's offer to neutralize Indo-China met Japanese contentions. He said that if it were accepted it might establish a new basis for continuation of the Hull-Nomura talks looking towards a general agreement. Grew and Welles both told the Japanese the freezing order, like the earlier abrogation of the American-Japanese commercial treaty, would at first be interpreted liberally by the United States.

Thus doors were again left open by the Roosevelt administration for the Japanese government to achieve peacefully its legitimate ambitions. But immediately reports were received that the Japanese were making demands on Thailand of the same sort which had preceded invasion of southern Indo-China.

Roosevelt promptly on July 31 told the Japanese government through Welles and Nomura that in the judgment of the United States government "there was not the remotest threat of danger to Japan nor the slightest justification for Japan alleging" that concessions by Thailand were necessary as a means of assuring a Japanese source of raw materials or as a military precaution. But Roosevelt again offered Japan a constructive alternative: he said his offer to neutralize Indo-China should now be regarded as embracing Thailand in order to give Japan the same guarantees and security in that area.[16]

Just as the offer regarding Indo-China had been backed up by the freezing order, so now the President's offer regarding Thailand was backed up on August 1 by an embargo against the export of aviation gasoline. The stated purpose was "in the interest of national defense," and merely on that ground the order was long overdue. In the opinion of most Americans it was also long overdue as an economic sanction against Japanese aggression, and the order was greeted with very wide public satisfaction.

## Japanese Responses

The aviation gasoline embargo brought two quick responses from the Japanese. First, Minister Wakasugi of the Washington Embassy asked Welles for an exact statement of the policies of the United States and the feelings of the American people towards Japan. He had been instructed to carry home a report on these subjects to his government. Welles answered succinctly that the policy of the United States was peace in the Pacific; renunciation by all powers of force and conquest; recognition of the rights of independent and autonomous peoples to independence; and equal opportunity and fair treatment for all, exclusive preference or privilege for none. Wakasugi said he was "unable to understand at all" the President's proposal regarding Indo-China. Welles clarified it for him, and the Minister said "he could not deny that what the President proposed, if consummated, would give security

to his own country and to the other nations in the Far East."
Wakasugi claimed to represent Premier Konoye's "personal establishment" in the United States. He departed forthwith for Tokyo.

The second response followed from the Japanese government
on August 6. Nomura asked Hull for an interview. Hull agreed.
Roosevelt was now at sea with Churchill. Conversations were resumed in Washington between Hull and Nomura. They did not
end until minutes after the bombing of Pearl Harbor.

Nomura apologized for his government's delay in answering the
President's proposal of July 24. Obviously it had required the
freezing order and the embargo on aviation gasoline to obtain
even the pretense of an answer. Nomura handed Hull a "Proposal
of the Japanese Government." Nomura called it a reply "in a
way" and "off the record" to the President's proposal. But it ignored the proposal to neutralize Indo-China. Instead the Japanese
government proposed to withdraw its troops from that country
only after a settlement of the China Incident. Meanwhile, Japan
would promise not to send troops into further regions of the
southwest Pacific area. It also offered to guarantee the neutrality
of the Philippine Islands, and to cooperate with the United States
to obtain for it such natural resources as the United States required. In return the United States was asked to suspend its
military measures in the southwest Pacific areas, and to advise
Great Britain and the Netherlands to do the same; to cooperate
with the Japanese government in obtaining natural resources it
required in the southwest Pacific area, especially in the NEI; restore normal trade between the United States and Japan; use its
good offices for direct negotiations between China and Japan for
the purpose of a speedy settlement of the China Incident; and
recognize a "special status" of Japan in Indo-China even after the
withdrawal of Japanese troops. Nomura furthermore gave Hull
to understand that if Chiang Kai-shek refused to negotiate, the
United States must discontinue its aid to China.[17]

The Japanese proposal of August 6 not only ignored the President's offer of July 24, it omitted most of the provisions in earlier
Japanese proposals which offered any ground for hope that the
Japanese government might alter its policy of menace and aggression. "Special status" for Japan in Indo-China was the sort of
phrase which, in American-Japanese understandings earlier in the
century, had been invariably interpreted by the Japanese to jus-

tify unlimited domination. Besides a blank check in China, Japan now asked the United States to approve Japanese domination of Indo-China, from which it could menace the Philippines and other areas while the United States must withdraw from the Philippines means of defense and ask the British and Dutch to do the same in their possessions.

Secretary Hull on August 8 told Nomura that the Japanese proposals were "lacking in responsiveness to the suggestion made by the President." For "convenience of reference" he repeated the President's proposal regarding neutralization of Indo-China and Thailand. Nomura asked whether it might not be possible for Roosevelt and Konoye to meet in the Pacific. Hull reviewed the American position once more, and declared that it now remained with the Japanese government to decide whether it "could find means of shaping its policies accordingly and then endeavor to evolve some satisfactory plan."

## The "Encirclement" Charge

Ambassador Halifax next day asked Hull, as British officers and Churchill were asking the Americans at Argentia, what aid the United States might give in case Singapore and the NEI were attacked. Hull would not make a commitment. He said that if further Japanese moves to the south occurred, the American and British governments "should naturally have a conference at once." [18] This emphasized the status of the conditional staff plans of the United States and Great Britain: the United States had no commitment to instrument them. The British wished to regard the invasion of southern Indo-China as a signal that American-British-Dutch planning should be carried to the point of commitments. The Roosevelt administration refused.

This refusal is a part of the record which Beard, Morgenstern, and the Minority Report ignore. Indeed, the fact of a British request on August 9, 1941, is sufficient proof of the falsity of the isolationists' contention that a commitment had already been made. The refusal also proved the falsity of Japanese claims that Japan was being "encircled." Hull told the American press on August 8, and repeated for Nomura's benefit, that "there is no occasion for any nation in the world that is law-abiding and peaceful to become encircled by anybody except itself." This made it quite clear that only *if* Japan itself forced unity upon the United States, Great Britain, and the Dutch, by committing aggression against them, would they proceed *thereafter* to "encircle" Japan to the best of their ability. Actually an American promise to the British and the Dutch to go to war if they were attacked would not have merited the term "encirclement of Japan." That term imputes aggressive designs to the encircling powers, whereas the design proposed by the British was purely defensive. But the Roosevelt administration refused to face Japan even with a circle of powers committed to act together for defense in circumstances other than a direct attack by Japan against the United States itself.

## *The Bases of Decision*

Hull sent the Japanese proposal of August 6 to Roosevelt at sea. Thereupon the Atlantic Conference considered the problem of Japan in the specific context of possible replies. Beard, Morgenstern, and the Minority Report entirely ignore the background which is found in the Hull-Nomura conversations. But the decision obviously cannot be understood except in the light of those conversations. The actual position of American-Japanese relations may be summed up on the basis of those facts narrated above which were known to Roosevelt, as follows:

1. Japan's professed desire to reach a diplomatic settlement with the United States was dishonest. When it found that the United States was willing to discuss terms proposed by Japan, it withdrew precisely those of the terms which made discussion possible, and left only those which would give American support to Japan in carrying out its imperialist program. Japan refused to consider the President's suggestion of July 24, which would have satisfied all of Japan's professed aims. *Japan in the spring and summer of 1941 would accept no diplomatic arrangement which did not give it everything that it might win in the Far East by aggression, without the trouble and expense of military campaigns.*

2. The Japanese invasion of southern Indo-China proved in action that, for the Japanese government, diplomacy, even conceived of solely as an instrument of aggression, was a less desirable weapon than direct military action.

3. Japanese occupation of bases in southern Indo-China could have no other purpose than preparation for a major southward advance into territories of the United States, Great Britain, or the Netherlands.

In this situation Roosevelt could not regard further conversations with the Japanese as any longer useful for any other purpose than postponing Japanese aggression against the Philippines-Malaya-NEI area. Churchill, however, lacked the Americans' experience of the Hull attempts to reach agreement with Japan, and told Roosevelt that if further discussions took place between the United States and Japan, there was "a reasonable chance that Japanese policy might be modified and that a war in the Pacific might be averted." Roosevelt saw no such chance. According to Forrest Davis and Ernest K. Lindley, friends of the President, Roosevelt answered: "I think I can baby them along for three months." [19] Welles's account of the President's answer is different: according to him, the President believed that by continuing conversations "any further move of aggression on the part of Japan which might result in war could be held off for at least thirty days."

Either way, President Roosevelt's lack of hope that further conversations could do more than postpone new Japanese aggressions is made to seem thoroughly sinister in the accounts of Beard, Morgenstern and the Minority Report. Beard implies that Roosevelt was ready to deliver an "ultimative" statement to Japan provocative of war.[20] Morgenstern is more plain: the President was convinced that "war was inevitable." Therefore Morgenstern finds it "difficult to see" what meaning attached to the subsequent Hull-Nomura conversations. Evidently postponement of the inevitable moment in order to improve the defenses of the country or countries Japan would attack has no meaning for Morgenstern. He goes on to state that Roosevelt and Churchill had "virtually precluded any constructive resolution of the problems between the United States and Japan." [21]

It is notable in this statement that not Japan in the preceding six months' conversations but Roosevelt and Churchill are pictured as being guilty of "virtually precluding" any "constructive resolution." Roosevelt had decided that war was "inevitable" for no reason apparent in Morgenstern's account except his general anxiety for war. His plan for continuing conversations with Japan was merely quixotic; conversations would have no meaning because Roosevelt and Churchill were now close to success in their plot to frustrate Japanese desires for a "constructive," peaceful, agreement between the United States and Japan. Beard entirely ignores the Hull-Nomura conversations prior to the Atlantic Conference. Morgenstern's few references to those conversations impress the reader that reasonable Japanese offers were countered by stubborn unreasonableness in order to avoid agreement and provoke war. The dominant motive of Hull in partially rejecting the Japanese draft proposals, which was to avoid appeasement of Japan and, all the more so, to avoid support of Japanese aggression and punishment of its victims, Morgenstern never mentions.[22]

The Minority Report is more cautious in its language but identical in its implications. President Roosevelt is described as "certain" at Argentia that the United States would become involved in the war, and Roosevelt's own actions and plans are the only facts in evidence which the Minority offers to explain Roosevelt's strange certainty.[23]

Perhaps it is excusable to repeat that it was Japan's conduct in the Hull-Nomura conversations coupled with its invasion of southern Indo-China, its occupation of bases there obviously pointed towards the Philippines-Malaya-NEI area, and its menacing attitude towards Thailand that led Roosevelt to believe war was "inevitable" in the sense that further aggressions by Japan were inevitable. Neither Roosevelt nor Churchill believed that Japan wanted to fight both their countries at the same time.[23a]

But whether Roosevelt further believed that if Japan confined its aggressions to non-American territory—a course obviously dictated by Japanese self-interest—the United States would nevertheless enter the war, does not appear in the record. What is clear in the record is Roosevelt's refusal to make any promise to Britain that the United States would enter the war under such circumstances. A plausible guess may be that Roosevelt intended to leave the decision to the event: if Japan attacked the NEI or Singapore, the response of the American people, the strength of their desire to declare war against Japan, would be a main factor in his decision whether to ask Congress for war. Americans' response could not be foretold; therefore Roosevelt, who synchronized policy with public opinion in all things, could not foretell his own action in so momentous a matter as breaking his anti-war pledge. Meanwhile, all the evidence points to the conclusion that he was determined to avoid making his decision before the event.

Churchill proposed to Roosevelt, on August 9 and 10, that the United States, Great Britain, the Netherlands, and possibly the Soviet Union, should make simultaneous and parallel declarations to Japan that a further aggressive move would bring war with all of them. The evidence of Roosevelt's reply is clear enough in the Welles Memorandum: he rejected Churchill's proposal. But Welles himself before the Investigating Committee, and Hull before that Committee and in his *Memoirs*, later stated that the President and Churchill did agree to make a parallel declaration. Still, Welles when pressed by the Committee said he merely "took it for granted" that Churchill joined the agreement, but he did not remember the President making a "specific statement" that an agreement was reached.[24]

The best evidence of the existence of a Roosevelt-Churchill agreement to make parallel declarations is in Hull's *Memoirs*. There he states that Sir Ronald Campbell, British Chargé, handed him on August 30 two alternative drafts of a warning Britain intended to send Japan. Hull suggests that he advised the British to tone down the warning to eliminate a threat of war if Japan moved. But Hull says nothing about the outcome, whether the British accepted his advice or, indeed, sent a warning at all.[25] The question of Dutch and Soviet parallel warnings disappears entirely from the record immediately after Churchill proposed their participation.

In the confused state of the evidence, it will be convenient here to assume that Roosevelt and Churchill did agree at Argentia that they would make warning declarations to Japan. Beard, Morgenstern and the Minority Report accept the existence of such an agreement as proved, which is hardly true: the most that can be said is that its existence cannot be disproved. But even assuming that it did exist, the isolationists abuse their readers with falsifications of known facts.

Chief of these known facts is that the declaration Roosevelt made to Nomura on August 17, following the Atlantic Conference, was *not* the declaration that Churchill on August 9-10 had asked him to make. On this point all authorities agree. The Welles Memorandum contains a full statement of the alternative declaration Roosevelt proposed and later, with modifications suggested by Hull, delivered to Nomura. The changes which Roosevelt and Hull installed in the declaration removed whatever "ultimative" character may be ascribed to Churchill's original.

## An Ultimatum?

Since the charge that Roosevelt and Churchill delivered any number of ultimatums or "ultimative" declarations to Japan runs through the whole isolationist thesis, definition of the term, which the isolationists never discuss, is necessary. The word "ultimatum" in diplomatic usage has a clear-cut meaning understood by all governments. A declaration of one government to another is not an ultimatum unless it contains *all* of the following:

1. A demand or demands of the issuing government upon the other government. A proposal of terms desired by the issuing government for incorporation in an agreement with the other government, such terms to be the subject of further negotiation, does not constitute a "demand," and a document containing such a proposal is not an ultimatum for the obvious reason that it is not the "last" statement of the issuing government.

2. A time limit. The demand or demands of the issuing government must be fulfilled by the other government within a period of time specified in the issuing government's declaration. It will be seen that otherwise the declaration would not be "ultimate" because the other government could procrastinate without end.

3. A statement, however "diplomatically" worded, that if the demand or demands of the issuing government are not met by the other government within the time specified, the issuing government will make war against it.

This definition is not a mere matter of diplomatic metaphysics. Common sense is all that is needed to understand that the word ultimatum must be reserved for the kind of declaration which is genuinely the ultimate diplomatic act of a government before it goes to war, if its demands are not met. The declaration, by its nature, must *end* the possibility of further negotiation. Surrender without war, or war, are the only alternatives facing a government that receives an ultimatum from another. Any door left open in a declaration by one government to another for further diplomatic negotiations between them removes from the declaration the character of an ultimatum. Since this is true, it is impossible to say what the terms "ultimative," "tantamount to an ultimatum," and "ultimative in character," which Beard and Morgenstern apply to numerous American and British documents and speeches directed to Japan, may mean, because if a declaration is not the *last* one, it may well turn out to be the *first* one of a long new series of declarations and counterdeclarations, conversations and negotiations between the two governments. That is precisely what happened after Roosevelt delivered to Japan the declaration he discussed with Churchill at Argentia.

Beard always cautiously uses such meaningless terms; Morgenstern, after using "tantamount to an ultimatum," gives it up in favor of the unadorned word, "ultimatum." Both of course wish to place on Roosevelt the burden of war guilt which traditionally attaches to a government or leader who issues an ultimatum. Only one procedure can merit heavier guilt, that is, a surprise attack without an ultimatum or declaration of war. That Japan was guilty of this procedure is not discussed by the isolationists: they are content to find Roosevelt guilty of issuing "ultimative" declarations and ultimatums which, in their minds, sufficiently explain why it was that a war occurred. The reader is intended to conclude that the Japanese government, warned by ultimatums or ultimatum-like declarations, sensibly forestalled a forthcoming attack by attacking first and, justifiably, without warning.

The truth is that not even Churchill's original draft proposal of an American declaration to Japan was an ultimatum. It contained no time limit. It was simply a *warning*, that *if* Japan committed a new aggression, even though that aggression was not directed against United States territory, the United States would take *countermeasures*. These countermeasures might *lead* to war. If Japan attacked any third power "in consequence of such counter measures or of their support of them," the President would seek authority from Congress to give aid to such power. This was very different from saying that the United States would make war against Japan if it committed a new aggression. "Authority from Congress to give aid" to third powers did not necessarily mean a declaration of war, although it was a very strong hint. But the declaration could have contained a direct threat of war and still it would not have been an ultimatum, lacking as it did a time limit within which demands for action by Japan must be fulfilled, and hedged about as it was by the contingency that Japanese aggression against a third power must be the "consequence of American countermeasures." The countermeasures which might lead to war, and the aid to a third power for which authority would be asked from Congress, were not specified, but there would obviously come to mind as countermeasures United States naval protection of British and Dutch communications in the southwestern Pacific and reinforcement of British and Dutch bases in that area. The authority for which Congress would be asked could hardly be less than war.

## Roosevelt Again Opens the Door

Roosevelt told Churchill on August 11 that he would add to the proposed declaration a concrete offer by the United States to continue American-Japanese conversations looking towards a general settlement. The offer was that Japan should make a promise to carry out immediately, instead of contingently upon a successful general settlement, the items of its August 6 proposal which provided that Japan would withdraw its troops from French Indo-China and would not occupy further areas to the south. If Japan would make this promise beforehand, the United States would, while making it clear that the other items in the Japanese proposal of August 6 were in general unacceptable, nevertheless in a friendly spirit explore the possibility of a general settlement between the two governments. A modified version of Churchill's warning would be appended to the American offer and would be made conditional upon Japan's refusal of that offer. Welles reported this conditional and modified version of Churchill's warning as follows:

The President would further state [to Nomura] that *should Japan refuse to consider* [the offer to renew negotiations] and undertake further steps in the nature of military expansions, the President desired the Japanese Government to know that in such event in his belief various steps would have to be taken by the United States notwithstanding the President's realization that the taking of such further measures might result in war between the United States and Japan.

Thus the President dropped the most ominous clause of Churchill's version: the threat to ask Congress for authority to give aid to a third power. This came too close to a promise by Roosevelt to Churchill to break his anti-war pledge if Japan attacked a third power. Roosevelt not only made the warning conditional upon Japanese refusal of an American offer to continue conversations, but watered it down to a simple warning of "various steps" which would not require authority from Congress. These "further measures" might *result* in war but would not themselves constitute war.

Roosevelt thus removed from the declaration the last one of the three components of an ultimatum. He invited further conversations between the United States and Japan. Leaving the door open to further negotiation was particularly necessary in the case of Japan because otherwise the warning, although not an ultimatum, contained a suggestion that if Japan committed new aggressions, American countermeasures would be *designed* to leave Japan little alternative except to attack the United States, and therefore was a challenge which the Japanese could not ignore without "losing face." Churchill commented that for this reason Roosevelt's suggestion appeared to him to "cover the situation very well."

The President's plan at the same time avoided any suggestion that the United States would appease Japan. The demonstration of Japanese bad faith during the earlier conversations was not ignored. Before conversations would be resumed by the United States, Roosevelt would require Japan to give evidence of a desire to modify its policy of aggression by making a specific promise to withdraw from Indo-China and a general promise to refrain from new aggressions to the south. Roosevelt ingeniously installed one of the requirements of an ultimatum, a demand upon the other party, as an only alternative not to *war*, or even to *countermeasures which might lead to war*, but as the only alternative to *no further conversations*. And the demands were only for *promises* by Japan. Carrying out the specific promise to withdraw from Indo-China was not required prior to further conversations.

Welles suggested that the Japanese be required to promise to refrain from aggression not only in the southwestern Pacific but in the whole Pacific region, which would exclude an attack against the Soviet Union and any new moves in China. Roosevelt agreed. He asked Churchill whether he might tell the Japanese that the British government had assured him it had no aggressive intentions against Thailand. Churchill said he heartily concurred.

Welles wanted this amplified to include a statement that the British government supported Roosevelt's proposal for the neutralization of Indo-China and Thailand. Churchill and Roosevelt agreed.[26]

Assuming that it was understood at the Conference that Britain would also make a warning declaration to Japan, this understanding cannot be called an "agreement" having the meaning of a Roosevelt "commitment" to Britain to issue an "ultimatum" to Japan that the United States would go to war if Japan committed a new aggression against territory not belonging to the United States. An accurate description of the outcome of the Churchill-Roosevelt talks on Japan is that Roosevelt and Churchill exchanged information of their intentions to issue warnings to Japan that countermeasures which might lead to war would follow if Japan committed a new aggression; the American warning was to be contingent upon Japanese refusal to accept an American offer to continue conversations looking towards a general agreement.

## Churchill's Warnings to Japan

Churchill in subsequent public statements, if not in a private and direct declaration to Japan, coupled a warning to Japan with a reference to renewed American-Japanese conversations. In a radio address on August 24 he pointed out the Japanese threat to southwestern Pacific areas and said: "It is certain that this has got to stop. Every effort will be made to secure a peaceful settlement. . . . If these hopes should fail, we shall, of course, range ourselves unhesitatingly at the side of the United States." [27] On November 10 he said publicly that "should the United States become involved in war with Japan a British declaration will follow within the hour." [28]

## Roosevelt's Warning to Japan

Churchill's warnings were stronger than his original version discussed at Argentia, insofar as they dropped reference to countermeasures which might lead to war, in favor of a direct warning of war. But Roosevelt watered down his declaration after the Conference still further. He substituted the word "conflict" for "war." Then he turned it over to Hull for comment. On August

15, Welles returned to Washington ahead of the President. He carried a copy of the declaration. Hull and his subordinates studied it. Hull felt that the declaration "might be misinterpreted in Japan and treated as a challenge" to incite the people of Japan to immediate war. He removed the conditions Roosevelt wanted to lay down—that Japan must promise to withdraw from Indo-China and to refrain from new aggressions if it wished to renew conversations with the United States. No promise to the United States was asked for. Instead, the Japanese government was merely asked to consult its own feelings and:

In case the Japanese Government feels that Japan desires and is in position to suspend its expansionist activities, to readjust its position, and to embark upon a peaceful program for the Pacific along the lines of the program and principles to which the United States is committed, the Government of the United States would be prepared to consider resumption of the informal exploratory discussions which were interrupted in July and would be glad to endeavor to arrange a suitable time and place to exchange views.

This was incorporated in a written statement to be handed Nomura. The warning, on the other hand, was removed to an oral statement, thereby subtracting from it some metaphysical degree of strength. And the paragraph containing the warning was revised by Hull to remove all reference to war *or* conflict.

In Hull's redraft, the President's July 24 proposal to neutralize Indo-China, and Japan's continued military expansion were first referred to. Then the sympathy of the United States government for Japanese professions in favor of "a fresh basis for amicable and mutually profitable relations" was reiterated. But, the last sentence of the penultimate paragraph read: "This Government feels at the present stage that nothing short of the most complete candor on its part, in the light of evidence and indications which come to it from many sources, will at this moment tend to further the objectives sought." The crucial conclusion followed:

Such being the case, this Government now finds it necessary to say to the Government of Japan that if the Japanese Government takes any further steps in pursuance of a policy or program of military domination by force or threat of force of neighboring countries, the Government of the United States will be compelled to take immediately any and all steps which it may deem necessary toward safeguarding the legitimate rights and interests of the United States and American nationals and toward insuring the safety and security of the United States.[29]

The Hull redrafts were accepted by Roosevelt and delivered by him in that form to Nomura on August 17.

Step by step the original Churchill conception of a warning to Japan had been weakened until in its final form it was a rather mild warning that if Japan failed to accept an unconditional American offer to renew conversations, and committed new aggressions, the United States would take steps to protect its interests and security.

The Minority Report noted that the warning paragraph referred to Japanese domination of "neighboring countries" and not only to the territory of the United States.[30] It is certainly true that Roosevelt did not adhere to the isolationist strategy of ignoring aggressions against non-American territory no matter how untenable militarily such aggressions would make American territory. If his warning of August 17 to Japan was stronger than any action he had taken prior to new aggressions by Hitler and Mussolini, it was because the United States had stronger treaty commitments in the Far East than in Europe, and owned territory there besides. Japanese occupation of bases in southern Indo-China brought the Philippines into focus as a next target of aggression more directly than American territory had ever before been menaced. Lend Lease, furthermore, had made the strategy of forehandedness the policy of the United States. Aid to Britain and other defenders obviously required aid in defending positions in the Pacific which they depended upon for survival, and Roosevelt in his warning did not threaten more than measures "short of war" which he was authorized to take under the Lend Lease Act and his Constitutional authority as Commander-in-Chief.

Mild as it was, the August 17 warning to Japan was second only to the Atlantic Charter as a product of the united front established by Roosevelt at Argentia. Without making a "dangerous challenge" to Japan, Roosevelt and Hull, by warning the Japanese against new aggressions in "neighboring countries," served notice that the United States would aid to an undefined extent any victim of aggression. The unity of the Dutch and British could be taken for granted because they were already allies in the war against Hitler. The willingness of those two powers to support the United States if it alone should be attacked could also be taken for granted, and Churchill, to remove any doubts, made an overt public promise. What was not certain was whether the United States in the event most likely to occur, that is, Japanese attack against non-American territory, would stand idly by or hit back.

The final version of the American declaration made clear that the United States would take action stronger than existing measures. "War" or "conflict" were not mentioned, but they were most definitely not ruled out. Thus Roosevelt and Hull established a maximum degree of unity with other powers menaced by Japan without making the commitment to go to war if non-American territory was attacked, which would have violated Roosevelt's anti-war pledge.

Just as the very fact of the Roosevelt-Churchill meeting was a more effective demonstration of Anglo-American unity than any particular wording of the Atlantic Charter, so the fact that the Roosevelt warning to Japan issued from the Atlantic Conference was a better demonstration of a united front than any particular wording of the declaration. Nomura had been asked while Roosevelt was still at sea to present himself at the White House for a conference immediately upon the President's return. This left no doubt that Roosevelt would present Japan with the product of discussions with Churchill.

Nomura seemed to expect, on August 17, an extremely important new statement of American policy. Before the President transmitted his oral or written statements, the Japanese drew from his pocket and read a prepared instruction from his government. In it Premier Konoye was represented as desiring so earnestly the preservation of peaceful relations that he was willing to meet President Roosevelt midway geographically between Japan and the United States to "sit down together and talk the matter out in a peaceful spirit." Had Roosevelt prepared an ultimatum, this instruction was well designed to place Japan on record as making an honorable last effort to forestall it.

But Roosevelt proceeded to make the oral statement of warning and, after a pause to let it sink in, he read the written statement offering to renew conversations. Then he handed copies of both to Nomura. Discussion followed in which Roosevelt agreed in principle to a meeting with Konoye and said it might be arranged for about October 15. Thus Roosevelt opened the door to peaceful settlement still wider. But at the same time he told Nomura that Japan should make a clearer statement of its position before preparations for the conference began.[31]

This latter remark of Roosevelt's became in following days a condition without which he refused to meet Konoye. Upon its reasonableness hinges judgment of the location of responsibility for the failure to hold the meeting and, in the opinion of isolationists, responsibility for the fall from power of Prince Konoye, "the last of the moderates."

# 16.

## *"Shoot on Sight"*

$B$EFORE THE PROJECT OF A ROOSEVELT-KONOYE MEETING failed, a radical change occurred in the American relation to the European war. The United States entered a period of limited and undeclared war with the President's order to the Navy on September 11 to "shoot on sight" in American defense waters.

This order complemented in the military sphere the advance in political action against aggression represented by the Atlantic Charter. It was all the more remarkable because support of the President in Congress had receded dangerously in the debate on extension of Selective Service. Roosevelt had agreed with considerable reluctance, at the insistence of Stimson and Marshall, to make the fight for extension. Isolationists were able to arouse powerful sentiment against it by appealing for the return of the drafted boys to the arms of their mothers. Passage of the bill by the margin of one vote in the House of Representatives was a warning signal that echoed and re-echoed during the next months. It meant that every legitimate means of strengthening policy by exercising Executive authority was preferable to risking tests in Congress which might destroy administration policy altogether. It confirmed Roosevelt's wisdom in refusing to commit himself to ask Congress for a declaration of war except in case of attack against territory of the United States. This was a conclusion interventionists were unwilling to accept, but their purpose was to influence public opinion and Congress, and it was the President's responsibility to avoid the debacle that would follow a defeat in Congress.

Senator Wheeler interpreted the vote in the House as follows:

"This vote clearly indicates that the Administration could not get a resolution through the Congress for a declaration of war." [1] He was probably right. Lord Beaverbrook visited the United States after the Atlantic Conference to observe opinion for Churchill. He reported that there was no chance of the United States entering the war until forced to do so by an attack on its territory. He expected this could not happen until after Britain and Russia had been defeated. The British leaders believed furthermore that Hitler, not Japan, would attack the United States, but only after he had perfected his victory in Europe. These viewpoints, authenticated in British documents studied by Robert Sherwood, are proof that the British leaders had won no "commitment" from Roosevelt that he would break his anti-war pledge. They foresaw the possibility of British defeat without United States entry into the war. Some of the enthusiasm created by the Atlantic Conference ebbed away. [2]

## A New United Front

Roosevelt used his existing authority under the Constitution and the Lend Lease Act to carry forward his policy. In spite of steady Russian retreat before the Nazi onslaught, he worked vigorously to extend aid to the Russian people and the Red Army. On August 18, 1941, he approved a second list of supplies to be sent. An inter-governmental committee including Harry Hopkins and Ambassador Oumansky worked in Washington. Consultations with Lord Beaverbrook, the British Minister of Supply, resulted in an Anglo-American mission to Moscow to work out long-range plans. W. Averell Harriman headed the American delegation. Conferences began in Moscow on September 29 and within two days the terms of a nine-months' supply program had been agreed upon. The American contribution amounted to about a billion dollars.

This was no small achievement, because during September a movement had developed in and out of Congress to prevent United States aid from going to Russia. Congress had under consideration the second appropriation for Lend Lease. Isolationist Congressmen saw in the unpopularity of the Soviet Union and Communism an opportunity to restrict the law by forbidding the President to use any of the new appropriation to help Russia. Stettinius and others argued strongly against such a blow to Russian morale and in favor of the President's discretionary power. The movement to ban aid to the Soviet Union failed.[3]

Stettinius and Hopkins became chief organizers of aid to Russia. They met opposition high in the ranks of administration officials. British tanks and planes reached the Russian front before American machines did. The Russians continued to pay cash for their purchases in the United States until November, 1941.[4]

Roosevelt was acutely aware of the unpopularity of the Soviet Union in the United States. He worked especially to placate Catholic sentiment. The press had noted the absence from the Atlantic Charter of two of the President's Four Freedoms: freedom of religion and freedom of information. In his message to Congress on August 21, transmitting the joint declaration for the record, the President said those two freedoms were included of necessity because of world need.[5] In September, Roosevelt told Oumansky that it would be highly useful if Moscow would make a demonstration of religious freedom in the Soviet Union. The Soviet government complied by making public gestures of benevolence towards religion. Father Braun, the only American Catholic priest in Russia, observed improvements in the Soviet toleration of religion, and attributed the change to Roosevelt's influence.[6]

On September 3, 1941, Roosevelt sent Myron C. Taylor on a second mission to Pope Pius XII to explain the administration's view of the necessity to support Russia against Hitler. Taylor carried a letter in which the President drew the vital distinction between Russia and Germany upon which his policy rested:

In my opinion, the fact is that Russia is governed by a dictatorship, as rigid in its manner of being as is the dictatorship in Germany. I believe, however, that this Russian dictatorship is less dangerous to the safety of other nations than is the German form of dictatorship. The only weapon which the Russian dictatorship uses outside of its own borders is communist propaganda which I, of course, recognize has in the past been utilized for the purpose of breaking down the form of government in other countries, religious belief, et cetera. Germany, however, not only has utilized, but is utilizing, this kind of propaganda as well and has also undertaken the employment of every form of military aggression outside of its borders for the purpose of world conquest by force of arms and by force of propaganda. I believe that the survival of Russia is less dangerous to religion, to the church as such, and to humanity in general than would be the survival of the

German form of dictatorship. Furthermore, it is my belief that the leaders of all churches in the United States should recognize these facts clearly and should not close their eyes to these basic questions and by their present attitude on this question directly assist Germany in her present objectives.[7]

Pope Pius XII in his written answer to the President did not touch upon the critical issue. But in private discussion with Taylor and in public statements he made a distinction between atheistic communism and the Russian people which suggested that the Catholic Church would not oppose the Russians' right to defend themselves against aggression. Taylor also discussed the Atlantic Charter with the Pope, and the latter in an address on Christmas Day, 1941, stated essential conditions of world order under moral law which seemed to confirm the principles of the Charter.[8] The Catholic hierarchy in the United States subsequently did not place itself officially in opposition to aid to Russia, and eminent Catholic laymen gave positive support to the policy.[9]

Fundamentally it was the fight Russians made to defend their land that brought aid from the United States and support for such a policy from all but the most single-minded opponents of communism as the sole threat to American institutions. Roosevelt was among those who maintained optimism even when the Red Army suffered disasters in the south and the north and seemed about to give way before Moscow. On October 30, 1941, he cabled Stalin that he had approved shipments amounting to one billion dollars to be financed under Lend Lease without interest charges, repayments to begin five years after the war. On November 7, the defense of the Soviet Union was formally declared vital to the defense of the United States under the terms of the Lend Lease Act. On June 11, 1942, a Master Lend Lease Agreement placed Russian aid in the same framework as aid to Britain and China.[10]

During November the Battle of Moscow reached its fearful climax. On December 7, in a synchronization of events that largely escaped Americans concerned with their own crisis, the Red Army began the counterattack before Moscow which was one of the great turning points of the Second World War. Still, for several years, Russia was in the broadest sense fighting defensively, and remained in the position of supplicant for material aid and for a second front in Europe.

It is of great importance in studying the policy of President Roosevelt to note that during this period, when Russia was in the position of supplicant and the United States in the position of giver, Roosevelt worked to win political concessions from the Soviet government in the same way that he worked to obtain them from Great Britain. When the first glimmer of hope appeared in the Russian fighting, the Soviet government began at once to show interest in an enlarged territorial position after the war. Demands were made to Britain for agreements looking towards settlement of boundaries with annexations by Russia of territories won during the period of the Nazi-Soviet Pact. The situation became tense and Foreign Minister Anthony Eden planned to leave for Moscow on December 7, 1941, in order to discuss postwar problems. The British had kept Washington informed of these developments. On October 1, adherence by the Soviet government to the terms of the Atlantic Charter had been announced. But later Ambassador Maisky in London told Ambassador Winant he believed the Soviet government should have been consulted beforehand about its terms.[11]

Now on December 5, Roosevelt and Hull sent a message to Eden which laid out the lines of American policy towards Soviet ambitions until the Yalta Agreement in 1945. It asserted that the test of American good faith would be the fulfillment of the program of aid to Russia. The Atlantic Charter represented the attitude of the Soviet government as well as the United States and Great Britain on postwar problems. The United States government opposed any agreements on specific terms of postwar settlement, particularly concerning individual countries, because they might jeopardize common aims looking towards an enduring peace. *"Above all, there must be no secret accords . . . the constitutional limitations to which this Government is bound must be kept in mind."* [12] This matched the Administration's effort, as shown most clearly in the Roosevelt instructions to Hopkins,* to obtain British adherence to the policy of anti-imperialism. What was most feared was a degeneration of Allied diplomacy like that of the First World War when secret imperialist treaties gravely interfered with the possibility of Wilson carrying out his program for a stable peace.

In negotiations that extended into 1942, the British showed

* See above, p. 363.

willingness to make a secret agreement with the Soviet government if Roosevelt would consent. Hull put up powerful opposition which the President supported. The British used the American objection as a lever to obtain Soviet consent to the omission of all territorial provisions in the Anglo-Soviet alliance treaty of May 26, 1942. Thus the first round was won for anti-imperialism. But the Soviet leaders obtained promises that a second front would be opened soon, and this could be regarded as compensation for their failure to obtain Britain's confirmation of the Soviet gains under the Nazi-Soviet Pact.[13]

Only in 1945, at the Yalta Conference, when the Soviet Union had obtained Lend Lease aid to the amount of more than ten billion dollars, after the second front had been opened, the Rhine crossed, and victory in Europe was certain, did Roosevelt consent to violation by the Soviet Union of the principle of anti-imperialism. The United States was then the supplicant for Soviet aid in the war against Japan, which Roosevelt's military advisers told him would require two more years and invasions, costly in American lives and material, of the Japanese islands and the Asiatic mainland. The Soviet government was at last in the position of giver, and Stalin extorted from Roosevelt betrayal of the anti-imperialist clause of the Atlantic Charter. First Roosevelt consented, in June, 1944, to an Anglo-Russian division of Europe into spheres of influence, applicable only to "war conditions," and only for a three-months' trial.[14] This division became permanent.

Then in February, 1945, at Yalta, Roosevelt made a secret agreement with Stalin to use his influence to obtain Chinese consent to restoration to the Soviet Union of Tsarist imperialist positions in China.[15] In this agreement Roosevelt violated one of the central principles of his foreign policy—a principle for which he had fought consistently and successfully, not only in the policy of the United States, but of every other nation he could influence during the preceding twelve years. No excuse of his physical weariness or explanation of the need for Soviet aid against Japan can wipe out the blemish on Roosevelt's record. But the Soviet government must be named as the prime mover in the betrayal, and the British government preceded the American government in giving way to Soviet imperialism. Roosevelt was guilty of optimism that a violation of anti-imperialist principle in limited areas would encourage Sovet adherence to the principle of collective security on the basis of ample Soviet frontiers. In 1950 his optimism has not quite been proved to have been absolutely unfounded. The Soviet government has not shown the unlimited and untameable aggressiveness of Nazi Germany.

In 1941 the Roosevelt administration set out to liquidate the Soviet suspicion of the capitalist world which had inspired Soviet policy after the interventions in the Russian Revolution and civil war and after the Munich Agreement. Capitalist governments doubtless had equal reason to allow suspicion of the Soviet government to inspire their policies, but Roosevelt determined to take the initiative in destroying the mutual antagonisms which fed on each other. Sherwood writes:

The repeated warnings of possible Russian perfidy that Roosevelt received in 1941 and throughout the years that followed served only to make him increase his efforts to convince the Russians of America's incontestable good faith.[16]

Russia was the severest test of Roosevelt's belief in the doctrines of internationalism, that good faith by one nation will engender good faith in others, and that the possibility of peaceful cooperation among nations must be absolutely exhausted before recourse is had to other means of maintaining security. Only future history will finally determine whether his action at Yalta instrumented his belief by means of a justifiable compromise with principle, or amounted to a "Munich" productive not of peace but war.

However mistaken his final act in American-Russian relations may be judged now or hereafter to have been, it is clear that Roosevelt in 1941 was the chief architect of a united front among the Soviet Union, Great Britain, and the United States.

### Execution of Task (b) (2)

This political development was matched in the military sphere by Roosevelt's decision in September to strengthen naval policy in the North Atlantic. It will be remembered that on July 26, 1941, after the occupation of Iceland, the Navy under Western Hemisphere Defense Plan 4 began to escort convoys of United States and Icelandic merchantmen to Iceland. Execution of Task (b) (2) of Plan 4, which authorized merchantmen of other nations to join such convoys, had been postponed. The waters east of Iceland were a Combat Zone under the Neutrality Act. Therefore Lend Lease cargoes in American ships had to be transferred to ships of other flags at Iceland before they could be carried on the last leg of their journey. Execution of Task (b) (2) would not end this requirement. Repeal of the combat zone clause of the Neutrality Act was necessary if American merchantmen were to proceed beyond Iceland. But Task (b) (2) would permit British and other foreign merchantmen to join American convoys to Iceland, where British naval escorts and land-based aircraft would take over the job of protecting the ships on the last leg.

On August 13, 1941, instructions were issued to the United States Navy preliminary to the order to execute Task (b) (2).[17] The date suggests that the decision was reached at the Atlantic Conference. No question exists that the President had constitutional authority to order execution of Task (b) (2). But he had said that convoys meant shooting, "and shooting comes awfully close to war." Therefore his antiwar pledge seemed to be involved and he did not order execution of Task (b) (2) until after a United States naval vessel, the destroyer *Greer,* was attacked by a German submarine on September 4, 1941.

As it happened, the *Greer* was not engaged in escorting a convoy but in carrying mail to Iceland. The exact nature of the incident was the subject of much dispute and investigation. The President, on September 11, described it publicly as follows: "I tell you the blunt fact that the German submarine fired first upon this American destroyer without warning, and with deliberate design to sink her." He called this "piracy—legally and morally," and not the first nor the last act of piracy committed by the Nazi government against the American flag. He specified the *Robin Moor* sinking in May and the sinking on September 6 of the merchant ship *Steel Seafarer* in the Red Sea.[18]

Isolationists fixed upon the *Greer* incident to convince the public that no basis existed for the President's accusations against Germany. Senator David I. Walsh obtained from Admiral Stark a detailed description of the incident. The *Greer* had been informed by a British plane of the presence of a submerged submarine ten miles ahead. The destroyer trailed the submarine and broadcast its position in conformity with standard practice of the

Neutrality Patrol. The British plane dropped depth charges and left. The submarine fired a torpedo at the *Greer*, missing it by about a hundred yards. The destroyer then dropped eight depth charges. The submarine fired another torpedo which missed. Two hours later, the *Greer* dropped more depth charges, without known results. After searching for several more hours, the American ship proceeded to Iceland.[19]

Clearly the *Greer* had been attacked while pursuing patrol duties. Broadcasting information had been initiated in 1939, and "trailing" had started after the President's declaration of unlimited emergency in May, 1941. But Stark's report made the tactical position of the *Greer* seem less defensive than the President had stated in his September 11 speech, and isolationists made the most of it. Beard finds in the Stark report an explanation for the President's failure to ask Congress for a declaration of war. He implies that Stark by exposing "realities" frustrated the President's desire to exploit deceptive "appearances." [20]

But if the President had been seeking grounds to break his antiwar pledge he could have found them in the *Robin Moor* and *Steel Seafarer* sinkings, which presented no difficulty in proving that Germany had "attacked." Such grounds for American entry into the war Roosevelt himself had ruled out long before when he advocated measures in the Neutrality Acts designed to avoid "incidents" by prohibiting American travel and shipping in combat zones. Such incidents had led to American entry into the First World War; they had been called flimsy excuses in retrospect, and Roosevelt was determined to avoid this, like many others of Wilson's "mistakes."

The President made this very clear in his speech on September 11:

Our type of democratic civilization has outgrown the thought of feeling compelled to fight some other nation by reason of any single piratical attack on one of our ships. . . .
It would be unworthy of a great nation to exaggerate an isolated incident, or to become inflamed by some one act of violence. But it would be inexcusable folly to minimize such incidents in the face of evidence which makes it clear that the incident is not isolated, but part of a general plan.

The body of the President's speech was devoted to description of
that general plan. Seizure of control of the oceans by Hitler was
the chief item stressed:

> To be ultimately successful in world mastery Hitler knows that he
> must get control of the seas. He must first destroy the bridge of ships
> which we are building across the Atlantic, over which we shall con-
> tinue to roll the implements of war to help destroy him and all his
> works in the end. He must wipe out our patrol on sea and in the air.
> He must silence the British Navy.

Roosevelt called it "simple arithmetic" that the United States
Navy could be an invincible protection only if the British Navy
survived. Otherwise the Axis powers would possess two or three
times the potential naval power of the Americas.

American action in defense of freedom of the seas, and use of
the seas to insure delivery of Lend Lease cargoes to Britain were
the grounds of Roosevelt's "shoot on sight" order. He called the
Nazi submarines and raiders "the rattlesnakes of the Atlantic,"
and explained: "when you see a rattlesnake poised to strike you
do not wait until he has struck before you crush him." The new
policy he called "active defense:"

> In the waters which we deem necessary for our defense American
> naval vessels and American planes will no longer wait until Axis sub-
> marines lurking under the water, or Axis raiders on the surface of the
> sea, strike their deadly blow—first.
>
> Upon our naval and air patrol—now operating in large numbers
> over a vast expanse of the Atlantic Ocean—falls the duty of maintaining
> the American policy of freedom of the seas—now. That means, very
> simply and clearly, that our patrolling vessels and planes will protect
> all merchant ships—not only American ships but ships of any flag—
> engaged in commerce in our defensive waters. . . .
>
> It is no act of war on our part when we decide to protect the seas
> which are vital to American defense. The aggression is not ours. Ours
> is solely defense.
>
> But let this warning be clear. From now on, if German or Italian
> vessels of war enter the waters, the protection of which is necessary for
> American defense, they do so at their own peril.
>
> The orders which I have given as Commander in Chief to the United
> States Army and Navy are to carry out that policy—at once.
>
> The sole responsibility rests upon Germany. There will be no shoot-
> ing unless Germany continues to seek it.[21]

In accordance with the President's public announcement, Task
(b) (2) of Western Hemisphere Defense Plan 4 was ordered executed
on September 16. On October 11, Plan 5 superseded Plan 4, and
it remained in effect until after Pearl Harbor. The new Plan
placed British and Canadian escort vessels under the strategic direction of the United States in the Western Atlantic. Passages of
the President's September 11 address were cited and the "shoot
on sight" order was incorporated in Task (a):

Protection against hostile attack United States and foreign flag
shipping other than German and Italian shipping by escorting, covering, and patrolling as circumstances may require, and by destroying
German and Italian Naval, Land, and Air Forces encountered.

In Task (d) it was determined that the normal right of a belligerent to capture enemy merchant shipping would not be exercised. A preliminary statement in the Plan specified that the
United States was "not at war in the legal sense, and therefore
does not have any of the special belligerent rights accorded under
United States law to States which are formally at war." [22]

## A Limited, Undeclared War

It was natural that after the "shoot on sight" order the United
States was described by many as being "in" the war. But its position was actually like that of the United States in 1798 during
the Undeclared War against France, and Roosevelt himself frequently pointed out the precedent. Then, too, the United States
Navy had fought enemy warships but did not capture enemy
merchantmen. The area of conflict was restricted in 1798 to the
West Indies as it was restricted to Atlantic waters outside Combat
Zones in 1941. Congress raised an army then also.

Roosevelt satisfied some of his critics when he acted on one
more item in the precedent of 1798. President John Adams had
been given specific authorization by Congress for the order to
"shoot on sight;" Roosevelt on October 9 asked Congress to repeal sections of the Neutrality Act that forbade the arming of
American merchant ships and their entry into belligerent ports.
Such action would authorize Roosevelt to wage limited, undeclared war on the sea.

Beyond that point, the analogy between 1798 and 1941 broke down. Congressional authority was not necessary for President Adams to order the Navy to use force, any more than Roosevelt needed it. Congress in 1798 nevertheless went through the form of giving Adams such authority. It was dominated by pro-war Federalists, and President Adams' statesmanship consisted in preventing them from precipitating an unnecessary declared war. He obtained from France full satisfaction of American grievances.

Such a denouement in 1941 would have been possible only for an administration willing to abandon Britain and give consent to Axis conquests. Plan 5 contained the following statement: "The operations which will be conducted under this plan are conceived to form a preparatory phase for the operations of Navy Basic War Plan Rainbow No. 5." The Rainbow Plan was for use when war should be declared.[23] This was an expression of Roosevelt's conviction, made known to his associates at the time of the Atlantic Conference, that war was inevitable. In the isolationist thesis, Roosevelt's conviction that war was inevitable is made to appear as proof that his measures were designed to provoke war. Fundamental to Roosevelt's thinking was the belief that the Axis leaders could not be "provoked" into adding the United States to their list of enemies until Russia, Britain and NEI had been conquered. This was a thoroughly reasonable belief at the time. It proved to be unsound only because Hitler and Tojo were overconfident that Russia was defeated. Hitler announced the "final defeat" of the Red Army on October 3, 1941. He said: "This enemy is already broken and will never rise again." [24] This was the moment when Hitler demanded that his Axis partner should attack the United States. His purpose was to distract the United States during the next period while he accomplished the defeat of Britain.

American Lend Lease aid to Britain was the policy that caused Hitler to decide on the moment for war against the United States. The details of American naval tactics to help protect Lend Lease shipments to Britain were significant only insofar as they showed that the United States would not be intimidated into abandoning the Lend Lease program.

The Japanese leaders calculated that the possibility of Roosevelt asking Congress for a declaration of war if Japan invaded the southwest Pacific was too great a risk. They were confident not only that Russia was defeated but also that if they incapacitated the American fleet at Pearl Harbor, they could quickly conquer the whole southwest Pacific area. With Russia and Britain defeated, and United States sea power broken, the Axis would rule Europe and Asia and could organize both continents at leisure for a final conflict with the isolated Western Hemisphere.

The nub of the matter is that the Axis wrote off Russia too soon, while Roosevelt remained confident that Russia was far from defeat. All the information of Japanese intentions, derived from Magic as well as Japanese public acts and private diplomacy, pointed to Japanese invasion of areas in the southwest Pacific, probably excluding the Philippines. Roosevelt believed that war was inevitable because he believed the United States should and would aid the British and the Dutch when the Japanese attacked them. He refused to make any commitment regarding the precise nature of American aid in that event: he kept his hands entirely free to shape his future policy in close harmony with the development of events and of American public opinion. But he felt certain that new proofs of the unlimited scope of Japanese aggressiveness, and realization that Britain, if defeated in Asia and Australia and the Pacific, could not hold out in Europe, would produce new currents of opinion in America which would radically change his obligations under his antiwar pledge.

In the meantime, the last thing Roosevelt wanted was to "provoke" war. Two facts, apart from all other considerations, destroy the isolationist thesis. Roosevelt had at hand incidents of Nazi attack on American shipping quite sufficient to justify violation of his antiwar pledge if he had been interested in provoking war. His address of September 11 showed that he was chiefly concerned to *avoid* war as a result of such incidents. More serious incidents followed. Yet the President in his Navy Day address on October 27, 1941, again showed that he would exploit no incidents, however severe, to take the country into war. The truth of the situation was that Hitler was attempting to provoke Roosevelt into a blunder on either one of the two sides of his dilemma: by giving way to the interventionist demand for a declaration of war, which would throw the country into a paralyzing last-ditch fight between isolationists and internationalists with grave risk of a victory in Congress for the former; or by giving way to the isolationist demand to retreat from the policy of aid to Britain, which would suit Hitler quite as well. Roosevelt refused to be provoked into taking either course.

The other fact that does not square with the isolationist thesis is that Roosevelt was determined to concentrate American aid against Hitler and avoid distraction in the Far East. This ruling strategic plan makes nonsense of the isolationist image of a Roosevelt who provoked attack against the United States by Japan. Had he wanted war, he would hardly have rejected the ready-made excuses which Hitler offered him to fight the *kind* of war his strategy required, and at the same time have maneuvered the Japanese into forcing on the United States the kind of war Hitler wanted it to fight, that is, one which would give Hitler maximum time to defeat Russia and Great Britain.

This consideration, like many others, is obscured by the gigantic miscalculation of the Axis leaders that Russia in the fall of 1941 was defeated. But it must be remembered that the period after Pearl Harbor, while the United States was on the defensive in the Pacific, seemed to the Axis leaders sufficient time for mopping-up operations in Russia and for the launching of a campaign against the British Isles, before Lend Lease aid could make them impregnable and while the American Navy was elsewhere engaged. This, Hitler's plan for world victory, Roosevelt was determined to frustrate by allowing nothing to distract the United States from concentrating its effort on aid to Britain. If isolationists allow no other motive to be imputed to Roosevelt, they must at least admit his consistent adherence to his "Hitler first" strategy—a strategy they themselves were loudest in publicizing because they believed it to be mistaken.

### *"Our Primary Task"*

Roosevelt's next step in strengthening American support of Britain was predicated on his refusal to exploit Nazi attacks on American shipping to ask Congress for a declaration of war. Formerly he had advocated clauses of the Neutrality Act which were intended to prevent such attacks. They were ineffective because Nazi submarines operated far beyond the combat zones American merchantmen were forbidden to enter. Furthermore, Roosevelt had declared in his September 11 address that attacks on American vessels would not be used as Wilson had used them, as a reason for an American declaration of war. Therefore the prohibitions only weakened American efforts to support Britain, without making less likely United States entry into the war.

The President on October 9 asked Congress to repeal "crippling provisions" of the Neutrality Act. Repeal, he said, "will not leave the United States any less neutral than we are today, but will make it possible for us to defend the Americas far more successfully and to give aid far more effectively against the tremendous forces now marching toward conquest of the world." He named the arming of merchant ships and abolition of combat zones as specific purposes he had in mind.[25]

This proposal meant that armed American merchant ships would carry contraband into Allied ports. Under the old code of international law, contraband cargoes were subject to capture by the enemy of the country of their destination, and armed ships were subject to attack without warning. The modern code made aid to the victims of aggression an obligation, but it was still true that sending armed ships with contraband cargoes into Allied ports was an "act of war" in the sense that Roosevelt had defined it in January, 1941: it meant shooting, and shooting came "awfully close" to war.

From this point of view, Roosevelt's request to Congress to repeal sections of the Neutrality Act was a request for authorization which would absolve him of his implied promise to commit no "act of war" under Lend Lease. It was a request for authority to wage an undeclared naval war, and for approval of the "shoot on sight" order of September 11-16. This is emphasized by Roosevelt's rejection of a suggestion made to him by Secretary Hull. In July, Hull had told Welles and Roosevelt that delay by Congress might be avoided by obtaining legal opinions that the Lend Lease Act had altered the Neutrality Act. Hull in his *Memoirs* writes that it was Hitler who "forced the issue" by sinking American ships early in September.[26] It does not follow, however, that these sinkings "forced" the President to ask Congress for authority he might well have found in the Lend Lease Act. Rather the President's action argued that he wished to give full opportunity to Congress and people to debate and decide whether an undeclared naval war should be waged to insure delivery of Lend Lease cargoes to defenders against aggression.

Once the President had made clear that sinkings of American ships would not be offered by him as reason for a declaration of war, repeal of prohibitions in the Neutrality Act became a measure, like Lend Lease itself, well calculated to prevent American entry into the war. This was because Nazi sinkings of unarmed American ships in waters close to the Western Hemisphere were much more likely to inflame American sentiment in favor of war than shooting between American and Nazi armed ships in waters close to Europe. The President's program would leave him no grounds for a request to Congress for a declaration of war if sinkings multiplied: he asked for authority to wage undeclared naval war, and sinkings were to be expected.

This viewpoint was accepted by Congressmen who supported repeal. For example, Representative Walter A. Lynch, a Democrat of New York, said:

No one in this House is more opposed to war than I. . . .

It is because I want to keep war from our land that I shall vote to arm American merchantmen. If an armed American merchantman, on the high seas, sinks a German submarine or surface raider in self-defense, war is not inevitable. If German submarines or surface raiders continue to sink unarmed American ships, war, in my opinion, is inevitable.[27]

Isolationists saw the measure as one more proof that Roosevelt was intent upon provoking Germany into war. Doubtless a great deal of ambiguity was inherent in a state of undeclared naval war. Isolationists, however, transformed ambiguity into oversimplification in their chant: "This is war."[28]

The President on October 27, Navy Day, made an address over the radio which contained his chief statement of policy during the period of undeclared war. On October 17 the United States destroyer *Kearny* had been torpedoed several hundred miles southwest of Iceland with a loss of eleven crewmen's lives. More merchant ships had been sunk. These events indicated more plainly than anything Roosevelt could say the meaning of his request to revise the Neutrality Act.

Americans in majority did not regard the sinkings as reason for entry into the war. They supported the President's policy of force in the Battle of the Atlantic and accepted the casualties that followed. This left the isolationists in a dilemma from which they tried to escape by joining in the interventionists' demand that the President ask Congress for a declaration of war. General Robert E. Wood, head of the America First Committee, issued a public appeal a few days after the attack on the *Kearny* for the President to ask Congress for a vote on war.[29] Isolationists also circularized families of the men who had lost their lives on the *Kearny* with messages containing statements such as: "Your dear son was sent to his death by the murdering imbecile head of our Government," and with cartoons depicting the hanging of Uncle Sam by Roosevelt and "Me, too, Willkie." [30]

Roosevelt in the Navy Day Address, his last important one before Pearl Harbor, clung to the method he had used ever since the failure of his Quarantine the Aggressor speech in 1937: *one step at a time*, a step dictated by necessities of the moment, designed to command the support of all but the extreme isolationists, a step *forward* towards the goal of internationalism in foreign policy. The House of Representatives had already voted favorably on the arming of merchant ships. Beard complains that the administration "hurried" the bill through the House under a gag rule.[31]

Contrary to the Beardian thesis, the President again, as always, explained his policy to the public and Congress fully and carefully. He said on October 27, "America has been attacked." Beard, following prognostications of the eminent *New York Times* columnist, Arthur J. Krock, finds in this statement evidence that the President intended to use the torpedoing of the *Kearny* as reason to abandon his antiwar pledge under the terms of the proviso in the 1940 Democratic Platform, "except in case of attack." The President's intention was frustrated, Beard argues, because details of the attack on the *Kearny* showed that the destroyer was on convoy duty and had been engaged in depth-bombing German submarines before it was torpedoed. Incidentally, Beard attempts to sustain his thesis that the administration lied regarding convoys. In a footnote he cites portentously Secretary Knox's denial of Senator Wheeler's charge that the Navy was convoying ships to Great Britain.[32] The Navy only escorted convoys as far as American-occupied Iceland.

Beard's picture of the President whipping up an excuse to abandon his antiwar pledge and then frustrated by the facts of the *Kearny* incident is purely imaginary. In his Navy Day Address the

President used the *Kearny* incident not to justify entry into the war but to win support for his program of using force to defend the freedom of the seas. He had made clear as early as May 27, 1941, that the entry of Nazi submarines and raiders into waters considered vital to the safety of the Western Hemisphere was itself an aggression, an "attack." Iceland had been occupied because it was a strategic outpost of the Western Hemisphere. He had also made it clear on September 11 that "incidents," not merely shooting affrays but sinkings of unarmed American merchant ships, would not be used as reason for the United States to enter the war.

Now in his Navy Day Address he called the *Kearny* torpedoing an "attack" in the sense that the position of the United States Navy in waters between the United States and Iceland was defensive, designed to protect the freedom of the seas. The entry of Nazi warships into those waters was offensive, designed to forbid American use of those waters:

The purpose of Hitler's attack was to frighten the American people off the high seas—to force us to make a trembling retreat. This is not the first time he has misjudged the American spirit. That spirit is now aroused.

If our national policy were to be dominated by the fear of shooting, then all of our ships and those of our sister republics would have to be tied up in home harbors. Our Navy would have to remain respectfully —abjectly—behind any line which Hitler might decree on any ocean as his own dictated version of his own war zone.

Naturally, we reject that absurd and insulting suggestion. We reject it because of our own self-interest, because of our own self-respect, because, most of all, of our own good faith. Freedom of the seas is now, as it has always been, a fundamental policy of your Government and mine.

Here was no suggestion that Roosevelt wanted the public to regard the *Kearny* incident as more than a challenge to the American right to use the ocean highways. He described elements of the Nazi plan for world conquest that directly threatened Americans, then announced, more flatly than ever before, the policy of helping to destroy Hitlerism and the policy of American entry, after the victory, into a world system of collective security:

Very simply and very bluntly, we are pledged to pull our own oar in the destruction of Hitlerism.

And when we have helped to end the curse of Hitlerism, we shall help to establish a new peace which will give to decent people everywhere a better chance to live and prosper in security and in freedom and in faith.

Far from proposing that the United States, to carry out those policies, should enter the war, Roosevelt reaffirmed that producing and delivering the arms for men fighting on the battle fronts was "our *primary* task." Nazi defiance of the American will to deliver the arms did call for new measures: "I say that we do not propose to take this lying down." Not only would the orders to the Navy to shoot on sight stand, but the area and tactics of the naval war should be extended. He spoke approvingly of progress through Congress of the revision of the Neutrality Act, and said:

Our American merchant ships must be armed to defend themselves against the rattlesnakes of the sea.

Our American merchant ships must be free to carry our American goods into the harbors of our friends.

Our American merchant ships must be protected by our American Navy.

It can never be doubted that the goods will be delivered by this Nation, whose Navy believes in the traditions of "Damn the torpedoes; full speed ahead!"

The President ever since the Fall of France had defined American defensive *strategy* as requiring offensive *tactics*. Now he restated this conception: "The first objective of that [total national] defense is to stop Hitler." To accept so active a policy as one which could properly be called defensive, it was necessary only to agree that the predominant fact of the world situation was aggression by the Axis nations.

In the perspective of the American defeats at Pearl Harbor and for months thereafter, one must view Roosevelt's attitude towards the question of American readiness for war in the fall of 1941 as unduly optimistic. He said:

The lines of our essential defense now cover all the seas; and to meet the extraordinary demands of today and tomorrow our Navy grows to unprecedented size. Our Navy is ready for action. . . .

Our new Army is steadily developing the strength needed to withstand the aggressors.

If he was too optimistic regarding the readiness of the armed forces to support the risks of even his cautious policy of one forward step at a time, the greater risks of a declaration of war might have proved more disastrous than the event. Admittedly a declaration of war would likely have alerted the fleet at Pearl Harbor as it was not alerted on December 7, and would in a thousand ways have invigorated production and military effectiveness. But the lesser request for Congress to expand measures of undeclared naval warfare met severe opposition, and a request for a declaration of war for the sake of its invigorating effects would have invited a prolonged, bitter, and divisive debate, in which isolationists would wield the powerful emotional weapon of Roosevelt's abandonment of his pledge, with demoralizing effects upon people and armed forces, and risk of defeat which would discredit the administration and turn the nation back to isolationism.

## Slowly but Surely

Forward towards internationalism slowly, but forward surely was Roosevelt's decision. Isolationists called this forward movement a drive towards war, but insofar as it did involve use of force, Roosevelt measured his steps in strict time to the pace of people and Congress and left it for the Axis to prove that the pace was too slow.

On October 27 the President also designated forward steps in areas other than the Battle of the Atlantic. He explained the reasoning which, on November 7, would bring Russia within the coalition of nations receiving Lend Lease aid:

Nobody who admires qualities of courage and endurance can fail to be stirred by the full-fledged resistance of the Russian people. The Russians are fighting for their own soil and their own homes. Russia needs all kinds of help—planes, tanks, guns, medical supplies, and other aids—toward the successful defense against the invaders. From the United States and from Britain, she is getting great quantities of those essential supplies. But the needs of her huge army will continue—and our help and British help will have to continue.

The other day the Secretary of State of the United States was asked by a Senator to justify our giving aid to Russia. His reply was: "The answer to that, Senator, depends on how anxious a person is to stop and destroy the march of Hitler in his conquest of the world. If he were anxious enough to defeat Hitler, he would not worry about who was helping to defeat him."

This remained the administration's answer throughout the war, and it satisfied most Americans; indeed they were eager to welcome Russia into the coalition of peaceful nations cooperating against aggression.

Roosevelt called production the chief task of the American people in which they must take giant forward steps:

Upon our American production falls the colossal task of equipping our own armed forces, and helping to supply the British, the Russians, and the Chinese. In the performance of that task we dare not fail.[33]

The naval war in the Atlantic intensified until it could not be doubted that Hitler was determined to risk an American declaration of war rather than permit the delivery of Lend Lease cargoes. Besides sinking merchant vessels, Nazi submarines sank the United States destroyer *Reuben James,* on October 31, with a loss of one hundred and fifteen lives. Roosevelt reaffirmed his position that the United States should accept the risks of the naval campaign without using losses as a basis for a declaration of war. When a reporter asked: "Will this first actual sinking [of an American warship] make any difference in the international relations of the United States?" the President replied that he did not think so: "The destroyer was merely carrying out its assigned task." He also hinted that the Germans, too, were suffering losses.[34] It was Hitler, not Roosevelt, who found the German-American undeclared naval war of 1941 unprofitable, and it was Hitler's blunder to conceive that a declared war would be preferable for Germany.

It was on the ground that the naval campaign was in fact the best stratagem for the United States that Roosevelt and Hull urged Congress to revise the Neutrality Act. The House in October had repealed section 6, which forbade arming of merchant ships. The Senate, after Roosevelt's Navy Day Address, repealed sections 2 and 3, prohibiting American ships from entering belligerent ports and combat zones, as well as section 6. Opposition to repeal of sections 2 and 3 developed in the House. Roosevelt and Hull sent letters to House leaders on November 13 urging repeal of all three sections. That same day the House passed the Senate measure by the close vote of 212 to 194. The President signed it on November 17.[35]

This revision of the Neutrality Act signified formal approval by Congress of the President's policy of using force to insure delivery of Lend Lease cargoes to allies abroad. It demolishes the charge that the President exercised illegal and unconstitutional authority, in Beard's words, to "initiate war at will." [36] The President had made known to the public item by item his developing policy, with ample, even redundant explanations of each step, and he had asked Congress and obtained by normal procedure authority which a specific law had withheld from him. American democratic processes functioned with exemplary thoroughness in the famous episodes that resulted in repeal of the arms embargo, enactment and extension of Selective Service, enactment of Lend Lease, and now finally the repeal of provisions of the Neutrality Act restricting the naval campaign to deliver Lend Lease cargoes. The last measure fully justified the President in violating his virtual pledge, in January, 1941, to avoid naval escorts because they would lead to shooting, and shooting came "awfully close to war." Shooting had occurred, people and Congress were firm in its justification, and the President had proved that he would not use fatalities resulting from naval protection of Lend Lease cargoes to violate his pledge against "sending our boys into the European trenches." He had developed so effective a lot of measures short of war that his policy could even be justified to interventionists during the last days before Pearl Harbor as being more effective in helping to win the war than if he had asked for a declaration.

# 17.

## *Roosevelt and Konoye*

W HILE THE PRESIDENT BY NOVEMBER, 1941, HAD PROVED
that American losses in the Battle of the Atlantic would not lead
him to break his antiwar pledge, the Axis leaders gave him no
chance to show whether he would also adhere to his pledge if
Japan attacked territory of the Netherlands or Great Britain.

Ample evidence exists to prove that Roosevelt feared a Pacific
war because it would interfere with the primary task of defeating
Hitler by aiding Britain and Russia. He and Hull faced the final
diplomatic encounters with the Japanese determined to avoid giving Japan any justification for war. But they were equally firmly
determined to avoid appeasement of aggression at the expense of
the territories and rights of third powers. The Hull-Nomura talks
prior to the Atlantic Conference had convinced Roosevelt that the
Japanese government would be satisfied with nothing less than
American diplomatic, political, economic and moral cooperation
with Japan in its program of domination over China and conquest
of territories to the south. Therefore the most that could be hoped
for in the new round of talks was postponement of new Japanese
aggressions.

### *Raid or Sabotage?*

As for administration estimates of where the blows were likely
to fall, it appears certain that a transpacific raid to Hawaii was
considered to be less likely than undercover sabotage of the fleet
there by Japanese agents, while main blows were directed against
Thailand and Singapore. On June 17, 1940, when the Fall of
France caused fear in Washington that Japan would burst out in

new directions, General Marshall ordered General Herron, in command at Hawaii, as follows: "Immediately alert complete defensive organization to deal with possible transpacific raid."[1] But standard dispositions of fleet and air units in such an alert were of precisely the sort that made them most vulnerable to sabotage. These dispositions called for dispersal and concealment to avoid presenting to raiders close groupings of planes and ships. This reduced the value to raiders of particular targets, but it also increased the danger of sabotage because it spread thin the guards assigned to protect planes and ships against saboteurs. The anti-raid alert was relaxed a month later.

On February 7, 1941, General Marshall wrote to General Short, the new commander at Hawaii, in terms that showed his indecision whether a raid or sabotage was the greater danger. He placed sabotage first: "The risk of sabotage and the risk involved in a surprise raid by air and by submarine constitute the real perils of the situation."[2] By May, Marshall had gone over completely to the conception that sabotage was the danger. On May 3 he wrote to President Roosevelt: "In point of sequence, sabotage is first to be expected and may, within a very limited time, cause great damage. On this account, and in order to assure strong control, it would be highly desirable to set up a military control of the islands prior to the likelihood of our involvement in the Far East."[3]

This estimate remained unchanged up to the moment of the Japanese raid, and it is the essential reason why that raid was successful. The Army and Navy were alerted on December 7 against sabotage; ships and planes were concentrated in close groups, amounting to "sitting duck" targets for the Japanese. The Minority Report of the Joint Committee to Investigate the Pearl Harbor Attack and the writings of Beard and Morgenstern are loaded with implications that Roosevelt and his subordinates in Washington *desired* the disaster at Pearl Harbor, that this is the essential reason for their failure to order the Hawaiian commanders to alert their forces against a Japanese raid rather than against sabotage.

## Preliminary Considerations

The isolationists' chief material in evidence is the series of Magic intercepts which, they assert, made plain to officials in Washington during the last days before the attack that the Japanese had in fact dispatched the raiding force to Hawaii. The correctness of this assertion will be examined in the next chapter. Here several preliminary considerations will be noted. The isolationist thesis has never been driven (in print) beyond the level of implication and innuendo to its necessary overt conclusion: that the leaders in Washington who received copies of Magic intercepts and had ultimate responsibility for the conduct of the armed forces in Hawaii, a group that included President Roosevelt, Secretaries Hull, Stimson and Knox, General Marshall and Admiral Stark, deliberately exposed the soldiers and sailors, the warships and planes at Pearl Harbor to maximum injury and death at Pearl Harbor on December 7. The isolationist thesis requires one to believe that it was for *this reason alone* that they failed to order an alert against the Japanese raid by planes and submarines. Or, stated another way: Roosevelt, Hull, Stimson, Knox, Marshall and Stark refrained from ordering an alert against the Japanese raid they knew was coming because such an alert would reduce the casualties and damage the raid would cause, and therefore reduce the value of the event as an incentive to war.

There exists in law a rule that accusations which are beyond the capacity of human credence need not be refuted. This would seem to be such an accusation. It is difficult to believe that isolationists have failed to draw the obvious conclusion from their case for any other reason than that stating it refutes it. They are satisfied to create suspicion of an absolutely incredible crime by leaders, at least some of whom, all Americans revere.

If the motive of an investigator of events prior to Pearl Harbor is to draw from the evidence inferences that are probabilities rather than impossibilities, those events become understandable and, with the benefit of hindsight, not without implications of errors in judgment by the responsible officials in Washington. The error that explains all lesser errors is that the Roosevelt administration failed to estimate the extreme daring and foolhardiness in aggression of the Japanese leaders. Roosevelt himself was accustomed to accusations that he exaggerated the scope of Axis designs: his error turned out to be that he underestimated their scope. This was a reasonable error. Japan in 1941 was generally regarded as "bogged down" in China, its forces overextended, its Russian flank exposed, and its military power gutted by shortage of raw materials. For Japan to attempt to improve its situation by thrusting towards the raw material sources of the NEI was reasonable enough, but to attack the United States before it had opportunity to exploit those raw materials was totally unreasonable. Japanese Navy leaders, as late as mid-October, 1941, opposed the Pearl Harbor expedition because Japan lacked oil enough to carry out naval tasks in a war with the United States. Postwar investigations have shown that the Konoye Cabinet fell from power on this issue.[4]

## Japanese Fear of Russia

It should also be considered that Roosevelt's opinion, expressed at the Atlantic Conference, that war was inevitable, like any opinion, could be modified by developments. Japan's fear of Russia, reflected in its anxiety for a Roosevelt-Konoye meeting after the President delivered his warning and offer to renew conversations to Nomura on August 17, was such a development. The President had agreed in principle to the meeting, but had asked that Japan make a clear statement of its position before preparations began. He had gone so far as to name October 15 as a tentative date for the meeting. Nomura on August 23, before his government answered the President's statements of August 17, pleaded with Hull for an earlier date than October 15 for the Roosevelt-Konoye meeting. He said his government was afraid some agreements might be reached in the September American-Anglo-Russian conference in Moscow that would be "detrimental" to Japan. The Japanese regarded shipments of American supplies to Vladivostok as designed to build up Soviet strength in Siberia where it menaced Japan. Hull answered that American aid to Russia was directed exclusively against Germany, but added: "Of course, if Japan should project herself militarily into the Russo-German situation—which I hope she will not—an entirely different question will be presented." [5]

Nomura thus represented Japanese fear of a Soviet-American rapprochement which would leave Japan exposed in the north greatly to the detriment of plans for southward invasions. He "contented himself with laughing very heartily" when Hull asked him whether he did not think the Russo-Japanese Neutrality Pact of April, 1941, gave Japan all the assurance of Russia's peaceful attitude Japan desired.[6]

Japanese fear of Russia was reasonably assessed at face value by the American Chiefs of Staff. They made a report to the President on September 11, entitled "Joint Board Estimate of United States Over-all Production Requirements," which reveals that they saw Russia in the north checkmating Japanese moves to the south, and that they took for granted that the Japanese would be completely occupied between north and south without inviting completion of the circle in the east by the United States. For example, this important document states:

It is unlikely that Japan will simultaneously attempt a major effort to the Northward and to the Southward, because of her lack of equipment and raw materials.

All the more so, the Joint Board implied throughout the report, Japan would not simultaneously attempt a major effort to the eastward.

The Chiefs of Staff believed the United States should enter the war against Germany. But they believed that even that commitment would not weaken the United States in relation to Japan; on the contrary, they proposed that the United States should participate in the European war *"while holding Japan in check pending future developments."* Extreme limits of direct danger to the United States from Japan were defined as dependent, for one thing, upon results in Europe favorable to Japan. In that situation, *after* Hitler defeated Russia, Japan "might" engage in "submarine and raider action against United States naval forces and United States and British lines of communication in the Central and Eastern Pacific Ocean." In a situation even more favorable, that is, were Japan to defeat China and Russia and succeed in controlling Thailand, Malaya, and the NEI, it would work for peace for the purpose of organizing the "East Asia Co-Prosperity Sphere." In that event: "Almost inevitably the Philippine Islands would ultimately pass under Japanese hegemony." [7]

This notable document pictured the United States as being capable, with Britain, Russia and China, of determining the sequence of events. The United States and its friends held the Axis powers in double pincers: Germany between Russia and Britain supported by the United States; Japan between Russia, China, Malaya-Australia and the NEI supported by the United States. Therefore the United States and its friends were regarded as capable of exercising the initiative in determining new developments of the global situation in such fashion as would close the double pincers. But the Joint Chiefs did not consider that Germany and Japan were equally able to picture the global situation as placing them in control of double pincers with which they could checkmate Russia in the east while destroying her in the west, break the British Empire in two, and attack the United States from the Pacific in order to undermine its campaign in the Atlantic.

For the immediate future it depended solely upon the question which side would in fact exercise the initiative to determine which side would wield the pincers. The American Chiefs of Staff believed the United States should join the war in Europe while holding Japan in check in the east: they wanted to wield the pincers. But they failed to estimate that if the United States did not *immediately* seize the initiative, the Axis would do so. Roosevelt consequently did not realize that the final moment for decision whether to break his antiwar pledge had arrived in September. He believed that moment would only arrive when Japan might play the strongest card it seemed to possess: attack northward or southward. His reasoning, that refusal to enter the European war made possible more effective American contributions to the defeat of Hitler, has been discussed in the previous chapter.

Either way, Roosevelt and his advisers believed to the end that Japan would at most only be able, and dare, to launch a limited offensive to the south *or* the north and that a Japanese offensive in either direction necessarily precluded a simultaneous offensive against the United States.

## The Appalling Paradox

Nothing in the report of September 11 suggests that the Joint Chiefs imagined Japan would dare to move into the central and eastern Pacific so long as Russia and Britain stood on its northern and southern flanks, that is, so long as Hitler had not subjugated them. The Joint Chiefs wanted the United States to enter the war in Europe, but they did not expect that to affect the current situation. Immediately following the proposal, the report stated: "Necessarily, only small Army contingents are now sufficiently equipped and trained for immediate participation in offensive operations." [8] The military leaders saw United States entry into the war as having immediate effects chiefly upon morale in the armed forces and civilian production. When the Japanese chose their date for the attack on Pearl Harbor they *wrongly* judged that the condition named in the American Joint Chiefs of Staff report of September 11 had been met: but Hitler was *not* successful in Europe. America, the Japanese calculated, could be diverted to the Pacific and Britain cut off from the Far East to help Hitler finish off the British homeland. The American leaders, on the other hand, *rightly* judged that the condition prior to which the Japanese would not attack the United States had not been met, and the Russian counteroffensive on December 7 bore them out.

Thus may be understood the appalling paradox that Roosevelt and Hull were right in their belief that the United States was playing from strength in the final conversations with Japan even though the Japanese were actually planning the attack on Pearl Harbor. Each side set out to "baby along" the other, the Americans to postpone if not prevent Japanese aggression to the south or the north, the Japanese to prepare an attack on the United States as a "sanction" if appeasement could not be extorted from it. In the isolationist thesis attention is concentrated exclusively on the disaster at Pearl Harbor to prove that Roosevelt and Hull were victims—by implication, eager victims—of Japanese policy. But the outcome of the war is a better criterion by which to judge which side was the victim of Japanese policy.

## The Japanese Stiffen Their Terms

Playing from strength, Roosevelt and Hull were determined to avoid appeasement. The Japanese government answered Roosevelt's proposal on August 28. It insisted that the Roosevelt-Konoye meeting be held prior to any negotiations and as quickly as possible. In response to the President's request for a clear statement of its attitudes and plans, the Japanese government presented, besides usual protestations of peaceful intentions, several qualifications containing obvious escape clauses. It would not withdraw its troops from Indo-China until the China Incident was "settled," or a "just peace" was established in East Asia. It would take no military action against Russia so long as Russia "does not menace Japan or Manchoukuo." It would not use military force against a neighboring country "without provocation." How those phrases could be interpreted by the Japanese to claim American support for past and future aggressions was obvious from former Japanese practice. It was even made clear in the same communication, in a paragraph describing recent Japanese aggressions:

When a nation is obstructed in the path of natural and peaceful development, or when the means of its existence is threatened, not only is it imperative that that nation should take defensive measures, but it is also required to do so for the maintenance of a just peace. This was the motivating policy of the Japanese Government.

Then the Japanese made a charge, only slightly veiled, that, while Japan was defensive in its policy, it was the United States that was guilty of threatening weaker powers. This would make some "feel compelled to consider defensively their relations with the United States." The United States was furthermore warned to "avoid any action that might give rise to a fear of menace to Japan through collaboration with the Soviet Union." These assertions more than counterbalanced a statement that the Japanese action in Indo-China was not a "preparatory step for military advance into neighboring countries," and that this pledge would "suffice to clarify also Japan's intentions toward Thailand." [9]

Roosevelt chose to respond as favorably as possible. He complimented Konoye, through Nomura, on the "spirit of his communication." He spoke encouragingly of a meeting with Konoye, but stated that he preferred Alaska as the scene rather than Hawaii. Nomura immediately afterwards suggested to Hull the date September 21-25. He hinted that Germany was inciting Japan against the United States.

President Roosevelt, according to Hull, "would have relished a meeting with Konoye, and at first he was excited at the prospect." But Hull insisted that agreement on essentials must be reached before the meeting, and the President "instantly agreed that it would be disastrous" to hold the meeting otherwise. Hull in his conversation with Nomura on August 28 made this condition known to him. A Roosevelt-Konoye meeting, he said, should have as its purpose "the ratification of essential points already agreed to in principle." [10]

It may be observed here that this is valuable cautionary procedure in organizing a business meeting between heads of state. Bickering and risk of failure incident to any international negotiation is tolerable only if the officials engaged do not embody the ultimate sovereignty of their nations. Even between two governments so tightly bound in friendship and cooperation as Great Britain and the United States, preliminary agreement on essentials was necessary before Roosevelt and Churchill met at Argentia. This was the meaning of Roosevelt's instructions to Hopkins for his meeting with Churchill prior to the Conference: "Economic or territorial deals—NO. . . . No talk about war." Chamberlain had failed to obtain such preliminary agreement with Hitler before Munich. Roosevelt failed to obtain preliminary agreement with Stalin before Yalta.

The mistake was not made in 1941. Nomura himself admitted that with regard to Japanese troops in North China there would be "real difficulty." He accurately defined the difficulty. It arose because, as Hull noted:

it was the idea of the Japanese Government that we [the United States government] exercise our good offices in bringing the Chinese and Japanese together leaving China and Japan to reach a direct settlement among themselves whereas the United States Government desired to discuss with Japan the basic terms on which peace was to be concluded.

Coupled with Nomura's admission that Japanese troops in North China constituted a "real difficulty," this meant that Japan would insist on a "peace" with China that would leave Japan in military occupation of part of China, and the United States in entering an agreement with Japan at a Roosevelt-Konoye meeting must consent to Japanese imposition of such a "peace" on China.

Hull answered that in order to exercise good offices between Japan and China, the United States must have the confidence and friendship of the Chinese government before *and after* the event. Nomura thereupon proposed that the whole question of China should be ignored by Roosevelt and Konoye. Were there not, he asked Hull, other questions apart from China which could be disposed of "with a view to tiding over a critical situation?" The absurdity of this Nomura admitted by recalling that his government made withdrawal of its troops from Indo-China dependent on solution of the China Incident. Nomura ended the conversation with a statement that he recognized the reasonableness of Hull's position but had misgivings as to how far his government could go because of "internal political difficulties." Still he assured Hull that Konoye had great courage and was ready to assume great risks.[11]

In following days the Japanese begged for speedy arrangements and at the same time demanded preliminary actions by the United States government that far surpassed what the United States asked. Ambassador Grew in Tokyo was asked by Foreign Minister Toyoda to appeal to his government to take three steps without which Toyoda feared Konoye would meet "serious obstacles" in his efforts to bring about an understanding: 1) no delay in the Roosevelt-Konoye meeting; 2) give up sending tankers to Russia by the Pacific route at least pending the outcome of the meeting; 3) also pending the meeting, suspend the order freezing Japanese assets in the United States. Grew answered that he was "under no illusion" that his government would agree to the "preposterous requests" in points (2) and (3).[12] And indeed this effort showed that the "moderate" Konoye government expected the United States to abandon aid to Russia and resume aid to Japan while the Japanese government should make no preliminary concessions and receive a blank check for the Roosevelt-Konoye meeting.

That it was a blank check the Japanese required is supported by evidence of Konoye himself in his memoirs, which were uncovered in 1945. There Konoye revealed that in August, 1941, when he told Army leaders of his desire to meet Roosevelt, the militarists made him promise that if Roosevelt failed to "understand" Japan, and was resolved to go on with his present policy, Konoye would quit the meeting determined to "make war on the United States." [13]

Although this was not known by Hull at the time, it justified his suspicion that Japan would accept no agreement short of consent to the past and future program of the Japanese extremists. Points (2) and (3) of Toyoda's message to Grew repeated the pattern of the conversations earlier in the year: when the Japanese found the United States willing to discuss a given plan for agreement, they stiffened their terms. Furthermore, rumors in the American press raised an outcry against appeasement of Japan. This, if nothing else, imposed caution on the administration.

## Ideal Principles and Their Practical Application

Still Roosevelt and Hull did not close the door. On September 3, Nomura went to the White House for the answer to Konoye's letter of August 28. The President, in Secretary Hull's presence, assured Konoye that the United States government was prepared to proceed "as rapidly as possible" towards completion of arrangements for a meeting. But he had to take account of developments in the United States as well as Japan, and he could not avoid recognizing that some quarters in Japan raised obstacles to successful collaboration. Therefore he felt it necessary to suggest that:

we take precaution, toward ensuring that our proposed meeting shall prove a success, by endeavoring to enter immediately upon preliminary discussion of the fundamental and essential questions on which we seek agreement. The questions which I have in mind for such preliminary discussions involve *practical application* of the principles fundamental to achievement and maintenance of peace. . . .

The President also made an oral statement to Nomura reiterating the four fundamental principles originally offered by Hull on April 16. Adherence to courses in harmony with these principles, the President said, would bring Japan more benefit than any other course, and only upon the basis of such principles could an agreement be reached which would be effective. He attempted to pin down the vague assurances Japan had given on August 28:

The Government of the United States understands that [those assurances] exclude any policy which would seek political expansion or the acquisition of economic rights, advantages or preferences by force.

This oral statement also pinned down the practical matters at issue by referring Nomura to the "divergences of view" which "remained unreconciled" when the earlier round of conversations was interrupted in July. Pleas that the United States should "understand" the difficulty of the Japanese government in holding in check its populace and military leaders, Roosevelt answered as follows:

It goes without saying that each Government in reaching decisions on policy must take into account the internal situation in its own country and the attitude of public opinion therein. The Government of Japan will surely recognize that the Government of the United States could not enter into any agreement which would not be in harmony with the principles in which the American people—in fact all nations that prefer peaceful methods to methods of force—believe.[14]

In conversation, Roosevelt and Hull repeatedly emphasized the necessity for Japan to state its position regarding three points at issue: evacuation of Japanese troops from China, nondiscrimination in commerce, and interpretation of Japanese obligations under the Axis alliance. Nomura said Konoye wanted to discuss these points at the meeting with Roosevelt. But it was made clear to Nomura that "several days should be consumed" by the Japanese government before the meeting in "clarifying and stating strongly" its position, and that the Japanese government should also work to educate and organize public opinion in support of the proposals for a peaceful settlement. Nomura was told that after the United States received assurances justifying a meeting, it would discuss the matter with the British, the Chinese, and the Dutch, because there was no other way to establish peace, confidence, and friendliness in the Pacific or to rebuild a suitable economic structure.[15] This meant that Roosevelt would not dispose of the property of other governments in a bilateral agreement with Konoye—an elementary but necessary warning. Secretary Hull during following days gave assurance to the Chinese that the United States would not consider any arrangement that permitted the continuation of aggression in China.

The United States had now restated its position. It had dropped specific references to Indo-China and Thailand. Japanese invasion of southern Indo-China had disrupted the earlier conversations, and Roosevelt had offered neutralization as a solution of the status of those territories. Now in September the American administration by avoiding emphasis of the new aggression that had disrupted the conversations proved once more that it would erect no obstacle to a general settlement with Japan.

## New Escape Clauses

Confusion among the Japanese leaders followed the American offer of September 3. The next day Nomura handed Hull a statement containing a proposed draft agreement in terms quite vague, but he presently withdrew it because it was submitted "without the approval of the Japanese government." In Tokyo on the afternoon of September 5, Konoye invited Grew to a secret meeting that night, but then he withdrew the invitation.[16]

On September 6, Nomura handed Hull a draft proposal from his government. It was riddled with escape clauses. Japan promised not to make any military advance against areas adjoining Indo-China or southward "without any justifiable reason." Another version read that Japan would make no advance to the north. Hull asked repeatedly for clarification but never received it. The interpretation and execution of the Axis alliance by Japan would be "independently decided." Japan would withdraw its armed forces from China in accordance with unspecified agreements between Japan and China. Japan would not restrict the economic activities of the United States in China "so long as pursued on an equitable basis." But the "reciprocal" undertakings of the United States contained no escape clauses. It would be required to stop aid to China; suspend military measures in the Far East and southwestern Pacific, that is, end the defense program in the Philippines, and stop aid to Australia, British possessions, and the NEI; resume exports to Japan, and discontinue the freezing order against Japanese funds, these acts to be reciprocated by Japan; and permit Japanese ships to use the Panama Canal.[17]

Trade arrangements made crystal clear Japanese intentions in China. The United States and Japan would make reciprocal commitments to carry on trade in the southwestern Pacific area on a nondiscriminatory basis and help each other obtain raw materials there. But no such arrangement would be made regarding China: in that country Japan would not restrict United States economic activities "so long as pursued on an equitable basis." The United States had sufficient influence in the southwestern Pacific to obtain raw materials for Japan, therefore Japan installed no escape clause for either government for that area but asked for reciprocity. In China no reciprocity was offered, and the United States was asked to rely on Japanese judgment whether United States economic activities there were "equitable," with an obvious inference that Japan, after establishing "peace" with China, would be in control of all of that country.

The September 6 draft would make the United States help Japan consolidate positions in Asia already won by aggression and abandon present and future victims of Japanese imperialism. The American obligations would be inescapable, while Japanese obligations would be subject to Japanese interpretation of wide-open escape clauses. Furthermore, if the United States accepted this draft it would compromise the program of aid to Britain and Russia as well as abandon aid to China. Japan would exercise a right to decide whether the policy of the United States towards Germany was "offensive." Its demand that American shipments to Vladivostok be stopped had already indicated how this right would be exercised.

If interim shifts of front by the Japanese be disregarded, they had now offered the United States five draft proposals for agreement on the following dates: April 9, May 12, June 15, August 6, and September 6. After the first "unofficial" draft of April 9, each draft required more cooperation by the United States in Japanese aggression than the one preceding.

Hull decided that the Japanese proposals of September 6 "fell short of any possibility of acceptance." He saw only a remote chance of reaching agreement. His "major hope" was to postpone Japan's next advance, which would "probably" bring war in the Pacific.[18] Foreign Minister Toyoda tried to transfer the conversations to Tokyo. Hull objected, but the Japanese nevertheless made important statements originally to Grew in Tokyo, and discrepancies between documents received in Washington from Grew and from Nomura added to the confusion. Several weeks passed before the confusion following Nomura's error in presenting the September 4 draft without approval of his government was straightened out.[19]

On September 22, Toyoda handed Grew the text of basic terms of peace Japan proposed to establish with China. These terms were less acceptable than the list Japan had earlier proposed. In the new terms no limits were named for the "certain areas" of China in which Japan would continue to station troops after "peace." During the summer, Hull had signified willingness to eliminate the question of recognition of Manchuria from the agreement and leave it for later decision. Now Japan installed "Recognition of Manchoukuo" in its list of terms for peace with China. These items, besides repetition of the former requirements that the Japanese puppet government in Nanking be "fused" with the government of Chiang Kai-shek, and the wide-open clause that economic activities of third powers in China would not be restricted by Japan "so long as they are pursued on an equitable basis," made the new terms more unacceptable than ever.[20]

## Grew Proposes "Constructive Conciliation"

The most important comment, during the whole period, on the Roosevelt-Hull conduct of negotiations with Japan was made on September 29 by Ambassador Grew in a report to Secretary Hull. This report raised the question whether there was not a vista open to the Roosevelt administration located somewhere between the road of appeasement and the road of refusal to appease which might end in war. Grew asserted that such a vista existed. He called it "constructive conciliation," and located it between "the method of progressive economic strangulation" of Japan by American sanctions, and the method of "so-called appeasement." Grew rejected appeasement as a possible course. He saw the United States government as choosing "constructive conciliation" as evidenced by its continual willingness to negotiate any issues with Japan. He firmly believed the United States now had the opportunity to stop Japan's expansion without war or an immediate risk of war, and that failure to use the opportunity would face the United States with a greatly increased risk of war.

Grew warned Hull that Japan might deliberately decide on war with the United States in response to American action in the Pacific. He stressed that Japanese reactions could not be measured, nor Japanese actions predicted, by any Western measuring rod. Therein lay the danger of insisting on detailed and satisfactory preliminary commitments from Japan prior to a Roosevelt-Konoye meeting. Such insistence would cause the conversations to drag on until Japanese elements favorable to a rapprochement decided agreement was hopeless and that the United States was only playing for time. The abnormal sensitiveness of the Japanese would bring serious results, probably including "unbridled acts," and danger of war. Konoye would fall and a military dictatorship ready for a head-on collision with the United States would take over. Grew raised the question whether the consequences of a failure to hold the Roosevelt-Konoye meeting would not be worse than a failure of the meeting to achieve complete success. He considered that face value must be placed on confidential statements to him that the Japanese government could not "define its future assurances and commitments more specifically than hitherto stated," because Matsuoka in July, after retiring as Foreign Minister, had told the German Ambassador in detail the course of conversations with the United States, and it was feared that supporters of Matsuoka remaining in the Foreign Office would reveal to the Germans and to Japanese extremists any information that would make the position of the Konoye cabinet untenable.

Nevertheless Grew had been told that Konoye in direct negotiations with President Roosevelt could offer him assurances that "will not fail to satisfy the United States." The truth of this, Grew said, he could not determine. But he did not consider it unlikely because Japan had shown, by entering into formal negotiations with the United States, readiness to make its adherence to the Axis alliance a dead letter.

In conclusion Grew gave his opinion that the United States would not reach its objective by insisting in preliminary conversations that Japan provide "the sort of clear-cut, specific commitments which appear in any final, formal convention or treaty." Confidence must be placed in the good faith of Konoye and his supporters

to mould Japan's future policy upon the basic principles they are ready to accept and then to adopt measures which gradually but loyally implement those principles, with it understood that the United States will implement its own commitments *pari passu* with the steps Japan takes. . . .

This was what Grew meant by "constructive conciliation," and it was, he asserted, the only alternative to wholesale military defeat of Japan. The Ambassador ended by deferring to "the much broader field of view of President Roosevelt and Secretary Hull," and he expressed "full awareness" that his own approach was "limited to the viewpoint of the American Embassy in Japan." [21]

Secretary Hull makes no reference in his *Memoirs* to this significant report. It must engage the attention of anyone attempting to judge the Roosevelt-Hull policy. In the absence of comment by Hull, it may nevertheless be ventured to estimate his and Roosevelt's view of Grew's proposal on the basis of their known actions and general views. Hull in close contact with Roosevelt prepared a comprehensive statement to the Japanese government which he handed to Nomura on October 2. It amounted to an answer to Grew.[22]

Grew's proposal for "constructive conciliation" was vitiated by a basic error of fact. Roosevelt and Hull did not refuse to hold the meeting with Konoye because, as Grew stated in his report, the Japanese failed to provide beforehand "the sort of clear-cut, specific commitments which appear in any final, formal convention or treaty," or because "moderates" in the Japanese government could not "define its future assurances and commitments more specifically than hitherto stated" for fear of pro-German officials. The Japanese government in its communications of September 6 and 22 had satisfied Roosevelt's and Hull's request for preliminary statements of its attitudes and purposes. Roosevelt and Hull refused to hold the meeting with Konoye for a quite different reason, namely, that *the Japanese proposals were unacceptable as a basis for agreement.* They meant nothing else than United States appeasement of Japan, which Grew himself had ruled out as a possible policy for the United States. In fact, they meant more than appeasement, they required United States cooperation with Japan in aggression.

Grew in his report emphasized Japan's agreement to American general principles for peace in the Pacific. He ignored the fact that the practical measures Japan proposed transformed those principles into their opposites. Grew asked Roosevelt and Hull to have faith that the Japanese government would adopt measures which would "gradually but loyally" implement those principles. But Konoye's first step in implementing them was to destroy them and ask the United States to help install opposite principles. If Roosevelt had met Konoye on the basis of the Japanese proposals, he himself would have been guilty of bad faith had he then refused to sign an agreement with Konoye to implement United States cooperation with Japan in aggression.

Postwar investigations of the International Military Tribunal for the Far East have brought to light documentary proof that Grew's belief that the Konoye government could be satisfied short of appeasement was mistaken. That government had adopted in October, 1940, and carried out step by step a program of aggression in which diplomacy was used merely as a weapon alternate to military action to achieve expansion.[23]

## A Set of Contradictions

Hull's worst suspicions of Japan were correct. In his communication to Nomura on October 2 he reiterated the four principles to which Japan claimed to subscribe. He specifically stated that the United States government had no purpose of discussing details. Rather it was the set of contradictions between principles avowed and applications proposed by the Japanese government that caused the difficulty. They were, he said, "a source of disappointment." He pointed them out one by one. He asked for further clarifications of the Japanese proposals:

From what the Japanese Government has so far indicated in regard to its purposes this Government derives the impression that the Japanese Government has in mind a program which would be circumscribed by the imposition of qualifications and exceptions to the actual application of those principles.

If this impression is correct, can the Japanese Government feel that a meeting between the responsible heads of government under such circumstances would be likely to contribute to the advancement of the high purposes which we have mutually had in mind?

Hull ended with strong assurances that the President hoped a meeting with Konoye could be held.[24]

## Wakasugi's "Mistake"

Convincing evidence presently came from the Japanese themselves that it was they who made impossible Grew's "constructive conciliation," that they insisted upon appeasement as the only purpose of a Roosevelt-Konoye meeting. Japanese officials in Tokyo and Washington consumed many hours in explaining to Americans that the October 2 statement mystified them because Hull had not made known precisely what the United States would consider proper bases for a Roosevelt-Konoye meeting. But Ambassador Nomura on October 9 admitted in a conference with officials of the State Department that he himself had noted "some contradictions" of the agreed-upon principles in the Japanese proposals for implementing them. He thereupon made a frank justification of those contradictions:

Mentioning that the Japanese public had suffered the sacrifices of four years of war, the Ambassador said that his Government would *necessarily* have to present to the Japanese people some *reward* for that sacrifice or some *attractive alternative gain.*

The Americans replied that Japan stood to gain more by following a "progressive and constructive program of peace in the entire Pacific than by any other course," but the Japanese showed no comprehension of that alternative.[25]

Nomura was no diplomat, and his inadvertencies of the sort quoted above probably explain his virtual supersedure in November by Kurusu. But he had only put into words what was apparent to Hull if not to Grew: that Japan allowed the United States no alternative to appeasement.

Attempts of other Japanese officials, quite skilled in diplomacy, to plead ignorance of American desires and mystification by the statement of October 2, also broke down. The Minister-Counselor of the Japanese Embassy, Wakasugi, had recently returned from Japan, and, on October 13, in conversation with Under Secretary Welles, he at first repeated the refrain that the Japanese government found it impossible to learn what "in reality" were the desires of the United States. Then Wakasugi not only specified those desires with the greatest clarity, but seemed to promise that the Japanese government would satisfy them. He said the Japanese promise in the draft proposal not to undertake further aggressive action could be made without the qualification "save for justifiable reasons," because that phrase "was entirely unnecessary and could readily be withdrawn." He said the Japanese government would be "entirely willing" to meet the American objection to omitting China from the commitment in favor of commercial equality in the Pacific region. Wakasugi asked whether the United States could not agree to leave to Japan "discretion" in interpreting its obligations under the Axis alliance. He realized a new Cabinet might interpret its obligations differently, but the present one was the only Cabinet which could be set up that would desire to remain at peace with the United States if the United States entered the European war. He said that the Japanese government was "willing to evacuate all of its troops from China." Welles thought he had misunderstood this last statement, but Wakasugi repeated it twice. Welles was furthermore assured that all the "controlling" Japanese Generals and Admirals fully supported the Japanese government in desiring to make a "comprehensive and satisfactory" agreement with the United States.

Wakasugi emphasized to Welles that he spoke "unofficially." But his statements on aggression, trade, and evacuation of China hit the precise points of the chief objections of Hull and Roosevelt to the Japanese proposals of September 6 and 22, and, since he had just returned from Japan, where he had presumably learned the views of his government, his statements to Welles on October 13 demolished the pretense that the Japanese did not understand what the United States "in reality" wanted.

Wakasugi said he believed his government must reach a final decision within twenty-four or forty-eight hours. Grew was informed of Wakasugi's remarkable statements to Welles. On October 15 he talked with the Japanese Vice Minister for Foreign Affairs "off the record," but, as Grew reported to Washington, "along lines largely parallel to" the Wakasugi-Welles conversation on October 13.[26] A day later, October 16, the Konoye cabinet fell and the "Pearl Harbor" government took power with General Hideki Tojo as Premier and Shigenori Togo as Foreign Minister.

Wakasugi promptly changed front. He had appointments with Welles on October 16 and 17, and the Under Secretary took him to Hull for conversations on both days. According to Secretary Hull's memorandum, Wakasugi "sought to keep in harmony with his talks with Under Secretary Welles," but he actually hedged on the main points of evacuating China, nondiscrimination in the whole Pacific, and interpretation of the Axis alliance. The net result was to return the situation to the impasse preceding Wakasugi's strange statements to Welles on October 13. The tone of Hull's memorandum makes obvious the Secretary's impatience with Wakasugi's zigzag. If the October 13 "unofficial" statements meant anything, the new government of Tojo repudiated them. Hull wrote: "The upshot . . . left us with the view that the new Japanese Government would have to speak next and before we had further serious conversations with their representatives here." [27]

The October 13 statements of Wakasugi might have been taken more seriously but for several circumstances. Toyoda had already told Grew on October 10 that because Ambassador Nomura seemed "very fatigued," a diplomat of wide experience would be sent to Washington to "assist" him.[28] This was as much as to say that the existing Japanese delegation in Washington was repudiated. The fall of the Konoye Cabinet was already in sight. Japan was sending large new contingents of troops into Indo-China, building new air bases there, and displacing the Vichy French administrators with Japanese officials. This, as the Japanese government was told, constituted "a complete negation of the spirit and letter of the undertakings which the Japanese Government expresses willingness to assume." [29] Magic intercepts showed that Germany, after Roosevelt's September 11 "shoot on sight" order, applied extreme pressure on the Japanese government. One of Foreign Minister Toyoda's last acts was to send Nomura instructions, amounting to a weak version of German demands, that the United States be warned of trouble with Japan if the United States continued to "attack" the Axis powers.[30]

In the light of these ominous events, Wakasugi's statements to Welles take on the appearance of a mistake arising from the confusion attendant upon the impending fall of Konoye. Far from working for agreement with the United States, the Konoye government in the main was attempting to stave off its overthrow by conceding to the demands of the militarists. The "mistake" is nevertheless an extremely valuable part of the record. First, it proves that the Japanese knew precisely what was necessary to bring about a Roosevelt-Konoye meeting and settlement with the United States. Second, the "mistake" and Japan's draft proposals prove that the Japanese consciously designed the escape clauses in the draft proposals to leave no room for Grew's policy of "constructive conciliation" short of American cooperation to help Japan win the fruits of aggression.

### The Last Chance?

The coming to power of Tojo ended talk of a meeting between Roosevelt and the Japanese Premier. The administration in its efforts to maintain the secrecy of the negotiations, efforts insisted upon by the Japanese who feared the effects of publicity in rousing the militarists,[31] had publicly denied that Prince Konoye had "invited" Roosevelt to a Pacific conference. It was true that the stage of issuing an invitation was never reached. Beard treats the administration's uncommunicativeness as part of its plot to deceive the public by maintaining false "appearances." [32] In his exposition of the "realities" of the affair, Beard declares that Roosevelt and Hull not only pursued the "usual policy" of secrecy, but employed "dilatory" methods. Ambassador Grew's arguments in favor of "constructive conciliation" are Beard's chief evidence in support of his implication that Roosevelt and Hull wanted no reasonable settlement with Japan. But it is noteworthy that after carefully implanting in his reader's mind suspicion that Roosevelt and Hull deliberately rejected a reasonable opportunity for a settlement with Japan, Beard disclaims responsibility for arousing such suspicion by remarking that sufficient documents are not available for judgment. He admits that it is possible to find bases for argument *for*, as well as against Roosevelt's refusal to meet Konoye. Beard excuses his own failure to use the documents that are available because the " 'solution' of this insoluble 'problem' " lay outside the "purposes and limitations" of his book. After calling the Roosevelt-Konoye affair "momentous in the history of American relations with Japan," Beard's evasion of the problem, which would seem to be no more insoluble and is far more adequately documented than most of the problems he claims to solve, is disappointing.[33]

Perhaps Beard had been discouraged by the statement in the Minority Report of the Pearl Harbor Joint Committee, that to go into the issue of the wisdom of the Roosevelt administration in its conduct of relations with Japan,

would involve the committee in the complexities of history extending back more than 50 years and in matters of opinion which cannot be settled by reference to anything as positive and definite as the Constitution, laws, and established administrative practices of the United States government.[34]

Besides, the question was excluded by the terms of the Committee's instructions. But the Committee did not fail to develop information on the subject in order to "understand the questions involved."

Morgenstern, more bold than Beard, examined evidence found by the Committee and other documents, and came to very clear conclusions. "Diplomacy," he writes, "failed because diplomacy was not employed to avert war but to make certain its coming." His chief "evidence" is that administration officials were aware that imposition of economic sanctions against Japan involved a risk that Japan would use force to obtain the raw materials it needed. This is certainly true, but it is a long distance from this to the statement that the administration imposed sanctions *because* the policy contained a risk of war. Morgenstern set out to prove more: that the Roosevelt administration made *certain* that war would result.

Perhaps one example of Morgenstern's interpretations will suffice to illustrate his extreme version of the isolationist thesis regarding the Roosevelt-Konoye meeting. He writes that Hull's statement to Nomura that preliminary terms would be discussed with China, Britain, and the Netherlands "demonstrated unmistakably that this country already had an alliance, admitted or not, with China and the western imperialisms and was conducting its diplomacy much more with the view to protecting their interests than its own." Hull's actual purpose was to assure China, Britain, and the Netherlands that the United States would not betray to Japan their rights or territories. The American policy involved was antiappeasement, which had been proclaimed time and again by Roosevelt and Hull as a policy designed primarily to serve the self-interest of the United States.[35] Incidentally Beard, although he approved Morgenstern's book, found in the documents reason to "put a stop to the vulgar saying: 'The United States was raking British chestnuts out of the fire.' "[36]

It cannot be admitted that with Konoye's fall the last chance of avoiding war with Japan disappeared. If the Roosevelt administration had been willing to support Japan's past and future program of aggression, the Tojo government would very likely have been happy to drop the plan to attack the United States, at least temporarily. The actions of Roosevelt and Hull lead one to assume that they believed the risk of new Japanese aggressions was preferable to a profoundly immoral Far Eastern Munich. History had proved that appeasement was not only immoral but also that aggressors could not be permanently appeased. The most that could have been accomplished by a Far Eastern Munich was to postpone a little longer new Japanese aggressions. This was no temptation for Roosevelt and Hull because it would be more than balanced by the degradation of the American and all free peoples, because it would violate the American commitment in the Lend Lease Act to aid peaceful nations against aggression, and because it was in any case politically impossible: the great majority of the American people long since had given up indifference to immorality in international relations.

# 18.

## Roosevelt and Pearl Harbor

THE FALL OF THE KONOYE GOVERNMENT LED ADMIRAL Stark to send a war warning on October 16, 1941, to Admiral Husband E. Kimmel in command of the Pacific fleet and to Admiral Thomas C. Hart in command of the Asiatic fleet. The first inference in this warning was that war between Japan and Russia was "a strong possibility." But, the warning continued:

Since the United States and Britain are held responsible by Japan for her present desperate situation, there is also a possibility that Japan may attack these two powers. In view of these possibilities, you will take due precautions, including such preparatory deployments as will not disclose strategic intention nor constitute provocative actions against Japan.[1]

This reflected the estimate of Washington authorities that Japan was most likely to attack Russia at the penultimate moment of Hitler's conquest, in like manner as Mussolini had attacked France. The Pacific commanders were given enough information regarding diplomatic developments to lead them to believe that they knew the situation, but not enough to judge it as effectively as the leaders in Washington. Magic intercepts, the best source of information regarding Japanese intentions, were not transmitted to the commanders. Copies went to only nine persons in Washington, including President Roosevelt, Secretaries Hull, Stimson and Knox, General Marshall and Admiral Stark. General Marshall later said this was necessary to guard a military secret of incalculable value.

## *"No Abrupt Change"*

The war warning of October 16 was virtually withdrawn on October 20. General Short was told that tension between the United States and Japan continued, "but no repeat no abrupt change in Japanese foreign policy appears imminent." [2] This reflected an assurance by Konoye to Grew on October 17 that the new Japanese government would not break off the negotiations with the United States but "exert its utmost in continuing [them] to a successful conclusion. . . ." [3]

On October 24, Wakasugi told Welles that he had instructions to inform the United States that his government desired to continue the conversations without delay. He had been told to ask whether the United States had any counterproposals to make to the Japanese proposals of September 27. Welles answered that recent statements of prominent officials of the Japanese government and Army and Navy were not conducive to agreement. He pointed especially to a public statement of a responsible Japanese naval officer that the Japanese Navy was "itching to fight" the United States Navy. The result, Welles said, was "disastrous" in its effect upon American opinion. As for American counterproposals, Welles said it did not seem to him that any were called for. Still, if misunderstandings had arisen because of phraseology in the Japanese proposals of September 27, Hull and he were willing to consider any changes in the phraseology which the Japanese might suggest.

Welles opened up an attractive vista to the Japanese. He said that an agreement on economic principles might be reached first of all. He wondered if the new Japanese cabinet members understood the practical advantages to Japan of the economic policies set forth by Secretary Hull:

Surely . . . they must recognize, if they understood it, how much Japan would profit if, for example, British imperial preferences were abolished and Japan could trade with all the Pacific nations, including Canada, Australia and New Zealand, on the same terms on which England could trade.

Wakasugi did not deny Welles's statement that Japan had prospered and became a great power during the period when its relations with the United States and Britain were amicable, and that Japan had lost by turning to Hitler's sinister slogan of "have and have not nations," and by claiming "economic encirclement."

The next day Grew in Tokyo learned from a "reliable Japanese informant" that the Japanese Emperor, just prior to the fall of Konoye, had in an unprecedented action ordered the Army and Navy leaders to "obey his wishes" that there should be no war with the United States. Tojo was "committed to a policy of attempting to conclude successfully the current Japanese-American conversations." Japanese leaders believed that removal of Japanese troops from China and Indo-China was the chief difficulty, but that even this could be done if the United States did not insist that they be withdrawn "at once." [4] The Americans had time and again assured the Japanese they did not expect "miracles" in the way of immediate withdrawals.

## New Danger Signals

Hull was placed on guard by certain ominous developments. Japan continued to reinforce Manchuria and Indo-China. The Japanese showed extreme urgency in their attitude towards the American conversations. A Magic intercept of a message from Foreign Minister Togo to Nomura dated October 21 showed intransigence:

"Our country has said practically all she can say in the way of expressing of opinions and setting forth our stand. We feel that we have now reached a point where no further positive action can be taken by us except to urge the United States to reconsider her views. . . . We urge, therefore, that, choosing an opportune moment, either you or Wakasugi let it be known to the United States by indirection that our country is not in a position to spend much more time discussing this matter." [5]

Such a signal could not but make the Roosevelt administration wary that Japanese gestures towards reaching an agreement were a blind. Hull warned Nomura on October 28:

"The Japanese Government must know that in whatever direction they might make a rash move, whether south or north, this might well have immediate and incalculable consequences." [6]

The British estimate of probabilities is shown in a request of Ambassador Halifax to Hull, on October 29, that the United States and Britain should notify Japan that they would fight if Japan blockaded Vladivostok or attacked Russia. This revived the attempt of the British at the Atlantic Conference to obtain a commitment from the United States that it would enter the war if Japan attacked a third power. Hull refused. He was only willing to warn Japan that blockade action against Russia "would have to be treated by this country and by Great Britain as the beginning of an unlimited program of conquest by force." Halifax said he would refer the question to his government.[7] This evidently came to nothing, but Hull had already issued a comparable warning to Japan.

Foreign Minister Togo on November 3 sent Saburo Kurusu, former Japanese Ambassador to Germany, to Washington to "assist" Nomura. He had signed the Axis alliance in Berlin. In spite of this, Ambassador Grew saw no reason to believe that Kurusu was "any more friendly to the Nazis than to us." [8]

Grew sent a report to Hull and Welles on November 3 which, as he wrote in his diary, he hoped history would not overlook if war occurred.[9] He did not renew his September 29 proposal that "constructive conciliation" be the policy of the United States. Once more he ruled out appeasement of Japan. But he did give full credit to the sincerity of the Tojo government in "seeking conciliation with the United States." He reasoned that Japanese pro-Axis elements had gained power following the Fall of France. But after the signing of the Axis alliance, Germany's failure to invade Britain and its attack against the Soviet Union, coupled with the strong policy of the United States, had strengthened moderate elements and led the Japanese government to seek conciliation with the United States. If this effort failed, Grew wrote that he foresaw:

a probable swing of the pendulum in Japan once more back to the former Japanese position or even farther. This would lead to what he has described as an all-out, do-or-die attempt, actually risking national hara-kiri, to make Japan impervious to economic embargoes abroad rather than to yield to foreign pressure. It is realized by observers who feel Japanese national temper and psychology from day to day that, beyond peradventure, this contingency not only is possible but is probable.

This turned out to be a correct prediction. But Grew offered no advice as to how the United States might fend off Japan's "do-or-die attempt." It was his opinion that strengthening economic sanctions would not avert war. But he believed the primary question was whether American national interests justified war in case the first line of national defense, diplomacy, failed.[10]

Since appeasement of Japan, including the relaxation of economic sanctions, was ruled out, the only possibility Grew saw for a peaceful solution is found in his assertions that Japanese "moderate elements" were still in power, that the Japanese government actually sought conciliation with the United States.

If Hull could agree with this on November 3, his belief vanished two days later. A Magic intercept of Togo to Nomura read:

"Because of various circumstances, it is absolutely necessary that all arrangements for the signing of this agreement be completed by the 25th of this month. I realize that this is a difficult order, but under the circumstances it is an unavoidable one. Please understand this thoroughly and tackle the problem of saving the Japanese-American relations from falling into a chaotic condition."

Secretary Hull observes in his *Memoirs* that this meant Japan had "already set in motion the wheels of her war machine. . . ." This and other signs Hull read as proof that Japan was turning to new aggressive advances in the South Seas, "including war with the United States if we did not sign the agreement she required." [11]

Grew himself saw similar evidence in the Japanese press. On November 5 he noted in his diary a list of seven demands which the *Japan Times and Advertiser* said the United States should adopt to make "restitution" to Japan. Besides bald versions of demands already made officially by the Japanese government, this one was laid down:

Acknowledge Japan's Co-Prosperity Sphere and leadership of the western Pacific, letting Manchuria, China, Indo-China, Thailand, the Netherlands Indies and other states and protectorates establish their own political and economic relations with Japan without interference of any kind.

This newspaper was known to be the organ of the Japanese Foreign Office. Grew believed that it printed these demands to intimidate American isolationists and pacifists and force the United States to make an agreement on Japan's terms. Considering that the statements of American isolationists, Grew wrote:

are splashed across the front pages of the Japanese press under big headlines, it is no wonder that the Japanese people believe that they represent the majority of American public opinion.

The American Ambassador, who had been consistently more optimistic than leaders in Washington, now wrote:

I have about given up hope of the Washington conversations' making any progress, but if the door can be kept open and a complete breakdown avoided, it may be that we can tide things over until the inevitable crack in Germany and the German Army begins, and then the problem will gradually solve itself. This is about the best we can hope for now.[12]

This remote hope came within one day of possible fulfillment. The "crack" in the German Army was opened a month hence, on December 7, the day the Red Army launched its great counteroffensive in front of Moscow. If that counteroffensive had begun earlier, or if Japan had fixed a later date for the attack on Pearl Harbor, Grew's hope might have been fulfilled.

## To Gain Time

To keep the door open in order to seize the last chance of tiding things over became the purpose of the Roosevelt administration in the last round of conversations with Japan. Hull warned the President and Cabinet on November 7 that "we should be on the lookout for a military attack by Japan anywhere at any time." This led to warning speeches to the public by Secretary Knox and Under Secretary Welles.[13]

But Hull's warning to the Cabinet did not lead to a new warning by authorities in Washington to commanders in the Pacific for two more weeks. Secretary of War Stimson has written that since August, 1941, the General Staff had been developing an important new strategic concept regarding the Philippine Islands.

Formerly the Islands had been regarded as an "unprotected pawn" certain to fall easily to Japan early in a war. But General Douglas MacArthur had been recalled in July to active duty in the United States Army after building up the Philippine Army for the Commonwealth, and he was highly optimistic that his forces could hold the Islands. Also, proponents of air power believed that if a force of the new B-17 heavy bombers, the Flying Fortresses, could be sent to the Philippines, the Islands could be defended and the Japanese could be prevented from moving south through the China Sea. Stimson on October 6 told Hull the Army needed three months to build up the Philippines.[14]

Concentration on the task of building up defenses of the Philippines, as the point were the United States was most likely to be attacked by Japan, evidently preoccupied Washington authorities during the weeks following Hull's warning to the Cabinet. The Secretary of State set out to provide the commodity his colleagues demanded of him—time.

He did this by holding up to the Japanese an attractive picture of the benefits Japan would derive from liberal economic policies and cooperation with the United States to instrument them, and the "position of moral leadership" it would win if it made a liberal settlement with China. Nomura on November 7 handed Hull "new" draft proposals for an agreement. They contained the usual escape clauses. Instead of rejecting them outright, Hull, on November 12, told Nomura that it would be helpful if the Tojo government would confirm the statement Wakasugi made on October 13 to Welles that the Japanese government was willing to omit the escape clauses from its draft proposals.[15]

Three days later Hull handed Nomura the draft of a proposed joint American-Japanese declaration on economic policy. This document was remarkable as evidence that the United States did not merely hold open the door to a settlement with Japan, but offered a specific invitation to the Japanese to enter an era of prosperity as well as peace. President Roosevelt on November 10 had told Nomura that the purpose of the American government was "to do its best in the spirit of fair play to contribute to establishing a basis for peace, stability, and order in the Pacific area." Nations, Roosevelt added, must think "one hundred years ahead," but he also recognized the value of taking into account "actual human existence," and spoke of a *modus vivendi* between Japan and the United States.[16]

Hull's proposed declaration instrumented the President's words. Under it the United States and Japan would cooperate in urging all nations to liberalize their trade policies in order to give all nations an opportunity to secure the commodities each country needed "for the safeguarding and development of its economy." The United States and Japan would each make its "appropriate contribution" towards creation of liberal international relations. As important steps, they would take measures to normalize economic relations between themselves, begin discussions for a reciprocal trade agreement, and apply any defense restrictions on exports to each other in a friendly spirit. Complete economic independence would be restored to China, and in that country as well as the other Pacific areas Japan and the United States would seek no preferential or monopolistic economic rights but urge programs of economic development with full and equal opportunity for all outside nations to participate in them.

Hull told Nomura that this economic declaration was subject to agreement on other points involved in a peaceful settlement.[17] By making a constructive and detailed proposal to solve the economic problem which the Japanese claimed justified their policy of military aggression, Hull took the longest step possible towards meeting Japan half way. Besides this, his suggestion that the October 13 statements of Wakasugi be confirmed exploited to the utmost the only constructive proposal by Japan which could be found in the record.

### Kurusu

Kurusu arrived in Washington on November 17 and was immediately presented to Hull and Roosevelt. Hull distrusted him and was convinced that he knew the plans of his government and played a double role of trying to press the United States to accept Japan's terms or, failing that, would try to lull the administration with talk until Japan was ready to strike. An oral statement to Hull by Nomura ignored the request that Wakasugi's October 13 statements be confirmed. An "explanation" declared that the escape clauses in the Japanese draft proposals for an agreement were used

only in order to express the qualification which is due to and necessary for a sovereign state and were not intended to limit or narrow
down in any way the peaceful intentions of the Japanese Government.[18]

This was very different from Wakasugi's offer to withdraw the
clauses.

The President told Kurusu that the policy of the United States
in relation to Germany was one of self-defense. Kurusu said Germany had not "up to this time" asked Japan to fight; that Japan
was serving "a desirable purpose" without fighting. This evidently
meant that Japan was keeping large bodies of Soviet troops and
large portions of the British and American Navies diverted from
Europe and the Atlantic. The President and Hull found it necessary to explain that not the United States but Japan was the aggressor in the Pacific. Kurusu said he was not familiar with commercial policy and had not examined Hull's proposal on that
issue. He repeated the perennial Japanese complaint that troops
could not be withdrawn from China "at once." The President in
turn repeated the American answer that "the question ought to
be worked out in a fair way considering all of the circumstances.
. . ." And he promised that "at a suitable stage," after Pacific questions had been determined, the United States might bring Japan
and China together to settle remaining questions or details.[19]

### "East Wind Rain"

Secretary Hull wrote in his *Memoirs* that the situation now
"could not have been more tense." The day before Kurusu arrived,
a Magic intercept from Togo to Nomura rejected Nomura's suggestion that the Japanese government ought to "wait and see what
turn the war takes and remain patient." Togo replied that he was
"awfully sorry to say that the situation renders this out of the
question. I set the deadline for the solution of these negotiations
. . . and there will be no change." That deadline, November 25,
was a week off. Nomura grasped at the President's mention on
November 10 of a *modus vivendi* between Japan and the United
States. In an intercepted message to Tokyo on November 19,
Nomura stated: "I think that it would be better to fix up a temporary 'truce' now in the spirit of 'give and take' and make this

the prelude to greater achievements to come later." Tokyo answered on November 20: "Under the circumstances here, we regret that the plan suggested by you . . . would not suffice for saving the present situation." [20]

This interchange demonstrated two things about the *modus vivendi,* which was presently discussed in Washington: that even the "moderate" Nomura meant it to be preliminary not to peace but to "greater achievements," that is, conquest; and that his government was not interested in a truce which would require postponement of the attacks it had planned. If one speaks of the realities of the situation, as they were exposed to Roosevelt and Hull in the intercepted Japanese messages, it was Japan that issued an ultimatum, including demands, a deadline, and threat of aggression if the demands were not met in the specified time; and for the United States it was, in Hull's words, "a case of signing on the dotted line or taking the consequences." [21]

Ambassador Grew, on the same day that Kurusu arrived in Washington, sent Hull another warning of "the need to guard against sudden Japanese naval or military actions in such areas as are not now involved in the Chinese theater of operations." He said that the intelligence activities of his Embassy were practically restricted to "what could be seen with the naked eye," and that Washington must not depend upon him for any advance information. Troop dispositions, however, indicated new operations either in the southwest Pacific, or Siberia, or both.[22] Actually of course the Japanese were organizing the raiding force that attacked Pearl Harbor, as well as other forces designated for points in the southwest Pacific, including the Philippines. But it is notable that Grew in Tokyo evidently saw no reason to warn Washington against more than the "normal" targets of Japan: the southwest Pacific and Siberia.

Nor did Magic intercepts give the administration leaders a more accurate picture of Japanese military intentions. The most specific intercept was the famous "east wind rain" message of November 19 from Tokyo to the Japanese Embassy in Washington. In it a complete breakdown of the conversations was foreseen, and a code for future use was designated:

In case of emergency *(danger of cutting off our diplomatic relations),* and the cutting off of international communications, the following warning will be added in the middle of the daily Japanese language short wave news broadcast:

(1) In case of Japan-U.S. relations *in danger:* Higashi No Kazeame [east wind rain].

(2) Japan-U.S.S.R. relations: Kitanokaze Kumori [north wind cloudy].

(3) Japan-British relations: Nishi No Kaze Hare [west wind clear].[23]

The prevailing expectation in Washington was that the Japanese would move into Thailand and southward towards Malaya and the NEI, with a possible attack against the Philippines to protect their flank; or, less likely than the southward move, they might move against Siberia. The words italicized in the message quoted above indicate that the code was to be used in a situation amounting to less than a Japanese surprise attack against one or more of the three great powers, that is, *danger,* not certainty, that *diplomatic relations* would end. In another message on the same day, Tokyo warned that if relations with the United States were *"becoming dangerous,"* the word "Higashi" would be used at the beginning and end of Japan's intelligence broadcast." [24]

It may be conjectured that the Japanese government used such "mild" terms out of caution, not wishing to reveal its actual plans in any message sent abroad. Furthermore, Admiral T. S. Wilkinson, Director of Naval Intelligence, believed that the Germans knew in October, 1941, that the United States had solved the Japanese code and had warned the Japanese government.[25] It would be an obvious ruse of the Japanese to send plausible but misleading information in the useless code. If Washington officials were suspicious that the Japanese knew their code was broken, they would not accept intercepts at face value.

It seems doubtful that one may fairly base judgments of the actions of the Roosevelt administration upon the premise that the Magic intercepts gave leading officials accurate foreknowledge of Japanese actions. Not only was there no reference in the intercepts to an impending Japanese attack upon any American territory, but the intercepts were probably read with considerable skepticism. Responsible officials in Washington could be expected to rely chiefly on known Japanese military and naval movements and an estimate of "logical" probabilities. Both pointed to Japanese attack upon the Philippines as the most extreme probability, and Magic intercepts did not contradict this estimate.

The chief item used by Morgenstern to support the isolationist thesis that Washington officials knew beforehand Pearl Harbor would be attacked is a series of intercepts beginning September 24, 1941, of messages between Tokyo and the Japanese Consul General in Honolulu. These messages conveyed the anxiety of Tokyo for data regarding the exact locations of warships in Pearl Harbor, and the reports of the Consul General containing full information. Morgenstern neglects to mention that such information was well within the requirements of a Japanese plan of sabotage by Japanese agents. The authorities at Pearl Harbor were prepared against that danger. But Morgenstern himself does not claim to find in any message prior to one dated 7:22 P.M., December 6, and another of a few hours later, 12:42 A.M., December 7, material that "gave away" the secret of a bombing raid. In these messages the Consul General *for the first time* spoke of air defenses at Hawaii and observed: "I imagine that in all probability there is considerable opportunity left to take advantage for a surprise attack. . . ." Morgenstern then comments that after a December 4 intercept of an "east wind rain" execute message, and the long series of Japanese messages from Honolulu to Tokyo, "there could be no question where the attack would come."

This slurs over his own admission that, not the "long series of messages," but only those sent within the last twelve hours before the Japanese planes appeared over Pearl Harbor at dawn on December 7 actually pointed to raiding planes rather than sabotage. The fact that the two messages which did expose the secret were not decoded until December 8, Morgenstern calls "Washington's excuse. . . ." But Morgenstern himself makes this excuse seem extremely plausible. He describes how the "give-away" messages were intercepted in San Francisco and copies mailed to Washington. Hearing of this, Army Signal Intelligence Service ordered the messages to be sent to Washington on a new teletype machine which had been installed that day. When the messages arrived in Washington, translators were called to night duty. But the final and very lengthy Japanese diplomatic message was then being intercepted, and the translators worked on it instead. Other messages less indicative of Japanese attack were processed even more slowly.[26]

Such is the best evidence Morgenstern can find that for Washington officials "there could be no question where the attack would come," with its implication that commanders at Pearl Harbor were not ordered to shift from preparations against sabotage to preparations against air attack because Roosevelt, Hull, Stimson, Knox, Marshall, and Stark preferred the more serious loss of life and damage to the fleet that would result from mistaken preparations. For such a terrible implication, Morgenstern at the crucial point can do no better than verify the plain reason why Washington officials did not receive the "give-away" messages in time, and call the reason an "excuse."

## The Wrong Foot

Another grave accusation of the isolationists is that Roosevelt and Hull so conducted negotiations with Kurusu as to coerce the Japanese into attacking the United States. The assumption is made that if the United States refused to make an agreement with Japan, this amounted to coercion of the Japanese and created a situation in which not the Japanese but Roosevelt and Hull were responsible for the Japanese attack that followed. A necessary corollary of the argument is that Kurusu and the Tojo government did in fact "urgently desire" not merely *an* agreement with the United States but one that should have been accepted by Hull and Roosevelt. Charles A. Beard proves at great length that the Japanese did "urgently desire" *an* agreement, which was doubtless true. If the Tojo government could gain the objectives of its aggressive program with the cooperation of the United States, it is difficult to believe that sheer quixoticism would have led it to reject such an arrangement and risk defeat in war instead. Even this, however, it may be noted in passing, was the choice of Mussolini when France and Britain offered him his price if he would take it without war.

Beard finds in a Japanese proposal on November 20 for a "truce" or *"modus vivendi"* an opportunity for Hull, knowing that it was Japan's "last effort," that the American Army and Navy needed time for preparations, and that a two-front war should "if humanly possible" be avoided, to use "supreme diplomatic ingenuity," and "supreme statesmanship" to "keep conversations going. . . ." Hull on November 26 rejected the Japanese proposal. In Beard's view, Hull "for reasons which are nowhere explicit" failed the supreme test of his career and answered the Japanese with what Beard calls "an ultimative notice." [27]

It is now possible to state certain facts of the situation which were not available to Beard. They suggest that he was too hasty in condemning Hull's statesmanship without sufficient data regarding the possibility that it was Japanese statesmanship, or lack of it, that was responsible for the failure of diplomacy and outbreak of war. After the war, the International Military Tribunal for the Far East found in the Japanese archives the story of Japanese purposes and plans. On November 5, an Imperial Conference decided that if the United States did not accept Japan's terms by November 25 (later extended to November 29), Japan would attack the United States. On November 10, the task force which had been organized and trained to bomb Pearl Harbor was ordered to the Kurile Islands and the date of December 7 was fixed for the attack. On November 22, the task force was ordered to proceed from the Kuriles to Hawaii. These actions were taken *before Hull answered Japan's "last offer" of November 20*. Foreign Minister Togo described the Japanese terms of November 20 as an "ultimatum." [28]

In short, Beard's mistake is that he puts the shoe on the wrong foot. Hull was incapable of issuing an "ultimative notice" to the Japanese after November 20 for the reason that Japan had already issued an ultimatum to the United States on that date, and proceeded to carry out its military threat within two days, before Hull answered its diplomatic threat. Beard would make the Roosevelt administration appear guilty of an aggression in diplomacy which he believes "explains," if it does not excuse, the subsequent Japanese aggression at Pearl Harbor. Actually it was Japan that was guilty of diplomatic as well as military aggression against the United States. Hull knew from Magic intercepts that the Japanese proposals of November 20 constituted an ultimatum involving demands, a deadline, and threat of attack. The only thing he did not know was that the attack was directed at Pearl Harbor or any American territory.

## The Modus Vivendi

The Japanese on November 20 offered a draft proposal for a "temporary agreement." In the light of the rejection by the Japanese government, on November 19, of Nomura's suggestion in favor of such an agreement, this proposal must be regarded as the sheerest of hypocrisies designed to occupy the time while the Japanese task force proceeded to Hawaii. Two of the chief issues on which the United States desired settlement, namely, Japan's obligation under the Axis alliance, and economic policy in China and the Pacific regions, were left for later consideration. On remaining issues, Japan offered to make one concession, withdrawal of Japanese troops from southern to northern Indo-China, in return for United States cooperation with Japan in securing the fruits of aggression in China. Japan asked the United States to stop giving aid to China and to restore economic relations with Japan, including delivery to Japan of a required quantity of oil, while Japan made "peace" with China. Kurusu had admitted to Hull that "peace" with China would involve the stationing of Japanese troops there for an indefinite period. Besides providing Japan with American oil to help it impose its will on China, the United States was asked to "cooperate" with Japan in obtaining for it oil and other materials in the NEI. Japan would promise to make no armed movement southward, but offered no guaranty against aggression northward.[29]

Hull considered that the proposals called for "virtually a surrender" by the United States. He asked Kurusu and Nomura, as he later wrote:

what they thought would be the public reaction in the United States if we were to announce tomorrow that we had decided to discontinue aid to Great Britain. There was no reply. "In the minds of the American people," I continued, "the purposes underlying our aid to China are the same as the purposes underlying aid to Great Britain. . . ."[30]

Hull regarded the situation as virtually hopeless. But the military leaders pleaded with him for more time, and therefore Hull and State Department officials sought desperately to work out some counterproposal to keep the conversations going. For a few days a three-months' *modus vivendi* was considered. It is noteworthy that it was while Hull worked on this scheme, that the Japanese task force was ordered on November 22 to proceed eastward through the north Pacific to reach Hawaii by December 7. No inkling of this reached American observers or officials in Washington, but ominous movements of Japanese forces into positions where they were poised for attacks against Thailand, Malaya, the NEI, and possibly the Philippines or Guam, were known in detail. On November 24, Army and Navy commanders in the Pacific were warned that a Japanese "surprise aggressive movement in any direction including an attack on the Philippines or Guam is a possibility." [31] This was interpreted in Hawaii to require no change in preparations against sabotage as the chief danger.

President Roosevelt, Secretary of the Treasury Morgenthau, and other officials helped Hull explore the possibility of a *modus vivendi*, and he consulted the representatives of Great Britain, China, the Netherlands, and Australia. A Magic intercept from Tokyo to Kurusu and Nomura on November 22 extended the deadline from November 25 to 29. One phrase in it provides the first reason why Hull in the end decided not to make a counterproposal for a *modus vivendi*. The Japanese Ambassadors were instructed: "Stick to our fixed policy. . . ." This could only mean that nothing but complete American surrender to the Japanese proposals would satisfy Tojo. It confirmed Hull's belief that no arrangement that the United States could accept would be acceptable to Japan. The intercepted message ended: "This time we mean it, that the dead line absolutely cannot be changed. After that things are automatically going to happen." [32]

The second reason why Hull decided against the *modus vivendi* is that the government of China objected to it and obtained wide support for its objection, including that of Churchill. The final American draft of the *modus vivendi* called for mutual pledges that the United States and Japan would not advance in the Pacific area by force or threat of force; Japan would withdraw its troops from southern Indo-China, and also reduce its forces in northern Indo-China to 25,000—a number thought to preclude a campaign to close the Burma Road; the United States would allow limited quantities of American oil, cotton, and other commodities to go to Japan and it would buy Japanese goods; the United States would urge Britain, Australia, and the Netherlands to resume trade similarly with Japan; and the United States affirmed its fundamental position that any settlement between Japan and China must be based upon the principles of "peace, law, order, and justice." Attached to this three-months' *modus vivendi* was a ten-point proposal for a permanent agreement.[33]

The *modus vivendi* drawn up by Hull meant temporary appeasement of Japan insofar as it would give temporary United States approval to Japanese conquests and relax the economic sanctions which the United States, Britain, Australia and the Netherlands had imposed against Japan during preceding months. The plan must be regarded as a product of the desperation of the Roosevelt administration in its fight for time. Had it been offered to Japan, it would have been a violation of the administration's principle of no compromise with aggression.

Only agreement by China, the government which would be the chief victim of this appeasement, that the time which might be gained would be worth the sacrifice, would have justified such an offer to Japan. China refused to agree. Churchill supported the Chinese view. After hectic discussions, the decision was reached on the night of November 25 to make no counterproposal of a *modus vivendi* but to answer the Japanese only with the ten-point proposal for a permanent settlement.[34]

## On the Rock of Principle

In this decision the Roosevelt administration met the supreme test of its statesmanship in service of the policy of collective security against aggression. Beard's statement that the decision was made "for reasons which are nowhere explicit"[35] is nonsense; Beard himself recites the evidence that the Chinese government violently opposed the *modus vivendi*. He ignores another contributing factor, that is, the futility of offering to Japan, in the face of the intercepted instructions to the Ambassadors to "stick to our fixed policy," an American *modus vivendi* which would have required Japan to retreat from its "fixed policy," especially in the matter of the number of troops to be left in northern Indo-China. Beard does not wish to admit that the one thing which might have justified temporary appeasement of Japan was the consent of China. The Roosevelt administration refused to make a deal with Japan affecting China's fate without its consent. It refused to ignore the rights of China as Chamberlain had ignored those of Czechoslovakia at Munich.

On the rock of this principle, the last possibility of Roosevelt and Hull attempting to postpone the deadline in Japan's ultimatum collapsed. Actually, no such possibility existed. But the administration believed that a possibility still existed that Japan would only attack non-American territory, leaving room for a choice by the United States whether it should enter the war.

No one but an absolute pacifist would argue that the danger of war is a greater evil than violation of principle. It must be concluded that the isolationist thesis involves denunciation of the Roosevelt-Hull decision against the *modus vivendi* because of the nature of the principle involved. The isolationist believes that appeasement of Japan without China's consent violated no principle worth a risk of war. The internationalist must believe that the principle did justify a risk of war. In short, subjective and *a priori* attitudes ultimately determine judgment of the Roosevelt-Hull policy. If an observer can be imagined to exist who is "neutral" as between the attitudes of isolationists and internationalists, he might conclude that it did not matter whether or not the Roosevelt administration offered the *modus vivendi* because the Japanese government was certain to reject it.

## A Third Choice?

By means of innuendos rather than overt statement, Beard implies that the Roosevelt administration had a third choice besides appeasement or refusal to appease, and took it: war. He combs the record to find "war-like" statements of the leaders in Washington, and presents them in sinister array entirely out of context. The President and his Cabinet on November 25, Beard writes, "discussed war, not prospects of peace. . . ." In Beard's vocabulary, discussion of war is synonymous with a desire for war. Secretary Stimson wrote in his diary regarding a meeting of the "War Council" with Roosevelt on November 25, which was attended by him and Hull, Knox, Marshall, and Stark, that Roosevelt brought up the likelihood that the Japanese, notorious for surprise attacks, would attack the United States within two days:

and the question was what we should do. The question was how we should maneuver them into the position of firing the first shot without allowing too much danger to ourselves. It was a difficult proposition.

Beard quotes this and Stimson's later amplification to the Joint Congressional Committee:

In spite of the risk involved, however, in letting the Japanese fire the first shot, we realized that in order to have the full support of the American people it was desirable to make sure that the Japanese be the ones to do this so that there should remain no doubt in anyone's mind as to who were the aggressors.

These, and many variations of the theme in discussions in Washington, Beard assembles to suggest that the administration wanted war with Japan. He entitles his final chapter, dealing with the outbreak of war: "Maneuvering the Japanese into Firing the First Shot." [36]

The part of the Japanese government in maneuvering itself into firing the first shot is not discussed by Beard. The situation as he describes it leads a reader to believe that it was the United States that took the initiative for war during the weeks preceding December 7, while Japan was coerced into beginning a war it had sought to avoid. Stimson's word "maneuver" is magnified out of all relation to the actual position of the two governments in which Japan, of course, exercised the initiative and the United States was forced into a war it had sought to avoid. After creating suspicion in the reader's mind that Stimson and the other leaders knew that the Japanese intended to attack Pearl Harbor, and that they wanted the attack to occur, Beard makes Stimson's use of the word "maneuver" appear to have been an affirmation of the administration's knowledge and desire. But, as has been shown, the administration thought exclusively in terms of a Japanese movement southward. The question was whether the President should ask Congress for a declaration of war *prior* to a Japanese attack on the Philippines or Guam, in order to avoid giving Japan the advantage of a surprise attack, or wait until Japan attacked United States territory, that is, "maneuver" Japan into firing the first shot. Despite much discussion, no final decision to ask Congress for a declaration of war was made. The other course, waiting while Japan might attack the United States, was a "maneuver" only in the sense that it involved avoidance of any action that would make the United States even *seem* to provoke or justify an attack by Japan. Whereas Beard makes the word appear to mean that the administration took positive actions to coerce the Japanese into attacking, it actually meant that the United States should do nothing that would give Japan an excuse for war.

## The Southward Expedition

Beard calls the United States reply on November 26 to the Japanese proposal of November 20 an "ultimative notice." Morgenstern calls it more simply an "ultimatum." [37] The Minority Report of the Joint Congressional Committee declares that Japan "treated" the answer "as an ultimatum," and that Hull on November 28, if not on November 26, knew that it would so treat it. [38] Dramatic proof came on November 25 that it was Japan that had not only issued an ultimatum on November 20 but proceeded to carry out its new program of aggression without waiting for an answer from the United States. On the afternoon of the 25th, intelligence reports to Secretary Stimson stated that five Japanese divisions were moving southwards from Shantung and Shansi towards Indo-China or points beyond. [39] If more evidence were needed by the administration that the Japanese government had no intention of accepting any *modus vivendi* or any arrangement that would inhibit its program of conquest, this provided it. The President and Hull were sent copies of the report. Morgenstern avoids assessing this intelligence report at its face value by noting that on the next day, when Hull discussed with Stimson his decision to reject the *modus vivendi,* he "did not refer to the Japanese troop movement." Morgenstern notes that when the President on the 26th heard of the troop movement from Stimson, he said it "changed the whole situation, because it was an evidence of bad faith on the part of the Japanese. . . ." But, writes Morgenstern, the Hull answer to Japan that day had already "changed the whole situation." [40]

The United States was actually incapable of "changing the whole situation" no matter what it did short of an attack against Japan, and even this in the circumstances would have been an offensive action only on the level of tactics: Japan had already seized the initiative of the offensive on the higher level of strategy. The Japanese aggressive movement southward was obviously launched well before the Japanese government expected any reply to its proposal of a *modus vivendi*. News of it in Washington merely *confirmed* one of the premises upon which the decision was made to reject the *modus vivendi:* that Japan acted in bad faith. Beyond this, it is clear now that Japan was willing to expose its bad faith by moving an expedition southward in plain view because it served as a screen for its more stunning act of bad faith in sending the expedition to Pearl Harbor.

Considering the scope of Japanese bad faith, what was hidden from Washington as well as what was exposed, one may call suspicion of Japan, which was the fundamental source of Chinese and all other opposition to the *modus vivendi,* the highest statesmanship. Had the *modus vivendi* been accepted, the lowering of guard and injury to morale among all anti-Axis peoples and governments would have invited disaster much more severe than actually occurred. Japan in its diplomacy and its military actions had already launched new aggressions against every Pacific power before the United States had an opportunity to accept or reject the *modus vivendi.* To search in such a situation for ignorance among Washington officials of the full scope of Japanese aggression in order to fix war guilt on them is ludicrous, especially in view of the charge by the same critics that Washington officials should have been more suspicious than they were of Japanese intentions at Pearl Harbor.

Even if Hull's November 26 answer to Japan had been an ultimatum, it would have been a nullity because Japan had issued one earlier and was acting on it. While it is conceivable that the orders to the Pearl Harbor expedition, and even the southward expedition, could have been rescinded during the days that remained prior to December 7, it is still true that the very act of sending those expeditions in the directions of their respective targets while "negotiations" proceeded in Washington constituted a threat of war signifying not merely bad faith but that those negotiations took place under the sanction of a Japanese ultimatum.

## The Message of November 26

Hull's answer on November 26 was a refusal to surrender to the Japanese ultimatum. This was implicit in his rejection of the Japanese proposal for a *modus vivendi.* But he did not entirely reject that proposal, and he offered Japan a draft plan for an agreement on all points at issue as a basis for continued negotiations. This took away from his answer all character of a challenge to Japan to carry out its threat of war. Hull did not expect the Japanese government to accept his constructive proposal for an agreement, and he warned the armed service chiefs that Japan could be expected now to attack, but this was not, as the isolationists charge, proof that he regarded his answer as an "ultimatum." It was proof that he judged correctly that Japan would attack if the United States did not entirely surrender to Japan's ultimatum.

Hull's draft proposal for an American-Japanese agreement contained ten points. None of them was unacceptable or disadvantageous to a Japanese government mindful of the real interests of Japan: 1) a multilateral nonaggression pact among the governments principally concerned in the Pacific; 2) an agreement among the governments principally interested to respect the territorial integrity of Indo-China and equality of economic opportunity in that country; 3) no support of any Chinese government except the national government of Chiang Kai-shek; 4) relinquishment of extraterritorial rights in China by the United States as well as all other powers; 5) a liberal trade agreement between the United States and Japan; 6) mutual removal of freezing measures; 7) stabilization of currency values between the dollar and the yen; 8) an agreement that neither country would interpret an agreement with a third country in a way that would conflict with the fundamental purpose of establishing peace; 9) both governments would use their influence to lead other governments to accept and carry out the principles of this American-Japanese agreement; 10) Japan would withdraw its forces from China and Indo-China.

This draft proposal was accompanied by an explanation that the United States government regarded "some" but not all of the points in the Japanese *modus vivendi* of November 20 as in conflict with the fundamental principles to which each government had committed itself. The American draft proposal was not offered as the only terms of agreement the United States was willing to accept. Hull explained to Nomura and Kurusu that it was offered as *"one practical exemplification of a program which this Government envisages as something to be worked out during our further conversations."* [41]

To sum up: the American answer to Japan on November 26 did not reject *all* of the terms of Japan's proposed *modus vivendi;* the American draft proposal was not offered as the *only* terms of agreement the United States would accept; the United States made *no demands* upon Japan; the American draft proposal contained many offers that the Japanese had often admitted were advantageous to Japan because they would satisfy Japanese demands for security and prosperity—most significantly, an offer to end United States economic sanctions against Japan; it named *no deadline* for an answer by Japan; it contained *no threat of force or war* or other penalty if Japan refused to accept the American proposal; it specifically *invited* Japan to *continue negotiations;* it *promised to consider* new Japanese proposals, in the usual manner of a peaceful power, in the course of further negotiations.

To call such a proposal an "ultimatum" or an "ultimative notice" is to murder the meaning of the word. If, as the Minority Report asserts, the Japanese war lords "treated" this answer "as an ultimatum," evidence is available, in Togo's description of the Japanese terms of November 20 as an ultimatum, which proves that he, at least, had for some days already accepted the fact which American isolationists reject: that to the Japanese government belonged the responsibility for war that accrues to a government guilty of issuing an ultimatum. When the Japanese Foreign Minister admits responsibility, it seems excessive for Americans to find the Japanese innocent and their own government guilty.

## The War Warnings of November 27

Having rejected the Japanese ultimatum, and expecting nothing from his own conciliatory offer, Secretary Hull told the heads of the Army and Navy that in his opinion the Japanese were "likely to break out at any time with new acts of conquest, and that the matter of safeguarding our national security was in the hands of the Army and Navy." [42] War warnings were accordingly sent out on November 27 from Washington to the commanders in the Pacific. Judgment of responsibility for the unpreparedness of the forces at Pearl Harbor is of concern in this book only because the isolationist criticism of the conduct of foreign relations by the Roosevelt administration includes a heavy implication that it deliberately maximized the disaster for purposes of inciting the American people to war. The evidence gathered by the Joint Congressional Committee shows that no "plot," but a complex of misunderstandings, errors in judgment, and inadequate liaison among commanders in the field, and between them and officials in Washington, adequately explain the disaster. The Majority Report of the Committee summarized its findings as follows:

The evidence before the Committee reflects an unusual number of instances where military officers in high positions of responsibility interpreted orders, intelligence, and other information and arrived at opposite conclusions at a time when it was imperative for them to estimate the situation and to arrive at identical conclusions.

Admiral Kimmel [in the war warning of November 27] was ordered to execute an *appropriate defensive deployment* [which would have taken the Fleet out of Pearl Harbor]. Everyone in Washington in testifying before the committee seems reasonably certain as to just what this meant; Admiral Kimmel did not feel that it required his doing anything greatly beyond what he had already done, even though he knew that Washington knew what he had previously done. In using [on November 27] the words "this dispatch is to be considered a war warning" everyone in Washington felt the commander in chief [Kimmel] would be sharply, incisively, and emphatically warned of war; Admiral Kimmel said he had construed all the messages he had received previously as *war warnings*. Everyone in Washington felt that upon advising Hawaii [beginning December 3] the Japanese were destroying their codes it would be understood as meaning "war in any man's language;" Admiral Kimmel said that he did not consider this intelligence of any vital importance when he received it.

The War Department warned General Short [on November 27] that hostilities were possible at any moment, meaning armed hostilities; General Short felt that sabotage was one form of hostilities and instituted an alert against sabotage only. Washington ordered the commanding general to undertake [air] reconnaissance; the latter took for granted that the War Department had made a mistake and proceeded in effect to ignore the order on the basis of this assumption. General Short was instructed to report the measures taken by him pursuant to departmental orders. He replied that his department was alerted against sabotage and that he had effected liaison with the Navy; the Director of War Plans saw the reply and took for granted the commanding general was replying to a different warning concerning subversive activities, at the same time suggesting that some of his subordinates may have interpreted the reply to mean that, in effecting liaison with the Navy, General Short had necessarily carried out the order to conduct reconnaissance.

General Short said he thought the order given Admiral Kimmel to execute a defensive deployment necessarily required distant reconnaissance; the commander in chief did not so interpret the order. Admiral Kimmel saw the warning General Short received and took for granted the Army would be on a full [anti-air raid] alert designed to protect the fleet base.

This well-nigh incredible lack of mutual understanding between the two commanders in Hawaii is the central explanation of the Pearl Harbor disaster. But the Majority Report places secondary responsibility upon the highest officials in Washington, who allowed their subordinates in Hawaii to fail to carry out the intended purposes of the orders they issued:

As has been seen, an objective consideration of the warnings received by the Hawaiian commanders indicates they were adequate. But on the basis of the disaster, in the future *adequacy* cannot be regarded as sufficient. Dispatches must be unmistakably clear, forthright, and devoid of any conceivable ambiguity.[43]

The Investigating Committee was composed of ten members, four of them Republicans and the rest Democrats. Eight members signed the Majority Report. One of the eight, Representative Frank B. Keefe of Wisconsin, submitted "Additional Views." He summarized his views as follows:

I think it is true that none of the military chiefs at Washington or Hawaii thought the attack would come at Pearl Harbor. I conclude that they all thought it would come first in the Far East. Obviously this was a fatal mistake, and I agree that the mistake was without proper justification and that neither Hawaii nor Washington should be excused from criticism for having made it. I think that the facts in this record clearly demonstrate that Hawaii was always the No. 1 point of danger and that both Washington and Hawaii should have known it at all times and acted accordingly. Consequently I agree that the high command in Hawaii was subject to criticism for concluding that Hawaii was not in danger. However, I must insist that the same criticism with the same force and scope should apply to the high command in Washington. It is in this respect that I think the tenor of the committee report may be subject to some criticism.[44]

Taking into account this qualification made by Representative Keefe, all of the Democrats and half of the Republicans on the Investigating Committee rejected the isolationist thesis regarding the Pearl Harbor attack. The members of the Committee did not divide on party lines but according to prior attitudes towards the internationalist foreign policy of the Roosevelt administration. Senators Owen Brewster of Maine and Homer Ferguson of Michigan, who signed the Minority Report, were well known for their isolationist views.

"Shadings" of interpretation are certainly present in the Majority Report. But this is quite a different matter from the distortions and errors of fact in the Minority Report, a number of which have already been noted. The purpose of those distortions and errors is clearly to support the thesis that President Roosevelt and his immediate subordinates deceived the American public that their objective was peace and defense, while they plotted entry into the war by means of secret commitments to allies, provocative and aggressive acts of war, rejection of fair proposals for peaceful agreement made by the Japanese government ending with the November 26 proposal which Japan justifiably treated as an ultimatum, and deliberate exposure of the armed forces and the fleet at Pearl Harbor to maximum injury in order to incite the American people to war.

It is, then, surprising that the formal list of "Conclusions of Fact and Responsibility" in the Minority Report does not embody the conclusions stated above which proceed logically from the argument of the Minority Report as a whole. Instead, quite mild assertions are made that Washington officials did not adequately discharge their responsibility to inform and direct the commanders at Hawaii with sufficient precision and energy to prepare them against the actual danger.[45]

This is an anticlimax. The "Conclusions" of the Minority Report are no more than a detailed confirmation of the paragraph quoted above from the "Additional Views" of Representative Keefe—who was willing to sign the Majority Report. They amount to an admission of bankruptcy for the isolationist thesis. It was perhaps for this reason that Beard and Morgenstern found it necessary to refurbish that thesis in their books.

### "Winds Execute"

One of the few disputed factual questions in the Pearl Harbor Investigation was whether American Army and Navy monitors prior to December 7 did receive an "execute" message from Japan in the "Winds" code, warning Japanese agents abroad of war with the United States and Britain and peace with Russia. The Majority Report of the Committee states that:

the preponderate weight of [evidence] indicates that no genuine execute message was intercepted by or received in the War or Navy Departments prior to the attack on Pearl Harbor. Investigation conducted in Japan strongly indicates no execute message was dispatched before the attack and the British and Dutch, who were also monitoring for an execute message, have advised that no such message was intercepted. A reasonable construction of the code is that it was designed for use in the event ordinary commercial channels of communication were no longer available to Japan, a contemplation which did not materialize prior to Pearl Harbor. The fact that a message "West wind clear," applying to [rupture with] England, was broadcast after the attack tends to confirm this conclusion.[46]

Beard at the conclusion of his argument against the finding of the Majority Report on the "Winds execute" controversy, makes the highly significant statement that the putative message of December 4 in any case did not necessarily mean war. He states it as his opinion, based on a careful study of the vast mass of evidence, that high officers of the Navy Department did receive a message on December 4 or 5 "which they regarded as a winds execute message and at the time did believe that it meant *either a breach in diplomatic relations with Japan* or war." [47] This admission of the ambiguity of the code itself is not subscribed to by Morgenstern. He states that a "Winds execute" message baldly meant war. Then he devotes two chapters to a tendentious review of the evidence and concludes that a message was actually received and circulated among leading officials in Washington. He explains contradictory evidence by a "campaign of intimidation" against Army and Navy officers "sensitive to prospects of promotion. . . ." [48] The "Conclusions" of the Minority Report, consistently with their repudiation of the full-blown isolationist thesis, contain this statement regarding the "Winds execute" affair: "Admittedly the evidence is confusing and conflicting, but. . . ." and there follows a review of indications that the message was received.[49]

For the student of the charge that the Roosevelt administration deliberately maximized the disaster at Pearl Harbor in order to overwhelm isolationist opposition to entry into the war, a charge that requires more than "confusing and conflicting" evidence if it is to be accepted as truth, the essential point in the Winds affair may be found in the fact which Beard partially admits and Morgenstern denies: that the Winds code itself contained no ref-

erence to war, only to *"danger* of cutting off our *diplomatic relations."* Therefore, even if Washington officials did believe that a
genuine "Winds execute" message had been detected in Japanese
news broadcasts, there was no reason for them to interpret it as a
more definite warning of an attack against the United States than
the floods of information regarding the Japanese armada sailing
southwards through the China Sea.

## The Plan of November 28

Another disputed factual question in the Pearl Harbor Investigation bears more directly on Roosevelt's foreign policy. It involves the isolationist charge that the Roosevelt administration
made a commitment to Great Britain to go to war even if Japan
only attacked non-American territory. During the months after
the refusal of General Marshall and Admiral Stark to approve the
ADB report because it contained implications of such a commitment, the British tried to meet their objections to it, and in November, Admiral Hart, commander of the United States Asiatic
Fleet, and Admiral Phillips, the British Far Eastern commander,
held discussions on the matter. On November 5 and 27, Marshall
and Stark submitted to the President a recommendation that he
should adopt the program of the rejected ADB report *not* because
any commitment had been made to another government, but because American interest required it. This would mean that the
United States would enter the war if the Japanese attacked British
territory, or the NEI, or if the Japanese moved forces into Thailand west of 100° east longitude, or south of 10° north latitude, or
into Portuguese Timor, New Caledonia, or the Loyalty Islands.

The Joint Congressional Committee received in evidence a
message sent on December 5 (December 6, Singapore time) by Captain John M. Creighton, United States naval attaché at Singapore,
to Admiral Hart in Manila, as follows:

Brooke-Popham [British Air Marshal at Singapore] received Saturday
from War Department London: "We have now received assurance of
American armed support in cases as follows: A) we are obliged execute
our plans to forestall Japs landing Isthmus of Kra or take action in
reply to Nips invasion any other part of Siam [Thailand]; B) if Dutch
Indies are attacked and we go to their defense; C) if Japs attack us the
British. Therefore without reference to London put plan in action if

first you have good info Jap expedition advancing with the apparent intention of landing in Kra, second if the Nips violate any part of Thailand. Paragraph. If NEI are attacked put into operation plans agreed upon between the British and the Dutch." [50]

The Congressional Committee found no substantiating evidence for the truth of this report picked up in Singapore that London had received "assurance." Captain Creighton testified that he had little remembrance of his message, and that it must have been based on hearsay and rumor. His duty as a naval observer for the United States required him to pick up any and all information he could and relay it to higher authorities. Admiral Hart relayed the information to Admiral Stark in Washington. He knew of nothing to substantiate the report, and since the project of supporting the British against Japan would require action on his part, his ignorance of it would be strange, if Creighton's information were true. His dispatch to Stark stated: "Learn from Singapore we have assured Britain armed support under three or four eventualities. Have received no corresponding instructions from you." Admiral Stark testified before the Congressional Committee that Creighton's report may have been based on a misconception as to the state of Anglo-American discussions regarding the ADB report. [51]

But the best indication of the falseness of Creighton's information is found in discussions in Washington on the question of what the United States should do if the Japanese southward expedition only attacked non-American territory. That was the situation Washington officials considered most likely to materialize. The outstanding fact that emerges from the voluminous evidence of the administration's discussions is that *no final decision* was reached prior to December 7. A tentative plan involving several successive steps, but *not necessarily* including armed support of the British or Dutch if the Japanese only attacked non-American territory, had been partially carried out by December 7, and further instrumentation of this program had been planned for days following December 7. Discussions leading up to this program and the plan itself were incompatible with a commitment to the British or the Dutch, and they were also incompatible with a definite expectation that the Japanese would attack Pearl Harbor or any other American territory. This will be evident from an examination of those discussions and of the program.

Opinion in the administration was at first divided on the question of what should be done if the Japanese attacked only non-American territory. Secretary Stimson was eager to seize the military advantage that would accrue to the United States if it struck the Japanese armada from the Philippines without warning, but he was overruled by the War Council on November 28. Out of the discussion emerged the outline of what became the President's program. Stimson described the discussion in his diary:

It was now the opinion of everyone that if this [Japanese-China Sea] expedition was allowed to get around the southern point of Indochina and to go off and land in the Gulf of Siam, either at Bangkok or further west, it would be a terrific blow at all of the three Powers, Britain at Singapore, the Netherlands, and ourselves in the Philippines. *It was the consensus of everybody that this must not be allowed.* Then we discussed how to prevent it. It was agreed that if the Japanese got into the Isthmus of Kra, the British would fight. It was *also agreed* that *if the British fought, we would have to fight.* And it now seems clear that if this expedition was allowed to round the southern point of Indochina, this whole chain of disastrous events would be set on foot of going.

It further became a consensus of views that rather than strike at the force as it went by without any warning on the one hand, which we didn't think we could do; or sitting still and allowing it to go on, on the other, which we didn't think we could—that the only thing for us to do was to address it a warning that if it reached a certain place, or a certain line, or a certain point, we should have to fight. The President's mind evidently was running towards a special telegram from himself to the Emperor of Japan. This he had done with good results at the time of the *Panay* incident, but for many reasons, this did not seem to me to be the right thing now and I pointed them out to the President. In the first place, a letter to the Emperor of Japan could not be couched in terms which contained an explicit warning. One does not warn an Emperor. In the second place it would not indicate to the people of the United States what the real nature of the danger was. Consequently I said there ought to be a message by the President to the people of the United States and I thought that the best form of a message would be an address to Congress reporting the danger, reporting what we would have to do if the danger happened. The President accepted this idea of a message but he first thought of incorporating it in the terms of his letter to the Emperor. But again I pointed out that he could not publicize a letter to an Emperor in such a way; that he had better send his letter to the Emperor separate as one thing and a secret thing, then make his speech to the Congress as a separate and a more understandable thing to the people of the United States. This was the final decision at that time and the President asked Hull, and Knox and myself to try to draft such papers.[52]

Thus the plan of November 28 contained three steps; first, to send an appeal to Emperor Hirohito; second, to send a message to Congress which would not ask for a declaration of war but would describe the necessity for a warning to Japan that if the armada in the China Sea moved in the direction of an attack against territory of a third country, the United States would have to fight; and third, to address such a warning to Japan. The second and third steps were evidently to be taken more or less simultaneously. In any case, the import of the message to Congress was not to be a request for war *following* a Japanese refusal of the warning, but an announcement and explanation of the warning itself.

The discussion Stimson describes clearly shows that the administration had no previous commitment to the British or the Dutch to enter the war, because the decision itself was still under discussion on November 28. A plan was adopted which made decision on United States entry into the war contingent upon further efforts to stop the Japanese armada by peaceful methods, and presumably it was contingent also upon a favorable reception by Congress and the American people of the warning message.

### "A Little Respite"

On December 1, intelligence reports changed the situation. Word was received in Washington that the Japanese expedition in the China Sea was landing near Saigon in southern Indo-China.[53] This indicated that at least for the time being the Japanese would not transgress the lines Washington regarded as decisive. It caused the President to insert a new step in his plan which would be taken before any of the others. He asked the Japanese government, through Sumner Welles, on December 2, for a reply to the question what it intended by the new occupation of southern Indo-China. The reply was not received until December 5. Then the Japanese said the movement was "precautionary." [54]

A new re-enforcement of southern Indo-China was sufficiently grave as an admission of Japanese bad faith in conducting negotiations with the United States to lead the Japanese to expect that the United States would break relations, and this provides a reasonable interpretation of the state of mind in which Washington officials received information in Magic intercepts, and possibly in the disputed "Winds execute" message of December 4, that heralded an approaching crisis.

At the same time, such re-enforcement was likely at best only to delay for a short time a Japanese attack on territory beyond Indo-China. Therefore the President on December 2, after telling Stimson of the preliminary step he had taken, indicated to him that he still planned to take the further three steps, and would perhaps back up the address to Congress with a speech to the country. Stimson himself, however, regarded the report that the Japanese were landing near Saigon as giving the administration "a little respite." [55]

On Saturday, December 6, the day after receipt of the evasive reply of the Japanese government, intelligence reports were received shortly before noon in Washington that indicated the December 1 reports had been in error: the Japanese armada was moving on around the southern tip of Indo-China and westward towards Thailand. A landing was fourteen hours away.[56]

## The Appeal to Hirohito

During the remaining hours before news came that Pearl Harbor was being bombed, the crisis for Washington officials was occasioned by an imminent attack by Japan against Thailand. The Japanese expedition approaching Hawaii, in the absence of distant air reconnaissance, remained hidden. Magic interception of the Japanese reply to the November 26 draft proposal of the United States occurred during the night of Saturday. Copies were circulated to administration officials on Sunday morning, December 7. A final intercept instructed the Japanese Ambassadors to present the answer to Hull at one o'clock that afternoon, the moment bombs were to fall on Pearl Harbor.[57]

But this Japanese message was not a declaration of war, it did not even break off diplomatic relations with the United States, it merely notified the American government that the Japanese government considered it "impossible to reach an agreement through further negotiations." [58] Contentions in the Minority Report, and by Beard and Morgenstern, that Magic interception of the message still gave time for Washington officials to warn Hawaii against attack, break down because the "zero hour"—one o'clock—synchronized very well with the expected attack against Thailand, and this was doubtless the Japanese intention. In the light of all that had preceded, it was to be expected that Japan should break off negotiations for an agreement with the United States at the same moment that it launched the very act of aggression against Thailand which it had been the chief effort of Roosevelt and Hull in the conversations since July, 1941, to prevent.

It seemed to the leaders in Washington during the afternoon of December 6, and until the Pearl Harbor news arrived at two o'clock the next afternoon, that they still had a choice: whether or not to enter the war when the Japanese attacked Thailand. No final decision had been reached regarding an actual war message to Congress because it would in any case be contingent upon the results of the three steps planned on November 28. Immediately after receipt of the news that the Japanese expedition was heading for Thailand, President Roosevelt turned to the next step: an appeal to Emperor Hirohito.

This famous message is popularly regarded as an appeal by Roosevelt designed to fend off an attack by Japan against the United States. It was not that, because Roosevelt believed that Thailand, and Thailand alone, was the Japanese target. What he wished to fend off was this aggression which, although it was not directed against United States territory, was so injurious to American interest that it might lead the United States to go to war against Japan. Having in mind the fact that an American-Japanese war was Hitler's strategy to defeat Russia and Britain by diverting Lend Lease aid from them, and that American strategy required concentration on the fight against Hitler, Roosevelt was determined to exhaust every possibility of avoiding the necessity to fight Japan.

The appeal to Hirohito was dispatched to Tokyo at nine o'clock at night on December 6. The President reminded Hirohito that almost a century ago the President of the United States had addressed an offer of friendship to the Emperor of Japan. Now he felt he should address him because of the "deep and far-reaching emergency which appears to be in formation." Developments in the Pacific area contained "tragic possibilities" threatening to destroy the beneficial influences of the long peace between Japan and the United States. The people of the United States had eagerly watched the conversations between the two governments and hoped that the conflict between Japan and China could be ended. Americans had hoped, he wrote:

that a peace of the Pacific could be consummated in such a way that nationalities of many diverse peoples could exist side by side without fear of invasion; that unbearable burdens of armaments could be lifted for them all; and that all peoples would resume commerce without discrimination against or in favor of any nation.

Roosevelt said he hoped it would be clear to the Emperor that in seeking these great objectives "both Japan and the United States should agree to eliminate any form of military threat." He then reviewed the movement of Japanese troops into Indo-China even though no attack had been made or contemplated by a third country. New movements during recent weeks of Japanese military, naval and air forces were in such large numbers that "a reasonable doubt" was created regarding their defensive character. Their numbers and direction led the people of the Philippines, the NEI, Malaya, and Thailand to ask whether Japan intended to attack in one or more of these directions. Roosevelt said he was sure Hirohito would understand the fear of all those peoples and why the American people looked askance at the establishment of bases so heavily manned and equipped as to threaten "measures of offense." In a separate paragraph he said: "It is clear that continuance of such a situation is unthinkable." The peoples of the area could not sit "either indefinitely or permanently on a keg of dynamite." He gave absolute assurance that the United States would not invade Indo-China if all the Japanese forces were withdrawn, and he thought the same assurance could be obtained from the governments of the NEI, Malaya, and Thailand. He would even ask for such assurance by the government of China. "Thus a withdrawal of the Japanese forces from Indo-China would result in the assurance of peace throughout the whole of the South Pacific area." The appeal ended:

I address myself to Your Majesty at this moment in the fervent hope that Your Majesty may, as I am doing, give thought in this definite emergency to ways of dispelling the dark clouds. I am confident that

both of us, for the sake of the peoples not only of our own great countries but for the sake of humanity in neighboring territories, have a
sacred duty to restore traditional amity and prevent further death and
destruction in the world.[59]

## No Commitment

On the afternoon of Saturday, December 6, when the message
to Hirohito was made ready, a Magic intercept of a message from
Togo to Nomura was delivered to Hull. It stated that the Japanese reply in fourteen parts to the American proposal of November 26 would be received by Nomura probably the next day, and
that a later message would state the time when Nomura should
deliver it to Hull. An earlier intercept had declared that the November 26 proposal could not be accepted by Japan as a "basis
for negotiations." When the answer arrived, the negotiations
would be "de facto ruptured." [60] On that Saturday also the Navy
Department informed officials that the Japanese Embassy had destroyed its codes.[61]

Late in the afternoon, the possibility emerged that the next
step in the administration program for meeting the crisis, that is,
a warning message to Japan, would be taken in parallel with
warnings by Great Britain and the governments of the British
Dominions. Prime Minister Churchill had earlier proposed to the
Dominions that they unite with Great Britain to warn Japan:

that if Japan attempts to establish her influence in Thailand by force
or threat of force she will do so at her own peril and His Majesty's
Governments will at once take all appropriate measures. Should hostilities unfortunately result the responsibility will rest with Japan.

The Australian government accepted Churchill's proposal "subject to conditions that President gives prior approval to text of
warning as drafted and also gives signal for actual delivery of
warning."

Australian Minister Casey discussed the subject with President
Roosevelt late in the afternoon of December 6 and learned that
the Churchill proposal coincided with the next step of the President's plan. That evening Casey described the Roosevelt plan in
a message to the Australian government:

1. President has decided to send message to the Emperor.
2. President's subsequent procedure is that if no answer is received by him from Emperor by Monday evening (December 8).
    (a) he will issue his warning on Tuesday afternoon or evening.
    (b) warning or equivalent by British or others will not follow until Wednesday morning, i.e., after his own warning has been delivered repeatedly in Tokyo and Washington.

Evidently the Australian initiative led Churchill to send Roosevelt a copy of the proposed British warning with a request for comments. Senators Ferguson and Brewster ferreted out information of the whole episode, and documents from the President's personal files and from the records of the Australian government were made available to the Investigating Committee. The paper containing Churchill's request for comments came from the British Embassy in Washington and bore the date December 7, 1941. To it was attached a sheet which gave the text of Churchill's proposed warning.[62]

The purpose of the Senators was to find evidence which would prove the existence of a Roosevelt commitment to Churchill to go to war in case Japan attacked non-American territory. In their Minority Report they make no reference to the episode. The evidence actually proved that no such commitment existed. But this did not deter Charles A. Beard. He is unable to link the documents in the case with the many commitments he charged Roosevelt with making earlier in the year. That charge in Beard's text is now forgotten. But he makes up a new brief that Roosevelt, on December 6, for reasons unstated, found it necessary to make a new commitment to the British, or at least to Australia, on that Saturday afternoon.

Churchill's proposed warning to Japan, Beard calls "in effect" an "ultimatum," in spite of the fact that it contained no time limit and made *Japanese* use of force the condition upon which Britain would, not declare war, but take "all appropriate measures." Then, if war resulted, the responsibility would rest with Japan.

Having asserted that the proposed British warning was an ultimatum, with accompanying implications of war guilt, Beard sets out to prove that Roosevelt made a "commitment" to Minister Casey regarding procedure to be followed in carrying out the *British* proposal. He makes no reference to the well-established fact that an American warning to Japan had been planned as early as November 28. Beard goes farther: he asserts that in his conference with Casey on the afternoon of December 6, Roosevelt "agreed" to send a message to the Japanese Emperor. Then he asks the portentous question: Was the President's message to the Emperor framed to meet his "commitment" to Casey, or was it an "independent action?" The answer, Beard decides, must be "conjectural" because a letter to Hirohito had been "discussed" for many days prior to December 6 by Roosevelt, Hull, Stimson, and Knox.[63]

Thus Beard does his best to rescue for his thesis an image of Roosevelt making a commitment to a foreign government to issue an ultimatum. The "ultimatum" was never sent because Japan violently intervened in the procedure, but this in Beard's book is insignificant compared with the revelation of Roosevelt's guilty intention. The facts in the case are, once more, imbedded in Beard's own text, and, sifted out from his distortions, they plainly show that when Roosevelt was told of the proposed British warning, he merely *informed* Casey that the American government had already planned to issue a warning to Japan as part of a program that included a message to the Emperor as an antecedent step. If the plan had been carried out, it would have amounted to no more than "parallel action" of the sort which was traditional in Anglo-American dealings with Japan.

The most revealing aspect of Beard's charge is that in the crucial events of December 6 he can find no evidence of a Roosevelt commitment to Churchill. Beard does not attempt to call Australia's move to obtain parallel action by the United States in issuing a warning to Japan, even when distorted by the words "commitment" and "ultimatum," evidence that Roosevelt had promised Churchill to enter the war if Japan attacked non-American territory. Thus Beard himself abandons one of the main charges in his indictment of the President.

## No Foreknowledge

Another main charge in the isolationist thesis collapses in the face of the Roosevelt-Casey evidence. This one is Morgenstern's chief preoccupation: that Roosevelt and other officials in Washington knew beforehand that the Japanese were about to attack Pearl

Harbor. Why Roosevelt, if he knew what impended at Pearl Harbor, should have been concerned to find a *casus belli* at Thailand an indefinite number of days after a warning which was planned for delivery to Japan two days *after* the attack on Pearl Harbor, presents a conundrum for Morgenstern which he dismisses as follows:

> *It is only curious* that as late in the day as this Roosevelt should still have been worrying lest the Japanese fail to provide the necessary incident.

Then Morgenstern proceeds casually to ignore this "curiosity" of Roosevelt's behavior and reassert his thesis.[64] But Morgenstern's failure to offer any explanation of the "curiosity" is actually an abandonment by him of his thesis that the Roosevelt administration provoked, expected, and maximized the Pearl Harbor attack because it wanted a *casus belli*. The same thing may be said of the failure of Senators Brewster and Ferguson to mention the Roosevelt-Casey episode in their Minority Report after they worked so vigorously to obtain the evidence regarding it. The terms of their indictment of the President are more guarded than those of Beard and Morgenstern, confined as they are to charges that the President and his subordinates did not convey proper orders and information to the Hawaiian commanders, and therefore they are not under the embarrassment of reporting that their investigation into the episode revealed the falsity of a more serious indictment.

The Minority Report, however, exploits its failure to mention the Roosevelt-Casey episode in order to strengthen its basic charge of Presidential failure to order proper defensive dispositions at Hawaii in time for the impending attack. After December 2, the Report states, the President "fully abandoned" the plans to send a warning to Japan and a message to Congress. He "only turned" to carry out the plan to make an appeal to Hirohito, and this was done "after it was too late." The President then "adhered" to the plan of "waiting for Japanese action." This comes very close to the charge that the President consciously allowed the Pearl Harbor attack to provide him with a disastrous *casus belli*.[65] The fact, which Senators Brewster and Ferguson themselves unearthed, is, of course, that the President did plan on December 6 to issue the warning to Japan, and this was linked from the beginning with the plan to address Congress.

## A Final Question

For the student of Roosevelt's policy, one question remains. In the expected event that the Japanese expedition moving westward towards Thailand would not immediately attack the Philippines, would the President have followed up unsatisfactory Japanese replies to his letter to the Emperor of Japan and his warning to the Japanese government with a request to Congress for a declaration of war? The issue would involve a climactic test of Roosevelt's adherence to his policy of collective security, on the one hand, and his antiwar pledge, on the other. No evidence is available for an answer except Stimson's diary record that the group present at the meeting on November 28 "agreed" that if the British fought, the United States would have to fight. The three-step plan that was then adopted was designed both to fend off the necessity to fight and to present the American Congress and public with an opportunity to judge the issue.

It may be stated with considerable confidence that if public and Congress with something approaching unanimity had asked for war, Roosevelt would have broken his antiwar pledge. But in the more likely case, that isolationism still commanded a strong minority in and out of Congress, who denied that a Japanese attack on non-American territory and British entry into the Pacific war justified American entry, it must remain purely conjectural whether the President nevertheless would have asked Congress for a declaration of war. The disappearance from the record of all discussion by him of what might follow a failure of his warning to deter Japan suggests that he left the decision for the event.

# *Epilogue*

 T HE CHIEF LESSON THAT PRESIDENT ROOSEVELT DREW FROM
the Japanese attack on Pearl Harbor was the lesson of internationalism. In his War Message to Congress at noon on December
8, 1941, he said:

I believe I interpret the will of the Congress and of the people when
I assert that we will not only defend ourselves to the uttermost but will
make very certain that this form of treachery shall never endanger us
again.[1]

This statement might have been understood to apply only to
military measures, but on December 9, in a radio address to the
nation, the President amplified it:

In my message to the Congress yesterday I said that we "will make
very certain that this form of treachery shall never endanger us again."
In order to achieve that certainty, we must begin the great task that
is before us by abandoning once and for all the illusion that we can
ever again isolate ourselves from the rest of humanity.

In these past few years—and, most violently, in the past few days—
we have learned a terrible lesson.

It is our obligation to our dead—it is our sacred obligation to their
children and our children—that we must never forget what we have
learned.

And what we all have learned is this:

There is no such thing as security for any nation—or any individual
—in a world ruled by the principles of gangsterism. . . .

The true goal we seek is far above and beyond the ugly field of battle. When we resort to force, as now we must, we are determined that

this force shall be directed toward ultimate good as well as against immediate evil. We Americans are not destroyers; we are builders.

We are now in the midst of a war, not for conquest, not for vengeance, but for a world in which this Nation, and all that this Nation represents, will be safe for our children. . . .

We are going to win the war, and we are going to win the peace that follows.[2]

A long step towards "the true goal" was taken on New Year's Day, 1942, when the representatives of twenty-six nations, comprising the overwhelming majority of the inhabitants of the world, signed the United Nations Declaration. This Declaration created a united front against aggression among the United States, Great Britain, the Dominions including India, the Soviet Union, China, Belgium, Czechoslovakia, Greece, Luxemburg, the Netherlands, Norway, Poland, Yugoslavia, and the nine Latin American Republics which had already declared war. Cordell Hull with exemplary caution had first obtained assurances from these governments that they had no secret agreements in violation of the anti-imperialist aims of the coalition.[3]

The signatory governments pledged themselves to employ their full resources in war against the Axis, to coöperate with each other, and not to make a separate armistice or peace with the enemies. They also subscribed to the principles of the Atlantic Charter, including the eighth point in favor of a "permanent system of general security." Thus the United Nations Declaration was no ordinary war alliance but a promise that victory would be used to create a new international order.[4]

Within a few weeks after the Pearl Harbor disaster, President Roosevelt had made it yield compensation by advancing his true goal of internationalism. The United Nations Declaration was the central act of his twelve years' labor to create a new foreign policy for the United States. When he died in April, 1945, Congress and the people were virtually unanimous in favor of American entry into a world organization for collective security. President Roosevelt had already planned to cap the imminent victory over Hitler with the San Francisco Conference to draw up the United Nations Charter.

American entry into the United Nations completed President Roosevelt's work. Then the work of realizing his vision of world peace under international moral law began. That vision is still a distant prospect. But President Roosevelt had demonstrated how it could be approached steadily despite compromises and defeats. His vision is worthy of humanity's patient labor. If it is ever realized, whenever men gather to honor the architects of their happiness, they will gratefully remember the work of Franklin Delano Roosevelt.

# Reference Notes

## Chapter 1—Introduction

1. (Yale University Press, New Haven, 1946).
2. (Yale University Press, New Haven, 1948).
3. See, for examples of the use the isolationist press makes of Beard's work: "FDR Tactics Menace U.S., Beard warns," *Chicago Daily Tribune*, April 3, 1948; and the editorial in the *New York Daily News*, April 12, 1948.
4. Beard, *American Foreign Policy*, 40-3.
5. *Ibid.*, 1-2n.
6. See *The Open Door at Home, a Trial Philosophy of National Interest* (The Macmillan Company, New York, 1935).

## Chapter 2—Roosevelt and the "New Neutrality"

1. Franklin D. Roosevelt, "Our Foreign Policy: A Democratic View," *Foreign Affairs*, VI (July, 1928), 573-86.
2. Beard, *Roosevelt and the Coming of the War*, 444.
3. Henry L. Stimson and McGeorge Bundy, *On Active Service: In Peace and War* (Harper and Brothers, New York, 1948), 292-3.
4. *The Public Papers and Addresses of Franklin D. Roosevelt: With a Special Introduction and Explanatory Notes by President Roosevelt* (Random House, New York, 1938), II, 11-6.
5. Raymond Moley, *After Seven Years* (Harper and Brothers, New York 1939), 69, 78-9, *The Memoirs of Cordell Hull* (Macmillan, New York, 1948), I, 155.
6. *Papers of F. D. Roosevelt*, II, 187.
7. Beard, *American Foreign Policy*, 127-8.
8. His first message was dated April 5 and addressed to both houses. *Peace and War: United States Foreign Policy: 1931–1941* (United States Government Printing Office, Washington, 1942), 11, 23.
9. Beard, *American Foreign Policy*, 129-30.
10. Keith Feiling, *The Life of Neville Chamberlain* (Macmillan, London, 1946), 322-4.
11. *Memoirs of Cordell Hull*, I, 176-7.
12. *Ibid.*, 336-8, 346-7.

13. Beard, *American Foreign Policy*, 151.

14. *Ibid.*, 165.

15. On the next page Beard quotes the "drag us into war" sentence without explanation, as something "He also maintained." *Ibid.*, 166.

16. Feiling, *Chamberlain*, 272.

17. *Papers of F. D. Roosevelt*, V, 8-18.

18. Beard, *American Foreign Policy*, 169-70.

19. *Papers of F. D. Roosevelt*, V, 285-92.

20. *Memoirs of Cordell Hull*, I, 478.

21. Feiling, *Chamberlain*, 325.

22. *Memoirs of Cordell Hull*, I, 491.

23. *Ibid.*, 506.

24. *Papers of F. D. Roosevelt* (Macmillan, New York, 1941), 1937, 192-3.

25. *Loc. cit.*

26. Winston S. Churchill, *The Second World War: The Gathering Storm* (Houghton Mifflin Company, Boston, 1948), 248.

27. *Ibid.*, 212-5.

28. *Memoirs of Cordell Hull*, I, 481-2, 517.

29. *Ibid.*, 511.

30. *Ibid.*, 512.

31. *Ibid.*, 512-3.

32. *Ibid.*, 513.

33. *Ibid.*, 513.

34. *Ibid.*, 516-7.

35. *Ibid.*, 517.

36. *Loc. cit.*

37. *Infra*, pp. 282 ff.

38. Feiling, *Chamberlain*, 394.

39. Beard, *American Foreign Policy*, 180-1.

40. *Memoirs of Cordell Hull*, I, 509.

41. *Ibid.*, 531-4.

42. Whitney H. Shepardson and William O. Scroggs, *The United States in World Affairs* (Harper and Brothers, New York, 1939), 1938, 209-11.

43. *Memoirs of Cordell Hull*, I, 536.

44. *Ibid.*, 541.

45. *Ibid.*, 544-5.

46. *Papers of F. D. Roosevelt*, 1937, 406-11.

47. *Memoirs of Cordell Hull*, I, 545.

48. *Papers of F. D. Roosevelt*, 1937, 422-3.

49. Department of State, *Press Releases*, 1937, no. 417, pp. 254-5.

50. *Peace and War: United States Foreign Policy, 1931–1941*, 381-3.

51. *Papers of F. D. Roosevelt*, 1937, 423.

52. Royal Institute of International Affairs, *Documents on International Affairs* (Oxford University Press, London, 1939), 1937, 49.

53. *Papers of F. D. Roosevelt*, 1937, 437.

54. Royal Institute, *Documents*, 1937, 51.

55. *Memoirs of Cordell Hull*, I, 550-1.

56. *Ibid.*, 554-5.

57. *Papers of F. D. Roosevelt*, 1937, 424.

58. *Memoirs of Cordell Hull*, I, 556.

59. Beard, *American Foreign Policy*, 207.

60. Sumner Welles, *The Time for Decision* (Harper and Brothers, New York, 1944), 64-6. *Memoirs of Cordell Hull*, I, 546.

61. *Ibid.*, 546-8.
62. Welles, *Time for Decision*, 66.
63. *Loc. cit.*
64. Churchill, *The Gathering Storm*, 251.
65. Quoted in *ibid.*, 252.
66. Feiling, *Chamberlain*, 336.
67. Quoted in Churchill, *The Gathering Storm*, 253.
68. *Loc. cit.* Welles, *Time for Decision*, 68.
69. Quoted in Churchill, *The Gathering Storm*, 253.
70. Welles, *Time for Decision*, 68.
71. *Papers of F. D. Roosevelt*, 1938, 69. Italics added.
72. Beard, *American Foreign Policy*, 212.
73. *Ibid.*, 214.
74. Churchill, *The Gathering Storm*, 251.
75. Beard, *American Foreign Policy*, 215-6.
76. Quoted in *Memoirs of Cordell Hull*, I, 574. Italics added.
77. Welles, *Time for Decision*, 66.
78. *Documents on American Foreign Relations: January 1938–June 1939*, edited by S. Shepard Jones and Denys P. Myers (World Peace Foundation, Boston, 1939), 276-7.
79. The Stimson Doctrine was inapplicable to *Anschluss* because no new government (as Manchoukuo) or new title of an old government (as the Italian Empire) was created and available for recognition. By recognizing that Austria was henceforth a part of Germany, the United States included the extinguished nation with Germany in the American blacklist of powers that discriminated against United States trade. Germany therefore received no benefits from Austria's former unconditional most-favored-nation status in trade with the United States.
80. *Memoirs of Cordell Hull*, I, 303-6.
81. Royal Institute, *Documents*, 1938, I, 409.
82. Churchill, *The Gathering Storm*, 310-2.
83. *Documents on American Foreign Relations: 1938–1939*, ed. Jones and Myers, 19-23.

## *Chapter 3—Munich: The Turning Point*

1. *Documents on American Foreign Relations: 1938–1939*, ed. Jones and Myers, 23-6.
2. *Ibid.*, 459-61.
3. *Papers of F. D. Roosevelt*, 1939, 364-5.
4. *Ibid.*, V, 8-18.
5. *New York Times*, September 18, 25, 1938.
6. *Ibid.*, September 3, 1938.
7. Churchill, *The Gathering Storm*, 304.
8. *New York Times*, September 23, 1938.
9. *Memoirs of Cordell Hull*, I, 590-2.
10. *Papers of F. D. Roosevelt*, 1938, 531-2. Italics added.
11. *Documents on American Foreign Relations*, 1938–1939, ed. Jones and Myers, 289-92.
12. *Ibid.*, 293-4.
13. *Ibid.*, 288-9.
14. *Ibid.*, 288.
15. *Ibid.*, 296.
16. *Ibid.*, 292.

17. *New York Times*, "News of the Week," October 2, 1938.

18. *Memoirs of Cordell Hull*, I, 592.

19. *Ibid.*, 594.

20. For Hull's statement: *Documents on American Foreign Relations, 1938–1939*, ed. Jones and Myers, 297. For Roosevelt's extremely aloof comment: *New York Times*, October 1, 1938. The Department of State a few weeks later flatly denied that the Roosevelt messages made the United States accessory to the Munich Agreement. *New York Times*, "News of the Week," October 23, 1938.

21. Beard, *American Foreign Policy*, 219-20. The date, September 27, which Beard uses should be September 26, as it is the first Roosevelt letter from which he quotes.

## Chapter 4—The Primacy of Foreign Danger

1. *New York Times*, October 1, 1938.

2. *Ibid.*, "News of the Week," October 2, 1938.

3. *New York Times*, October 1, 1938.

4. *Ibid.*, October 4, 1938.

5. *Ibid.*, October 5, 1938.

6. *Ibid.*, October 6, 8, 1938.

7. *Ibid.*, "News of the Week," October 9, 1938.

8. *New York Times*, October 10, 1938.

9. *Ibid.*, October 12, 1938.

10. *Memoirs of Cordell Hull*, I, 624-5. See below, p. 112.

11. *New York Times*, October 15, 1938.

12. *Ibid.*, October 16, 1938.

13. Anne O'Hare McCormick, "As He Sees Himself," *New York Times Magazine*, October 16, 1938.

14. *New York Times*, October 17, 1938.

15. *Ibid.*, October 23, 1938.

16. *Ibid.*, "News of the Week," October 23, 1938.

17. Joseph Borkin and Charles A. Welsh, *Germany's Master Plan* (Duel, Sloan and Pearce, New York, 1943), 193, 219, *et passim*.

18. *Papers of F. D. Roosevelt*, 1938, 563-6.

19. *Ibid.*, 584-93.

20. James A. Farley, *Jim Farley's Story: The Roosevelt Years* (Whittlesey House, McGraw-Hill Book Company, New York, 1948), 142-57.

21. *Ibid.*, 163.

22. *Papers of F. D. Roosevelt*, 1938, 597.

23. Shepardson and Scroggs, *The United States in World Affairs, 1938*, 115-6.

24. Feiling, *Chamberlain*, 389-90.

25. *Events Leading up to World War II* (USGPO, Washington, 1945), 170-2.

26. *Memoirs of Cordell Hull*, I, 518-30.

27. *Papers Relating to the Foreign Relations of the United States: Japan: 1931–1941* (USGPO, Washington, 1943), I, 803-4.

28. *Ibid.*, 820-6. *Memoirs of Cordell Hull*, I, 569-70.

29. *Ibid.*, II, 1140-2.

30. *Documents on American Foreign Relations: 1938–1939*, ed. Jones and Myers, 116-21.

31. *Memoirs of Cordell Hull*, I, 610.

32. *Ibid.*, 500.

33. *Ibid.*, 601-8.

34. Shepardson and Scroggs, *The United States in World Affairs: 1938*, 376-7.
35. *Memoirs of Cordell Hull*, I, 611.
36. Beard, *American Foreign Policy*, 220. Italics added.

## Chapter 5—The Fight Against the Arms Embargo: Failure

1. Henry DeWolf Smyth, *Atomic Energy for Military Purposes* (Princeton University Press, Princeton, 1945), 45-7.
2. Joseph Harsch in *Christian Science Monitor*, January 7, 1939. Shepardson and Scroggs, *United States in World Affairs: 1939*, 11-5.
3. *Loc. cit.*
4. Feiling, *Chamberlain*, 392, 394-5.
5. *Papers of F. D. Roosevelt, 1939*, 1-12. Italics added.
6. Beard, *American Foreign Policy*, 224.
7. *Memoirs of Cordell Hull*, I, 613.
8. *Papers of F. D. Roosevelt, 1939*, 70-4.
9. Shepardson and Scroggs, *United States in World Affairs, 1939*, 120-3.
10. Beard, *American Foreign Policy*, 36-9.
11. *Memoirs of Cordell Hull*, I, 624-6.
12. Shepardson and Scroggs, *United States in World Affairs, 1939*, 101-6.
13. *Ibid.*, 104-5.
14. *Papers of F. D. Roosevelt, 1939*, 111-3.
15. *Ibid.*, 154-7.
16. *Memoirs of Cordell Hull*, I, 613-4.
17. Feiling, *Chamberlain*, 399-400.
18. *Memoirs of Cordell Hull*, I, 642.
19. Shepardson and Scroggs, *United States in World Affairs, 1939*, 76-7.
20. *Documents on American Foreign Relations, 1938–1939*, ed. Jones and Myers, 306-9.
21. *Memoirs of Cordell Hull*, I, 620.
22. *Documents on American Foreign Relations, 1938–1939*, ed. Jones and Myers, 309-26.
23. *Nazi-Soviet Relations, 1939–41*, edited by Raymond J. Sontag and James S. Beddie (Department of State, USGPO, 1948), 2.
24. *Ibid.*, 1-2.
25. Feiling, *Chamberlain*, 403. Churchill, *The Gathering Storm*, 362-77.
26. *Nazi-Soviet Relations, 1939–41*, 15.
27. *Memoirs of Cordell Hull*, I, 643-5.
28. *Congressional Record*, Appendix, Vol. 84, Pt. 14, p. 2327.
29. *Memoirs of Cordell Hull*, I, 645-8, 655-6.
30. Shepardson and Scroggs, *United States in World Affairs, 1939*, 85.
31. *New York Herald Tribune*, July 12, 1939.
32. *The French Yellow Book* (Reynal and Hitchcock, New York, 1940), 145-6, 163-4.
33. *Memoirs of Cordell Hull*, I, 200, 656.
34. Churchill, *The Gathering Storm*, 391.
35. *Papers of F. D. Roosevelt, 1939*, 380-1.
36. Beard, *American Foreign Policy*, 232-4.
37. *Papers of F. D. Roosevelt, 1939*, 381-7.
38. *Memoirs of Cordell Hull*, I, 649-53.
39. *Papers of F. D. Roosevelt, 1939*, 387-8.
40. *Ibid.*, 391.
41. Beard, *American Foreign Policy*, 234.

## Chapter 6—The Fight Against the Arms Embargo: Success

1. *Memoirs of Cordell Hull*, I, 627-33.

2. Shepardson and Scroggs, *United States in World Affairs, 1939*, 261-4.

3. *Memoirs of Cordell Hull*, I, 635-9. Shepardson and Scroggs, *United States in World Affairs, 1939*, 265-70.

4. *Ibid.*, 265-6, 268.

5. *Ibid.*, 267-8.

6. *Memoirs of Cordell Hull*, I, 655-7. Italics added.

7. Churchill, *The Gathering Storm*, 395-6. Shepardson and Scroggs, *United States in World Affairs, 1939*, 140-1.

8. *Events Leading up to World War II*, 202-14. *Papers of F. D. Roosevelt*, 1939, 444-50. Shepardson and Scroggs, *United States in World Affairs, 1939*, 139-53. Churchill, *The Gathering Storm*, 395-400. *Memoirs of Cordell Hull*, I, 654-65.

9. *Memoirs of Cordell Hull*, I, 676.

10. *Papers of F. D. Roosevelt*, 1939, 460-4.

11. *Memoirs of Cordell Hull*, I, 677. Churchill, *The Gathering Storm*, 423.

12. *Papers of F. D. Roosevelt*, 1939, 464-78.

13. Shepardson and Scroggs, *United States in World Affairs, 1939*, 162.

14. *Memoirs of Cordell Hull*, I, 685.

15. Shepardson and Scroggs, *United States in World Affairs, 1939*, 339.

16. *New York Times*, Sept. 15, 1939.

17. *Ibid.*, Oct. 21, 1939.

18. *Ibid.*, September 16, 1939.

19. Porter Sargent, *Getting Us Into War* (P. Sargent, Boston, 1941), 130. James F. Byrnes, *Speaking Frankly* (Harper and Brothers, New York, 1947), 7-8.

20. Shepardson and Scroggs, *United States in World Affairs, 1939*, 167.

21. *Papers of F. D. Roosevelt*, 1939, 512-22.

22. Beard, *American Foreign Policy*, 235-7.

23. *Memoirs of Cordell Hull*, I, 684.

24. *New York Herald Tribune*, October 25, 1939.

25. *New York Times*, September 21, 1939.

26. *Ibid.*, October 14, 1939.

27. *Congressional Record*, Vol. 85, Pt. 1, p. 411.

28. *Ibid.*, 411-42. Dorothy Thompson, *New York Herald Tribune*, October 18, 20, 23, 1939; Eleanor Roosevelt, *New York World Telegram*, October 19, 1939.

29. Beard, *American Foreign Policy*, 238-60. *Congressional Record*, Vol. 85, Pt. 1, p. 442.

30. *New York Times*, October 2, 1939.

31. Stimson and Bundy, *On Active Service*, 317.

32. *Memoirs of Cordell Hull*, I, 692-7.

33. *Papers of F. D. Roosevelt*, 1939, 556-7.

34. Beard, *American Foreign Policy*, 264.

35. Churchill, *The Gathering Storm*, 440-1.

36. Shepardson and Scroggs, *United States in World Affairs, 1939*, 221. *Memoirs of Cordell Hull*, I, 679-82.

37. *Memoirs of Cordell Hull*, I, 688-90.

38. *Documents on American Foreign Relations: 1939–1940*, II, ed. Jones and Myers, 115-9.

39. *Ibid.*, 119-21.

40. *Ibid.*, 121-30.

41. Shepardson and Scroggs, *United States in World Affairs, 1939*, 194, 206.

42. Welles, *The Time for Decision*, 210-4; *Memoirs of Cordell Hull*, I, 692; Shepardson and Scroggs, *United States in World Affairs, 1939*, 197-9, 209-11.

43. *Documents on American Foreign Relations, 1939–1940*, ed. Jones and Myers, 100-21.

44. Farley, *Jim Farley's Story*, 152-3, 164.

45. *Ibid.*, 174-80.

46. *Ibid.*, 181-8; 196, 200-1.

47. Frances Perkins, *The Roosevelt I Knew* (Viking Press, New York, 1946), 126-8.

48. Broadus Mitchell, "War to the Rescue," *Depression Decade: From New Era Through New Deal: 1929–1941* (Rinehart and Company, New York, 1947), 361-403.

49. *Statistical Abstract of the United States: 1939* (USGPO, Washington, 1940), 371, 377-8, 389, 774.

50. *Ibid.*, 371, 737.

51. *Ibid., 1942*, 371.

52. Mitchell, *Depression Decade*, 371.

53. Farley, *Jim Farley's Story*, 199; *Papers of F. D. Roosevelt, 1939*, 586-7.

## Chapter 7—The "Phony" War

1. *Memoirs of Cordell Hull*, I, 701.

2. *Papers of F. D. Roosevelt, 1939*, 538-9; *Memoirs of Cordell Hull*, I, 702-3.

3. *Ibid.*, 703-5. *Documents on American Foreign Relations, 1939–1940*, ed. Jones and Myers, 132.

4. *Memoirs of Cordell Hull*, I, 704-5.

5. *Papers of F. D. Roosevelt, 1939*, 587-8.

6. *Documents on American Foreign Relations, 1939–1940*, ed. Jones and Myers, 385-6.

7. *Papers of F. D. Roosevelt, 1939*, 588-9.

8. Churchill, *The Gathering Storm*, 543-7.

9. *Ibid.*, 560-1, 573-4. Shepardson and Scroggs, *United States in World Affairs, 1940*, 35-6, 40-3.

10. *New York Herald Tribune*, February 20, 1940.

11. *Memoirs of Cordell Hull*, I, 707.

12. Bullitt has recently written that Roosevelt "had been so angered by Stalin's aggression against Finland that he had used his influence to have the Soviet Union expelled from the League of Nations." William C. Bullitt, "How We Won the War and Lost the Peace," *Life*, August 30, 1948, p. 91. The frankly tendentious purpose of Bullitt's article, its many errors on known matters of fact, the documentation and scholarly ambience of Hull's *Memoirs* and Hull's superior responsibility have led to decision in favor of Hull in this case of flat contradiction between two actors in the scene. *Memoirs of Cordell Hull*, I, 709-10.

13. Shepardson and Scroggs, *United States in World Affairs, 1940*, 26.

14. *Papers of F. D. Roosevelt, 1940*, 49-51.

15. *Memoirs of Cordell Hull*, I, 743. Shepardson and Scroggs, *United States in World Affairs, 1940*, 33-4.

16. *Memoirs of Cordell Hull*, I, 743.

17. *Papers of F. D. Roosevelt, 1940*, 92-4.

18. *Memoirs of Cordell Hull*, I, 743-5.

19. *Ibid.*, 733.

20. Shepardson and Scroggs, *United States in World Affairs, 1939*, 224.

21. *Memoirs of Cordell Hull*, I, 734-6.

22. *Ibid.*, 720-3.

23. Shepardson and Scroggs, *United States in World Affairs, 1939*, 397.

24. *Documents on American Foreign Relations, 1939–1940*, ed. Jones and Myers, 249-60.

25. *Memoirs of Cordell Hull*, I, 723-30. Joseph C. Grew, *Ten Years in Japan* (Simon and Schuster, New York, 1944), 289-312.

26. Shepardson and Scroggs, *United States in World Affairs, 1940*, 149-59.

27. *Ibid.*, 380.

28. Waverley Root, *The Secret History of the War* (Charles Scribner's Sons, New York, 1945), I, 622 ff.

29. *Ibid.*, Author's Note.

30. *Memoirs of Cordell Hull*, I, 731-2.

31. *Papers of F. D. Roosevelt*, 1939, 606-9.

32. *Ibid.*, 609-11.

33. *Wartime Correspondence between President Roosevelt and Pope Pius XII*, with an Introduction and Explanatory Notes by Myron C. Taylor (Macmillan Company, New York, 1947), 21-31.

34. *Memoirs of Cordell Hull*, I, 731-2.

35. Welles, *The Time for Decision*, 73.

36. *Memoirs of Cordell Hull*, I, 737-8.

37. *Papers of F. D. Roosevelt*, 1940, 1-10. Italics added.

38. Welles, *Time for Decision*, 73-4.

39. *Ibid.*, 76-7.

40. *Ibid.*, 74.

41. *Memoirs of Cordell Hull*, I, 737-8.

42. *Papers of F. D. Roosevelt*, 1940, 77.

43. *Memoirs of Cordell Hull*, I, 738-9.

44. *Papers of F. D. Roosevelt*, 1940, 103. Italics added.

45. *Memoirs of Cordell Hull*, I, 739-40.

46. *Nazi Conspiracy and Aggression*, Office of United States Chief of Counsel for Prosecution of Axis Criminality (USGPO, Washington, 1946), I, 743-8.

47. Welles, *Time for Decision*, 73-147. Robert E. Sherwood, *Roosevelt and Hopkins: An Intimate History* (Harper and Brothers, New York, 1948), 137.

48. *Memoirs of Cordell Hull*, I, 746-50.

49. *Papers of F. D. Roosevelt*, 1940, 154-5.

50. Smyth, *Atomic Energy*, 46-8.

51. *Papers of F. D. Roosevelt*, 1940, 10-24.

52. *Ibid.*, 8-10. Italics added.

53. *New York Times*, October 26, 1939.

54. Sherwood, *Roosevelt and Hopkins*, 94-8, 117, 170.

55. Farley, *Jim Farley's Story*, 214.

56. *Ibid.*, 220.

57. *Ibid.*, 223-6.

58. *Ibid.*, 225-7. *Memoirs of Cordell Hull, passim.*

59. Sherwood, *Roosevelt and Hopkins*, 172.

60. *Ibid.*, 172-3.

61. Farley, *op. cit.*, 233.

62. Bascom N. Timmons, *Garner of Texas: A Personal History* (Harper and Brothers, New York, 1948), 262.

63. *Ibid.*, 259.

64. *Papers of F. D. Roosevelt*, 1939, 410-4.

65. Timmons, *Garner of Texas*, 260.

66. *Ibid.*, 270. Italics added.

67. Farley, *op. cit.*, 212.

68. *Papers of F. D. Roosevelt*, 1940, 162.

## Chapter 8—"Behind Walls of Sand"

1. *Papers of F. D. Roosevelt*, 1940, 157.
2. *Memoirs of Cordell Hull*, I, 752-3.
3. *Ibid.*, 754-6.
4. *Ibid.*, 756-8.
5. *Ibid.*, 759-60.
6. *Ibid.*, 769.
7. *Papers of F. D. Roosevelt*, 1940, 184.
8. *Memoirs of Cordell Hull*, I, 764.
9. *Papers of F. D. Roosevelt*, 1940, 189.
10. Winston S. Churchill, *The Second World War: Their Finest Hour* (Houghton Mifflin Company, Boston, 1949), 25-6.
11. *Ibid.*, 23.
12. *Ibid.*, 24-5.
13. *Memoirs of Cordell Hull*, I, 765-6.
14. *Papers of F. D. Roosevelt*, 1940, 191.
15. Beard, *American Foreign Policy*, 268.
16. *Papers of F. D. Roosevelt*, 1940, 198-205. Italics added.
17. *Memoirs of Cordell Hull*, I, 767.
18. Edward R. Stettinius, Jr., *Lend-Lease: Weapon for Victory* (Macmillan, New York, 1944), 48.
19. *New York Times*, May 20, 1940.
20. Perkins, *The Roosevelt I Knew*, 384.
21. Sherwood, *Roosevelt and Hopkins*, 158-9.
22. Smyth, *Atomic Energy*, 48.
23. Sherwood, *Roosevelt and Hopkins*, 152-5.
24. *Papers of F. D. Roosevelt*, 1940, 230-40.
25. *Ibid.*, 241.
26. *Ibid.*, 250-3.
27. Churchill, *Their Finest Hour*, 118.
28. *Papers of F. D. Roosevelt*, 1940, 259-64.
29. *Memoirs of Cordell Hull*, I, 784-5. Sherwood, *Roosevelt and Hopkins*, 143.
30. *Papers of F. D. Roosevelt*, 1940, 262-3.
31. *The Ciano Diaries: 1939–1943*, edited by Hugh Gibson (Doubleday and Co., New York, 1946), 212-63.
32. *Memoirs of Cordell Hull*, I, 777-84. *Events Leading up to World War II*, 239-41.
33. Shepardson and Scroggs, *United States in World Affairs*, 1940, 88-94.
34. *Papers of F. D. Roosevelt*, 1940, 266-7. Prior quotations from *Memoirs of Cordell Hull*, I, 765-76, 787-91; *Events Leading up to World War II*, 244.
35. *Memoirs of Cordell Hull*, I, 771.
36. *Ibid.*, 791.
37. *Ibid.*, 791-3.
38. William L. Langer, *Our Vichy Gamble* (Alfred A. Knopf, New York, 1947), 45-6.
39. *Ibid.*, 47-9. Quotation from Italian Staff Report, June 18, 1940, *Graziani Papers, Ibid.*, 49.
40. Quoted, *Ibid.*, 50.
41. *Ibid.*, 50-5.
42. *Memoirs of Cordell Hull*, I, 796.
43. Sherwood, *Roosevelt and Hopkins*, 148-9.
44. *Memoirs of Cordell Hull*, I, 798-800.

45. Sherwood, *Roosevelt and Hopkins*, 146-7.
46. Stimson and Bundy, *On Active Service*, 318-9.
47. *Ibid.*, 323-30.
48. *Ibid.*, 331.
49. *New York Times*, July 3, 4, 1940.
50. Sherwood, *Roosevelt and Hopkins*, 151, 162, 165.
51. *Memoirs of Cordell Hull*, I, 793.

## Chapter 9—"Because America Exists"

1. Churchill, *Their Finest Hour*, 25.
2. Stimson and Bundy, *On Active Service*, 324.
3. Farley, *Jim Farley's Story*, 232-3.
4. *Memoirs of Cordell Hull*, I, 855, 858 *et passim*.
5. *Ibid.*, I, 858-61.
6. Farley, *Jim Farley's Story*, 246-58.
7. Beard, *American Foreign Policy*, 268.
8. *Papers of F. D. Roosevelt*, 1940, 286-91.
9. Sherwood, *Roosevelt and Hopkins*, 179.
10. *Ibid.*, 176.
11. *New York Times*, June 27, 1940.
12. Beard, *American Foreign Policy*, 290-1.
13. Byrnes, *Speaking Frankly*, 10-1. *Memoirs of Cordell Hull*, I, 862.
14. Beard, *American Foreign Policy*, 289.
15. Farley, *Jim Farley's Story*, 289-92.
16. Russell Lord, *The Wallaces of Iowa* (Houghton Mifflin Company, Boston, 1947), 475-6.
17. Perkins, *The Roosevelt I Knew*, 133.
18. Farley, *Jim Farley's Story*, 293-4.
19. Sherwood, *Roosevelt and Hopkins*, 178-9.
20. *Papers of F. D. Roosevelt*, 1940, 293-303. Italics added.
21. Beard, *American Foreign Policy*, 294.
22. *Ibid.*, 294.
23. Lord, *The Wallaces of Iowa*, 479-80.
24. *Papers of F. D. Roosevelt*, 1940, 315-7.
25. *Ibid.*, 1940, 327-8.
26. *Ibid.*, 473-5.
27. Shepardson and Scroggs, *The United States in World Affairs*, 1940, 245.
28. Churchill, *Their Finest Hour*, 400-1.
29. Shepardson and Scroggs, *United States in World Affairs*, 1940, 257-8.
30. Churchill, *Their Finest Hour*, 402.
31. Sherwood, *Roosevelt and Hopkins*, 175-6.
32. Churchill, *Their Finest Hour*, 409.
33. *Papers of F. D. Roosevelt*, 1940, 375-85, 391-407. *Memoirs of Cordell Hull*, I, 831-43. Shepardson and Scroggs, *United States in World Affairs*, 1940, 256-64. Churchill, *Their Finest Hour*, 398-416. Sherwood, *Roosevelt and Hopkins*, 174-6.
34. *Memoirs of Cordell Hull*, I, 834. *Papers of F. D. Roosevelt*, 1940, 331.
35. *Memoirs of Cordell Hull*, I, 791-2, 821-6. Hull's statement (p. 826) that "the Act of Havana never had to be applied" is an error. He himself writes (II, 1051) regarding the occupation of Dutch Guiana that it was arranged "in keeping with the procedure established at the Havana Conference in 1940."
36. *Ibid.*, I, 827-9.

37. *United States Statutes at Large*, Vol. 54, Pt. I, Ch. 365, pp. 396-7.

38. *Papers of F. D. Roosevelt*, 1940, 466.

39. *Memoirs of Cordell Hull*, I, 888-916. *Papers Relating to the Foreign Relations of the United States: Japan: 1931–1941* (USGPO, Washington, 1943), II, 53-116, 164-73, 211-29, 280-97. Langer, *Our Vichy Gamble*, 78-9. Churchill, *Their Finest Hour*, 337, 497-8. Shepardson and Scroggs, *United States in World Affairs*, 1940, 149-86.

40. Sherwood, *Roosevelt and Hopkins*, 189.

41. *Papers of F. D. Roosevelt*, 1940, 499-506.

42. Sherwood, *Roosevelt and Hopkins*, 189-90.

43. *Papers of F. D. Roosevelt*, 1940, 504.

44. *Ibid.*, 522-3.

45. *New York Times*, October 31, 1940.

46. *Papers of F. D. Roosevelt*, I, 789.

47. *Ibid.*, 1940, 517.

48. Sherwood, *Roosevelt and Hopkins*, 191.

49. *Ibid.*, 187-91.

50. Shepardson and Scroggs, *United States in World Affairs*, 1940, 324-28.

51. Perkins, *The Roosevelt I Knew*, 126-7.

52. *Papers of F. D. Roosevelt*, 1940, 530-9.

53. Churchill, *Their Finest Hour*, 553.

## Chapter 10—The Vichy Policy

1. The views of critics of the Vichy policy "from the left" are stated elaborately in Waverley Root, *The Secret History of the War*, II, 189 ff. *et passim*. Their thesis is stated more succinctly in Robert Bendiner, *The Riddle of the State Department* (Farrar & Rinehart, New York, 1942).

2. Langer, *Our Vichy Gamble*, 69-73.

3. *Ibid.*, 76.

4. Root, *Secret History of the War*, II, 252n.

5. *Ibid.*, 194.

6. Churchill, *Their Finest Hour*, 507-18.

7. Root, *Secret History of the War*, II, 193 *et passim*.

8. *Memoirs of Cordell Hull*, I, 853-4. Langer, *Our Vichy Gamble*, 139-40.

9. *Memoirs of Cordell Hull*, I, 819.

10. *Ibid.*, 849-51.

11. Langer, *Our Vichy Gamble*, 102-4.

12. *Memoirs of Cordell Hull*, I, 851, 882.

13. Langer, *Our Vichy Gamble*, 118-20. *Memoirs of Cordell Hull*, I, 883-4.

14. Churchill, *Their Finest Hour*, 508-9.

15. Chevalier, *Procès du M. Pétain*, 254-5, cited in Langer, *Our Vichy Gamble*, 120.

16. *Memoirs of Cordell Hull*, II, 948-9.

17. *Loc. cit.* Langer, *Our Vichy Gamble*, 120-1.

18. *Memoirs of Cordell Hull*, I, 874-82.

19. Department of State, *The Spanish Government and the Axis* (USGPO, Washington, 1946). Langer, *Our Vichy Gamble*, 91-2, 126-7.

20. Robert D. Murphy, "Visit to North Africa," cited in Langer, *Our Vichy Gamble*, 128-9. *Memoirs of Cordell Hull*, II, 949-50.

21. Renée Pierre-Gosset, *Conspiracy in Algiers: 1942–1943* (The Nation, New York, 1945), Chs. I, II.

22. *Memoirs of Cordell Hull*, II, 948-52. Italics added. Langer, *Our Vichy Gamble*, 129-36.

23. *Memoirs of Cordell Hull*, II, 948-66. Langer, *Our Vichy Gamble*, 137-61.


## Chapter 11—Lend Lease

1. Sherwood, *Roosevelt and Hopkins*, 224.
2. Churchill, *Their Finest Hour*, 557-67.
3. Stettinius, *Lend-Lease*. 62-3, 70.
4. *Papers of F. D. Roosevelt*, 1940, 605-7.
5. Stettinius, *Lend-Lease*, 65.
6. *Papers of F. D. Roosevelt*, 1940, 633-44.
6a. Beard, *American Foreign Policy*, 321-2.
7. *Papers of F. D. Roosevelt*, 1940, 541-3.
8. *Ibid.*, 663-72.
9. *Ibid.*, 281-5.
10. Charles A. Beard, *President Roosevelt and the Coming of the War: 1941: A Study in Appearances and Realities* (Yale University Press, New Haven, 1948), 15-6. Beard in a footnote (p. 16) refers readers to Hearings of the Senate Committee on Foreign Relations for Secretary Stimson's "attempt to provide some sanction of international law for the Lend Lease Act."
11. *Congressional Record* (77th Congress: 1st Session), Vol. 87, Pt. 10 (Appendix), pp. A 178-9.
12. *Papers of F. D. Roosevelt*, 1940, 711-2.
13. *Memoirs of Cordell Hull*, II, 925.
14. *Hearings before the Committee on Foreign Relations*, on S. 275 (77th Congress, 1st Session), Pt. 1, pp. 34-6.
15. Stettinius, *Lend-Lease*, 67-70.
16. Beard, *Roosevelt*, 29-30.
17. *Senate Hearings*, on S. 275, Pt. 1, p. 43.
18. *Ibid.*, 30.
19. *Ibid.*, 204.
20. *Ibid.*, 211.
21. *Ibid.*, 89-90, 115.
22. Beard, *Roosevelt*, 32-3.
23. *Hearings on S. 275*, Pt. 2, pp. 307-17.
24. *Ibid.*, Pt. 1, p. 203.
25. *Ibid.*, Pt. 2, pp. 307-17.
26. *New York Times*, August 5, 1940.
27. *Hearings on S. 275*, Pt. 2, pp. 490-4.
28. *New York Times*, March 12, 1941.
29. *Ibid.*, March 16, 1941.


## Chapter 12—The Convoy Conundrum

1. *Papers of F. D. Roosevelt*, 1940, 460-7.
2. *Ibid.*, 633-44.
3. *New York Times*, January 22, 1941.
4. Beard, *Roosevelt*, 98n.
5. *Ibid.*, 429. Italics added.
6. *New York Times*, April 18, 1941.

7. Beard, *Roosevelt*, 83.
8. *Memoirs of Cordell Hull*, II, 945-6.
9. Sherwood, *Roosevelt and Hopkins*, 291-2.
10. *New York Times*, April 26, 1941.
11. *Development of United States Foreign Policy: Addresses and Messages of Franklin D. Roosevelt* (77th Cong: 2nd Sess.), Senate Document No. 188, pp. 101-9.
12. Beard, *Roosevelt*, 103.
13. Stimson and Bundy, *On Active Service*, 364-76. Author's italics.
14. *New York Times*, April 23, 1941.
15. Stimson and Bundy, *On Active Service*, 364-81. Italics added.
16. (Devin-Adair, New York, 1947).
17. Beard, *Roosevelt*, 342n.
18. *Memoirs of Cordell Hull*, I, 906-7.
19. *Ibid.*, 909.
20. *Ibid.*, 911-2.
21. *Ibid.*, 913-6.
22. *Hearings* before the Joint Committee on the Investigation of the Pearl Harbor Attack (79th Cong: 1st Sess.), Vol. 84, Pt. 14, Exhibit 9, pp. 972-3. (Hereafter referred to as JCC, *Hearings*.) Beard states (p. 420n.) that the Congressional Committee "for reasons of its own" did not print every one of Admiral Stark's letters to Admiral Kimmel, and he warns students of history to "be on guard against basing conclusions solely on the voluminous *printed* record of the Congressional Committee on Pearl Harbor." To clinch the matter, Beard cites the letter of April 3, 1941, in which Stark wrote: "The question as to our entry into the war now seems to be *when*, and not *whether*." The letter was printed by the Congressional Committee. See JCC, *Hearings*, Pt. 33, Ex. 73, p. 1375. Professor Samuel Eliot Morison drew this error by Beard to my attention.
23. JCC, Majority *Report of the Joint Committee on the Investigation of the Pearl Harbor Attack* (79th Cong: 2nd Sess.), Senate Document 244, pp. 168-71; *Hearings*, Vol. 84, Pt. 15, Exhibit 49, pp. 1485-1550.
24. JCC, *Hearings*, Vol. 82, Pt. 5, pp. 2332-3.
25. JCC, *Majority Report*, 169. *Report of ABC-1*, *Hearings*, Vol. 84, pp. 1485-1550. *Hearings*, Vol. 81, Pt. 3, pp. 1052-3.
26. *Report of ABC-1*, *Hearings*, Vol. 84, pp. 1485-1550.
27. JCC, Minority *Report*, pp. 506-8.
28. JCC, *Majority Report*, 172n.
29. Morgenstern, *Pearl Harbor*, 104. Italics added.
30. *Ibid.*, 109. Italics added.
31. Beard, *Roosevelt*, 442.
32. *Ibid.*, 443-4.
33. *Ibid.*, 446.
34. JCC, Minority *Report*, 506-7. Italics added (except "or").
35. Morgenstern, *Pearl Harbor*, 113-6. Italics added.
36. Beard, *Roosevelt*, 447-9. Morgenstern, *Pearl Harbor*, 111-6.
37. *Memoirs of Cordell Hull*, II, 935-9.
38. *Messages of Roosevelt*, 94-5.
39. *Memoirs of Cordell Hull*, II, 927, 943.
40. JCC, *Hearings*, Vol. 90, Pt. 26, p. 265. Cf. Stimson and Bundy, *On Active Service*, 386-7.
41. JCC, *Majority Report*, pp. 173-4. Italics added.
42. JCC, Minority *Report*, pp. 543-44.
43. Morgenstern, *Pearl Harbor*, 92-3.
44. *Ibid.*, 94-5.

45. JCC, *Hearings*, Pt. 5, p. 2293.
46. *Messages of Roosevelt*, 103-4.
47. Sherwood, *Roosevelt and Hopkins*, 296-7.
48. *Memoirs of Cordell Hull*, II, 942.
49. Sherwood, *Roosevelt and Hopkins*, 295-9.

## Chapter 13—America and Russia

1. *Nazi-Soviet Relations: 1939–1941*, ed. Sontag and Beddie, 217-59.
2. *Memoirs of Cordell Hull*, II, 967-73.
3. *New York Times*, November 16, 24, 27, 1940; June 6, 9, 10, 1941.
4. *Ibid.*, June 23, 1941.
5. Sherwood, *Roosevelt and Hopkins*, 293-4, 374, 390.
6. *New York Times*, June 23, 1941.
7. *Ibid.*, June 25, 26, 1941.
8. Stettinius, *Lend-Lease*, 120-4.
9. Sherwood, *Roosevelt and Hopkins*, 303-4. Italics added.
10. *Memoirs of Cordell Hull*, II, 946-7. Sherwood, *Roosevelt and Hopkins*, 290.
11. *New York Times*, July 4, 1941.
12. Stimson and Bundy, *On Active Service*, 372-3.
13. *New York Times*, July 8, 1941.
14. JCC, *Hearings*, Pt. 5, pp. 2292-7. *New York Times*, September 12, 1941.
15. Beard, *Roosevelt*, 435.
16. Sherwood, *Roosevelt and Hopkins*, 308-48.

## Chapter 14—The Atlantic Conference

1. (Harper and Brothers, New York, 1946).
2. Sherwood, *Roosevelt and Hopkins*, 359. Beard, *Roosevelt*, 453n.
3. *Ibid.*, 242.
4. Beard, *Roosevelt*, 479-80.
5. Welles, *Where Are We Heading?* 12.
6. *New York Times*, December 20, 1944.
7. Sherwood, *Roosevelt and Hopkins*, 311.
8. *Ibid.*, 227.
9. Welles, *Where Are We Heading?* 6-17. *Messages of Roosevelt*, 112-3.
10. Sherwood, *Roosevelt and Hopkins*, 367.
11. Beard, *Roosevelt*, 476n. Beard italicizes the two words in the quotation from Welles (*Where Are We Heading?* 18), in which Welles states a common charge against Roosevelt.
12. Morgenstern, *Pearl Harbor*, 122.
13. Root, *Secret History of the War*, II, 304-6, 313-4. Italics added.
14. *Ibid.*, I, 471.
15. JCC, *Hearings*, Pt. 14, Ex. 22C, pp. 1295-6.
16. *Messages of Roosevelt*, 112.
17. JCC, *Hearings*, Vol. 84, Pt. 14, Exhibit 22B, pp. 1269-71.

## Chapter 15—Roosevelt and Japan

1. *Memoirs of Cordell Hull*, II, 982-4.
2. Joseph W. Ballantine, "Mukden to Pearl Harbor," *Foreign Affairs*, XXVII (July, 1949), 659-60.

3. *Papers Relating to the Foreign Relations of the United States: Japan: 1931–1941* (USGPO, Washington, 1943), II, 398-402, 420-5, 439-40. *Memoirs of Cordell Hull,* II, 984 ff.

4. *Foreign Relations: Japan,* II, 432-4.

5. *Memoirs of Cordell Hull,* II, 1002.

6. *Foreign Relations: Japan,* II, 446-54.

7. *Ibid.,* 457. Italics added.

8. *Ibid.,* 458.

9. *Memoirs of Cordell Hull,* II, 1009.

10. *Foreign Relations: Japan,* II, 485-505.

11. *Memoirs of Cordell Hull,* II, 1013.

12. Ballantine, "Mukden to Pearl Harbor," 661.

13. Morgenstern, *Pearl Harbor,* 132.

14. *Ibid.,* 132.

15. *Foreign Relations: Japan,* II, 522-30, 266-7.

16. *Ibid.,* 530-40.

17. *Ibid.,* 540-50.

18. *Ibid.,* 550-3. *Memoirs of Cordell Hull,* II, 1017.

19. Forrest Davis and Ernest K. Lindley, *How War Came,* (Simon and Schuster, New York, 1942), 10.

20. Beard, *Roosevelt,* 457-8, 487.

21. Morgenstern, *Pearl Harbor,* 121.

22. *Ibid.,* 127-38.

23. JCC, Minority *Report,* pp. 14-5.

23a. Sherwood, *Roosevelt and Hopkins,* 316.

24. JCC, *Hearings,* Vol. 81, Pt. 2, pp. 541, 548.

25. *Memoirs of Cordell Hull,* II, 1023.

26. JCC, *Hearings,* Pt. 4, pp. 1784 ff.

27. *New York Times,* August 25, 1941.

28. *Ibid.,* November 11, 1941.

29. *Memoirs of Cordell Hull,* II, 1018-20. *Foreign Relations: Japan,* II, 556-9.

30. JCC, Minority *Report,* 509.

31. *Foreign Relations: Japan,* II, 554-9. *Memoirs of Cordell Hull,* II, 1019-20.

## Chapter 16—"Shoot on Sight"

1. *New York Times,* August 14, 1941.

2. Sherwood, *Roosevelt and Hopkins,* 368-9.

3. Stettinius, *Lend-Lease,* 125-6.

4. *Ibid.,* 128. Sherwood, *Roosevelt and Hopkins,* 395, 400.

5. *Congressional Record* (77th Congress, 1st Session), Vol. 87, Pt. 7, p. 7223.

6. *Memoirs of Cordell Hull,* II, 976-7. Sherwood, *Roosevelt and Hopkins,* 391-3.

7. *Wartime Correspondence between President Roosevelt and Pope Pius XII,* 61-2.

8. *Ibid.,* 58-9, 63-4.

9. Sherwood, *Roosevelt and Hopkins,* 384, 398.

10. *Ibid.,* 396-8. Stettinius, *Lend-Lease,* 130.

11. *Events Leading up to World War II,* 299. *Memoirs of Cordell Hull,* II, 1165-7.

12. *Loc. cit.* Italics added. Sherwood, *Roosevelt and Hopkins,* 401-2.

13. *Memoirs of Cordell Hull,* II, 1165-74.

14. *Ibid.,* 1455-8.

15. Byrnes, *Speaking Frankly,* 42.

16. Sherwood, *Roosevelt and Hopkins*, 400.
17. JCC, *Hearings*, Vol. 82, Pt. 5, p. 2295.
18. *Messages of Roosevelt*, 114-5.
19. *Congressional Record* (77th Congress, 1st Session), Vol. 87, Pt. 8, pp. 8314-5.
20. Beard, *Roosevelt*, 138-42.
21. *Messages of Roosevelt*, 114-9.
22. JCC, *Hearings*, Vol. 52, Pt. 5, p. 2296.
23. JCC, *Loc. cit.*
24. *New York Times*, October 4, 1941.
25. *Ibid.*, October 10, 1941.
26. *Memoirs of Cordell Hull*, II, 1046-7.
27. *Congressional Record* (77th Congress, 1st Session), Vol. 87, Pt. 7, p. 7966.
28. A convenient group of extracts from isolationist speeches is in Beard, *Roosevelt*, 165-72.
29. *New York Times*, October 23, 1941.
30. Sherwood, *Roosevelt and Hopkins*, 381-2.
31. Beard, *Roosevelt*, 159.
32. *Ibid.*, 142-8.
33. *Messages of Roosevelt*, 120-4.
34. *New York Times*, November 1, 1941.
35. *Events Leading up to World War II*, 303. *Memoirs of Cordell Hull*, II, 1050-1.
36. Beard, *Roosevelt*, 590.

## Chapter 17—Roosevelt and Konoye

1. JCC, *Hearings*, Vol. 84, Pt. 15, Exhibit 52, p. 1594.
2. *Ibid.*, Exhibit 53, pp. 1602.
3. *Ibid.*, Vol. 81, Pt. 3, pp. 1092-3.
4. Ballantine, "Mukden to Pearl Harbor," 663.
5. *Memoirs of Cordell Hull*, II, 1020-1.
6. *Loc. cit.*
7. Quoted in Sherwood, *Roosevelt and Hopkins*, 410-2, 414-5. Italics added.
8. *Ibid.*, 415.
9. *Foreign Relations: Japan*, II, 572-5.
10. *Memoirs of Cordell Hull*, II, 1021-2, 1025.
11. *Foreign Relations: Japan*, II, 576-9.
12. *Ibid.*, 579-82.
13. Quoted in *Memoirs of Cordell Hull*, II, 1025-6.
14. *Foreign Relations: Japan*, II, 588-92: Italics added.
15. *Loc. cit.*
16. *Ibid.*, 597-601.
17. *Ibid.*, 608-9. *Memoirs of Cordell Hull*, II, 1028-30.
18. *Memoirs of Cordell Hull*, II, 1028-30.
19. *Ibid.*, 1030.
20. *Foreign Relations: Japan*, II, 633. *Memoirs of Cordell Hull*, II, 1031-2.
21. *Foreign Relations: Japan*, II, 645-50. Also in Grew, *Ten Years in Japan*, 436-42.
22. *Memoirs of Cordell Hull*, II, 1033. *Foreign Relations: Japan*, II, 656-61.
23. Ballantine, "Mukden to Pearl Harbor," 659.
24. *Foreign Relations: Japan*, II, 656-61.
25. *Ibid.*, 676, Italics added.
26. *Ibid.*, 680-6.

27. *Ibid.*, 687-9.
28. *Memoirs of Cordell Hull*, II, 1034.
29. *Foreign Relations: Japan*, II, 668.
30. *Memoirs of Cordell Hull*, II, 1034.
31. *Ibid.*, 1024.
32. Beard, *Roosevelt*, 189-92.
33. *Ibid.*, 190, 496-506.
34. JCC, *Report of the Joint Committee*, Minority *Report*, 497.
35. Morgenstern, *Pearl Harbor*, 128, 139-40.
36. Beard, *Roosevelt*, 504n.

## Chapter 18—Roosevelt and Pearl Harbor

1. JCC *Hearings*, Vol. 90, Pt. 26, Hart Inquiry, Exhibit 6, p. 487.
2. *Ibid.*, Vol. 82, Pt. 7, p. 2933.
3. *Foreign Relations: Japan*, II, 691.
4. *Ibid.*, 692-8.
5. Quoted in *Memoirs of Cordell Hull*, II, 1055.
6. *Loc. cit.*
7. *Ibid.*, 1056.
8. Grew, *Ten Years in Japan*, 471.
9. *Ibid.*, 470.
10. *Foreign Relations: Japan*, II, 701-4.
11. *Memoirs of Cordell Hull*, II, 1056-7.
12. Grew, *Ten Years in Japan*, 471-4.
13. *Memoirs of Cordell Hull*, II, 1058. *New York Times*, November 12, 1941.
14. Stimson and Bundy, *On Active Service*, 388-9.
15. *Foreign Relations: Japan*, II, 729.
16. *Ibid.*, 718, 736-7.
17. *Ibid.*, 736-7.
18. *Ibid.*, 738-43. Hull's remark in his *Memoirs* that his request for confirmation was answered in the "affirmative" by Nomura evidently applies to the September 6 and 25 Japanese draft proposals *including the escape clauses*. *Memoirs of Cordell Hull*, II, 1062-3.
19. *Foreign Relations: Japan*, II, 740-3.
20. JCC, *Hearings*, Vol. 83, Pt. 12, Exhibit 1, pp. 129, 137-8, 158, 160. *Memoirs of Cordell Hull*, II, 1063.
21. *Loc. cit.*
22. *Foreign Relations: Japan*, II, 743-4.
23. JCC *Hearings*, Vol. 83, Pt. 12, Exhibit 1, p. 154. Italics added.
24. *Ibid.*, 155. Italics added.
25. *Ibid.*, Vol. 81, Pt. 4, p. 1815, cf. p. 1861.
26. Morgenstern, *Pearl Harbor*, 248-51.
27. Beard, *Roosevelt*, 506-16.
28. Ballantine, "Mukden to Pearl Harbor," 662-4.
29. *Foreign Relations: Japan*, II, 748-9, 755-6.
30. *Memoirs of Cordell Hull*, II, 1070-1.
31. JCC, *Hearings*, Vol. 84, Pt. 14, Exhibit 37, p. 1405.
32. *Memoirs of Cordell Hull*, II, 1074.
33. *Ibid.*, 1072-3, 1077-81.
34. *Ibid.*, 1074-81.
35. Beard, *Roosevelt*, 515.

36. *Ibid.*, 517-9, ff.
37. Morgenstern, *Pearl Harbor*, 288 *et passim.*
38. JCC, Minority *Report*, 563-4.
39. JCC, *Hearings*, Vol. 83, Pt. 11, pp. 5433-4.
40. Morgenstern, *Pearl Harbor*, 288.
41. *Foreign Relations: Japan*, II, 764-70. Italics added.
42. *Memoirs of Cordell Hull*, II, 1087.
43. JCC, *Majority Report*, 259-60.
44. *Ibid.*, 266-A.
45. JCC, Minority *Report*, 503-6.
46. JCC, *Majority Report*, 191-2.
47. Beard, *Roosevelt*, 536. Italics added.
48. Morgenstern, *Pearl Harbor*, 198-222.
49. JCC, Minority *Report*, 526.
50. JCC, *Majority Report*, 170n.
51. JCC, *Hearings*, Vol. 84, Pt. 14, Exhibit 40, p. 1412; *Majority Report*, 170-1.
52. JCC, *Majority Report*, 178. Italics added.
53. JCC, *Hearings*, Vol. 83, Pt. 11, p. 5427.
54. *Foreign Relations: Japan*, II, 778-84.
55. JCC, *Majority Report*, 178; *Hearings*, Vol. 83, Pt. 11, p. 5427.
56. *Ibid.*, Vol. 84, Pt. 14, Exhibit 21, p. 1246.
57. *Memoirs of Cordell Hull*, II, 1095.
58. *Foreign Relations: Japan*, II, 792.
59. *Ibid.*, 784-6.
60. JCC, *Majority Report*, 433; *Hearings*, Vol. 84, Pt. 12, Exhibit 1, p. 195.
61. *Ibid.*, Vol. 83, Pt. 12, p. 236; *Majority Report*, 435.
62. JCC, *Hearings*, Vol. 83, Pt. 11, pp. 5164-6; *Majority Report*, 428-31. Hull
relates that Churchill had suggested to Roosevelt a warning to Japan in a cable
dated November 30, that is, two days after the Americans had decided to issue a
warning. *Memoirs of Cordell Hull*, II, 1092.
63. Beard, *Roosevelt*, 544-8.
64. Morgenstern, *Pearl Harbor*, 298. Italics added.
65. JCC, Minority *Report*, 513.

## Epilogue

1. *Messages of Roosevelt*, 126.
2. *Ibid.*, 131-2.
3. *Memoirs of Cordell Hull*, II, 1116.
4. *Documents on American Foreign Relations*, 1941–1942, ed. Leland M. Goodrich
(World Peace Foundation, Boston, 1942), IV, 203, 208-9.

# Index